COMMERCIAL CONTRACT LAW

This book focuses on the law of commercial contracts as constructed by the US and UK legal systems. Leading scholars from both sides of the Atlantic provide works of original scholarship focusing on current debates and trends from the two dominant common law systems. The chapters approach the subject areas from a variety of perspectives – doctrinal analysis, law and economic analysis, and social-legal studies, as well as other theoretical perspectives. The book covers the major themes that underlie the key debates relating to commercial contract law: role of consent; normative theories of contract law; contract design and good faith; implied terms and interpretation; policing contract behavior; misrepresentation, breach, and remedies; and the regional and international harmonization of contract law.

Contributors provide insights on the many commonalities, but more interestingly, on the key divergences of the United States' and United Kingdom's approaches to numerous areas of contract law. Such a comparative analysis provides a basis for future developments and improvements of commercial contract law in both countries, as well as in other countries that are members of the common law systems. At the same time, insights gathered here should also be of interest to scholars and practitioners of the civil law tradition.

Larry A. DiMatteo is the Huber Hurst Professor of Contract Law & Legal Studies at the Warrington College of Business Administration and Affiliated Professor at the Levin College of Law at the University of Florida.

Qi Zhou is a Lecturer at the University of Sheffield, School of Law.

Séverine Saintier is a Senior Lecturer at the University of Sheffield, School of Law.

Keith Rowley is the William S. Boyd Professor of Law at University of Nevada, Las Vegas, William S. Boyd School of Law.

Commercial Contract Law

TRANSATLANTIC PERSPECTIVES

Edited by

LARRY A. DIMATTEO
University of Florida

QI ZHOU
University of Sheffield

SÉVERINE SAINTIER
University of Sheffield

KEITH ROWLEY
University of Nevada, Las Vegas

CAMBRIDGE UNIVERSITY PRESS
Cambridge, New York, Melbourne, Madrid, Cape Town,
Singapore, São Paulo, Delhi, Mexico City

Cambridge University Press
32 Avenue of the Americas, New York, NY 10013-2473, USA

www.cambridge.org
Information on this title: www.cambridge.org/9781107028081

First published 2013

Printed in the United States of America

A catalog record for this publication is available from the British Library.

Library of Congress Cataloging in Publication data

Commercial contract law : transatlantic perspectives / [edited by] Larry A. DiMatteo, University of Florida, Qi Zhou, University of Sheffield, Séverine Saintier, University of Sheffield, Keith Rowley, University of Nevada Las Vegas.

pages cm

Includes index.

ISBN 978-1-107-02808-1 (hardback)

1. Contracts – United States. 2. Contracts – Great Britain. 3. Commercial law – United States. 4. Commercial law – Great Britain. 5. Common law – United States. 6. Common law – Great Britain. I. DiMatteo, Larry A., editor of compilation.

K840.C655 2013

346.4102′2–dc23 2012044080

ISBN 978-1-107-02808-1 Hardback

Robert Bradgate

Edward Bramley Professor of Commercial Law Emeritus

This scholarly book brings together commercial and contract law scholars from both the United States and the United Kingdom. The impetus for this project was a symposium held on 9–10 September 2011 to celebrate the lifetime achievements in this field by Robert Bradgate, Edward Bramley Professor of Commercial Law Emeritus at the University of Sheffield, United Kingdom.

Brief Contents

Contents

Contributors

Peter A. Alces is the Rita Anne Rollins Professor of Law at The College of William & Mary School of Law. He practiced law in Chicago and taught at the University of Texas, Graduate School of Business, and the University of Alabama, School of Law. He has been a visiting professor at the University of Illinois, Washington & Lee University, Washington University, and University of Texas Law Schools. He is the author of a number of books and articles, including *Commercial Contracting*; *The Law of Suretyship and Guaranty*; *Bankruptcy: Cases and Materials*; *Cases, Problems and Materials on Payment Systems*; *The Commercial Law of Intellectual Property*; *Sales, Leases and Bulk Transfers*; *The Law of Fraudulent Transactions*; and *Uniform Commercial Code Transactions Guide*. He was Editor-in-Chief of the *Journal of Bankruptcy Law and Practice*, 1991–2005. He is a member of the American Law Institute and the Association of American Law Schools' Section on Commercial and Related Consumer Law; he was adviser to Restatement (Third) of the Law of Suretyship and Guaranty.

T. T. Arvind was appointed professor of commercial law at the University of Newcastle on September 1, 2012. Prior to that, Dr Arvind was a lecturer in Law at the University of York, School of Law. He is a qualified attorney in India, where he practiced law with a leading commercial practice for many years before coming to Britain to pursue a career in academia. Dr Arvind joined York Law School in 2007, after five years as a lecturer at the University of East Anglia, Norwich. His research focuses on using evolutionary and historical approaches to analyze current legal questions, and specifically on the intellectual, social, economic, and other influences that shape legal change. He recently completed an analysis of the reaction of lawyers and judges in developing countries to the introduction of transplanted harmonised laws, and a study of the factors that influenced the diverse responses of the German states to the Code Napoleon at the beginning of the nineteenth century (for which he won the SLS Best Paper Prize in 2009). He was awarded the ICLQ Young Scholar Prize in 2010.

Richard Austen-Baker is a senior lecturer in Law at the University of Lancaster. He came to academia after practicing as a barrister. His research interests are in common law, particularly contracts (history, theory, and doctrine), commercial law, and the law of torts as well as the common law remedies. He recently published a book in the field of implied terms and is currently expanding his research in the field of relational contract theory.

Jean Braucher is the Roger C. Henderson Professor of Law at the University of Arizona, James R. Rogers College of Law. She serves as Vice-President of the National Consumer Bankruptcy Rights Centre and, since 2010, as Director of the National Association of Consumer Bankruptcy Law. Her research interests are contract and consumer law. Her most recent work is *Contracts: Law in Action* (with Stewart Macaulay, John Kidwell, and William Whitford) (3d ed. 2010 & 2011).

Curtis Bridgeman is the James Edmund and Margaret Elizabeth Hennessey Corry Professor of Law and Associate Dean for Academic Affairs, Florida State University College of Law. His scholarship explores the structure and philosophy of contracts and commercial and bankruptcy law. He has written about contract formalism, the specification of rules of contract law, and the role of planning and practical reasoning in contract law. Bridgeman teaches Contracts, Commercial Law, Creditors' Rights, Jurisprudence, and Philosophy of Private Law.

Roger Brownsword is Professor of Law and Director of TELOS at King's College London and an Honorary Professor of Law at University of Sheffield School of Law. As a researcher, Professor Brownsword writes in the fields of contracts and the common law, legal theory, bioethics and the regulation of technology in the UK as well as Australia, Brazil, Canada, Denmark, France, Germany, the Netherlands, Singapore, and the United States. Most recently, Professor Brownsword has acted as a specialist adviser to the House of Lords Select Committee on Stem Cells and the House of Commons Science and Technology Committee. Professor Brownsword is a member of the Editorial Board of *Modern Law Review*.

David Campbell is Professor of International Business Law at Leeds University School of Law. He holds degrees from Cardiff (BSc Econ), Michigan (LLM), and Edinburgh (PhD). He is a Fellow of the Chartered Institute of Arbitrators. He has taught at various UK law schools as well as in Australia, Hong Kong, New Zealand, Spain, and the United States. His research interests are for remedies for non-performance of contractual obligations as well as regulatory theory.

David Capper is a reader at Queen's University of Belfast School of Law. After practicing at the Bar of Northern Ireland for five years he was appointed to the post of Lecturer in Law at Queen's University Belfast in 1989 and was promoted to

Reader in June 2002. In 1990–91 he was Visiting Assistant Professor of Law at the University of Detroit Mercy in Detroit, Michigan. He is the Queen's University constituency representative on the council of the Society of Legal Scholars in Great Britain and Ireland and was a member 1995–2001 (vice-chair 1997–2001) of the Lord Chancellor's Legal Aid Advisory Committee for Northern Ireland. He also serves as a lay member of the Institute of Chartered Accountants in Ireland's Insolvency Licensing Committee and is company secretary of SLS Legal Publications (NI) Ltd. Since 2001 he has been Editor of the *Northern Ireland Legal Quarterly*.

James Devenney was appointed professor of commercial law at the University of Exeter School of Law in 2011. He also held posts at the University of Wales, Cardiff, and the University of the West of England, Bristol. His main research interests are contract law, consumer law, and commercial law. He is currently working on a research project on the European Draft Common Frame of Reference with the Institute of European and Comparative Law at the University of Oxford and Humboldt Universität, Berlin, Germany. He is also involved in a three-year project, Credit & Debt: Protection of Vulnerable Consumers in Private Law (Undue Influence, Unconscionability & Good Faith), which is being funded by the EU.

Larry A. DiMatteo is the Huber Hurst Professor of Contract Law & Legal Studies at the Warrington College of Business Administration at the University of Florida, as well as an Affiliated Professor of Law at the Levin College of Law and at the Center for European Studies both at the University of Florida. He holds a JD from Cornell University, LLM from Harvard Law School, and a PhD from Monash University (Australia). He is the author of numerous books and articles on contract law, international sales law, international patent law, legal history, and legal theory. He is the 2011–12 University of Florida Teacher-Scholar of the Year. He also was awarded a 2012 Fulbright Professorship.

Roger Halson is Professor of Contract Law at the University of Leeds. He has previously taught at Hull, University College London, and Nottingham. He has written extensively in the field of contract law, especially remedies, and his work has been cited by the House of Lords as well as by appellate courts overseas.

Martin A. Hogg is a senior lecturer at the University of Edinburgh, School of Law. Following two years qualifying as a Solicitor with Dundas & Wilson CS in Edinburgh, he was appointed as a Lecturer at the Faculty of Law at Edinburgh in 1995. In 2004 he was appointed Senior Lecturer. He has previously held office as Associate Dean of the Faculty of Law, as well as Director of Undergraduate Studies and Director of Teaching of the Law School. He currently chairs the Law School's Board of Studies. His main areas of research lie in all aspects of the law of obligations, with a current particular emphasis on comparative obligations theory, causation, and the concept of damage. He is the Scottish Reporter for the *European Tort Law Yearbook*, published annually by the European Centre of Tort and Insurance Law. He also serves as Assistant Editor of *Edinburgh Law Review*.

Thomas W. Joo is a professor of Law at the University of California, Davis, School of Law, specializing in corporate governance, contract law, white-collar crime, and critical race theory. Prior to joining the UC Davis faculty, Professor Joo was a clerk in the chambers of the Honorable Wilfred Feinberg of the U.S. Court of Appeals for the Second Circuit and an associate at Cleary, Gottlieb, Steen, and Hamilton in New York. He currently serves as an Executive Committee Member of the Section on Contracts of the Association of American Law Schools. His most recent work is *Corporate Governance: Law, Theory & Practice* (Carolina Academic Press 2004, 2d ed. 2010).

Mel Kenny is Professor of Commercial Law at De Montfort University. He was previously a Reader at Leicester University School of Law. Mel has worked at the Universities of Leipzig (1990–97), Bremen (1997–2001 and 2005–07), Lucerne (2001–05), Durham (2007–08), and Leeds (2008–10) and joined the De Montfort Law School in 2012. In recent years his research has centered on three highly charged legal topics: the 'Europeanisation' of national private law systems and the associated calls for codification and consolidation; the comparative assessment of the treatment of surety agreements across Europe, and the general issue of consumer protection. He is Co-editor of a new series of edited collections, the first volume of which is titled *Unconscionability in European Private Financial Transactions: Protecting the Vulnerable* (Cambridge University Press 2011).

Nancy S. Kim is Professor of Law at California Western University School of Law in San Diego. Professor Kim joined the faculty in fall 2004. Prior to that time, she was Vice-President of Business and Legal Affairs of a multinational software and services company. After graduating from law school, she was a Women's Law and Public Policy Fellow at Georgetown University Law Center and a Ford Foundation Fellow at the UCLA School of Law. Kim is a past recipient of the Wiley W. Manuel Award for pro bono services for her work with the Asian Pacific American Legal Center. Kim currently serves on the executive committee of the Section on Internet and Computer Law of the American Association of Law Schools. Her scholarly interests focus on culture and the law, contracts, women and the law, and technology.

Charles L. Knapp is the Joseph W. Cotchett Distinguished Professor of Law at the University of California Hastings College of the Law. He came to Hastings in 1998 from New York University Law School, where he had been a faculty member since 1964 and was the Max E. Greenberg Professor of Contract Law. Besides his years of service at NYU, he has been a visiting professor at Harvard, the University of Arizona, Brooklyn Law School, and the University of Copenhagen. His principal teaching and research interest is contract and commercial law. Along with Hastings Professor H. G. Prince and Professor Nathan Crystal, he is the co-author of a widely used casebook, *Problems in Contract Law*, published by Aspen and now in its sixth edition.

Juliet P. Kostritsky is the John Homer Kapp Professor of Law at Case Western Reserve University Law School. She is a member of the American Law Institute. Her research interest includes contract and commercial law and she teaches the courses on contract, property, and commercial paper. Her recent research focuses on the interpretation of contract.

Hector L. MacQueen is a professor of Private Law at Edinburgh University and currently serves as a Scottish Law Commissioner. Professor MacQueen has previously held visiting appointments at Cornell University in the United States, the University of Utrecht in the Netherlands, and Stetson University College of Law. He has been a Fellow of the Royal Society of Edinburgh since 1995 and was elected a Fellow of the British Academy in 2006. In October 2008 he was elected Vice-President (Humanities) of the RSE for a three-year term. Professor MacQueen's work in obligations is mainly concerned with the law of contract and unjustified enrichment. He is the author or co-author of three standard student texts and is the Scottish Editor of the last three editions of *Atiyah's Sale of Goods*.

Zoe Ollerenshaw is a senior lecturer in law at University of Sheffield School of Law. Her research interests are contract and commercial law. She qualified as a Solicitor in 1987 and worked in private practice specializing in commercial law, intellectual property, and IT law for leading international law firms. She returned to academia in 2000. She is a member of the Sheffield Institute for Commercial Law Studies (ICLS).

Keith Rowley is the William S. Boyd Professor of Law at UNLV's William S. Boyd School of Law, where he teaches contract law, commercial law, economics and the law, and law and popular culture. He is an elected member of the American Law Institute and currently serves as chair of the AALS Section on Contracts; as Developments Reporter for the ABA Business Law Section's Uniform Commercial Code Committee; and as U.S. liaison to the Contract, Commercial, and Consumer Law Section of the Society of Legal Scholars. He has previously chaired the AALS Section on Commercial and Related Consumer Law and the Sales Subcommittee of the ABA Business Law Section's UCC Committee.

Djakhongir Saidov is a senior lecturer in law at the University of Birmingham, School of Law. He joined Birmingham Law School in September 2004. Prior to joining Birmingham, Dr Saidov taught at the Norwich Law School, University of East Anglia. He also practiced law in Tashkent, Uzbekistan. He received his LLB from the University of World Economy and Diplomacy (Uzbekistan) and his LLM with distinction and PhD from the University of East Anglia. His research and teaching interests are in the fields of international commercial law and law relating to international oil and gas operations. His recent publications include *The Law of Damages in International Sales – the CISG and Other International Instruments* (Oxford, Hart Publishing 2008) and 'A ULIS Echo in the CISG World' *Lloyd's Maritime and Commercial Law Quarterly* [2010, pp. 201–07].

Séverine Saintier is a senior lecturer at the University of Sheffield, School of Law. Prior to her current position, Dr Saintier worked in Liverpool University (1997–2003). She joined the Sheffield School of Law as a Lecturer in 2003 and was promoted to Senior Lecturer in 2008. She obtained a Maîtrise in international business law, an LLM in English law in 1995, and a PhD in 2001 from Sheffield University. Her research interests are in the areas of commercial, agency, and comparative law. She has contributed the national notes for English law in the Mandate and Representation Title of Principles, Definitions and Model Rules of European Private Law: Draft Common Frame of Reference. Her second monograph in the field of commercial agency (co-authored with Jeremy Scholes) has been used by the House of Lords in the case of *Lonsdale* (2007). Dr Saintier has been the Director of the Sheffield Institute of Commercial Law Studies (ICLS) since 2007.

Qi Zhou is a lecturer at the University of Sheffield, School of Law, in the United Kingdom. Previously, he was a practicing attorney in the People's Republic of China. His research interests are in the areas of contract law, commercial law, and regulation, as well as law and economics. Dr Zhou is the convener of the contract, commercial, and consumer law group of the Society of Legal Scholars; a member of the Standing Committee of the UK Chinese Law Association; an Assistant Editor of the *Journal of International Trade and Policy*; and a member of the Sheffield Institute of Commercial Law Studies (ICLS). He has researched in such areas as efficient breach, remedies and unconscionable contracts, misrepresentation, and unilateral mistakes.

Foreword

It was a privilege for me to be invited to attend the symposium in Sheffield in September 2011 that has given rise to this book. I imagine the invitation was the result of my long association with the School of Law at Sheffield rather than any perception that I have current expertise in the comparative law of commercial contracts. However, I derived enormous benefit from my attendance.

The sharing of knowledge and expertise among legal experts from different jurisdictions is essential to the development of the law. It is also important that, at a time when the laws of the United Kingdom are more than ever influenced by developments in the European Union, we do not forget the heritage that we share with other common law jurisdictions, particularly in relation to our fundamental concepts and basic principles. One of the most formative and durable influences on my judicial career was the time I and other British judges and lawyers spent with American colleagues in Edinburgh, London, and Washington DC, in 1999 and 2000 as part of the Anglo-American Legal Exchange. The historical similarities in our respective laws bind us together and our more recent divergences enable each of us to see how our own laws and practices may yet develop.

And so to the world of commercial contracts. Notwithstanding their common origins, the laws of the United Kingdom have developed differently from those of the United States. Most noticeably, they have diverged in relation to the duty of good faith and the doctrine of unconscionability. American judges have been more interventionist than their British counterparts. In the United Kingdom, the biggest source of regulation and calibration of unequal bargaining power now derives from obligations imposed on the Member States of the European Union. However, even in areas where there are no or few such obligations, the judicial development of our law does not always replicate the approach of American courts. Thus, for example, our approaches to construction, to implied terms, and to remedies differ significantly.

All this makes the comparative methodology that permeates this book particularly useful. Leading scholars from the United States and from the United Kingdom have come together to bring their varied expertise to bear on these important issues. Their approaches are refreshingly diverse. Some contributions resemble ones with which I was familiar as a Professor of Law thirty years ago. Others, particularly the more theoretical ones, are expressed in a language with which I was previously unfamiliar. Taken together, the contributions provide a unique and extremely valuable set of insights into our respective commercial contract laws. The book will help academics and practitioners on both sides of the Atlantic, and in Continental Europe, to appreciate where there is hope for harmonisation or approximation and where there is not. It is a most stimulating collection that should enhance the understanding of all those concerned with the development of the law of commercial contracts, both within and beyond the academic world.

I congratulate the organisers and the contributors to the September 2011 symposium. It is entirely appropriate that it can now reach a wider audience through this original and excellent book, which is a fitting celebration of the achievements of Professor Robert Bradgate, which inspired it.

Maurice Kay
Vice-President, Court of Appeal Civil Division
Royal Courts of Justice
London

PART I

The Role of Consent

Part I begins with an introductory chapter that explains the purpose of the book. Put succinctly, the book seeks to compare the common law systems of the United Kingdom and the United States in the area of commercial contract law at the levels of theory, doctrine, and practice. The ultimate goal of the book is to highlight the differences between the two systems and to suggest areas that would benefit from law reform. Part I explores the core concepts of what makes certain promises legal or moral commitments. It also reviews the coherence of the views or roles of contract law as facilitator of the exercise of private autonomy versus contract as a regulatory regime that controls the free exercise of such autonomy. This analysis concludes that the dichotomy between immutable and default rules is a false one. Finally, this part analyzes the issue of whether a legal obligation under contract law is equivalent to a moral obligation to honor the contract. This analysis is done in the context of strategic mortgage defaults. Chapter 2 reviews six theories of contracts – exchange of promises, agreement in fact, reliance, assumption of legally binding obligations, relationship- or status-based, and transfer of rights. The chapter concludes that a number of these theories do not adequately explain contract law as currently practiced and should be discarded. The remaining theories can be subsumed under an "agreement plus intention" model. It also suggests that European contract law has moved more actively in the direction of this model, while American contract law has yet to make a full commitment. In the end, the chapter asserts that a pure form of such a model requires a reassessment of the doctrine of consideration and the area of third-party rights, as currently formulated. Chapter 3 questions the premise that a contract is the end product of the parties' will. Instead, contract law should be seen as a three-party exchange among the parties and the regulatory nature of judicial review. It makes the bold assertion that the distinction between immutable and default rules is a fallacy. The courts retain overarching power to modify, enforce, and even covertly avoid default rules. It concludes that there is no such thing as a self-enforcing contract, even if the parties opt out of the judicial system. Finally, courts often cloak their decisions in the veil of party consent in order to mask the exercise of regulatory control. Chapter 4 analyzes the morality of promise in the context of strategic mortgage defaults where the mortgage principal exceeds the value of the home. The morality of commitment implied in explicit promises holds that the breach of the promise to repay is inherently immoral in situations where the mortgagor has the financial means to pay. This chapter argues that the immorality of promise breaking in strategic default is avoidable if the promisor does not view the promise as a moral obligation. Because of the impersonal, distant nature of modern-day lending, the mortgagor does not view the promise to repay as a moral commitment, but as merely a legal commitment with legal consequences. As such, the moral imperative to repay when financially able is dampened, but not necessarily eliminated.

1

Transatlantic Perspectives

Fundamental Themes and Debates

Larry A. DiMatteo, Qi Zhou, and Séverine Saintier

This chapter provides the reasons and purposes for the writing of this book. It briefly discusses the importance of a comparative analysis of English and American common law in the area of commercial contract law. It also provides a roadmap of the collection of essays incorporated in the book by previewing the themes and topics covered in the book's remaining twenty-one chapters.

I. LEGACY OF ROB BRADGATE

This book is the product of a symposium held in September 2011 in honour of Rob Bradgate, Edward Bramley Professor of Commercial Law at the University of Sheffield School of Law. Professor Bradgate is a remarkable figure in English commercial law scholarship. He studied law at the University of Cambridge, joined the University of Sheffield as lecturer in law in 1989, obtained a Chair in Commercial Law in 2002, and was appointed Edward Bramley Professor of Commercial Law in 2008. He retired in 2010, becoming Emeritus Professor of Law. Professor Bradgate faithfully served the University of Sheffield School of Law for twenty-one years until his retirement. He has published widely in the fields of commercial law, specializing in commercial and consumer transactions. His book, *Commercial Law*, published by Oxford University Press, is regarded as one of the leading authorities on English commercial law. Professor Bradgate served as the convener of the contract, commercial and consumer law group of the Society of Legal Scholars for many years. He has worked tirelessly to build links, platforms, and opportunities for legal scholars around the world. Professor Bradgate wished to enhance communications among scholars on both sides of the Atlantic. The symposium was a step towards achieving this objective. It is, thus, fitting that the book be dedicated to such an outstanding person and scholar.

A. *Commercial Contract Law in the United Kingdom and United States*

Commercial contract law evolved from commercial practice. It is shaped and developed constantly by interactions between commercial transactions and judicial decisions. The international and dynamic features of commercial contracting make it one of the most fascinating topics in the scholarship of contract law. Although the United States and the United Kingdom share the same common law tradition, commercial contract law in the two countries differs in many ways. Common law lawyers and scholars in both camps share the same foundational principles and concepts in almost all areas of law. They "speak" the same legal language. America's embrace of *Hadley v. Baxendale* in 1854, seventy-one years after its independence, attests to the fact of the overwhelming commonality of their contract laws. However, like any other branch of a legal tradition, American law has forged its own path – still solidly rooted in English common law – which has led to divergence and variations between the two in areas of substantive law. It is important to emphasize that most of the time, the differences have been more a matter of degree than of kind, but now and then significant divergences have appeared. This book focuses on the law of commercial contracts as constructed by the American and UK legal systems in order to survey the nuances of those differences. It brings together prominent legal scholars from the US and the UK including representatives from Scotland, Wales, and Northern Ireland.

1. Statutory Interventions into the Common Law

One formulaic difference is that in the area of the international commercial sale of goods the US is a signatory to the United Nations Convention on Contracts for the International Sale of Goods (CISG), and the UK is not. Another stark reality is the UK's membership in the European Union. As such, numerous EU Directives and Regulations have pre-empted the working of the common law. The US's federal and state governments also intervene in numerous areas of private law pre-empting the existing common law. Often times these interventions are undertaken with the intention to modernize, simply, or codify what has been created by the common law but has grown chaotic over time. The most popular example of this codification and modernization of the common law is the American Uniform Commercial Code (UCC), which substantially harmonized vast areas of commercial law among the fifty American states. The English Sale of Goods Act did the same but does not capture the many areas of commercial law, such as negotiable instruments, documents of title, secured transactions, wire transfers, and so forth, found in the UCC. Thus, some of the differences between UK and US commercial contract law are associated with various legislative enactments. However, it should be kept in mind that these statutory initiatives remain embedded in the common law system. As such, it is the courts that determine the ultimate meanings and scope of these interventions into the common law. In essence, the statutory incursions into the common law are captured by the common law.

In the United States, federal intervention has a more harmonizing effect since federal statutes are interpreted by a unified court system. But, at the state level there are fifty separate common law systems (not including the District of Columbia and US territories or possessions). Therefore, the ubiquity of the UCC masks the differences of interpretation created by the self-contained state court systems. The same can be said about the more substantial differences between English and Scottish law. This book touches upon some of these differences, but its main focus is on the broader conceptualizations of commercial contracts from the different perspectives of scholars from the American, English, and Scottish legal traditions, along with the views of scholars from Northern Ireland and Wales.

2. Divergence, Convergence, and Law Reform

Some of the differences between UK and American law are seen at the level of meta-principles. The two most obvious are the duty of good faith (and fair dealing) and the doctrine of unconscionability. The role of the duty of good faith continues to expand in the United States from its humble beginnings in sales and negotiable instrument law to employment law and landlord-tenant law. One of the key forces behind this broadened use in the United States has been the impact of the American UCC. The impact of the UCC on American commercial law is generally understood as the harmonization of law among the fifty American states. But equally important is the fact that numerous principles codified in the UCC, such as the duty of good faith and fair dealing, as well as the doctrine of unconscionability, have been applied by analogy to other areas of contract law. In essence, this process of analogizing has worked to change the common law of contracts in a way not found in the United Kingdom. Along with the duty of good faith, the doctrine of unconscionability is more fully developed in the United States than in the United Kingdom.

History indicates that such divergence may be more a matter of evolutionary lag than of a permanent schism. The common law continues to evolve to respond to the rapidly changing transactional landscape. In this way, English common law's moving to a greater use of the principles of good faith and unconscionability is possible, if not, likely. An analogy can be offered in the area of contract interpretation. Just as both systems have moved away from formalistic interpretation of contracts to various uses of contextual evidence, the speed of this change in interpretive methodology has varied between the US and UK. Although the US may have moved more quickly to embrace contextualism, the movement is apparent in both systems. That said, many years have passed since the decision in *Hadley v. Baxendale*, and, in practice, the two systems have become more distant from each other, more so than is the case among the UK and the English Commonwealth countries. This fact makes such comparative discussions as represented by the contributions in this book all the more important, because with divergence comes the opportunity to learn from perspectives and roads taken by the related system. This leads to a better understanding of the variations in the common law systems, as well as comparative benchmarks for future reforms.

B. *Major Themes*

Unconscionability and good faith are only the more grandiose and obvious examples of the differences between the US and UK common law. There are many more subtle disparities – seen at the doctrinal level, as opposed to the level of meta-principles discussed previously – such as the judicial attitude toward contractual interpretation, legal remedies for misrepresentation and breach of contract, and rules relating to implied terms. This book examines a number of important topics of commercial contract law in both countries. The eminent scholars from both the UK and the US who have contributed to this undertaking present their latest research on the most important issues of comparative commercial contract law.

The broader conceptualizations noted previously provide the framework for the comparative analyses in this book. The chapters analyse various themes and topics at levels of theory, doctrine, and practice. In the area of contract theory, analyses are offered on competing theories of contract law, as well as its core concepts – the role and conceptualization of promise and consent. Normative offerings of what the law should be include chapters on a "naturalistic" approach to contracts, the role of contracts in a "networked" world, and the continued role of equity in contract law. So as not to get completely lost in the theoretical and normative realms, the book changes focus to analyse the freedom incumbent in private law as stressed in a chapter on reasonability and contract design. As noted previously, the general duty of good faith has been more openly embraced in US contract law, but mostly rejected in English contract law. A chapter is offered that presents a relational approach to the duty of good faith.

The pivotal role of the judiciary is studied in chapters on implied terms and contract interpretation, and subsequently in chapters reviewing some of contract law's policing doctrines. The foundation of contract law is the principle of freedom of contract. Put simply, private parties create their own law through the contract. Courts mostly play the neutral role of arbiter of disputes but essentially are under a duty to enforce the agreed upon bargain strictly. However, unfettered freedom leads to abuse and overreaching. Because of such misbehaviour, contract law's primary function of facilitating private ordering is accompanied by a secondary regulatory function. This secondary function of contract law primarily regulates impermissible conduct through the policing of unfair terms. This policing, often premised upon the belief that the unfair terms are generally a product of bargaining power and informational disparities, takes two forms – long-standing common law policing doctrines and more recent legislative enactments.

The major area of policing in which differences are apparent is the regulation of unfair terms and the protection of perceived weaker parties. Consumers for the most part have been the beneficiaries of this regulation. Much of this is due to the UK's membership in the EU, which has been active in enacting directives in many areas, such as distance contracts, products liability, privacy protection, and guarantees. One chapter is devoted to conceptualising the remedial scheme for calculating the remedy for the termination of a commercial agency relationship, something which does not exist in the United States. Another chapter examines the regulation of unfair terms under the Draft Common Frame of Reference (DCFR). An American scholar visits the issue of the regulation of unfair terms in software contracts. The scholar speaks to the lack of express regulation of unfair terms in software contracts in the United States and explores avenues for such regulation. Finally, the general policing doctrine of unconscionability is the subject of another chapter. The chapter reviews the American experience in the use of this doctrine in regulating "unconscionable" terms and contracts. This is an area of divergence between American and English common laws. The unconscionability doctrine is more liberally recognized in the United States, although it is important to realize that the doctrine in the United States is almost exclusively used for purposes of consumer protection and plays little role in commercial contracts. Thus, in the area of commercial contracts, American and English laws are very much aligned on this issue.

Two chapters focus their attention on the more targeted, traditional policing doctrine of misrepresentation. One chapter reviews an increasingly chaotic English jurisprudence involving the different types of misrepresentation and suggests the development of an integrated system to replace the current complexity of misrepresentation law. Another chapter re-examines the nature of damages in cases of fraudulent misrepresentation. Another author provides a comparative analysis of damages awarded for documentary breaches under English law and the CISG. This part concludes with an examination of the role (or lack thereof) of the "performance interest" under English and Scottish laws.

Finally, in response to regionalization and globalization, the move towards greater harmonization of laws has become more pronounced and heavily analysed. The movement of EU harmonization of law has advanced into the area of private law including the areas of general contract and sales law. The issues discussed include the difficulties and issues relating to the harmonization of default rules, as opposed to mandatory rules. The most recent attempt at the Europeanization of private law – Proposed Common European Sales Law or CESL – is analysed and critiqued, and, finally, a review of the current state of the international harmonization of sales law as represented by the CISG is offered. The rest of this chapter provides additional information, albeit brief, on the material covered in this book.

1. Topical Preview

At the risk of being redundant, this section provides added detail of the specific topics covered in the book by way of introduction. It provides not only the specific topics but the key issues addressed in those topical areas.

2. Consent and Promise

Part I presents a theoretical inquiry into the role of consent in contract law. In Chapter 2, the author ventures into the quagmire of the many different competing theories of contract law. He points out the interconnections between the different theories and offers an innovative new theory. This theory explains the role of consent though an "agreement plus intention" model. He asserts that this model borrows from the best of the competing theories and offers a consensus model of the bindingness of some, but not all agreements or promises. Chapter 3 questions the premise that the contract is created by the parties' will. Instead, the author asserts that the illusion of party-willed consent is a result of a conflation between consent and efficiency. Therefore, contractual consent is best understood as the product of a three-party interaction among the parties and a judge. From this perspective the idea of self-enforcing contracts becomes illusory. Courts continue to cloak their decisions in the veil of party consent when, in fact, contractual interpretation is merely an exercise of regulatory control. In Chapter 4, the author poses a number of provocative questions including whether mortgage contracts, notably the promise to repay the loan, should be considered as enforceable promises and whether strategic defaults should be considered immoral acts. The deflation of housing prices in the ongoing financial crisis has left many homeowners with the dilemma of continuing to make mortgage payments on homes that are worth less than the principal of the mortgage loan. In such cases, should the mortgage contract, given the traumatic change of circumstances, generate the same expectation of repayment as is found in other contracts?

3. Theories of Contract, Networks, and Equity

Part II challenges conventional contract theories, in particular the classical contract model and the supremacy of the freedom of contract paradigm. In Chapter 5, the author explains that new research findings in neuroscience provide valuable insights into contract law and questions the validity of conventional contract theories. In fact, he argues that contract doctrine fails to reflect the normative commitments represented by consequentialist and deontological theories of human agency. In Chapter 6, the author argues that existing contract law fails to deal adequately with the world of network contracts. As such, it needs to be reformed. First, in contract interpretation a contract that is part of a network of contracts needs to be interpreted on the basis of the context of the network. Second, the interface between network contracting and the regulation of consumer transactions needs to be reflected in contract doctrine. Finally, in Chapter 7, the author examines the role of equitable principles in regulating trust and fiduciary relationships as the basis to support the argument that equitable principles continue to play a major role in the construction of commercial contracts and in the application of commercial contract law. In essence, equity is playing an increasing role in regulating commercial transactions, thereby replacing some functions of contract law.

4. Discrete and Relational Contracting

Part III focuses on the problems and issues presented by online contracting and the role of good faith in the renegotiation of relational contracts. Chapter 8 deals with the phenomenon of mass consumer online agreements and the importance of the necessity for contract law to confront the distinction between offline and online contracting. The author explores the importance of contract design in protecting consumers in online transactions. The core argument is that the online contract's form and manner of presentation are as important as the contract's content. The manipulation of the design of online contracts impacts the quality of consent. The contract drafter can mask the bindingness of the contract and manipulate consumer behavior through design. Therefore, the courts should consider contract design in online consumer contracts in the interpretation and enforcement of the terms of the contract, and the degree of their bindingness. Chapter 9 moves from the discreteness of online consumer transactions to the area of long-term, relational contracting. The author examines the expanded role that the concept of good faith should play in the context of relational contracts. The author argues that the duty of good faith should be more broadly recognised in English contract law, especially in the role of regulating long-term contracts, where dramatic changes in circumstances and expectations often require good faith renegotiation.

5. Implied Terms and Contract Interpretation

Part IV critically evaluates two judicial techniques of contract regulation, namely, implied terms and interpretation. Chapter 10 continues the analysis of the good faith theme of the previous chapter by making the unique argument that the implication of contract terms in English law is often used as a technique to reach minimal thresholds of good faith (despite the lack of a good faith doctrine in English common law). However, the author asserts that because of the limited recognition of the duty of good faith in English contract law, the technique of implied terms cannot be employed to its full extent. The requirement of neutrality largely restricts the discretion of judges to use implied terms as a regulatory method. Chapter 11 reviews different theoretical approaches to contractual interpretation, arguing that none of the existing approaches is satisfactory; and, therefore, a more adequate theoretical method of contractual interpretation is needed. The author advances a law and economics or consequentialist approach to contract interpretation. This approach is represented by a simple question: Given the words the parties used, what is the best (surplus maximizing) interpretation of the bargain? Interestingly, this question leads the author to conclude that the new formalism advanced by some law and economics scholars actually works to decrease party-generated surpluses (increases inefficiency in contract interpretation). Instead, purposivism, contextualism, and consequentialism are forms of interpretation most likely to reduce costs and create surpluses.

6. Contract Law's Regulatory Function

Part V further studies the regulatory function of contract law discussed above in relationship to the regulatory function of implied terms. Chapter 12 investigates the impact of EU law on national contract laws. It examines the EU Directive 86/653 on self-employed commercial agents and its implementation in France, Germany, and the UK. The author shows that the countries' implementations possess substantial variance due to their different perspectives on the protections needed in the principal–commercial agent relationship, as well as the meanings of "compensation" and "indemnity." It concludes by offering an innovative approach to unifying the two forms of recovery under the Directive. Chapter 13 reviews the development of the concept of unconscionability in American contract law and further illustrates how it is used to regulate contractual relationships. The author gives a historical accounting of the doctrine in the United States, assesses the continuing feasibility of the procedural-substantive unconscionability dichotomy, and anticipates future developments in the application of the doctrine. Chapters 14 and 15 offer different perspectives on the important issue of the regulation of standard contract terms. Chapter 14 presents a comparative analysis of legal rules governing unfair contract terms between the US and the UK, critically evaluating the different regulatory approaches employed in the two jurisdictions. It examines the shortcomings of the American Law Institute's Principles of Software Contracts and the EU Directive on Unfair Contract Terms in Consumer Contracts. In the end, each initiative possesses a number of strengths that should be combined to regulate unfair terms better. Chapter 15 provides a broad view of the consolidation of European private law. It examines the past and current attempts at EU private law harmonization and finds that the litany of initiatives have been contradictory in numerous ways. The chapter then focuses on the regulation of unfair contract terms in relationship to the Draft Common Framework Reference (DCFR). It then offers an assessment of the areas of private law harmonization that may be feasible in the short term by using a multi-dimensional approach.

7. Misrepresentation and Breach

Part VI explores legal remedies in contract law for misrepresentations and breach of contracts. Chapter 16 performs a comparative analysis of Australian, UK, and US laws relating to the remedies of rescission and damages for misrepresentation. The author finds the UK approach of awarding damages for misrepresentation to be unnecessarily expansive and argues for repealing the UK Misrepresentation Act of 1967. In its place, he proposes a coherent system of legal remedies for misrepresentation in which the use of rescission and the awarding of damages are clearly delineated by limiting the awarding of damages to cases involving torts (deceit and negligent misstatement). Chapter 17 continues on a similar theme but focuses on the specific area of fraudulent misrepresentation. It looks at the laws of England and Wales in determining that the current law is applied in an overly aggressive way. The previous chapter looked at the law of misrepresentation outside the area of tort and found that the awarding of damages in these areas was overly expansive. Here, the author argues, similarly, that within the tort of intentional misrepresentation the courts have been overzealous in punishing defendants and suggests ways of reforming this area of law. Chapter 18 compares the legal remedies for the documentary breach in international sales contracts by comparing English law and the CISG. In so doing, the chapter illustrates the strengths and weaknesses of the two legal regimes. The comparison is drawn in the context of international commodities trading. On one hand, it is argued that English law is superior because of the precision of its rules while the CISG's open-textured rules are not suitable to speedy decision making in such volatile markets. On the other hand, it is these same open-textured rules that allow the CISG to respond to the peculiar needs of businesses in various unique trade sectors. Chapter 19 provides an intriguing analysis on the enforceability of "keep upon" clauses in England and Scotland. Through this comparative analysis, the authors argue against the expanded use of the specific performance remedy more generally in the law.

8. Contract and Sales Law Harmonization

Part VII examines current trends in the harmonization of contract law. The first three chapters focus on the Europeanisation of private contract law. These chapters review the differences between unifying mandatory and default rules, the pitfalls of private law harmonization in Europe, and the feasibility of the Proposed CESL. Chapter 20 argues that the current efforts to harmonize European contract law are inherently flawed because they fail to note the crucial distinction between mandatory and default rules. It suggests that the focus on the development of harmonized default rules, if not doomed to failure, is likely to only have a marginal impact. The real obstacle to trans-border trade in Europe is the variations in mandatory rules. The chapter therefore concludes that it is in the area of mandatory national laws that the harmonization effort would produce the greatest benefits.

Chapter 21 reviews the proposed Common European Sales Law (CESL) from a number of perspectives: first, whether there is a need for harmonization in European Internet trading and whether the CESL serves that end; second, whether two national laws on a given subject can co-exist. It uses the example of the evolution of Scottish sales law in relationship to English sales law. More importantly, the Scottish mixed system of common and civil law is mined to build a framework for analysing the first attempted harmonization of European contract law through an EU Regulation. Third, it compares the proposed CESL with the UK Sale of Goods Act. In the end, the author sees the CESL as a useful experiment in European private law harmonization – "it would provide an interesting experiment with which to test the claim that the variety of domestic laws in the European Union is a barrier to the achievement of a single market." In practice, it may serve as a means of filling the perceived need to reduce obstacles to cross-border trading by Internet and small- and medium-sized business enterprises. Because of the CESL's optional nature, the chapter concludes that no harm would be caused with its passage while significant benefits would be obtained if businesses widely elected to opt in to the law.

Chapter 22 assesses the current state of the Convention on Contracts for the International Sale of Goods (CISG) effort to harmonize international sales law and draws some valuable implications for the international harmonization of contract law. It provides an analysis of whether there has been a substantive convergence in CISG jurisprudence. The chapter confronts the possible "future" roles of the CISG in harmonizing international sales law. The areas analyzed include whether there is likely to be a continuance of current trends towards substantive convergence, whether the CISG will gain greater operational usefulness, whether the CISG will be used as evidence of customary international law, and whether it will continue to be used as a model for the modernization of domestic sales and contract laws.

II. CONCLUSION

In summary, this book presents comparative perspectives on important issues of commercial contract law. Leading scholars from the United States and all parts of the United Kingdom provide works of original scholarship focusing on the current debates and trends from both sides of the Atlantic. It is the hope that this book will open communications between commercial and contract law scholars from the two dominant common law systems and begin a dialogue so that we may learn from each other. The chapters in the book approach the subject area from a variety of perspectives – doctrinal analysis, law and economic analysis, social-legal studies, as well as other theoretical perspectives. The book covers the major themes that underlie the key debates relating to commercial contract law: role of consent; normative theories of contract law; contract design and good faith; implied terms and interpretation; policing contract behavior; misrepresentation, breach, and remedies; and the regional and international harmonization of contract law.

The comparative nature of the book allows for an assessment of the current state of commercial contract law in the United States, United Kingdom, and to some extent Europe. In the end, the assessment provides opinions on the strengths and weaknesses of the current national and European approaches to two major issues of contract law – how commercial contract law should be reformed to remain relevant given the rapidly changing context of modern commercial practices and whether harmonization of the different contract law regimes is a worthwhile effort. The contributors provide insights on the many commonalities, but more interestingly, the key divergences of the United States and United Kingdom's approaches to numerous areas of contract law. Such a comparative analysis provides a basis for future developments and improvements of commercial contract law in both countries, as well as other countries that are members of the common law systems. At the same time, insights gathered here should also be of interest to scholars and practitioners of the civil law tradition.

2

Competing Theories of Contract

An Emerging Consensus?

Martin A. Hogg

This chapter opens by noting the bewildering array of contract theories that appear to exist in Anglo-American law, contrasting this with the essentially uniform contract theory of the mixed legal system of Scotland. The question posed is whether there is any way through the jungle of competing theories, and whether any consensus is emerging as to the way forward. In answering those questions, the chapter proceeds by considering three major issues: (1) Do any one of the competing theories of contract law describe the law as it is actually formed and applied? Any of those that fail to do so should not be given significant scholarly attention. (2) Do what seem like competing theories actually possess various degrees of commonality? (3) In terms of the recognition of underlying commonalities, is there an emerging consensus as to how an ideal, harmonised, cross-national contract law might take shape? This undertaking will rely heavily on provisions of both the American Restatement (Second) of Contracts and the Draft Common Frame of Reference (DCFR).

The competing major contract theories of contract that will be considered include (1) contract as an exchange of promises; (2) contract as an agreement in fact; (3) contract as based upon the reasonable expectations or reliance of the parties (consequentialism); (4) contract as based upon the assumption by the parties of legally binding obligations; (5) contract as based upon the relationship or status of the parties, such as in an agency or trust relationship; and (6) contract as based upon a transfer of rights between the parties. Each theory will be reviewed for their strengths and weaknesses. The author asserts that only the first two have engendered any widespread adherence by courts, and thus are the only two that can seriously claim to reflect a broad-based understanding of the basis for contract law. The others, while attracting occasional support from courts, have largely been the preserve of academic scholarship. The one exception is the impact of reliance theory on certain areas of contract law.

The chapter also analyses the competing theories of contract in reference to the poles of will/autonomy and consequence/effect. However, such a metric does not properly explain transfer theories of contract law. Such theories are best understood by referencing a third pole, characterised by the content and rights of the contract relationship. The chapter suggests that some theories can be grouped as different views of the same rationale. For example, will theory (promise), agreement, and assumption of obligation should be merged through a revitalised will theory. This new will theory would be based upon the idea that contract is an expression of the parties' will by which they assume, through the medium of agreements or promises, obligations having their source in the normative power of the state.

The final part of the chapter suggests that a consensus is merging in Europe as to the proper characterisation of contract law, as an emanation of the parties' wills in terms of agreement plus intention to be bound as found in the DCFR and the Principles of European Contract Law (PECL). In contrast, such a consensus has not been firmly established in US common law. The doctrine of consideration and the current American view of privity present obstacles for a purely intention-based theory of the common law. Projects like the DCFR present opportunities to reconsider the reach of the doctrine of consideration and third party rights (privity).

I. INTRODUCTION

To a Scots lawyer, the array of competing contract theories, which seek to win over academics, practitioners and judges in some jurisdictions, is a fascinating reminder of a vibrancy of contract theory and discourse largely lacking from Scots private law. Since the publication in 1681 of Stair's magisterial Institutions of the Law of Scotland, Scottish legal thought has held a largely unchallenged view that a contract is based upon an agreement of the parties intended by them to give rise to obligations binding at law.[1] The twin pillars of agreement and intention to be bound – or, as Stair somewhat differently put the intentional element, a manifestation of 'engagement', such being conduct going beyond mere 'desire' or 'resolution'[2] – provided a theory of contract which has proved both uncontroversial and stabilizing. Reliance has had a limited role in Scots contract law (mostly in relation to misrepresentations and to a limited form of pre-contractual liability),[3]

[1] '*Pactum* or paction ... is the consent of two or more parties, to some things to be performed by either of them; for it is not a consent in their opinions, but a consent in their wills, to oblige any of them': James Dalrymple, Viscount Stair, INSTITUTIONS OF THE LAW OF SCOTLAND, I.x.6 (2nd ed. 1693; reprinted, Edinburgh & Yale University Presses: New Haven, CT, and Edinburgh, 1981). This definition – focusing on an agreement, which discloses a consent to be bound – is discussed further later.

[2] Stair, *Id.* I.x.2.

[3] This form of pre-contractual liability arises where B makes an implied, but false, assurance that a contract exists between A and B, which assurance A relies upon to its detriment: for discussion of this form of liability, see Martin A. Hogg, PROMISES AND CONTRACT LAW: COMPARATIVE PERSPECTIVES (Cambridge University Press: Cambridge, 2011), at 197–200.

because it was not required to perform the function it has often played in the Common law in softening injustices caused by application of the doctrine of consideration and a strict approach to privity of contract. Scots law knows no such doctrine of mutual consideration: all agreements intended seriously to give rise to legal obligations are enforced (subject to any requirements of form) whether they be onerous or gratuitous in nature. The same applies to unilateral promises[4]: these are enforceable undertakings in Scots law, and are recognized as a separate class of voluntary obligation alongside contract. This has had the perhaps unsurprising effect of tending to limit talk of 'promissory liability' to unilateral promises alone, and of encouraging the idea of agreement, rather than promise, as the natural explanation for the basis of a contract. Despite such a traditional separation of promissory and agreement language, it is of course possible to characterize agreement as the end process reached by a process of promising, and more will be said of such an approach later.

While the waters of contract theory may have been calm in Scotland, in other systems, among them England and, even more so, the Common Law jurisdictions of the United States, the battles between competing theories of contract law are well known. To the outside observer of such systems, the ideas of promise and agreement, as two separate characterizations of contract, appear to have sat rather awkwardly alongside each other for some considerable time. Many of the leading Common law contract treatises seem to hedge their bets by providing dual descriptions of contract in both agreement and promise-based terms, while adding commentary on how, additionally, reliance explains the bases of certain exceptional forms of contractual liability. When one adds to this the arguments of 'transfer theorists' and 'relational theorists' of contract, as well as the emerging arguments of 'neo-virtue' contract ethicists, it begins to look as if contract has become the playground of legal theorists intent on showing off their new toys. Is there any way through the maze of competing contract theories? Indeed, what are the hopes of any consensus emerging of the direction in which to move the law?

These questions will be addressed in what follows in a three-part analysis. First, there is a review of the strengths and weaknesses of the major competing theories of contract – not all theories describe the law as it actually is; those which fail to do so ought not to command our adherence; second, there is a consideration of whether there are some connections between these differing theories of contract which have hitherto been ignored; and third, there is an examination of whether there is an emerging consensus as to how an ideal, harmonized, cross-national contract law might look, taking in to consideration the provisions of both the Restatement

4 Again subject to any requirements of form (such requirements being set out principally in the Requirements of Writing (Scotland) Act 1995).

(Second) of Contracts[5] and the Draft Common Frame of Reference (the 'DCFR'),[6] the latter almost certainly destined to be implemented legislatively, at least in part, in the proposed Common European Sales Law.[7]

II. THE COMPETING THEORIES OF CONTRACT

There follows a consideration of the main contenders for the most fitting explanation of the binding force of contracts. This discussion is premised on the assertion that theories of contract law, which are merely or largely suggestions of how contract might be conceived of in an ideal world ought not to command our adherence or respect. We are not designing a legal system from scratch and, unless we propose abolishing all existing jurisprudence and establishing a wholly new legal system without any connection to what has gone before, any contract theory which seeks our loyalty ought at least to provide a coherent explanation of the law as it is, one therefore (in systems based upon the idea of precedent) that is capable of explaining the decisions of the courts.

With that in mind, what are the contenders for what might be called a 'general theory of contract', one capable of providing a broad basis upon which the enforceability of contractual relationships as a whole could be said to rest? While certain theories that some might consider as viable contenders may be omitted from what follows, the discussion will be confined to a consideration of the following significant theories of contract:

1. Contract as based upon the promises of the parties
2. Contract as based upon the agreement of the parties
3. Contract as based upon the reliance of the parties
4. Contract as based upon the assumption by the parties of legally binding obligations
5. Contract as based upon the transfer of rights between the parties
6. Contract as based upon the relationship existing between the parties

A. *Contract as Based upon Promises*

One of the greatest difficulties encountered when researching the institution of promising is the common failure of those writing about promise to define their

[5] American Law Institute, RESTATEMENT OF THE LAW: CONTRACTS, SECOND (American Law Institute Publishers: St. Paul, Minnesota, 1981–96).

[6] Christian von Bar and Eric Clive (eds.), PRINCIPLES, DEFINITIONS AND MODEL RULES OF EUROPEAN PRIVATE LAW: DRAFT COMMON FRAME OF REFERENCE (Sellier: Munich, 2009).

[7] COM(2011) 635 final.

terms, most notably the term 'promise' itself. Without agreed terms, people often talk at cross-purposes, imagining that their own understanding of what a promise is, is shared by others. One possible definition of a promise is:

> a statement by which one person commits to some future beneficial performance, or the beneficial withholding of a performance, in favor of another person.[8]

In so defining the term, certain types of conduct are excluded from the category of promises, such as a commitment made by a party only to itself, a statement, which does not relate to a performance in the future, or an undertaking to harm rather than benefit another.[9]

There is an ancient tradition of esteeming promise-keeping that can be traced back to Plato and Aristotle, and doubtless even before.[10] This practice of promise-keeping appears to be a universal phenomenon of human societies,[11] and as a result has been reflected in the law of civilizations both ancient and modern. As a result of the influences of both Roman law (in which one kind of promise, the stipulatio, was a principal plank of contract law)[12] as well, later, of the canon law,[13] in which the act of promising manifested in whatever form so long as supplemented by an oath was sufficient to ground liability, the idea of the promise was utilized both to explain contractual liability and to justify the idea that all contracts should be enforced (pacta sunt servanda[14]). Though the idea of the contract as promise came to be somewhat eclipsed in the Common law by that of bargain and agreement, all Common law systems retain a form of promissory liability (whether through use of the seal or the device of the deed), and agreements are often still analyzed as an exchange of promises: I promise to do x in exchange for your promise to do y. The Restatement (Second) of Contracts grounds its definition of contract in the idea that a contract is a promise or a set of promises.[15] In more recent times, the idea of 'contract as promise' was revived by Charles Fried in his work of the same name, who emphasized the moral basis of contract as promise: we enforce contracts because they are promises, and we enforce promises because morality dictates that that is the right thing to do.[16]

[8] Martin A. Hogg, PROMISES AND CONTRACT LAW, *supra* note 3, at 6.

[9] The component requirements of a promise, and hence things which do not qualify as promises, are discussed in greater detail, *id.* at 10–25.

[10] *Id.* at 68 ff.

[11] Contrary arguments that there are a few societies, such as Tonga and Iran, where the idea of promising is unknown are unconvincing: see *id.* at 52–6.

[12] *Id.* at 111 f.

[13] *Id.* at 79 ff.

[14] On the origins of the maxim, see *id.* at 82, and sources footnoted there.

[15] RESTATEMENT (SECOND) CONTRACTS, s.1.

[16] See Charles Fried, CONTRACT AS PROMISE (Cambridge, MA: Harvard University Press, 1981), at 16.

There are, of course, well-known objections to the idea of contract as promise. A principal one is that it creates an illegitimate link between the moral worth of promises and their normative force: morality is not law, and vice versa. This criticism has proved a powerful one, and reflects a general sense in modern thought that more must be provided by way of explanation for why promises ought to be honored than just our sense that it is morally right to do so. We live in a post-modern age where a shared morality, even a shared view that promises ought to be honored, is becoming increasingly a thing of the past. There are various responses that might be made to this paradigm shift. One is to attack it head on, either in an entirely reactionary way which posits turning the clock back to a prior way of thinking (a tactic unlikely to succeed in anything other than radically reformulated Western societies) or else by positing neo-virtue ethicist arguments for holding to promises and thus contracts.[17] An alternative approach is largely to accept that grounding contract in a mere moral sense that we should honor our promises is insufficient to justify the normative force of contracts, but, at the same time, to argue that the form of the promise (a voluntary undertaking by which the promisor binds him- or herself to a beneficial performance in favor of another) is still a perfectly accurate description of the elements of a contract, albeit that the normative force of such a contract must be located beyond the mere moral sense or will of the promisor. In other words, on this view we need to get beyond the idea of 'contract as promise' as necessarily implying a promissory theory of contract which stresses the morally binding nature of promises. For a generation of contract scholars brought up on Fried's variety of promissory theory that may be difficult, but not impossible, to do. How might this shift to a new species of promissory theory be achieved?

A reconfigured promissory theory of contract might conceive of promising as the mechanism by which an obligational relationship comes into being, while acknowledging that the normative force of the relationship derives from the determination by the state that such a promise-based relationship is to give rise to obligations, and that the obligations so incurred will be such as are assumed by the parties but moderated and supplemented by community values embodied in common law rules and legislative provisions. In other words, a promissory view of contract might be developed in which contract is seen as undertaken voluntarily by parties through the form and medium of promising, such parties in promising subjecting themselves to obligations which have their force in the normative power of the legal sovereign. A promise on this view is simply a manifestation of consent to the imposition of obligations by the legal system.

This new approach to contract as promise – locating normative force in a source other than the mere moral sense of the parties – can also provide an answer to a

[17] Of which there are a number of proponents, of whom Alasdair Macintyre is perhaps one of the best known.

second common criticism of the idea of contract as promise: that normative force cannot be located within the individual will alone, and thus cannot be located in a promise, which is, after all, an act of the will. This objection was popularized by the Enlightenment philosopher Dave Hume, who objected to the idea of the human will as a normative power.[18] To argue that contracts are enforceable because they are acts of the human will was, so Hume argued, a merely sentimental ex-post facto rationalization of the desirable outcome that, in reality, most contracts are honored by contracting parties. However, taking a similar line to that which was just argued in relation to the first objection, Hume's argument can be countered by accepting that the will itself is not the normative force of contractual (or unilateral promissory) obligations. On the contrary, the promisor is merely consenting to the imposition by the law of obligations upon him. Legal systems may respect the free will of parties in entering into contracts (and unilateral promises) without it being necessary to conceive of the will as itself the source of the normative force of the relationships entered into.[19]

A third objection to the idea of contract as being promissory in nature is that the idea of promise is inherently unilateral, whereas contract, by contrast, is a bilateral undertaking.[20] In fact this is an argument that would chime with many Scots lawyers: in Scots law the language of promising is reserved for a voluntary obligation conceived of as distinct from that of contract, namely the unilateral promise.[21] Such a taxonomy presupposes a concept of the promise which is inherently unilateral and of the contract as inherently bilateral. However, this peculiar jurisdictional approach to one side, in a wider jurisdictional context (especially within Common law discourse) it is quite possible to argue that, while promising is indeed a unilateral act, because promises may be made conditionally (I promise to do x if you promise to do y), an exchange of conditional promises is a perfectly rational and logical way of describing the congruence of two unilateral acts in such a way that they produce a bilateral relationship. Likewise, an accepted unilateral promise is a perfectly rational and logical description of a gratuitous contract (a contract formed by one party making a promise which is then simply accepted by the other), an analytical approach favored by the Spanish Scholastic School and taken up by Stair in his description

[18] See David Hume, A Treatise of Human Nature, III.ii.5 (John Noon: Edinburgh, 1739).

[19] This argument is explored in greater depth in Martin A. Hogg, Promises and Contract Law *supra* note 3, at 88–91.

[20] By unilateral is meant 'constituted by one party' and bilateral, in consequence, 'constituted by two parties.'

[21] In the Scots conception of such a promise, the promisor must intend immediately to be bound when making the promise (in the same way as a promisor in English law may immediately bind himself unilaterally by putting his promise in deed form); if the promisor does not intend immediately to be bound, then the promise is not a unilateral promise but a promise requiring acceptance before it will bind, in other words an offer.

of an offer as a 'promise ... pendent upon acceptation'.[22] So, while it is true that a promise is a unilateral act, so long as the promisor does not intend immediately to be bound on making a promise (in which case it will be a genuine unilateral promise), it is possible to argue that a promise made conditionally upon acceptance (or some counter-promise) of the promisee, albeit a unilateral act of the promisor, may be the means by which a bilateral contractual relationship is constituted.

A fourth objection is that, it is said, contract as promise is circular: if I promise on the condition that you promise, I am therefore (it is argued) not promising unless and until you do, but, as you are also waiting for that to happen, the result is that there is a stalemate, with each of us waiting for the other to promise first. The reality, however, is that this does not happen: because an offeree has already had the benefit of receiving the offeror's conditional promise, such offeree has no reason to wait further, and that offeree's acceptance therefore concludes the contract. This objection therefore does not capture the reality of contract formation process.

Lastly, it is said that promises cannot explain so-called simultaneous transactions, such being those where the undertaking of liability appears to occur simultaneously with performance.[23] This is said to be problematic because, as mentioned earlier, a promise relates to a future commitment: one cannot promise what one is doing at the very moment the promise is made. One such simultaneous transaction is said to be an immediate purchase of goods in a shop, where the offer to purchase occurs simultaneously with the handing over of the price and the acceptance of the offer occurs simultaneously with the handing over of the goods to the buyer. The promissory theorist Stephen Smith, concerned that such transactions appear to lack any promises made by the parties, suggests that they cannot therefore be contracts,[24] a conclusion which flies in the face of the recognition by all legal systems of such transactions as contractual. In reality, many such apparently simultaneous transactions in fact contain promises of a future performance, even if such performance happens only a few moments later (such as payment tendered by a credit or debit card which must be electronically authorized by the issuer).[25] In genuinely simultaneous transactions there is, however, admittedly a problem of analysis: they do appear to lack promises of future performance (save ones that might be implied into the contract), and so are anomalous for a promissory theory of contract. It may be that, for such transactions, one must look for a theory which bases the contract on an agreement (conceived of in non-promissory terms) between the parties, or

[22] INST. I.x 6.

[23] The problem is discussed in Stephen A. Smith, CONTRACT THEORY (Oxford University Press: Oxford, 2004), at 62–3, and also in Martin A. Hogg, PROMISES AND CONTRACT LAW, *supra* note 3, at 215–17.

[24] Stephen Smith *Id.* at 62–3.

[25] Martin A. Hogg, PROMISES AND CONTRACT LAW, *supra* note 3, at 216.

an assumption of obligation by the parties, rather than an exchange of promises. If that is true, then the idea of contract as promise would be unable to explain every instance of contract.

Most of the objections mentioned previously do not strike home, save perhaps (for some contracts) the last one, and promissory theory remains valuable in emphasizing the voluntary acceptance of commitment which is the essence of contract, as well as the importance both of objectively manifested declarations of will and the value of personal responsibility (we are evidently most responsible for those things which we undertake voluntarily). However, promissory theory must be careful not to venture too far, and to seek to claim that promise can or should explain the whole content of all contracts. For instance, implied terms conceived of as promises are a fiction stretched too far: it is more honest and transparent to accept that many implied terms simply do not depend upon the will or promises of the parties, but are imposed for policy considerations determined by legislatures or the courts. Nor can promissory theory realistically claim any more that the obligatory force of a contractual promise must be seen as deriving from the human will – we are not after all, as it were, law-makers for ourselves; rather promise need be conceived of as no more than the voluntary faculty through which the parties submit to the imposition of duties upon them by the law. Conceived of in this way, promise still seems an (if not the only) apposite way to describe the nature of contracts, whether of an entirely private or else commercial type, and as a theory it has valuable historical connections to the earlier tradition of promise as the pre-eminent form of voluntary liability, a tradition only later supplanted by that of the agreement.[26] Moreover, as has already been hinted at when describing the way in which the offer and acceptance process can be described in promissory terms, it is perfectly possible to conceive of agreement as the result reached by the mechanism of promising. More is said of this idea in the next section.

B. *Contract as Based upon Agreement*

On this view, a contract is essentially an agreement between the parties, to do or abstain from doing something, which agreement the parties intend to give rise to binding obligations on both of them or conceivably (in systems like Scotland where a gratuitous contract is possible) only on one of them. The agreement is typically considered as arising through a process of mutual exchange of proposed terms called offer and acceptance (though the exchange might equally be called one of conditional promises), but it is possible to conceive of agreement as being reached by other

[26] See further on this history, Martin A. Hogg, Promises and Contract Law, *supra* note 3, chs. 2 and 3.

means (for instance, through both parties assenting to a document prepared by a third party). Agreement has proved a very popular analysis for the nature of contract, both in national systems (such as Scotland, South Africa, England, and France[27]) and in model law. In the Principles of European Contract Law (the "PECL"),[28] the reaching by the parties of a 'sufficient agreement' is (together with the further requirement of an intention by them to be legally bound) the requirement for the existence of a contract.[29] Similarly, in the DCFR, a contract is defined as "an agreement, which is intended to give rise to a binding legal relationship or to have some other legal effect."[30] The utilization of the idea of agreement in these two influential documents is a telling sign within current European contract thinking of agreement as the preferred way of characterizing contract. In both the PECL and DCFR, the promise narrowly defined as a form of unilateral undertaking or unilateral juridical act is conceived of either as a sort of anomalous contract (one concluded without acceptance), as in the PECL, or as a separate species of valid but non-contractual juridical act, as in the DCFR.[31]

The criticisms of agreement-based theory are well known. First, it has been said that it suggests an internal mental meeting of the minds, an impractical requirement which has had to be tempered by an emphasis upon objective, external manifestations of agreement. This tension however is one that runs throughout the whole of contract law, not just contract theory: it colors the rules on formation of contract, error, and interpretation, among other areas of the law. Ultimately the argument that an agreement theory of contract law is undermined by a preference for objective manifestations of consent rather than the determination of actual subjective agreement is rather unpersuasive. Subjective agreement on every aspect of a contract is unlikely in the vast majority of cases ever to be present. Most contracting parties, especially in commercial contracts, simply do not actively ponder all the terms of their proposed agreement in their minds at the time of contracting. Many contracts are entered in to on a standard form basis, or, if negotiated, have their terms drawn up and argued over by legal representatives rather than the parties themselves. In such cases, a search for genuine subjective agreement on the whole terms of the contract would be fruitless. At best, a signature has to serve as an objective manifestation or token of agreement. The practical reality is that the human (or the corporate) mind is usually too elusive to evaluate: courts must inevitably look to

27 See the *Code Civil*, Art. 1134–1.

28 Ole Lando and Hugh Beale (eds.), PRINCIPLES OF EUROPEAN CONTRACT LAW (Revised edition, Kluwer Law International: The Hague, 1999–2003).

29 PECL Art. 2:101(1).

30 DCFR Art. II. – 1:101(1).

31 The proposed Common European Sales Law does not make specific provisions for unilateral promises, given that sales contracts are bilateral promises.

objective manifestations of the will.[32] It is a strength, not a weakness, of agreement theory that it does so.

Second, it is frequently objected that the idea of agreement requires to be supplemented by an intention to be bound to the agreement (by contrast with the promise, which presupposes in its definition an intention to be bound), leading some to conclude that what is crucial is not in fact the agreement of the parties but any form of conduct – agreement being merely one – which demonstrates obligatory intent. It is, however, possible to define agreement in such a way that it includes the idea of obligatory intention (or consent) within the definition. Indeed, this is exactly what Stair did for Scots law when he defined a contract as requiring 'the consent of two or more parties, to some things to be performed by either of them; for it is not a consent in their opinions, but in their wills, to oblige any of them'.[33] Stair places the emphasis in the idea of agreement both on 'the things to be performed' (i.e. the terms) as well, crucially, as on the binding nature of the intended terms: it is an agreement, which must disclose obligatory intent. Thus put, agreement need not be seen as requiring to be supplemented by any extra element, though admittedly it is necessary to explain this understanding of agreement in a way which seems unnecessary with a promise (one can conceive of defining agreement without an obligatory element, but not so with promise). So, while it is true to say that a contract must necessarily demonstrate an intention by the parties to be bound, we can go further than describing it simply as an act by which parties bind themselves (for there are many such types of act) and say that it is 'an agreement by which parties intend to bind themselves' or one in which they 'consent to be bound'. That at least has been the traditional approach of Scots law, which has not felt there to be any deficiency in the idea of agreement so conceived. There are obvious parallels with the consent theory of US contract law espoused by Randy Barnett,[34] though a certain amount of hard work has to be done to coalesce such a theory with the position of the Restatement (Second) of Contracts that '[n]either real nor apparent intention that a promise be legally binding is essential to the formation of a contract'.[35]

32 For a classic judicial application of the objective approach, see *Embry v. Hargadine, McKittrick Dry Goods Co.* 127 Mo. App 383, 105 S.W. 777 (1907). The judgment of the court suggests a preference for what might be called 'subjective objectivity', i.e., an objective manifestation of consent by one party judged from the reasonable perspective of the other party.

33 INST. I.x.6.

34 Randy Barnett, *A Consent Theory of Contract* (1986) 86 COLUMBIA LAW REVIEW 269. His theory is usefully summarized for those new to US Contract Law in ch. 3 of Randy Barnett, THE OXFORD INTRODUCTIONS TO US LAW: CONTRACTS (Oxford University Press: Oxford, 2010).

35 §21. The section continues by stating that 'a manifestation of intention that a promise shall not affect legal relations may prevent the formation of a contract,' thus placing the onus on parties to overcome a presumption against legal enforcement of apparent contracts. See further on intent to contract in US law, Gregory Klass, *Intent to Contract*, 95 VIRGINIA LAW REV. 1437, (2009).

Third, it has been said that, like promise, agreement cannot explain the whole content of many contracts, especially those into which terms are imposed by statute or the common law (the idea of the implied agreement of the parties to such terms being an unconvincing fiction). This is a valid point, but one to which a response has already been suggested in relation to promissory theory: will-based theories, whether promissory or agreement in nature, need not attempt to explain the whole content of contracts as stemming from the will of the parties. All that they need do is (1) to demonstrate that the existence of the contract was the result of a voluntary exercise of the will, and (2) to explain the content of the express terms of the contract, in so far as these are not struck down or over-ridden by statute or public policy. External moderation of the contract's content is, especially in Europe, a growing feature of modern contract law. Such external moderation of contracts reflects a normative reality that parties submit to the imposition of obligations whose content is ultimately determined by the state.

The traditional arguments against agreement-based theories are weak. This may explain in part why, in many jurisdictions, the idea of an agreement intended to be binding on the parties remains the most commonly adopted explanation for contract law. In Scotland, an agreement-based explanation of contract is the sole judicially accepted theory for the basis of contract, albeit that many recent decisions of the courts have emphasized the necessity of demonstrating that it be an agreement which the parties intended to bind themselves to at law.[36] It is interesting to ask why in Scotland this agreement-based theory has gone unchallenged for over 300 years: it may be that a small jurisdiction produces less appetite for legal theory (though the contributions of Hume, Kames, and latterly MacCormick, suggests that legal theory is not a topic without interest to Scots thinkers); it may be that a system of so-called Institutional Writers (i.e. writers treated as authoritatively stating the law) – of which Stair is the foremost – produced a degree of reverence towards institutional contract theory which was lacking in other precedent based jurisdictions (this may well be so, given the adulatory terms in which later writers and courts have talked of Stair); largely, it seems to be because, Scots law having reserved the language of promise for the unilateral promise, an agreement theory of contract is perceived to make most sense of why the law respects contractual undertakings, and has yet to be confronted by a different theory capable of explaining the nature of contract more convincingly. It is a theory, which certainly chimes with Scottish Enlightenment thinking on the importance of the rational will and its place within human relations.

[36] See, for instance, *Aisling Developments Ltd v. Persimmon Homes Ltd* [2008] CSOH 140, 2009 SLT 494; *Baillie Estates v. Du Pont (UK) Ltd* [2009] CSOH 95 (affd. [2009] CSIH 95).

C. *Contract as Based upon Reliance*

If promissory theories tend to be deontological and moral in nature, then reliance theories of contract focus upon the effect produced by party conduct and the equity of having regard to such effect.[37] A reliance view of contract (such as that of Patrick Atiyah's) posits that contractual obligations flow from the detrimental reliance of parties (as well, in Atiyah's grand scheme of obligations law, from the conferral of benefits).[38] Reliance theory has proved especially attractive to the Common law in explaining why some types of promise, not meeting the requirements of consideration or proper form, can nonetheless give rise to liability. The need for such reliance-based explanations of liability is much diminished in systems not requiring mutual consideration for a valid contract and/or readily freely enforcing unilateral promises: there is, for instance, little need for a common law doctrine of promissory estoppel, or for a statutory equivalent such as §90 of the Restatement (Second) of Contracts,[39] if unilateral promises lacking an acceptance, and variations to contracts lacking consideration, can be enforced. An ideal system of private law would surely provide for enforcement of such unilateral promises (which more obviously and fitly explain the nature of many transactions too often shoe-horned into the borrowed clothing of bilateral contracts)[40] as well as contracts unsupported by mutual consideration. The PECL and DCFR models for a possible single European contract law provide to this effect. Where such a model prevails, the case for a general reliance theory of contract law loses almost all of its force: it cannot explain the enforcement of unilateral promises or contracts where no reliance has followed from the making of the contract (so-called executory contracts), yet such promises and contracts are enforced in the law of many legal systems, to the evident disapproval of Atiyah. Atiyah's grand benefit and reliance theory simply fails to explain the nature of such legal systems as they are, and for that reason cannot be accepted as an adequate general theory of contract. At best, reliance can explain some exceptional forms of liability, as model codes tend to provide, and as the law of misrepresentation and some aspects of the law of damages indicate.

37 Apart from reliance, there are other consequentialist explanations of contract, for instance, explanations based upon the most economically efficient use of the parties' resources, but only reliance-based explanations will be considered in this text.

38 See, for instance, Patrick S. Atiyah, Essays on Contract (Oxford University Press: Oxford, 1986), at 21.

39 §90(1) states: 'A promise which the promisor should reasonably expect to induce action or forbearance on the part of the promisee or a third person and which does induce such action or forbearance is binding if injustice can be avoided only by enforcement of the promise. The remedy granted for breach may be limited as justice requires.'

40 See Martin A. Hogg, *Promise: The Neglected Obligation in European Private Law*, 59 International & Comparative Law Quarterly 461 (2010).

D. Contract as Based upon the Assumption of Legally Binding Obligations

The idea of a contract as a voluntary assumption by parties of obligations imposed by the law in consequence of such assumption is not in fact a new one, though it has been re-popularized by Brian Coote in his recent work Contract as Assumption.[41] As an idea it attempts to blend the element of the voluntary conduct of the parties – they must proactively wish to assume liability – with the notion that, ultimately, it is the legal sovereign which imposes the duties resulting from the voluntary assumption[42] – something being 'assumed' suggests a taking on of duties which exist externally and which are superimposed upon the parties' relationship. Avoiding talk of promising or agreement, the theory does not seek to limit the types of conduct which might give rise to such assumption – these are multifarious, and may arise through promising, agreeing, or some other conduct objectively manifesting the desire to be bound. There are elements of this theory in Stair, with his view that parties must move beyond either desiring something and resolving to do something, to the crucial stage of demonstrating 'engagement' (contractual commitment).

The assumption theory has attractive aspects to it: as was suggested earlier in relation to the promissory and agreement theories of contract, will-based theories are best defended when they see the will merely as the means by which parties may consent to the imposition of obligations which derive their normative force from without the parties' relationship. On the other hand, the assumption theory of contractual liability, in concentrating on the mechanism by which duties arise (a voluntary assumption), does not tell us very much about the nature of the duties assumed. To say that a duty has been assumed does little more than tell us that there exists a duty stemming from some variety of free conduct of the parties in accepting the imposition of the duty: but so put, we might be describing unilateral promises, marital obligations, duties deriving from the taking up of an office (e.g. from being director of a company), as well as contractual duties, among others. Unless we know something more about the nature of what was assumed – that it was an agreement to perform some mutual undertakings – we cannot arrive at a complete theory of the nature of contractual duties.

The idea of assumption of obligation is a broad one; ultimately, many of the duties imposed upon human beings could be described in assumption terms. The theory looks almost like a substitution for the idea of free will, rather than as a focused basis for describing the nature of contractual liability.

[41] Brian Hoote, CONTRACT AS ASSUMPTION (Hart Publishing: Oxford, 2010).

[42] The conceptualization of contract in some systems is somewhat difficult to reconcile with this view. Thus the provision of the French *Code civil* (Art. 1134–1) that '[a]greements lawfully entered into take the place of the law for those who have made them' suggests that the law is ousted by the parties' agreement rather than the law's being the source of obligations assumed by the contracting parties.

E. Contract as Based upon the Transfer of Rights

The 'transfer theory' of contract sees contracts as deriving their force from the fact that they embody a transfer of rights from A to B. Whilst such a description plainly fits many contracts, it presupposes that the rights in question pre-exist the formation of the contract. That does not always hold: if I contract to clean your windows, there are no pre-existing rights, which I am transferring to you by contracting with you. Your right to have your windows washed does not exist until we conclude the contract; before that point I merely have a liberty – to undertake or not to undertake to wash your windows – which I have exercised by undertaking to wash them and thereby to bind myself in contract.

The transfer theory cannot explain the field of contract as a whole, although it is possible to discern rights-transfer language embedded in other theories of contract. In Barnett's consent-based approach to contract law, for instance, the language of value-enhancing rights transfers features, as indeed does the language of reliance on such transfers.[43] The effect is that, within Barnett's consent-based theory of contract, elements of both transfer and reliance theories are used to explain features of the law without being used to explain the normative force of contract law in general. This is a largely unobjectionable borrowing of the language of other theories to explain elements of contract law, though there are still dangers inherent in so doing, such as the danger that, even without using the idea of transfer to explain the normative force of contract, the suggestion is still conveyed that all contracts involve a transfer of rights. Such a characterization may be true of all contracts of sale, but it is not true of contracts for services, where rights only come into existence when the service-provider undertakes to perform the services. Caution requires to be shown when borrowing ideas and language from one theory of contract and embedding them in another.

F. Contract as Based upon Relationship

On this theory, what gives contract its force, and determines its content in specific cases, is the relationship which exists between parties who contract. One of the leading advocates of relational contract theory, Ian Macneil, saw contract as relations in which exchange occurs between people.[44] The nature of a relationship of exchange

[43] 'To ensure that a rights transfer is value-enhancing for *both* parties, both parties must assent to transfer their rights to each other': Randy Barnett, THE OXFORD INTRODUCTIONS TO US LAW: CONTRACTS, *supra* note 32, at 71.

[44] See, for instance, Ian Macneil, *Relational Contract Theory: Challenges and Queries*, NORTHWESTERN UNIVERSITY LAW REV. 877, at 878, (1999). Such a theory of relationships of exchange as the nature of contract would evidently find it difficult to accommodate the gratuitous contract, where one party undertakes to perform without receiving anything in exchange.

is often wider and deeper than appears merely from the interaction of the parties in a specific instance of exchange: each may be relying upon societal, commercial or industry norms, or the parties may have a pre-existing relationship which will properly help to determine how the present transaction ought best to be understood.

Before critiquing this theory of contract, it must be acknowledged, in Macneil's defense, that he self-consciously asserted that he was not attempting to craft a general explanation of the normative basis of contracts, but rather to explain contractual relations in the real world.[45] Nonetheless, given Macneil's attempts to map out comprehensively the various types of relationship which can be called contractual, and his usage of the term 'relational contract theory', it is not illegitimate to seek to explore whether his theory does have anything to say about the normative basis for contractual relationships in general. In fact, Macneil asserts that there are various characteristics of contractual behavior which are normative in nature, including (amongst others) reciprocity (getting something back for something given), flexibility, contractual solidarity, and harmonization with the social matrix (which is to say, supra-contractual norms).[46] These norms do not posit a single basis for the nature of contract, but rather assert certain features of common contractual behavior as normative, on Macneil's view because of their repetitive nature: '[s]ince repeated human behavior inevitably creates norms, these behavioral categories are also normative categories'.[47] This clearly locates the normative force of contract law in the positive behavior of contracting parties, which resonates to some extent with traditional will-based theories of contract, given that they traditionally locate normative obligational power within the parties' conduct, specifically conduct manifesting their will to bind themselves.

As an approach focusing on the reality of relationships, it is not surprising that the relational theory is less formalistic than other theories; it may offer solutions to problems at the pre-contractual stage, solutions which other theories find it hard if not impossible to provide; and it justifies calling some things 'contracts' which, according to classic theories of contract would not be, such as a number of common forms of 'heads of understanding' used in construction partnering projects. Relational theory may be argued to have played a role in giving the ideas of 'good faith' and 'trust' a greater prominence in Common law and mixed legal systems, and may also be argued to have scored something of a victory in recent developments in the English legal approach to interpretation of contracts: Lord Hoffmann's 'contextualized' approach to contractual interpretation has more than a ring of relational theory about it.[48]

45 *Id.* at 879, 880.

46 *Id.* at 879–80.

47 *Id.* at 879.

48 See speech of Lord Hoffmann in *Investors Compensation Scheme Ltd* v. *West Bromwich Building Society* [1998] 1 WLR 896, [1998] 1 All ER 98.

Some of these may be welcome developments in contract law. However, the principal problem for relational theory arises when one attempts to use it to answer specific questions in relation to discrete contracts, such as the time a contract was formed, whether a specific term forms part of such a discrete contract, and the entitlement to exercise a contractual remedy in specific circumstances. Using the touchstone of the parties' wider relationship provides no evident answer to such questions (and, Macneil might have replied, it was not intended to), nor do the specific normative behavioral traits of parties provide any obviously clear answer. Whilst relational theory may be useful in reminding us that many contracts are part of a wider relationship between parties which may throw light upon the contract in question, as a general theory of contract it will not do. In that conclusion, Macneil would doubtless have agreed: he was arguing for the importance of understanding contract within its relational framework, not in trying to posit a single, general normative basis upon which contracts rest.

G. *Conclusion on Competing Theories of Contract*

Of the theories discussed previously, only the first two (the promissory and agreement-based theories) have engendered any widespread adherence by courts, and they are thus the two theories which compete for the claim of best reflecting the understanding of courts about what they are doing when they enforce contracts. The others, while attracting occasional support from some courts, have largely been the preserve of academic discussion, albeit that reliance thinking has crept in to contract law as an additional factor in certain limited fields, and that it can be said that the idea of assumption of obligation (or consent to the imposition of obligation) reflects the element of an intention to be bound which features in agreement-based theory. The fact that the idea of an assumption of obligation, while insufficient as a stand-alone explanation of contract, has featured within agreement-based theories indicates that it is not impossible to detect cross-streams of influence between the various theories considered. In the following section therefore, there is an examination of whether these various cross-streams can be drawn together in an explanation of contract law capable of uniting the disparate concerns underlying the spectrum of theories.

III. CONNECTIONS BETWEEN COMPETING THEORIES OF CONTRACT

In reading academic treatments of discrete contract theories, connections with other theories, as well as the historical merging of certain theories into others, are often overlooked. Looking for such connections and historical developments may, however, assist in finding a way through the theoretical maze.

TABLE 2.1. *A bipolar taxonomy of contract theories*

WILL/AUTONOMY	CONSEQUENCE/EFFECT
Promissory theory	Reliance theory
Agreement theory	Relational theory
Assumption of obligation theory	

What connections between the various theories of contract are discernible? One area of inter-theory connectivity is discernible when one examines whether specific contract theories emphasize (on the one hand) party autonomy and the will, or (on the other) the consequences and effects upon parties of contracting. Using these two criteria, it is possible to classify contract theories as indicated in Table 2.1.

The promissory, agreement, and assumption of obligation theories, each rest[49] upon a belief that contracts derive their normative force from a voluntary exercise of the will of the contracting parties: such parties, in objectively demonstrating contractual intent, indicate a willingness to be bound to an obligation-creating relationship (the same might be said of a unilateral promisor in relation to unilateral promise). By contrast, reliance and relational theories of contrast emphasize the consequences or effect of contracting (they produce reliance, or they reflect a relationship of exchange existing between the parties) as critical in determining the nature of contract.

Where does transfer theory fit in to this picture? As a theory which emphasizes both the element of the will (the transfer of rights intended by transferor and transferee) as well as of effect (the focus is on the result intended, the transfer of the rights in question), transfer theory may be placed somewhere between these two poles. Essentially, its prime focus is on the content of contracts, as revised Table 2.2 indicates.

The three types of will-based theory listed have been advanced, at various times, as distinct, separate theories, albeit linked by their focus on the will. Such distinct conceptualization misses an opportunity to draw the strands together. As suggested earlier in the discussion of these theories, it is possible to draw together the three theories by positing contract as an agreement, reached through the process of promising, by which the parties intend to assume, or to have imposed upon them, obligations. So stating matters is not merely a neat academic trick which conflates the three into a convenient catch-all theory, but it can be argued to disclose the developmental stages of a will-based contract theory. Though the following broad

[49] At least, as traditionally conceived. A new approach to conceiving of normative force in will theories is advocated later.

TABLE 2.2. *A tripolar taxonomy of contract theories*

WILL/AUTONOMY	CONSEQUENCE/EFFECT
Promissory theory	Reliance theory
Agreement theory	Relational theory
Assumption of obligation theory	

CONTENT (RIGHTS)
Transfer Theory

brush description glosses over the historical details,[50] one can in the theory of voluntary obligations trace an early legal and moral focus on the act of promising (reflected in promissory theory) which came in time to be replaced by a greater mercantile emphasis upon agreement (reflected in agreement theory), such agreement coming eventually to be seen within the context of an increasing subjugation of parties' transactions to external regulation and thus, ultimately, as the mechanism by which parties might subject themselves to obligations deriving their force not from their own will but from their assent to duties whose normative force lies in the authority of the legal sovereign (reflected in assumption of obligation theory).

It is suggested that these three grand ideas of voluntary obligation, developed slowly over time, lying at the core of the three will theories of promise, agreement and assumption, are capable of being reflected in a single, revitalized will theory, containing within itself the marks of each of the historical developments described. If a nomenclature is needed for such a revitalized will theory in order to distinguish it from classical will theory, then the term 'co-operative will theory' might well be found suitable: in such a revitalized will theory, the contracting parties are (under the increased influence of external normative considerations) expected to show more by way of co-operation with each other than under classical will theory, as well as to co-operate (in the exercise of their will) with the restrictions placed upon the will by external norms, rules and values. In such a co-operative will theory, the nature of contract may be described in the following way:

> An agreement, based upon the promises[51] of the parties, disclosing the intention of the parties to bind themselves to obligations which have their normative force in, and which are moderated by, the legal sovereign (i.e. the state).

[50] The historical development is explored in much greater detail in chapters 2 and 3 of Martin A. Hogg, PROMISES AND CONTRACT LAW, *supra* note 3.

[51] Or, in cases where no future performance of the parties is pledged (as may possibly be the case with simultaneous transactions, discussed earlier) some other, non-promissory, conduct indicating an intention to be bound.

Such a co-operative will theory would offer a number of benefits to modern contract law over other theories, including the following benefits:

(i) It offers the best explanation for the recognition by modern courts of a doctrine of freedom of contract which is tempered by increasing external control and regulation of such freedom. Traditional promise or agreement-based theories, in locating the normative force of contracts in the promises or agreement of the parties, cannot explain why the will of the parties is very often over-ridden by reference to external normative considerations. They cannot, for example, satisfactorily explain such features of contract law as the imposition of implied terms into classes of contract without regard to the will of the parties,[52] the 'completion' of contract by courts where parties appear still to be at odds on essentials of the relationship (for instance the price),[53] and restraints placed upon party autonomy justified by reference to duties of 'good faith'.[54] Such increasing external normative restraints have been described within a European legal context as 'tightening protective standards', and as leading to 'an increasingly inseparable combination and mix of those parts of contract law which have enabling character (facilitative law) and the regulatory parts, establishing and safeguarding (market) order'.[55] The co-operative will theory is capable of explaining such aspects of the external legislative and judicial moderation of agreements in the context of a continued respect for the autonomy of the parties as determinative of the existence of a contract, the greater part of its content, and the conditions for remedial entitlement.

(ii) In retaining the central element of a voluntary exercise of the will of the parties as the constitutive means for the assumption of their duties, co-operative will theory provides an important continued emphasis upon the values of personal liberty and responsibility. Continued judicial emphasis upon the importance of a free choice as lying at the root of contractual obligation is one important bulwark against growing government tendencies (on both sides of the Atlantic) to diminish the sphere of personal autonomy. An ever greater proportion of people's lives is subject to government control and regulation, much of it justified in protective, paternalistic terms with which it is difficult

[52] So-called terms implied in law.

[53] As occurred, for instance, in the Scottish case of *Avintair v Ryder Airline Services* 1994 SC 270, 1994 SLT 613.

[54] Whilst English law has traditionally been antagonistic to good-faith-based duties or remedial restraints being imposed upon contracting parties, a duty of good faith and fair dealing in both performance and enforcement is contained in the RESTATEMENT (SECOND) CONTRACTS, §205.

[55] See Stefan Grundmann, *The Future of Contract Law*, EUROPEAN REV. OF PRIVATE LAW 490, at 500–509, 527 (2011).

to disagree without appearing to be indifferent to the ill effects which sometimes arise from the self-interested exercise of personal freedom. Yet history has many lessons for us of the consequences of radically restricting personal, including contractual, freedom, and of blunting the consequences of personal responsibility. The largely stagnant economies of the former Soviet bloc testify to the dire economic and social consequences, which resulted from the near absence of any contractual freedom. While such ill effects were never visited upon Western democracies to such an extent, economic stagnation in those democracies during the 1960s and 1970s went hand-in-hand with a growing attack upon contractual freedom and on the importance of party autonomy and responsibility. The consequentialist contract theories popular among academics in those decades sought to downplay the will as the crucial element in contractual formation and content, and cast undertakings to perform duties as giving rise not to genuine responsibility to perform such duties but merely to pay damages if any loss resulted. Yet those academic attempts failed ultimately to produce a sea-change in judicial thinking: courts continued to recognize the central element of the human will in determining the existence of, and content of, voluntary obligations, albeit at the same time softening some of the perceived hard edges of self-interest. The continued value placed by courts on party autonomy, given the economic and social benefits such autonomy brings, is recognized in the co-operative will theory.

(iii) In abandoning earlier attempts by will-based theories to explain the whole content of contract by reference to the will of the parties, the co-operative will theory sensibly rejects highly fictional attempts to explain things such as terms implied into classes of contract as deriving from the presumed intention of the parties. Such attempts by will-based theories in the past were in great part responsible for such theories falling out of favor: in attempting to explain too much of contract law, they seemed to undermine the idea of the will as having any useful function to play in contract theory. By recognizing that normative forces reside outside the will of the parties, and by therefore allowing for regulation and control of contractual content and remedial entitlement by reference to legislative provisions and common law norms, the will is given a reduced and more practical territory to occupy.

(iv) Co-operative will theory recognizes the importance and legitimacy of tempering personal contractual freedom by reference to external societal norms such as good faith, equity, non-oppression and reasonableness. Few today, except perhaps strict libertarians, would argue that the wholly unfettered will of contracting parties is capable of providing the most equitable form of contractual liability. In an age where, for instance, standard form, small print agreements have become the norm in consumer contracts, a complete

> absence of any control of the use of such contract form would be likely to lead to a near universal abuse of the position of the party controlling such terms. The case for modifying the rules on what becomes part of the contract and/or for substantive control of certain types of unfair terms has been largely won, at least on the European side of the Atlantic. Indeed, on both sides of the Atlantic, common law external controls on contract formation, content, and remedial entitlement have always operated through a combination of both legal and equitable default rules. However, earlier manifestations of contract theory have failed sufficiently expressly and coherently to marry the justification for such external controls with respect for party autonomy. Where the line should lie between the two will doubtless continue to be a hotly debated issue between libertarians and paternalists, but that the two are capable of being integrated into contract theory is a major benefit of the co-operative will theory.

For the preceding reasons (amongst others), it is suggested that co-operative will theory is capable of explaining modern European contract law well. It also presents itself as a credible model for explaining US Common law, which, while it has traditionally shown a greater respect for the personal autonomy of contracting parties (as befits the constitutional libertarian tradition of the United States), has increasingly to explain statutory incursions into such contractual freedom, even if at present they remain less far-reaching.

A revitalized, co-operative will theory of the type described previously would not merely enable the various strands of the disparate will theories to be married, it would also allow the concerns underlying consequentialist theories of contract law to be addressed. Co-operative will theory recognizes the legitimacy of such concerns through stressing that the normative force of contracts derives from a source external to the parties' own will, and that, in consequence, their determination of the content and effect of contracts may be moderated to reflect externally determined normative considerations. Table 2.2 may be amended to represent how co-operative will theory is capable of marrying respect for the will with a concern for equitable moderation traditionally associated with consequentialist theories (see Table 2.3). In effect, co-operative will theory straddles the divide between the traditionally conceived will and consequential families of contract theory.

Is co-operative will theory likely to prove attractive to courts and scholars? It is worth stressing that it is not suggested that systems with a settled and unchallenged view of contract theory (like Scots law) need necessarily adopt a co-operative will theory incorporating all of the elements of the three existing variations of will theory. A contract theory, like that of Scots law, based upon the notion of agreements disclosing obligatory intent would not necessarily have to add in the extra element of promise as the mechanism to reach agreement if that were thought to be an unnecessary

TABLE 2.3. *Co-operative Will Theory*

WILL/AUTONOMY		CONSEQUENCE/EFFECT
Promissory theory Agreement theory Assumption of obligation theory	⇨ *Co-operative will theory: will as the means to assume, through agreements/ promises, obligations having their force in, and moderated by, the legal sovereign.* ⇦	Reliance theory Relational theory
	CONTENT (RIGHTS)	
	Transfer Theory	

accretion (and a potentially somewhat confusing one, given the separate obligation of promise already recognized in the law). However, all legal systems having some variety of will-based theory as their general contractual theory face the challenge of explaining consequentialist elements of contract law and the increasing state regulation of contracts. Adoption of a co-operative will-based theory which (whether or not it draws expressly in its formulation upon all three historic developmental strands of will theory) conceives of the will as the faculty of assuming obligations deriving their normative force from a source beyond the parties themselves, and one therefore which can accommodate and explain external regulation of contractual content, will prove necessary for any system which hopes to continue to utilize the will as a central element in contract theory as the twenty-first century progresses.

It is noteworthy that, in what has been said about co-operative will theory, it has not been suggested that the traditional doctrines of consideration and privity of contract should have any role to play. These doctrines always proved difficult to accommodate within a theory of contract said to rest upon the human will, for why should the human will, if it is indeed the determinative force in contract, be restricted by a requirement that both parties must have given consideration under the contract or a rule that third parties cannot be the beneficiaries of enforceable contractual rights if the contracting parties so will? Ultimately, there is no convincing answer to this question save to recognize that, whatever other constraints may be justifiable on the will of contracting parties, a requirement of mutual consideration and a denial of third party rights are not among them. The challenge this poses for the Common law of contract is considered in the following, final section.

IV. FUTURE DEVELOPMENTS OF CONTRACT THEORY: AN EMERGING CONSENSUS?

Finding a consensus among academics on contract theory has proven an elusive hope in most jurisdictions; followers not just of will theories but of the other varieties of contract theory flourish in University law schools, ensuring that new adherents of these competing theories arise in successive generations. Yet while this may be true of academia, in the emerging European new ius commune will theory appears largely to predominate in the minds of policy makers and practitioners, a will theory based either upon the twin pillars of agreement and intention to be bound (in both English and Scots thinking, albeit with some contemporaneous conceptualizations in 'promissory' terms in England), or, to the same effect if expressed slightly differently, upon the concurring declarations of will of the parties intended to have binding effect (in the Germanic tradition).

Such a consensus is evident from the adopted texts of recent pan-European contract projects, where it is an agreement-based expression of the will, which has been utilized in the definition of contract. Both PECL[56] and the DCFR[57] adopt such an agreement approach in their provisions, each of these projects representing a cross jurisdictional consensus that the proper theoretical basis for contract lies in the idea of an agreement intended by the parties to be binding. The relevant provision of the proposed Common European Sales Law repeats the agreement-based definition of the DCFR.[58]

Other emerging consensuses about contract law are discernible in the text of the PECL and the DCFR, among them that

(1) Freedom of contract is the foundational principle of the law of contract,[59] a view which further supports the consensus that it is an exercise of the free will of the parties which triggers the imposition of contractual obligations;
(2) The intention of a contracting party is to be judged objectively, by considering how such a party's conduct would have appeared to a reasonable person in the position of the other party[60];
(3) Contracts do not require mutual consideration in order to be valid and enforceable (in other words, a gratuitous contract is entirely possible);
(4) A unilateral promise is to be given legal effect, if seriously intended by a promisor to have such effect[61];
(5) Despite the statement in the Principles preceding the text of the DCFR that "[a]nother ingredient of contractual security is the protection of reasonable reliance and expectations in situations not covered by the doctrine of contractual loyalty", the role given to reliance is in fact quite restricted – it explains

56 PECL Art. 2:101(b).
57 DCFR Art. II.-1:101(1).
58 Proposal for a Common European Sales Law, COM(2011) 635 final, Art. 30(1).
59 DCFR Principle 3 ('Freedom of contract the starting point'), and Art. II.-1:102(1); PECL Art. 1:102.
60 DCFR Art. II.-4:102; PECL Art. 2:102. In German law, this is referred to as the doctrine of the 'objective horizon' of the recipient of a contractual declaration, or *Empfängerhorizont*.
61 DCFR Art. II.-1:103(2); PECL Art. 2:107.

liability for misrepresentations,[62] it plays a limited role in the rules on the revocation of offers[63] and the crystallization of third party rights,[64] and it forms part of a rule preventing inconsistent dealing which is contrary to the good faith principle.[65] No greater role is needed for reliance on account of the DCFR's/ PECL's enforcement of gratuitous contracts and unilateral promises; and

(6) Freedom of contract is properly restrained, in the name of community values and societal well-being, through other restraining devices, such as inequality of bargaining power and abuse of a dominant position. The good faith principle manifests itself in various specific ways, such as in a duty to negotiate in good faith,[66] a requirement that a court interpret contract terms in good faith,[67] as part of the test for judging whether a term in a contract is unfair (and thus potentially invalid),[68] and, significantly, as a required characteristic of a party's conduct in the performance of its obligations and in the exercise of its rights or remedies under the contract.[69] These checks on freedom of contract can evidently not be explained by reference to the will of the parties, hence the need for a theory of contract such as the co-operative will theory suggested earlier capable of marrying the will with external normative controls. No theory can, however, explain where exactly the boundary properly lies between freedom of contract and such external restraints: this remains, in all legal systems, a matter of on-going debate.

These emerging consensuses are largely uncontroversial for civilian systems and for the mixed legal system of Scotland, though Common law jurisdictions are confronted with a challenge to the fundamental doctrines of consideration and privity and to the need to employ gap fillers such as promissory and proprietary estoppel. They are also confronted by a challenge to the noted tendency of the Common law to force essentially unilateral undertakings into the bilateral form of contract: if someone promises to reward another for doing something, why not simply accept that this is a unilateral promise and treat it as such? Characterizing such an act as a 'unilateral contract' or an 'option contract', with the added difficulty of how to ensure that the offeror does not seek to revoke the offer once the offeree has begun to perform, unnecessarily complicates matters. If such an act is seen as a unilateral

62 DCFR Art. VI.-2:207.

63 DCFR Art. II.-4:202(3)(c).

64 DCFR Art. II.-9:303(3).

65 DCFR Art. I.-1:103(2): "It is, in particular, contrary to good faith and fair dealing for a party to act inconsistently with that party's prior statements or conduct when the other party has reasonably relied on them to that other party's detriment."

66 DCFR Art. II.-3:301(2).

67 DCFR Art. II.-8:102.

68 DCFR Art. II.-9:403–5.

69 DCFR Art. III.-1.103.

promise, and enforced as such, the promisor is irrevocably bound to fulfill the terms of the conditional promise of reward as and when the condition is fulfilled.[70] Unilateral promise provides a useful model for a number of features of both private and commercial transactions which are currently rather awkwardly made to take contractual form in order to overcome the general unenforceability of unilateral promises in the Common law.[71]

Will the distinctive attitude of the Common law withstand the current pressure upon it from harmonization projects? The prediction of the success of the DCFR as a politico-legal enterprise is beyond the scope of this paper,[72] but the promulgation of such projects at least presents a good opportunity for debates between Common, Civilian and Mixed system lawyers as to the core elements of a contract doctrine which accurately describes the nature of contract in modern Western legal systems, elements shorn of any adornment unnecessary for, or inconsistent with, the putting into effect of the intention of the parties.[73] While it has been suggested that co-operative will theory can perform that task, it is also suggested that such a theory does not require the doctrine of mutual consideration, the non-enforcement of seriously intended unilateral promises, nor the prevention of contracting parties from conferring enforceable rights upon third parties to contracts if they so desire.

V. CONCLUSION

A contract debate which might lead to a re-thinking by Common Law jurisdictions of the need for these restrictions on the autonomy of contracting parties would be a welcome one. English law to some extent, and US Common Law more so,[74] have historically been largely unreceptive to doctrinal development resulting from

[70] Barnett favors seeing so-called unilateral contracts such as that in *Carlill* v. *Carbolic Smoke Ball Co.* [1893] 1 Q.B. 256 as unilateral promises, binding when made, rather than as offers accepted by conduct (see Randy Barnett, THE OXFORD INTRODUCTIONS TO US LAW: CONTRACTS, *supra* note 32, at 82), albeit that he cannot bring himself to treat a unilateral promise as a separate species of voluntary obligation, but rather characterizes such cases as contracts made by way of unilateral promise.

[71] For discussion of such transactions, see Martin A. Hogg, 'Promise: The Neglected Obligation in European Private Law', *supra* note 37.

[72] And, at the time of writing, only a modest beginning to implementation of the CFR project has been proposed, namely, the Common European Sales Law referred to earlier, supra note 7.

[73] The requirement of consideration causes, for instance, an insurmountable problem for the Common Law in definitively recognizing a gratuitous relationship of agency as a contract, even if such a characterization would otherwise reflect the intentions of principal and agent.

[74] 'American cases rarely cite foreign materials. Courts occasionally cite a British classic or two, a famous old case, or a nod to Blackstone; but current British law almost never gets any mention ... American lawyers and jurists have been, on the whole, extremely parochial': Lawrence M. Friedman, AMERICAN LAW IN THE TWENTIETH CENTURY (Yale University Press: New Haven, CT, 2004), at 575.

external legal influence. Such insularity is in contrast to the experience of the mixed legal system of Scotland, which in contract law (as in many other parts of private law) has been markedly shaped by non-native doctrinal influences. Though some such influences were, in retrospect, brought to bear in a way which did not properly respect existing law or structures, the end result has been a law of contract which is outward looking and ready to be creative in its search for appropriate solutions to perceived problems, whatever (or wherever) their source might be. In an increasingly globalized world, contractual insularity is going to be increasingly impracticable. A Common Law which was more receptive to doctrinal and theoretical developments resulting from a comparative legal dialogue would be a law more likely to continue to be attractive as the lex contractus for commercial as well as private parties. The transatlantic conversation which led to publication of the present work might fruitfully be just the start of a reconnection of US contract law with the rest of the Common law world and indeed with other legal traditions.

3

Contracts, Courts, and the Construction of Consent

Thomas W. Joo

Anglo-American contract law sometimes acknowledges that the legal construct of "objective consent" is distinct from actual subjective consent. But contract law also labors to obscure this distinction and conflate the two concepts – indeed, the very term "objective consent" performs this function. Economic analysis of law sometimes engages in a similar conflation by treating the efficiency of an arrangement – as determined by a judge (or an academic theorist) – as a perfect proxy for subjective consent to that arrangement.

Basing contractual obligations on judicial assessments of outward phenomena means contract law depends at least in part on judges' subjective notions of policy and fairness. Conflating this court-centered process with subjective consent is descriptively inaccurate. It is also faulty normative reasoning, as it invokes simple libertarian rhetoric to justify a more complex, statist process. The conflation problem is especially relevant with respect to form contracts, which fit uneasily with traditional notions of subjective consent. Courts and theorists should avoid the easy invocation of "consent" as the basis of contract law and instead be more specific in disclosing– and defending – the normative assumptions behind their prescriptions.

I. INTRODUCTION

Contract law is fundamentally oxymoronic in that it involves the state enforcement of "consensual" commitments. That is, contractual obligations are said to have distinctive legal status because they are voluntarily assumed. But that voluntary quality is, paradoxically, invoked to legitimate the use of state power to coerce individuals into honoring such obligations. Theorists sometimes argue that contracting parties consent in advance to precisely such a state encroachment on their liberty.[1]

[1] *E.g.*, *Richard* A. Posner, *Are We One Self or Multiple Selves? Implications for Law and Public Policy*, 3 LEGAL THEORY 23, 34 (1997).

However, this theoretical justification raises the question of whether any person can truly "consent" to waive the liberty of his "future self," whose preferences are unknown at the time of contracting.[2]

The paradox deepens: not only does the state enforce "consensual" obligations; it also defines what constitutes "consent." Because consent cannot be directly observed, the "objective theory" of contract looks to outward manifestations of intent. Without the ability to read minds, it is impossible to base law purely on the parties' actual subjective intentions. As far back as the sixteenth century, a discussion of contracts in a legal text noted, "The intent inward in the heart, man's law cannot judge."[3] The objective theory does not solve this problem; it sidesteps it by redefining "consent" independently of subjective intention. Oliver Wendell Holmes famously stated that "the law has nothing to do with the actual state of the parties' minds. In contract, as elsewhere, it must go by externals, and judge the parties by their conduct."[4] The Second Restatement of Contracts puts it even more bluntly: "The conduct of a party may manifest assent although he does not in fact assent."[5] The more the law succeeds in avoiding the practical difficulties of identifying subjective intent, the less relevance the "consent" inquiry has to the putatively fundamental question of party autonomy. The objective theory has traditionally located consent in "reasonable" manifestations of assent and "reasonable" contract terms. A contemporary variation replaces the "reasonable" with the economically "rational" or "efficient."

In hard cases, an objective analysis of contractual consent cannot reliably tell us whether the parties actually intended to be obligated or what they understood the terms of their obligations to be. Indeed, the court may simply be forced to decide what it thinks the obligations between the parties *should* be. The argument that there is a tension between "objective consent" and the libertarian theory of contract is of course not a new one.[6] The aim of this chapter is not to rehash that argument, but to examine how legal rhetoric attempts – with much success – to disguise the

2 Derek Parfit, *Later Selves and Moral Principles, in* PHILOSOPHY AND PERSONAL RELATIONS 137 (A. Montefiore ed. 1973). Even if intent to be legally bound is possible in theory, American contract doctrine does not require it. AMERICAN LAW INSTITUTE, RESTATEMENT OF THE LAW, SECOND, CONTRACTS § 21 ("Neither real nor apparent intention that a promise be legally binding is essential to the formation of a contract."). English law nominally requires such intent, although that requirement has been characterized as a "doctrinal fiction." Gregory Klass, *Intent to Contract*, 95 VIRGINIA L. REV. 1437, 1453–60 (2009).

3 Quoted in Joseph M. Perillo, *The Origins of the Objective Theory of Contract Formation and Interpretation* 69 FORDHAM LAW REVIEW 427, 432 (2000).

4 Oliver Wendell Holmes, Jr., THE COMMON LAW 242 (Mark DeWolfe Howe ed., Little, Brown: Boston 1963).

5 RESTATEMENT (SECOND) OF CONTRACTS § 19(d).

6 *E.g.*, Stephen Hedley, *Keeping Contract in Its Place – Balfour v. Balfour and the Enforceability of Informal Agreements*, 5 OXFORD J. LEGAL STUDIES 391, 393 (1985) ("the tests ostensibly aimed at discovering the parties' intentions almost invariably lead the courts to impose their view of a fair solution to the dispute").

tension by conflating "contract" (in the sense of consensual bargains) with "contract law" (i.e., rules created by legislatures and courts). Corporate law manipulates the rhetoric of "contract," taking advantage of the word's associations with consent to enhance the legitimacy of corporations and corporate law on libertarian grounds while disguising their nonconsensual aspects.[7] So too does contract law employ the rhetoric of "consent" to justify the role of the state and disguise the nonconsensual aspects of contract law itself. This both reflects and reinforces the belief that "freedom of contract" can and should be the organizing principle of contract law. Indeed, it is contract law's skillful use of libertarian rhetoric that give it the rhetorical clout that other legal subfields, such as corporate law, draw upon.

The legitimating power of "freedom of contract" rhetoric derives from two independent theoretical postulates: first, a categorical commitment to individual liberty and, second, a consequentialist theory that consensual transactions enhance utility. Economists since Adam Smith have argued that the "invisible hand" of the market allocates resources efficiently, and that consensual obligations (*i.e.*, market transactions) thus further both individual liberty *and* social welfare. The pairing of these categorical and consequentialist justifications can provide consent-based contract theory with dual sources of legitimacy. But this duality can be destabilizing if the law must choose between the two values of liberty and efficiency. Some theorists and, occasionally, courts, believe a court should identify and enforce not consensual bargains, but arrangements that would be most welfare-enhancing, or "economically efficient." Rather than face the choice between the values of liberty and efficiency, however, many theorists and judges have tried to avoid it by arguing that consent is always efficient. The consensual bargain *is* the efficient allocation. From this, some argue that a court should limit itself to identifying consent, because this is sufficient to serve both liberty and efficiency.

But this argument sends us full circle back to the problem discussed previously. Actual consent is often impossible to identify via factual inquiry, and thus must be identified using normatively loaded "objective standards" that drain "consent" of its libertarian meaning. The supposed identity of consent and efficiency is sometimes invoked as a solution to this problem. If the efficient allocation and the consensual bargain are necessarily the same, the law can find the consensual bargain by identifying the efficient allocation. This is hardly a solution, however. Rather, it is another iteration of the same problem. That is, the "efficient" allocation is at least as difficult to identify and normatively contingent as the "consensual" bargain. It is merely a new type of "objective" measure of assent.

7 Thomas W. Joo, *Contract, Property, and the Role of Metaphor in Corporations Law*, 35 UC Davis L. Rev. 779 (2002).

This chapter will consider how the rhetoric of United States contract law disguises the oxymoron of "objective consent," in particular, how it does so by conflating consent with efficiency. In recent decades, libertarianism and free-market economics have gained renewed influence on politics, legal theory, and jurisprudence. This trend has been particularly pronounced in – but by no means limited to – the U.S. After all, British thinkers like Smith pioneered the notion of the convergence of liberty and efficiency. Courts and theorists on both sides of the Atlantic should move away from the empty invocation of "consent" as a justification for contract enforceability and instead be more specific in disclosing, and defending, the normative criteria they use to construct their prescriptions. The difficulty in maintaining the distinction between consent and efficiency, and, more broadly, between contracting and contract *law*, is also important for other nations to observe as they develop market-centered legal and economic institutions.

II. CONFLATION OF EFFICIENCY AND CONSENT

Under a libertarian approach to contract, the moral basis for enforcing a contractual obligation lies in the fact that the obligation was freely assumed. This party-centered approach to contract can be contrasted with a consequentialist approach that considers the benefits to society. Welfare economics, for example, suggests that bargains should be enforced because – and only insofar as – they are efficient; that is, that they increase *overall* economic welfare.

This economic principle does not tell us what institution is best qualified to identify efficiency. Ian Ayres argues that "nothing in economics can define what beginning premises or assumptions are empirically reasonable," and he declares himself relatively "sanguine about the capacity of courts or legislatures" to reach efficient results.[8] Similarly, Richard Posner has argued that "in many cases a court can make a reasonably accurate guess as to the allocation of resources that would maximize wealth."[9] Melvin Eisenberg has recognized that courts faced with enforcing contracts sometimes have to choose between consent and efficiency (among other values), and that efficiency should take precedence in such cases.[10] This approach,

[8] Ian Ayres, *Valuing Modern Contract Scholarship*, 112 YALE L.J. 881, 887 (2003).

[9] Richard A. Posner, THE ECONOMICS OF JUSTICE 62 (Harvard University Press: Cambridge, Mass. 1981).

[10] Melvin Eisenberg, *The Bargain Principle and Its Limits*, 95 Harvard L. Rev. 741, 752–54 (1981). While "efficiency" is mainly associated with market-conservative economic views, Eisenberg invokes it to justify substantive unconscionability doctrine, which is generally associated with consumer protection. He argues that courts should invalidate contract provisions that provide for substantively inefficient exchanges even if there were no defects in the bargaining process – that is, even if the contract was "freely" entered into.

then, seeks normative legitimacy in economic efficiency, not consent, and entrusts courts to identify efficiency.

Alan Schwartz has argued that this kind of active role for courts in identifying superior outcomes makes contract law unacceptably "court-centered."[11] Similarly, Randy Barnett has argued that if the enforceability of a promised exchange is made to depend on a court's evaluation of its efficiency or other consequentialist metrics, then contract law has no distinct identity at all.[12] It would simply consist of state allocation of resources based on societal benefit. Indeed, he argues, if courts pursue "efficiency" rather than consent, they could just as well uphold "efficient thefts": stealing would be justified as long as the thief put the stolen goods to a more productive use than the owner would have.

Many commentators, however, argue that there is no danger of conflict between consent and efficiency or between parties' intent and court-centeredness. They argue that consensual bargains are by nature efficient; thus it is unnecessary to choose between the consented-to arrangement and the efficient one.[13] This idea that the free pursuit of individual self-interest increases overall social welfare dates back at least as far as Adam Smith:

> Every individual ... neither intends to promote the public interest, nor knows how much he is promoting it.... By directing ... industry in such a manner as its produce may be of greatest value, he intends only his own gain, and he is in this, as in many other cases, led by an invisible hand to promote an end which was no part of his intention.[14]

Conservative free-market theorists take this argument further and hold that bargaining is the *only* way to identify efficient allocations.[15] According to this theory, "The marginal cost and benefit curves associated with a prospective realignment of resources are not known by the government. Each affected individual knows his benefit or cost, and, in the absence of high exchange cost, this information would

11 Alan Schwartz, *The Myth That Promisees Prefer Supracompensatory Remedies: An Analysis of Contracting for Damage Measures*, 100 YALE L.J. 369, 407 (1990) ("The question now, it seems, is whether defenders of court centeredness can show how their commitment to it is reconcilable with Contract Law's parallel commitment to party autonomy.").

12 Randy Barnett, *A Consent Theory of Contract*, 86 COLUMBIA L. REV. 269, 299 (1986).

13 Jules Coleman, *The Normative Basis of Economic Analysis: A Critical Review of Richard Posner's* The Economics of Justice, 34 STANFORD L. REV. 1105, 1108 ("The libertarian's emphasis on free exchange and the utilitarian's concern for welfare maximization are both exemplified by Pareto superior moves to Pareto optimal outcomes.").

14 Adam Smith, THE WEALTH OF NATIONS, Book IV, Ch. II.

15 E.g., Ludwig von Mises, *Economic Calculation in the Socialist Commonwealth* (1920), reprinted in COLLECTIVIST ECONOMIC PLANNING 87, 104 (Friedrich A. Hayek, ed., Ludwig von Mises Institute: Auburn, Ala. 2009) ("As soon as one gives up the conception of a freely established monetary price for goods of a higher order, rational production becomes completely impossible.").

be transmitted to others in the form of market negotiations. The primary problem of the government *is* the estimation problem."[16] Under this view, free markets, in which each individual bargains to maximize her individual utility, are the only way to maximize individual and thus social utility. Consensual bargaining is the necessary and sufficient condition for efficiency. Party-centeredness thus serves both liberty and efficiency. Third parties such as judges or legislators cannot hope to identify efficient allocations of resources.

Richard Posner's more recent work has applied these premises to contract doctrine. Rejecting his earlier arguments in favor of judicial determinations of efficiency, he has frequently argued, in effect, that if a court thinks a consensual bargain is inefficient, the court must be wrong. If a consensual bargain has been made, it must be efficient. Because the bargain is both consensual and efficient, the court has no ground to refuse to enforce it.[17] Posner initiated an entire subgenre of law-and-economics scholarship devoted to explaining how voluntary arrangements that appear inefficient are in fact efficient. For example, while many see gratuitous promises as economically nonproductive transfers of wealth, Posner has argued that they may in fact enhance welfare.[18] The common law is skeptical of contract provisions that stipulate "penalties" for breach (that is, consequences in excess of expectation damages). Some commentators have defended this rule on the ground that penalties inefficiently overdeter breaches of contract.[19] Posner, however, has argued (in his capacity as a judge) that such clauses, as the product of consensual bargaining, should be presumed to be economically efficient:

> The parties (always assuming they are fully competent) will, in deciding whether to include a penalty clause in their contract, weigh the gains against the costs – costs that include the possibility of discouraging an efficient breach somewhere down the road – and will include the clause only if the benefits exceed those costs as well as all other costs.[20]

The theory that consent is proof of efficiency makes it unnecessary to make the hard normative choice between the two values when enforcing consensual bargains. It facilitates an ideological alliance between consequentialist free-market economists and categorical libertarians. *If* individual bargaining *always* produced efficient outcomes, a finding of consent would also be a finding of efficiency, and such a

[16] Harold Demsetz, *Some Aspects of Property Rights*, 9 J. L. & ECONOMICS 61, 68 (1966).

[17] Richard A. Posner, ECONOMIC ANALYSIS OF LAW 105 (5th ed., Aspen Law & Business: New York 1998).

[18] Richard A. Posner, *Gratuitous Promises in Economics and Law*, 6 J. LEGAL STUDIES 411 (1977).

[19] *E.g.*, Kenneth W. Clarkson et al., *Liquidated Damages v. Penalties: Sense or Nonsense?* 1978 WISCONSIN L. REV. 351.

[20] *Lake River Corp. v Carborundum Co.*, 769 F.2d 1284, 1289 (7th Cir. 1985). The court, per Judge Posner, nonetheless rejected the penalty clause in question pursuant to the state-law rule.

finding would make it possible to avoid choosing between the two values. Normative arguments based on liberty and the efficiency of bargaining could both be raised without conflict. This could be referred to as the "reductionist" approach to the categorical-consequential divide.

But even assuming the validity of this principle, employing it requires a method of identifying consent. The court-centered approach silently assumes that a court can identify the normatively preferable (e.g., the most efficient) contract or term. The party-centered approach recognizes the implausibility of this assumption, but requires its own silent assumption about a court's abilities – that courts are competent to identify when, and on what terms, a consensual bargain has been struck.

This assumption would be plausible if consent were an empirical fact whose existence a court could determine through fact-finding. But consent is a subjective, internal event. It cannot be directly observed and thus requires more than mere evidence gathering; indeed determining the existence of consent is not a purely empirical exercise. As noted previously, because the critical subjective aspect of consent cannot be observed, a workable legal definition of consent requires redefining the notion in an "objective" way that replaces much, if not all, of its fundamental libertarian content with the court's normative preferences as to bargaining procedure and content.

Some theorists argue that conservative free-market theory suggests a way to identify consent: if consensual bargains are indeed the *only* route to efficiency, then identifying the efficient contractual arrangement would also identify the consented-to bargain. Under the so-called "hypothetical bargain" approach, "the parties will be deemed *ex post* to have consented *ex ante* to the term that would have been most rational for them to specify; in short, rationality implies consent."[21] This approach, which might be called "reverse reductionism," attempts to answer Barnett's charge of statism by focusing on efficiency but characterizing it as no different from consent. But of course it substitutes the impossible task of identifying subjective consent with the equally elusive – and even more obviously court-centered – goal of identifying "efficiency."

The conflation of consent and efficiency is only a slight variation on the traditional objective theory, which similarly conflates consent and "reasonableness." As noted above, Holmes and the Restatement have candidly declared subjective intent legally irrelevant to "objective consent." But more often, courts and theorists applying the objective model engage in reverse reductionism: they seek libertarian legitimacy for their decisions by claiming "objectively reasonable" arrangements describe the subjective intent of the parties. A 1921 New York case, *Jacob & Youngs v.*

[21] John C. Coffee, *The Mandatory/Enabling Balance in Corporations Law: An Essay on the Judicial Role*, 89 Columbia L. Rev. 1618, 1623 (1989).

Kent,[22] is a classic example that prefigured the contemporary "hypothetical bargain" formulation. There, the court argued that its "objective" reasoning identified the parties' true intent, even though that reasoning contradicted what would seem to be the objective manifestation of the parties' intent: the literal text of their written agreement.

The contract at issue required a builder to construct a home. The contract specified that the builder was to use plumbing pipe made by the Reading Manufacturing Company. When the builder had completed the home, the owner's architect refused to supply a completion certificate because some of the pipe was not manufactured by Reading. The architect then instructed the builder to replace the pipe, but the builder refused. The owner had by this time paid some 95 percent of the $77,000 contract price but refused to pay the remaining balance, for which the builder sued.

The court found that Reading pipe and the pipe actually used in the construction were of equivalent value, and that replacing the pipe would be extremely costly. Making full payment conditional on the builder's perfect compliance with the contract specifications, the court stated, would be unduly harsh. The doctrine of substantial performance is intended to prevent such unfair results. Under that doctrine, the builder should receive the full contract price less an allowance for the value of the defect. The court acknowledged that the normal measure of this allowance would be the cost of repairing the work to conform to specifications. Indeed, in language that the court ignored, the written agreement seemed to expressly require such repair.[23] The court nonetheless stated that if the cost of repair is "grossly and unfairly out of proportion to the good to be attained," the allowance should be measured instead by the difference in *value* between the defective work and the work expected, which the court found to be "nominal or nothing." The court thus ordered the owner to pay the builder in full.

The holding turns upon the court's normatively laden determination that the owner had no right to compensation for the cost of repair because that cost would be "grossly and unfairly out of proportion to the good to be attained." That is, repair

[22] 230 NY 239 (1921).

[23] The agreement required the builder "*to take down* all portion of the work which the Architect shall…condemn as…*in any way* failing to conform to the drawings and specifications, and shall make good all work damaged or destroyed thereby." Richard Danzig, The Capability Problem in Contract Law 109 (Foundation Press: New York 1978) (excerpting the contract). Even more specifically, it further stated that work "the *material*…of which…is not fully in accordance with the drawings and specifications, *in every respect*, will be rejected and *is to be immediately torn down, removed and remade or replaced*." E. Alan Farnsworth, et al., Contracts: Cases and Materials 645 fn. a. (7th ed., Foundation Press: New York). The same clause further gave the owner the option to waive actual replacement and instead receive money "equivalent to the difference in value of the work as performed and as herein specified."

would be unjustified because it would generate less benefit for the owner than it would consume in terms of the builder's resources. This characterization is of course closely analogous to the contemporary concept of "efficiency."

As Alan Schwartz has argued, the court's reasoning can be characterized as a "court-centered" calculation of social welfare. A dissenting judge argued that the owner "had a right to contract for what he wanted."[24] The court, however, insisted that its decision *did* reflect the parties' intent. Because it would be unjust to deny the builder full payment due to a trivial deviation, the court reasoned, the parties *could not have intended* such a result:

> From the conclusion that promises may not be treated as dependent to the extent of their uttermost minutiae without a sacrifice of justice, the progress is a short one to the conclusion that they may not also be so treated without a perversion of intention. Intention not otherwise revealed may be presumed to hold in contemplation the reasonable and probable.[25]

This reverse-reductionist rhetoric subtly effaces the role of social welfare concerns, and of the court, in determining the content of the parties "contractual" obligations. The court claims that by introspectively identifying the "reasonable" contract, it has not only identified the set of obligations that is normatively best for society, but has *also* identified the parties' actual, subjective intent.

There are three basic problems with this type of reverse-reductionist approach. First, and most obviously, "reasonableness" cannot be consistently or objectively defined. It is a policy-based normative conclusion by another name. The court's interpretation of the *Jacob & Youngs* contract could be called "reasonable." It may not follow the literal words of the contract, but it mitigates potential harshness and waste. However, the literal reading of the contract is also "reasonable" for other reasons – it is more consistent with the parties' observable manifestations of intent. That is, "reasonableness" varies according to normative preferences. Second, due to the policy significance of defining "reasonableness," it is not clear that courts are the best institution to construct and apply such definitions. In *Jacobs & Young*, the court presumed to know that the builder valued the final installment payment more highly than the owner valued the correct brand of pipe. Finally, even if courts can define and identify the reasonable arrangement, it does not follow that the parties actually agreed to that arrangement. Even if most people act reasonably most of the time, it is obvious that many people act idiosyncratically and unreasonably much of the time. Moreover, the court's definition of "reasonable," like the contemporary definition

[24] *Jacobs & Young*, 230 N.Y. 239, 245 (McLaughlin, J., dissenting). Furthermore, although the court asserted that the cost of repair was grossly disproportionate to the difference in value, the builder had, according to the dissent, offered no evidence as to the cost of repair.

[25] *Id.*

of "efficiency," looks to the *overall* benefit generated by the transaction. But equating this with intent portrays parties as unrealistically altruistic. "Reasonable" (or "economically rational") parties would likely prefer, and at least sometimes obtain, bargains that maximize their *own* gains (or "rents"), even at the expense of overall gains. In *Jacobs & Young*, for example, awarding the owner the cost of repair would arguably overcompensate the owner. The court saw that as evidence that the parties could not have intended that result. But the cost of repair would obviously be preferable to the owner, and the builder might have consented to it (perhaps in exchange for some other concession in the contract).

While *Jacob & Youngs* is fairly extreme in its rejection of the parties' expressed intent, its disguising of "court-centered" decision-making as "party-centered" is not. It is hardly controversial that any objective approach to intent (that is, any practicable approach to intent) requires a court to impose meanings onto parties' actions in order to construct "consent." This is a practical consequence of our inability to read the parties' minds. But while contract theory and jurisprudence acknowledge this fact, they generally fail to confront how this concession to practicality undermines the legitimacy of consent-based theories of contract enforceability. Instead, they more often try to square the circle with rhetoric designed to suggest that legal obligations constructed from externally imposed standards (such as "reasonableness" or "efficiency") were in fact subjectively consented to. Such contortions are an attempt to avoid the tension between the categorical libertarian justification for enforcing contracts and instrumental justifications such as economic efficiency.

III. ILLUSORY NATURE OF PARTY-CENTRISM

The tension between consent and efficiency is highlighted in the jurisprudence of standard-form contracts, especially those made between sophisticated commercial entities and lay consumers. On the one hand, a given consumer often lacks actual knowledge of a form contract's terms and thus arguably lacks actual intent to agree to them. Yet the enforceability of form contracts can generate social benefit by facilitating the smooth functioning of a mass consumer economy. Thus consent and efficiency potentially militate in opposite directions.

This problem is illustrated by a trio of U.S. cases in which different courts applied different analyses for nearly identical form contracts. *Klocek v. Gateway, Inc.*,[26] *Hill*

[26] 104 F. Supp. 2d 1332 (D. Kan. 2000). *Klocek* was a federal trial court decision in an individual federal action; plaintiff brought a motion for class certification, but the court found the pro se plaintiff was not an adequate class representative. Although the complaint survived a motion to dismiss in this opinion, it was subsequently dismissed for failing to meet the amount-in-controversy requirement for federal diversity jurisdiction. *Klocek v. Gateway, Inc.*, 2000 U.S. Dist. LEXIS 21854 (D. Kan. 2000).

v. Gateway 2000, Inc., [27] and *Brower v. Gateway 2000, Inc.*, [28] each involved the enforceability of arbitration clauses in form contracts. *Hill* in particular illustrates a reverse-reductionist use of efficiency to infer consent. The cases involve forms the Gateway[29] computer company provided to customers who ordered personal computers on the telephone or in a Gateway store.[30] When the customer later took delivery of the computer, the box contained Gateway's form stating that by retaining possession of the computer, the customer would consent to an arbitration clause and other terms.[31] These terms had not been mentioned at the time of the order. Gateway argued that the customer, by keeping the computer, had assented to Gateway's arbitration clause. *Klocek* rejected this argument on the ground that the customer's order was an offer to purchase, and Gateway's shipment constituted an acceptance of the terms of the order, forming a contract without the arbitration clause. *Hill* and *Brower*, however, found that Gateway's shipment constituted an offer to sell subject to an arbitration clause, and the customers had accepted this offer by retaining the computers.

The *Klocek* court found that the customer had not assented to the arbitration clause. According to the court, the customer offered to buy the computer over the phone. Article 2 of the Uniform Commercial Code (UCC)[32] typically views consumer sales transactions as initiated by a consumer's offer to buy goods, which the seller may accept by shipping or promising to ship.[33] The court held that Gateway's shipment of the product with additional terms constituted an acceptance containing "additional or different terms" under UCC § 2–207, and one that was not "expressly conditional" on the consumer's assent to the additional terms. Under § 2–207, such a response to an offer constitutes an acceptance of the offer made by the consumer. Thus Gateway, by shipping the computer, accepted the consumer's offer to purchase, which lacked an arbitration provision.

27 105 F. 3d 1147 (7th Cir. 1996). *Hill* was a federal appellate court decision in a federal class action.

28 676 N.Y.S.2d 569 (App. Div. 1998). *Brower* was the decision of a New York intermediate appellate court in an individual state-law action.

29 The company was known as Gateway 2000, Inc. until 1998, when it changed its name to Gateway, Inc.

30 In *Hill* and *Brower*, the customers had ordered the computer over the phone and received the product in the mail. In *Klocek*, the record was unclear whether the customer had purchased over the phone or in person at a Gateway store.

31 In *Brower* and *Hill*, the terms in the box gave customers 30 days to return the computer if they did not agree to the terms; in Klocek, the terms gave the customer 5 days.

32 Article 2 of the UCC, which has been adopted by 49 of the 50 American states, governs domestic contracts for the sale of movable goods.

33 "[A]n order or other offer to buy goods for prompt or current shipment shall be construed as inviting acceptance either by a prompt promise to ship or by the prompt or current shipment of conforming or non-conforming goods. . . ." UCC § 2–206. Presumably Gateway's telephone operators responded to phone orders with a "prompt promise to ship."

Hill v. Gateway, however, found that mutual assent occurred at a later point in the transaction, and that the customers had thus assented to the arbitration clause. This contrast illustrates the fact that party-centrism merely instructs a court to enforce "consensual" bargains without restricting the court's power to define "consent." While *Klocek* treated the formation question as a simple one, *Hill* characterized it as difficult. *Hill* suggested that conventional fact-finding and doctrine with respect to "objective manifestations" could not answer whether the customers assented to arbitration by failing to return the computers, or whether the customers and Gateway had already consented in the phone call to a contract with no arbitration clause.[34] Rather than analyzing, or even describing, the actual words used by the parties over the phone,[35] the court provided a lengthy, and entirely non-empirical, discussion of the relative efficiency of outcomes under the different theories of formation. While *Klocek* suggested that Gateway would have had to articulate the arbitration clause at the time of ordering in order to make it part of the contract, *Hill* rejected such a requirement on the ground that it would be inefficient:

> Practical considerations support allowing vendors to enclose the full legal terms with their products [after payment].... If the staff at the other end of the phone for direct-sales operations such as Gateway's had to read the four-page statement of terms before taking the buyer's credit card number, the droning voice would anesthetize rather than enlighten many potential buyers. Others would hang up in a rage.... Writing provides benefits for both sides of commercial transactions. Customers as a group are better off when vendors skip costly and ineffectual steps such as telephonic recitation, and use instead a simple approve-or-return device. Competent adults are bound by such documents, read or unread.[36]

That is, the customer's promise to pay and the seller's promise to deliver in the phone call did not constitute an offer and acceptance. Rather, they merely set the stage for a later offer by Gateway, which included additional terms and which the customer could accept by retaining the computer (or reject by sending it back).[37] Significantly, the court did *not* assert that such was the parties' mutual subjective understanding of the formation process at the time of the phone call.[38] Nor did it

[34] The court held that UCC § 2–207's rules of variant acceptance did not apply, on the ground that 2–207 applies only to a "battle of the forms" and the Gateway transaction involved only one form. This conclusion is baffling as a doctrinal matter, however, as §2–207 makes no mention of "forms" at all. *Klocek*, 104 F.Supp. 2d at 1339.

[35] Because *Gateway* was a class action, it was probably impractical, if not impossible, to analyze the actual words used in each transaction.

[36] *Hill*, 105 F. 3d at 1150.

[37] "Gateway shipped computers with the same sort of accept-or-return offer ProCD made to users of its software." *Id.*

[38] Again, *Gateway* was a class action; thus it would be all but impossible to assess subjective intent with respect to every transaction.

characterize the phone call as an "objective manifestation" of such an understanding. Rather, the court argued that it would be *more efficient* to send written terms in the box with the computer and have the customers keep the computer if they agreed to the terms and return the computer if they did not.[39] The "approve or return" device was better for the parties' welfare, and thus, the court argued, it was the applicable method of formation.

The customer's retention of the computer would not have signaled consent to arbitration had the *Hill* court applied *Klocek*'s UCC-based approach to the formation of sales contracts,[40] which would locate offer and acceptance at the time of ordering. This is not to say that the UCC more accurately describes the parties' actual intent. Indeed, the *Klocek* court's UCC approach, no less than the *Hill* court's efficiency approach, redefines "consent" in a nominally "objective" way without any real attempt to determine subjective intent. In both *Klocek* and *Hill*, courts used the rhetoric of party-centered analysis even as they made outcome-determinative choices about how to define consent. *Klocek*'s apparently mechanical application of the UCC's offer-and-acceptance doctrine disguises important, difficult determinations, such as whether the customer indeed intended to make an offer by placing an order, and, if so, whether Gateway's shipment of the computer was or was not "expressly conditional" on the customer's assent to arbitration.[41]

Both courts, then, disguise the role of the law and of the court by using party-centered rhetoric. *Klocek* applies statutory definitions of "objective" manifestations of "consent." *Hill* uses efficiency arguments to establish the terms in the box as the offer and the customer's retention of the computer as the appropriate method of acceptance, and thus set up a nominally "party-centered" conclusion: the customer's retention of the product manifests assent to the arbitration clause, despite that clause's late appearance in the formation sequence.[42] This is a complex

[39] Elsewhere in the opinion, the court also stated that Gateway's advertisements gave customers constructive notice that the terms disclosed over the phone were incomplete and thus that no contract had yet been formed. "Gateway's ads state that their products come with limited warranties and lifetime support," though they said nothing about arbitration. The court implies, unconvincingly, that the customers should have figured from the ads that the sale might also be subject to other terms and conditions (such as arbitration) even if not disclosed during the phone order. *Hill*, 105 F. 3d at 1150.

[40] See the discussion of UCC §§ 2–206 and 207, *supra* notes 33–34 and associated text.

[41] *Klocek* notwithstanding, an argument could be made that the arbitration clause should have been enforceable under the "expressly conditional" rule of UCC 2–207. Gateway's shipment instructed the consumer to return the computer if she did not assent to additional terms, such as the arbitration clause. Thus, it could be characterized as "expressly conditional" on the consumer's assent to arbitration, and buyers who retained possession could be said to have thereby assented to arbitration. *See* Thomas W. Joo, *Common Sense and Contract Law: Fear of a Normative Planet?* 16 TOURO L. REV. 1037, 1039 n. 8 (2000).

[42] Many theorists refer to *Hill* as having introduced "rolling contract formation," in which one party can unilaterally introduce terms even after mutual assent has been reached. While *Hill* does seemed to have opened the door to this practice, the decision itself clearly identifies a discrete moment of

and subtle conflation of efficiency and consent, but not an unfamiliar one. It is the modern equivalent of the claim in *Jacob & Youngs* that the necessity of avoiding economically wasteful construction manifested to the court an "intention not otherwise revealed." Similarly, *Hill* claims that the need to avoid the waste of the seller's resources, which would ultimately reduce the welfare of both consumer and seller, reveals the true mutual intent of the parties.

Hill's reverse-reductionist reasoning suffers from the same problems that afflict the "reasonableness" standard seen in *Jacob & Youngs*. First, "efficiency" cannot be easily defined. For example, the Pareto and Kaldor-Hicks models, the most commonly cited competing definitions, have differing views about the role of negative externalities in defining "efficiency." Second, even if efficiency can be defined, it is not clear that courts are the appropriate institution to construct or apply the definition. If efficiency consists in maximizing utility, then any third party presuming to identify the efficient allocation must presume to know the parties' utility functions. As discussed, market conservatives refuse to believe any third party, least of all a state actor such as a judge, has that ability. Third, even assuming that courts can identify the most efficient (or "reasonable") arrangement, it does not necessarily follow that that arrangement was consented to. It is sometimes suggested that efficient allocations are literally consented to, on the theory that "everyone would consent to Pareto improvements."[43] But, as Jules Coleman has argued, "the consent argument for Pareto superiority either fails or is best understood as a definition of rational self-interest."[44] Individuals do not always choose to act in ways that would maximize their measurable material welfare. This may be due, for example, to moral reservations about seeking advantage or ignorance or indifference to the material gain. Equating Pareto superiority with choice is a tautology based on "defining the Pareto rankings in terms of hypothetical choices"[45] – that is, it means choosing *for* people, not implementing their choices.

The legitimacy of judges' policy-based decisions requires some explanation of why judges are qualified to make such decisions. If policy decisions are based on general wisdom and experience, it might be argued that judicial appointment (or election) processes screen for those characteristics. But it is harder to believe that courts have the ability (or even the incentive) to identify the most economically efficient general rules or specific arrangements.

formation (the expiration of the return period) at which terms appear to have become fixed and after which no further terms were introduced. What appears to be "rolling formation" is merely postponed formation.

[43] Jules Coleman, Book Review, *The Grounds of Welfare:* Fairness Versus Welfare, 112 YALE L.J. 1511, 1519 (2003).

[44] *Id.*

[45] *Id.*

It is hardly clear, for example, what qualified the *Hill v. Gateway* court to opine that "customers as a group are better off when vendors skip costly and ineffectual steps such as telephonic recitation, and use instead a simple approve-or-return device."[46] This is an *empirical* assertion, but the court cites no data in support. Even if a court were to embark on a data-driven analysis, it is unclear that the court would have the required expertise. As another example, economic theorists have argued that when the parties' intended outcome is unclear in a given case, courts should apply a default interpretation that will incentivize efficient outcomes in the future. The default interpretive rules that economic commentators recommend in the name of efficiency vary widely, however, some recommend that a court identify what the majority of contracting parties would have preferred (the "hypothetical bargain" approach referred to previously). Others argue for "penalty default rules" that parties would *not* prefer, on the theory that such rules will incentivize clearer drafting in the future, creating efficiency gains that outweigh the short-term efficiency costs of the immediate decision.[47] It is unclear how courts could be expected to sort through these considerations and properly evaluate the utility of a default-rule principle,[48] or even why they would attempt to approach the problem that way.[49]

What might qualify judges to make efficiency evaluations? Justice Byron White of the U.S. Supreme Court, dissenting in a securities-law case, argued that economic theories, particularly new ones, are "nothing more than theories" and are thus too unreliable for judges to use in decision making.[50] Courts lack the resources of other institutions, such as Congress, to investigate and determine what new economic theories imply for the law. It might be argued that the evaluation of relative efficiency is a species of factual determination that a trial court could make on the basis of expert testimony about empirical economic observations. Even assuming that to be true, courts rarely even attempt it. *Hill*, for example, drew conclusions about the effect of

[46] This is not to slight the technical prowess of the author of *Hill*'s author, Judge Frank Easterbrook, who was a pioneer of law-and-economics scholarship even before his appointment to the bench. But it is unclear how even the ablest economist could reach the quoted conclusion without reference to any data.

[47] Ian Ayres & Robert Gertner, *Filling Gaps in Incomplete Contracts: An Economic Theory of Default Rules*, 99 YALE L. J. 87 (1989).

[48] Alan Schwartz, *The Default Rule Paradigm and the Limits of Contract Law*, 3 SOUTHERN CALIFORNIA INTERDISCIPLINARY L. J. 389, 416 (1993) (arguing that courts do not have the necessary information to craft efficient default rules).

[49] "There is no reason why the prediction must be that contract law is efficient; this seems to be an accident of intellectual history. One could imagine a different theory, along the lines of public choice, that holds that contract law reflects the self-interested decisions of judges to implement policy preferences. Indeed, such an approach has been used by political scientists to explain judicial interpretation of statutes and constitutional provisions." Eric Posner, *Economic Analysis of Contract Law After Three Decades: Success or Failure?* 112 YALE L. J. 829, 834 n. 9.

[50] *Basic v. Levinson*, 485 U.S. 224, 254 (1988).

contract formation rules on the utility of customers and sellers without consulting any evidence, and thus implies grander assumptions about judges' abilities.[51]

Efficiency-based judging needs an explanation of why judges are qualified to perform economic analysis. This would require a complex political-science analysis of who judges are, how they become judges, and to whom they are accountable. In the United States at least, the answers to these questions vary by jurisdiction. Some judges are elected, while some are appointed. Rules on eligibility, nomination and confirmation processes, and removability also vary. Merit-based nomination and appointment systems might be more qualified to identify technocratic ability (such as efficiency-minded judges), but free and fair judicial elections would confer greater democratic legitimacy on explicitly policy-based decisions.

IV. CANDOR IN THE JUDICIAL CONSTRUCTION OF CONSENT

By obscuring the role of the court and portraying contract lawmaking as party-centered, cases like *Hill* avoid questions about the legitimacy of judges' policy-based thinking. *Brower v. Gateway*,[52] a New York state appellate court decision concerning the same Gateway form contract, is much more candid about the role of the court. On the one hand, the court purported to find party consent to the arbitration clause, but, on the other, that consent did not prevent the court from rejecting some elements of the clause on policy grounds. The court explicitly followed *Hill* in finding that "the contract . . . was formed and acceptance was manifested not when the order was placed but only with the retention of the merchandise beyond the 30 days specified in the Agreement enclosed in the shipment of merchandise."[53] Like *Hill*, *Brower* found that the customers gave their informed consent to the terms; in doing so, *Brower* (unlike *Hill*) explicitly considered and rejected plaintiff's arguments of procedural unconscionability.[54]

But *Brower* nonetheless gave partial relief to the customer that departed from the party-centered principle. Despite having found a bargained-for agreement to the arbitration clause, *Brower* refused to enforce the clause as written, on the basis of *substantive* unconscionability alone.[55] The clause required arbitration under the

51 The same can be said of the California court's conclusions about late fees in *UCAN v. AT&T*, *infra*, and of Judge Posner's ruminations on the efficiency of liquidated damages clauses in *Lake River v. Carborundum*, discussed *supra*, though those were merely dicta.

52 676 N.Y.S.2d 569 (App. Div. 1998).

53 *Id.*, at 571.

54 "As to the procedural element, a court will look to the contract formation process. . . . [D]espite appellants' claims to the contrary, the arbitration clause is in no way 'hidden' or 'tucked away'. . . nor is the option of returning the merchandise, to avoid the contract, somehow a 'precarious' one." *Id.*, at 573–74.

55 "While it is true that, under New York law, unconscionability is generally predicated on the presence of both the procedural and substantive elements, the substantive element alone may be sufficient to render the terms of the provision at issue unenforceable." *Id.*, at 574.

rules of the International Chamber of Commerce (ICC), which required a $4,000 advance fee, of which $2,000 was non-refundable. The court found this fee excessive (particularly in light of the relatively low cost of Gateway products) and remanded the case to the trial court for the appointment of a substitute arbitrator.

Party-centeredness can only answer a very narrow range of problems. For example, it would foreclose *Brower*'s refusal to enforce an assented-to choice of arbitration forum. It cannot answer more common questions like the dispute between *Hill* and *Brower*, on the one hand, and *Klocek*, on the other: whether and when consent occurred. Defining consent "objectively" is the only way to make a consent theory workable beyond cases where consent is obvious. But paradoxically, "objectivity" necessarily strips away much of the core liberal-individualist meaning of "consent." Like all rules, any "objective" theory is indeterminate due to the limitations of fact finding and definitions of "objective consent." But of course all rules are contestable in these senses. The real problem with the legal construction of consent is that to the extent "consent" is constructed and attributed by courts (or legislators), it loses the unique characteristics that supposedly distinguish "consent" from "law." This is a "problem" at the level of existing libertarian contract theory: the absence of subjective assent does not make "contract" obligation uniquely problematic. After all, subjective assent is not required for non-contractual legal liability.

The focus on consent in both *Hill* and *Klocek* is at least nominally consistent with the party-centered principle. But by identifying terms as substantively unfair and striking them down on that ground, *even though* they were consented to, *Brower* openly rejects the party-centered principle. This rejection of party intent is of course inherent in courts' ability to void contracts based on substantive unconscionability or violations of public policy. Many commentators disapprove of such doctrines for this very reason, but as a descriptive matter, such doctrines are always available to potentially trump any party-centered analysis. Moreover, as noted above, even nominally party-centered judgments turn upon court-centered choices. Thus *Brower* differs from *Klocek* and *Hill* less in its court-centeredness than in its candor about its court-centeredness.

The U.S. Supreme Court demonstrated a lack of such candor in *AT&T Mobility LLC v. Concepcion*, a recent opinion also involving an arbitration clause in a consumer form contract.[56] The clause in question required arbitration of all disputes but precluded class arbitration. A lower federal court struck down the clause on the ground that its preclusion of class actions and class arbitration was unconscionable under applicable state-law precedent. The Supreme Court, however, held that the state-law doctrine was preempted by a federal statute, the Federal Arbitration Act. The Court held that the clause must be upheld "as written" because the act

56 131 S. Ct. 1740 (2011)

favors "affording parties discretion in designing arbitration processes."[57] According to the Court, the state-law analysis applied by the lower court favored class arbitration such that the consumer's right to arbitrate class disputes would be "manufactured ... rather than consensual."[58] But the Supreme Court's conclusion assumes, without analysis, that the customer had indeed consented to the clause "as written." The Supreme Court did not address the lower court's concern that such consent was absent because the consumers had limited choice due to unequal bargaining power.[59] This is not to say that the lower court was necessarily correct in this assessment. Rather, the point is that the Supreme Court ignored the contested nature of "consent," invoking the word as the end of the discussion rather than acknowledging it as a central disputed concept in unconscionability analysis – a concept with respect to which the Court made fundamental but unspoken assumptions. The Court employed party-centered "consent" rhetoric to obscure the court-centered nature of its decision.

Concepcion is naïve (if not disingenuous) in its insistence that consumers who sign form contracts with arbitration clauses actively participate in "designing the arbitration process." In contrast, the *Gateway* opinions, for all their shortcomings, recognize and struggle with the attenuated nature of consent in the form-contract context. In form contracts, the "agreement" is not produced by a process of give-and-take negotiation, but presented by one side as a take-it-or-leave-it proposition. In the case of consumer forms, the author of the form is likely to be more sophisticated and the consumer is unlikely to have actually read or understood the dense and complex terms of the form. On the one hand, it is argued that by signing the form, the consumer has objectively manifested consent to all the terms, read or unread. The consumer is not literally forced to give assent, and she always has the choice not to contract at all. On the other hand, critics argue that a consumer could not have subjectively consented to, or be reasonably understood to have consented to, terms she did not read or understand. Furthermore, even if she had choice with respect to the contract, it was severely constrained by the lack of opportunity to bargain over the terms.

Karl Llewellyn is credited with a compromise analysis of form contracts that continues to dominate today. He argued that a consumer assenting to a "boilerplate"

57 *Id.*, at 1749.

58 *Id.*, at 1751.

59 Indeed, section 2 of the Federal Arbitration Act specifically states that arbitration clauses "shall be valid, irrevocable, and enforceable, *save upon such grounds as exist at law or in equity for the revocation of any contract.*" 9 U.S.C. § 2 (2011). The plaintiffs thus argued that the lower court's application of state-law unconscionability doctrine was consistent with the Act, but the Court disagreed. The lower court had applied a state-law precedent that applied a stringent unconscionability analysis to arbitration clauses in contracts of adhesion. The Supreme Court chose to view this precedent as a specifically anti-arbitration rule rather than as an application of general contract law principles. *Concepcion*, 131 S. Ct. at 1748.

contract specifically assents to a handful of explicitly negotiated terms and also gives "a blanket *assent ... to any not unreasonable ... terms* the seller may have on his form."[60] Whether the consumer has read the terms is irrelevant, as long as the consumer had the opportunity to do so.

Llewellyn's approach tries very carefully to fit form contracts into traditional notions of notice and informed consent. *Hill, Brower* and *Klocek* implicitly follow this approach. Despite their differences, all the opinions assume that customers can give "blanket assent" to reasonable terms. Thus all the decisions concern themselves with whether, and when, the customer gave such assent, and what terms were knowable by the consumer at that time; none is concerned with whether the terms were explicitly bargained over or even whether they were *actually* known to the consumer. *Klocek* argues that formation occurred on the phone, and the customer thus gave "blanket assent" to the terms disclosed at that time (and only to those terms). *Hill* and *Brower* argue that the formation occurred later, and the customer gave "blanket assent" to the terms disclosed at that later time, which included the arbitration clause. In Llewellyn's terms, *Brower* could be said to differ from *Hill* in that it found certain details of the arbitration clause "unreasonable" and thus not subject to the consumer's "blanket assent."

The focus on a discrete moment of consent can create a hurdle for some form contracts, however. According to *Klocek*, for example, terms that the consumer sees only after purchase may be revealed too late to be part of the contract with the seller. *Hill* avoids this problem by relocating formation to a later moment in time. Sales contracts are typically formed when a seller accepts a buyer's advance payment or promise to pay, not when the buyer subsequently takes delivery and retains possession. In addition to its efficiency arguments in favor of this later time of formation, *Hill* appealed to "consent" and party-centeredness by suggesting that the buyers had constructive *notice* that the contract would be formed by a subsequent accept-or-return process. That is, the unusual formation process was not being foisted upon them by the court in retrospect, but was understood by the parties at the time they transacted. In an earlier opinion, *ProCD v. Zeidenberg*, the same judge had held that a notice on the outside of a retail software package informed the buyer that the software would be subject to a restrictive license whose terms would be found inside the box.[61] Since the buyer was on notice that he did not know the terms of his contract with the manufacturer at the time of purchase, he was on notice that a contract could not have been formed at that time. Such advance written notice was absent in *Hill*, in which the purchase took place over the phone. Nonetheless, the

[60] Karl N. Llewellyn, The Common Law Tradition: Deciding Appeals 370–71 (Little, Brown: Boston 1960) (emphasis added).

[61] 86 F.3d 1447, 1450 (7th Cir. 1996).

Hill court found notice elsewhere: in vague statements in Gateway's advertisements (despite the lack of evidence that the plaintiff buyers had seen the ads).[62]

Other sellers might provide even less notice that terms will arrive later and, consequently, that contract formation will occur later. So if advance notice is necessary (as *ProCD* and *Hill* suggest, but do not state) some accept-or-return contracts may fail. Commentators have thus created a more flexible and sophisticated theorization of "consent" in accept-or-return form contracts that would make advance notice unnecessary. While *ProCD, Hill,* and their progeny simply located the traditional discrete moment of formation later in time (and argued that buyers had constructive notice that this would be so), the theory of "rolling contracts" extrapolates from *ProCD* and *Hill* a more radical theory: that there is no discrete moment in the formation process at which the door is closed to new terms. Robert Hillman, for example, has complained that a focus on the time of formation is "a dead-end debate."[63] The court in *Klocek* argued that the door was closed to further terms after the contract formed on the phone. But, Hillman argues, whether the customer receives notice of additional terms before or after the contract is "formed" is irrelevant because the time of formation is not necessarily determinative of the enforceability of terms. From the point of view of consent theory, he argues that parties rarely have any actual intent as to the precise time they become legally bound. Further, modern "relational" contract doctrine recognizes that contracts are relationships in which mutual expectations evolve over time rather than springing into existence at a single discrete moment.[64] Most important, since one of the core assumptions of form contracts analysis is that most consumers *do not* read or understand forms, whether they are available before or after the "time of formation" simply cannot have any practical relevance.[65] Thus, Hillman argues, Llewellyn's theory of blanket assent should apply even to terms sent later in time. According to Hillman, Llewellyn's qualification of "blanket assent" should continue to apply: it extends only to terms that are not unreasonable. Hillman's logic is unassailable: the time of formation should not matter *if* we accept the blanket assent principle, under which enforceability is based entirely on substantive "reasonableness" and not on notice of or subjective assent to any particular

[62] According to the court, some Gateway advertisements stated that its computers were sold with "limited warranties and lifetime support." 105 F.3d at 1150. Although the ads apparently said nothing about arbitration, the very vagueness of these statements, according to the court, put the customers on notice that the shipment "would include *some* important terms, and they did not seek to discover these in advance." *Id.*

[63] Robert A. Hillman, *Rolling Contracts*, 71 FORDHAM L. REV. 743, 757 (2002).

[64] For example, a buyer who knew additional terms would be in the box might have " impliedly agreed...to delegate to Gateway the right to establish the terms." Furthermore, even if a contract had been formed at the time of purchase, the UCC allows for modifications without consideration. *Id.*, at 754.

[65] *Id.*, at 757.

term. But the fact that enforceability is based on the substance of the obligation and not on its voluntary assumption underscores the fact that the subjective, libertarian aspect of consent has disappeared from the analysis. The basis for enforcing the "reasonable" terms cannot be consent, as there is none; indeed the set of "reasonable" terms is unknown at the time of formation. Indeed, they are unknown to *either* party, for even the author of the form contract does not know which of its terms will bind itself or the customer until a *court* rules on their reasonableness. For example, the Gateway company thought that its form terms meant disputes were subject to arbitration under ICC rules. That turned out to be true with respect to the members of the *Hill* class action, but not with respect to the individual plaintiffs in *Brower*.

While Hillman, like Llewellyn, emphasizes the terminology of "consent," in fact the "rolling contract" theory points out the unimportance of actual agreement to anything: if the customer is bound to terms she is not going to read, not only is it irrelevant *when* the customer receives them, but it is also irrelevant *whether* the customer ever receives them. All that matters is whether they are reasonable: that is, whether a *court* eventually finds them reasonable.

In his influential critique of the "blanket assent" theory, Todd Rakoff argued that consent to unread terms was the equivalent of "handing over a blank check," a kind of conduct one would not expect to see "as a matter of course in ordinary commerce."[66] Thus, he argued, there is no consent to unread terms, "reasonable" or not, and they should thus be presumptively unenforceable. In response, Randy Barnett has argued that just as a soldier can commit herself today to obey future orders that she does not know, a party signing a form contract without reading it can consent to be legally bound to terms without knowing their details.[67] But there is a difference between what parties could or should be bound to and what they can plausibly said to have actually consented to. Even granting that it is *theoretically possible* (as Barnett insists) that *someone could* "consent" to as-yet unknown terms, that is simply not the same as *finding*, as an *empirical* matter, that a *particular* party in a particular case actually intended to give her consent to unknown terms. But many consumers may be unaware that there are any important terms in the fine print, or they may believe (however incorrectly or unjustifiably) that they cannot be bound to terms they have not read.

Barnett further argues that blanket assent does not require a consumer to sign a truly "blank" check, because it limits the reach of "blanket" assent to *reasonable* terms only. While this addresses the potential for unlimited delegation to the party drafting the form, it undermines the fundamental notion of "consent." As argued

[66] Todd D. Rakoff, *Contracts of Adhesion: An Essay in Reconstruction*, 96 HARVARD L. REV. 1174, 1200 (1983).

[67] Randy Barnett, *Consenting to Form Contracts*, 71 FORDHAM L. REV. 627, 636 (2002).

previously, basing enforceability on reasonableness means establishing the content of the agreement by an *ex post* court evaluation based on factors other than subjective agreement.

Rakoff objected to the blanket assent theory and argued that the enforceability of terms should require actual knowledge and understanding of and consent to each term of a form agreement. Rakoff can be criticized for applying an impracticably high standard of subjective assent for enforceability. But despite his disagreement with Llewellyn, Hillman, Barnett and *Hill* about the enforceability of form contracts, Rakoff's fundamental normative assumption is essentially the same: that consent is the *sine qua non* of enforceability. The impracticability of Rakoff's approach illustrates the impossibility of *any* workable individualist, libertarian theory of consent to form contracts. Indeed, Rakoff's deconstruction of "consent" raises questions outside the form-contract context as well. His doubts about the quality of subjective agreement may apply, in varying degrees, to the formation of any contract. For example, there is some degree of bargaining-power disparity between any two parties. Moreover, even "negotiated agreements" between sophisticated parties often involve terms, including boilerplate, that the parties may not have read or understood at the time of formation.[68] Such terms are nonetheless enforceable, subject to a court's review of their "reasonableness" under such rubrics as unconscionability and public policy. This suggests that something like a "blanket assent" argument, with all its attendant shortcomings, may be required to explain "consent" to many contracts that are not standard-form contracts.

"Blanket *assent*" is simply not convincing as a description of subjective party intent. Blanket consumer obligation to unread terms (subject to some limitations of fairness) is far more convincing as a matter of economic policy. Nearly all consumer contracts today are standard forms. Lack of subjective agreement notwithstanding, the functioning of the consumer economy would seem to require some legally enforceable relationship between the consumer and the seller. *Hill,* then, despite its speculative nature and confounding party-centered rhetoric, got it right insofar as it recognized that form contracts *must* rely on policy grounds for their enforceability. Indeed, this may be true of all contracts.

A California case, *Utility Consumers Action Network v. AT&T* ("UCAN"),[69] provides a good example of a court candidly using an economic analysis on its own terms, independent of consent-based rhetoric. UCAN, a consumer advocacy group, challenged fees charged for late payment of cable television bills. The cable

[68] *Cf.* John C. Coates IV, *Explaining Variation in Takeover Defenses: Blame the Lawyers*, 89 California L. Rev. 1301 (2001) (arguing that antitakeover provisions in a company's corporate charter may derive from borrowed boilerplate provisions unsuited to the company in question).

[69] 135 Cal. App. 4th 1023 (2006).

provider, AT&T, stated those fees in the form contracts signed by its customers. According to the Second Restatement of Contracts, liquidated damages are permissible in amounts "reasonable in light of the anticipated or actual loss caused by the breach and the difficulties of proof of loss. A term fixing unreasonably large liquidated damages is unenforceable on grounds of public policy as a penalty."[70] UCAN conceded that AT&T's actual harm would have been difficult to prove and that AT&T had made a reasonable effort to estimate its anticipated harm before setting its late fees. But UCAN argued that California case law requires something more than the Restatement test. A number of California cases state that liquidated damages must reflect a "reasonable endeavor by the parties" to estimate actual damages.[71] UCAN argued that this language requires mutual efforts *by both parties* to estimate actual damages. Thus, as the court put it, "UCAN contends that a sum selected by only one party in that party's preprinted form contract is invalid." UCAN implicitly argued that the Llewellyn model of "blanket assent" to form contracts did not apply to liquidated damages provisions such as late fees. California case law, UCAN argued, required actual negotiations between the seller and the customer, resulting in actual subjective assent.

The California Court of Appeal (the state's intermediate appellate court) rejected this interpretation of the law. It argued that California's "reasonable endeavor" test does not require "bilateral negotiations," but merely "reasonableness of the sum of liquidated damages."[72] The court cited Williston for support of this approach: "The chief, almost the only means, of determining whether the parties in good faith endeavored to assess the damages is afforded by the amount of damages stipulated for...."[73] But in this quote, Williston makes the reverse-reductionist argument that consent can be inferred from efficiency: that is, the reasonableness of the amount is relevant insofar as it implies a "reasonable endeavor" by both parties. In short, Williston presumed the necessity of consent, but UCAN concedes that there was *no* bilateral endeavor, and holds that none is necessary. Whatever its normative desirability, this analysis is more candid and realistic than *Concepcion*'s naïve assertion that a consumer's signature on a form evidences bilateral participation in "designing" the contractual arrangement.

70 RESTATEMENT (SECOND) OF CONTRACTS § 356. Under California statute, the requirement that actual damages be difficult to estimate applies only to consumer contracts. CALIFORNIA CIVIL CODE § 1671(d); *see also UCAN*, 135 Cal App 4th at 1029. In non-consumer contracts in California, liquidated damages clauses are valid unless a party can prove that the clause was "unreasonable" at the time entered into. CALIFORNIA CIVIL CODE § 1671 (b).

71 *UCAN*, 135 Cal. App. 4th at 1029 (citing *Rice v. Schmid* 18 Cal.2d 382, 385–386 (1941)).

72 *Id.*, at 1035.

73 *Id.*, at 1034 (citing Samuel Williston, CONTRACTS, vol. 3, § 779 (2d ed. 1936)).

The UCAN court maintained that non-negotiated late fees are economically justified:

> Requiring a large enterprise to negotiate the terms of a late fee provision with thousands or hundreds of thousands of potential customers would effectively make it impossible to provide for late fees, even when they are warranted by the impracticability of determining damages and even when the amount selected by the business was designed to do no more than cover its damages and bore the proper relationship to the amount of such damages. We refuse to endorse such an interpretation of the reasonable endeavor requirement.[74]

The court's economic argument may be convincing (despite its lack of explicit empirical support), but it is not the same as a subjective agreement argument. The court makes no argument that the parties mutually understood or agreed that the obligation to pay fees would not require negotiation. Moreover, the court makes the validity of a liquidated damages provision dependent on an *ex post* judicial evaluation of the normative desirability of alternative damages, and *not* on parties' *ex ante* consent to an alternative damages regime. Unlike *Hill*, the *UCAN* court is forthright about its economic analysis and does not try to disguise it as a consent-based analysis. "It is the end result which counts," the court stated, "not the number of parties who took part in reaching that result."[75] While *UCAN*'s economic analysis raises questions about institutional competence akin to those raised by the "reasonableness" and "efficiency" determinations discussed, its candor about its reasoning moves those questions to the fore rather than hiding them behind the rhetoric of party-centrism.

V. CONCLUSION

The discourse about "default" and "mandatory" (or "immutable") rules in contract assumes the law has two kinds of rules: those it allows parties to change by agreement, and those it does not.[76] It then asks whether and to what extent rules of contract law should be default or mandatory in character. But as a descriptive matter, true "default rules" may not exist in contract law. Although contract purports to replace or supplement the obligations of public law with "private law," every such attempt is subject to judicial review. In the past few decades, American corporate law scholarship has developed a consensus that corporate law in the United States is largely "contractual" – that is, "consensual." Many background legal rules are defaults that

[74] *Id.*, at 1038.

[75] *Id.*, at 1039.

[76] E.g., Ian Ayres and Robert Gertner, *Strategic Contractual Inefficiency and the Optimal Choice of Legal Rules*, 101 YALE L.J. 729 (1992).

may be changed by putatively consensual devices such as corporate charters, and even to the extent that rules are mandatory, the American federal system allows corporate constituents to choose their state of incorporation, in effect allowing them to select much of the regulatory regime to which they are subject. But John Coffee has urged theorists to look at the mandatory-default question in another way: "What is most mandatory in corporate law is not the specific substantive content of any rule, but rather the institution of judicial oversight."[77] The same can be said of contract law generally: parties may have apparent freedom to design their obligations, but in the end, a court decides.

Parties sometimes attempt to opt out of the legal system by making their obligations enforceable exclusively through formal non-legal institutions such as arbitration or through informal means, as when parties draft a "gentleman's agreement" that declares itself legally unenforceable. But such putative opt outs are always subject to challenge in court: again, the court gets the last word. In some cases, of course, informal non-legal sanctions, such as loss of professional reputation and future business, can make contractual commitments at least partly self-enforcing. But the availability and effectiveness of such sanctions vary widely from case to case. Moreover, they cannot compensate victims of breach; at best, they may disincentivize breaches that offer little gain.[78]

If party-centeredness is largely illusory, is the court's role in "contract" law any different from its role in other areas of law? The need to satisfy the stylized rhetoric of "consent" may place *some* limits on the range of actions a court can take without jeopardizing its legitimacy. The existence of cases like *Brower* shows that such a rhetorical convention is insufficient to entirely prevent courts from using open-ended policy and equity-based approaches. But refusal to enforce terms once they are said to have been "consented to" is recognized as a departure from the general rule and must be justified by protestations that the circumstances are exceptional. Note also that *Brower* used substantive unconscionability only to reject the arbitration *forum*; it used a party-centered analysis to enforce the broader obligation to arbitrate.

Consent rhetoric, however stylized, enjoys special legitimating power in contract cases. Cases that depart from this model may be more likely to be confined

[77] John C. Coffee, *The Mandatory/Enabling Balance in Corporations Law: An Essay on the Judicial Role*, 89 Columbia L. Rev. 1618, 1619 (1989).

[78] Stewart Macaulay's classic empirical research on "relational sanctions" suggested that reputational sanctions can actually operate to excuse, rather than enforce, obligations. He found that, at least in some industries at the time, both buyers and sellers believed buyers were entitled to "cancel" their purchase contracts. Thus sellers did not generally sue when buyers repudiated, and tended to accept limited settlements based on out-of pocket costs rather than expected profit. Stewart Macaulay, *Non-Contractual Relations in Business: A Preliminary Study*, 28 American Sociological Rev. 55 (1963). In such a situation, non-legal sanctions would be more likely to discourage a seller from enforcing contractual expectations than to discourage a buyer from breach.

to their facts and less likely to serve as precedent. This local preference for stylized consent rhetoric may have some constraining effect that distinguishes contract law from other areas of law. In other areas of the law, say environmental regulation, the analogue of consent may be statutory direction, the analogue of constructed consent may be statutory implication, and the analogue of unconscionability may be disregarding the statute for purposes of equity or policy. Such cases are also likely to enjoy less legitimacy than cases that "follow the statute."

Of course, this is a very soft constraint on courts. Empowering courts to make decisions of any sort implicitly incorporates the assumption that they are for some reason the appropriate institution to do so. The orthodox story is that we trust trial courts for their fact-finding ability, and appellate courts for their knowledge of the law (which embodies policy decisions that are made by legislatures or the common law tradition, not by individual courts). As we have seen, courts sometimes openly reject the legal principle of party-centeredness in favor of other legal principles, such as unconscionability. But as we see in cases from *Jacobs & Young* to *Hill* to *Concepcion*, they typically purport to be driven by party-centeredness while obscuring the fact that they are actually making other kinds of determinations, such as "efficiency." The conflation of efficiency with consent obscures a deep, fundamental issue: the relative normative importance of efficiency and consent. This question is far beyond the scope of this chapter or this book. Suffice to say that in order for this question to receive proper consideration, it should be highlighted rather than obscured.

4

Are Mortgage Contracts Promises?

Curtis Bridgeman

This chapter addresses the issue of whether strategic mortgage defaults are immoral. In a strategic default a homeowner defaults on his mortgage contract even though he could afford to make the payments with relative ease – a decision that may sometimes make financial sense when property values have declined so much that a borrower owes more on a home mortgage than the home is worth. The initial premise seems rather obvious: that homeowners who had borrowed hundreds of thousands of dollars, promised to pay it back, and were able to pay it back quite easily should actually do so unless someone could show otherwise.

However, there are numerous critics of the preceding proposition. Many critics felt that either the contracts in question did not contain promises, or else they contained a merely "business" arrangement that could be broken at any time so long as one was willing to suffer the consequences, especially in states where the remedies upon default were limited. What seems odd about these arguments is that they ignored the specific language in the contracts whereby the borrower explicitly promises to pay back the amount borrowed plus interest. Much more attention was paid to the remedies available in the event of breach, or in some cases the language of other contracts that allowed promisors to cancel by paying a fee. That focus makes sense for a legal argument, but it seems that anyone interested in the moral obligation could not ignore the explicit promise.

This chapter analyses the argument that these contracts do not contain promises despite the explicit promissory language. Very briefly put (for now), the reason is that a promise, according to one leading way of thinking, is by definition a situation when a person knowingly undertakes a moral commitment to do (or refrain from doing) a certain deed and in so doing invites the promisee to trust that she will do that deed. Importantly, the trust involved in promising is a special sort of trust. In promising, the promisor invites the promisee to believe that the promisor not only will do the deed, but that the promisor also sees herself as taking on a moral commitment to do the deed, and that for that reason the promisee can trust that the promisor will do the deed.

There was a time, the author believes, when mortgage contracts were promises in this sense. When borrowers were more likely to borrow from a local bank and make their promise to a local banker who was likely to hold the mortgage, borrowers likely saw themselves as taking on a moral commitment. The chapter argues that borrowers are more likely to see themselves as merely assuring lenders that they can be trusted because they are taking on a legal commitment, with legal consequences. Although mortgage contracts still contain promissory language, that alone is not sufficient to constitute a promise. What is required is a context that makes clear that the would-be promisor is offering assurances that she sees herself as morally committed, not just subject to sanctions. In today's world of mortgage brokers, remote mortgage holders, and impersonal credit scores, borrowers are much more likely to see themselves as merely making themselves vulnerable to legal sanctions. Whether strategic default is morally defensible is, of course, a further question. But if it is, it may be because borrowers are simply not making promises in the relevant sense.

I. INTRODUCTION

The recent boom and bust in the U.S. housing market have generated much discussion about strategic default in the popular press. This practice, where a homeowner defaults on his mortgage contract even though he could afford to make the payments with relative ease, may make financial sense when property values have declined so much that the borrower owes much more on the mortgaged property than its market value. It is impossible to know what percentage of defaults in any given year are strategic, though one suspects the percentage must be small, as most who default are probably simply unable to pay. Recently, some legal academics have defended the practice, arguing that strategic default is morally acceptable. In a recent article I offered a critical response to these arguments.[1] My article did not offer an original argument that strategic default is immoral; rather I showed how several arguments defending the practice are misguided. I took it as rather obvious that a homeowner who had borrowed hundreds of thousands of dollars, promised to pay it back, and was able to pay it back quite easily should actually do so. To say that others did not find this point so obvious would be an understatement.

Many of the criticisms my article received were either the result of kneejerk anti-bank sentiment or else a failure to appreciate that I was only addressing those situations where a borrower truly could afford to pay with relative ease (however

[1] Curtis Bridgeman, *The Morality of Jingle Mail: Moral Myths about Strategic Default*, 46 Wake Forest L. Rev. 123 (2011).

defined) but chose not to. But a more interesting line of objection emerged: many of the critics felt that either the contracts in question did not contain promises or else they contained merely a "business agreement" that could be broken at any time so long as one was willing to suffer the consequences – especially in states where the remedies upon default were limited (e.g., in "non-recourse" states, where deficiency judgments are not available, leaving lenders to look only to the value of the house in the event of default). What struck me as odd about these arguments is that they ignored the specific language in mortgage contracts whereby the borrower explicitly promises to pay back the amount borrowed plus interest. Much more attention was paid to the remedies available in the event of breach, or in some cases the language of other contracts that allowed promisors to cancel by paying a fee. That focus makes some sense for a legal argument, but it seemed to me that anyone interested in the moral question could not ignore the explicit promise.

After much reflection, I now think I understand why people do not see these contracts as constituting promises, despite the fact that they contain explicit promissory language. According to one leading way of thinking, a promise means knowingly undertaking a moral commitment to do (or refrain from doing) a certain deed and, in so doing, inviting the promisee to trust that the promisor will do that deed.[2] Importantly, on this view, the trust involved in promising is a special sort of trust: the promisor invites the promisee to believe that the promisor not only will do the deed, but that the promisor also sees herself as taking on a moral commitment to do the deed and assures the promisee that *for that reason* (perhaps among others) the promisee can trust that the promisor will do the deed. This is distinct from other ways in which the promisor may convince the promisee that the promisor can be trusted. For example, a promisor may mention that he would fear retribution from the promisee's relatives, or that his friends would think poorly of him if he were to break his promise, or that he has a side bet with a third party that he will do the deed, and so on.

There was a time, I believe, when mortgage contracts *were* promises. When borrowers were more likely to borrow from a local lender and make their promise to a local lender who was likely to hold the mortgage, borrowers likely saw themselves as taking on a moral commitment to repay the loan and as communicating such an intention to the lender. Now, I will argue, borrowers are more likely to see themselves as merely taking on a legal commitment with legal consequences. Although mortgage contracts still contain promissory language, that alone is not sufficient to constitute a promise. Promising requires a context that makes clear that the would-be promisor is offering assurances that she sees herself as giving herself a moral reason to perform, and not just reassuring the promisee that she has other

[2] T. M. Scanlon, What We Owe to Each Other, ch. 7 (1998).

kinds of reasons to perform. In today's world of mortgage brokers, remote mortgage holders, and impersonal credit scores, borrowers are much more likely to see themselves as merely making themselves vulnerable to legal sanctions.

So it may be the case that despite the promissory language in mortgage contracts, borrowers today do not make promises when they enter into a typical mortgage contract. It does not follow, though, that strategic default is morally permissible. I will argue that would-be strategic defaulters are morally required to keep their non-promissory agreements for precisely the same moral reason that promises give moral obligations. The philosopher Timothy Scanlon has argued (persuasively, to my mind) that promises are merely one member of a family of obligations that arise from what he calls the principle of fidelity.[3] That principle, roughly speaking, forbids people to fail to live up to expectations they have intentionally created in others in situations where the others desire an assurance that an actor will do a specified deed. One way of giving such assurances is to promise, but the principle is not limited to promising, as I will explain. It is wrong to break one's promises because it is *generally* wrong to give assurances and then fail to live up to those assurances. The moral obligation does not depend on the presence of a promise.

II. WHY DO PEOPLE MAKE PROMISES?

To understand what promises are, it might be useful to begin by understanding what promises do. In short, promises give the promisee an assurance that the promisor will do (or refrain from doing) a specified act.

Suppose that we are farmers who own adjacent parcels of land and that a stream runs across both of our parcels.[4] Suppose further that I would like to build up the banks of the stream on my land in order to prevent flooding, but that I cannot do so without assistance. I therefore solicit your help. Suppose that you and I have no particular ties of friendship or family to one another that create a duty to help each other. I propose that if you will help me build up the banks of the stream on my land, then I will help you build up the banks of the stream on your land. With no reason to trust one another, though, you might worry that you may help me with the banks on my land, only to have me renege on the deal and refuse to help you with the banks on your land. (Of course, you could insist that we work on the banks on your land first, but then I would have the same doubts as to whether you would help me later.)

3 *Id.*

4 I borrow this illustration and much of the related discussion in this and the following paragraph from Scanlon, *see id.* at 297, who appears to have been inspired by Hume, *see* David Hume, A TREATISE OF HUMAN NATURE 520–21 (L. A. Selby-Bigge ed., Clarendon Press, 1888) (1739).

What I need to do is convince you that I will still have a reason to help you with your banks after you have already helped me with my own. We can imagine many possible reasons that I might cite in order to convince you. For example, I might point out that it would be economically bad for me if the stream floods your land, because the runoff would flow onto my adjoining land.[5] Or, I might convince you that I will perform for sentimental reasons, that is, because I would be emotionally moved by your willingness to help. Or, I might convince you that I have a side bet with a third party that I will keep all of my commitments for a year. Or, I might convince you that I am a "stern Kantian moralist" and offer a promise to help you if you will help me.[6]

In all four examples, I give you a reason to believe that I will help you if you will first help me. But only the last case is a promise, because only in the last case do I convince you that you can trust that I will perform because I am willing to give myself a moral duty to perform. There is a difference between saying, "You have reason to believe that I will do X because [in the first example] I will have an economic interest in doing X," and "You have reason to believe that I will do X because I hereby promise to do X and thus give myself a moral commitment to do X." What is different about promising is that promises supply a self-imposed moral reason to perform that did not exist prior to the promise.

For the moment, we can be agnostic about what grounds the moral duty to keep a promise. For now, all we are trying to understand is what a promise is. Therefore, it does not matter exactly why promises provide moral obligations – whether, for example, one really is a "stern Kantian moralist," is a utilitarian, or has some other explanation for why promises create moral obligations. The point is simply that when one promises one takes on a moral obligation to do the specified act, and, very often, the point of the promise is to convince the promisee that one sees oneself as having a moral obligation to do the specified act.

It is possible, of course, that my promise could give me both self-interested reasons and moral reasons to perform. Having promised, I incur a moral duty to perform, and thereby have a moral reason to perform regardless of what is in my own best interests; at the same time, my promise may make it in my own best interests to perform in order to avoid social sanction or some other negative consequence. Promising might give me multiple reasons to perform, and therefore give the promisee multiple reasons to believe I will perform. The presence of these non-moral reasons to perform does not, however, mean that I have not made a promise.

5 Scanlon's example differs from Hume's in that Hume's farmers were simply to help each other harvest crops; thus, the failure to harvest the second farmer's crop would be unlikely to harm the first farmer once his own crops were harvested.

6 See Scanlon, *supra* note 2, at 297–98.

Although it is easy to imagine how it would be useful for me to give myself a reason to perform in this manner, thereby perhaps convincing you to cooperate with me, there has been much debate about whether I can do so. There mere fact that I would welcome a moral obligation does not mean that I can have one just by willing it to be so, and Hume claimed to find the idea that I could as mysterious as the doctrine of transubstantiation.[7] But that debate is not our concern here. All we need for now is to note that, if I can convince you that I see myself as taking on a moral obligation to perform, and you believe that I take my moral obligations seriously, then you will have some reason to trust me and cooperate with me.

Of course, even if you are not bothered by Hume's challenge, you may simply not believe that I am a moral person. In that case, even if I promise, you may not be ready to trust me. But this lack of trust is a problem that contract law can overcome. If you and I live in a society that enforces contracts, then you may have reason to believe that I will perform even if you do not trust me to live up to my moral obligations. Indeed, as I have argued at length elsewhere, this is precisely contract law's purpose.[8] Contract law does not aim to enforce our moral obligations as such; rather, it provides trust so that we can cooperate with one another in situations like the one I have described. You can have a certain amount of confidence that even if I will not live up to my moral obligations, I will live up to my legal obligations – if for no other reason than that there will be bad consequences for me if I do not.

III. ARE CONTRACTS PROMISES?

Typically people make promises and contracts for the same reason: to convince another person that they will do a specified act. However, just because people typically make contracts and promises for the same reason does not mean that they are the same thing. Both Restatements of Contracts define a contract as a promise that the law will enforce.[9] But while it may have once been the case that most contracts contained promises, it has never been the case – at least not in modern times – that

7 I shall farther observe, that since every new promise imposes a new obligation of morality on the person who promises, and since this new obligation arises from his will; 'tis one of the most mysterious and incomprehensible operations that can possibly be imagin'd, and may even be compar'd to *transubstantiation*, or *holy orders*, where a certain form of words, along with a certain intention, changes entirely the nature of an external object, and even of a human creature. Hume, supra note 4, at 524 (emphasis in original, footnote omitted).

8 Curtis Bridgeman, *Contracts as Plans*, 2009 U. Ill. L. Rev. 341 (2009).

9 More precisely (and awkwardly), the Restatements define contracts as promises "for the breach of which the law gives a remedy, or the performance of which the law in some way recognizes as a duty." Restatement of Contracts § 1 (1932); Restatement (Second) of Contracts § 1 (1979).

every enforceable contract necessarily contains a promise. Consider, for example, Michael Pratt's example of Rudy the Electrician.[10] Rudy is an "eccentric, earnest, solitary sort who takes pains to minimize moral claims others have on him."[11] Thus, Rudy will only work with customers who accept his disavowal of any promissory obligation to complete the agreed-upon work and will make only purely legal commitments. In Pratt's example, a customer named Eliza signs an agreement with Rudy plainly stating that the two intend to enter into a legally binding exchange agreement but do "not intend to bind [themselves] morally...; these are contractual undertakings, not promises."[12] The point, according to Pratt, is that this agreement should be understood as a binding contract even though there is no promise-based moral obligation underwriting it.

Although people like Rudy are surely rare, it is certainly the case that such an agreement would be enforceable in contract law. And for good reason: Rudy and Eliza would like to enter into a mutually beneficial arrangement in conditions where they have no particular reason to trust one another. The law can easily provide such trust, and it is the goal of contract law to do so. The fact that they are not entering into moral commitments is of no moment. Contract law is not really concerned with moral obligations anyway. This was part of what Pratt was trying to show (as a counterexample to Charles Fried's promise theory of contract),[13] but there is plenty of doctrinal evidence for the proposition as well.[14]

Of course, a much more likely scenario would be an electrician simply promising to do the work, taking on both a moral and a legal commitment. Indeed, the Rudy example is a bit fanciful not just because it is hard to imagine someone with Rudy's peculiar reservations about moral commitments, but also because it is hard to imagine the expression of such commitments not giving Eliza great pause. In a more ordinary scenario, she might expect Rudy to be motivated both by a moral commitment and by a legal commitment (as well as a concern about his own reputation). And, in fact, with such low-stakes transactions, the costs of enforcing a legal commitment may be so high that a customer would rationally look for non-legal reasons to trust the electrician. But, the fact that there are ordinarily multiple reasons to perform, and to trust another to perform, arising from the same agreement does not mean that those reasons are not distinguishable. There is no necessary tie between contract and promise.

10 Michael G. Pratt, *Contract: Not Promise*, 35 FLA. ST. U. L. REV. 801 (2008).

11 *Id.* at 807.

12 *Id.* at 807–08.

13 Charles Fried, CONTRACT AS PROMISE: A THEORY OF CONTRACTUAL OBLIGATION (1981).

14 *See, e.g.*, Curtis Bridgeman, *Reconciling Strict Liability With Corrective Justice in Contract Law*, 75 FORDHAM L. REV. 3013, 3015–20 (2007).

IV. ARE MORTGAGE CONTRACTS TYPICALLY PROMISES?

We should begin by noting the fact that mortgage contracts clearly contain promissory language. This is a fact that has been sometimes ignored in the debate about strategic default. One oft-discussed article cited cancellation provisions in cell-phone contracts and cavalierly claimed that mortgage contracts are "no different in principle" from cell-phone contracts without citing any language from mortgage contracts or attempting to explain how the explicit promissory language in mortgage contracts looks nothing like a cancellation clause.[15] In my first article on strategic default, I took the promissory language from mortgage contracts at face value, considered it obvious that they contained promises, and proceeded to the question of under what circumstances one might be excused from performing such a promise.[16]

But saying (or signing one's name to) the words "I promise" is neither necessary nor sufficient for promising. What we must do is interpret those words in the context in which the speaker (or signer) uttered them. In the right context, one can promise without saying the words "I promise" – as, for example, one might do if one were asked if one promised and replied, "I do." Similarly, in some contexts uttering the words "I promise" will not constitute a promise at all. For example, an actor uttering the words "I promise" as a character on stage would not herself be undertaking a promissory obligation. Our question, then, is whether the words "I promise to pay" constitute a promise in the context of borrowing money to buy a house (or using one's house as collateral for a loan).

There may have been a time when the typical mortgage contract did include a promise. In an era where lending transactions took place on a much more localized level than is now currently the case, it seems natural to think of mortgage contracts as containing promises. Borrowers were likely to know their banker, or at least the bank president, personally, and a person's personal reputation among her peers in the community was at stake with each transaction. A borrower who looks his lender (or its representative) in the eye and sees that person in the community – and perhaps is more likely to be aware of the ill effects of a failure to pay for that lender – seems more likely to consider the loan transaction a moral commitment.

To be sure, even in small-town America of fifty years ago mortgage contracts were not *only* promises. Bankers made sure to get both a promissory note and a mortgage on the house (though I have been loosely referring to both agreements here as "mortgage contracts"). Securing the loan with collateral provided additional assurance to lenders that the lender would be protected if the borrower failed to pay

[15] Brent T. White, *The Morality of Strategic Default*, 58 UCLA L. Rev. Discourse 155, 158 (2010), *available at* http://www.uclalawreview.org/pdf/discourse/58-8.pdf.

[16] *See* Bridgeman, *supra* note 1, at 140–42.

(whether she could afford to pay and chose not to, or was simply unable). Even unsecured loans were typically memorialized in a legally binding, written agreement rather than just by handshake, giving the lender some assurance of recourse to law if necessary. But this does not mean that the borrower did not also take on a moral commitment, and communicate this commitment to the lender in order to assure the lender that the borrower would have not only legal, but also moral reasons to repay the loan.

But there is some reason to think that modern mortgage contracts do not constitute promises in most transactions today the way they used to, at least in the United States. Home loans are often brokered by third parties who have no stake in the loan, and the rights to payment are often sold on the mortgage securities market soon after, or even before, the transaction is finalized. Lending decisions are based more on credit scores and loan-to-value ratios than a personal relationship with the borrower. Banks have become larger and larger, and a high percentage of home loans are made by national or even international lending institutions.

Of course, the lender – who almost always provides the paperwork – still includes promissory language in the contract the borrower signs. But it is not at all clear that lenders make any special effort to ensure that borrowers actually see themselves as taking on a moral commitment. And borrowers, in turn, may see themselves as mere customers of the bank who are judged by their credit scores and income, but not seen as individuals in any personal way. To the degree that they believe the banks see the transaction as devoid of promises, they themselves are more likely to see it that way as well.

That is not to say that borrowers in these transactions no longer see themselves as taking on serious commitments. Rather, my point is that they may be more likely to see themselves as taking on only legal commitments, not moral ones. They know they are giving the bank assurances that they will perform, but the assurances take the form of putting themselves on the hook legally to repay the money (or potentially forfeit the home). In this context, the words "I promise to pay" (if the borrower even notices those words) do not necessarily mean what they would mean if uttered to a friend. Instead, in this context, they may well mean something like "You can be assured that I will pay, because I am hereby making myself vulnerable to legal sanctions if I do not." That is not at all the same as saying "You can be assured that I will pay, because I see myself as taking on a moral commitment to pay."

I do not know whether this way of thinking is an accurate description of our current practices. In fact, I still feel that the presence of promissory language is strong prima facie evidence that a promise has been made. But, supposing that this view, or something much like this view, is correct, would it then be morally permissible to default strategically on a home mortgage on the grounds that one had not actually promised to perform?

V. IF MODERN MORTGAGE CONTRACTS ARE TYPICALLY NOT PROMISES, IS STRATEGIC DEFAULT MORALLY ACCEPTABLE AFTER ALL?

Let us begin with a reminder about what I mean by the term "strategic default." I use that term to refer only to cases where borrowers who can comfortably afford to pay choose not to do so, most likely because on balance they find it not in their interest to do so (presumably because the consequences of default are considered less onerous than the price of paying off the loan). I do not include those who cannot afford to pay their loan in this definition. (And their case would be an easy moral case as well, because one is not morally required to do what one is unable to do: "ought" implies "can.") I also leave it to others to decide how to define what "comfortably" means. It is surely an interesting question whether one is required to sacrifice retirement savings to pay off an underwater mortgage, for example, but that is not our question here. I am only concerned with the question of whether it is ever wrong to walk away from one's mortgage when one could easily pay, leaving the bank with the house but ignoring any deficiency between the value of the home and the unpaid debt. Those who talk of a "right" to walk away or an unwritten "put option" in a mortgage contract would apparently deny this.[17] For the sake of simplicity, let us also assume that the lender was guilty of no particular malfeasance in the loan transaction, e.g. lying to the borrower or falsifying paperwork.[18] In short, let us assume the best-case scenario: a sophisticated borrower who made a well-informed decision to borrow, was not cheated in the transaction, and now has the ability to pay the mortgage back with relative ease even though it is not in her best financial interests to do so.[19]

Suppose, then, that what I have suggested here is correct: borrowers who enter into mortgage contracts today typically are not actually promising to perform. Rather, they see themselves as making themselves vulnerable to legal sanctions in order to induce banks to loan money, but not as making a moral commitment to pay back the money. The banks seek a reason to believe that borrowers will pay the money back, but the kind of reason they seek is not a moral commitment, but rather merely a legal commitment. Borrowers, in turn, give legal commitments, but do not understand the promissory language to which they agree (if they notice it at

[17] *See, e.g.*, Brent T. White, *Underwater and Not Walking Away: Shame, Fear, and the Social Management of the Housing Crisis*, 45 Wake Forest L. Rev. 971, 1006, 1011–12 (2010).

[18] Surely the banks were guilty of some more general malfeasance, but that is a point I discussed elsewhere. *See* Bridgeman, *supra* note 1, at 133–40.

[19] Some have argued to me that this case rarely, if ever exists. That may be so, though I am not so sure. But it is a useful exercise to figure out the moral boundaries in easy cases first, no matter how uncommon such easy cases are in practice. If we can do so, then we will be in a better position to tackle the more difficult cases, such as borrowers who can afford to pay, but not very comfortably.

all) as constituting an act of giving themselves a moral reason to perform in order to gain the bank's trust. If that is correct, does it mean that it is acceptable for borrowers to default strategically? I will argue no: Strategic default is immoral even for non-promissory contracts.

First, let us return to the question we passed over earlier: why it is that promises create moral obligations. This is a topic on which much has been written, far too much to survey here. Utilitarians, of course, argue that promises give moral obligations because (or to the extent that) breaking promises reduces overall welfare.[20] Others argue that it would be unfair for individuals to benefit from the practice of promising while undermining that very practice by breaching.[21] And Kantians argue that breaking one's promises violates the categorical imperative.[22]

For my part, I would like to return to Tim Scanlon, who I think has given the most persuasive account of why promises create moral obligations. For Scanlon, promissory obligations are "one special case of a wider category of duties and obligations regarding the expectations we lead others to form about what we intend to do."[23] When we make a promise we invite the promisee to expect that we will do what we say. Very often the promisee has reason to want us to do the promised act, and also reason to want to be assured in advance that we will do the promised act.

Scanlon posits a handful of moral principles which he claims govern (though not necessarily exclusively) our giving of assurances.[24] For example, he argues that it would generally be wrong of me to manipulate you by inducing you to do something I want you to do (e.g., help me build up the banks of my stream) by leading you to believe I will do something that you want me to do (e.g., help you to build up the banks of your stream) when I actually have no intention of doing any such thing.[25] Even absent intentional manipulation it would be wrong of me carelessly to lead you to form a false belief about my intentions, and if I do lead you to such a belief then I owe it to you to take steps to prevent losses you may incur due to my carelessness. Most importantly, if I do knowingly and intentionally lead you to believe that I will do a specified act that you want to be assured I will do, then I owe it to you to do that act.

Scanlon offers a contractualist argument for the truth of these moral principles, buttressed by a series of thought experiments. This is not the place to review those arguments in any detail. Much else has been written about them, and while I find

[20] *See, e.g.*, Neil MacCormick, *Voluntary Obligations and Normative Powers I*, 46 PROC. ARISTOTELIAN SOC'Y SUPP. 59, 73 (1972).

[21] *See, e.g.*, John Rawls, A THEORY OF JUSTICE 303–05 (rev. ed. 1999).

[22] *See, e.g.*, Immanuel Kant, GROUNDING OF THE METAPHYSICS OF MORALS 40 (Lewis White Beck trans. & ed. 1959); Fried, *supra* note 13, at 14–19.

[23] Scanlon, *supra* note 2, at 295.

[24] *Id.* at 296–309.

[25] *See id.* at 297–98.

them largely compelling, one need not buy into his entire account in order to see how it helps to illuminate the question we face here. It is important, however, to note one key feature of Scanlon's account: the moral principles do not apply only to promises, but also to any method of giving the sought-after assurances.

Consider first a simple case. Suppose I want you to give me money. In order to induce you to do so, I hatch an elaborate plan to make you believe that if you give me money, I would be so overwhelmed with gratitude that I would return the favor by giving you much more money later – something I, in fact, have no intention of doing. My plan need not even involve direct communication between us, much less my giving of a promise to you. I might instead plant stories in the local newspaper, hire actors to say things around you that lead you to form a false belief about my intentions and tendencies, and so on.[26] Such a plot would be morally wrong, and it would be wrong for the same reason that offering a lying promise (i.e., a promise I have no intention to keep at the time I make it) would be wrong. It would manipulate you in an unacceptable way that uses you and fails to show you proper respect as a person of equal moral standing. Whether I manipulate you with a lying promise or an elaborate, non-promissory scheme is of little moment.

More realistic examples are actually easy to find. Many standard-form consumer transactions try to skate a thin line between commitment and non-commitment. Credit card companies would very much like their consumers to believe that their rates will not rise, but they avoid commitments whenever possible and prefer to reserve the right to change terms at any time. Airlines encourage the belief that your flight will leave at a specified time (both by posting that time and by touting their own reliability), but in the fine print (these days in the "terms and conditions" on their Web sites) specifically claim that the schedules are not part of the contract. It is an open question whether such agreements involve promises at all.[27] But to the extent such representations are intended to mislead hearers about the speaker's (or anyone's) intentions or commitments, they are manipulative and immoral in the same way that lying promises are.

Presumably most contracts do not contain lying promises. No doubt, most borrowers in the mortgage context do intend to repay the loan at the time they make the contract, even if they are not promising to do so. But they have still led the lender to expect their performance. In fact, they have induced the lender to hand over a large sum of money in expectation of that performance. Having done so, borrowers incur a duty to repay the money as they assured the lender they would, whether they assured the lender by means of a contract, a promise, both, or by some other means.

[26] This is similar to Scanlon's example about the farmer dropping hints at the feed store. *See id.* at 305.

[27] *See* Curtis Bridgeman & Karen Sandrik, *Bullshit Promises*, 76 Tenn. L. Rev. 379 (2009).

To see that this is so, recall the agreement between Rudy the electrician and Eliza, his customer. They agreed that Rudy would perform services for pay, and further agreed that their agreement was legally enforceable but that it did not constitute a promise. Suppose that after reaching this agreement, Rudy performs the agreed-upon services, but Eliza, without justification or explanation, refuses to pay.[28] Is it morally wrong of her to refuse?

It seems to me quite clear that it is. She has intentionally led Rudy to believe that if he provides her the electrical services she needs she will pay him for his work. The fact that she used a legal commitment rather than a promise to lead him to this belief matters little. The reason it would be wrong of her to promise to do it and not perform is because it is *generally* wrong intentionally to induce someone to form expectations about your future conduct in order to get them to do what you want and then fail to live up to those expectations.[29] Promising is one way of inducing those expectations, but only one. Making contracts is another.

The Rudy and Eliza example may be particularly tricky, though, if Rudy has expressed his desire to avoid not only any promissory commitments, but any mutual moral commitments whatsoever. To my mind it would still be wrong of Eliza to breach once she has led him to expect performance. That is especially true once she has allowed him to perform the work on her house.[30] I am not sure that our duty to show others equal concern and respect can be so easily waived by agreement in the way that our duty not to punch each other can be waived by boxers who step into the ring.

But even if doubts remain about Rudy and Eliza, mortgage contracts are not nearly so difficult. The parties do not expressly agree that there will be no moral commitments of any sort. On the contrary, the explicit language is promissory. I have suggested here that typical borrowers these days may well not understand themselves as making any sort of promise despite that language, but that does not mean that the context calls for a complete waiver of all moral obligations. It just means that borrowers may not be trying to assure the lender that they can be trusted because of a promise. Instead, they are trying to assure the lender in other ways. The goal, though, is the same: to induce the lender to expect performance so that the lender will hand over a large sum of money. Having accomplished this goal, a borrower is morally required to do as he said he would do unless he can provide a justification for not doing so, such as an inability to pay, or proof that he was lied to in the original agreement.

[28] If you like, you can further suppose that, for some reason, the agreement turns out not to be legally enforceable – perhaps Rudy lost the signed document and their jurisdiction requires a signed document for enforcement.

[29] *See* Scanlon, *supra* note 2, at 298.

[30] One might argue that her duty is limited to reimbursement for his time and labor if that amount is lower than the contract price.

One might object that the moral principles Scanlon identifies are grounded in our general duties to show equal concern and respect to other persons, acknowledging their moral worth as individuals, and that we do not owe these duties to abstract entities like banks. But this objection is based on willful myopia. It is true that lending institutions are not themselves people (despite Mitt Romney's claim that "corporations are people, too"), but they are owned by people, and their financial transactions have direct impact on the well-being of their human investors. Insurance fraud is not acceptable just because the titular victim is an abstract entity rather than one's neighbor, and the same is true for strategic default.

One might also object that, in this context, the agreement does not call for full performance, but rather either performance or the surrendering of the home as collateral. This argument might be especially appealing in non-recourse systems. But true non-recourse systems are actually quite rare in the United States.[31] And, even in the non-recourse states, the contractual language does not usually give the borrower the right to walk away from any deficiency. Of course, we have been discussing how one should perhaps read beyond the explicit promissory language to the background context, which may well be based on legal obligations, but not moral commitments. That does not mean, however, that we may read anything we like into the context. Unless it can be shown that, when borrowers assure lenders of performance, they are really assuring them of either performance or merely surrendering the collateral – despite no language to that effect, and indeed a good bit of language to the contrary – then it would be a huge stretch to argue that the agreement is really a non-promissory assurance that the borrower will either pay the loan back or surrender the house and walk away from any remaining balance.[32] Even the Holmesian "option theory of contract," which sees all contractual duties as merely the duty either to perform or pay damages, does not go so far, because the Holmesian version includes the duty to pay expectation damages.[33] Reading mortgage contracts as mere "catch me if you can" assurances goes well beyond an interpretive exercise.

VI. CONCLUSION

I have tried to explain a broadly held intuition that mortgage contracts, at least in today's mortgage industry, do not really contain promises despite their promissory language. My explanation is that promises, by definition, involve an assurance that the promisor can be trusted at least in part because the promisor is taking on a moral commitment to perform. While many contracts may contain such promises, it may

[31] *See* Bridgeman, *supra* note 1, at 126–27.

[32] For more discussion of the interpretation of mortgage agreements, see *id.* at 140–50.

[33] *Id.* at 145.

be the case that most commercial transactions between consumers and large companies, including agreements between consumers and large lending institutions, no longer do. It may be mutually understood that these transactions are impersonal and more reliant on legal remedies than on promissory commitments.

I have also argued, however, that even if this is true as an empirical matter, it does not make borrowers free, morally speaking, to engage in strategic default. It is wrong to induce others to lend money by assuring them that they will be repaid and then refuse to repay the money without justification, whether one induces them by means of a promissory assurance or a legal assurance. The wrong involved in breaking promises is just one example of a failure to respect others by failing to live up to the assurances one has given, by whatever means.

Both lessons may well go far beyond the mortgage context. Our commercial transactions are dominated more and more by interactions with large companies rather than friends and neighbors. (At most, our friends and neighbors may be representing those companies.) These transactions are seldom negotiated on an individual basis, certainly beyond the most basic terms, and seem to be becoming less and less personal. That may mean that promising is a less central feature of our contracting experience than ever before. But modern contract law was never aimed at policing promissory morality to begin with. Nor does the absence of promising free us of all moral responsibility toward our contracting partners. Whether promises are present or not, contracting still commonly involves reassuring other parties that we will act a certain way in the future, and inviting those parties to trust that we will do so. Having invited that trust, and often profited from it, we still owe it to the other party to perform as planned unless we can establish some special justification.

PART II

Normative Views of Contract

Part II looks at three views of contract most easily summarized as natural law theory, theory of networked contracts, and the equitable theory of contracts. All three views contest the classical contract model and the unfettered supremacy of freedom of contract. Chapter 5 asserts that contract law is based on a normative calculus (deontological-consequentialist) and that contract doctrine should forward these normative commitments. The chapter shows the normative weaknesses of contract doctrine in the areas of formation of agreement and risk allocation. The chapter argues that both deontological and consequentialist theories of contracts have shortcomings. It asserts that a fuller understanding of human agency is needed, based upon the findings of neuroscience, to rationalize all of contract law.

Chapter 6 notes that classical contract law was challenged in the twentieth century by mass consumer sales and standard form contracting. It suggests that in the twenty-first century a new challenge has arisen – that of network contracting. Both commercial contractors and consumers form networks of contracts electronically and non-electronically. The chapter seeks to answer this question: What are the implications of this networked world for the law of contract? In the end, it concludes that contract law will need to be reformed to regulate contracts that have network effects.

Finally, Chapter 7 re-enters the debate over the role of equity in the application of contract law. The chapter's focus is solely on commercial transactions and the role of the principles of equitable trusts and fiduciary duties in resolving commercial disputes. The chapter first examines the use of equitable principles by parties in certain quasi-commercial transactions. It asserts that a careful reading of the case law shows factors that trigger the use of equitable principles in the name of contract law. It concludes that the recognition of this phenomenon will allow the myopic contract-only view of commercial transactions to be reformulated to openly recognize the relational-contextual elements courts use in resolving commercial contract disputes.

5

Naturalistic Contract

Peter A. Alces

The theoretical bases of contract generally are dependent on either deontological or consequentialist normative commitments, or some combination of the two. Contract doctrine should instantiate (or at least not frustrate) the operation of the normative calculus. The chapter assesses whether contract doctrine is deficient in forwarding such normative commitments. At the least, the normative inquiry is opaque as it relates to contract doctrine. The chapter describes the normative impotence of contract by focusing on the two foundations of consensual liability: allocation of risk and formation of agreement. The material on mistake, impracticability, and the modification of contract doctrine depicts how risks are allocated. The chapter draws from the most recent United States Supreme Court arbitration decisions to illustrate the failure of the agreement principle.

The chapter suggests that contract law doctrine can only make sense if we take account of the fundamental bases of the normative considerations we actually bring to the resolution of a contract controversy. Those bases are best revealed in recent neuroethical and evolutionary inquiries into the constitution of the human agent's normative commitments.

Finally, the chapter describes the apposite contract doctrine and surveys, summarily, the commentary that reveals the normative quandaries. It engages primarily apposite consequentialist theory but also suggests the limits of a deontological perspective that is subject to the same deficiencies as utilitarian analyses. From those premises apposite neuroscience findings are considered to see what, if anything, a more sophisticated sense of human agency can do to refine either the formation or application of doctrine. Ultimately, the chapter concludes that contract doctrine fails, at least in crucial ways and at crucial junctures, in relation to the preceding normative commitments.

I. INTRODUCTION

This chapter posits an empirical, reductionist approach to the persistent questions that contract law presents.[1] The object is either to resolve the questions or to appreciate better the barriers to their resolution. There is currently a naturalistic turn in the psychological[2] and philosophical[3] (and perhaps even jurisprudential[4]) literature, an emerging sense that real insights may be gained by drilling down rather than by looking heavenward. The tension is persistent; perhaps there is nothing new under the Sun.[5] Developments in the hard sciences, most notably neuroscience, have accommodated this new perspective; the relation between neuroscience and this new empiricism is at least coincident, and likely more than "coincidental" (in the colloquial sense).

But the argument here is not entirely dependent on the current (or, for that matter, even foreseeable) efficacy of neuroscientific insights. The argument does depend on a sense that neuroscience can – indeed, already has – affect our appreciation of what it means to be "human." We may anticipate that developments in the apposite science will be deliberate, even gradual, but we cannot rule out operation of something like "Moore's law,"[6] whereby advances proceed at a geometric rate. We could even conclude that the relationship between neuroscience and the law has been perennial: there are, after all, conceptions of capacity in the contract law not wholly unrelated to what we might term "folk neuroscience."[7] Ultimately, though, the most essential premise is that what we learn about human agency informs what we can know about our law generally, no less our contract law specifically.

1 Although the focus here is on contract law, this approach may offer insights into other areas of the law, or to the law more generally.

2 *See, e.g.*, Joshua D. Greene, *The Secret Joke of Kant's Soul*, 3 MORAL PSYCHOLOGY at 35 (2008); Richard Joyce, THE EVOLUTION OF MORALITY (MIT Press: 2006); Marc D. Hauser, MORAL MINDS: HOW NATURE DESIGNED OUR UNIVERSAL SENSE OF RIGHT AND WRONG (Little Brown: 2006); Jonathon Haidt, THE HAPPINESS HYPOTHESIS (Arrow books: 2006).

3 *See generally*, John M. Doris, LACK OF CHARACTER (Cambridge University Press: 2002).

4 *See, e.g.*, Michael Freeman, *Introduction: Law and the Brain*, 13 LAW AND NEUROSCIENCE: CURRENT ISSUES 1 (Michael Freeman ed., 2011); Semir Zeki & Oliver R. Goodenough, *Law and the Brain: An Introduction*, 359 PHIL. TRANS. ROYAL SOCIETY LONDON BIO. SCI. 1775 (2004). Thus far, attention has focused on the criminal law. *See, e.g.*, Owen D. Jones & Robert Kurzban, *Intuitions of Punishment*, 77 CHICAGO L. REV. 1633 (2010).

5 In the painting *School of Athens* (1511) by Raphael, Plato is depicted pointing upward, toward heaven. Next to him, Aristotle is depicted pointing downward, toward the Earth.

6 Moore's law is the application of exponential growth to the field of microchip technology; it predicts that computer processing speed capabilities double every eighteen months.

7 *See*, e.g., RESTATEMENT (SECOND) OF CONTRACTS §§ 12, 14–15 (discussing capacity to contract, including provisions regarding age and insanity); *cf.* MODEL PENAL CODE § 4.01 ("A person is not responsible for criminal conduct if at the time of such conduct as a result of mental disease or defect he lacks substantial capacity either to appreciate the criminality of his conduct or to conform his conduct to the requirements of the law.").

This chapter's naturalistic inquiry into the premises of contract liability is built around seven assertions, or stages of inquiry, that do not divide neatly into separate sections. The parts that follow will respond to these assertions in terms that constitute the naturalistic argument, and that challenge extant normative explanations of the doctrine:

1. The doctrine: All (or virtually all) of contract (at least the most interesting questions) resolves into either risk allocation or agreement (enough agreement?);
2. With regard to those issues, current doctrine accommodates "smuggling";
3. A conception of human agency that is more refined, more accurate than either consequentialism or deontology would impact contract doctrine and our appraisal of normative contact theory (it would be striking if that were not true);
4. Neuroscience could inform that refinement, but needs first to overcome fundamental theoretical challenges: most prominently, is the human agent nothing more than a situs of neurons firing? Does morality supervene on naturalistic phenomena? (The non-naturalist dilemma);
5. Neuroscience seems to confirm that we are consequentialists using deontology as a heuristic[8];
6. There is affinity between deontology and dualism (herein of "naturalistic fallacy");
7. This reductionist perspective could provide a guide to better doctrine and the basis to critique normative theories of contract.

Those assertions do not so much provide the organizing principle of this chapter as they posit a framework that will ultimately support the chapter's conclusions.

The purpose of this chapter is to describe in broad outline the contours of the inquiry built around these central assertions. The goal (in a later work) will eventually be to construct and justify these assertions fully, but for now the object is merely to offer a glimpse of the whole in order to accommodate appreciation of the fit among the parts.

II. ESSENTIAL NORMATIVITY OF CONTRACT DOCTRINE

The contract doctrine is composed in such a way as not just to accommodate but also actually to encourage normative analysis in the application of law to fact: it is not merely the product of a particular normative commitment (or stacking or

[8] *See* Laurence Tancredi, HARDWIRED BEHAVIOR: WHAT NEUROSCIENCE REVEALS ABOUT MORALITY 133 (Cambridge University Press: 2005) ("The brain at its most basic is designed to obtain rewards and avoid punishment.").

interrelation of normative commitments). Normative contract theory, at least in most of its iterations, has assumed that contract makes sense, can be rationalized in either consequentialist or deontic terms: we can interpret the doctrine as vindicating either an efficiency criterion (Pareto[9] or Kaldor-Hicks[10]) or some non-consequentialist duty,[11] typically in a Kantian sense of autonomy.[12] "Theories" of contract proliferate, even like Topsy. And, not surprisingly, most of the conversation explains what is wrong with each elaboration of preceding consequentialist or deontic perspectives.[13] There is much more smoke than light, and the smoke obscures, as smoke will.[14] While more epistemic theory has joined the conversation in other areas of the law, most notably the criminal law,[15] the pertinence of neuroscientific inquiry to contract has not been explored. This chapter is an effort to fill that gap in the literature and, in the process, to assert the importance of a more empirical perspective to all of law.

Richard Joyce has located our morality in our affective reactions, and so ultimately in the evolutionary forces that framed our emotions. We celebrate and denigrate because we are predisposed to find some things grand and others grotesque on account of forces operating on our forebears a couple of hundred thousand years ago.[16] Other evolutionary psychologists reach the same conclusion and are able to build an empirical structure that would describe the progress from emotion *to*

9 Given an initial allocation of goods, a "Pareto improvement" is a change to the allocation such that at least one individual is better off, while no other individual is worse off. A system is considered Pareto efficient when no further Pareto improvements can be made – that is when no individual's situation can be made better off without making another individual's situation worse. Richard A. Posner, ECONOMIC ANALYSIS OF LAW 12–13 (6th ed., Aspen Publishers: 2003).

10 Unlike Pareto efficiency, Kaldor-Hicks efficiency allows for improvements that may leave some individuals worse off, but which the parties would still make even if the beneficiaries of the improvement were required to compensate those individuals. Thus, an optimal result can be reached by arranging compensation from those that are made better off to those that are made worse off, so that all are better off than they were before. *Id.* at 13.

11 For examples of the non-consequentialist perspective, see generally, Charles Fried, CONTRACT AS PROMISE: A THEORY OF CONTRACTUAL OBLIGATION (Harvard University Press: 1981); Randy E. Barnett, *A Consent Theory of Contract*, 86 COLUM. L. REV. 269 (1986); Peter Benson, *The Unity of Contract Law*, *in* THE THEORY OF CONTRACT LAW: NEW ESSAYS 118 (Peter Benson ed., 2001).

12 *See, e.g.*, Fried, *supra* note 11; Thomas M. Scanlon, *Promises and Contracts*, *in* THE THEORY OF CONTRACT LAW: NEW ESSAYS 86 (Peter Benson ed., 2001).

13 *See, e.g.*, Peter A. Alces, A THEORY OF CONTRACT LAW: EMPIRICAL INSIGHTS AND MORAL PSYCHOLOGY 75–114 (2011) (discussing elaboration of normative theory of contract from deontic and consequentialist perspectives, and showing how each elaboration attempts to demonstrate the shortcomings of the preceding consequentialist or deontic arguments).

14 *See generally* Peter A. Alces, *Unintelligent Design in Contract*, 2008 U. ILL. L. REV. 505 (2008) (reviewing different normative theories of contract); Alces, *supra* note 13.

15 *See, e.g.*, Adam Kolber, *The Subjective Experience of Punishment*, 109 COLUM. L. REV. 182 (2009); Amanda C. Pustilnik, *Violence on the Brain: A Critique of Neuroscience in Criminal Law*, 44 WAKE FOREST L. REV. 183 (2009); Jones & Kurzban, *supra* note 4.

16 Joyce, *supra* note 2, at 7–8.

morality *to* law in empirical terms. What we find repulsive we deem immoral and what we find immoral we make illegal. That is not to suggest some lack of rationality. Just the contrary: our emotional reactions are heuristics supporting *generally* rational reactions, at least those reactions that would have been rational on the savannah (else *we* would not have forebears and would not be – though perhaps others would).[17] We thrive as a species, and have certainly won the competition for survival with other species, because of our ability to communicate (which accommodates collaboration).[18] And that communication can take normative form, in our ethics and morals. We exploit the salience of emotional reaction and moral opprobrium to normative effect.

In his generally troubling THE DISENCHANTMENT OF SECULAR DISCOURSE,[19] Steven Smith posited "smuggling," an idea about how values (normative analyses) are necessarily imported into the application of law to facts, the space within which doctrine operates. Smith tells us that, even despite ourselves (notwithstanding doctrine's efforts to objectify normativity), our discourse "smuggles in" normative considerations surreptitiously;[20] we cannot avoid such considerations because "our deepest convictions rely on such notions."[21] There is no reason to concede that these notions are real, have any reality referent beyond their deontic tug. It is enough for present purposes to appreciate that we understand and talk about our emotional reactions in normative terms, and that is true whether those reactions resonate with something more substantial than evolutionarily programmed neural excitation. Smith's point is that there is something irresistible about this kind of smuggling; doctrine cannot constrain it: "We have little choice except to smuggle such notions into the conversation – to introduce them incognito under some sort of secular disguise."[22]

In the contract law, as in all areas of the law, there are several junctures that could facilitate such values smuggling, and it would not be particularly worthwhile to rehearse all or even most of them here. It suffices to rely on two central contract issues that reveal the normative dynamic: risk allocation and conceptions of agreement. (Indeed, it may be that all of contract ultimately resolves into one of those questions or some combination of the two, but it is not necessary to reach

[17] *See, e.g.*, *id.*; Haidt, *supra* note 2.

[18] On the role of conscience in cooperation, see Lynn Stoudt, CULTIVATING CONSCIENCE: HOW GOOD LAWS MAKE GOOD PEOPLE (Princetown University Press: 2011).

[19] Steven D. Smith, THE DISENCHANTMENT OF SECULAR DISCOURSE (Harvard University Press: 2010) (relying on the supernatural to explain human normativity).

[20] Certainly, the smuggling is sometimes explicit as well, as in the use of the term "justice" in the Restatement, Second of Contracts. *See* Peter A. Alces, *On Discovering Doctrine: Justice in Contract Agreement*, 83 WASH U. L. Q. 471, 483 (2005).

[21] Smith, *supra* note 19, at 26.

[22] *Id.* at 26–27.

that conclusion here.)[23] "Efficiency" and "promise" can do only so much work; the doctrine will have to distill those conceptions in terms of risk allocation and agreement.

That insight (or, at least assertion) vindicates reliance on particular aspects of doctrine, ultimately, to manifest the pertinence and power of an empirical perspective. Consider first allocation of risk:

The "mistake" doctrine in contract distinguishes cases of mistaken value (no contract avoidance) from the parties' mistake as to the character of the contract subject matter (contract avoidance). If buyer and seller disagree as to the value of the Mustang that is the subject of their transaction, well, that is just how markets work: get the assets to the party who values them more. But if A thinks she is selling a car and B thinks he is buying a horse, then mistake doctrine intervenes to relieve the parties from their misunderstanding, even if B would have wanted, after the fact, to take advantage of what turned out to be a very good price for a car. The canonical cases describe that value-character distinction.[24] But the dichotomy, particularly its vagueness, provides the means for a court's values to be smuggled in.

When a marriage dissolves and the court must determine whether the settlement agreement was the product of mistake,[25] and so avoidable on that basis, how should it characterize one party's misapprehension of an "account" that was actually the subject matter of a Ponzi scheme? Is that a mistake of value (surely the funds deposited by a Ponzi scheme victim are value-less or nearly so) or a mistake of characterization (are the funds even an "account")? More essentially, does the value-character dichotomy do the work that the doctrine would have it do? Or is it merely a means for the court to describe its conclusions in terms that can then claim a doctrinal imprimatur? Whatever the doctrine does endeavor to isolate, is it clear that the value-character dichotomy provides the means to instantiate that object? Those questions suggest the salience of smuggling.

[23] Charles Fried, for example, argues that the majority of contract law can be explained by positing the "promise principle" of agreement as the moral basis for contract. Those portions of the doctrine which cannot be accounted for by the promise principle (because parties only *seem* to agree, as in mistake and frustration), Fried claims are largely explained by principles of risk allocation. *See* Fried, *supra* note 11, at 57–62.

[24] *Compare Sherwood v. Walker*, 33 N.W. 919, 923 (Mich. 1887) ("[A] party who has given an apparent consent to a contract of sale may refuse to execute it … if the assent was founded, or the contract made, upon the [mutual] mistake of a material fact."), *with Wood v. Boynton*, 25 N.W. 42, 45 (Wis. 1885) ("In the absence of fraud or warranty, the value of the property sold, as compared with the price paid, is no ground for a rescission of a sale.").

[25] *Simkin v. Blank*, 80 A.D.3d 401 (N.Y. App. Div. 2011) (reformation of a divorce contract to reflect that "accounts" held in Bernard Madoff's Ponzi scheme were not actually assets, despite both parties' mistaken belief that they were).

Next consider impracticability, the contemporary iteration of what began as an "impossibility" doctrine.[26] The apposite Restatement and Uniform Commercial Code provisions focus on the occurrence of a contingency the nonoccurrence of which was a "basic assumption" upon which the parties contracted.[27] That formula leaves a good deal of room for smuggling, and the language of the cases bears that out.[28] The issue – again, as in the case of mistake – concerns allocation of risk: indeed, it is axiomatic that mistake and impracticability concern the same calculus, just at different times.[29] Mistake is pertinent with regard to the parties' understanding of the facts as they existed at the time of contracting, and impracticability pertains to the parties' understanding of the likely course of events post contract formation. But the analysis is the same, and there would seem to be no reason, other than historical accident,[30] for the ostensibly divergent formulations.

[26] John Edward Murray, Jr., MURRAY ON CONTRACTS § 112 (5th ed. Lexis Nexis: 2011) (discussing the evolution of the traditional "impossibility" doctrine into the modern and more lenient concept of "impracticability").

[27] U.C.C. § 2–615 (2011) ("[Delay or non-delivery does not constitute breach] if performance as agreed has been made impracticable by the occurrence of a contingency the non-occurrence of which was a basic assumption on which the contract was made."); RESTATEMENT (SECOND) OF CONTRACTS § 261 (1981) ("[Party is not in breach if] a party's performance is made impracticable without his fault by the occurrence of an event the non-occurrence of which was a basic assumption on which the contract was made.").

[28] *See, e.g.*, *Kilgore Pavement Maint., LLC v. W. Jordan City*, 257 P.3d 460, 462 (Utah Ct. App. 2011) ("A finding of impossibility or impracticality excuses a party from performing unless the party has assumed the risk of the event."); *Aluminum Co. of Am. v. Essex Grp., Inc.*, 499 F. Supp. 53, 72 (W.D. Pa. 1980) ("The focus of the doctrines of impracticability and of frustration is distinctly on hardship."); *Redland Co., Inc. v. United States*, 97 Fed. Cl. 736 (Fed. Cl. 2011) (holding that even if performance is possible, it is impracticable if it can be performed "only at an excessive and unreasonable cost, or when all means of performance are commercially senseless.").

[29] *See, e.g.*, Paul J. Gudel, *Relational Contract Theory and the Concept of Exchange*, 46 BUFF. L. REV. 763, 781 (1998) ("Both economists Posner and Rosenfield and liberal theorist Fried agree on the basic approach to this issue [of mistake, impracticability, and impossibility]: a court confronted with this problem is confronted with a problem of allocating to one of the parties a risk that the parties did not at the time of agreement allocate themselves."); H. Ward Classen, *Judicial Intervention in Contractual Relationships under the Uniform Commercial Code and Common Law*, 42 S.C. L. REV. 379, 398 (1991) ("Each of these doctrines [mistake, impracticability, and impossibility] is limited by the notions of allocation and assumption of risk."); Mark P. Gergen, *A Defense of Judicial Reconstruction of Contracts*, 71 IND. L.J. 45, 47 (1995) ("I propose that we reorder the way we think about the doctrines on impracticability, mistake, penalties, forfeiture, and good faith … by recasting them around the principles of unselfish performance and loss alignment.").

[30] *See, e.g.*, Alces, *supra* note 14, at 505 ("Because doctrine is a matter of historical accident rather than 'divine' inspiration, efforts to explain doctrine as an outgrowth of some coherent and fundamental purpose are necessarily unavailing, and ultimately obfuscatory."); Nathan B. Oman, *A Pragmatic Defense of Contract Law*, 98 GEO. L.J. 77, 115 (2009) ("General Contract Law has frequently been seen by contract theorists as a historical accident born of an formalism whose basis was ultimately more aesthetic than functional.").

Finally, the modification principles confirm the centrality of risk allocation to the contract doctrine. The parties will often respond to "the occurrence of a contingency the non-occurrence of which was a basic assumption" upon which their contract was founded by modifying, or attempting to do so. It is not surprising, then, that the modification doctrine shares DNA with mistake and impracticability.[31] If the change in circumstances that prompts the attempt to modify would inure disproportionately to the advantage of one party (as is likely the case, particularly if a court is called into the fray), then the counterparty may try to change the terms of the contract to adjust the parties' relative rights and duties into better balance, or at least into a balance more in line with the allocation at the time of contracting. That effort could, though, from the perspective of the beneficiary of the original allocation, look like extortion, and indeed it may be extortion if the party seeking the modification tries to take what an objective observer might deem to be unconscientious advantage of the changed circumstances. The canonical cases, again, illustrate the tension the modification doctrine would modulate.[32] If the party seeking the modification is trying to avoid the consequences of a risk that party assumed at the time of contracting, the law should not brook such a reallocation. But if the party seeking the modification is merely seeking an adjustment that would essentially preserve the deal, the allocation of risk upon which the parties (in some fictional sense, perhaps) agreed, then there is no reason for a court to resist the modification.

The problem is that the doctrine actually obscures the normative calculus, so courts smuggle. Interestingly, what began as smuggling has now worked its way into the black letter, thanks to the legal realism of Karl Llewellyn.[33] In fact, the apposite UCC provision, Section 2–209, is just part of a patchwork available to courts eager to escape the doctrinal incongruities of the consideration doctrine.[34] Courts and

[31] *See* Richard A. Posner & Andrew M. Rosenfeld, *Impossibility and Related Doctrines in Contract Law: An Economic Analysis*, 6 J. LEGAL. STUD. 83 (1977).

[32] *See Alaska Packers' Ass'n v. Domenico*, 117 F. 99, 102 (9th Cir. 1902) ("[T]he party who refuses to perform, and thereby coerces a promise from the other party to the contract to pay him an increased compensation for doing that which he is legally bound to do, takes an unjustifiable advantage of the necessities of the other party."); *Angel v. Murray*, 322 A.2d 630, 635 (R.I. 1974) ("[C]ourts will not enforce an agreement that has been procured by coercion or duress and will hold the parties to their original contract regardless of whether it is profitable or unprofitable.").

[33] *See* UCC. § 2–209 (2011).

[34] Murray criticizes the consideration doctrine as historical accident: "[I]t is clear that consideration was not a well-planned, rationally conceived device for deciding which promises are enforceable," and from an early time the doctrine was manipulated by the courts to validate their normative analyses. Murray, *supra* note 26, at § 54. For example, performance of a pre-existing duty was regularly held not to be consideration when the courts believed one party was extorting another, even if agreement existed between the parties. *See, e.g.*, *Alaska Packers*, 117 F. at 102. On the other hand, courts were willing to accept a pre-existing duty as consideration if it appeared that unforeseen circumstances

legislatures have provided means to cut through the consideration underbrush to reach results more candidly consistent with the allocation of risk premise that actually supports the operation of the law when circumstances change, and, to be honest, change in ways the parties did not foresee or which it would have been irrational for them to investigate before the fact. Even the allocation of risk formula, though, remains a bit opaque: the question really is whether it would have been efficient to impose a pre-contract duty to investigate on one party rather than the other. If the cost of such an investigation would have exceeded the benefits – the likelihood that an unlikely but possible occurrence would eventuate – then the court will more probably find one of the available grounds to enforce the negotiated[35] modification.[36]

The agreement calculus, too, incorporates smuggling into the normative foundations of contract. This is an area of the law that has attracted a good deal of attention in recent years, both in the courts and in the commentaries. Three cases, in particular, and the critical appraisal they have engendered capture the tension: does "agreement" require understanding, real appreciation of what you are getting yourself into along with an authentic, voluntary undertaking? Alternatively, is what we have come to consider "consent" ostensible agreement enough? Or, what if "agreement" is not binary, a 1 or a 0? Is there a third alternative: are there degrees of agreement so that what may be "enough" agreement in one context may not be enough in the next? The doctrine is strikingly opaque on this.[37] The decisions seem to rely on empirical

would make contract on the original terms inequitable to the performing party. *See, e.g., Angel*, 322 A.2d at 635. Comment a to UCC. § 2–209 (2011) explains its purpose is to "protect and make effective all necessary and desirable modifications of sales contracts without regard to the technicalities which at present hamper such adjustments," eliminating the doctrinal incongruities and replacing them with an intent-based validation of modifications. For the remainder of this "patchwork," *see also infra* note 36.

35 The modification of a contract must be at least ostensibly the product of agreement in order for the modification doctrine to operate. *See Asmus v. Pacific. Bell*, 999 P.2d 71 (Cal. 2000) (holding that employees' assent to employer's unilateral contract modification was evidenced by the fact that they continued to work for their employer).

36 The doctrine supports at least five methods of enforcing contract modification: (1) New consideration, *see Clyde Rudd & Assocs., Inc. v. Taylor*, 225 S.E.2d 602 (N.C. Ct. App. 1976); (2) Unforeseen circumstances, *see Brian Const. & Dev. Co., Inc. v. Brighenti*, 405 A.2d 72 (Conn. 1978); (3) Non-uniform statutory modification, *see* La. Civ. Code Ann. art. 1906 (2011); (4) UCC 2–209 modification, *see* UCC. § 2–209 (2011) (consideration requirement eliminated, only agreement between the parties is required to bind them to the modification); (5) *Solum id fac*, "just do it," *see Schwartzreich v. Bauman-Basch*, 131 N.E. 887 (N.Y. 1921) (modification on equitable grounds without doctrinal justification).

37 *See* Peter A. Alces, *Contract Reconceived*, 96 Nw. U. L. Rev. 39, 47 (2001) ("To decide whether a promise is enforceable, within the Restatement structure, you cannot follow the formation rules and say, for instance, Contract = Agreement + Bargain + Consideration, because Offer and Acceptance are constituents of Bargain and also constitute 'manifestation of mutual assent,' or Agreement.").

conclusions not clearly supported by the available evidence. There are apposite canonical cases.

In *Carnival Cruise Lines, Inc. v. Shute*,[38] the United States Supreme Court, sitting in admiralty jurisdiction,[39] considered the case of cruise passengers injured on their voyage who sought to bring suit against the cruise line in the passengers' home jurisdiction, notwithstanding the choice of venue provision in the form ticket "contract" pursuant to which the passengers "agreed" to litigate any claims against the cruise line in a venue across the country.[40] The Court acknowledged that the term in issue would not reasonably be the subject of negotiation between the cruise line and its customers.[41] But that did not matter. In light of the costs that the clause in issue saved the cruise line (which savings *could*, of course, be passed along to its passengers), there were efficiency reasons to uphold the enforceability of the agreement.[42] Now that does not really have much to do with "agreement," if we understand "agreement" to have something close to its familiar sense.

The *Carnival Cruise* conclusion seemed to be based on "folk economics," efficiency assertions at best vaguely related to facts "on the ground," so to speak. But the trend continued in Judge Easterbrook's opinion for a panel of the United States Seventh Circuit Court of Appeals in *ProCD, Inc. v. Zeidenberg*.[43] The case concerned a "shrink wrap" license that attempted to limit the licensee's rights by the interposition of terms arguably provided by the licensor post contract. Judge Easterbrook, in an opinion that displayed a (to be charitable) curious understanding of the Uniform Commercial Code,[44] reasoned that a contract could be formed

[38] 499 U.S. 585 (1991).

[39] *Id.* at 590. The Supreme Court has no unique or particular common law contract competence. Since the Court in *Erie R.R. Co. v. Tompkins*, 304 U.S. 64 (1938), held that federal courts lack the power to create general federal common law, federal courts must apply state contract law. So the Court rarely decides contract cases except where Article III confers federal jurisdiction, as in admiralty. U.S. Const. art. III, § 2.

[40] Mrs. Shute, a Washington State native, embarked on a Carnival cruise from California and was injured in international waters off the Mexican coast. The forum selection clause on the back of her ticket provided that all claims were to be litigated in Florida, a forum in which she was "physically and financially incapable" of pursuing litigation. *Carnival Cruise*, 499 U.S. at 585.

[41] *Id.* at 593 ("[I]t would be entirely unreasonable for us to assume that respondents – or any other cruise passenger – would negotiate with petitioner the terms of a forum-selection clause in an ordinary commercial cruise ticket.").

[42] *Id.* at 594 ("Finally, it stands to reason that passengers who purchase tickets containing a forum clause like that at issue in this case benefit in the form of reduced fares reflecting the savings that the cruise line enjoys by limiting the fora in which it may be sued.").

[43] 86 F.3d 1447 (7th Cir. 1996).

[44] "[Judge Easterbrook] concludes, erroneously, that Section 2–207 is irrelevant because there was only one form in issue and he understands Section 2–207 to be a battle of the forms provision." Alces, *supra* note 12, at 46; *See also* Roger C. Bern, *"Terms Later" Contracting: Bad Economics, Bad Morals, and A Bad Idea for A Uniform Law, Judge Easterbrook Notwithstanding*, 12 J.L. & Pol'y 641, 642–43(2004) (noting Easterbrook's errors).

before all of its terms were finally set. That conclusion challenged the conceptions of agreement upon which a good deal of the doctrine would seem to be premised. Whether the move Easterbrook described is just the realization of contract by status foreshadowed by Grant Gilmore[45] or whether it stretches the consent concept beyond the breaking point, it is clear that *ProCD* and cases joining the conversation about form contracting[46] have refocused the inquiry into the nature of consensual liability.

The latest (but surely not the last) contribution to the conversation about consent is another United States Supreme Court decision, this time the Court's construction of a federal statute, the Federal Arbitration Act. In *AT&T Mobility LLC v. Conception*,[47] the Court upheld the enforceability of a waiver of the right to proceed by way of class action in arbitration. The decision seems striking: it would effectively deny consumers access to the only effective means to seek redress of their contract-based grievances. But while the decision may appear to devastate the rights of subordinate parties in contracts of adhesion, it is not inconsistent with the thread that connects *Carnival Cruise*, *ProCD*, and similar precedent.[48] It would seem clear, though, that form contracting has pulled contract (kicking and screaming?) into the twenty-first century. Modern technologies may have rendered classical contract conceptions incoherent, and "agreement" in any familiar sense may be a casualty, or at least no longer recognizable.

For present purposes – the hypothesis that an "empirical morality" would compel reconsideration of the contract doctrine and its operation – the point of reviewing the risk allocation and agreement doctrine and cases is to support development of a framework that would provide the means to appreciate better the assumptions about human agency that contract doctrine would vouchsafe. The allocation of risk and agreement dimensions of contract law reveal predominantly normative but also factual questions: how do human agents allocate risk? What does it mean to agree? So we may expect courts to consult normative conceptions, consequentialist and nonconsequentialist, in deciding cases. Similarly, those who would compose restatements of the doctrine would not be able to avoid normative inquiry. It is as though the consequentialist-deontic "battle" is fought out each time a question of mistake, impracticability, modification, or agreement arises. It is the normative-centric nature of the inquiry that formulates the doctrine, and all of contract, so nicely on the head of a pin. But it is not enough to appreciate the essential normativity of the contract

45 Grant Gilmore, The Death of Contract (Ohio State University Press: 1974).

46 *See Hill v. Gateway 2000, Inc.*, 105 F.3d 1147 (7th Cir. 1997); *Klocek v. Gateway, Inc.*, 104 F. Supp. 2d 1332 (D. Kan. 2000); *Brower v. Gateway* 2000, Inc., 246 A.D.2d 246 (NYSD. 1998).

47 131 S. Ct. 1740 (2011).

48 *See* cases cited *supra* note 46.

doctrine; what ultimately matters is the fit of that doctrine with the normativity of the human agent.

III. MINIMUM CONTENT OF NATURAL CONTRACT LAW

An empirical morality, a perspective that would proceed from naturalistic premises, does not sit comfortably with deontic theory generally. Proponents of what could be termed "brain law" can make sense of consequentialism; that, after all, is the vernacular of evolutionary theory.[49] But the attractions of armchair intuition notwithstanding,[50] it is worthwhile to consider the assumptions about human agency that are central to deontic theories. Certainly if deontic theory gets them wrong, then we would not be surprised to find that the conclusions flowing from such fundamental error would be fallacious. It is important, then, to review the places from which representative deontic theories begin. It may be that an empirical morality could reveal flaws in deontic conceptions of human agency that would undermine the normative conclusions proceeding from the misconceptions. If advances in neuroscientific techniques ultimately lead to refinement of our idea of what it means to be human, then we may expect that a more empirically sophisticated account of human agency than can be intuited from the armchair might impact the law generally, and the contract law specifically. But no less significantly, if advances in our understanding of human agency *did not* lead to reconceptualization (if not just reconsideration) of the fit between the human agent and legal doctrine, *that* would be quite important, and certainly worthy of legal theorists' attention.

While it would not be possible to survey all of the deontic theories of human agency in this chapter, it is possible to provide a synopsis that identifies the common ground, or common assumptions. Such a synopsis would be all the more powerful the more disparate the conclusions of those whose normative theory proceeds from such common ground. The extent of their ultimate disagreement may say something about the areas of agreement. For exemplary purposes, then, it is worthwhile to consider the foundations of particularly prominent analytical moral philosophy that premises conclusions about the law on suppositions about human agency.

H. L. A. Hart, a positivist,[51] may have been the most important analytical legal philosopher of the twentieth century. His "minimum content of natural law" posited

[49] *See* S. S. Schweber, *The Genesis of Natural Selection-1838: Some Further Insights*, 28 BIOSCIENCE 321, 324–25 (1978) (discussing Adam Smith's influence on Charles Darwin).

[50] After all, Einstein's theory of relativity must have owed something to his armchair, so too even Darwin's evolutionary theory.

[51] Legal positivists hold that law serves strictly a societal coordination function, without reference to morality or the common good. *See* Leslie Green, *Legal Positivism*, THE STANFORD ENCYCLOPEDIA OF PHILOSOPHY, http://plato.stanford.edu/archives/fall2009/entries/legal-positivism (Edward N. Zalta ed., last updated Jan. 23, 2003).

certain truths about human agency that would, necessarily, determine the contours of the law. He offered five constituents of that "minimum content":

1. Human vulnerability: since "men are both occasionally prone to, and normally vulnerable to, bodily attack," legal systems have the command "Thou shall not kill."[52]
2. Approximate equality: legal systems must take into account the fact that no man is so strong that he can always dominate other men.[53]
3. Limited altruism: since men are neither angels nor devils their legal system must be based in a system of mutual forbearances as, otherwise, great harm could come to social life.[54]
4. Limited resources: food, clothes, and shelter are scarce resources making "some minimal form of the institution of property" necessary.[55]
5. Limited understanding and strength of will: sanctions are needed to "*guarantee* that those who would voluntarily obey shall not be sacrificed to those who would not because except in very small, closely-knit societies, submission to the system of restraints would be folly if there were no organization for the coercion of those who would then try to obtain the advantages of the system without submitting to its obligation."[56]

Hart's crucial idea here is that our conception of law – how it works, how it fails, its efficacy generally, even the structure of doctrine – depends, or should depend, on law's fit with the human agent, human thriving. We need not take issue with Hart's catalog; what matters more is that he recognized that such a catalog, or something very much like it, was indispensable to a conception of law. Law that does not conform to the authentic human agent that would be its subject and object is ultimately inefficacious and may not even be law at all.[57]

Hart's "minimum content" has attracted attention (though perhaps not as much as you might expect, given its fundamental significance). There have been both supporters[58] and critics,[59] and it will be necessary for an empirical morality to take

[52] H.L.A. Hart, The Concept of Law 190 (Clarendon Press 1961).

[53] *Id.*

[54] *Id.* at 191–92.

[55] *Id.* at 192.

[56] *Id.* at 193.

[57] "In the absence of this content men, as they are, would have no reason for obeying voluntarily any rules; and without a minimum of co-operation given voluntarily by those who find that it is in their interest to submit to and maintain the rules, coercion of others who would not voluntarily conform would be impossible." *Id.* at 189.

[58] *See, e.g.*, Anthony T. Kronman, *Hart, Austin, and the Concept of a Legal System: The Primacy of Sanctions*, 84 Yale L.J. 584 (1975).

[59] *See, e.g.*, Richard A. Epstein, *The Not So Minimum Content of Natural Law*, 25 Oxford J. Legal Stud. 219 (2005); S. B. Drury, *H. L. A. Hart's Minimum Content Theory of Natural Law*, 9 Political Theory 533 (1981).

account of the commentary. Engagement of those perspectives, though, must maintain focus on a hypothesis this study is testing: the dependence of normative theory on a conception of human agency (and so the importance of getting that conception right).

A prominent natural law theorist of the Thomistic tradition,[60] John Finnis, premised his theory on "basic forms of human good," which do not track but are certainly redolent of Hart's appreciation of the fundamental.[61] Finnis's final basic good is religion, "a recognition (however residual) of, and concern about, an order of things 'beyond' each and every man."[62] Now the point is not that Finnis is likely wrong here, though that case may be made; the point instead is in the nature of his finding. Given that millions of people want nothing to do with religion[63] (indeed, many finding it not merely benign but even malignant[64]) on what basis can Finnis conclude that religion is somehow basic "however residual"? This is not to say that Finnis is wrong: perhaps secularists are somehow cut off from authentic human thriving. Even if that is the case, and Finnis is right (to any extent), would we not benefit from an understanding of the source of his conclusion? And could not more thoughtful attention to the nature of what it means to be human, the type of insight to which empiricism (neuroscience) might contribute, be pertinent to the support for such a conclusion? But it is not necessary to draw too much attention to the religious value. It would seem that Finnis's other values, in the tradition of Hart's "minimum content of natural law," depend on an understanding of human agency that we need not rely on intuition alone to inform.

While John Finnis discovered his basic forms some thirty or so years ago, and Hart his minimum content some fifty years ago, contemporary accounts of human thriving continue to posit non-empirical foundations of normative theory, notwithstanding

60 *See* John Finnis, AQUINAS: MORAL, POLITICAL, AND LEGAL THEORY (Oxford University Press: 1998).

61 *See generally*, John Finnis, NATURAL LAW AND NATURAL RIGHTS (Oxford University Press: 2011). Finnis's basic forms of life are: Life, Knowledge, Play, Aesthetic Experience, Friendship, Practical Reasonableness, and Religion. *Id.* at 86–90.

62 *Id.* at 90.

63 One estimate places the number of secularists at just over one billion people. Hilmar Schmundt, *Going Godless: Does Secularism Make People More Ethical?* SPIEGEL ONLINE, *available at* http://www.spiegel.de/international/spiegel/0,1518,777281,00.html. Another source estimates that "non-religious" people make up 16% of the world population. *Major Religions of the World Ranked by Number of Adherents* ADHERENTS.com, *available at* http://www.adherents.com/Religions_By_Adherents.html.

64 There is no need here to catalog the atrocities committed in the name of religion. As particularly prominent examples, *see, e.g.*, Thomas Aquinas, SUMMA THEOLOGICA Part II-II, Question 11, Article 3 (observing that heretics "deserve not only to be separated from the church by execution, but also to be severed from the world by death."); Thomas More, DIALOGUE CONCERNING HERESIES (1529) (burning of heretics just and necessary); John Calvin also supported the death penalty for heretics. Davison M. Douglas, *God and the Executioner: The Influence of Western Religion on the Death Penalty*, 9 WM. & MARY BILL RTS. J. 137, 153 (2000); Martin Luther promoted anti-Semitic views. Martin Luther, ON THE JEWS AND THEIR LIES (1543).

the progress in neuroscience over the last decade or so.[65] Amartya Sen and Martha Nussbaum have developed a "capabilities" approach to normative theory. Sen discovered ancient sources of his premises,[66] which would support an argument of the capabilities' venerability. Nussbaum too is able to rely on ancient sources to like effect.[67] Nussbaum's elaboration of the core capabilities provides a catalog quite similar to Finnis's, though it lacks his reference to the supernatural.[68]

A theory of empirical morality, or a theory of how empirical morality must matter to normative legal theory, needs to take account of the Hart, Finnis, Sen, Nussbaum and like catalogs of human goods and values. The argument of those philosophers has to be that an appreciation of what is essential to human thriving must be part of our normative theory; if the world were run by dogs, their laws would be different. So it does make sense to take account of the essentially human in order to reach conclusions about human thriving and so human normative theory. The question for Hart, Finnis, Sen, and Nussbaum must be, then, why their catalogs are accurate. What insights might an empirical morality offer that they do not appreciate?

That analysis would be informed by consideration of the contributions of those who have commented on the fundamental values approaches, and also by the findings of evolutionary psychologists and neuroscientists themselves. The literature heretofore has not pursued that opposition, and it may be that a measure of the intuitive and empirical continuities and discontinuities could inform our understanding and the operation of legal doctrine. At this juncture, it would be necessary to formulate the neuroscientific state of the art: what can the empirical perspective do? And, every bit as important, what can it *not* (at least yet) do?

IV. LIMITS OF EMPIRICISM?

Can we rely on the empirical findings neuroscience would provide to resolve normative questions? Can we reach conclusions about the deontic-consequentialist divide by discovering neurological differences revealed in the course of the two types of reasoning? Is the divide metaphysical? Essential? A "natural kind?"[69] Would it

[65] V. S. Ramachandran, THE TELL-TALE BRAIN: A NEUROSCIENTIST'S QUEST FOR WHAT MAKES US HUMAN xii (W. W. Norton Company Ltd: 2011) "Brain science has advanced at an astonishing pace over the past fifteen years[.]").

[66] Amartya Sen, *Human Rights and Asian Values*, Sixteenth Morgenthau Memorial Lecture on Ethics & Foreign Policy, 1997, at 19–23 (discussing the edicts of third-century B.C.E. Indian Emperor Ashoka, and writings of fourth-century B.C.E. thinker Kautilya).

[67] Martha C. Nussbaum, CREATING CAPABILITIES 125–129, 132–33, 141 (Belknapp, Harvard University Press: 2011).

[68] *Id.* at 17–45.

[69] *See* Brian Bix, LAW, LANGUAGE, AND LEGAL DETERMINACY 136–140 (Clarendon Press:1993).

correlate to a physical difference, in process at least? Or, is the distinction instead a human normative device?

In what has become an infamous contribution to the basic moral psychology literature, Joshua Greene claimed to be able to isolate consequentialist from non-consequentialist "reasoning" in the human cognitive system.[70] He relied on functional magnetic resonance imaging, fMRI. While it will be necessary to consider at length the limitations of Greene's analysis and conclusions, for present purposes, it is worthwhile to reflect on what could be at stake in Greene's neuroscience. His method may be valuable as the source of a thought experiment even if it turns out to be dubious as an empirical matter.

Imagine, as Greene did,[71] that we could isolate, very certainly, the part of the brain process responsible for consequentialist reasoning from the separate part responsible for deontic reasoning. Further, imagine that we could apply some metric to compare the relative acuity of the two distinguishable processes so that we could conclude that one region, and so one process, relies on emotion and the other on rationality. Now, once we enlist evolutionary theory to support the conclusion that emotion is less reliable, and is just a heuristic to guide fitness decisions more certainly accurate 150,000 years ago on the savannah than today in the urban metroplex,[72] then we may be able to support a consequentialist over a deontic worldview. Indeed, framed in just that way, deontology is a heuristic for consequentialism and would counsel "welfare" analyses when we are able to do the math. The thoughtful responses to Greene's thesis suggest that caution would be prudent. It may be that neuroscience confirms we are all consequentialists, at least by nature. That might not tell us whether we *should* be deontologists, any more than understanding the bases of anti-social behaviors excuses them. We need not conclude that we are determined by our nature, or should be. But we would need to find the normative source of such a rebellion against our natural propensities. From that perspective, we would turn to what neuroscience can do once we come to terms with its limitations, at least the limitations that maintain in the current state of the field.[73] Even if neuroscience transforms our intuitions about free will and determinism,[74] will that matter to our law? Or will our law remain the same, if perhaps just a bit more grudgingly so? It is one thing to understand better why the violent criminal is violent; it is quite another to transform understanding into the basis of acquittal. Further, while neuroscientific

[70] Greene, *supra* note 2, at 41–46.

[71] *Id.*

[72] Joyce, *supra* note 2, at 222.

[73] *See* Stephen J. Morse, *Lost in Translation? An Essay on Law and Neuroscience*, 13 LAW AND NEUROSCIENCE: CURRENT LEGAL ISSUES 529 (Michael Freeman ed., 2011).

[74] *See* Joshua D. Greene & Jonathan Cohen, *For the Law, Neuroscience Changes Nothing and Everything*, 359 PHIL. TRANS. ROYAL SOCIETY LONDON BIO. SCI. 1775 (2004),

insights could refine our evidence law, and certainly lead to treatments for those whose deficiencies impair their ability to function in social settings, how would it matter to the legal doctrine more generally? While there may be answers to those questions, it will likely be necessary to consider the doctrine in light of what *may* transpire in the future. Even if neuroscience eventually supports a radical reconception of what it means to be human, we will need to decide how much "what it means to be human" matters to different areas of the law, like contract. In fact, it may demonstrate more about the power of empirical morality if we see its room for operation in the contract law, an area not as obviously susceptible to neuroscientific clarification as the criminal or even tort law.

The object of legal doctrine generally and perhaps contract particularly is to accommodate planning.[75] Contract law structures transactions or makes it possible for the parties to structure transactions in order to maximize or vindicate what they will. In that way, contract liberates as much as it constrains, something Hume understood as a means to make sense of obligation.[76] Neuroscience can certainly tell us about human preferences and how those preferences are ordered. Behavioral economics, also understandable as a neuroscientific insight, has confirmed that doctrine depends on a conception of rationality that may be incomplete, to say the least.[77] If the legal doctrine rests on inaccurate assumptions about human agency, then we may expect that the law's coordination function would be undermined.[78]

There are, however, conceptual challenges to naturalism that, at least, suggest caution. Is it true that neuroscience tells us anything important about what it means to be human? It is at the point we consider that question that we must confront the dualist challenge, in a form not much evolved since the dawn of the Enlightenment.

V. DUALISM

While naturalism denotes many things, a complex worldview, perhaps nothing better demonstrates the commitment of the perspective than its monism: the idea that all there is, or all we can know, are physical properties subject to physical laws. Naturalism rejects dualism, the idea that there is more than can "meet the eye" (in

[75] *See* Curtis Bridgeman, *Contracts as Plans*, 2009 U. Ill. L. Rev. 341 (2009).

[76] *See* David Hume, A Treatise of Human Nature, Part 2 *Of Justice and Injustice*, Sect. 5 *Of the Obligation of Promises* (Norton & Norton eds., 2000).

[77] *See generally*, Cass R. Sunstein, Behavioral Law and Economics (Cambridge University Press: 2000); Daniel Kahneman and Amos Tversky, Choices, Values, and Frames (Cambridge University Press: 2000).

[78] Terrence Chorvat & Kevin McCabe, *The Brain & the Law*, 359 Phil. Trans. Bio Sci. 1727 (2004).

a generous sense). Dualism, in its several iterations,[79] would draw a line between the firing of neurons or chemical reactions that, at some level, *indicate* thought and the something else that *constitutes* thought, in humans, at least.

Though surely not the only statement of the substance dualist position, perhaps the most famous would be Rene Descartes's "Je pense, donc je suis." That pithy phrase captures a sense of self by reference to an ability to discern something else, a division between mind and body, the idea that mind is more than body, more than neurons and chemicals. There is, per dualism, a mind-brain divide. We might understand the elegant function of the brain, a physical entity, but that would not provide us access to the soul, or even the mind for that matter. At the time, Cartesian dualism was a triumph of Enlightenment rationality, philosophy over theology, the bête noire of the philosophers.[80] While we are certainly painting with a very broad brush here, it is safe to say that Descartes's effort was a step forward, an effort to rely on human rationality rather than divine inspiration to formulate human agency.

Today the intellectual battlefield, such as it is, is not a site of standoff between theology and philosophy, though certainly theologians would have a dog in the fight.[81] Instead, the opposition is between naturalism and non-naturalism, both of which may be conceived as philosophical commitments. If we are to rely on naturalistic principles to inform our conception of human agency and thus our understanding of law's operation on and with human agents, we need to take account of the problem dualist perspectives present for an empirical morality. Normative perspectives dependent on deontology may, necessarily, entail dualism, or at least rely on dualist-like conceptions that present the same challenge for empirical jurisprudence as Cartesian metaphysics (and its elaborations) pose for naturalism generally. If that is right, and the idea requires subsequent further elaboration, then, we may free ride (in a non-pejorative sense) on the naturalist critique of dualism as we promote an empirical jurisprudence.

Such an investigation would necessarily entail consideration of the debate between contemporary philosophers and neuroscientists who believe that there is a mind-brain divide, dualists, and those who appreciate what we term "mind" as a manifestation of the brain as physical organ, monists. The question has, in fact, resonated in the legal scholarship. It will be necessary to trace the contours of the debate, and to take account of how the questions matter to naturalistic jurisprudence, even

79 The Stanford Encyclopedia of Philosophy offers a catalog of the different phases of dualism. *See* Howard Robinson, *Dualism*, THE STANFORD ENCYCLOPEDIA OF PHILOSOPHY, http://plato.stanford.edu/archives/fall2003/entries/dualism (Edward N. Zalta ed., last updated Aug. 19, 2003).

80 *Id.*

81 *See, e.g.*, Smith, *supra* note 19; Joseph Vining, THE SONG SPARROW AND THE CHILD: CLAIMS OF SCIENCE AND HUMANITY (University of Notre Dame Press: 2004).

as applied quite specifically to the contract law. Preliminarily, it is worthwhile to afford a sense of the tension.

There is perhaps no more comprehensive statement of the modern dualist perspective than that offered by M. R. Bennett (a neuroscientist) and P. M. S. Hacker (a philosopher) in their PHILOSOPHICAL FOUNDATIONS OF NEUROSCIENCE.[82] At the outset, it is important to recognize that neuroscientists are not all monists. Bennett is, his protestations to the contrary notwithstanding, a dualist.[83] So even those whose work reflects an intellectual commitment to the mechanistic can and do question whether all there is *is* that which we can see, even if only under an electron microscope. Bennett and Hacker's argument is premised on their discovery of the so-called mereological fallacy: succinctly, the confusion of a part with the whole, that is, the brain with the "human being." They repeat throughout their book what amounts to a mantra: the brain does not (decide, act, promise, etc.); the "human being" does.[84] In the course of their argument, they wage a focused and sustained attack on the work of naturalists, particularly Daniel Dennett[85] and John Searle.[86]

The Bennett and Hacker assault on naturalism has been more recently repeated in the work of two law professors, Michael Pardo and Dennis Patterson.[87] The

[82] Curiously, Bennett and Hacker deny that they are dualists. Maxwell R. Bennett & Peter M. S. Hacker, PHILOSOPHICAL FOUNDATIONS OF NEUROSCIENCE 111 (Blackwell Publishing: 2003).

[83] Like Pardo and Patterson, Bennet and Hacker skirt dangerously close to substance dualism when they posit that the subject of perception is the "person," a concept equally dualistic to the Cartesian "mind" that they are trying to eliminate. *See infra* note 96.

[84] "But [neuroscience's] discoveries in no way affect the conceptual truth that these powers and their exercise in perception, thought and feeling are *attributes of human beings*, not of their parts – in particular, *not of their brain*." Bennet & Hacker, *supra* note 82 at 3. "Ascribing mental states to the brain makes no more sense than ascribing them to the kidneys.... What go on *in* the brain are neural processes, which need to occur in order for the person, whose brain it is, to be going *through* the relevant mental processes ...." *Id.* at 112.

[85] Bennett and Hacker devote an entire appendix to attacking Dennett's work, *see id.* at 413.

[86] Bennett and Hacker's second appendix wages a similar attack on Searle's naturalism, *see id.* at 436.

[87] Michael S. Pardo is an Associate Professor at the University of Alabama School of Law. Dennis Patterson is a Professor of Law at the European University Institute in Florence, Italy, Professor of Law and Philosophy at Rutgers University, and Professor of Jurisprudence and International Trade at Swansea University in Wales. Their recent article *Philosophical Foundations of Law and Neuroscience*, 2010 U. ILL. L. REV. 1211 (2010) [hereinafter *Philosophical Foundations*], argues that neuroscience's utility in the law is based upon a "problematic premise" misconstruing the relationship between mind and brain. Another, *More on the Conceptual and the Empirical: Misunderstandings, Clarifications, and Replies*, 4 NEUROETHICS 215 (2010), critiques the claims of the leading proponents of neuroscience's explanatory powers for law and ethics, notably Walter Glannon and Thomas Nadelhoffer. Pardo and Patterson have also collaborated on two forthcoming papers challenging the application of neuroscience to law in a variety of issues: *Minds, Brains, and Norms*, NEUROETHICS (forthcoming) and *Neuroscientific Challenges to Retributivism, in* THE FUTURE OF PUNISHMENT (Thomas Nadelhoffer ed., Oxford University Press, forthcoming). Both papers criticize the explanatory role of neuroscience in ethics and law. Pardo and Patterson are also writing a forthcoming book, the title of which captures their dualism: MINDS, BRAINS, AND LAW (Oxford University Press, forthcoming).

Pardo/Patterson recapitulation of Bennett and Hacker resolves to not much more than these four points, at least for purposes of this chapter:

1. The mind cannot be reduced to the brain because that would eliminate the possibility of a person's choosing what to do, rather than just obeying the dictates of the brain.[88]
2. Neuronal activity may correlate with a physical activity, but behavior determines what it means to engage in an activity.[89]
3. We cannot attribute activities of the person to activities of the brain; the person believes; the brain does not.[90]
4. How can neuroscience possibly account for legal disagreement if it just examines the brain?[91]

While Bennett and Hacker concluded that the brain and the "human being" are distinct entities, Pardo and Patterson instead juxtapose the brain and the "person." It is not clear how the move from "human being" to "person" is an innovation, and that obscurity undermines efforts to isolate the contribution that Pardo and Patterson would make to the debate.

Pardo and Patterson, though, do bring the naturalism question into focus in the legal context. Perhaps because Pardo is an evidence and criminal law teacher,[92] the examples they rely upon are drawn from the evidence and criminal law. But it is also true that the typical arguments in favor of importing findings from neuroscience to the law arise in the criminal law setting.[93]

Both Bennett and Hacker's book and Pardo and Patterson's reprise of it have been the subject of response from naturalists. Dennett and Searle contributed to a slim volume that considered the Bennett/Hacker argument and Dennett/Searle responses side by side.[94] While that colloquy is valuable, and merits attention in due course, for now it suffices to say that Dennett and Searle more convincingly refute Bennett and Hacker than offer any new insights into naturalism, which was, after all, not their object. Responses to Pardo and Patterson, perhaps

[88] *See Philosophical Foundations*, *supra* note 87 at 1220.

[89] *See id.* at 1226–27.

[90] *See id.* at 1225.

[91] *See id. at* 1250.

[92] *See Law School Directory, Michael S. Pardo*, University of Alabama School of Law (Nov. 07, 2011), http://www.law.ua.edu/directory/People/view/Michael_S._Pardo.

[93] *See, e.g.* Susan A. Bandes, *The Promise and Pitfalls of Neuroscience for Criminal Law and Procedure Conclusion*, 8 Ohio St. J. Crim. L. 119, 120 (2010) ("Most prominently, neuroscience has weighed in on the nature of the basic requirements for criminal responsibility, including free will, voluntariness, *mens rea*, and mental competency.").

[94] Maxwell Bennett, Daniel Dennett, Peter Hacker & John Searle, Neuroscience & Philosophy: Brain, Mind & Language (Columbia Univ. Press: 2007).

because they were not responses to ad hominem attacks,[95] more directly engage the naturalist-dualist divide.[96]

Pardo and Patterson's critics have replied in terms that would also be responsive to Bennett and Hacker; for example: a conscious activity, such as behavior (that would matter to the law) does not alone explain whether someone has the capacity to "conform his conduct to social norms."[97] The pertinence of that observation to capacity issues in contract is clear. Further, dysfunction in the brain can undermine a person's "ability to follow social and legal rules"; "we must know about the neural underpinning in order to know that an agent has or lacks the relevant capacity."[98] And finally, it is not clear that knowledge is rooted in behavior, as Pardo and Patterson suggest; whether someone knows something does not depend on whether he can communicate that knowledge. Walter Glannon, focusing on the lie detection setting, concludes that the Pardo and Patterson attack "confuses two questions: (1) can brain regions lie? and (2) can one detect willful lying of a person by looking at sub-personal indicators in their brains?"[99]

Perhaps most helpful is the clarification that critics of both Bennett and Hacker and Pardo and Patterson offer. While the anti-naturalists describe their argument as conceptual,[100] their critiques actually devolve into semantic quibbling. The

95 Dennett praised some of the content of Bennett and Hacker's work, but ultimately found it to be a "quite remarkably insulting attack on me." *Id.* at 75.

96 "As for the claim about 'substance dualism,' however, we do not see how this follows from what we have said." Michael S. Pardo & Dennis Patterson, *More on the Conceptual and the Empirical: Misunderstandings, Clarifications, and Replies*, 4 NEUROETHICS 215 (2010). Pardo and Patterson, like Bennett and Hacker before them, protest that they are not dualists, but the protests are not convincing. Pardo and Patterson describe a middle path between materialism and dualism by proposing that "mind" is merely the aggregate of a person's intellectual abilities, making it a function of the physical "brain." *Philosophical Foundations*, *supra* note 87, at 1249. Since "mind" is now a collection of properties rather than a separate *ousia* they can claim to have avoided the dualistic premise of non-physical substance. However, they cross the ontological divide by positing that the "person" that thinks and feels is not the "brain" which performs these concomitant functions (firing neural synapses, etc.). *Id.* at 1249. "Personhood" is the non-physical entity linked to the now materially grounded "mind." But on what grounds can this "person" be said to exist, if it is a non-physical entity? Only by recourse to non-physical substance, the defining characteristic of dualism. Hence Glannon points out that Pardo and Patterson come "dangerously close to … substance dualism." Walter Glannon, *Brain, Behavior, and Knowledge*, 4 NEUROETHICS 191 (2010) [hereinafter *Brain, Behavior, and Knowledge*]. Their method is linguistically distinct but functionally identical to Cartesian dualism; they substitute "person" and "brain" for "mind" and "body," but dualism by any other name is still dualism.

97 *Brain, Behavior, and Knowledge* at 194.

98 *Id.* at 193.

99 *Id.*

100 For Pardo and Patterson, *see Philosophical Foundations*, *supra* note 87, at 1222 ("We explain why the question of what the mind is and what the various psychological categories under discussion are (e.g., knowledge, intention, rationality), are conceptual rather than empirical questions."). For Bennett and Hacker, *see* Bennett et al., *supra* note 94, at 4 ("Empirical questions about the nervous system

anti-naturalists rely on Wittgenstein's language theory to support their conclusion that the language we use conveys truths that naturalism would obscure.[101] Here critics of Pardo and Patterson can borrow from Dennett and Searle: "Just because the criteria we traditionally relied on when talking about mental activities such as knowing, deciding, intending, and lying were behavioral, it doesn't follow that neural criteria could not possibly be adopted in the future in light of developments in neuroscience."[102]

Given the relative nascence of the neuroscience that could matter to law, writ large, there is a danger of confusing the conceptual and the empirical. That is, limitations of the extant science may compromise the conceptual argument. We cannot, given the state of brain science, make confident claims about *how* the empiricism of neuroscience can change our understanding of what it means to be human. The deontic-consequentialist divide can still make sense in ways it might not once we better understand a present mystery such as consciousness.[103] All, or virtually all, of our normative conclusions are certainly some amalgam of the deontic and the consequentialist. So there must be something more fundamental than either discrete normative perspective; we must be motivated by something that is manifest in the deontic-consequentialist "choice." Neuroscience can, at least conceptually, reveal that "something" more fundamental.

But so far we have not yet certainly discovered that something. That failure, for now, may be a function of the limitations of our empirical method. While we can now *see* the concentration of hemoglobin in different parts of the brain,[104] we do not *yet* know what to make of the migration of such concentrations. There is, also, enough bad science to disparage the good science,[105] no matter how cautious the

are the province of neuroscience .... By contrast, conceptual questions ... are the proper province of philosophy.").

101 *See Philosophical Foundations*, *supra* note 87, at 1222 n. 62.

102 Thomas Nadelhoffer, *Neural Lie Detection, Criterial Change, and Ordinary Language*, 4 NEUROETHICS 205, 210 (2011).

103 For helpful discussions of consciousness, *see generally* Nicholas Humphrey, SOUL DUST: THE MAGIC OF CONSCIOUSNESS (Princetown University Press: 2011); Nicholas Humphrey, SEEING RED: A STUDY IN CONSCIOUSNESS (Harvard University Press: 2009); V. S. Ramachandran, A BRIEF TOUR OF HUMAN CONSCIOUSNESS 39 (Pi Press: 2004).

104 This is how fMRI scans work, giving real-time data of brain function by monitoring levels of oxyhemoglobin in different parts of the brain. When a portion of the brain engages in neural activity, it sets off a chemical reaction that briefly changes the local concentration of oxyhemoglobin in the blood. These changes can be picked up by a magnetic resonance imager by injecting a paramagnetic contrast agent into the blood; the result is that the portion of the brain engaging in neural activity can be made to "light up" on the screen. P. M. Matthews, & P. Jezzard, *Functional Magnetic Resonance Imaging*, 75 J. OF NEUROLOGY, NEUROSURGERY, & PSYCHIATRY 6 (2004).

105 Joshua Greene, for example, has been criticized for founding deep philosophical conclusions upon scientifically shallow data. "Greene has very recently acknowledged that a statistical reanalysis of the results of this first study shows that the study's results are dubitable." Richard Dean, *Does Neuroscience Undermine Deontological Theory?* 3 NEUROETHICS 43 (2010).

claims of the new science's promoters. It is not particularly problematic that our current methods confront apparently insurmountable obstacles. The history of science is the history of our overcoming what once seemed to be insurmountable obstacles. The real problem is that our current empirical limitations can frustrate our conceptual aspirations (which may or may not ultimately be realized). To be more concrete, consider lie detection: it is not clear that it is even possible to detect any but the most basic types of deception on a neuronal level.[106] So it may be that neuroscience's focus on the neuron will be of limited utility for law. That is an empirical challenge. But it would be a conceptual challenge if we were to infer from the limitations of extant methods that neuroscience *cannot* detect the kind of deception that would matter to the law. It would seem, though, that insofar as we do rely on objective determinants of veracity,[107] something other than the declarant's account of her state of mind, we do recognize the *conceptual* possibility that scientific method can, eventually, provide a means that may be currently beyond our imagination.

The empirical limitations to our application of neuroscience are daunting, and it is neuroscience itself that has revealed those limitations. For example, we possess limited understanding of the physical link between brain activity and behavior; we do not fully understand how brains interact with environmental, cultural, social, economic, and other forces to produce behavior; we do not understand how or the extent to which higher-order brain functions can be localized in particular sites of the brain; also, there is great neural variation within and among human populations, so identifying "normal" would be problematic; and, so far, researchers have been unable to reproduce results reliably over time and across different experimental settings.[108] Indeed, right now, the science may be better at discovering new mysteries than in solving those we have already discovered.

But insofar as the state of the science has revealed more about how the brain works[109] (and how it fails to work when it fails to work[110]) it would be premature, at least, to find conceptual barriers where there are only empirical challenges. A

[106] Jay D. Aronson, *The Law's Use of Brain Evidence*, 6 Annu. Rev. L. Soc. Sci. 93 (2010).

[107] "[E].g., respiratory, electrodermal, cardio-vascular, and vasomotor activity." Charles R. Honts, *Psychophysiological Detection of Deception*, 3 Current Directions in Psychol. Sci. 77 (1994).

[108] *See* Aronson, *supra* note 106; Laura Capraro, *The Judicial Role of Emotions in the Decisional Process of Popular Juries*, *in* 13 Law and Neuroscience: Current Legal Issues 407 (Michael Freeman ed., 2011).

[109] *See generally* Debra A. Gusnard et al., *Medial prefrontal cortex and self-referential mental activity: Relation to a default mode of brain function*, 98 Proc. Nat'l Acad. 4264 (2001); Don M. Tucker, *Lateral Brain Function, Emotion, and Conceptualization*, 89 Psychol. Bull. 19 (1981).

[110] *See generally* John D. Herrington et al., *Localization of Asymmetric Brain Function in Emotion and Depression*, 47 Psychophysiology 442 (2010); Robert L. Kahn et al., *Memory Complaint and Impairment in the Aged: the Effect of Depression and Altered Brain Function*, 32 J. of Am. Med. 1569 (1975).

"smart phone" would have been impossible, and maybe only barely conceivable, a decade ago. The goal should be realism tempered with imagination. And the current dilemma with which nascent neuroscience confronts law is how to strike the balance. We already have come to appreciate the limits of "eyewitness" testimony,[111] and the operation of biases that undermine efficiency analyses.[112] Those discoveries do not just concern evidence but can impact the formation and operation of doctrine as well. Indeed, it would be important (and quite remarkable) if the better appreciation of human agency neuroscience could provide *would not* impact the doctrine. That itself would be an important normative discovery.

Consider once more the agreement calculus. Contract cares about agreement, the combination of the subjective and objective that justifies, on some grounds, the imposition of liability. Agreement has normative significance in contract law: it is "efficient" to enforce deals that are the product of agreement because agreement assures that goods and services will move to those who value them more,[113] Pareto or at least Kaldor-Hicks moves. It also seems right, in a deontological sense, to hold transactors to what they have agreed to and to relieve them from deals to which they have not, in fact, in reality, agreed.[114] But our current conception of agreement, not a model of clarity in any event,[115] is based on a "folk psychology"[116] of meeting minds to some extent or another. It is not difficult to imagine how neuroscience could shed light on agreement, both as an evidentiary matter and, more importantly for present purposes, as a conceptual matter (and the two are related).

So far as evidence is concerned, consider a thought experiment. Assume that we have identified the neural reactions that are operative within a neural bargaining module.[117] From there, it is not difficult to *imagine* that the manifestations of bargaining in the parties to a formal agreement could be revealed in a neural signature, different in substance from the signature designed to serve an ostensibly

[111] *See, e.g.*, Brian L. Cutler, Steven Penrod, MISTAKEN IDENTIFICATION: THE EYEWITNESS, PSYCHOLOGY, AND THE LAW (Cambridge University Press: 1995); Jennifer L. Devenport, *Eyewitness Identification Evidence: Evaluating Commonsense Evaluations*, 3 PSYCHOL. PUB. POL'Y & L. 338, 361 (1997).

[112] *See generally* C. Edwin Baker, *The Ideology of the Economic Analysis of Law*, 5 PHIL. & PUB. AFF. 3 (1975).

[113] *See* Joseph William Singer, *The Reliance Interest in Property*, 40 STAN. L. REV. 611, 709 (1988); Charles K. Rowley, *Wealth Maximization in Normative Law and Economics: A Social Choice Analysis*, 6 GEO. MASON L. REV. 971 (1998).

[114] *See generally*, Eric E. Wilson, *Kantian Autonomy and the Moral Self*, 62 REV. OF METAPHYSICS 355 (2008); Fried, *supra* note 10; Barnett, *supra* note 11.

[115] *See* Alces, *supra* note 37, at 39.

[116] "Folk psychology" refers to "[t]he collection of psychological principles and generalizations which … underlies our everyday explanations of behavior." Stephen Stich & Shaun Nichols, *Folk Psychology: Simulation or Tacit Theory?* 3 PHIL. ISSUES 225, 227 (1993).

[117] On the possibility of a "bargaining module," *see* Leda Cosmides & John Tooby, *Can a General Deontic Logic Capture Facts of Human Moral Reasoning? How the Mind Interprets Social Exchange Rules and Detects Cheaters, in* 1 MORAL PSYCHOLOGY 53, 53 (Walter Sinnott-Armstrong ed., 2008).

similar but essentially different purpose in the current law. (We have already seen this in moves toward devices that would seem to indicate real understanding in contract better.)[118]

At some point neuroscience could intimate and eventually confirm that "agreement" itself is a strained (at best) concept that does not accomplish what our normative understanding of the doctrine assumes that the concept in fact does accomplish. It may be that there is no such thing as "agreement," as contract conceives it. Instead what there is could be a range of coincidence that is dependent on dynamic uncertainties. If agreement does not work the way we have come to believe it works (perhaps because we want or need to believe that it works that way, to justify some conception of the normative status quo), then arguments for continued reliance on the concept are undermined. We would not say that a dog "has agreed" to anything because agreement as we understand it can have no meaning for a dog. Now if we discover that agreement does not, cannot, mean what we think it means for human agents, then its role in contract comes into question, or, at least, should be subject to reconsideration.

Keep in mind, here, though, that I am *most certainly not* suggesting that neuroscience will disclose that we are no more able to agree than is the family pet. That is neither likely the case nor the point of this conceptual observation. For now it suffices to say that if neuroscience could help us overcome our biases, our species-specific hubris, then neuroscience could impact upon our legal doctrine.[119] Also, neuroscience could demonstrate how agreement made more sense when deals were conducted at arms' length and how, empirically, that model does not work in contemporary form contracting environments. Though it would be premature to reach any conclusion, we could decide that agreement has become so attenuated, so removed from what we imagine the concept meant two hundred years ago, that we need new social structures to make sense of our enforcement of promises. Granted, this work has already begun in behavioral economics.[120] But it is likely that neuroscience will continue to demonstrate limitations of our current conceptions, ways in which our folk psychology misses the mark that are significant to legal doctrine. It could be that "agreement" as conceived by contract law is prototypical folk psychology, based on a dualistic conception of "mind" that neuroscience will undermine.

Stephen Morse has made clear how the limitations of the current science may undermine our enthusiasm for neuroscientific inquiry applied to law, essentially an empirical

[118] *See, e.g.*, Principles of the Law of Software Contracts § 2.02 (2010).

[119] As, of course, it already has: consider capacity to contract requisites, a rough form of neuroscience. *See* Restatement (Second) of Contracts § 12 (1981).

[120] *See, e.g.*, Essays on Contract Theory and Behavioral Economics (Daniel Gottlieb ed., Massachusetts Institute of Technology: 2009).

response to the conceptual claims of naturalism.[121] He acknowledged that it has become clear that Cartesian dualism is wrong, but Morse despairs that it is not (yet?) clear how the brain enables the mind.[122] The current state of the science can provide only crude information about a person's ability or inabilities that may help determine his or her capacities.[123] It is his conclusion that neuroscience will not fundamentally change how the law operates, a conclusion that is shared by some neuroscientists,[124] that presents the real challenge for the empirical normative perspective. It is a view premised on what Morse and others conclude is a necessary limitation on neuroscience and what neuroscience can tell us about what it means to be human.

The dialog among deontologists, naturalists, and those anywhere on the deontic-naturalist continuum necessarily concerns dualism, however cast.[125] But that dialectic (which, ultimately, is what it is) resolves into the tension surrounding the so-called naturalistic fallacy, the perhaps mistaken belief that "is equals ought." Contemporary normative empiricists assert, at least after a fashion, that "is" does equal "ought," but a good deal depends on what we mean by "is" and "ought."

VI. IS NATURALISM FALLACIOUS?

In his magisterial *Principia Ethica*,[126] G. E. Moore asserted that it is erroneous to equate what *is*, say a pleasant feeling, with what is *good*. Moral properties, such as goodness, cannot be reduced to physical properties. That is a simplistic rendering of Moore's idea that does justice neither to the subtlety of his observations[127] nor to the erudition of those who have criticized and elaborated on his ideas.[128] But the simple equation suffices for present purposes: describing the normative difference between the deontic and naturalist perspectives.

Sam Harris, a somewhat notorious naturalist,[129] understands the challenge presented by Moore's identification of the naturalistic fallacy: "introspection offers no

[121] Morse, *supra* note 73, at 539.
[122] *Id.* at 546–47.
[123] *Id.* at 539.
[124] Greene, *supra* note 2, at 41–46.
[125] *See supra* note 79.
[126] G. E. Moore, PRINCIPIA ETHICA (Barnes and Noble Books,1903).
[127] For thoughtful elaborations, *see, e.g.*, Michael Ridge, *Moral Non-Naturalism*, THE STANFORD ENCYCLOPEDIA OF PHILOSOPHY, http://plato.stanford.edu/archives/spr2010/entries/moral-non-naturalism/ (Edward N. Zalta ed., last updated Jun. 26, 2008); Allen Gibbard, *Normative and Recognitional Concepts*, 64 PHIL. AND PHENOMENOLOGICAL RES. 64, 153 (2002); William K. Frankena, ETHICS 85–86 (Prentice Hall: 1973).
[128] *See, e.g.*, Ridge, *supra* note 126; Bernard Williams, ETHICS AND THE LIMITS OF PHILOSOPHY 121–22 (Fontana Press: 1985).
[129] *See generally* Sam Harris, THE END OF FAITH (WW Norton Company Ltd: 2004); Sam Harris, LETTER TO A CHRISTIAN NATION (Alfred A. Knopf 2006). Harris is perhaps best known for his strident atheism.

clue that our experience of the world around us, and ourselves within it, depends upon voltage changes and chemical interactions taking place inside our heads.[130] And yet a century and a half of brain science declares it to be so."[131] It would seem to run contrary to our conceptions of self to reduce what we are to what can be translated into nothing more than physical reactions that are not so much mysterious as they are complex. Harris would ground all human normativity in "human thriving," an idea that, he acknowledges, does not accommodate a neat calculus.[132]

Patricia Churchland, another prominent neuroscientist and normative naturalist, resonates with Harris's conclusion and offers elaboration pertinent to the is-ought tension. The naturalist response to those who conclude naturalism is itself fallacious is a question: if our nature does not determine goodness, what does?

> Morality can be – and I argue is – grounded in our biology, in our capacity for compassion and our ability to learn and figure things out. As a matter of actual fact, some social practices are better than others, some institutions are worse than others, and genuine assessments can be made against the standard of how well or poorly they serve human well-being.[133]

The deontic response must reside in dualism: there must be some source of the good that goes beyond (in a sense, at least) human thriving. Either that or "human thriving" must be construed in such a way as to make room for something like Finnis's religious "good." [134]

But the naturalist view would not equate "is" with "ought" in order to argue that what brings us pleasure is necessarily good. Naturalism instead would likely say that the perspective of human thriving goes beyond such a simplification. What may be good for the individual could be, net, not so good for the greater number. We would not equate individual pleasure with corporate good. Surely, though, it is true that what inures to the net benefit of humankind, construed in evolutionary terms, that is, reproductive success, is a viable measure of goodness. The naturalistic equation works only so long as what leads to evolutionary success confers pleasure, in Finnis's "goods," or Sen-Nussbaum's "capabilities" terms. And it is not clear that all of those goods or capabilities result in reproductive success.

[130] We might add: and nothing more than voltage changes and chemical interactions.

[131] Sam Harris, The Moral Landscape: How Science Can Determine Human Values 158 (Free Press 2010).

[132] Harris notes that not all cultural values can be easily worked into his theory: "certain cultures are less suited to maximizing well-being than others .... [T]he ruthless misogyny and religious bamboozlement of the Taliban [is] an example of a worldview that seems less than perfectly conducive to human flourishing." *Id.* at 43.

[133] Patricia S. Churchland, Braintrust: What Neuroscience Tells Us about Morality 200 (Princetown University Press: 2011).

[134] *See* Finnis, *supra* note 60.

The work of deontology, however, is not complete with the demonstration that there is more to life, to life well lived, than reproductive success. It may be that the goods' and capabilities' appeal to hedonistic goals is not so different from reproductive success after all. If beholding a sunset, or writing or reading a wonderful poem, or realizing an ambition, for example, causes joy that bears no direct or even indirect relation to reproductive success, those experiences may be different in kind from sex but no more ethereal, no less grounded, ultimately, in our neural composition. That is, all that deontology may demonstrate is that a greater range of sensations (elicited by a broader range of sources) may matter to human thriving. It would not have so demonstrated that there is any greater good than human pleasure. Further, it would then be possible for naturalists in the strictest Darwinian tradition to find a connection between our ostensibly pure aesthetic sense and reproductive success.[135] But that is not to suggest that our sense of rapture is inauthentic, that goods and capabilities do not appeal to us in ways that seem celestial. It is to say, though, that we need not wrap ourselves in some supernatural mystery to celebrate certain things, or have to divorce such things from the terrestrial in order to appreciate their power over us.

To concretize the foregoing deontic-naturalist tension better, consider the familiar "brain in a vat" thought experiment. Robert Nozick posited the "Experience Machine."[136] Imagine there were a machine that could reproduce all, really all, of our experiences and provide our brains the identical stimulation that the actual experiences would provide. Would we opt to be plugged in? Nozick said we would not:

> First, we want to do certain things, and not just have the experience of doing them.... A second reason for not plugging in is that we want to be a certain way, to be a certain sort of person.... Thirdly, plugging into an experience machine limits us to a man-made reality, to a world no deeper or more important than that which people can construct.[137]

John Finnis, too, writing from a dramatically different[138] perspective, reached not just a similar but the same conclusion with regard to the same thought experiment:

> On reflection, is it not clear, first that you would not choose a lifetime of "thrills" or "pleasurable tingles" or other experiences of that type? But, secondly, is it not clear that one would not choose the experiences of discovering an important theorem, or

[135] "The solution to the problem of aesthetics, I believe, lies in a more thorough understanding of the connections between the thirty visual centers in the brain and the emotional limbic structures (and of the internal logic and evolutionary rationale that drives them)." Ramachandran, *supra* note 103, at 59.

[136] Robert Nozick, ANARCHY, STATE AND UTOPIA 42–45 (Basic Books 1974).

[137] *Id.* at 43.

[138] Nozick approaches the problem from the libertarian perspective, *see id.*, while, Finnis examines it from the standpoint of natural law, *see infra* note 139.

> of winning an exciting game, or of sharing a satisfying friendship, or of reading or writing a great novel, or even of seeing God … or any combination of such experiences? The fact is, is it not, that if one were sensible one would not choose to plug into the experience machine at all.[139]

Both Nozick and Finnis suffer from an apparent lack of imagination, which is particularly curious in Finnis's case. Could Finnis imagine a god who could manipulate (or design) neural matter in such a way as to constitute experience in a certain way? Surely we must realize that what we experience is determined by the "limitations" of our sensory and neural equipment. There is not yellow or blue light in some essential sense. There are, though, frequencies that our occipital lobe interprets as yellow or blue. The same is true of sound frequencies or gustatory phenomena, some of which do not exist at all for us, but which our dogs are very aware of and which may determine their actions. So the dog's *experience* is not the same as our *experience*, and the difference between the two is solely determined by empirically salient differences between species.

Further, there is no way for Finnis or Nozick to know, to a certainty, that we are *not* in what amounts to an experience machine, essentially no more than brains in a vat. That is not to suggest we are living in a "matrix," but it is to assert that we are necessarily constrained by conceptions and, therefore, *experiences* that can be dreamt of in our philosophy. It is, indeed, particularly curious that Finnis, the natural lawyer who believes in the supernatural, was not able to comprehend a necessary consequence of appreciating the (relatively) limited nature of our endowments (relative vis-à-vis those of an omnipotent deity, that is). And contemporary neuroscience would seem to confirm the limited range of our sensibility, as well as our frequent failures to appreciate those limitations.[140]

If the ideas of Finnis and Nozick matter at all to the normativity of law, and there is reason to believe that, at least for some, they might,[141] then ultimately their

[139] John Finnis, NATURAL LAW AND NATURAL RIGHTS 95 (Cambridge University Press: 1980). What Finnis means by "sensible" may be crucial; if his analysis were correct then recreational drug use, for example, would not exist.

[140] We can learn more about how the brain works when we better understand the sources of its malfunction. Consider phantom limbs, for example: V. S. Ramachandran details a series of cases of anosognosia, a condition experienced by patients who have been paralyzed on one side of their body and will vehemently maintain they are not in fact paralyzed; they believe they are moving their immobile arm, leg, etc. Understanding that malfunction leads to better understanding of neural pathways. *See* Ramachandran, *supra* note 103, at 33–38 (2004).

[141] *See, e.g.*, Peter Benson, *The Basis of Corrective Justice and Its Relation to Distributive Justice*, 77 Iowa L. Rev. 515 (1992) (positing Nozick's entitlement theory as a basis for distributive justice); Mark R. Discher, *A New Natural Law Theory as a Ground for Human Rights?* 9 Kan. J.L. & Pub. Pol'y 267 (1999) (arguing from Finnis's natural law theory to a theory of legal standards of minimal treatment for human beings); Stephen Macedo, *Homosexuality and the Conservative Mind* 84 GEO. L.J. 261 (1995) (arguing Nozick and Finnis's work as a moral basis against legal discrimination of homosexuals).

epistemology may matter to specific bodies of law, such as contract. And it would seem that the Finnis-Nozick perspective, as least insofar as the brain in the vat idea is concerned, could resonate with regard to the allocation of risk and agreement premises of contract, dependent, as they are, on conceptions of human agency and human thriving. The challenge that remains is to understand how inquiry on this very abstract level could matter to law generally, and matter specifically to the law of contract. How does the law of consensual relations depend upon conceptions of human agency? And why would our conception of human agency's dependence on the deontic-naturalist dialectic determine the form and function of the legal doctrine?

VII. SO WHAT?

Reconsider now the point of departure in this chapter: much (if not all) of what we understand to be foundational to contract resolves to allocation of risk or agreement (and, indeed, now it may even be clear that we could find some more fundamental source for both allocation of risk and agreement). The doctrine that tries to capture those two dynamic inquiries focuses on the parties' state of mind, and ability both to understand and to anticipate. Those abilities may be uniquely human. They certainly contemplate complex neural function, a level of consciousness that other beings cannot replicate in any way even approaching a similar level of sophistication. The fact that we can place our neural functioning on a scale, that we can compare what we can do with what other living things cannot, provides us a sense of our limitations too. (Indeed, it may be that the sense of human limitations provided the basis of the supernatural.)[142] Similarly, our appreciation of the range of our capabilities, the differences among us, also confirms our limitations.

Insofar as the doctrine really begins rather than settles the normative analysis in contract, we cannot determine the resolution of trouble cases (or even anticipate the contours of their resolution) until we appreciate the contours of human agency. How could we determine whether minds have met until we take account of the ability of minds to meet? How could we determine whether a particular contingency was foreseen unless we can determine that it was foreseeable, given the competence of human agents? What does it mean for a human to thrive? It may well be that the calculus provided by the doctrine does not align with what neuroscience can tell us about human agency. This chapter begins the inquiry into what neuroscience reveals about human agency that would matter to the efficacy and normativity of

[142] *See generally* Pascal Boyer, RELIGION EXPLAINED (Basic Books 2001); Lee A. Kirkpatrick, ATTACHMENT, EVOLUTION, AND THE PSYCHOLOGY OF RELIGION (The Guildford Press: 2005); David Sloan Wilson, DARWIN'S CATHEDRAL (University of Chicago Press: 2002).

contract doctrine: further work will endeavor to fill the gap left by deontic and consequentialist theory.

Neuroscience can, at least as a conceptual matter, tell us more about what it means to be human than we yet know. At some level, perhaps not yet glimpsed, neuroscience may provide the basis of an empirical morality, a normative system authentically and thoroughly considerate of human capacities. Just imagine that we could, again as a conceptual possibility, come to understand that it is the firing of certain neurons at certain levels of intensity and at a certain frequency that determines human thriving. If we could then calibrate our legal doctrine, including our contract doctrine, to yield results consonant with human thriving so conceived, would we not want to do so?

6

Contract in a Networked World

Roger Brownsword

In the second half of the twentieth century, the doctrines of the classical law of contract, together with the underlying philosophy of freedom of contract, were found wanting in a mass consumer marketplace. In the early years of the twenty-first century, there are new challenges for contract law as business contractors form networks, as networks of connected contracts become more common, and as the consumer marketplace migrates to networked electronic environments. What are the implications of this networked world for the law of contract?

In this chapter, it will be argued that contract doctrine needs to be reformed so that it makes explicit provision for contracts having network effects. There are two respects in which contract law should be coded for networks: first, where contractors act on the assumption that their transactions will be interpreted and applied in a way that is sensitive to their network characteristics; and, second, where the recognition of network effects is in line with the purposes that direct the regulation of consumer transactions. As for the philosophy of freedom of contract, it will be argued that the classical value of self-governance is as important as ever, but that with the burgeoning of e-commerce, there is an agenda of emerging questions that highlights new challenges and opportunities for contractual autonomy.

I. INTRODUCTION

Although it is not yet a feature of mainstream contract thinking, there has been, for some time, an interest in the idea of network contracts, or of contracts with network effects.[1] There are many reasons for being attracted by the idea that there should be

[1] See, e.g., John N. Adams and Roger Brownsword, *Privity and the Concept of a Network Contract* 10 LEGAL STUDIES (1990) 12; John N. Adams and Roger Brownsword, KEY ISSUES IN CONTRACT (London: Butterworths, 1995) Ch. 5; and John N. Adams, Deryck Beyleveld, and Roger Brownsword, *Privity of Contract – the Benefits and the Burdens of Law Reform* 60 MODERN LAW REVIEW 238 (1997). Recently, there has been a small explosion of the contractual networks literature, including:

an explicit doctrinal coding for networks – for example, that such a coding would develop the shape of contract thinking in a way that moves it more closely into alignment with networking forms of economic organisation and business practice; that it would present the opportunity to specify distinctive and desired legal effects – particularly effects that tend towards the heightening of cooperative contractual obligations and the recognition of connected third-party interests; that it would facilitate a more appropriate framing of questions concerning the fairness of exclusion and limitation clauses in connected contracts[2]; and that, by releasing courts from the shackles of classical contract thinking, doctrinal recognition of networks would reduce the artificiality (and increase the transparency) of judicial reasoning.

However, if the apparently attractive idea of network contracts is to be translated into a robust and workable doctrine, two important questions demand our attention. First, there is the question upon which I will focus in this chapter, namely: in what way, or in what circumstances, are network contracts or network effects to be treated as arising? Are network contracts to be treated as arising because the law recognises a certain pattern of transactional connection (such as the familiar hub and spoke pattern of franchising, or the chains of carriage and distribution, and so on) or because the individual contracts are bound together (and explained) by a common organising purpose (as in construction projects or the financing of consumer sales); or do such networks arise because the lead contractors so declare? Putting this in a somewhat different way: do network effects arise by way of regulatory imposition (including occasional judicial declaration), or by virtue of explicit adoption by the contracting parties, or by reference to implicit practice-based expectation? Second, there is the question of the range of network effects. What kind of special effects are encompassed by networks? Twenty years ago, much of the interest in networks was galvanised by the restrictive privity principle that was, formally at least, a fundamental feature of English contract law. However, there are reasons for thinking that network effects might extend well beyond a relaxation of the restrictions on third-party claims or defences, to encompass intensified responsibilities (based on principles of cooperation and loyalty) between the parties to the network. So, for example, if a franchisor, by contracting for all network franchisees, is able to obtain discounts

Fabrizio Cafaggi, *Contractual Networks and the Small Business Act: Towards European Principles?* 4 EUROPEAN REVIEW OF CONTRACT LAW 493 (2008); Fabrizio Cafaggi (ed.), CONTRACTUAL NETWORKS, INTER-FIRM COOPERATION AND ECONOMIC GROWTH (Cheltenham: Edward Elgar, 2011); Marc Amstutz and Gunther Teubner (eds.), NETWORKS: LEGAL ISSUES OF MULTILATERAL COOPERATION (Oxford: Hart, 2009); Gunther Teubner, *'And if I by Beelzebub Cast Out Devils,...': An Essay on the Diabolics of Network Failure* 10 GERMAN LAW JOURNAL 395 (2009); and Gunther Teubner, NETWORKS AS CONNECTED CONTRACTS (Oxford: Hart, 2011) (translated by Michelle Everson, and with an exceptionally helpful introduction by Hugh Collins).

2 See, e.g., Roger Brownsword, *Network Contracts Revisited* in Marc Amstutz and Gunther Teubner (eds.), NETWORKS: LEGAL ISSUES OF MULTILATERAL COOPERATION (Oxford: Hart, 2009) 31.

for goods to be supplied by the network, is it not arguable that a fair share of this discount should be passed on to the individual franchisees;[3] or, again, is it not arguable that a franchisee who has an otherwise clear right to terminate in the face of a serious breach by the franchisor might be required to exercise some restraint for the sake of the other franchisees? Although I will not pursue this second question in a sustained way in this chapter, I will proceed on the assumption that network effects are not limited to a relaxation of the privity principle.

To clarify and to ground our thoughts in relation to the focal question of when network contracts or network effects arise, we can consider three test cases: first, a competition between private contractors of the kind litigated in the case of *Clarke v. Earl of Dunraven: The Satanita*[4] (where there were potentially some difficulties in constructing or inferring contractual relationships between the competitors); second, a case of consumer protection such as that in *OFT v. Lloyds TSB Bank plc*[5] (in which the House of Lords held that the protection given to credit card holders by section 75(1) of the Consumer Credit Act 1974 extends to more complex modern credit networks as well as to transactions made with overseas suppliers); and, third, *New Zealand Shipping Company Ltd. v. A. M. Satterthwaite & Co. Ltd.: The Eurymedon*,[6] which we can treat as a representative commercial case, in this instance involving the carriage of goods by sea, but it could equally well be an example from construction or franchising (where the commercial purpose will be effected through a cluster of contracts).

Stated summarily, our conclusions are the following. First, given that the European consumer marketplace is nowadays a densely regulated zone (where transactional obligations are contractual only in a severely attenuated sense), the relevant question is whether the regulatory purposes (whatever they might be) are likely to be advanced by introducing particular network effects – or, if we were to be more critical, the question would be whether some specified *legitimate* regulatory purposes would be assisted by the introduction of networks. Either way, at any rate within the context of European law, so far as consumer contracts are concerned, network effects arise by way of regulatory imposition and the classical law of contract is relevant only to the extent that it is adopted or adapted by

[3] Some examples are given in Gunther Teubner, NETWORK AS CONNECTED CONTRACTS *supra* note 1. In his introduction, Hugh Collins cites the South African Supreme Court of Appeal case of *Seven Eleven Corporation of SA (PTY) Ltd v Cancun Trading No 150 CC*, Case No 108/2004, 24 March, 2005; and, in Chapter 4, Teubner discusses at length the *Apollo* (Optik) case, OLG Bremen WRP 2002, 224; OLG Düsseldorf WRP 2002, 235; OLG Frankfurt 23 July 2002–11 U (Kart.) 55/00; OLG Frankfurt 23 July 2002–11 U (Kart.) 42/00. BGH Pressemitteilung No 64/2003.

[4] [1897] AC 59.

[5] [2007] UKHL 48. For discussion, see Hugh Collins, *Introduction to Networks as Connected Contracts* in Gunther Teubner, NETWORK AS CONNECTED CONTRACTS *supra* note 1, at 38–40.

[6] [1975] AC 154.

regulators.[7] Second, in the heartland of commercial contracting, we are in a zone that is subject to co-regulation. Here, once public policy has been taken into account, the function of the law of contract is to support self-regulation, to offer contractors a range of governance options, and to formulate default rules for cases where the contractors fail to order their own transactions. It follows that contract law should be flexible enough to permit such contractors to opt for transactional rules that have network effects; and, in the absence of explicit adoption, such effects should be recognised where they are implicitly embedded in business practice.[8] Finally, in the zone of purely private contracting (where explicit adoption or rejection of network effects is less likely to occur), the underlying pattern is much as in commercial contracting. Hence, provided that regulators do not rule out networks on public policy grounds, the default position might or might not be in favour of networks. Where the default is not in favour of network effects, then the parties might nevertheless switch the default either by explicit or by implicit signals (and, vice versa, where the default is in favour of networks). While judges might be entrusted with a discretion to declare that the contracts of private contractors should be treated as having network effects (where this is necessary in order to give effect to the implicit reasonable expectations of the parties), the occasions for having to rely on such a discretion might be (and, so far as possible, should be) minimised by paying careful attention to the default rules for this class of contracting.

The chapter has four principal parts. First, we outline three test cases (one private, one consumer, one commercial) for network effects; second, we consider whether, in relation to consumer contracts, the basis for network effects is regulatory imposition or contracting party adoption; third, we ask the same question in relation to commercial contracts; and, finally, we again ask this question but now in relation to purely private contractual arrangements.

II. THREE TEST CASES

In its classical form, the English law of contract assumes that the standard marketplace deal is a discrete spot transaction: A and B make their exchange; there is neither context nor continuity. This assumption militates against taking into account any relational elements in the dealings between the parties – which, in turn, can

7 Compare Roger Brownsword, *Regulating Transactions: Good Faith and Fair Dealing* in MODERNISING AND HARMONISING CONSUMER CONTRACT LAW (Geraint Howells and Reiner Schulze (eds.), Munich: Sellier, 2009) 87; and *The Theoretical Foundations of European Private Law: A Time to Stand and Stare* in THE FOUNDATIONS OF EUROPEAN PRIVATE LAW (Roger Brownsword, Hans Micklitz, Leone Niglia, and Steven Weatherill (eds.), Oxford: Hart, 2011) 159.

8 Compare the analysis in Roger Brownsword, *Regulating Transactions: Good Faith and Fair Dealing*, *supra* note 7.

make it difficult to draw on the background to read co-operative obligations into the particular transaction.[9] It also militates against locating the particular transaction in a context of connected contracts that, as a set, reflect and articulate the underlying (commercial) purpose of the deals. Nevertheless, there are occasions when the courts, even without a jurisprudence of network contracts, are able to declare what are, in as many words, network effects. In this section, we can introduce three such instances of implicit network thinking.

A. Clarke v. Dunraven

Somewhat surprisingly, *Clarke v. Dunraven* is a case that has a place in the classical canon of contract law. Far from being a convenient illustration of the joining of offer and acceptance to form an agreement between the parties, it is a case in which commentators struggle to find an account of offer and acceptance that smoothly fits the facts. If *Clarke v. Dunraven* has a point to prove, it is not entirely clear what that point is.

Briefly, the facts of the case were that the Mudhook Yacht Club organised a regatta on the Clyde. While the competitors were manoeuvring their yachts to get into position for the start of the fifty mile race for the Muir Memorial Challenge Cup, there was a collision: one yacht, the *Satanita*, ran into and sank another, the *Valkyrie*. The question was whether the owner of the *Satanita* should pay to Lord Dunraven, who was the owner of the *Valkyrie*, the limited damages set by the Merchant Shipping Act Amendment Act 1862 or "all damages" as provided for by the competition rules. Although each entrant had signed a letter to the club secretary agreeing to be bound by the competition rules, there was no explicit and direct contractual relationship (incorporating the competition rules) between the competitors themselves.

At first instance, Bruce J. held that, even if there was a contract between the competitors, it was not so express as to override the statutory limitation. However, this decision was reversed by the Court of Appeal, the owner of the *Satanita* being held liable for "all damages"; and the view of the Court of Appeal was duly upheld by the House of Lords. According to Lord Esher M.R. (in the Court of Appeal), it was a condition of entering the race that each yacht-owner "must enter into an obligation with the owners of the yachts who are competing, which they at the same time enter into similarly with you."[10] The puzzle, however, is quite how the competitors

[9] Compare Roger Brownsword, *Suisse Atlantique* in LANDMARK CASES IN THE LAW OF CONTRACT (Paul Mitchell and Charles Mitchell (eds.), Oxford: Hart, 2008) 299. Even where the court is sensitised to the relational dealing between the parties, there still might be a reluctance to embrace a cooperative ethic: see, e.g., *Baird Textile Holdings Ltd v. Marks and Spencer plc* [2001] EWCA Civ 274.

[10] [1895] P. 248, at 255.

entered into contractual relationships with one another. To fit these facts into the classical contractual matrix, we need to ask who was offering what when, and then we should ask how and when the offer was accepted.

The best traditional account of the contracting process as between the competitors runs along the following lines. The first entrant [A], when agreeing with the club to be bound by the competition rules, made an offer to every subsequent entrant to be bound by the competition rules in return for those subsequent entrants' also agreeing to be so bound. The second entrant [B], when agreeing with the club to be bound by the competition rules, (i) made an offer to each and every subsequent entrant to be bound by the competition rules in return for those subsequent entrants also agreeing to be so bound, and (ii) accepted the offer made by the first entrant [A]. The third entrant [C], when agreeing with the club to be bound by the competition rules, (i) made an offer to each and every subsequent entrant to be bound by the competition rules in return for those subsequent entrants also agreeing to be so bound, (ii) accepted the offer made by the first entrant [A], and (iii) accepted the offer made by the second entrant [B]. And, so on.[11] For pragmatists, this is the only sensible view, but, for contract purists, this analysis stretches to breaking point the classical understanding of contractual formation – the main problem being that the entrants are being treated not only as offerors (in relation to fellow competitors) when they had no awareness that they were acting in this role but also (the first entrant apart) as acceptors of offers of which they were unaware.[12]

If the common law jurisprudence had featured the idea of a contractual network, it would have been simplicity itself to have treated the complex as constituting a network, one of the effects of which was that the competitors could enforce the competition rules directly against one another. Moreover, such a characterisation might have been defended equally well by saying either that there is a general rule that competitions are to be treated as having third-party network effects unless the

[11] Compare Gunther Teubner, *'And if I by Beelzebub Cast Out Devils,...': An Essay on the Diabolics of Network Failure supra* note 1 at 404–405:

Some scholars try to construct a "network contract" and base it on the traditional law of agency with mutual authorisations between all participants. When a new member enters the network, he is supposed to strike a multilateral agreement with all the other members who in their turn are supposed to have given their authorisation in advance. This somewhat monstrous construct disregards the social peculiarities of networks and therefore imposes greatly exaggerated requirements on the legal formation of networks.

[12] To this day, even in the most modern of texts, the puzzle persists. See, e.g., Andrew Burrows, A Casebook on Contract (Oxford: Hart, 2007) at 56:

It is unclear whether the judges thought that the contract was formed when sending in an entry for the race or when the yachts began to race. On either view, how could the (bilateral) contract between each yacht-owner be analysed in terms of offer and acceptance? Apart from problems over acceptance in ignorance of an offer, it would seem to require one to say, absurdly, that each yacht-owner was at the same time making an offer to the others and accepting their offers.

organisers clearly signal otherwise (in effect, opting out from the default rules), or that competitions are to be treated as having such network effects where the organisers clearly signal that this is their intention (in effect, opting in).[13]

Granted, in *Clarke v. Dunraven*, the nature of the particular competition rule at issue might give one reason to pause, for this was a rule that increased the obligations that otherwise applied in the case of collisions at sea. Even if a general rule licensing competitors to hold one another to the competition rules is plausible, it is not so obvious that the general rule should also endorse intensified responsibilities in competitions. Rather, the reason why the competitors raced under these conditions of heightened obligation was because the competition organisers had so stipulated. In other words, without over-elaborating the analysis, we might treat the third-party network effects as a feature of the default rules for competitions without also treating the heightened obligation in this way – competitors who wanted to race on such terms would need to signal this explicitly.[14]

In *G. Percy Trentham Ltd. v. Archital Luxfer Ltd.*,[15] Lord Steyn remarked that the modern courts "ought not to yield to Victorian times in realism about the practical application of rules of contract formation."[16] On the evidence of *Clarke v. Dunraven*, even the Victorian courts, it seems, were capable of taking a realistic view. Nevertheless, if the idea of network effects had been embedded in Victorian contract doctrine, the dispute in *Clarke v. Dunraven* surely would have been settled or disposed of quietly in the lower courts.

B. *OFT v. Lloyds TSB*

Under the provisions of section 75(1) of the Consumer Credit Act 1974, a creditor who is party to a debtor-creditor-supplier agreement is jointly and severally liable with the supplier for the latter's misrepresentation or breach of contract in relation to a transaction (with the creditor) that is financed by the credit arrangement.[17] In 1974, consumer use of credit cards was (by today's standards) at a relatively low level, it was largely domestic, and it was all off-line. With the increasing use of credit cards to support consumer transactions, and particularly with the development and growth

[13] Compare the forthright approach by Rigby LJ [1895] P. 248, at 262:

> It appears to me that all that is necessary to constitute a contract between the yacht owners is to bring home to each of them the knowledge that the race is to be run under the Yacht Racing Association rules, and that they, the one and the other, deliberately enter for the race upon those terms.

[14] Whether or not this was the competitors' intention was the principal point that was argued on the final appeal to the House of Lords.

[15] [1993] 1 Lloyd's Rep 25.

[16] *Id.*, at 29.

[17] Section 75(3) of the Act disapplies the protection afforded by section 75(1), inter alia, where the cash price is under £100 or over £30,000.

of on-line shopping, the question for the courts in *OFT v. Lloyds TSB* was whether the protections in section 75(1) applied where a UK consumer, using a credit card issued by a UK card issuer, dealt with a foreign supplier. Even though a protective scheme with application to foreign suppliers would expose UK card issuers to some 29 million suppliers worldwide, and even though the credit infrastructure no longer maps on to the tripartite debtor-creditor-supplier template of the 1970s, the House of Lords ruled that section 75(1) so applied.[18]

The changing nature of the credit infrastructure is described by Lord Mance in the following way:

> Large-scale consolidation has led to card issuers becoming members of one of the two main international credit card networks, VISA and MasterCard. Under the rules of these networks, certain card issuers are authorised to act as "merchant acquirers." … They contract with suppliers … to process all such supply transactions made with cards of the relevant network.… Suppliers do not become members of the network, but contract with merchant acquirers to honour the cards of the network.… Where the merchant acquirer is itself the issuer of the card used in a particular transaction, the transaction is tripartite.… But in the more common (and in the case of a foreign transaction inevitable) case of use of a card issued by a card issuer other than the merchant acquirer who acquired the particular supplier, the network operates as a clearing system, through which the merchant acquirer is reimbursed by the card issuer.[19]

At all levels, however, the courts were clear that the fact that 1970s-style three-party networks have been overtaken by four-party networks did not derail the legislative intention that consumers should be given the protection envisaged by section 75(1).[20]

We should not overstate the significance of the court's talking the talk of networks. Credit card arrangements are networked; such is the economic reality; but it does not follow that there is a special doctrinal coding for networks. In the *OFT v. Lloyds TSB* case, the fact that networks are involved is not seen as legally significant; it is simply a matter of whether the legislative purposes encompass credit card–supported transactions with foreign suppliers.

To put network thinking to the test, imagine that section 75(1) had never been enacted. Imagine, then, a case such as *David Boyack v. The Royal Bank of Scotland*[21] – a case alluded to by Lord Hope in the *Lloyds TSB* case – where Mr Boyack, having

[18] Seemingly, even with such a large exposure, the value of credit card transactions with foreign suppliers is less than 10% of that of domestic transactions. See [2007] UKHL 48, para 23.

[19] [2007] UKHL 48, para 23.

[20] *Id.*, at para 24.

[21] At the time of *OFT v. Lloyds TSB*, pending in the Sheriff Court at Kirkcaldy: see [2007] UKHL 48, at paras 10–11 (Lord Hope).

used a credit card (issued by RBS) to buy a clock in Dubai, now alleged that the contract was induced by misrepresentations made by the seller, and contended that RBS (qua card issuer) should be treated as jointly and severally liable for the supplier's misrepresentation. Without the support of section 75(1), Mr Boyack would need to claim (i) that, for the purposes of the law of contract, debtor-creditor-supplier arrangements (whether three or four-party schemes) should be treated as networks and (ii) that one of the network effects is to increase the responsibility of credit card issuers in relation to their card holders, specifically by securing the rights of card holders arising from any card-facilitated sale.

Whether or not a court, without the direct support of legislation, should declare a network with these particular effects in a consumer case of this kind is a question to which we will return.[22]

C. The Eurymedon

The factual background in *The Eurymedon* was a familiar one. Stated simply, A (the owner of goods) contracted with B (a carrier) for the carriage of the goods from Liverpool to Wellington; and B contracted with C (stevedores) to unload the goods when they arrived in Wellington. As a result of C's carelessness, the goods were damaged, and A sued C for compensation. By way of defence, C relied on various exemptions and limitations of liability that were written into the carriage contract (the contract between A and B). If, at that time, English law had not operated with a doctrine of privity of contract, there would have been no difficulty in allowing C, who was clearly an intended beneficiary of the relevant contractual provisions, to plead this defence. However, with privity standing between C and the protective clauses, the Privy Council needed to find a contractual connection between A and C.

Introducing the majority's opinion, Lord Wilberforce famously remarked that commercial deals (including the complex of contracts at issue) are often put together in ways that do not correspond particularly well to the classical model:

> The whole contract is of a commercial character, involving service on one side, rates of payment on the other, and qualifying stipulations as to both. The relations of all parties to each other are commercial relations entered into for business reasons of ultimate profit. To describe one set of promises in this context as gratuitous, or nudum pactum, seems paradoxical and is prima facie implausible. It is only the precise analysis of this complex of relations into the classical offer and acceptance, with identifiable consideration, that seems to present difficulty,

[22] Later at IIIB(c).

> but this same difficulty exists in many situations of daily life, eg sales at auction; supermarket purchases; boarding an omnibus; purchasing a train ticket; tenders for the supply of goods; offers of rewards; acceptance by post; warranties of authority by agents; manufacturers' guarantees; gratuitous bailments; bankers' commercial credits. These are all examples which show that English law, having committed itself to a rather technical and schematic doctrine of contract, in application takes a practical approach, often at the cost of forcing the facts to fit uneasily into the marked slots of offer, acceptance and consideration.[23]

Having signalled that a practical approach was to be taken, how were the facts to be forced into the appropriate slots? According to Lord Wilberforce:

> There is possibly more than one way of analysing this business transaction into the necessary components; that which their Lordships would accept is to say that the bill of lading brought into existence a bargain initially unilateral but capable of becoming mutual, between the shippers and the stevedore, made through the carrier as agent. This became a full contract when the stevedore performed services by discharging the goods. The performance of these services for the benefit of the shipper was the consideration for the agreement by the shipper that the stevedore should have the benefit of the exemptions and limitations contained in the bill of lading.[24]

The artificiality of this analysis did not go unnoticed by the minority members of the judicial panel,[25] and nor has it gone unnoticed by contract commentators.[26] Rather like the analysis in *Clarke v. Dunraven*, we have (in *The Eurymedon*) B acting as agent of A to transmit an offer by A to C, in circumstances where A did not know that it was making such an offer and where C, in performing its work for B, did not realise that, at the same time, it was accepting an offer made by A. Nevertheless, as in *Clarke v. Dunraven*, where the practical sense of the arrangements gives a clear steer, the purity of the classical law of contract has to yield to pragmatism.

If the Privy Council had been able to tap into a jurisprudence of network contracts, it might have been much easier to allow C to plead the defence. One view would be that, where commercial contracts are connected by a common purpose[27]

[23] [1975] AC 154, at 167.

[24] *Id.*

[25] Viscount Dilhorne and Lord Simon.

[26] See, e.g., Andrew Burrows, A CASEBOOK ON CONTRACT *supra* note 12 at 480. Having outlined the reasoning of the majority, Burrows asks:

> Was the reasoning artificial in (i) regarding the unloading of the goods as consideration for the exclusion of liability and (ii) treating the carriers as agents for the stevedores in receiving the offer of a unilateral contract?

[27] Compare Gunther Teubner, *'And if I by Beelzebub Cast Out Devils,...': An Essay on the Diabolics of Network Failure supra* note 1 at 406; and Cordula Heldt, *Internal Relations and Semi-Spontaneous Order: The Case of Franchising and Construction Contracts* in Amstutz and

and fit a common pattern (as in carriage or construction), then they should be treated as a network unless there is a clear contrary intention – and that one of the network effects is to license third-party claims and defences within the network.[28] Alternatively, one might want to rest the argument on the intentions of the contractors – in which case, we would be looking for signals from the contractors that they intend to adopt a network (with standard network effects) or that they at least intend to adopt some particular network effect.

D. *Reasonable Expectations*

Before we proceed, we should observe that, in each of the three cases discussed, we might be encouraged to say that if network effects are included, they serve to support the reasonable expectations of particular parties – the expectations of the competitors that the race rules applied inter se; the expectations of credit card users that when they buy from, say Amazon, they are protected by their card companies; and the expectations of downstream contractors in carriage contracts that they operate within the framework set by the head contract. So encouraged, we might suppose that the adoption of networks is very much in tune with the perceived purposes of the modern law of contract. However, this rather begs the question of whose expectations are decisive and why particular expectations are judged to be reasonable.[29] Is it from the standpoint of the regulators or as between the parties that the expectation is so judged? Are expectations reasonable because they are based on an explicit signal given either by the regulators or by co-contractors; or are they reasonable because they are in line with the sectoral assumption (in carriage, or shipping, or construction, or whatever); or is it because they are based on a practice that has spontaneously evolved in a particular way to a point that now implicitly encourages and supports the relevant expectation?[30] Accordingly, before we draw the conclusion that there is some congruence between networks and the protection of reasonable expectations, we need to take a harder look at each class of contract that is represented by our three test cases.

Teubner (eds.), NETWORKS: LEGAL ISSUES OF MULTILATERAL COOPERATION, *supra* note 1, at 137.

[28] Compare Lord Wilberforce's even bolder approach in *Port Jackson Stevedoring Pty Ltd v Salmond & Spraggon (Australia) Pty Ltd: The New York Star* [1981] 1 WLR 138.

[29] See, further, Roger Brownsword, *After Investors: Interpretation, Expectation and the Implicit Dimension of the "New Contextualism"* in THE IMPLICIT DIMENSIONS OF CONTRACT (David Campbell, Hugh Collins, and John Wightman (eds.), Oxford, Hart, 2003) 103.

[30] In practice, this will be the most problematic and controversial kind of case. See further text later at IV(iv); and compare Gunther Teubner, *'And if I by Beelzebub Cast Out Devils,...': An Essay on the Diabolics of Network Failure supra* note 1 above, and Heldt, *supra* note 27.

III. THE BASIS FOR NETWORK EFFECTS: CONSUMER CONTRACTS

We can start by considering the appropriateness of networks and of particular network effects in the sphere of consumer contracting. We can take this in two stages: first, we will state rather summarily our view that the law of contract has been displaced from this sphere, this inviting us to think instead in terms of the regulation of consumer transactions; and, second, we will review cases such as *OFT v. Lloyds TSB* in this light.

A. *The Nature of the Modern Regulation of Consumer Transactions*

For some time, it has been clear that the general law of contract has crafted a special set of rules to cover consumer transactions – for example, this is a sector that is distinguished by a high level of control over allegedly unfair terms and unfair commercial practices,[31] by a high threshold for the incorporation of terms,[32] by an unquestioned (and non-excludable) right of rejection where goods are not of satisfactory quality or reasonably fit for purpose,[33] and by the recognition of consumer surplus in making awards of damages.[34] When we say that the modern law has retreated somewhat from the classical principles of freedom and sanctity of contract, it is in relation to consumer contracts that we find the clearest evidence of such a retreat. However, with the systematic programme of single market consumer protection that has emanated from Brussels, it is time to move on from the concession that the law of consumer contracts represents a set of exceptions to the general law of contract. The idea of the bifurcation of contract law no longer does justice to the actuality.

In our view, we should now replace the idea that consumer transactions in Europe are covered by a special division of the law of contract with the idea that the consumer marketplace, and the transactions made therein, represents a particular regulated zone.[35] In short, we should view consumer transactions as a class of regulated transactions. This new (regulatory) paradigm might not sound so very different; but, it reflects two fundamental shifts in our thinking.

[31] See the Directive on Unfair Terms in Consumer Contracts 1993/13/EC and the Unfair Commercial Practices Directive 2005/29 EC.

[32] In English law, the best example from a clutch of cases is *Thornton v Shoe Lane Parking Ltd* [1971] 2 QB 163.

[33] In English law, see section 14 of the Sale of Goods Act 1979, reinforced by section 6(2) of the Unfair Contract Terms Act 1977.

[34] Seminally, see *Jarvis v. Swan's Tours Ltd* [1973] QB 233 and Case C-168/00 *Simone Leitner v. TUI Deutschland* [2002] ECR-I-2631.

[35] See Roger Brownsword, *The Theoretical Foundations of European Private Law: A Time to Stand and Stare* in THE FOUNDATIONS OF EUROPEAN PRIVATE LAW, *supra* note 7 at 159.

The first shift is to appreciate that, as with any regulatory enterprise, our evaluations need to start with the purposes that either are being pursued or that should be pursued by regulators. If transactions in the consumer marketplace are to be regulated, the question is, 'For what purpose is the regulation introduced?', that is, what are regulators trying to achieve – or, to be more critical, what purposes should regulators pursue? It is only then that we can consider whether particular regulatory initiatives and interventions are fit for purpose. As Hugh Collins has put it:

> Once legal discourse reorients itself towards the instrumental reasoning of welfarist regulation, it must observe closely the consequences of regulation in order to ascertain whether the objectives are being achieved. The trajectory of legal evolution alters from the private law discourse of seeking the better coherence for its scheme of principles to one of learning about the need for fresh regulation by observations of the consequences of present regulation. Information about the world, especially market practices, has to be gathered and reconstituted in a form which enables the legal discourse to adjust its own internal operations and regulatory outcomes. Within this new form of legal reasoning, what the law actually does, its social and economic effects, becomes crucial to the dynamic operations of the legal system.[36]

In other words, it is no longer relevant to ask how well some modification to consumer law fits with the general law of contract; rather, we need to focus on whether we are trying to do the right thing in relation to consumer transactions and whether our interventions are effective.[37] It is not coherence with the general law of contract that now controls; it is coherence with the (actual or the critically justified) regulatory objectives.

The second shift is to assess the appropriateness of some legal change by locating it in the broader landscape of the regulatory environment. Not only is this a matter about which I have written at length elsewhere, it is also less pressing for present purposes,[38] so it will not be rehearsed again here. Suffice it to say that regulators have many strategies available for the channelling of conduct.[39] Law in general, and

[36] Hugh Collins, REGULATING CONTRACTS (Oxford: Oxford University Press, 1999) at 8. I take it that, although Collins talks here about "welfarist" regulation, his point is of general application.

[37] For a comparable case, consider the limited regulatory effectiveness of European law in relation to the use of consumer data (e.g., by supermarkets who operate loyalty card schemes): see EC Health and Consumers Directorate-General, *Data Collection, Targeting and Profiling of Consumers for Commercial Purposes in Online Environments* (Brussels, 05.03.2009, SANCO/B2/GA/SR/GR), at 23–24.

[38] See, the references *supra* note 7 above; Roger Brownsword and Han Somsen, *Law, Innovation, and Technology: Before We Fast Forward – A Forum for Debate* 1 LAW INNOVATION AND TECHNOLOGY, 1 (2009); and Roger Brownsword and Morag Goodwin, LAW AND THE TECHNOLOGIES OF THE TWENTY FIRST CENTURY (Cambridge: Cambridge University Press, 2012) Ch 2.

[39] Seminally, see Lawrence Lessig, CODE AND OTHER LAWS OF CYBERSPACE (New York: Basic Books, 1999), Ch 7; and Lawrence Lessig, *The Law of the Horse: What Cyberlaw Might Teach* 113 HARVARD LAW REVIEW 501, 507–514 (1999).

contract law in particular, is just one mode of regulation. In some regulatory environments, law is critical; in others it is not; and, as the evolution of eBay illustrates, the relative importance of law can change over time.[40]

Once we start viewing transactions in the European consumer marketplace through a regulatory lens, it becomes apparent that regulators are seeking to put consumers in a position where they are able to make free and informed choices, and where they have the confidence to deal in any part of the single market, but without this amounting to a wholly unacceptable burden on business.[41] To a considerable extent, regulators have pursued these objectives by imposing a raft of responsibilities on suppliers. Possibly, it is something of an over-simplification to say this, but, from a regulatory viewpoint, this looks very much like a command and control strategy (with suppliers as the principal regulatory targets and consumers as the principal beneficiaries).

Given this perspective, if it is proposed that networks or network effects should be taken up in the regulation of consumer transactions, the only question is whether giving consumers third-party rights, or increasing the obligations of suppliers, or the like, is in line with the current regulatory objectives. Or, if we are to challenge the prevailing regulatory purposes, the question is whether such innovation would assist whatever objectives we think that regulators should be pursuing.[42]

B. *Networks and* OFT v. Lloyds TSB

In the light of the preceding, what would we now make of the issues arising in *OFT v. Lloyds TSB*? What should we make of the legislative adoption of the protection given by section 75(1) of the Consumer Credit Act 1974? What should we make of the courts' approach, confirming the application of the section to foreign suppliers? And, what would we make of the hypothetical proposition, in the *Boyack* case, that even in the absence of a provision such as section 75(1), network effects should be adopted?

1. The Legislative Approach

Assuming that the regulatory purpose is to protect consumers against more powerful suppliers and to encourage confidence in the credit card economy, section 75(1)

[40] See, e.g., the discussion in Jack Goldsmith and Tim Wu, Who Controls the Internet? (Oxford: Oxford University Press, 2006).

[41] Where regulators have less interest in encouraging consumers to cross borders, and where consumers themselves are perfectly happy to shop at home, the shift from contract to regulation might be less marked (such might be the case, for example, in countries such as Singapore).

[42] Compare Gralf-Peter Calliess, *Fitness Clubs: Consumer Protection between Contract and Association* in Networks: Legal Issues of Multilateral Cooperation, Amstutz and Teubner (eds.), *supra* note 1, at 241. Whilst we might think it appropriate for regulators to shield consumers against terms that are truly unfair and unreasonable, Calliess argues that regulators and judges also need to be sensitive to holding consumers to their obligations as members of clubs.

makes sense. The legislative scheme assumes that card issuers will be able to indemnify themselves against retailers. Given that most retailers are in no position to argue with card issuers, this means that the risk is being shifted from one vulnerable group (consumers) to another (especially small business retailers),[43] but, if the latter are in breach of contract, there is no reason why they should escape their obligations.

2. The Courts' Approach

The approach taken by the courts in the *Lloyds TSB* case is reasonably straightforward. The House of Lords tries to align itself with the regulatory objectives as articulated in the legislative scheme – which, barring some overriding constitutional question, is precisely what it should do.

To this, there is one caveat: if, in practice, UK card issuers are less well able to indemnify themselves against foreign suppliers, then it needs to be considered whether exposing card issuers to such a risk is consistent with the regulatory objectives. Again, this is a question that the court considered, concluding that card issuers have the resources to handle risks of this kind – or, at any rate, that card issuers are much better placed than card holders to cover themselves against such risks.[44] Putting this in the context of the current network arrangements, Lord Mance said:

> That, in today's market, arrangements between card issuers and overseas suppliers under schemes such as VISA and MasterCard are indirect (rather than pursuant to a direct contract as is still the case with American Express and Diners Club) is a consequence of the way in which the VISA and MasterCard networks have developed and operate. Likewise, the fact that the rules of these networks give card issuers no direct choice as to the suppliers in relation to whom their cards will be used. The choice of suppliers is, in effect, delegated to the merchant acquirers in each country in which these networks operate, and provision is made, as one would expect, to ensure and monitor the reliability of such suppliers in the interests of all network members. That network rules may not provide all the protections that they might, eg by way of indemnity and/or jurisdiction agreements, is neither here nor there. They could in theory do so, and it is apparent that there are some differences in this respect between different networks. The Crowther Report and 1974 Act proceed on the basis of a relatively simple model which contemplated that card issuers would have direct control of such matters. A more sophisticated worldwide network, like VISA or MasterCard, offers both card issuers and card holders considerable countervailing benefits. Card issuers make a choice, commercially inevitable though it may have become, to join one of these networks, for better or worse.[45]

[43] Compare, Roger Brownsword, *Judicial Revision of Abusive Contractual Terms: Credit Card Fraud and Charge-Back Clauses* Revista De Direito Bancario, Special Edition, (Proceedings of the First International Symposium of Banking Law: *Banking Law and the Globalization of the Financial System*, Sao Paulo, Brazil, 1998) 668.

[44] See [2007] UKHL 48, para 29.

[45] [2007] UKHL 48, para 30.

Moreover, "it was a principal theme" of the legislative background that "creditors would have a strong contractual and commercial influence over their suppliers and that, where resort could not be had to such suppliers, losses were better borne by creditors, who could spread them over the public at large, than by debtors."[46] In other words, even though the de facto choices of card issuers are not entirely free, as stakeholders in the networks in which they choose to participate, they are much better able than their card holders to bear the financial risks of participation.

3. The *Boyack* Hypothetical

In our hypothetical case based on *Boyack*, we would need to consider whether the regulatory objectives would be advanced by the adoption of network effects, particularly by giving the consumer the option of pursuing a claim, based on the supplier's default, against the credit card issuer. At once, it might be objected that such an imposition of liability on the non-defaulting credit card issuer smacks of the kind of thinking that we have in tort where employers are held to be vicariously liable for the defaults of their employees. Such an imposition, it might be objected, cannot be contemplated in a regime of contract law. However, this objection belongs in another age. Contract law, as we have argued, is no longer relevant to the regulation of consumer transactions. The only question is whether the doctrinal moves that we are debating are likely to help or to hinder the regulatory objectives. It is for this reason that we have a problem where regulators (as in the hypothetical) have not explicitly declared their objectives.

In the absence of explicit regulatory guidance, how should the courts proceed? One option would be to default to leaving the law alone, thus passing the responsibility back to the regulators. Another option would be to draw on the hints given by regulators as to their purposes in the light of which the courts would construct what they judge to be the most coherent or the most reasonable objectives against which to assess the suitability of a network innovation. Fortunately, because Brussels is rarely reticent about its regulatory purposes in the area of (European) consumer protection, we are unlikely to find ourselves in a regulatory void.[47] Granted, support

[46] *Id.*, at para 39.

[47] By way of illustration, consider the regulatory objectives expressed in Recitals 4 and 5 of Directive 2011/83/EU (on consumer rights) OJ L 304/64, 22:11:2011. *Inter alia*, Recital 4 states: "The harmonisation of certain aspects of consumer distance and off-premises contracts is necessary for the promotion of a real consumer internal market striking the right balance between a high level of consumer protection and the competitiveness of enterprises, while ensuring respect for the principle of subsidiarity." Then, in Recital 5, we read:

The cross-border potential of distance selling, which should be one of the main tangible results of the internal market, is not fully exploited. Compared with the significant growth of domestic distance sales over the last few years, the growth in cross-border distance sales has been limited. This discrepancy is particularly significant for Internet sales for which the potential for further growth is high. The cross-border potential of contracts negotiated away from business premises (direct selling)

for consumer dealing in Dubai might not be part of the current regulatory agenda in Brussels, but, if Mr Boyack had bought his clock in Paris, the regulatory hints might be sufficient to justify adopting such network effects as would encourage consumers such as Boyack to give Parisian suppliers a second chance.

4. Beyond *OFT v. Lloyds TSB*

Moving beyond the *OFT v. Lloyds TSB* case, there are a number of possible network effects that we might want to consider in relation to consumer transactions. For example, what if consumers were able (as in product liability claims) to leapfrog over their immediate suppliers (say, where those suppliers had gone out of business) to pursue a claim for breach of contract against an upstream producer (particularly where the supply chain was strongly integrated)[48]; or why not afford consumers who use debit cards or cheques to make their purchases the same kind of protection that obtains under section 75(1); or should there be other kinds of heightened obligation to be assumed by suppliers into the consumer marketplace (always bearing in mind that the voluntary assumption of such obligations by top-end retailers might be a feature of the regulatory environment); and so on? Each proposal invites careful consideration relative to the regulatory purposes and, if a network effect would seem to assist those purposes, then (but only then) should it be adopted.

IV. THE BASIS FOR NETWORK EFFECTS: COMMERCIAL CONTRACTS

Elsewhere, we have argued that it is in the field of commercial transactions that we find the paradigm of contractual obligation, the parties engaging in private ordering not just by entering into a transaction but by agreeing to the rules that should govern their dealing.[49] Accordingly, we can start by stating quite shortly what role

is constrained by a number of factors including the different national consumer protection rules imposed upon the industry. Compared with the growth of domestic direct selling over the last few years, in particular in the services sector, for instance utilities, the number of consumers using this channel for cross-border purchases has remained flat. Responding to increased business opportunities in many Member States, small and medium-sized enterprises (including individual traders) or agents of direct selling companies should be more inclined to seek business opportunities in other Member States, in particular in border regions. Therefore the full harmonisation of consumer information and the right of withdrawal in distance and off-premises contracts will contribute to a high level of consumer protection and a better functioning of the business-to-consumer internal market.

48 For such an example, see the decision of the Karlsruhe Court of Appeals, OLG Karlsruhe NZV 1989, 434, where it was held that the consumer purchaser of a car was not restricted to a claim against the now insolvent car dealer but, instead, could sue the Japanese importer (as the central node within the distribution system). See Gunther Teubner, NETWORKS AS CONNECTED CONTRACTS *supra* note 1 at 78 et seq.

49 See Roger Brownsword, *Contract, Consent, and Civil Society: Private Governance and Public Imposition* in CIVIL SOCIETY (Peter Odell and Chris Willett (eds.), Oxford: Hart, 2008) 5.

we see for the law of contract in what is, in effect, the co-regulation of commercial transactions. We will then suggest that, so to speak, the "Hoffmannisation" of the English law of contract is in line with, and indeed confirms, this reading. This will set up the basis for assessing the appropriateness of networks in commercial transactional settings. In the final section of this part of the chapter, we consider whether the contrast between a regulated zone of consumer transactions and a co-regulated zone of commercial transactions is too blunt, particularly bearing in mind the relative vulnerability of small businesses.

A. *The Nature of the Modern Regulation of Commercial Transactions*

Broadly speaking, we suggest that the modern approach to the regulation of commercial transactions is co-regulatory; the gist of such an approach is that it involves a public/private partnership. While the State sets the broad outlines of the regulatory environment in a way that secures the public interest, the detail is filled in by private regulators. Or, to put this another way, the state sets limits to a sphere of mandated private governance.

Applied to commercial transactions, the public interest side of co-regulation implies that, while some transactions might be subject to criminal prohibition, others might be discouraged or simply not enforced; that, while attempts to introduce or rely on some types of contractual term might be subject to criminal prohibition, others might simply not be enforced, and so on. In the regulatory mix, too, there will be measures that are designed to secure the public interest in competitive markets, respect for human rights, and the like. At all events, once the full set of public interest restrictions and limitations has been taken into account, contractors are left to make their own private arrangements. Essentially, these private arrangements may take one of two forms.

First, the parties may expressly elect to engage a particular set of rules to govern their dealings. When commercial parties engage the English or the New York law of contract as the applicable law for their transaction, they micro-manage their participation as co-regulators. Moreover, this is where we find a coalescence of the classical understanding of contract as voluntary obligation, of contract as being based on consent, and of contract as the expression of the parties' autonomy. In the real world of commerce, practice might deviate very substantially from this idealised view. Nevertheless, there is a background regulatory judgment here that the parties should be left to deal in accordance with their own rules.

Second, where domestic parties make no express choice of applicable law, the local law of contract applies as a default setting. Given what we would term a dynamic market-individualist approach (which typifies much of judicial thinking in commercial contract cases),[50] this default setting seeks out the regulatory backcloth that the parties have implicitly assumed to be applicable. Where that backcloth is represented by a trade standard form that is routinely used, the parties in effect submit themselves to the self-regulatory standards set by the sector. Where there is no standard form, there might nevertheless be various implicit customs and practices in the sector and, again, where this is the assumed backcloth, the parties submit themselves to the self-regulatory practice.

B. *The "Hoffmannisation" of Contract Law*

In a number of seminal judgments, most famously in *Investors Compensation Scheme Ltd v. West Bromwich Building Society*,[51] Lord Hoffmann has transformed the way that commercial contracts should be interpreted. In the *Investors Compensation* case, Lord Hoffmann declared that, in relation to commercial contracts, "contextual" interpretation should be preferred to an abstracted "literalism." Text, so to speak, has been replaced by context (or by text in context); and, as one commentator has put it, contextualism "is rapidly becoming the bible for the courts in contract interpretation disputes."[52]

Whereas literalism treats the words of a contractual agreement as having an abstracted life, or meaning, of their own (any context to be supplied being minimal), the fundamental feature of contextualism is that it seeks out the meaning that fits best with the context. In *Mannai Investments Co Ltd v. Eagle Star Life Assurance Co Ltd*,[53] where Lord Hoffmann prefigured the key aspects of his approach in *Investors*, he sketched his understanding of the relevance of context as follows:

> The meaning of words, as they would appear in a dictionary, and the effect of their syntactical arrangement, as it would appear in a grammar, is part of the material which we use to understand a speaker's utterance. But it is only a part; another part is our knowledge of the background against which the utterance was made. It is that background which enables us, not only to choose the intended meaning when a word has more than one dictionary meaning but also … to understand a speaker's meaning, often without ambiguity, when he has used the wrong words.[54]

[50] See Roger Brownsword, *Contract Law, Co-operation, and Good Faith: the Movement from Static to Dynamic Market-Individualism* in CONTRACTS, CO-OPERATION AND COMPETITION (Simon Deakin and Jonathan Michie (eds.) Oxford: Oxford University Press, 1997) 255; and Roger Brownsword, CONTRACT LAW: THEMES FOR THE TWENTY FIRST CENTURY, 2nd ed. (Oxford: Oxford University Press, 2006) Ch 7.

[51] [1998] 1 All ER 98.

[52] David W. McLauchlan, *The New Law of Contract Interpretation* (2000) 19 NEW ZEALAND UNIVERSITIES LAW REVIEW 147.

[53] [1997] 3 All ER 352.

[54] *Id.*, at 376.

Context, thus, plays an important corrective part in the process of interpretation. Hence, in *Mannai* itself, where a tenant purported to give notice to determine leases on 12 January 1995, when (to comply strictly with the terms of the leases) the tenant should have specified 13 January 1995, it mattered little why this mistake had been made. The critical point, as the majority ruled in *Mannai*, was that the landlord, receiving the notice, would have realised, *in this particular context*, that the tenant was intending to give notice in accordance with the terms of the lease and that a slip had been made in specifying 12 January rather than 13 January.

Similarly, in *Total Gas Marketing Ltd v. Arco British Ltd*,[55] Lord Steyn (who, along with Lord Hoffmann has been the principal author of the new contextualism) summarised the key idea in the following way: "[questions of interpretation] must be considered in the light of the contractual language, the contractual scheme, the commercial context and the reasonable expectations of the parties."[56]

More recently, Lord Hoffmann, in company with a unanimous House of Lords, has confirmed that the "context", for the purposes of interpreting a commercial contract, does not include the pre-contractual negotiations.[57] Nevertheless, even if the context stops at pre-contractual negotiations, all the indications are that contextualism itself does not stop at interpretation. Thus, in *Attorney General of Belize v. Belize Telecom Limited*,[58] Lord Hoffmann has taken the opportunity to explain how contextualism entails some revision of the traditional approach to implied terms. In the *Belize* case, relying on *Investors Compensation*, Lord Hoffmann explains that the implicit meaning of an instrument is that "which the instrument would convey to a reasonable person having all the background knowledge which would reasonably be available to the audience to whom the instrument is addressed."[59] According to Lord Hoffmann:

> It follows that in every case in which it is said that some provision ought to be implied in an instrument, the question for the court is whether such a provision would spell out in express words what the instrument, read against the relevant background, would reasonably be understood to mean.[60]

Moreover, the several stock litmus tests for implication – such as whether the implication goes "without saying", or is "necessary to give business efficacy to the

55 [1998] 2 Lloyd's Rep 209.

56 *Id.*, at 221. For his own part, Lord Steyn was particularly adept at applying such thinking to questions of implied terms: see, e.g., *Mosvolds Rederi A/S v Food Corpn of India* [1986] 2 Lloyd's Rep 68; and *Equitable Life Assurance Society v Hyman* [2000] 3 All ER 961

57 See *Chartbrook Limited v. Persimmon Homes Limited* [2009] UKHL 38, affirming the view in *Prenn v. Simmonds* [1971] 1 WLR 1381 where Lord Wilberforce, a proto-typical contextualist, ruled that pre-contractual negotiations are inadmissible.

58 [2009] UKPC 11.

59 *Id.*, at para 16.

60 *Id.*, at para 21.

contract", or would be self-evident to the officious bystander, and so on – must be read as articulations of the general test, namely, whether the proposed implied term would be an expression of "what the instrument, read as a whole against the relevant background, would reasonably be understood to mean."[61] While this does not speak directly to networks, it does signify that, where the working practice of contractors assumes more than minimal cooperation, this will be reflected in the terms that are implied.

However, the most radical implications of contextualism become apparent in the period-defining case of *Transfield Shipping Inc v. Mercator Shipping Inc*.[62] There, the charterers of a single-deck bulk carrier were in breach of contract by being some nine days late in redelivering the vessel to the owners. As a result of this late redelivery, the owners were put in a difficult position in relation to a new fixture of the vessel that had been agreed with another charterer. In order to retain this fixture, the owners agreed to reduce the daily rate by $8,000. The question was whether the owners were entitled to recover the loss of $8,000 per day for the duration of the new charter (a sum of $1,364,584.37) or merely the difference between the market rate and the charter rate for the nine day late redelivery (a sum of $158,301.17). The majority of the arbitrators and the lower appeal courts held that the owners were entitled to the higher amount: their reasoning was that the charterers must have known that the owners were likely to arrange a new onward charter, that market rates fluctuate, and that late delivery might reduce the profitability of the onward charter (i.e., the forward fixture). However, the House held unanimously (albeit with some hesitation) that the owners were restricted to the lesser sum.

According to Baroness Hale, the issue presented by the appeal "could be an examination question." Moreover, in response to the question,

> [t]here is no obviously right answer: two very experienced commercial judges have reached one answer, your lordships have reached another. There is no obviously just answer: the charterer's default undoubtedly caused the owner's loss, but a loss for which no-one has ever had to pay before. The examiners would surely have given first class marks to all the judges who have answered the question so far.[63]

Reflecting on the answers given by her colleagues, Baroness Hale identified two lines of reasoning in support of the lower sum.

One line of reasoning focuses on whether the particular type of loss was within the reasonable contemplation of the charterers. Following this line of thinking, the charterers "would expect that the owner would be able to find a use for his ship even if it was returned late. It was only because of the unusual volatility of the market at

61 *Id.*
62 [2008] UKHL 48.
63 *Id.*, at para 89.

that particular time that this particular loss was suffered. It is one thing to say ... that missing dates for a subsequent fixture was within the parties' contemplation as 'not unlikely'. It is another thing to say that the 'extremely volatile' conditions which brought about this particular loss were 'not unlikely'."[64]

The alternative line of reasoning "is that one must ask, not only whether the parties must be taken to have had this *type of loss* within their contemplation when the contract was made, but also whether they must be taken to have had *liability for this type of loss* within their contemplation then. In other words, is the charterer to be taken to have undertaken legal responsibility for this type of loss?"[65]

It is Lord Hoffmann who most clearly favours the alternative line of reasoning, but that is only half the story. The more important aspect of Lord Hoffmann's approach is the way in which he proposes that it should be determined whether a contract breaker has assumed responsibility for a particular type of loss. In a key section of his speech, Lord Hoffmann says:

> The case therefore raises a fundamental point of principle in the law of contractual damages: is the rule that a party may recover losses which were foreseeable ("not unlikely") an external rule of law, imposed upon the parties to every contract in default of express provision to the contrary, or is it a prima facie assumption about what the parties may be taken to have intended, no doubt applicable in the great majority of cases but capable of rebuttal in cases in which the context, surrounding circumstances or general understanding in the relevant market shows that a party would not reasonably have been regarded as assuming responsibility for such losses?[66]

Drawing a parallel with his own favoured contextual approach to the interpretation of contracts, Lord Hoffmann prefers the latter view. And, applying such a view, Lord Hoffmann finds that, relative to background market expectations in the shipping sector, "it is clear that [the parties] would have considered losses arising from the loss of the following fixture a type or kind of loss for which the charterer was not assuming responsibility."[67]

Transfield, thus, offers an important insight into the role of the modern law of contract. Contextualism is a particular expression of dynamic market-individualism;[68] and dynamic market-individualism is the expression of private governance in a larger co-regulatory regime. Stated simply, what this signifies is that the State sets certain public interest limits on the freedom of commercial contractors, but that,

64 *Id.*, at para 91.
65 *Id.*, at para. 92.
66 *Id.*, at para. 9.
67 *Id.*, at para. 23.
68 See Roger Brownsword, CONTRACT LAW: THEMES FOR THE TWENTY FIRST CENTURY, *supra* note 50 Ch 7.

within the (considerable) area of freedom left to them, such contractors may order their transactions as they wish. Where contractors do not signal their intentions, the law of contract offers a stock of default rules that can be applied. However, where it is either clear from the context, or the most reasonable interpretation of that context, that the contractors proceeded on the basis of certain rules, those rules (rather than the default rules of contract law) should be applied.

C. *Network Effects and* The Eurymedon

To what extent, should network effects be adopted in the commercial law of contract? First, networks and network effects should not be permitted (or, at any rate, their activities should be regulated) where this would be contrary to the public interest – for example, if networks were seen as having unacceptable anti-competitive effects, or unacceptable inefficiencies, or as being productive of unacceptable externalities, and so on. Secondly, once any public interest concerns have been dealt with, in the area where the contractors are free to privately order their dealings, the law should maximise their options. In the absence of any obvious reasons for public interest restriction on networks, the regulatory steer seems to be towards making it easy for contractors to opt for networks and network effects.[69] In other words, once any required public interest restrictions have been put in place, the regulatory approach should be one of facilitating the full range of private governance options.

After *Transfield Shipping*, however, we need to be particularly sensitive to the layering of the free zone. The general law of contract provides the default layer; but the contractors may construct alternative layers of governance either explicitly or by their implicit practice (by reference to the context). It follows that we might ask (i) whether networks should be taken up as part of the default layer or (ii) whether, assuming that networks have not been taken up by the default position, they nevertheless arise at some level of the alternative layering of governance. In response to the latter question, the position is straightforward where the parties expressly signal that their intention is to adopt network effects; such is their explicitly declared governance structure. However, in the absence of explicit signalling, it still might be argued that network effects should be applied because this would be to respect the implicit expectations of the parties – in the language of *Transfield Shipping*, this would be to draw on the context (sectoral or relational) in which the parties dealt.

To avoid any misunderstanding, let me spell out the complete three-stage design of a regulatory regime that addresses networks in this way. At the first stage, the public interest must be considered. Possibly, the public interest will dictate that

69 Compare, too, the discussion in *OFT v. Lloyds TSB Bank plc* [2007] UKHL 48, at para 36, concerning the variety of network provisions that might be adopted by the commercial parties.

networks should not be permitted; or, it might be that the public interest will be served by requiring the recognition of networks. Whatever the public interest determination, we move to the second stage if there is some room for contracting parties to self-govern in a networked way. At the second stage, the default setting has to be determined. Broadly speaking, that setting will be either for or against networks. Quite why the default setting should be tilted one way or the other merits regulatory attention (although this might be less important for commercial dealing, where the parties are legally advised, than for purely private dealing where the parties might be unaware that there is a default or that it can be switched). For the sake of illustration, let us suppose that the default is against network effects – as it would be in the classical English law of contract where the defaults are for privity of contract and adversarial dealing. At the third stage, with a default set against networks, it needs to be determined how the contractors may switch the default. Explicit signalling by the contracting parties is the clearest option; but a legal regime (even a regime with a classical legacy) might allow for implicit signalling and this is where, in practice, there are likely to be interpretive difficulties and controversial applications.

With these focusing comments, what should we make of the majority's approach in *The Eurymedon*? Had Lord Wilberforce talked the talk of networks and contexts, he would have said that the parties involved in carriage of goods by sea operate on the assumption that the liability of the parties who handle the goods is limited; and that the parties cover themselves with appropriate levels of insurance. Such an operational practice presupposes that the contracts have certain network effects (in relation to third-party claims and defences). Unless there is some public interest reason for restricting the parties' freedom to govern their dealings in this way, they should be permitted to do so. In other words, even if privity rules obtained as defaults, after *Transfield Shipping* we would say that the Hoffmann override applied and that network effects should be recognised.

What would we say about heightened obligations in commercial networks such as franchise schemes? Possibly, this might be a case in which there is an argument for building such cooperative principles into the default rules for this class of contracts. But, irrespective of this, if the express intention of the parties or if the implicit practice of franchising discloses a contextually supported reasonable expectation of co-operation, this kind of network effect should be applied.

D. *Beware the Classical Inheritance*

It has been suggested that contractual obligation is at its purest where the parties freely and explicitly agree to deal in accordance with certain framework rules. Transactions that are negotiated in accordance with the framework rules are binding because this is the effect of agreeing to such rules. If the parties have the option of adopting network effects as part of their framework understanding (as part of their private governance structure), then they self-regulate for such effects; and it is clear why networks then rule and why their requirements are a matter of obligation.

The parties may signal their agreement to deal on a basis that includes network effects either by expressly adopting a governance structure that has the desired effects or by simply participating in a practice that is understood by all participants to have such effects – when we join in a game of soccer, we do not need to reaffirm that we are playing in accordance with the official rules of association football; and so it is with transactions, where the practice is clearly established. However, this presupposes (to borrow from soccer) a set-piece view of transactions, when the actuality is that transactional practices (just like the game of soccer) can be much more fluid with shifting patterns and practices. Accordingly, to do justice to networks, we must be careful not to stick too rigidly to the classical view of set-piece dealing.

What this means is that we must also allow for the possibility that network effects arise other than by regulatory prescription or express contractual promise, that they can arise by virtue of practice (and the expectations generated by practice). The dynamics of networks are such that, as Gunther Teubner has put it, there is "the expectation that expectations will change."[70] As we have put it on a few occasions already, networks can arise "implicitly". This, I accept, is a proposition that favours doctrinal flexibility over certainty; and we know that there will be different interpretations as to whether a transactional practice or a particular trading relationship has evolved to a point that takes it over the threshold for a network. Nevertheless, so long as we are trying to track the practice-based expectations of contractors, there will always be grey areas where, no matter how the legal characterisation goes, there will be scope for disagreement.

E. Big Businesses, Small Businesses, and Shopping Malls

Under a co-regulated arrangement, commercial contractors are free to punch their weight. This means that more powerful contractors will strike hard bargains with less powerful contractors. Provided that the public interest has been secured, we might simply shrug our shoulders and conclude that this is the nature of the market. Unless we are to switch to a stronger regulatory approach, as with consumers, small

[70] Gunther Teubner, *'And if I by Beelzebub Cast Out Devils,...': An Essay on the Diabolics of Network Failure*, *supra* note 1 at 407. Teubner adds (ibid.):

> Such unspecified obligations that can be specified only after a certain period of time were not unknown in classical contract law, but only as secondary obligations opposed to the primary obligation that was expressly defined at the contractual conclusion. In the network, by contrast, primary obligations are defined by this type of deferred determination.

business contractors face a tough time. There is every reason to suppose that asymmetries of power will be exploited within networks just as without them.[71]

Consider a hypothetical shopping mall development. The developer lets a large unit to a major national retailer knowing that this will attract both customers and small businesses. However, the terms on which small businesses are brought into the shopping mall does them no favours. If the large retailer pulls out, the small businesses will be stranded. Is there anything in the idea of a network – particularly the idea that, in a network, the members share both the benefits and the burdens of their collective endeavours – that might assist them?[72]

If we start in the spirit of co-regulation, we must make sure that the contracts made at the mall are consistent with any relevant public interest considerations. One consideration might be the importance of the mall flourishing; it is no good for anyone if the mall is blighted by the withdrawal of a major retailer. Another consideration might be the importance of securing the confidence of small business people. But, how are these desiderata to be translated into legal principles?

If the public interest is sufficiently compelling, it might be reflected in the terms of the regulatory authorisation for the mall. Failing this, let us suppose that the developer and the major retailer are acutely aware of the considerations just identified. Accordingly, acting in a public-spirited way, they freely adopt network effects for the development and its contracts that respond to these concerns. Clearly, though, for the most part, this assumption is too good to be true; and, in the absence of such enlightened contractors, the burden of responsibility will lie with the ex ante prescriptions of regulators or the ex post rulings of courts.

If we think that regulators should be prescriptive in their protection of the interests of small business retailers, what do we think they should prescribe? If they prescribe a network effect that ties-in the major retailer, even when trading conditions are bad, this is likely to discourage investment by such retailers (who will see the risk as being loaded too heavily on their side); and, even if a tie-in is part of the deal, there might be difficulties in enforcing it.[73] Perhaps a more promising effect would be along the lines that major retailers should not make economic decisions without taking account of the stakeholding interests of smaller retailers. This is not a particularly demanding requirement but, where the default ethic is entirely one of short-term self-interest, it at least nudges doctrine towards a more cooperative approach.[74] A further possibility is to protect the smaller retailers by offering them

[71] In general, compare Gunther Teubner, *supra* note 1.

[72] On benefit sharing, see Reinhard Böhner, *Asset-Sharing in Franchise Networks: The Obligation to Pass on Network Benefits* in NETWORKS: LEGAL ISSUES OF MULTILATERAL COOPERATION Amstutz and Teubner (eds.), *supra* note 1 at 153.

[73] Compare *Co-operative Insurance Society Ltd v. Argyll Stores (Holdings) Ltd* [1998] AC 1.

[74] Compare Reinhard Böhner, *supra* note 72.

the option, where a major retailer pulls out of the mall, of pulling out themselves, or of renegotiating the terms of their contracts with the developers.[75]

If all else fails, we might turn, ex post, to the courts. Relying on standards of good faith and fair dealing, and exercising some control over unconscionable conduct, the courts might be able to deal with individual instances of unfair exposure. It must be conceded, however, that this, if not exactly an admission of regulatory defeat, is something of a last resort.

Unfortunately, there is no easy answer to the conundrum of how, within a network, the balance of individual and collective interest is to be struck. Indeed, as Gunther Teubner has emphasised, the very essence of networks is that they encourage *both* the maximisation of individual interest and good network citizenship.[76] Networks, so understood, necessarily involve a degree of productive discordance; and this is something that the courts should endeavour to reflect, rather than to resolve, in their decisions.

V. THE BASIS FOR NETWORK EFFECTS: PRIVATE CONTRACTS

Appeal court litigation of purely private transactions is relatively unusual. Nevertheless, it was transactions of this class – witness, cases such as *Tweddle v. Atkinson* [77] and *Beswick v. Beswick*[78] – that were the focus for the eventual relaxation of the privity rules in the Contracts (Rights of Third Parties) Act 1999. We should not assume, therefore, that disputes such as that in *Clarke v. Dunraven* are wholly exceptional. Even so, private transactions are not one of the more obvious targets for regulators.

Insofar as there is a background co-regulatory plan for purely private transactions, it probably mirrors that of commercial contracts. Accordingly, there will be some public interest regulatory restriction, for example, with regard to purely domestic agreements, surrogacy contracts, pre-nuptial agreements, and so on.[79] Such restrictions apart, the regulatory purpose will be to let the parties order their transactions in their own way. Hence, if competitors such as those in *Clarke v. Dunraven* wish to adjust the usual liability rules, public policy permitting, they should be free to do so.

75 I am indebted to my colleague John Phillips for this latter suggestion.

76 Gunther Teubner, *supra* note 1.

77 (1861) 1 B & S 393.

78 [1968] AC 58.

79 For a recent instance, concerning both pre- and post-nuptial agreements, compare *MacLeod v. MacLeod* [2008] UKPC 64 with the majority view in *Radmacher v. Granatino* [2010] UKSC 42, esp at paras 31–61. And, see Gunther Teubner, *'And if I by Beelzebub Cast Out Devils,...': An Essay on the Diabolics of Network Failure supra* note 1 at 415 (concerning the possible blocking of an exit option for powerful parties who wish to withdraw from their network responsibilities).

And, if they wish the rules to be enforceable horizontally as between the competitors, they should be free to do this too.

However, in the absence of legal advice, private transactors are unlikely to be aware of the full range of their legal options. And, we might assume that, in general, disputes between private transactors will need to be adjudicated by reference to the default rules. If this is correct, and if the default rules are not network sensitive (as they conspicuously were not so long as privity ruled), when they should be, regulators need to give this some attention. In this light, what should we make of the two key changes made by the Contracts (Rights of Third Parties) Act, 1999? First, for that class of transactions where the contracting parties intend to confer a benefit on a third party, the default position seems to be that the third party has a right of enforcement; in other words, the default is set for this particular network effect. The default may be switched, however, where the parties expressly so signal or where the circumstances (for which, perhaps, we should read context) indicate that no right of enforcement is contemplated. Second, in all other cases, including where the contract is simply of benefit to a third party, the default remains against network effects. Again, though, the default may be switched but only where the parties expressly signal that they are conferring a third-party right of enforcement.

Where the default rules are not appropriate, there is the question of whether judges might have a discretionary override to bring in network effects. While an unpredictable judicial discretion is not ideal, in this class of case, it probably can be tolerated.

VI. CONCLUSION

Although this is an essay in private law, it has been a discussion that has started in an unfamiliar place (with the regulation of transactions) and that has then proceeded in a somewhat tortuous way through consumer, commercial and purely private transactions. What are the principal conclusions with regard to network contracts and network effects? Are these ideas that we should embrace or reject?

First, in relation to consumer transactions, the utility and appropriateness of networks is to be judged entirely by reference to the regulatory objectives. If we accept the current regulatory objectives, the question is whether networks cohere with and assist the realisation of those objectives. If we reject the current regulatory objectives, we need to defend a different set of objectives and then assess the utility and appropriateness of networks relative to those revised regulatory objectives. In both cases, the question needs to be pursued with an awareness of the significance of legal provisions in the larger regulatory environment.

Second, in relation to commercial transactions, the first question is whether networks or network effects are compatible with public interest considerations (e.g., with competition policy, or with respect for human rights, and so on). If networks are not to be disallowed on public interest grounds, the question is whether they should be written into the default rules of contract law. However, where the general rules are simply defaults, and where express intention, context, and practice displace the defaults, the law should recognise networks and network effects wherever this is in line with the parties' reasonable expectations.

Third, with regard to purely private contracting (where explicit adoption of network effects is less likely to occur), the basic pattern is again co-regulatory. It might be more important here (than in commercial contracts) to attend to the default rules. Generally, though, we can entrust judges with a residual discretion to declare a group of contracts as having network effects where this is necessary in order to give effect to the implicit reasonable expectations of the parties.

Finally, there is plenty of unfinished business – for example, concerning the network protections that might be applied for the benefit of small businesses, the extent to which network effects might be incorporated into the default rules for commercial and for purely private transactions, how widely the effects of a network apply (the question of who has standing for network purposes),[80] the external liability of networked parties,[81] and how courts should respond where regulators have not given a clear steer as to their objectives in relation to consumer transactions. Before we can tackle this agenda, however, there needs to be a double revision to the general appreciation of contract law: first, we need to take on board the reality that many of the transactions that the law seeks to address are networked, that the discrete exchange of the classical law has been eclipsed by more complex and shifting forms of dealing; and, secondly, we need to grapple with the thought that the regulatory environment of which the law of contract is just one part is itself complex, dynamic, and networked – in short, that the regulation of networks is to be effected by a network of regulation.[82]

VII. CODA

In this chapter, I have done no more than hint at a further, highly abstract, question – namely, whether there is a significant connection between (both off-line and

[80] This is a question that should be clarified by regulators who provide for networks or by the lead contracting parties where they adopt networks as a feature of their private ordering.

[81] For a sophisticated discussion of this question, see Gunther Teubner, NETWORKS AS CONNECTED CONTRACTS, *supra* note 1 Ch 6.

[82] Compare Gunther Teubner, *'And if I by Beelzebub Cast Out Devils,...': An Essay on the Diabolics of Network Failure*, *supra* note 1 at 411.

virtual) contractual networks (whether viewed as a mode of business organisation or as a doctrinal response to this phenomenon, or both) and the various kinds of networks (social as well as infrastructural) that are found in on-line environments. A plausible and short answer to this question is that there is no connection; it is simply, as Hugh Collins puts it, that the word "network" is promiscuously used in a variety of contexts.[83] In a sense, I agree with this. However, we might suspect that there is a deeper thread of connection that takes us to the importance of self-governance. On the one hand, where parties to connected contracts sign up for network effects, this is an act of self-governance; and, in the same way, as David Post has highlighted, on-line communities can (and should be permitted to) seize the opportunity for self-governance.[84] When private ordering is being displaced not only by public regulation but also by imposed technological design, contract assumes a new significance as an important opportunity for self-governance. For the moment, we will have to pend this abstract question and leave our cryptic remarks hanging, but it is a question to which I intend to return.

[83] Hugh Collins, *Introduction to Networks as Connected Contracts* in GUNTHER TEUBNER, NETWORKS AS CONNECTED CONTRACTS (Oxford: Hart, 2011) 1, at 12–13.

[84] David G. Post, IN SEARCH OF JEFFERSON'S MOOSE (Oxford: Oxford University Press, 2009) esp. at 184–186.

7

Contract Transactions and Equity

T. T. Arvind

This chapter examines the role equitable principles play in the resolution of commercial disputes and explores the implications for our theoretical understanding of the basis and function of the law of contract. The focus is principally on situations where commercial transactions are dealt with using the principles of equitable trusts and fiduciary relationships. The chapter first discusses how marginal or peripheral contract-like transactions where the parties nonetheless intend to effectuate a commercial transaction, are dealt with by the law through the application of principles of equity. The analysis then looks at how equitable principles manifest themselves in the legal response to transactions that would typically be seen as contractual, and at how parties adopt and use these principles within the overall transactional and contractual framework.

Academic attempts to explain equity's role in commercial cases have, for the most part, either sought to remove equitable interventions from the transactional framework completely by treating them as a manifestation of property rights or of tort or civil wrongs, or to treat the interposition of equitable principles as being no different from the ordinary contractual response of implying terms in fact or law. It will be argued that these theories do not reflect the factors that judicial decisions use in the application of equitable principles in a transactional context, nor do they explain the range of contextual factors that appear to influence the way equitable principles are actually applied in commercial cases.

A closer examination of the case law shows a strong parallel between these factors and the concerns that have traditionally prompted equitable intervention. As such, the invocation of equitable principles in commercial contexts must be understood as a deliberate departure from the market-rationality basis of the transaction and which

I am grateful to Richard Hedlund, Juliet Kostritsky, Gary Wilson, Sarah Wilson and participants in the workshop at Sheffield University for their comments on earlier drafts of this chapter and on the conference paper.

is reflected in the law of contract, in favour of a more relational understanding of the transaction. The reasons for this departure – and for its exceptional character – reflect the traditional equitable jurisdiction over fraud and its preoccupation with conscience, and specifically equity's realisation that the unfettered application of strict rules of law can be destructive of the trust that is necessary for the effective functioning of commercial markets.

The open recognition of the application of equity to police commercial contracts has broader implications for how we understand and theorise about the legal response to problems arising in commercial transactions. Theories of commercial contracting implicitly treat contracts as being the sole legal image of the transaction, and the sole manner in which commercial transactions are reflected or modelled in the law. This chapter suggests that a contract represents one aspect – and only one aspect – of the transaction. Contracts, as the law understands them, are principally, instruments to regulate some aspects of the transaction. Whilst this aspect of the transaction is the one that most commonly comes to the fore in situations where the law intervenes in a commercial dispute, there are situations where other aspects of the transactional relationship assume greater prominence. The consequence is that if we seek to understand how the legal system reacts to the problems created by commercial transactions, the unit of analysis will need to be not the legal conception of the contract, but the broader legal representation of the transactional relationship of which contracts are a part. Correspondingly, theories of contract law must view the law of contract not in isolation, but as a component of the general legal response to the issues created by transactions which deals with one particular type of issue – the party-imposed regulatory framework – and which is embedded in a much broader system.

I. INTRODUCTION

The purpose of this chapter is to analyse the respective roles of contract law and principles of equity in commercial law. A puzzle with which theorists of the law of commercial contracts need to grapple is the increased role of equity in commerce. As commercial lawyers know very well, equitable concepts and remedies play a significant – and growing – role in cases arising out of commercial transactions.[1] Such use is exceptional, but it is nevertheless systematic. And, significantly, the

[1] As seen, not least, in the growing number of publications exploring the relationship between equity and commerce, e.g COMMERCIAL ASPECTS OF TRUSTS AND FIDUCIARY OBLIGATIONS (E. McKendrick ed., Oxford University Press: Oxford 1992); EQUITY IN COMMERCIAL LAW (S. Degeling and J. Edelman eds. Law Book Company: Sydney, 2005). Textbooks on equity have also begun to deal more expressly with commercial aspects. See e.g. Sarah Wilson, TODD & WILSON'S TEXBOOK ON TRUSTS (10th ed., Oxford University Press: Oxford: 2011) 459–483.

vast majority of the transactions to which it relates involve a contractual element. This means, in effect, that the courts have invoked, and continue systematically to invoke, equitable principles – and not principles of the law of contract – to resolve commercial disputes in transactions governed by a contractual framework.

Theories of commercial contracting, however, have for the most part paid little attention to these equitable principles or to their use by the courts. The implicit assumption is that these principles have few, if any, implications for the understanding of the law of contract, its function, or the principles upon which it is based. While a few equitable notions have received some attention – particularly the statutory doctrine of unconscionability as it exists in Australia and in the American UCC,[2] the remedies provided by promissory and proprietary estoppel,[3] the doctrine of 'clean hands'[4] and fiduciary relations and fiduciary duties[5] – the focus of this attention has for the most part been on accommodating these notions within the general conceptual framework provided by contract law.[6] Theoretical accounts of the law of commercial transactions, in other words, implicitly treat the idea of a 'contract' as being the sole legal image of the parties' transaction and the sole manner in which commercial transactions are reflected or modelled in the law. Equity is taken to follow this conception, and to play at best a peripheral role.

2 See e.g., Larry A. DiMatteo & Bruce L. Rich, *A Consent Theory of Unconscionability: An Empirical Study of Law in Action*, 33 Florida State University L Rev. 1067 (2006).

3 See e.g., Hugh Collins, The Law of Contract (Cambridge University Press: Cambridge 2003) 74–93; Elizabeth Cooke, *Estoppel and the Protection of Expectations*, 17 Legal Studies 258 (1997); Daniel A. Farber & John H. Matheson, *Beyond Promissory Estoppel: Contract Law and the "Invisible Handshake,"* 52 University of Chicago L Rev. 903 (1985).

4 See e.g., Leigh Anenson, *Treating Equity like Law: a Post-Merger Justification of Unclean Hands*, 45 American Business L. J. 455 (2008).

5 Most recently, in James Edelman, *When Do Fiduciary Duties Arise?* 126 Law Quarterly Review 302 (2010).

6 In England, at least, this has principally been due to the influence of Professor Birks's taxonomic project. Typical of this literature is the reluctance to engage with equity on its own terms. It is, for instance, argued that equity is purely a historical or jurisdictional category, which cannot coherently fit with the other private law categories. See e.g. Peter Birks, *Definition and Division: A Meditation on Institutes* 3.13, in The Classification of Obligations (P. Birks ed., Clarendon Press: Oxford 1997). Yet most equity jurists – including judges – themselves argue that the distinctiveness of equity lies not just in its historical origins, but in the fact that the primary focus of equity is redressing the consequences of unconscionable conduct. It is unclear why 'unconscionable conduct' should be any less suitable as the basis of a taxonomic category than 'unjust enrichment'. To say that 'we do this at law and that at equity' is no worse than to say 'we do this in tort and that in contract.' For an example of this approach, see Andrew Burrows, *We Do This at Common Law But That in Equity*, 22 Oxford Journal of Legal Studies 1 (2002). For a critical perspective on the attempt to forcibly assimilate equitable thinking to common law concepts, see Steven Hedley, *Rival Taxonomies Within Obligations: Is There a Problem?* in Degeling and Edelman, *supra* note 1, at 77. This presents a sharp contrast with the US, where the continued existence of equitable doctrines is more favourably viewed. See e.g. Douglas Laycock, *The Triumph of Equity*, 56 Law and Contemporary Problems 53 (1993).

Yet this view of commercial contracts misses the fundamental significance of the role played by equitable principles in shaping the legal response to commercial transactions. As will be shown in this chapter, the specific things equity is deployed to do are far from peripheral. Instead, they relate to issues, such as gap-filling and protecting expectations, that are generally taken to be part of the core functions of the law of contract, and are used to provide relief when the law of contract does not. Courts do this not just in consumer transactions or other transactions involving an imbalance of bargaining power – unconscionability in its traditional sense – but in cases involving complex commercial dealings between sophisticated parties.

Why is this happening? Why are courts choosing to invoke and apply principles of equity rather than principles of contract law to respond to contractual problems? This chapter argues that the invocation of equitable principles in a commercial context must be understood as a deliberate departure from the market-rationality understanding of the transaction that is reflected in the law of contract, in favour of a more relational understanding of the transaction.[7] The reasons for this departure and its exceptional character reflect the traditional equitable jurisdiction over fraud and its preoccupation with conscience, and specifically the equitable realisation that the unfettered application of strict rules of law can be destructive of the trust that is necessary for the effective functioning of commercial markets.[8] 'Conscience', in the sense it is used by courts applying equitable principles today, is principally a device to capture and represent in legal terms the 'embeddedness' of commercial transactions in a broader social context, and of market expectations in broader social expectations.[9]

As this chapter shows, re-examining the law of contract through this lens sheds considerable light on the direction English contract law has taken, and has fundamental implications for our understanding of the structure and basis of contract law and for theories of the relationship between the law and practice of commercial contracting. Far from being the sole legal image of the transaction, in legal terms, a contract represents one aspect – and only one aspect – of the transaction. Contracts, as the law understands them, are principally instruments to regulate some aspect of the transaction, ranging from very little to virtually all. Whilst this aspect of the transaction is the one that most commonly comes to the fore in situations where the law intervenes in a commercial dispute, there remain situations where other aspects

7 Compare Cornish and Clark's description of pre-fusion equity as "a refuge for those unfitted to a world of hard bargaining, or misled during their experience of it." William R. Cornish & George Clark, Law and Society In England 1750–1950, 202 (Sweet and Maxwell: London, 1989).

8 For the critique of process-oriented contract law in Lawrence E. Mitchell, *Trust, Contract, Process*, in Progressive Corporate Law 185–7 (L. Mitchell ed., Westview Press: Boulder 1995).

9 The language of 'embeddedness' is taken from the theoretical work of Karl Polanyi and, in particular, from his views on the relationship between markets and the broader society of which they are part. See further section III.

of the transactional relationship assume greater prominence, and where equitable principles are systematically deployed by the courts.

Section II discusses the role equitable principles play in the resolution of commercial disputes, by examining two leading English cases involving the application of the law of implied trusts. It is argued that both cases were, in essence, cases of contractual gaps and – on ordinary principles of contract law – should not have been decided the way they were. Section III considers the contrasting bases of equitable and contractual intervention in commercial disputes, making the argument that they represent fundamentally different approaches to understanding the parties' relationship. Section IV argues that the case law shows a reasonably clear set of considerations – or triggers – that appear to be associated with the invocation of equitable principles. These show resemblance to theories of network relations, suggesting that sound commercial logic underlies the role played by equity in commercial transactions.

II. EQUITY IN A CONTRACTUAL CONTEXT

Equity in a contractual context, is principally associated with the broad notion of 'unconscionable transactions' that has received statutory force in a number of common law jurisdictions, most notably the US (via the UCC) and Australia. England does not have any equivalent to these statutes. As a number of writers have documented, the express application of a broad doctrine of unconscionability was in retreat in England well before the Judicature Acts.[10] The Acts, and the decision in *Derry v Peek*,[11] effected such a comprehensive disappearance[12] that even the statutory regulation of unfair contract terms in English law is built upon the classically common law notion of reasonableness[13] (and, more recently, the continental notion of good faith[14]) rather than the equitable notion of unconscionability. Nonetheless, equitable intervention in commercial transactions has continued through a number of devices. The most studied of these is equitable estoppel, both in the form of proprietary estoppel – which only applies to promises concerning interests in land but can serve as a cause of action – and promissory estoppel, which applies to a broader

[10] See Michael Lobban, *Preparing for Fusion: Reforming the Nineteenth-Century Court of Chancery*, 22 LAW AND HISTORY REVIEW 389, 427, 565–600 (2004).

[11] (1889) LR 14 App Cas 337.

[12] See Michael Lobban, *Nineteenth Century Frauds in Company Formation: Derry v Peek in Context*, 112 LAW QUARTERLY REVIEW 287 (1996); Michael Lobban, *Commercial Morality and the Common Law: or, Paying the Price of Fraud in the Late Nineteenth Century*, in LEGITIMACY AND ILLEGITIMACY IN NINETEENTH-CENTURY LAW, LITERATURE AND HISTORY 119 (M. Finn, M. Lobban and J. Taylor eds., Palgrave: London, 2010).

[13] See e.g., Unfair Contract Terms Act 1977, s. 11.

[14] See e.g., The Unfair Terms in Consumer Contracts Regulations 1999 (SI 1999/2083).

range of promises but (in England) can only be a defence. Of equal importance, however, are the notion of the implied trust, and the notion of the fiduciary relationship. The conceptual problem presented by the use of these mechanisms in a contractual context is neatly illustrated by the case of *Barclay's Bank v Quistclose Investments*.[15]

The fact of *Quistclose* can be stated quite simply. A company called Rolls Razor had declared a dividend in favour of its shareholders totalling around £209,000. Unfortunately, the finances of the company were in a parlous state – it had no reserves left, and had significantly exceeded its agreed overdraft with Barclay's. At the time of the events leading to the litigation, the overdraft stood at £484,000 as against an agreed limit of £250,000. Barclay's put it on notice that it would not extend the overdraft by the amount necessary to pay the dividend. Rolls Razor began seeking financing of £1,000,000 to continue its activities. Preliminary negotiations with a financier suggested that funding might be forthcoming if they found money from elsewhere to pay the dividend. That money was obtained from Quistclose Investments (which was controlled by one of the people involved in Rolls Razor), subject to the condition "that it is used to pay the forthcoming dividend due on July 24 next." A special account (referred to in the litigation as "the dividend no. 4 account") was opened with Barclay's Bank. Rolls Razor deposited the money into this account, together with a covering letter that stated "We would like to confirm the agreement reached with you this morning that this amount will only be used to meet the dividend due on July 24, 1964." Unfortunately for Quistclose and Rolls Razor, the negotiations for the additional funding fell through, and the company entered liquidation before the dividend was paid. Quistclose requested a refund of the money, but Barclay's sought to set-off the credit balance in the special account against the debit balance in Rolls Razor's other accounts. The House of Lords held that a trust in favour of Quistclose had been created by the common intention of the parties, following the failure of the primary purpose of the loan. Because Barclay's knew of the primary purpose of the loan and its failure they had notice of the trust.[16]

As conventionally seen, the primary puzzle presented by this decision is that none of the discussions between the parties contained any mention whatsoever of a 'trust.' As a result most of the commentary on *Quistclose* has centred around identifying the type of implied trust that it created – whether it can be termed a resulting trust or a constructive trust[17] or whether it is some other form of beneficial interest.[18]

15 [1970] A.C. 567 (HL).

16 *Id.*, 582.

17 See e.g. Lord Millett, *The Quistclose Trust: Who Can Enforce It?* 101 LAW QUARTERLY REVIEW 269 (1985); Charles Rickett, *Different Views on the Scope of the Quistclose Analysis: English and Antipodean Insights*, 107 LAW QUARTERLY REVIEW 608 (1991).

18 Robert Chambers, RESULTING TRUSTS Ch. 3 (Clarendon Press: Oxford 1997).

More recently, academic commentators have also re-examined the question of whether the underlying principle in that case related to unjust enrichment rather than unconscionability.[19] A smaller number of commentators have examined the nature of security interest it creates, and its relationship to other types of security interests or charges in terms of policy, priority and regulatory requirements such as registration.[20] These perspectives, however, miss a point that is critically important to understanding the case's outcome as a legal response to a transactional issue. If we look at *Quistclose* through the lens of contract law, it seems strikingly obvious that the problem at the heart of *Quistclose* was a contractual gap. Specifically, there was an oral agreement between Quistclose and Rolls Razor for the loan of a sum of money, and it was also agreed that that money would be used for the specific purpose of paying the dividend. There were, however, none of the safeguards – whether by the creation of floating charges or other security interests or by the creation of operational restrictions on the account – that one often sees in loan agreements.

Even more fundamentally, there was a gap in the regulation of the relationship between Quistclose and Barclay's Bank – specifically, the absence of an inter-creditor agreement on their respective priorities and security interests in relation to the sums of money in the ordinary dividend no. 4 account. Barclay's would have had a security interest in that account under the banker's general lien and, in addition, they are likely to have obtained other covenants from Rolls Razor – for example, a requirement that Barclay's affirmative consent be obtained before the creation of a security interest over any account – under the terms and conditions pursuant to which the overdraft facilities were granted. Commercially, the issue of the priorities inter-se could have been dealt with either through an express inter-creditor agreement or, more simply, through an assent to the creation of a charge or lien. It was precisely this priority that was at issue in this case, but there was nothing we would even recognise as a contract as between Barclay's and Rolls Razor, and there was nothing in the wider documentation that dealt with the issue of priority.

The existence of these 'gaps' is understandable from a commercial perspective. Given the timeframe within which the events that lead to the litigation took place – days, rather than months – there was no time to obtain the waivers and consents from Barclays that would have been necessary to establish an effective security interest. Nonetheless, the absence of an agreement is significant from the point of view of contract law. Barclays had a security interest over the balance in any account, which Rolls Razor held with it. It would have relied upon this security interest in granting overdraft facilities to Rolls Razor. Contrast this, now, with the complete

[19] See e.g., Peter Birks, *Retrieving Tied Money* in THE QUISTCLOSE TRUST: CRITICAL ESSAYS 121 (W. Swadling ed., Hart Publishing: Oxford, 2004).

[20] See e.g., Michael Bridge, *The Quistclose Trust in a World of Secured Transactions*, 12 OXFORD JOURNAL OF LEGAL STUDIES 333 (1992).

absence of any attempt to create any form of safeguard – whether in the form of a security interest or otherwise – on the part of Quistclose. Given that the risk of Rolls Razor's insolvency – to the mitigation of which any security interest would have been directed – was eminently foreseeable at the time of the loan, it is extremely unlikely that a court would imply a term creating a security interest in Quistclose's favour into the contract between Quistclose and Rolls Razor.[21] If parties act in haste out of commercial imperatives, then they will almost certainly be taken to have assumed the commercial risks associated with their acts: the loss must lie where it falls. The effect of the invocation of equitable principles through the implication of a trust, therefore, was to grant a level of protection to a party in a contractual transaction whose effect was materially similar to that which the party could have obtained had the contract been appropriately drafted, hence putting it squarely in the realm of gap-filling, but which that party would plainly have been unable to obtain under the law of contract – not due to any deficiency in the law of contract, but because in the logic of the contract law, this would not have been seen as the sort of circumstance in which the court should intervene through the imposition of a novel term.[22]

This argument was actually put to the House of Lords in *Quistclose*. Counsel appearing for Barclay's Bank argued that there was a clear distinction between a relationship of debtor and creditor, and a situation where a person held money for another's benefit. Here, there was nothing in the documents to suggest that Quistclose was intended to retain 'property' in the money.[23] This argument will be recognisable to any contract scholar, but it was expressly rejected by the House of Lords. There was "surely no difficulty", Lord Wilberforce held, "in recognising the co-existence in one transaction of legal and equitable rights and remedies".[24] Indeed, he went on to add, "it would be to the discredit of both systems" if they could not accommodate such a "flexible interplay of law and equity."[25]

Whatever we make of the decision in *Quistclose*, it should be clear that it cannot be accommodated within a classic contractarian approach to the transaction. The House of Lords displayed a far greater willingness to add to what the parties had contractually agreed than one would see in a typical process of implying terms in contract law.[26]

[21] This is a point to be discussed in Section IV.

[22] Compare the point made in Sue Tappenden, *Commercial Equity: The Quistclose Trust and Asset Recovery* 2 JOURNAL OF POLITICS AND LAW 11 (2009).

[23] [1970] A.C. 567, 570.

[24] *Id.*, 581.

[25] *Id.*, 582.

[26] This point is worth emphasising, because there is a powerful trend in the literature on commercial equity that seeks to assimilate as much of it as possible within the categories of tort, contract and unjust enrichment. Treating the outcome as contractual is not possible without a radical revision of contract doctrine – which, as discussed in section II, is a hopeless task – and treating it as an exercise in the

Cases subsequent to *Quistclose* suggest that the courts are aware of the tension between the implication of terms and the implication of a trust, but nonetheless continue to use the device of implied trust where no relevant term would be implied. In *Neste Oy v Lloyd's Bank*,[27] Bingham J. spoke of the courts' "general disinclination … to see the intricacies and doctrines connected with trusts introduced into everyday commercial transactions."[28] That case involved the employment of a company called PSL by the claimants as their agents in the UK to pay liabilities – such as pilotage, towage, berthing charges, and so on – incurred by their ships at UK ports. PSL went into insolvency at a time when it held substantial funds that had been paid to it by Neste Oy for onward payment, and its bankers sought to exercise their right of set-off over those funds. Neste Oy challenged the bank's right to set-off, arguing that the funds were held in trust for it. The situation here is, as in *Quistclose*, marked by a contractual gap, or more particularly a failure by Neste Oy to contractually make arrangements to protect itself against PSL's insolvency, something it could have done. The court, as discussed previously, noted that courts were generally disinclined to introduce trusts into everyday transactions, and refused to imply a trust generally, distinguishing *Quistclose* on the basis that the parties, by not creating a separate account, had in effect assented to mingling Neste Oy's payments with PSL's general funds, unlike in *Quistclose* where the money had been kept separate. Nonetheless, it went on to find a different kind of trust – a constructive trust – in relation to the last payment made by Neste Oy. This payment was made two days before PSL went into insolvency, but not credited until after it resolved to cease trading. Under the circumstances, the court held, it would be 'against conscience' for PSL to retain the money, thus creating a constructive trust in favour of Neste Oy.[29]

In this case, the gap that was filled related to the relationship between Neste Oy and Lloyd's Bank. In the hypothetical costless world of perfect foreseeability which we use as our point of comparison to detect the existence of contract gaps, Lloyd's Bank and Neste Oy would have entered into an agreement documenting their priorities in the event PSL no longer had the ability to meet its debts. In the real world, agreements of that sort are rare, as are arrangements requiring payment agents such as PSL to maintain separate accounts for each of their customers. Transaction costs would make these unviable, certainly in the pre-computerised 1980s when this

reversal of unjust enrichment (as would seem to be the case under, for example, the Restatement (Third) of Restitution and Unjust Enrichment) simply shifts the justificatory question into a different pigeonhole without answering it. As discussed in section III, the outcome of *Quistclose* and similar cases is actually far easier to explain if one views them as instances of equity rather than unjust enrichment.

27 [1983] 2 Lloyd's Rep 658.

28 *Id.*, 665.

29 *Id.*

case was decided. That gap – the absence of a contractual framework dealing with the issue of Lloyds Bank's priority vis-a-vis Neste Oy – was the issue the court had to address.

What we see therefore is a situation where the courts systematically use principles of equity to fill contract gaps, and do so in a manner that has the effect of adding terms to the contract that simply would not have been implied into it had the court been applying the standard tests for the implication of terms. This raises the obvious question of how these two approaches fit together within the broader legal system, and whether they work well together. The next section compares the basis of these two modes of legal intervention in transactional disputes to analyse the role which equity plays in resolving transactional disputes and its general approach to such disputes, and to contrast this with the role and approach of the law of contract.

III. EQUITABLE PRINCIPLES AND CONTRACT LAW

A. *Restating the Issue*

The first problem in analysing the role which equity plays in the judicial resolution of transactional disputes is one of language. Conventional theories of the judicial role in the resolution of commercial disputes are built on and articulated in terms of contract gaps, or the contractual undertaking, or the contractual promise, or contractual reliance, which do not serve us well if we are seeking to explore the role not of contract law but of equity in transactional disputes.

Rephrasing the problem in Hohfeldian terms can, however, give us a more theoretically neutral perspective on what exactly courts are doing when they intervene in commercial transactions.[30] A court action brought in the context of a commercial transaction involves the assertion that the defendant owed the claimant an obligation. In the language of Hohfeld's fundamental jural conceptions, it involves the assertion of a claim and a correlative duty. The defence, to the extent that it seeks to counter this, necessarily involves the assertion of the jural opposite of a duty, namely, of a Hohfeldian privilege. Privileges, in the Hohfeldian conception, are free choices, whereas claims are constraints on choices.[31] The implication of this is that any obligation that exists in a transactional context is, to the extent it

[30] The adoption of a Hohfeldian perspective is particularly apposite because Hohfeld's most extensive discussion of his eight jural conceptions occurs in the context of a description of the relationship between rules of law and equitable principles. Wesley N. Hohfeld, *The Relations between Equity and Law* 11 MICHIGAN LAW REVIEW 537 (1913).

[31] This theme is developed more fully in Tt Arvind, THE LAW OF OBLIGATIONS: A NEW REALIST APPROACH Ch. 2. (Cambridge University Press: Cambridge forthcoming 2013).

obliges a party to act or refrain from acting in a particular way, first and foremost a restriction on commercial freedom. That is to say, it is a restriction that prevents parties from exercising free choice in relation to the conduct of their affairs by imposing a duty upon them and creating a correlative claim upon their conduct. The 'policy' question[32] that underlies legal intervention in commercial transactions is, therefore, one of the appropriateness of imposing such a restriction upon commercial freedom: is it, in a given dispute, appropriate to restrict the commercial freedom of a party to behave as they choose towards the other parties with whom they are transacting, and instead require them to follow a particular course of conduct towards those other parties?

From this perspective, what we call theories of commercial law or contract law are, in reality, proposals as to the approach we should adopt in answering this policy question – that, for example, only consensual restrictions should be imposed, or that restrictions should be imposed whenever someone relies upon their existence, or that efficient restrictions should be imposed. 'Doctrines' or 'rules' of contract law – frustration, breach, interpretation, repudiation, implication, mistake, remoteness, and so on – are the answers the legal system gives to this question in specific classes of circumstances. The question we need to ask in relation to equity is, therefore, in what circumstances does *equity* intervene to restrict the commercial freedom of a party against the setting of a commercial transaction, and how does this differ from the contractual approach? As we will see, both equity and the modern law of contract look to the surrounding context to answer this question, but they do so in fundamentally different ways.

B. The Contractual Solution

The main focus of the enquiry of the law of contract is the parties' agreement. The classical textbook account of the law of contract is that the legal approach to this question always begins with the parties' contract. Was a valid contract entered into and does it still subsist? What do the provisions of the contract tell us about this particular contingency? Are there any terms not expressly in the contract that nonetheless form part of it? Does the contract limit the liability of either party?

As most contract scholars now acknowledge, the terms in which the classical account describes contract law are an oversimplification. Nonetheless, the classical account makes an important point as to the basis upon which the courts decide

[32] In Hohfeld's terminology, 'rights,' 'duties' and so on were simple descriptors of jural relations. They told us nothing as to why the relations were the way they are. The *reasons* that explain or justify why the law recognises claims in certain situations but not in others are termed 'policy' in his system. The sharp polarisation between 'principle' and 'policy' that characterises modern debates about private law is, therefore, alien to Hohfeld's system – 'policy' encompasses them both.

whether or not to restrict a party's commercial conduct. If we take the terminology that the courts use in explaining their decisions seriously, the limits placed by the law of contract are based upon distinguishing between behaviour permitted under the contract and behaviour restricted by the contract. The process of drawing the distinction between behaviour permitted and restricted by a contract is not easy, and is certainly far more complex than the classical textbook account would suggest. Contracts are usually silent on key issues, and whilst it is a fairly sound principle to say that gaps should be filled with what the parties would have wanted or with the terms to which they would have consented, the trouble is that in very many cases it is virtually impossible to accurately estimate what the parties would have wanted – and, for that matter, even whether the parties would actually have agreed on any particular solution. In a functional sense, as distinct from a normative sense, this practical impossibility lies at the heart of what DiMatteo has called the subjective-objective dialectic in contract law.[33] Yet neither the subjective nor the objective position alters the essential character of the enquiry, which remains focused on the parties' contract.

For contract law, then, the key question is how we can use the incomplete instrument we have as a guide to determine whether unrestricted freedom of commercial action is appropriate in the context of the eventuation of a particular contingency. There has been a noticeable shift in the latter half of the 20th century in the way the English law of contract deals with this issue. The approach taken by the English courts in the first half of the 20th century is well represented by decisions such as *Arcos v Ronaasen*[34] and *Moore and Landauer*,[35] with their emphasis on providing a framework of certainty by strictly holding parties to their word. However, in a move that started in the 1960s, and reached a peak in the past decade-and-a-half, the upper judiciary restated and revised a number of doctrines that are at the heart of contract law – principles of contractual interpretation,[36] damages for repudiation,[37]

[33] Larry A. Dimatteo, CONTRACT THEORY: THE EVOLUTION OF CONTRACTUAL INTENT (Michigan State University Press: East Lansing 1998).

[34] [1933] AC 470. This case involved the sale by description of wood staves for making cement barrels, which were to be half-an-inch thick, but which actually were 9/16 of an inch thick. The arbitrator held that the goods met the description as they were merchantable and were fit for the intended purpose, but the House of Lords on a special case held that the goods did not meet the description and could be rejected.

[35] *Re Moore & Co Ltd. and Landauer & Co.'s Arbitration* [1921] 2 KB 519. This case involved the sale (by description) of tins of fruit, which were to be packed in crates of 30 tins each. Although the correct number of tins was delivered, half the cases contained only 24 tins. It was held that the purchaser could reject the goods as they did not meet the description.

[36] *Investor Compensation Scheme v. West Bromwich Building Society*, [1998] 1 WLR. 896, [1998] 1 All ER 98.

[37] *Golden Strait Corporation v. Nippon Yusen Kubishka Kaisha (The Golden Victory)* [2007] UKHL 12, [2007] 2 AC 353.

remoteness,[38] and the implication of terms[39] to name just a few. The general direction of these changes was away from certainty and strict performance.

The initial reception accorded to several of these decisions has been mixed. The revival of the category of innominate terms in *Hong Kong Fir*[40] after a long somnolence was met with alarm. The abandonment of the strict rule for the construction of notices in *Mannai v. Eagle Star*[41] was greeted by what can only be described as outrage: commercial practitioners hoisted a black flag over Lincoln's Inn,[42] and an editorial in a practitioner journal said that Lord Steyn's speech in that case came close "to the legal equivalent of blasphemy."[43] Shortly after the decision in *ICS v West Bromwich*,[44] whose essential point was that a commercial contract must be construed in keeping with its commercial context, a commentator speaking of Lord Hoffmann's decision acerbically observed: "It is hard to imagine a ruling more calculated to perpetuate the vast cost of commercial litigation."[45] Another, referring to the 'Hoffmann "school"', feared that its implication was that "the traditional barrier on the outskirts of a written contract has been largely dismantled."[46] The decision in the *Golden Victory*[47] was described as "the worst decision on any aspect of English commercial law" in a long time.[48] And the tone of some of the responses to the *Achilleas*[49] is at best one of resigned acceptance.

Looking at the commentary on these decisions, one is left with the impression that the principal source of this dissatisfaction is the difficulty one faces in reconciling these decisions with what we are led by contract theory to believe contract law is

38 *Transfield Shipping Inc v. Mercator Shipping Inc (The Achilleas)* [2009] 1 AC 61, [2009] 1 AC 61.

39 *Attorney General of Belize v Belize Telecom Ltd* [2009] U.K.P.C. 10; [2009] 1 W.L.R. 1988.

40 *Hong Kong Fir Shipping v. Kawasaki* [1962] 2 QB 26.

41 [1997] A.C. 749. The parties had entered into a lease of commercial premises, which contained a break clause permitting the lessee to terminate the contract on its third anniversary (and only on that date) by giving at least six months notice. Notice was given, but the letter giving notice erroneously gave the termination date as 12 January 1995 rather than 13 January 1995. The lessee contended that it was obvious that the notice was to have effect on 13 January, as that was the only day on which it could have effect. The case was appealed to the House of Lords, which by the narrowest of margins – a 3:2 split – and in the face of a strong dissent by the minority, found for the lessee.

42 Lord Steyn, *The Intractable Problem of the Interpretation of Legal Texts*, in COMMERCIAL LAW AND COMMERCIAL PRACTICE 123, 127 (Sarah Worthington ed., Hart Publishers: Oxford 2003).

43 Editorial, *Closing Time from House of Lords*, 18 Property Law Bulletin 14 (1997).

44 [1998] 1 WLR 896.

45 Christopher Staughton, *How Do the Courts Interpret Commercial Contracts?* 58 CAMBRIDGE LAW JOURNAL 303, 307 [1999].

46 Malcolm Clarke, *Interpreting Contracts – the Price of Perspective*, 59 CAMBRIDGE LAW JOURNAL 18, 19 (2000).

47 *Golden Strait Corporation v Nippon Yusen Kubishka Kaisha (The Golden Victory)* [2007] UKHL 12, [2007] 2 AC 353.

48 Sir Anthony Colman, quoted in Qi Zhou, *Damages for Repudiation: An ex ante Perspective on the Golden Victory* 32 SYDNEY LAW REVIEW 579 (2010).

49 *Transfield Shipping Inc v. Mercator Shipping Inc (The Achilleas)* [2009] 1 AC 61, [2009] 1 AC 61.

about, and the values it was said to espouse and to attempt to promote. In particular, they are hard to reconcile with the value of certainty and the importance of giving strict – almost literal – effect to the words of the contract, and what was considered to be the undesirability of introducing a wealth of extra factors for the court to take into account in shaping the scope of the parties' duties, adjusting the remedy or quantifying damages.

But if the new approach to contract law reflected by these cases is difficult to reconcile with the older theories, it is very hard to say what exactly the new approach *is* reconcilable with: what, in other words, is the theoretical basis on which they are built, and what deeper theoretical shift, if any in the judiciary's understanding of the role and function of contract law they represent. It was, for example, initially hoped that the decision in *ICS v. West Bromwich* – and especially the weight it placed on what it called the surrounding factual matrix – would open the doors to a more relational understanding of contract, but this is not what has happened.[50]

What, then, is the nature of the new approach to contract? The shift represented by these cases has been characterised by Brownsword as a shift from 'literalism' to 'contextualism'.[51] 'Contextualism' is a useful label to capture the essential question that the courts face in a situation where they are called upon to apply a contract to a particular contingency, in as much as it draws our attention to the centrality of the relationship between the contract as a document and the surrounding transactional context to which that document relates and which it attempts to regulate. But like 'relationality', the term 'contextualism' can conceal a range of approaches to the relationship between the contractual document and the transactional context.[52] Each of these possible approaches marks a different type of departure from literalism.

The question, therefore, is which specific type of departure from literalism the English judiciary has adopted. Lord Goff's dissent in *Mannai* gives us a useful starting point. He left little doubt as to why he was dissenting: the tenants could have protected themselves by adding a simple coordinate clause to the relevant sentence in the letter giving notice, stipulating that the notice would be effective on the stated day or, in the alternative, on the earliest day on which it could be effective under the contract. Commercial tenants frequently did so while issuing notices of termination. The fact that these tenants did not do so meant that they ought not to be treated as if they had done so.

50 Roger Brownsword, *After Investors: Interpretation, Expectation and the Implicit Dimension of the "New Contextualism,"* in IMPLICIT DIMENSIONS OF CONTRACT 103 (D. Campbell, H. Collins and J. Wightman eds., Hart Publishing: Oxford 2003). See in particular his analysis of *Baird Textiles v Marks and Spencer* [2001] EWCA Civ 274.

51 *Id.*

52 Brownsword makes much this point. See *supra* note 50.

The parallels between the terms of this dissent and the decisions in *Arcos* and *Moore* are obvious. The principle lying behind the holdings in both those cases was precisely that where commercial parties could have added words to protect themselves but did not do so, they will not be given that protection by the law. In *Arcos*, a simple 'approximately' would have sufficed. In *Moore*, an 'or other amount' would have had the same effect. The fact that the parties did not add those words meant that that they must be held to perform strictly in accordance with the terms to which they had agreed. This is exactly what Lord Goff would have had the court decide in *Mannai*.

The result is that if Lord Goff's dissent in *Mannai* represents a version of contextualism, and Brownsword has shown that it does, then so do *Arcos* and *Moore*. 'Context' in this version of the concept is principally a vehicle to ascertain whether commercial practice knows of ways in which one party can protect itself. If it does, and if that route was not taken, then the party will be left unprotected. If parties working in that area customarily do not take steps to protect themselves, that opens the door to a second enquiry – also contextual – into whether this pattern represents a common business assumption that one party would bear the risk (in which case a term would be implied) or whether it demonstrates the unforeseeability of the event in question possibility implicating frustration (an enquiry that, again, is also frequently contextual[53]), or whether the parties were mistaken, and so on through the many devices available to the law of contract, with the ultimate possibility being that the loss must lie where it falls. The key to this variety of contextualism is the significant scope it leaves for un-cooperative and opportunistic self-regarding behaviour, through its narrow and technical approach to the contract.[54]

The contextualism we see in the speech of Lord Hoffmann in *Mannai*, upon which he further built in *ICS v. West Bromwich* and again in the *Achilleas* and A-G *of Belize* is fundamentally different. What is striking about his ruling in *Mannai* is the way it parallels the approach of the English courts to the interpretation of statutes. Much of his language – including the reference to the 'matrix of fact' and the discussion of the limited relevance of the parties' intention[55] – has also been deployed in relation to statutory interpretation. His discussion of the 'common sense meaning' of contractual provisions bears a remarkably close resemblance to the well-known common sense construction rule, established in statutory interpretation for over a hundred years.[56] There are similarly strong parallels between the manner in which

53 E.g., *Ocean Tramp Tankers Corp v. V/O Sovfracht* [1964] 2 QB 226, *Davis v. Fareham UDC* [1956] AC 696.

54 In Mannai, for example, the landlords' actions were quite clearly driven by a desire to stop the tenant from using a contractual termination provision, which seemed like a bad bargain in the light of a fall in rental values. Similar factors are likely to have been at play in *Arcos* and *Moore and Landauer*.

55 [1998] 1 WLR. 896, 913.

56 *Gardner v. Jay* (1885) 29 ChD 50, 58 (Bowen LJ).

he justifies departing from the express words of the contract to the circumstances in which the courts hold a strained construction to be justified in relation to statutes.

In point of fact, these parallels have not escaped the courts – the analogy between the construction of contracts and statutes was expressly made by Lord Simon in the House of Lords in *Black-Clawson Ltd. v. Papierwerke* A.G.[57] A few years earlier, Lord Wilberforce had first begun the move away from the old canons of contract interpretation in *Prenn v. Simmonds*.[58] In *Black-Clawson*, Lord Simon drew upon this new approach. The courts, he said, should use an approach to the interpretation of statutes that was as broad as the approach to interpreting contracts described in *Prenn v. Simmonds*.[59] This should tell us something about the significance which the courts attach to a contract under the 'new contextualism', not least because we do not see these parallels in relation to the old approach to the construction of contracts and because we do not see these parallels in relation to the construction of other documents, such as documentary evidence. There is something, in other words, about the way contracts are perceived that leads the courts of England to draw a parallel between the effect of their provisions and the manner in which the application of their provisions to a particular factual context should be approached, and the corresponding processes in relation to statutes.

The shape of these parallels suggests that the approach to contractual documents, which the 'new contextualism' reflects, is most compatible with a judicial view of contracts as regulatory devices. Their purpose and effect are in law primarily seen as being the creation of a regulatory framework that will govern the parties' relationship, and in studying their impact upon a given transactional problem courts therefore do not approach them exclusively with a view to finding a provision that speaks directly to the matter at issue. If such a provision is found, the matter obviously rests there, but if – as is more frequently the case – no such provision exists, then the court can still decide the question within the context of the broad regulatory framework. Consent, to the extent it is relevant, is seen by the law as consent to a regulatory framework, not to individual duties. As Lord Hoffmann emphasised, the question is not what was in the parties' mind. The question is what a reasonable person would have thought.[60] This is not just a matter of proof or convenience: the reasonable person's understanding will apply even if that was not what was in one of the parties' mind. The two parties may not actually have had the same thing in mind, and to give effect to the intent of one over that of the other would be artificial.[61]

57 [1975] AC 591, 645–646.

58 [1971] 1 WLR 1381.

59 [1975] AC 591, 646.

60 [1998] 1 WLR. 896, 903.

61 Compare Lord Simon's treatment of the corresponding rule in the construction of statutes. *Black-Clawson Ltd. v. Papierwerke* A.G. [1975] AC 591, 645F.

The suggestion that the law embodies a regulatory understanding of contract also receives some support from two further sets of factors. The first consists of a few recent decisions of the Supreme Court as to the effect of agreements in more heavily regulated areas of law bordering contract. Consider, for example, the decision in *Radmacher v. Granatino*.[62] This case involved the legal effect of a pre-nuptial agreement. It had long been the law in England that agreements providing for future separation are contrary to public policy. This rule was abolished in *Radmacher*.[63] The Supreme Court held, instead, that the courts *should* "give effect to a nuptial agreement that is freely entered into by each party with a full appreciation of its implications unless in the circumstances prevailing it would not be fair to hold the parties to their agreement."[64]

The last qualification makes it hard to make sense of this judgment as an advancement of the cause of legal certainty – something it has been painted as doing. It does, however, make much more sense if one sees the decision as a move away from the classical understanding of a contract as an exchange for consideration – in which case it would indeed be difficult to see how an agreement in relation to future separation could be valid – to a new understanding of agreements as private regulatory frameworks, in which case a pre-nuptual agreement simply becomes an attempt by two parties to mutually regulate an aspect of a relationship that is also regulated by the law.[65] It is intrinsic to the nature of private regulation that it can be overridden by state regulation – as is true of any regulatory framework that is subject to a superior source of regulation – but subject to that qualification, there is no fundamental objection to widening the areas of interaction in which such arrangements are permitted outside the realm of economic exchange.

The second is the manner in which recent developments in contract have made that branch of law less distinctive, and drawn some of its doctrines closer to other areas of law. We have already seen that the new approach to interpretation shares much with the modern approach to statutory interpretation.[66] But this resemblance is even more striking when we compare other recent decisions to other aspects of the law of obligations. The ruling in *SAAMCO*[67] is so similar to tort that several

62 [2010] UKSC 42, [2011] 1 AC 534.

63 *Id.*, [52].

64 *Id.*, [75] (Lord Phillips).

65 This becomes particularly clear if we compare the decision of the majority, delivered by Lord Phillips, with the dissent of Lady Hale, who emphasises the status-based aspects of marriage over the aspect of agreement, and the incompatibility of that status with contract-based approaches. See esp. *Id.*, [132]–[140], [191]–[195].

66 The modern approach to statutory interpretation itself sprang out of a break in the inter-war period with the older approach to statutory interpretation, which was significantly less organic than the modern approach.

67 *South Australia Asset Management Corp v. York Montague Ltd* [1997] AC 191.

scholars spent a long time arguing that it was a tort case, until Lord Hoffmann, who delivered the leading judgment, explained (extra-judicially) that it was very much an application of the law of contract.[68] The decision in the *Golden Victory* has been much criticised, but in substance the approach is very similar to that that has been used in tort in relation to personal injuries in relation to supervening events,[69] as seen in *Jobling v. Associated Dairies*.[70] The effect of the rule in *The Achilleas*, too, is similar. This, again, is hard to explain under the conventional view of contract as exchange, but it makes much more sense under a view of contracts as private systems of regulation embedded within a broader legal system that has both facilitatory and regulatory dimensions.[71]

The contractual regulatory framework is brittle, particularly in a commercial context. Failure to comply with it does not attract sanctions that are in any way comparable to those attendant upon the failure to comply with an official state-created regulatory framework, and it is in consequence quite easily broken with – frequently, but not universally – very little pain.[72] The brittleness of contracts, again, makes more sense if we view them as a private regulatory framework rather than as reflecting a moral idea of promise or consent. It should come as no surprise that parties to a private regulatory framework are freer to fail to comply with its provisions than in the case of a state regulatory framework.

The reason that this point is important is that it sheds significant light on the nature and limits of the 'new contextualism.' Grounded as it is in a view of contracts as systems of regulation, it remains firmly anchored in an atomistic view of the relations that are the subject of the contract.[73] Context and the matrix of fact are only important to the extent they signal the problem the contractual provision in question was intended to address, or to the extent they signal that it is appropriate to adopt a strained construction of the instrument. Relationality and co-operation are only

68 Lord Hoffmann, *The Achilleas: Custom and Practice or Foreseeability?* 14 EDINBURGH LAW REVIEW 47, 58 (2010).

69 Not surprisingly, one of the most striking defences of the decision has come from a commercial lawyer who is also a tort theorist. Robert Stevens, *Damages and the Right to Performance: A Golden Victory or Not?* in EXPLORING CONTRACT LAW 171 (J. W. Neyers, R. Bronaugh & S. G. A. Pitel eds., Hart Publishing: Oxford 2009).

70 [1982] AC 794.

71 There is an obvious link here with the points made in the 1970s by, amongst others, Grant Gilmore and Patrick Atiyah, to the effect that the law of contract was approaching assimilation into tort. Whilst their reading of the trend went too far, the cases discussed here appear to be a clear continuation of the trend away from the classical account of contract, which they correctly identified.

72 David Campbell, *The Relational Constitution of Remedy: Co-operation as the Implicit Second Principle of Remedies for Breach of Contract*, 11 TEXAS WESLEYAN L. REV. 455 (2004–5).

73 Compare the argument made in Rob Merkin and Jenny Steele, INSURANCE AND THE LAW OF OBLIGATIONS (Oxford University Press: Oxford forthcoming 2013), Chapter 6, which looks at contracts as a mechanism of managing risk, particularly through facilitating market-based mechanisms of dealing with risk.

relevant to a contract in so far as the parties incorporate them into the regulatory framework. As we will see, it is this understanding of the contractual context that marks the principal divide between the contractual and equity-based approaches to transactional problems.

C. *The Equitable Approach*

Equity's starting point is strikingly different from that of contract. Part of the reason for the difficulty we face in theoretically accounting for equitable interventions in commercial transactions – to the extent that even equity's proponents are forced to pretend that it intervenes less than it does[74] – is that our analysis of commercial law (and, hence, of equitable intervention in commercial transactions) is built upon the theoretical concepts of the common law of contract. If we, for a moment, set aside all attempts to analyse equitable intervention through the eyes of common law, or redefine its concepts in common law terms, and look at it through what equity jurists claim its basis to be, then equity's main point is that you will not be permitted to exercise a right that you have acquired if it is against conscience to let you do so. In the contractual context, this therefore translates into a requirement that requires you to use your contractual rights, or any general Hohfeldian privileges the legal system may give you in relation to the subject matter of the contract, not for your own benefit, but for the benefit of the counterparty with whom you have chosen to transact.

This underlying principle is most explicit when equitable intervention takes the form of an implied trust, which is defined as a legal requirement that you hold the rights that are the subject of the trust for the benefit of the beneficiary, or an application of estoppel, which is expressly framed in terms of a party being prevented from exercising their strict legal rights. But it is also quite clear when we consider fiduciary duties or fiduciary obligations, another set of equitable obligations that are commonly invoked in the contractual context. The essence of a fiduciary duty is the equitable recognition of a 'legitimate expectation … that the fiduciary will not utilise his or her position in such a way which is adverse to the interests of the principal.'[75] Its chief characteristic is the duty of loyalty, requiring the fiduciary, amongst other things, to act for the benefit of his principal (and not his own), not to make a profit out of his trust, and not to allow his personal interests to conflict with his duties.[76] As with implied trusts, what distinguishes it from contractual duties is the breadth of

[74] See e.g. Paul D. Finn, *Fiduciary Law and the Modern Commercial World*, in COMMERCIAL ASPECTS OF TRUSTS AND FIDUCIARY OBLIGATIONS 7 (E. McKendrick ed., Oxford University Press: Oxford 1992).

[75] *Arklow Investments v. Maclean* [2000] 1 WLR 594, 598.

[76] *Bristol & West Building Society v. Mothew* [1998] Ch. 1, 18 (Millett L.J.). See also *Sinclair Investments v. Versailles Trade Finance* [2011] EWCA 347, [2011] 3 WLR. 1153.

these obligations, and the consequent insistence that commercial parties, acting in the course of a commercial transaction, must *subordinate* their interest to that of the people with whom they transact.

The contrast with the classical model of contractual duties – with their emphasis on self-motivated actors – is stark. The result is that the restraints which a fiduciary obligation places upon a party to a commercial transaction far exceed the scope of what a court would ordinarily be willing to recognise through the implication of a contractual term. Framing the basis of equitable intervention in these terms sheds light on a point on which courts have insisted when discussing equitable remedies – namely, that they impose obligations of a different character from ordinary contractual obligations, and that they do so with reference to the nature of the relationship between the parties. In other words, the courts in applying equitable principles to a given case usually begin by analysing the nature of the relationship between the parties,[77] and proceed from there to analyse the obligations that arise from the parties' expectations in the context of that relationship, rather than just the contractual document.[78] These are both points the courts have repeatedly emphasised. Thus, for example, they have refused to recognise obligations as fiduciary when the scope of the duties they impose are identical in every respect to duties imposed under a contract,[79] and they have refused to recognise implied trusts when the character of the relationship between the parties is no different from that in any commercial transaction.[80]

This in turn relates to the question of whether or not an equitable obligation should be recognised in a given case to a broader debate that is familiar in the context of commerce, namely, the question of the extent to which it is acceptable for a party to be self-serving in commercial transactions. In legal discussion, this question is usually framed in terms of either accepting or rejecting the idea that self-serving

77 Edelman has recently argued that fiduciary duties depend upon the scope of the parties' voluntary undertakings, rather than the relationship between the parties. The thrust of this argument appears to be more against the idea that fiduciary duties are of fixed effect in relation to fixed classes of relationship. For a more specific understanding of 'relationship' – in the sense of the relationship between the two specific parties, as is customarily used in relational theories of the law of obligations – it is difficult to see how the broad definition of 'undertaking' that Edelman adopts refers to anything different. Edelman, *supra note* 5. It is, in any event, as Edelman accepts, clear that the 'undertakings' that he argues form the basis of fiduciary duties are substantively different from the contractual terms.

78 The decision of the High Court in *John Youngs v. Aviva* [2011] EWHC 1515 is a good example of how these processes differ. Once the nature of the parties' relationship had been established with reference to the contractual documents, the nature of the fiduciary duties between the parties was then established solely by reference to that relationship, without any enquiry into the question of whether a reasonable person reading the document would come to conclusion that those duties flowed from the party's 'undertaking.'

79 See e.g. *In re Goldcorp* [1995] 1 AC 74 (PC).

80 *Neste Oy v. Lloyd's Bank* [1983] 2 Lloyds Rep 658.

behaviour in commercial contexts is inevitable and as a default position should not be constrained by the law. Equitable intervention, in contrast, of its nature implies a legal position that being self-serving is not acceptable in situations where equitable principles apply. Equally, contract law, as we have seen, draws the restrictions it places upon the ability of commercial parties to freely determine how they will act from the regulatory framework which the parties themselves put in place, and the broader legal framework within which that private regulatory framework is embedded. Equity, however, in its focus on restricting the ability of commercial parties to be self-regarding in their acts, looks to something other than the parties' contract. From where, then, does it draw its substantive propositions?

In the debate around the extent to which the law should permit individuals to be self-serving, theorists supporting a lighter touch typically invoke the notion of what Professors Adams and Brownsword memorably called 'market individualism', and in general treat this type of self-serving behaviour as not only inevitable but also acceptable because the purpose of contract law is seen as being the fostering of "*competitive* exchange".[81] Those who oppose this position typically either argue that the law should adopt a more 'moral' perspective protecting the 'performance interest',[82] or that it should adopt a more relational perspective focusing on the fact that self-serving behaviour is destructive of relations.[83] But neither the manner in which equity intervenes to restrict the ability of parties to be self-regarding, nor the situations in which it does so, are explicable by these two commonly taken positions.

Equity has traditionally justified the specific obligations it imposes through the device of 'conscience'. The equity jurisdiction, it used to be said in the days when it still was a separate jurisdiction, operated upon the defendant's conscience. This concept continues to be cited as being the basic principle of equity by bar, bench and academy.[84] As used in these modern day sources, it clearly refers to a social principle – not a commercial principle or a principle of efficient markets, but some

81 John Adams & Roger Brownsword, *The Ideologies of Contract*, 7 LEGAL STUDIES 205, 206 (1987). Adams and Brownsword contrasted this approach with what they called 'consumer-welfarism,' which in their account stood for principles of "fairness and reasonableness in contract." *Id.*, 210.

82 The most influential article in the English context has been Daniel Friedman, *The Performance Interest in Contract Damages*, 111 LAW QUARTERLY REVIEW 628 (1995), but others have taken the argument much further, calling for a complete revision of the law of contract remedies in the name of protecting the performance interest. See e.g. Charlie Webb, *Performance and Compensation: An Analysis of Contract Damages and Contractual Obligation*, 26 OXFORD JOURNAL OF LEGAL STUDIES 41 (2006). For a rejoinder to this approach, see David Campbell & Donald Harris, *In Defence of Breach: A Critique of Restitution and the Performance Interest*, 22 LEGAL STUDIES 209 (2002).

83 Most influentially, in the work of Ian MacNeil. See Ian MacNeil, THE NEW SOCIAL CONTRACT (Yale University Press: New Haven 1980).

84 E.g., Margaret Halliwell, EQUALITY AND GOOD CONSCIENCE IN A COMTEMPORARY CONTEXT (Old Bailey Press: London 1977); Alastair Hudson, EQUITY AND TRUSTS 3 (6th ed., Routledge; Abingdon 2010).

principle that is part of the wider social context.[85] The key issue that characterises equity's departure from the contractual framework is, therefore, the suggestion that the market is embedded in a broader social context, that its logic is consequently intelligible to those who are not part of the market or of transactions in the market, and that it is legitimate and appropriate for judges to take account of this 'embeddedness' and hence to draw upon it in deciding cases.

The language of 'embeddedness' requires some explanation, coming as it does from a school of thought that is not commonly invoked in relation to private law. The suggestion that market transactions are embedded in a broader social context is not a novel one – it is the mainstay of economic sociology. The framework for this concept comes from the work of Karl Polanyi.[86] The rise of the idea that markets could regulate themselves – in the form of what was literally seen as a "self-regulating market" – had the effect, he argued, of separating the economic sphere of everyday life from the political and social sphere of everyday life.[87] But this was an inaccurate picture. The economy is embedded in the political system – in that the free market cannot exist without continuous state intervention.[88] Equally, the economic order is simply an aspect of the social order. The notion of self-regulating markets driven by rational choice focusing on the pursuit of specific ends through the exchange of scarce commodities was based on a *formal* understanding of what was 'economic'. The *substance* of economic transactions, in contrast, could not be understood without a focus on the extent to which people depend on their fellows and on nature for their living, on the human motives behind exchange, and on the relationship between the process of exchange and the natural and social environments in which they took place.[89]

Polanyi's focus in his work was on what one might call macro-economics – and, in particular, on bringing the economy within the realm of what democratic institutions could regulate and control (rather than leaving it in ever greater part to the market to deal with), and on the consequences (destructive, he argued) of not doing so.[90] His work, therefore, focuses on very broad themes relating to the legitimate

85 See esp. Hudson's discussion, *Id.*, 1170–1177.

86 In particular, but not exclusively, his book THE GREAT TRANSFORMATION (Beacon Press: Boston 2001) (first published in 1944).

87 *Id.*, 74

88 *Id.*, 145–6.

89 This idea – which is central to understanding the meaning of 'embeddedness' in Polanyi's theory, is not developed fully in THE GREAT TRANSFORMATION. Polanyi presented a much fuller outline of the difference between the formal and substantive meanings of 'economics' a decade after he wrote THE GREAT TRANSFORMATION in Karl Polanyi, *The Economy as Instituted Process* in TRADE AND MARKET IN THE EARLY EMPIRES (K. Polanyi, C. Arensberg, & H. Pearson eds., Free Press: New York 1956).

90 Thus a central portion of his theory was concerned with the argument that the process of turning more and more things over to the market would be so potentially catastrophic that it would

extent of control over the market, and the form such control could take. This – more normative – portion of his work remains both controversial and difficult.[91] However, the concept of 'embeddedness' by itself has analytical relevance to the study of private law.[92] Polanyi argued – in a claim echoed in modern economic sociology – that commerce was simply a means of social operation, embedded in the broader social context, and not – as Fred Bloch puts it – 'an analytically autonomous economic sphere' with 'a logic and rationality of its own.'[93]

Concepts that we attribute to this supposedly autonomous rationality are in consequence also not exclusive products of market rationality. 'Expectation' – a term that, notably, is also used extensively in equity – is not simply a feature of market rationality. It is a broader social concept, and the economic expectations that are the subject of contract law build upon, and are a special case of, social expectations. The basis of the equitable approach to commercial transactions, in other words, is this notion of the relationship between market expectations and social expectations, an understanding that the former are embedded in the latter, and that, in consequence, there will necessarily be circumstances in which it is not only appropriate but necessary to look to these latter expectations.[94]

The classical law of contract and equity thus draw upon radically different criteria in classifying actions as either being within the legitimate scope of a party's commercial freedom, or as being an illegitimate breach of a Hohfeldian duty that they owe their counterparties. The principal criteria equity uses relate to the permissibility of self-serving behaviour, as distinct from co-operative behaviour directed towards

result in an inevitable counter-reaction that sought to check the development of the market (the "double movement," as he termed it). However, the resultant counter-measures were themselves not free from problem: because they were "incompatible with the self-regulation of the market, and thus with the market system itself" it would only further unbalance society. Polanyi traced, amongst other things, the rise of fascism in twentieth century Europe to the attempts in nineteenth century England to steadily expand the domain of the market and reduce the amount of democratic control over it.

[91] There is, for example, a heated debate as to whether disembedding can ever be successful even amongst those who actually draw upon his theories. See e.g. Richard Swedberg, PRINCIPLES OF ECONOMIC SOCIOLOGY 27–28 (Princeton University Press: Princeton 2003).

[92] As is most clearly evident from the work of Mark Granovetter and the subsequent work that has drawn upon it. See esp. Mark Granovetter, *Economic Action and Social Structure: The Problem of Embeddedness*, 91 AMERICAN JOURNAL OF SOCIOLOGY 481 (1985). It should be noted that the economic sociologists, whilst inspired by Polanyi's work, adapted the concept of embeddedness in a way that means its precise analytical relationship to Polanyi's work is not always straightforward.

[93] Fred Bloch, *The Writing of The Great Transformation*, 32 THEORY AND SOCIETY 275, 298 (2003).

[94] This is not necessarily confined to the specific relationship between the parties – it would seem that courts applying principles of equity are also prepared to look to the surrounding circumstances and the expectations of all affected parties in society, and the social desirability of favouring one class over others. See, for example, Sarah Wilson's analysis of the factors that are likely to have lain behind the very different decisions in the seemingly similar facts of *Re Kayford* and *Re Farepack*. Wilson, *supra* note 1, at 478–481.

what Campbell has called 'joint maximisation'.[95] The classical law of contract, in contrast, does not reject self-serving behaviour, and the limits it places on the free exercise of commercial choice in general do not distinguish between self-serving behaviour and co-operative behaviour. Instead, it classifies an action as being within the legitimate scope of a party's commercial freedom depending on whether the parties' contract permits or restricts that type of action. The essential nature of the difference is, therefore, that the law of contract proceeds by attempting to place the event or contingency that is the source of the dispute within the regulatory framework agreed upon by the parties. Equity makes no such attempt. It draws, instead, upon a broader conception of the relationship of the parties as a commercial relationship embedded in a social context, and of the expectations that inhere in that social-commercial relationship, in deciding whether or not a particular action falls within the limits of a party's legitimate commercial freedom.

IV. THE DOMAIN OF EQUITY

The importance of the point that contract and equity have fundamentally different starting points and approaches cannot be overstated. There is a general reluctance amongst commercial lawyers to concede a separate place to equity – or, more particularly, to equitable concepts – within commercial law.[96] Given the nature of the principles that lie behind equitable intervention, this is not surprising. The idea of compelling a commercial party to act not in what he considers to be his interest but in what an honest person would consider to be another's best interests sits uncomfortably with what theorists generally believe the role of law in commerce should be about.[97] As a result, commercial theorists have made heroic efforts to accommodate equitable principles within standard understandings of the law of contract. Of particular note are Langbein's attempt to recategorise all trusts as simply a species of contract between the settlor and trustee,[98] Edelman's attempt to recategorise all fiduciary obligations as a species of implied term,[99] and Collins's attempt to re-theorise equitable estoppel as representing a reliance-based conception of contract.[100] Given that, as having been argued, equity represents a fundamentally different approach, all such projects would seem to be doomed to failure.[101]

95 David Campbell and Donald Harris, *Flexibility in Long-Term Contractual Relationships: The Role of Co-operation*, 20 JOURNAL OF LAW AND SOCIETY 166 (1993).

96 See e.g. Lord Millett, *Equity's Place in the Law of Commerce* 114 Law Quarterly Review 214 (1998).

97 On this point, see Roy Goode, COMMERCIAL LAW IN THE NEXT MILLENNIUM (Sweet & Maxwell: London 1998)

98 John Langbein, *The Contractarian Basis of the Law of Trusts* 105 YALE LAW JOURNAL 625 (1995).

99 James Edelman, *When Do Fiduciary Duties Arise?* 126 LAW QUARTERLY REVIEW 302 (2010).

100 Hugh Collins, *supra* note 3.

101 To argue that 'fusion' requires the assimilation of equitable principles into contract is, in that sense, as misguided as arguing that 'fusion' requires the assimilation of the law of private nuisance into contract.

But it is also important not to overstate the nature or extent of this difference. We do not live in an era of jurisdictional conflicts, as in the time of Coke and Bacon. Nor do we live in a time where common law judges and equity judges in their separate courts have ended up adopting fundamentally different approaches to the question of the relationship between social expectations and commercial expectations. In the modern context where the jurisdictions are fused, the judges who decide cases under the law of contract are the same as those who decide cases applying principles of equity, and the application of equitable principles represents not a conflict of jurisdictions or a conflict of principles, but a perception that it is apposite to invoke these principles in relation to issues that could also have been resolved through the law of contract. In looking at the relationship between equity and contract, therefore, we should be focusing not on quixotic attempts to harmonise their principles, whether in the name of fusion or otherwise, but on the types of circumstances and questions that trigger their application, with a view to understanding how these two sets of principles fit together within the broader context of the legal system's response to issues arising out of commercial relations.[102]

Seen in this light, two things stand out about the manner in which the judiciary engages with principles of equity in a contractual context. The first is their manifest reluctance to let the invocation of these principles become commonplace – a point stressed by the English judiciary in recent litigation connected with the collapse of Lehman Brothers.[103] Equitable principles, they have stressed, should not be imported into "everyday commercial transactions",[104] nor should they "introduce the whole new dimension" of such principles merely because one party has placed reliance upon another.[105] This reluctance sits side by side with the second trend – their manifest reluctance to banish these principles from the realm of contractual transactions. This is perhaps most clearly evidenced by the fact that many of the leading cases on equitable remedies in transactional contexts are cases where the existence and basis of the remedy was reaffirmed, but the remedy was *not* granted on the facts.[106] What the cases reflect, therefore, is a judicial perception that there are and always will be situations in a transactional context where it is appropriate to be guided by principles of equity – and, hence, the equitable approach of co-operation and other-regarding action – rather than the contractual approach of self-regarding action tempered by a party-selected regulatory framework. The implication is clear.

[102] And, needless to say, also social relations more generally, although my focus in this paper is confined to their commercial application.

[103] *Pearson v. Lehman Brothers* [2010] EWHC 2914, upheld on appeal in [2011] EWCA Civ 1544.

[104] *Neste Oy v. Lloyd's Bank* [1983] 2 Lloyds Rep 658, 665 (Bingham J.)

[105] *In Re Goldcorp Exchange Ltd.*, [1995] 1 AC 74, 98 (Lord Mustill).

[106] Examples include *Bristol & West Building Society v Mothew* [1998] Ch. 1 and *In Re Goldcorp Exchange Ltd.*, [1995] 1 AC 74.

Such situations must remain exceptional, but equally the possibility of applying them must remain available.

Borrowing an analogy originally suggested by Sims to describe the use of conceptions of good faith in contracting,[107] it may make sense to visualise the domains of application of the classical contract approach, the 'new contextualism' of modern English contract law, and the ' embeddedness' approach of equity in terms of a bubble of concentric circles embedded in the surrounding social context, with cases pushed outwards and inwards by 'triggers'. In the middle of the circle, furthest removed from the surrounding social context, we have the pure market transaction, represented by the one-off market exchange, where substitute transactions are relatively easy to implement and where the principal commercial remedy for failure to perform is to procure substitute performance on the market with relatively little loss. Where procuring substitute procurement is costlier, the law's role is to ensure that the party not in breach gets the difference. This is the epitome of market rationality – of transactions between rational actors pursuing their self-interest, disinterested in and unswayed by the type of relational considerations, interpersonal dependence and indeed long-term uncertainties that affect social interaction. Legal decision making in relation to cases that fall within this circle represents a radical understanding of disembedding. Market rationality is so strong and so distinctive, that those who are not part of the market cannot and should not tamper with its systems of ordering itself. Only the market's own self-regulating systems should be given effect to, with the result that – as we saw in *Arcos v. Ronaasen* and *Moore and Landauer* and arguably is Lord Goff's dissent in *Mannai* – if it was possible for a transactor to take market-based measures to protect themselves and if they failed to do so, the law will not intervene to augment their rights.

Moving outwards from this centre moves the case deeper into the culture in which the market is embedded and further away from pure market rationality. In the second, intermediate, circle, one is still within the realm of market rationality, but here the question becomes more complex, and the role of contracts as instruments to regulate the parties' freedom of action in future contingencies assumes more weight. This is the position of the 'new contextualism,' seen in cases like *Mannai*, *ICS*, *The Achilleas*, and *Belize Telecom*. Market rationality is still distinctive, but not entirely separate from normal rationality. Judges can use their cognitive processes to understand market-based systems of ordering, and to engage productively with them in the process of judging. A judge's answer to the question of what a reasonable market player would make of a contract will, thus, be within acceptable bounds of error. Courts need not treat the contract with the reverence accorded to uninterpretable

[107] Vanessa Sims, *Good Faith in Contract Law: Of Triggers and Concentric Circles*, 16 Kings College Law Journal 293, 306–309 (2005).

texts based on a higher rationality. In cases where the contract is clear, the innermost circle will usually provide a sufficiently good approximation of this process to make a movement to outer circles unnecessary. But, as *ICS* and *The Achilleas* discuss, there will be cases where this movement is necessary, the principal trigger being the commercial (not moral) unreasonableness of the outcome, which would result.

The outermost circle, closest to the surrounding social context and encompassing both inner circles, is that occupied by equity. The cases in this circle are those in which the undersocialised understanding of transactions that one sees reflected in the two inner circles becomes so unrealistic that no functioning legal system could insist upon on it without significantly eroding even the minimal level of trust that is necessary for commerce.[108] In particular, the functional equivalents for trust and reliance – complex contractual systems of incentives and disincentives – that are the mainstay of contract theory,[109] whilst an acceptable model in many circumstances, fails to present an accurate image of the transactions. Instead, transactions here are seen as being fully embedded in the social context, and the expectations of a party as to the conduct of the other are closely related to general social expectations as to how people will conduct themselves. In consequence, the factors that are relevant to assessing the parties' expectations – and, hence, to the broader question of whether a party's commercial freedom should be restricted in relation to the action or thing that is the subject of the dispute – include the nature and extent to which one party is dependent on the other.

What, then, is the trigger that places a situation within this outermost category of exceptional cases where the application of equitable principles is appropriate? The fact that the same judges choose whether or not to apply equity suggests that it should be possible, through analysing the cases, to arrive at an understanding of the system of thought, or less generally the theoretical basis, upon which they distinguish cases where the application of equity is appropriate from those where it is not. Unfortunately, the existing literature offers little guidance as to the nature of this distinction or the principles that inform it. Equity traditionally speaks in terms of conscience, and cases such as *Westdeutsche Landesbank*[110] have justified refusing to invoke equitable principles on the basis that the defendant's actions were not against conscience, but there is little in the cases that directly that tells us *why* insisting upon the contractual framework would be against conscience in some cases but not others. To attempt to shift the analysis to a different framework, for example the unjust enrichment framework used by the Restatement (Third) to explain constructive

[108] See Mitchell *supra* note 8 for an elaboration of the argument that the literalistic, classical approach to contract would necessarily have the effect of eroding trust.

[109] The point that the classical law of contract is a functional equivalent for the role that would otherwise be played by trust has been made by Lawrence Mitchell. See *supra* note 8, at 196–198.

[110] *Westdeutsche Landesbank Girozentrale v. Islington London Borough Council* [1996] AC 669.

trusts (which, as we have seen, have been used in contractual contexts in cases such as *Neste Oy*[111]), presents even greater conceptual difficulties, as it is hard to see how a party can argue that the simple enforcement of a valid contractual framework to which he has voluntarily agreed has 'unjustly' enriched his counterparty at his expense.

Given the limitations of our existing theoretical understanding of the reasons why courts use equity in some contractual cases but not others, any attempt to address this question will need to take the form of a systematic analysis starting from first principles. A closer examination of the cases suggests that four factors in particular emerge as being of special relevance to a decision that it is appropriate to invoke principles of equity to afford a party a degree of protection which exceeds what they would get from a normal application of principles of contract:

A. A *Complex Transactional Web*

Equity tends to most often be invoked in situations where the specific transaction that is at issue is part of a more complex transactional web – where, in other words, one of the parties deals with the other for the purpose of dealing with a third party, or in the context of a transaction where third party intermediaries are very closely involved in relation to the same subject matter. Agency – one of the best established classes of fiduciary relationships – is perhaps the paradigmatic example. But the implied trust cases show much the same characteristic. The nature of this complexity is clearly distinct from the mere presence of a third-party sub-contractor, in that the *purpose* of the appointment of the principal contractor is not the appointment of the sub-contractor: in that situation, the involvement of the third party is incidental to the transaction, and the transaction as such could easily proceed with the main contractor doing the work himself. In the type of situation that bespeaks a complex transactional web, in contrast, this involvement is of the essence of the transaction and removing it would render it a different transaction where the issue that necessitates the invocation of equity would not arise.[112] The centrality of privity – and, thus, of the atomistic transaction – to the standard conception of a contract as a regulatory framework means, in effect, that the law of contract simply cannot deal with situations of this type, other than to say that the loss must lie where it falls.[113]

[111] *Neste Oy v. Lloyd's Bank* [1983] 2 Lloyds Rep 658

[112] This is obviously true of the two cases that were examined in detail in section III, but is also true of virtually all other implied trust and fiduciary duty cases. See, for example, *Twinsectra Ltd v. Yardley* [2002] UKHL 12, [2002] 2 AC 164 and *Re Kayford* [1975] 1 All ER 604.

[113] It is worth mentioning that equity's ability to deal with multi-party litigation was one of its principal attractions even in the 19th century. Whilst the issue was seen in procedural terms then, and the argument can be made that the underlying reason for both springs from the fact that equity is not based on an atomistic, discrete conceptualisation of commercial relations.

B. The Difficulty of Dealing with the Obligation

Closely related to the previous point, the invocation of equity also tends to be associated with situations where detailing the obligations in the contract would necessarily be complex. Here, *Quistclose* is perhaps the best example, but most equitable obligations have an analogous aspect. In *Quistclose* – and, for that matter, in most cases of implied trusts – the problems are typically logistical, of getting all creditors to discuss and agree on their priorities inter-se, or of creating operational structures that will not add unmanageable burdens to aspects of a party's every day functioning. In fiduciary relations, the problem is definitional. The courts have struggled to explain precisely what the components of the obligation of loyalty are, for example. It is easy to see why having to do this in a contract would also be problematic for parties.

C. A Relational Attempt to Deal with this Difficulty

Flowing directly from the previous point, the courts tend to look for some signs that the parties did not intend to let the loss lie where it fell, but were open to a relational approach. The things they treat as signifying such an attempt fall far short of what would be required in order for a term to be implied – in particular, the courts tend not to look for specific evidence of intent to create the particular form of structure that equitable intervention takes. Examples include the instruction in *Quistclose* and the creation of a separate account (and conversely, the impact of the absence of either of these in *Neste Oy*). Correspondingly, in relation to fiduciary relations, courts tend to look for the use of language that signals one of the equitable categories, or for the creation of a relationship that resembles one of the equitable categories. The absence of such language or such a relationship is almost universally fatal to a claim that a fiduciary duty existed, as in *Re Goldcorp*,[114] while its presence tends to lead to the creation of a fiduciary duty where the other factors are also present. These two aspects of equity's intervention are perhaps easiest to reconcile with a traditional default rules analysis – in that equity is filling a contractual gap that is created due to the difficulty and cost to the parties of drafting a customised rule to fill the gap, and that it looks for some evidence that the parties wanted a rule along these lines before it implies one. But the default rules approach nevertheless is harder to reconcile with the particular form of the rule – a duty to co-operate – and with the importance of the other two factors that the analysis in this paper suggests are treated as being relevant to the application of equitable principles.

[114] [1995] 1 AC 74

D. *Indeterminacy and Vulnerability*

Finally, the invocation of equity appears to be quite strongly associated with what Deakin and Michie described as "relationships of an indefinite duration"[115] – in other words, with transactions that differ significantly from the archetype of the discrete exchange typified by a one-off sale, and especially with those that involve some form of dependence or vulnerability.

Taken together, these present a picture of transactions that are relational, but that are palpably distinct from what are called relational contracts in that section of the literature that builds upon the insights of transaction cost economics, because the transactions to which equity responds do not necessarily involve situations where *both* parties depend on each other – something that appears to be fundamental to transaction cost theories of relational contracting.[116] Mutual dependence is sometimes present in transactions where equitable principles are invoked by the courts (for instance, in joint ventures), but these principles are equally common where only one party depends on another – as was the case in *Neste Oy* – and the language in which equitable principles are framed strongly suggests that a relationship of unilateral dependence is sufficient to trigger them. There are, equally, some similarities with what economic sociologists refer to as 'network' relations,[117] in particular in relation to the presence of the element of 'mutually supportive actions' that are seen as being fundamental to these relations. The type of dependence that tends to trigger the application of equitable obligations is not just the ordinary dependence upon the other's performance that one sees in a range of commercial transactions, but the specific dependence upon *resources* controlled by another that is characteristic of networks.[118] A fuller exploration of this relationship would require a much deeper analysis than there is space for in this paper, but there does prima facie appear to be a possible connection, and one which potentially could speak directly to the issue of 'embeddedness'.[119]

115 Simon Deakin and Jonathan Michie, *The Theory and Practice of Contracting*, in CONTRACTS, COOPERATION AND COMPETITION 1, 9 (Simon Deakin & Jonathan Michie eds., Oxford University Press: Oxford: 1997).

116 See e.g. Oliver Williamson, THE ECONOMIC INSTITUTIONS OF CAPITALISM 77 (Free Press: New York 1985).

117 Walter W. Powell, Neither Market nor Hierarchy: Network Forms of Organization, 12 RESEARCH IN ORGANIZATIONAL BEHAVIOR 295 (1990). Note that network relations, as the concept is used in economic sociology, differs in many fairly significant ways from what legal theorists refer to as 'network contracts.'

118 *Id.*, 303–305.

119 As Powell has explained, his work is sympathetic to "the view that economic exchange is embedded in a particular social structural context," but seeks to identify "a coherent set of factors" that make it meaningful to talk about the forms of exchange that are more social. *Id.*, at 300–301.

V. CONCLUSION

Returning to the point with which this chapter begins, one of the aims was to show that contracts are not the sole legal image of a commercial transaction, and that the law of contract is not the sole way in which courts respond to commercial transactions. The law of contract, as argued in this paper, is in its application to commercial transactions still principally grounded in the notion of market rationality – albeit a less extreme notion than the version that characterised decisions from the early part of the twentieth century.

The centrality of this notion places limits upon the flexibility afforded by the significant liberalisation that the 'new contextualism' ushered in. This does not, however, mark the limits of the legal system as a whole. As this chapter has tried to show, equity is built upon a more relational and social understanding of the transactional relationship – one that is grounded in the 'embeddedness' of market transactions in a social context, and is of particular relevance to complex transactional networks.

This has several implications. The first, descriptive, implication is that a decision by the law of contract not to intervene does not mean that the legal position is that the loss should lie where it falls – it may simply mean that this particular sort of problem is better tackled through equity. If we are to understand the legal response to disputes arising in the course of commercial transactions, including such core questions of contract theory as how the law responds to contract gaps, we cannot afford to ignore the role played by equity and equitable principles in shaping the legal response.

This leads on to the second, normative, implication. It would be argued that in normative work, we must recognise that contract law is only one of the tools available to the law – and that, in certain circumstances – the use of other tools may be more appropriate. As this chapter has tried to show, the role equity plays is both normatively justified and pragmatically necessary. Classical contract law simply lacks the flexibility to deal with the contract gaps that arise in complex transactions involving network relations. Dealing effectively with these issues requires the law to recognise the 'embeddedness' of the transaction in a broader network of relations, which itself is part of a broader social context, and reflects broader social expectations.

The final, analytical, implication relates to how we approach principles of equity and the law of contract. As this chapter has tried to argue, we sometimes seem to go too far in attempting to harmonise principles of equity with those of other branches of law. It may be more fruitful to our understanding of the law as a whole to accept not only that equity is built on different principles representing a different type of response, but that there appears to be some form of consistency in relation to the types of situations where the court invokes these principles, and those where it leaves the loss to lie where it falls. Equally, the classical focus on contracts as the sole legal representation of a commercial transaction has led us to misconceptualise what contracts are, which in turn has led contract theory down blind alleys – notably, the theory of the 'performance interest', or the attempted revival of promissory theories of contract. If we instead regard the law of contract as part of a continuum of legal responses, which includes equity, a rather different picture emerges, where contracts are a way of regulating relations between persons. This alternate picture of contract is far better able to accommodate not only the relational aspect of contract, but also – as discussed in section III – a range of other emerging issues in contract law.

The role judges have shaped for equity is remarkable in that it has come in the absence of theorisation. But the danger of this absence is that the use of equitable principles will whither away, as has happened more than once in the past, if the reasons for their use and the role they play remains as poorly understood as it currently is. The reluctance with which equity is invoked suggests that this is a real danger, which can only be combated by defending and explaining the role of equitable principles in commercial transactions. It is time to move to thinking in terms of a law of commercial transactions, of which the law of contract is a part.

PART III

Contract Design and Good Faith

The two chapters in this part examine the expanding roles that contract design and good faith play in contract law. Chapter 8 focuses on consumer online contracting and how it differs from offline transactions. It makes the novel proposition that the presentation of online contracts conveys meaning that should be considered by courts. Through the manipulation of Web sites, sellers can seriously impact consumer behavior and responses. Given this fact, sellers should be encouraged to use online contract design to educate consumers and to obtain meaningful consent. In order to encourage such seller behavior, the burden of proof should be shifted to the seller to prove consumer consent to the online terms. In order to meet the standard of proof, the reasonable person standard should be used to answer the following question: What would a reasonable person in the shoes of the drafting party have done to elicit assent from the other party?

Chapter 9 looks at the role of good faith in the renegotiation or variation in complex, long-term, relational commercial contracts. The recent financial crisis and economic downturn has required unprecedented modifications of long-term loan and supply contracts. Such "good faith" (often out of necessity) adjustments to complex contracts challenge the limited recognition of the duty of good faith in English common law. It concludes that relational contracting requires a reassessment of the common law's refusal to recognize a duty to renegotiate in good faith in certain contexts.

8

The Duty to Draft Reasonably and Online Contracts

Nancy S. Kim

Mass consumer online agreements lack many of the features of traditional contracts. Their unique characteristics compound the problems that are generally raised by contracts of adhesion. Online agreements are usually presented to the consumer in a way that obscures their legally binding nature. This chapter argues that courts should recognize the differences between online and offline contracts by considering a contract's form and manner of presentation in adjudicating contract disputes. The design of a contract shapes, expresses and reveals the parties' intent. "Clickwrap" and "browsewrap" agreements have the power to affect consumer behaviour, not through their terms (which most consumers do not read), but through their presentation and design.

The chapter concludes that courts should recognize contracting realities, such as consumer behaviour and contract design, in applying the standard of reasonableness in contract disputes.

I. INTRODUCTION

I have a closet that has a sliding door that tends to jump off its track. There is an easy fix, which is that I can simply lift up the door and put it back on the track. This does not prevent it from happening again. The act of lifting the door and fitting it back on the track takes less than a minute. I have little closet space in my house and too many clothes. Yet, this closet remains nearly empty, filled only with items that I rarely wear. I compensate for the disuse of this closet by cramming my clothes into my daughter's closet or stuffing them into my dresser's drawers. I do this to avoid using the closet with the skittish door.

This chapter suggests that online contracts are like closet doors. Businesses understand this, which is why they try to make them as unobtrusive as possible; the equivalent of a door that so easily slides open that there is no need to even note its existence. Businesses design contracts to benefit themselves. They minimize the prominence of contracts without reducing the terms they contain. On the contrary, they take advantage of the demure form of contracts greedily to stuff them full of terms that disadvantage the consumer. Many of these terms have nothing to do with what the consumer understands to be the bargained for exchange.

The physical design of a notice or contract can affect the behavior of the parties in the same way that the placement of windows affects the use of a room or a handle the use of a cup. The form of a contract can be a feature, a part of the offered product or service. Forms can shape user behavior and expectations by affecting the user experience. This chapter deliberately uses the term "form" instead of "contract" to distinguish between the physical embodiment, which contains terms, and the use of the physical embodiment, or form, to express legal rights and obligations. Contracts have the power to affect consumer behavior, not through their text (which most consumers do not read) but through their form and design. Online, contracts can do more than merely expressing rights and responsibilities in words.

This chapter advocates using contract's form as function. The form of a contract – its design and presentation – can provide a function other than to describe in words the legal rights and responsibilities of the parties. The form itself shapes, expresses and reveals the parties' intent and expectations. Awareness of the potential uses of contract's form creates expectations of how companies *should* use them. Companies have a choice in crafting the design of contracts, and courts should acknowledge the effects of that choice when they interpret and apply legal standards.[1]

Courts have applied traditional principles of contract law to online contracts with little or no allowance for the ways that the online contracting environment differs from the offline one. Mass consumer online agreements, however, lack many of the features of traditional contracts. They are weightless, obscure and ubiquitous – and thus easily ignored. They offer fine print in an environment where colorful images dominate over text. Legalese just cannot compete with clips of cute babies and funny animals. Web site visitors seek instant gratification and arresting images, and companies respond by making their Web sites easy to use and visually appealing. By contrast, they design their online agreements to meet legal requirements, not to compete for consumer attention. The online environment, the unique characteristics of

[1] For an interesting, and infuriating, account of how business specifically design contract forms and terms to deter consumers from reading, *see* Bob Sullivan, GOTCHA CAPITALISM (Random House: 2007). Sullivan discusses how AT&T specifically designed a mailer to be discarded, and not read. *Id.* at 8–11. He also discusses a government study that found that credit card companies write agreements that are unlikely to be understood by the average consumer. *Id.* at 41–45. Of course, companies also structure transactions and contract terms to exploit consumer misperceptions. *See* Stefano Della Vigna & Ulrike Malmendier, *Contract Design and Self-Control: Theory and Evidence*, THE QUARTERLY JOURNAL OF ECONOMICS, 353 (May 2004) (analyzing the "profit-maximizing contract design of firms if consumers have time-inconsistent preferences and are partially naïve about it").

digital agreements, and the discreet way they are presented, compound the problems that are generally raised by paper contracts of adhesion.

This chapter argues that the standard of reasonableness is erroneous as currently applied to online contract disputes. In determining whether an online agreement is enforceable, courts focus on whether the party disputing the agreement (the "non-drafting party") had "reasonable notice" of the agreement and manifested assent. If the non-drafting party was aware of the contract terms and "manifests consent" by clicking or continuing to use the Web site, courts typically find assent to the agreement.

There are several factors that encourage courts to enforce contracts in all but the most egregious cases. First, under the blanket assent theory of contracts, either the consumer consents to all the terms of the contract or none of them. Furthermore, the non-drafting party has a duty to read. Accordingly, as long as the non-drafting party manifests assent, for example by signing an agreement, then ignorance of any particular term contained in the document typically will not excuse performance. Another factor is that commercial transactions are viewed favorably in a credit-based economy. One of the fundamental purposes of contracts is to facilitate and encourage commercial transactions. Under blanket assent, a finding of non-consent would invalidate the transaction *in its entirety*. Furthermore, courts are uneasy with policing the substantive terms of a bargain, hence the maxim that "courts will not review the adequacy of consideration." Consequently, courts are reluctant to invalidate a contract unless the type of transaction or the contract terms are socially harmful or outrageous.

Much then depends upon whether notice was reasonable. Unfortunately the reasonableness inquiry is rigged against the non-drafting party because it focuses on the non-drafting party's conduct rather than that of the party who has control over the form of notice. Contract law imposes upon the non-drafting party a duty to read, *yet there is no corresponding duty to draft reasonably*. The reasonable notice inquiry involves a determination of whether a reasonable person would have seen the contract terms. If so, the consumer then has a duty to read the terms. In other words, reasonable notice means only that the Web site indicate the existence of an agreement, not that it reveal the terms contained in the agreement in a noticeable manner. The burden is on the consumer – the non-drafting party – to track down the contract terms, which are often dispersed via multiple hyperlinks across different interior Web pages. In this way, the determination of reasonable notice places the burden of the online contracting process on the party who has no ability to craft the notice or negotiate any of the terms.

This chapter argues that in evaluating the reasonableness of notice, courts should consider the drafting party's role and responsibility in contractual relationships by recognizing a duty to draft reasonably. Modern contract doctrine places the onus of reasonable notice on the wrong party – the party that has no ability to determine the form or design of the contract or notice is charged with reading all the terms regardless of where they may be located. Given online contracting realities, the relevant inquiry regarding whether notice was "reasonable" should include a determination of whether a reasonable drafting party would have designed the contract in the way it was presented. Was the contract designed to attract the user's attention? Or was the contract created in such a way as to obscure its legal nature given the overall design of the Web site?

II. MODERN CONTRACTS AND THE DIMINISHING OF CONSENT

In a well-known article, Arthur Leff puzzled over changes in contracts' form and grappled with the way that standard form contracts challenged the classical conception of contracts.[2] Leff emphasized the power conferred by a classification label, noting that to "call a thing a contract is to make a legal classification."[3] He argued that mass consumer contracts were misclassified:

> Seeing that consumer transactions were communicative (rather than, say, physically coercive), mercantile (rather than charitable or donative) and bounded (rather than status-relational), and so on, "the law" continued to class them as contractual. This overlooked the fact that these "contracts" were not the product of a cooperative process, but the creation (essentially) of only one of the parties. In other words, "the law" was classing consumer transaction as contracts on the basis of less than all the criteria which actually shaped that particular class.[4]

Leff noted that the creation of a new category – "contracts of adhesion" – was a "brilliant coup" as an analytic device but a "disaster" as a practical matter.[5] He pondered why contracts of adhesion were called contracts at all since they were the "products of non-bargaining, unilaterally manufactured commodities."[6] He concluded that contracts of adhesion must have been labeled "contracts" because they physically resemble contracts that are the product of the bargaining process.[7]

Leff proposed that the "paper-with-words which accompanies the sale of a product" be thought of "as part of the product."[8] In doing so, that paper would presumably be subject to the same regulatory control as the accompanying product, but

[2] Arthur Allen Leff, *Contract as Thing*, 19 AMER. UNIV. L. REV. 131 (1970).
[3] *Id.* at 132.
[4] *Id.* at 143.
[5] *Id.* at 142.
[6] *Id.* at 147.
[7] *Id.* at 147.
[8] *Id.* at 155.

Leff favored using this metaphoric shift to "increase the availability and quality of the information upon which buying (market) decisions are based."[9] Unfortunately, greater disclosure is not likely to resolve many of the problematic aspects of mass consumer transactions, especially when they take place online.[10] Leff, too, acknowledged that people do not read contracts and that clearer disclosure thus may not help them.[11] Yet, he concluded that a metaphoric shift in thinking of mass consumer "paper" as part of the product rather than as an agreement "might in time lead to a perception of disclosure not in the old contract-interpretation terminology, but in a more realistic context, more attuned to what happens at retail, to the ultimate production of more *actual* information disclosure,"[12] which might ultimately (and ideally) "increase the power of the market itself to control the price-quality mix."[13]

Leff made a strong argument for viewing a mass consumer contract as a "thing" rather than as an "agreement," but he recognized the limitations of his proposal:

> While my suggestion has been wholly serious, I am quite aware of the fragility of this kind of effort. Language has never been much of a match for sense perceptions except as an analytic, and analytics have a way of being quickly swallowed up in the resurgent [*sic*] real world of synthetics.... The real hope of an exercise like this is necessarily more modest than any total sensory transformation. It can aspire at most temporarily to smash the semantic box in which our current thinking is locked. The next step, and the harder one, is crafting a better cabinet out of the materials really available in a real world.[14]

9 *Id.* at 156.

10 *See* Danielle Kie Hart, *Contract Law Now – Reality Meets Legal Fictions*, 41 U. BALT. L. REV. 1, 75, 76 (2011) arguing that disclosure statutes "obscure more problematic forms of bargaining inequality" and may actually "prevent many contracts from being successfully challenged based on several of the modern contract policing doctrines."); Amy J. Schmitz, *Legislating in the Light: Considering Empirical Data in Crafting Arbitration Reforms*, 15 HARV. NEG. L. REV. 115 (reviewing credit card and wireless service contracts and noting that most of the arbitration terms were "buried in long form contracts, and often appeared in unnoticeable or small typeface.") *Id.* at 149. Schmitz also conducted focus group studies whose participants felt "demoralized and helpless" when faced with form contracts. *Id.* at 151. Participants in her focus group also reported that they often bypass links in e-contracts and they felt it was a "waste of time to read or retain any copies of form contracts because they have no choice but to accept them." *Id.* at 152. Schmitz concludes that "disclosures are not worth their cost if they fail to help consumers shop for goods and services." *Id.* at 165. *But see* Robert A. Hillman and Ibrahim Barakat, *Warranties and Disclaimers in the Electronic Age*, 11 YALE J. L. & TECH. 1 (2009) (arguing that "e-commerce exacerbates the problem of warranties and disclaimers" but that "disclosure of disclaimers...is the best of various imperfect solutions to the problem.") *Id.* at 27.

11 Arthur Leff, *Contract as Thing*, *supra* note 2 at 157.

12 *Id.*

13 *Id.*

14 Arthur Leff, *supra* note 2, at 157.

In this article, I suggest that contracts themselves be used as the tools to "smash the semantic box."[15] The most appropriate place to "smash the semantic box" is in the online environment because drafting parties can more easily manipulate the form of contracts to shape contracting behavior and coax true consent.

One of the most notable scholars to tackle the complicated issues of contractual consent and online contract is Margaret Jane Radin.[16] Radin notes that standard form contracts create many positive "network effects" that facilitate their adoption.[17] She observes, however, that contract standardization also has harmful effects, most significantly coercion or lack of choice.[18] She notes that to the extent that browsewraps purport to "bind everyone who accesses the website, with no choice on their part other than to forego that website, it is a standard that forecloses choice; and to the extent that the same standard form contract is used on many different websites, it becomes a more powerful standard, and the risk of lack of choice or coercion increases."[19]

Radin distinguishes between two models of contract, "contract-as-consent" and "contract-as-product."[20] She notes that "contract-as-consent" is the traditional contract model which involves a meeting of the minds or "at least voluntariness, or at least consent."[21] Yet, Radin observes that the traditional model does not correspond to reality, particularly online:

> Contracts in electronic commerce do not look like the traditional picture of meeting of the minds or autonomous consent. The process of contract formation involves the human/computer interface, not the interaction of two autonomous repositories of Kantian personhood.[22]

[15] *Id.*

[16] *See generally* Margaret J. Radin, *Humans, Computers and Binding Commitment*, 75 Ind. L. J. 1125 (2000) [hereinafter Radin, *Humans, Computers*]; Margaret J. Radin, *Online Standardization and the Integration of Text and Machine*, 70 Fordham L. Rev. 1125 (2002) [hereinafter *Online Standardization*]; Margaret J. Radin, *Regulation by Contract, Regulation by Machine*, 160 Theoreticaly and Inst. Econ. 1 (2004) [hereinafter Radin, *Regulation by Contract*]; Margaret J. Radin, *Boilerplate Today: The Rise of Modularity and the Waning of Consent*, 104 MICH. L. REV. 1223 (2006) [hereinafter Radin, *Modularity and Consent*].

[17] *See* Margaret J. Radin, *Online Standardization and the Integration of Text and Machine*, 70 Fordham L. Rev. 1125, 1130–1132.

[18] *Id.* at 1132–1135. She also mentions the possibility of "lock in" and "lock out." She suggests as an example of a legal "lock-in," doctrines that "cannot be changed because we have all learned them and built up systems around them, and it would be too costly to substitute a new regime." *Id.* at 1133. She suggest that an example of "lock-out" in the legal context might be a "novel legal argument" or a "particularly good form contract or pleading" that is patentable. *Id.* at 1134.

[19] *Id.* at 1135.

[20] *Id.* at 1139–1140; *see also* Margaret J. Radin, *Humans, Computers, and Binding Commitment*, 75 Ind. L. J. 1125 (2000).

[21] *Id.* Radin, *Humans, Computers*, *supra* note 20, at 1126.

[22] *Id.*

Radin's second model, "contract-as-product", views terms as part of the product being offered:

> The contract-as-product model is the typical model assumed by economists. In this model, the terms are part of the product, not a conceptually separate bargain; physical product plus terms are a package deal. The fact that a chip inside an electronics item will wear out after a year is not less and no more a feature of the item and its quality than the fact that the terms that come with the item specify that all disputes must be resolved in California under California law. In this model, unseen contract terms are no more and no less significant than unseen internal design features; and it is not remarkable that there is no choice other than the take-it-or-leave-it choice not to buy the package.[23]

Radin supposes that contract as "negotiated text" will be "significantly eroded in the online environment"[24] and that the "contract is merging into the product; the text is merging into functionality."[25]

Both Arthur Leff and Margaret Jane Radin struggled with the deterioration of consent in standard form contracts. They argued that the lack of consent and the standardization of contract terms create contracts that are products, rather than agreements that reflect the intent of the parties.[26]

III. DUTY TO READ

Consumer standard form contracts pose dangers of overreaching by the drafting party as they are usually offered on a take-it-or-leave-it basis, meaning that the consumer has no power to negotiate terms. The inability to negotiate terms is a primary reason that few consumers actually read the terms of standard contracts. Courts, however, impose a duty to read on non-drafting parties to a contract even, incongruously, consumers in the context of standard form contracts who are inclined *not* to read the terms because of the futility of doing so.[27] Because of the objective theory

[23] *Id.*

[24] *Id.*

[25] *Id.*

[26] Other scholars have discussed "contracts as products" as well. *See* W. David Slawson, *Standard Form Contracts and Democratic Control Over Lawmaking Power*, 84 HARV. L. REV. 529 (1971); Jeffrey W. Stempel, *The Insurance Policy as Thing*, TORT TRIAL & INSURANCE PRACTICE L. J. 813 (2009) (expressly applying the notion that insurance policies are "things" purchased by policyholders).

[27] *See* E. Allen Farnsworth, CONTRACTS, Fourth Edition, (2004) (Aspen Publishers) section 4.26 (noting that "(a) party that signs an agreement is regarded as manifesting assent to it and may not later complain about not having read or understood it, even if the agreement is on the other party's standard form.... And since the objective theory of contracts imposes no requirement that one intend or even understand the legal consequences of one's actions, one is not entitled to relief merely because one neither read the standard form nor considered the legal consequence of adhering to it.")

of contracts, a party who manifests assent to a contract may not later escape it by claiming that he or she did not read the terms. In the offline environment, a party manifests assent by signing a contract or by accepting a document where the act of doing so implies assent.[28] In the online environment, a party manifests assent by clicking on an icon that indicates acceptance to terms or by continuing to use a Web site after notice of the terms.

The critical issue regarding assent in the online context is whether there was "reasonable notice." Reasonable notice means either actual or constructive notice.[29] Furthermore, reasonable notice, actual or constructive, does not mean that all the terms must be visible. Courts have found reasonable notice even where some terms were not readily apparent as long as the user was aware that additional terms existed. For example, in one case, the court held that the user had assented by clicking "Accept" to the terms of an online agreement which were contained in a scrollable box even though the agreement was thirteen pages long.[30] As long as there is reasonable notice of an agreement, and express or implied assent, the failure to read the terms does not excuse the user. In another case, a court found that a "reasonably prudent internet user" would have had notice of the "existence of the terms" in a scrollable box:

> Plaintiff had to have had reasonable notice of the terms. By clicking "Yes, I agree to the above terms and conditions" button, Plaintiff indicated assent to the terms. Therefore, the requirements of an express contract for reasonable notice of terms and mutual assent are satisfied. Plaintiff's failure to read the Agreement, if that were the case, does not excuse him from being bound by his express agreement.[31]

Another court found reasonable notice where a hyperlink indicated the existence of terms and conditions, even though none of the terms was actually

[28] *See* Joseph M. Perillo, CALAMARI & PERILLO ON CONTRACTS, Sixth Edition, 9.41 (stating that the "duty to read is based upon the objective theory of contracts...a party who signs an instrument manifests assent to it and may not later complain about not reading or not understanding.... The same rule applies even without a signature if the acceptance of a document, which purports to be a contract implies assent to its terms. Thus, for example, the mere acceptance of documents such as bills of lading, passenger tickets, insurance policies, bank books and warehouse receipts may give rise to contracts based upon the provisions contained therein. The recipient has a duty to read.")

[29] *Southwest Airlines Co. v. BoardFirst, LLC* WL 4823761 at 5.

[30] *Forrest v. Verizon Communications, Inc.*, 805 A.2d 1007, 1010–11 (D.C. 2002); *see also Feldman v. Google, Inc.*, 513 F.2nd 229, 237 (2007) (finding notice where user clicked "Yes" to terms of seven paragraph agreement in 12 point font); *Caspi v. Microsoft Network, LLC* 732 A.2d 528 (1999) (finding reasonable notice where user had to click "I agree" to terms of scrollable agreement even though relevant precision was in the last paragraph).

[31] *Feldman v. Google, Inc.*, *supra* note 30 at 3.

visible on that Web page.[32] That court compared online to offline agreements, stating:

> The blue hyperlinks on the defendant's Web pages, constituting the five-step process for ordering the computers, should be treated the same as a multipage written paper contract. The blue hyperlink simply takes a person to another page of the contract, similar to turning the page of a written paper contract.[33]

The court did not, however, recognize the myriad ways in which online agreements differ from paper ones, or the ways in which the online environment differs from the physical one. The duty to read places the burden of online contract's form, such as the need to click on hyperlinks and scroll through textboxes, upon the party with no responsibility for, or power over, the creation of such form. Not surprisingly, businesses feel no great need to make reading more convenient; they need only make the existence of terms noticeable. One court upheld an agreement where the user clicked a box to indicate acceptance, even though the actual terms of the agreement were visible only by clicking on a separate link directly above the box.[34] The court stated that:

> [The plaintiff] DeJohn had an opportunity to review the terms of the Register.com Agreement by clicking on the hyperlink Register.com provided. The fact that DeJohn claims that he did not read the contract is irrelevant because absent fraud (not alleged here), failure to read a contract is not a get out of jail free card.[35]

In the online environment, businesses are free to experiment with contracting forms. Courts have accommodated contracting innovation by approving both clickwrap and browsewrap forms, provided that businesses provide notice of the existence of terms, even if the terms themselves are not visible. Reasonable notice and the duty to read imposes upon the consumer the obligation to chase down terms upon notice of their existence.

Recognizing a duty to draft reasonably would shift the burden of online contracting from consumers to the party in the best position to shoulder it – the Web site owner. As anyone who has ever clicked "I agree" without reading the terms (and that means anyone who has ever clicked "I agree") knows, this "manifestation of consent" reflects a very superficial and limited view of assent, one that requires neither that the non-drafting party understand the terms nor that the drafting party make an effort to make the terms understandable.[36] Businesses have the power to do more

32 *Hubbert v. Dell Corp.*, 844 NE 2d 965, 968 (2006).

33 *Id.*

34 *DeJohn v. The TV Corporation International*, 245 F.Supp. 2d 913, 915–916, 919 (C.D. Ill. 2003).

35 *Id.* at 919.

36 On the contrary, one researcher found that companies used "language to construct a biased version of reality" that helped them gain access to consumer data that "they would not have access to if

than simply meeting minimal notice requirements; they can enhance the online contracting experience through their technical control over the design of their Web sites. As Jacqueline Lipton noted, "along with Property rights come important responsibilities ... any kind of Property rights, including information property rights, should be tempered by necessary legal duties imposed on the right holder as an incident of property ownership."[37] Businesses have information property rights in their Web sites, and thus the power to shape their contracts. This power is both a right and a responsibility, which should confer upon businesses a duty to draft contracts reasonably.

IV. CODE AS LAW AND FORM AS FUNCTION

Some have questioned whether contract law is up to the task of governing online transactions.[38] This chapter adopts the view that while contract law continues to provide fundamental guiding principles, the application of those principles to online transactions and digital information could benefit from the insights of cyber law scholars.[39] In particular, while contract law may govern the transactions between parties offline, in the online environment, the construction of a Web site and the use of forms determines the structure of the transaction and, thus, the nature of relationships. Joel Reidenberg used the term "Lex Informatica" to express how "(t)echnological capabilities and system design choices impose rules on participants" and how those choices reflect information policy.[40] Reidenberg stated:

> For Lex Informatica ... the primary source of default rule-making is the technology developer and the social process by which customary uses evolve. Technologists design the basic infrastructure feature that create and implement information policy defaults.... In the legal regulatory regime, private contractual arrangements can be used both to deviate from the law's default rules and to customize the relationship between the parties. Such deviations are only available if the law permits freedom of contract and does not preclude the participants' actions: circumstances

users were fully informed about data handling practices. The opacity and vagueness contained in these policies precludes people from understanding them in their entirety or may even deter them from reading these documents altogether, thereby preventing informed consent." *See* Irene Pollach, *A Typology of Communicative Strategies in Online Privacy Policies: Ethics, Power and Informed Consent*, 62 J. Bus. Ethics 221, 232 (2005).

37 Jacqueline Lipton, *Information Property: Rights and Responsibilities*, 56 FL. L. Rev. 135, 180 (2004).

38 For a discussion of the issue of electronic contracting and contract doctrine, *see* Robert A. Hillman & Jeffrey J. Rachlinsky, *Standard-Form Contracting in the Electronic Age*, 77 N.Y.U.L. Rev. 429, 432 (2002) (finding that while the online environment "changes some of the dynamics of standard form contracting ... these difference do not call for the development of a radically different legal regime").

39 The author of course means cyber law scholars in addition to Margaret J. Radin.

40 Joel R. Reidenberg, *Lex Informatica: The Formulation of Information Policy Rules Through Technology*, 76 Texas L. Rev. 553, 554 (1998).

> exist in which the law may not permit customization. For example, public policy generally rejects contractual waivers of liability for intentional or reckless harms inflicted on others. Like a legal regime, Lex Informatica offers both customization of rules and inalienable rules. Customization for Lex Informatica occurs through technological configurations.[41]

Similarly, Lawrence Lessig pronounced that "code is law" in explaining how software and hardware regulate cyberspace in the same way that law regulates the physical world.[42] In his book *You Are Not a Gadget*, Jaron Lanier discussed the programming decisions responsible for the design and function of the World Wide Web and explained how these decisions later created social and cultural problems.[43] James Grimmelmann has suggested that the problem of privacy in social media should be considered as "one of safe product design"[44] and that when privacy harms are "preventable with better design choices or more careful programming, it makes sense to ask whether the site operator should be held accountable for them."[45] The observations of these and other cyber scholars articulate a reality that contract scholars often ignore – Web site design affects user behavior and shapes norms. Significantly, the design is deliberate[46] even if the consequences are sometimes unintended.[47]

Recent studies suggest how a strategic use of contract design may affect and shape user behavior and understanding. One study found that the decision of college students to reveal personal information online depended to a great extent upon contextual factors.[48] In one experiment in that study, the students were

[41] *Id.* at 568.

[42] Lawrence Lessig, CODE 2.0, at 5 (2006). *See also* James Grimmelmann, *Regulation by Software*, 114 YALE L. J. 1719 (2005) (arguing that software is a modality of regulation akin to physical architecture).

[43] Jaron Lanier, YOU ARE NOT A GADGET: A MANIFESTO 3 (Penguin Books: 2010) ("Software is ... subject to an exceptionally rigid process of 'lock-in.' Therefore, ideas [in the present era, when human affairs are increasingly software driven] have become more subject to lock-in than in previous eras. Most of the ideas that have been locked in so far are not so bad, but some of the so-called web 2.0 ideas are stinkers, so we ought to reject them while we still can.")

[44] James Grimmelmann, *Privacy as Product Safety*, 19 WIDENER L. REV. 793, at 795 (2010).

[45] *Id.* at 14. Grimmelmann, however, cautions against a direct application of products liability law to online privacy. *Id.* at 19. Rather, he suggests that products liability law may help illuminate how to consider the problems of online privacy and social networking sites. *Id.*

[46] Nick Wingfield, *Microsoft Quashed Effort to Boost Online Privacy*, WSJ, August 1, 2010 (reporting that in an effort to increase ad revenues, Microsoft decided to design it's browser to make it easier to track users online movements).

[47] Julie Angwin provides an interesting account of the decision of the social networking site, MySpace, to allow "Fakesters," (people using fake identities) as members in order to cultivate a free-wheeling, irreverent image. Julie Angwin, STEALING MY SPACE 59–63 (Random House: 2009). Consequently, MySpace, more than other social networking sites, became associated with sexual predators, ultimately resulting in increased scrutiny from law enforcement officials. *Id.* at 191–201.

[48] Leslie K. John, Alessandro Acquisti and George Loewenstein, *The Best of Strangers: Context dependent willingness to divulge personal information*, (draft)(available at http://ssrn.com/abstract-1430482)

randomly assigned so that some of them received an initial consent warning, which required a "click" of acknowledgement, whereas other students received no warning.[49] The students were then asked questions about academic integrity, including whether they had ever cheated.[50] The researchers found that those students who received a consent warning made significantly fewer affirmative admissions than those who had not.[51] The warning made the privacy concern more salient.

In a second experiment, the same researchers sought to test the impact of reducing the privacy concern. They recruited university students to complete a survey.[52] The "frivolous" version of the survey, intended to downplay privacy concerns, was called "How BAD Are U??" and had a picture of a cartoon devil icon.[53] The baseline version of the survey was entitled "Carnegie Mellon University Survey of Ethical Standards" and had a professional look.[54] The questions were the same on both versions and inquired about unprofessional behavior such as drug use and sexual activity.[55] They found that participants in the frivolous condition were on average 1.7 times more likely to admit to having engaged in the questioned behaviors than those in the baseline condition.[56]

In an unrelated study, researchers tested the impact of "textured" or visually enhanced end user software license agreements.[57] The researchers drew upon visual design strategies employed by popular media to attract reader attention.[58] In order to retain reader interest, they created visual variety by introducing new visual elements continually throughout the agreement.[59] These visual elements included vignettes and mini-narratives employing cartoon stick figures to enhance the readability of text.[60] They found that textured agreements increased the time spent on agreement screens from an average of seven seconds to an average of thirty-six to forty seconds.[61] They also found that longer reading times correlated strongly with greater retention of information from the agreements.[62]

49 *Id.* at 5.
50 *Id.* at 6.
51 *Id.*
52 *Id.* at 7.
53 *Id.*
54 *Id.*
55 *Id.*
56 *Id.*
57 Matthew Kay and Michael Terry, *Textured Agreements: Re-envisioning Electronic Consent*, Symposium on Usable Privacy and Security (SOUPS) 2010, July 14–16, 2010, Redmond, WA, USA. http://cups.cs.cmu.edu/soups/2010/proceedings/a13_kay.pdfhttp://dl.acm.org/citation.cfm?id=1837127.
58 *Id.* at 3.
59 *Id.* at 4.
60 *Id.* at 5.
61 *Id.* at 11.
62 *Id.*

These studies suggest that user behavior is heavily influenced by both context and visual design and support the idea of using contract's form to shape behavior.

Currently, drafting parties make it difficult for Web site visitors to locate the various components of a contract. The terms of use often contain hyperlinks to other terms, scattering an agreement across several Web pages and necessitating multiple clicks. It is easy for someone to get lost amongst the thicket of hyperlinks and fine print.

Let's take for example privacy policies. Web sites currently provide constructive notice to their users of their online tracking methods in privacy policies. The policies are typically accessible via a hyperlink located at the bottom of a Web site's home page and also via a hyperlink from the terms of use. The user constructively assents to the terms of the privacy policy in either a browsewrap or a clickwrap, which references it.

Amazon's design is typical. Amazon's conditions of use (found via a hyperlink at the very bottom of its home page) inform consumers that "(i)f you visit or shop at Amazon.com, you accept these conditions."[63] The second paragraph counsels the consumer to "(p)lease review our Privacy Notice, which also governs your visit to Amazon.com, to understand our practices."[64] A visit to the Privacy Notice requires returning to the home page, scrolling to the bottom, and clicking on a link. The Privacy Notice reveals that "(b)y visiting Amazon.com, you are accepting the practices described in this Privacy Notice."[65] In order to learn what information is gathered by Amazon, the consumer must click on another link. The information gathered is non-trivial and includes the following litany:

> name, address, and phone numbers; credit card information; people to whom purchases have been shipped, including addresses and phone number; people (with addresses and phone numbers) listed in 1-Click settings; e-mail addresses of Amazon Friends and other people; content of reviews and e-mails to us; personal description and photograph in Your Profile; and financial information, including Social Security and driver's license numbers.[66]

Amazon does not clearly explain for what purposes the information is gathered, coyly stating only that "(w)e use the information that you provide for such purposes as responding to your requests, customizing future shopping for you, improving our stores, and communicating with you."[67]

[63] http://www.amazon.com/gp/help/customer/display.html/ref=footer_cou?ie=UTF8&nodeId=508088 (last visited August 17, 2011)

[64] *Id.*

[65] http://www.amazon.com/gp/help/customer/display.html/ref=footer_privacy?ie=UTF8&nodeId=468496 (last visited August 17, 2011).

[66] http://www.amazon.com/gp/help/customer/display.html/ref=footer_privacy?ie=UTF8&nodeId=468496 examples (last visited August 17, 2011).

[67] http://www.amazon.com/gp/help/customer/display.html/ref=footer_privacy?ie=UTF8&nodeId=468496#examples (last visited August 17, 2011).

But the morass of contract terms does not end there. The Privacy Notice states that the site includes "third-party advertising and links to other Web sites." These third party advertisers may "automatically receive your IP address" and may use "cookies, JavaScript, web beacons ... and other technologies to measure the effectiveness of their ads and to personalize advertising content." Furthermore, Amazon does not control the information practices of these third party advertisers and so a consumer must contact them "directly for more information about their privacy practices."[68]

Given the complicated, modular nature of the online contract, it is highly improbable that the consumer intends to enter into a contract and equally improbable that the drafter intends for the consumer to read the contract.[69] As Ryan Calo has noted, the problem with notice as a regulatory strategy is that often the *form* of notice is inadequate.[70] In the next section, I explain how companies might employ transactional hurdles, visualization strategies and sensorial landscaping to fulfill a duty to draft reasonably.

A. *Transactional Hurdles or "Contracts as Checkout Line"*

The function of a supermarket checkout line is to provide an orderly means by which customers may purchase desired items from a store. Yet, the checkout line does more than ease customers to the next available cashier.[71] It signals the time it takes to complete a transaction. Customers generally seek the shortest line in order to save time.[72] If all lines are too long, a customer may decide to leave the store and return at a less busy time or purchase items at another store. Some customers may bypass a large discount store with long lines in favor of a local corner store with no line, even if they have to pay a premium for the convenience. While the prices at the discount store may be lower than at the corner store, some customers may view the time spent in line as an added, non-monetary cost, which offsets the price differential. Contracts, too, can act as virtual checkout lines, to signal the hidden costs of a transaction.

68 *Id.*

69 In the context of online privacy policies and contracts, Woodrow Hartzog has recommended that in addition to the terms of the contract, that courts consider "other representations made by the website and the context in which information was disclosed." Woodrow Hartzog, *Website Design as Contract*, 60 AMER. U. L. REV. 1635, 1671 (2011).

70 Ryan Calo, *Against Notice Skepticism in Privacy (and Elsewhere)* 87 NOTRE DAME L. REV. 101 (2012).

71 Retailers are trying new approaches to placate buyers' frustration with waiting in line. *See* Ray A. Smith, *Find the Best Checkout Line*, D1, WSJ, December 8, 2011. *Available at* http://online.wsj.com/article/SB10001424052970204770404577082933921432686.html.

72 *Id.* (noting that shoppers "tend to become impatient quickly and fail to take into account key indicators of what may slow down a line.").

Transactional hurdles can be incorporated into privacy policies, for example, to signalize the often hidden privacy costs of using a particular Web site. The Internet has enabled companies to track users' movements using ever more sophisticated methods. Customers are often unaware of the methods, and the extent, to which they are tracked and recorded online.[73] A Web site may keep a record of all of a customer's purchases, the addresses of every person to whom the customer sent a gift, and products viewed and not purchased.[74] It may also record the features used by the customer on the site; the links clicked; information about the customer's computer Internet protocol address, browser type and operating system; and date and time information.[75] The Web site may record not only information about the user's movements on the Web site, but information about the Web site that the user visited immediately *prior* to going to the Web site.[76] The *Wall Street Journal* recently reported on the rise of the online "tracking industry," which is developing more highly sophisticated and largely unregulated methods of compiling consumer data:[77]

> Some of the tracking files identified by the *Journal* were so detailed that they verged on being anonymous in name only. They enabled data-gathering companies to build personal profiles that could include age, gender, race, zip code, income, marital status and health concerns, along with recent purchases and favorite TV shows and movies.[78]

A recent study found that online consumers were willing to pay a premium to purchase products from Web sites with protective privacy policies.[79] On average, they were willing to pay 60 cents extra on a purchase of $15 to buy from a Web

73 *See* Joseph Turow et al., CONTRARY TO WHAT MARKETERS SAY, AMERICANS REJECT TAILORED ADVERTISING 21 (2009), *available at* http://graphics8.nytimes.com/packages/pdf/business/ 20090929-Tailored_Advertising.pdf (noting that consumers often misunderstand the meaning of privacy policies and information collection practices); *see also* Stephanie Clifford, *Groups Far Apart on Online Privacy Oversight*, New York Times, December 8, 2009 (discussing concerns from academics and policy makers that consumers know "very, very little" about how their personal information is gathered online and used).

74 *See* Natasha Singer, *Shoppers Who Can't Have Secrets*, New York Times, April 30, 2010 (noting a documentary filmmaker's receipt of a printout from Amazon.com which contained information regarding purchased and perused items and gifts).

75 *See*, for example, Gap.com's privacy policy, *available at* http://www.gap.com/customerService/info.do?cid=2331&mlink=5058,1806877,14&clink=180687.

76 *Id.* ("We may also track certain information about the identity of the website you visited immediately before coming to our site.")

77 Julia Angwin and Tom McGinty, *Sites Feed Personal Details to New Tracking Industry*, WSJ, July 31 2010.

78 *Id.*

79 Janice Y. Tsai, Serge Egelman, Lorrie Cranor and Alessandro Acquisiti, *The Effect of Online Privacy Information on Purchasing Behavior: An Experimental Study*, 22 INFORMATION SYSTEMS RESEARCH 254 (2011).

site with a protective privacy policy.[80] Despite what companies pretend, consumers value their privacy and would pay more to protect it; yet, they unwittingly acquiesce to myriad uses of their personal information because the law has been interpreted in such a way as to make it exceedingly easy to do so.

The notion of blanket assent has come to mean that one click suffices to "manifest consent" to all the terms of the agreement, provided there is "reasonable notice." "Manifestation of consent" has been collapsed into the requirement of "reasonableness of the notice" so that evidence of one is often taken to mean evidence of the other. For example, a noticeable hyperlink indicating Terms of Use can be constructively assented to by the consumer simply by remaining on the Web site. Similarly, a click to accept the terms of a clickwrap agreement manifests assent to even those terms that are accessible only via hyperlinks contained in the clickwrap, even if those hyperlinks have not been clicked upon.

But in reality, a consumer clicking "I accept" usually does not intend to agree to all the terms, especially not to those which are accessible only via hyperlinks.[81] A customer purchasing a book on Amazon believes the bargain consists of the exchange of money for product; that customer may not be aware that he or she has also agreed to the intrusive practices revealed – and constructively assented to – in Amazon's privacy policy.

Furthermore, to claim that a visible hyperlink constitutes reasonable notice assumes that customers typically click on hyperlinks. This assumption is unreasonable as it places too great a burden on the customer. For example, on Amazon's home page, there are more than a dozen visible hyperlinks. It seems unlikely that Amazon actually expected its customers to click on each one and read the terms. The burden then is placed on the customer to click on those hyperlinks that seem, by their labels, to contain relevant information. The customer, however, does not know which ones are actually relevant until he or she reads the terms. In addition to the Conditions of Use there are other hyperlinks that might contain legal obligations or conditions of interest to the customer, including the Privacy Notice, Shipping Rates & Policies, and Your Account hyperlinks. The notice of a customer's contractual obligations, in the context of the overall design of the Web site, is not reasonable in any meaningful sense.

A more reasonable way for drafting parties to provide notice of contract terms, such as terms governing collection of customer personal information, is to require a "click" for each use of such information. It is technologically easy for companies to incorporate transactional hurdles into their Web sites. Furthermore, clicking

[80] *Id.* at 263–264.

[81] *See generally* Nancy S. Kim, *Contract's Adaptation and the Online Bargain*, 79 U. Cin. L. Rev. 1372 (2011).

to indicate the relinquishment of each right, such as the selling of personal data, more accurately reflects the bargained for exchange, coming closer to Leff's vision of "contract as product." A product that requires multiple clicking before it may be purchased may prove less desirable than one that a customer can purchase with one or two clicks. Web sites then may be able to compete on contract terms in a real way. A multiple clicking requirement would look as follows:

We may use your personal information in the following ways:

- To process and fulfill your order, including to send you emails to confirm your order status and shipment, [click required]
- To communicate with you and to send you information by email, postal mail, telephone, text message, or other means about our products, services, contests, and promotions, [click required]
- To administer and fulfill our contests and other promotions, [click required]
- To help us learn more about your shopping preferences, [click required]

Companies realize the value of getting their online customers to the checkout faster.[82] An aggravating "click" slows down the transaction process and forces companies to decide whether the additional uses of customer information are worth the risk of losing a sale[83] in the same way that a long line increases the risk of customers leaving the store without purchasing anything. Given that one of the primary reasons that consumers shop online is convenience, multiple clicking will likely hinder the online shopping experience at a given Web site which seeks multiple uses of personal information. In the context of commerce, a study conducted by Kuan-Pin Chiang and Ruby Roy Dholakia indicates that "convenience influences consumers' intention to shop online. When consumers perceive shopping offline as inconvenient, they are more likely to shop on the Internet."[84] Lan Xia and Devanathan Sudharshan note that interruptions during an online transaction "may cause negative feelings"[85] and "consumers may attribute their negative feelings with a decision process to the medium, that is, the Web site instead of the product

[82] *See* Claire Cain Miller, *Closing the Deal at the Virtual Checkout Counter*, New York Times, Oct. 12, 2009, B4 (discussing the importance that companies place on getting online shoppers to the checkout faster).

[83] *Cf.* Ronald Mann and Travis Siebeneicher suggest that internet retailers should "design websites to balance the benefits of extracting purposeful assent with the burdens of complicating the purchase process." Ronald J. Mann and Travis Siebeneicher, *Just One Click: The Reality of Internet Retail Contracting*, 108 Columbia L. Rev. 984, 986 (2008). They state that "fewer than ten percent" of the 500 internet retailers that they surveyed have sales processes "that create enforceable contracts on their sites." *Id.* at 987.

[84] Kuan-Pin Chiang and Ruby Roy Dholakia, *Factors Driving Consumer Intention to Shop Online: An Empirical Investigation*, 13 Journal of Consumer Psychology 177, 181 (2003).

[85] Lan Xia and Devanathan Sudharshan, *Effects of Interruptions on Consumer Online Decision Processes*, 12 Journal of Consumer Psychology 265, 279 (2002).

itself."[86] When the online experience at one site is more unpleasant, the consumer may look for another online retailer even if the prices offered at the first site are lower than at a subsequent site that does not require multiple uses of personal information.[87] Not surprisingly, online retailers seek to shorten the time, and steps, required to complete a transaction. They seek to "shorten the checkout line" without imposing an additional burden on the consumer, the equivalent of offering Saks Fifth Avenue–level customer service at Ross "dress-for-less" discount prices. Yet, the consumer does pay a price – without knowing it. It is as if the Saks store employees pickpocketed their customers in the dressing rooms instead of charging high prices at the register. Multiple clicking or other transaction hurdles annoy customers; that is why businesses do not like them – and why they are an effective and reasonable means of providing notice.

Businesses may bypass future transactional hurdles for repeat customers by having them fill out a form that indicates assent to each acknowledged use. After this initial form is filled out, the customer can simply click once to indicate continued agreement to its terms.

B. *Visualization Strategies or "Contracts as Road Signs and Traffic Lights"*

Another way that companies can draft more reasonably is by using visualization strategies, which are better suited for the online environment. Businesses understand the need for compelling and appealing images on their Web sites, yet they communicate legal obligations in drab textual format and then scatter the text across several hyperlinked pages. In the image driven online environment, a contract should contain more than just words.

Companies can employ some of the same tactics that governments have used to alert drivers to road conditions. A Web site visitor, like a driver, has limited attention and competing stimuli. Important notices must be visible and visually oriented. For example, rather than this:

> You represent and warrant that you own or otherwise control all of the rights to the content that you post; that the content is accurate; that use of the content you supply does not violate this policy and will not cause injury to any person or entity; and that you will indemnify us for all claims resulting from content you supply.

[86] *Id.*

[87] A study conducted by Rick Andrews and Imran Currim found that online shoppers were less price-sensitive than traditional supermarket consumers. Rick L. Andrews and Imran S. Currim, *Behavioural Differences between Consumers Attracted to Shopping Online versus Traditional Supermarkets: Implications for Enterprise Design and Marketing Strategy*, 1 Int. J. Marketing and Advertising 38 (2004). *See also* Kuan-Pin Chiang and Ruby Roy Dholakia, *above at n* 85 at 182, (finding that "it is possible that price may not be the dominating factor for online shopping and may be dependent on product category").

a Web site could add a simple sign to indicate the provision is important, like this:

> ⚠ **You represent and warrant that you own or otherwise control all of the rights to the content that you post; that the content is accurate; that use of the content you supply does not violate this policy and will not cause injury to any person or entity; and that you will indemnify us for all claims resulting from content you supply.**

Stefania Passera and Helena Haapio advocate a user-centered approach to contract design that recognizes the importance of images. They argue for the visualization of contract terms through the use of flowcharts, drawings and graphics.[88]

In addition, companies should not use images in a misleading way. In an oft-cited case, *Specht v. Netscape Communications Corp.*,[89] the Second Circuit held that a customer's clicking on a button to download software did not constitute acceptance of contractual terms because notice of terms required scrolling to the bottom of the page and thus was not reasonably conspicuous.[90] To put it another way, clicking on an icon to download software is not associated in most consumer's minds with clicking "I accept" to the terms of an agreement.

Certain icons, such as seals, give an impression of reliability. As Woodrow Hartzog has pointed out, icons such as padlocks give the impression that the Web site is protecting information.[91] A reasonable drafting party would not use text to contradict the implied meaning of images.

C. *Sensorial Landscaping or "Contracts as Neighborhoods"*

One night many years ago, I was driving home on the freeway and realized that the needle on my gas gauge was hovering near the red "low fuel" indicator. I spied a gas station and took the next exit. As I pulled into the station, a quick glance around told me that I should get back on the freeway and take my chances at the next exit. The gas pumps were apparently working, but the station was dimly lit with fluorescent light. The mini-mart was open, but the attendant was safely ensconced behind bulletproof glass and did not look up. There were no customers filling their car with gas. The gas station was not quite deserted, however. There were a couple of men, lying against a fence, arguing and apparently very angry at each other but too drunk to stand up and fight properly. A car playing loud music sped by. I heard voices yelling

[88] Stefania Passera and Helena Haapio, *User-Centered Contract Design: New Directions in the Quest for Simpler Contracting*. In: Henschel, René Franz (ed.), Proceedings of the 2011 IACCM Academic Symposium for Contract and Commercial Management. The International Association for Contract and Commercial Management: Ridgefield, CT, pp. 80–97, *available at* http://www.iaccm.com/admin/docs/docs/HH_Paper.pdf.

[89] 306 F.3d 17 (2nd Cir. 2002).

[90] *Id.* 30–32.

[91] Woodrow Hartzog, *Website Design as Contract*, 60 AMER. U. L. REV.1635 (2011).

at each other somewhere across the street. Next to the gas stations was a lot filled with car parts and other junk, which was marked off with a chain link fence and razor wire even though it did not look as if there was anything to steal.

The chances are that nothing would have happened to me if I had filled up my car with gas at that station. But in some situations, the probability of the risk is less significant than the gravity of the risk should it occur. I still had at least fifteen miles before I ran out of gas. A rapid risk-benefit calculation told me to make a U-turn and try my luck at the next station.

There were signals that aided my calculation of the risks involved in stopping at that gas station: the dim lighting, the fighting men, the oblivious attendant, most of all, the razor wire around a junk lot and the bulletproof glass. These signals created an environment that made me feel unsafe.

Businesses, too, can create an atmosphere that alerts the user to the type of contracting "neighborhood" that it has entered. They can take advantage of the other features of the online environment, such as sounds and animation. Ryan Calo has recommended moving beyond text and symbols to incorporate design strategies that reference experience. He provides examples of "visceral notice" such as the clicking sound a camera makes to alert a subject of being recorded.[92] In the online context, he references social technology that incorporates anthropomorphic design. A pair of tracking eyes, for example, would effectively notify Web site visitors that their online movements were being tracked.[93] Contractual provisions that burden users, such as indemnification provisions and mandatory arbitration clauses, might have a jagged font and/or a jarring sound associated with them. On the other hand, clauses that merely explain the nature of the Web site would have plain text, the equivalent of a safe neighborhood for contracting parties. Sensorial signals alert consumers to the nature of the contract or contractual provisions and enable them to make the risk-benefit analysis necessary to informed, actual consent.

V. CONCLUSION

Businesses have the ability to use contracts in multiple ways. They are *already* designing contracts to guide consumer behavior. Unfortunately, the design often obscures, rather than highlights, the content, lulling consumers into complacency. This Article argues for a paradigm shift in the way courts evaluate mutual assent in the online environment. It proposes that drafting parties have a duty to draft reasonably and suggests what reasonable drafting might look like in the online environment. Awareness of the possible ways that companies might provide notice should prompt reconsideration of what it means for notice to be "reasonable."

92 Calo, *supra* note 70.
93 *Id.*

9

Managing Change in Uncertain Times

Relational View of Good Faith

Zoe Ollerenshaw

Given the economic downturn, various studies have indicated that complex, long-term relational contracts are commonly being renegotiated and varied in order to obtain cost reductions or to meet other strategic and tactical business needs. This chapter will seek to critically examine the doctrine of good faith in the variation of such contracts. It will use the relational contract paradigm to analyse how (if at all) the doctrine applies under English common law to the variation process. Using recent decisions it will consider how the doctrine of good faith seeks to regulate variation; how it understands and comprehends this area; what legal rules it applies and what assumptions it makes about the way parties should/might behave in such circumstances. In doing so this chapter will conclude that the current view of good faith under English common law does not meet the relational needs of such contracts upon their variation and will suggest that if the law is to meet the commercial needs of parties to relational contracts, it will have to reconsider the extent of any obligation to renegotiate in good faith.

I. INTRODUCTION

Since the economic downturn, various studies have suggested that a number of complex long-term outsourcing contracts are being renegotiated or varied in order to obtain cost reductions or to achieve other strategic or tactical business needs.[1] Many such contracts include within their governance structure mechanisms allowing variations to the contract to be negotiated to take account of such developments. Sometimes such 'change control clauses' expressly impose upon the contracting parties an obligation to negotiate such changes in good faith. However, English law has traditionally rejected a general principle of good faith and is "aloof and suspicious"[2]

[1] For examples see fns 5, 7 and 8 post.

[2] Ewan Mckendrick, Good Faith: A Matter of Principle, in Good Faith in Contract and Property 39 at p. 41 (ADM Forte ed., Hart Publishing: Oxford and Portland, Oregon, 1999).

of such a doctrine and the various "competing conceptions"[3] of it. Even where an express duty of good faith has been imposed, the English courts remain cautious to embrace it, permitting such a duty only to be recognised in limited circumstances and then only to have a limited effect. This chapter examines whether a relational theory of contract would allow a meaningful role to be given to good faith when it is imposed as an express duty in the variation of complex long-term outsourcing contracts. It does not do so in an attempt to further arguments that a general principle of good faith should be imposed on English law or to suggest a greater and more dynamic role of good faith within English law. Rather, it is context specific, suggesting that if such an express duty is imposed upon the parties the courts should be willing to confer a construct upon the duty that implicitly recognises the relational nature of such contracts.

This chapter will begin by explaining the types of the long-term relational contracts the subject of its enquiry, their complex nature and the variations that could be suggested to them, in particular those prompted by the current adverse financial environment. In doing so, some of the contractual governance devices that might be included within their terms will be discussed. It will then examine English case law and its limited recognition of a duty of good faith, which reflects a classical and individualistic view of English contract law. However, as will be shown, this does not reflect the co-operative model that occurs in practice in the behaviours shown by the parties to long-term relational contracts. In Section V, it will consider aspects of relational contract theory and the norms and behaviours identified within it. Having done so, this chapter will use a relational contract prism to suggest a particular construct of good faith.

II. LONG-TERM AND COMPLEX OUTSOURCING CONTRACTS

This chapter is concerned with the variation of and the negotiation of variations to long-term, complex outsourcing contracts. Under such agreements, businesses source the ongoing supply of services or the ongoing provision of goods and services from external suppliers under contracts that last for some time. Such outsourcing arrangements can cover the supply of information, communication and other technology or communication services and goods (Information and Telecommunication Outsourcing [ITOs]) or the provision of business processing services (such as human resources, payroll, legal, accounting or other business processes) (Business Processing Outsourcings [BPOs]). Such contracts can last for a number of years and may (but not always) have commenced with the transfer of internal resources,

[3] Roger Brownsword, Norma J. Hird and Geraint Howells, Good Faith in Contract: Concept and Context, in GOOD FAITH IN CONTRACT at p. 10 (R. Brownsword, N. J.Hird and G. Howells eds., Ashgate Publishing: Aldershot, 1999).

assets and personnel from the business customer to the outsource provider. Services provided under such contracts vary widely. Some services to be provided may, by their nature, be relatively low in value where a high volume of regular service and goods provision is required (such as the provision of desktop computer applications and ancillary goods to be supplied with them [such as the desktop computers]). Ready competition for the supply of such services may be available and regular benchmarking reviews may be included in the contract terms to reflect that competition. Conversely, some services to be provided may only be required occasionally, may be highly specialised or peculiar to the particular customer and/or may be high in value or associated risk to the customer or its business. The idiosyncratic costs of a transfer to the outsourcing partner (in the case of an initial transfer of internal resources, assets and personnel), the internal business and investment costs to a customer of remaining with a particular provider, and the costs of migration away from a provider or the re-integration of the services back to a customer's organisation can also be high. It was estimated that in 2008 the global ITO market was worth US$ 240 billion with a 5–8 percent growth per annum forecast for the next four years[4] and that the BPO worldwide market would potentially be worth US$ 350 billion in 2010.[5] Such outsourcing contracts vary in term, typically running from three to ten years.

Other long-term outsourcing contracts have arisen in the United Kingdom as a result of a continued trend for more private sector involvement in the provision of governmental functions and services[6] and from the Private Finance Initiative (PFI), under which different public projects such as schools, hospitals and public infrastructure projects were funded. In PFI arrangements private providers funded the building of the projects, and either they owned the resulting assets, whose use was leased back to relevant governmental bodies or organisations, or the PFI providers operated the resulting projects within a larger national infrastructure network. Lease-back arrangements often include ongoing outsourcing contracts for the provision of ancillary services such as maintenance, upgrading and cleaning services.

4 Taken from Leslie Willcocks & Mary Lacity, THE PRACTICE OF OUTSOURCING: FROM IT TO BPO AND OFFSHORING (Palgrave, London, 2009) as referred to at p. 8 in Leslie Willcocks & Andrew S Craig, Outsourcing in Difficult Time – Releasing Cost but Maintaining Control, LOGICA in association with the London School of Economics' Outsourcing Unit, 2010, available at http://www.logica.co.uk/we-do/outsourcing/related-media/thought-pieces/the-outsourcing-enterprise – -outsourcing-in-difficult-times/.

5 Leslie Willcocks & Andrew S Craig, Outsourcing in Difficult Time- Releasing Cost but Maintaining Control, LOGICA in association with the London School of Economics' Outsourcing Unit, 2010, at p. 11 availableathttp://www.logica.co.uk/we-do/outsourcing/related-media/thought-pieces/the-outsourcing-enterprise – -outsourcing-in-difficult-times/.

6 For examples see the white collar and professional services provided to local government authorities the subject of an empirical study funded by the ERSC. See P. C. Vincent-Jones, A. W. Harries, I. D Campbell and W. B. Seal, Conflict and Co-operation in Contracting for Professional Services: A comparative study, The Economic and Social Research Council, Award Reference R000236416, 1998.

There are £12.6 billion PFI contracts in the National Health Service (NHS) alone.[7] Such contracts typically last for twenty-five to thirty years, although the sunk costs of some projects mean such arrangements can last considerably longer.[8]

Long-term outsourcing contracts can be complex in their nature and include a 'thick' web of interfaces (and consequent relations) between the service provider and customer or between the service provider and third parties. For example, in an ITO to a multinational business the service provider may need to interface with different business units, divisions or subsidiary companies (any of which may be managed separately within the customer's organisation); supply services to different user groups (with different levels of need and sophistication of service); report to different customer managers for different services; agree to contract changes and variations with different negotiators, depending upon the complexity and potential risks associated with or cost of the proposed change (on either an informal or a formal basis); liaise with former colleagues (if assets, personnel or resources were transferred from the customer to the service provider); and work with remaining in-house suppliers and developers of information technology (IT) services (assuming not all IT services were outsourced to the provider). In addition to such internal interfaces, the service provider may need to interface with external parties, such as different external suppliers of other IT and/or communication services, utility and other service providers, and their own sub-contractors and sub-sub-contractors. In the case of public sector outsourcing projects, service providers face a similar complex web of external and internal interfaces with the addition of various contacts or requirements with different governmental organisations and reporting bodies.

In long-term complex outsourcing contracts, a detailed contract is usually put in place between the parties setting out the services to be provided and the costs to be charged. These will commonly include various governance structures to manage the supply of the services and goods and the complex interfaces arising from them. Given the length of the contracts, it is expected that changes to the services and goods to be supplied may well arise. Such contracts therefore include various devices to agree to changes to the services to be supplied and to negotiate any consequent amendments required to the outsourcing contract. Change is heavily planned for.

Whilst the impact of some changes may be relatively certain in advance (for example, scaled increases in demand for services from the customer), the effect of

7 Lizzy Davies & Helene Mulholland, PFI Schemes taking NHS trusts to brink of financial collapse, claims Lansley, in The Guardian, 29 September 2011, available at http://www.guardian.co.uk/politics/2011/sep/22/pfi-schemes-nhs-trusts-brink-financial-collapse?INTCMP=SRCH.

8 For further information on PFI projects, their scope, cost and the services provided under them see Private Finance Initiative; where did it all go wrong? in The Telegraph, 29 September 2011, available at http://www.telegraph.co.uk/health/healthnews/8779598/Private-Finance-Initiative-where-did-all-go-wrong.html.

some of them may be more uncertain. Developments in technology, changes to business processes or models as a result of technological developments or the acquisition or divestment of businesses by the customer may all lead to change. Other uncertain variations may be driven by the very nature of the outsourcing relationship put in place. For example, express requirements for continuous improvement to the services or for structural innovation in the services to be provided may be imposed. Other foreseen but uncertain changes may also need to be dealt with such as the imposition of new statutory requirements on governmental authorities. Some changes may be totally unforeseen – such as changes required to reflect structural changes in the customer's business market. Various reports and studies have indicated previously unforeseen changes are now being made to outsourcing contracts in the light of the prevailing economic circumstances.[9] For example, in relation to ITO and BPO contracts it is suggested changes could be made to delay the provision of planned new services or innovations; to reduce the number of outsourcing suppliers used by a particular customer; to 'bundle' the provision of services together with one supplier to enable price or efficiency savings; to introduce quicker or cheaper services/solutions; and even to reduce the service charges, reduce the contractual commitment to take certain quantities of services or to require service providers to provide more or improved services for the same price.[10]

To cope with variations – foreseen or unforeseen, certain or uncertain – change control mechanism procedures are inserted into outsourcing contracts. A hierarchy of such mechanisms may be included depending on the complexity, scope, cost and risk of the variation required. These may vary from relatively informal negotiation and approval devices in the case of small, low-risk, low-cost changes to escalation to higher management and formal approval procedures for far reaching changes. Some change mechanisms allow the intervention of a third party to help resolve differences in agreeing to the change. The contractual provisions inserted into such contracts dealing with such mechanisms vary considerably in their terms. Some have no obligation imposed upon the parties in relation to the conduct of their negotiations. Others impose obligations upon the parties to use their "reasonable" or "best endeavours" to try to agree such changes. Occasionally, some include an express obligation of good faith upon the parties to attempt to negotiate and agree the variations. It is that express imposition of a duty of good faith in agreeing a change which is the subject of this chapter.

Having considered the long-term complex outsourcing contacts that are the subject of this chapter, it is now necessary to consider how English contract law deals with an obligation of good faith.

[9] For examples see *supra notes*, 5, 7 and 8.

[10] See *supra note*, 5 at p. 11 onwards.

III. A LIMITED RECOGNITION OF GOOD FAITH

As indicated at the beginning of this chapter, English law has been reluctant to embrace the concept of good faith. Aloof and suspicious of a general doctrine of good faith[11]; even an express duty of good faith has been held to be unenforceable. So found the House of Lords in the case of *Walford v. Miles*,[12] which concerned the enforceability of 'lock-in' and 'lock-out agreements' entered into during the course of "subject to contract" negotiations. The lock-out agreement in question, an obligation not to enter into negotiations with any third party to dispose of a business to them, although not by itself objectionable, was held to be uncertain because it was unlimited in its duration. More importantly, the lock-in agreement – an obligation to continue to negotiate in good faith with the plaintiff with the view to agreeing to dispose of the business to him – was held to be inherently uncertain and contrary to law:

> the concept of a duty to carry on negotiations in good faith is inherently repugnant to the adversarial position of the parties when involved in negotiations. Each party to the negotiations is entitled to pursue his (or her) own interest, so long as he avoids making misrepresentations. To advance that interest he must be entitled, if he thinks it appropriate, to threaten to withdraw from further negotiations or to withdraw in fact, in the hope that the opposite party may seek reopen the negotiations by offering him improved terms.[13]

Lord Ackner went on to provide:

> A duty to negotiate in good faith is as unworkable in practice as it is inherently inconsistent with the position of a negotiating party. It is here that the uncertainty lies.[14]

In the preceding decision, it is clear their Lordships adopted a very formalist and individualistic approach, viewing contracting as an essentially competitive process. It is significant that in the preceding case the parties were in the process of negotiating the sale of the proposed business and that importantly no legally binding agreement was found to be in place between them. Rather, such an uncertain obligation given during pre-formation negotiations was held to be a bare agreement to negotiate, which, being an agreement to agree, was unenforceable. Following the formalist approach it has long been a principle of English law that agreements to agree have no contractual force. In *May and Butcher, Ltd v. Regina*[15] the Kings Bench

[11] See *supra note* 2.
[12] [1992] 2 WLR 174.
[13] Lord Ackner, *ibid.*, at 138.
[14] *Ibid.*
[15] [1934] 2 KB 17.

Division was asked to decide whether a series of letters for the supply by the Crown of old tentage constituted a binding contract when the price for the tentage to be supplied was not set but was to be agreed to by the parties. The arrangement was found to be too uncertain to be contractually binding for the want of an essential term. Lord Buckmaster stated:

> In my opinion there never was a concluded contract between the parties. It has long been a well recognized principle of contract law that an agreement between two parties to enter into an agreement in which some critical part of the contract matter is left undetermined is no contract at all. It is of course perfectly possible for two people to contract that they will sign a document which contains all the relevant terms but it is not open to them to agree that they will in future agree upon a matter which is vital to the arrangement between them and has not yet been determined.[16]

Viscount Dunedin held:

> To be a good contract there must be a concluded bargain, and a concluded contract is one which settles everything that is necessary to be settled and leaves nothing to be settled by agreement between the parties. Of course it may leave something which still has to be determined, but then that determination must be a determination which does not depend upon the agreement of the parties.[17]

From the preceding it would appear any change control clauses existing in an outsourcing agreement (or, indeed, in any other contract) where the parties must agree to the change proposed are inherently unenforceable as agreements to agree. However, that is not the case. English law has adopted a more pragmatic approach in the case of concluded and binding contracts. In those cases, as opposed to discussions leading up to the entering of a contract, they have held that reasonable terms can be implied to give effect to the intentions of the contracting parties. In *Hillas & Co, Ltd v. Arcos, Ltd*[18] the House of Lords held that in a contract for the supply of timber entered into in May 1930 which included an option for the customer to purchase 100,000 standards of timber for delivery in 1931 upon 'conditions and prices which show them a reduction of 5 per cent on the fob value of the official price list at any time ruling during 1931' was enforceable. As Lord Tomlin stated:

> The problem of a court of construction must always be so to balance matters that, without violation of essential principle, the dealings of men may, so far as possible, be treated as effective, and that the law may not incur the reproach of being the destroyer of bargains.[19]

16 *Ibid.*, at 20.
17 *Ibid.*, at 21.
18 [1932] All ER 494.
19 *Ibid.*, at 499.

Lord Wright went on to provide:

> It is, accordingly, the duty of the court to construe such documents fairly and broadly, without being too astute or subtle in finding defects; but on the contrary the court should seek to apply the old maxim of English law, verba ita sunt intelligenda ut res magis valeat quam pereat. That maxim, however, does not mean that the court is to make a contract for the parties, or to go outside the words they have used, except in so far as there are appropriate implications of law as for instance, the implication of what is just and reasonable to be ascertained by the court as a matter of machinery where the contractual intention is clear but the contract is silent on some detail.[20]

Interestingly, he continued by saying:

> Thus in contracts for future performance over a period, the parties may not be able nor may they desire to specify many matters of detail, but leave them to be adjusted in the working out of the contract. Save for the legal implication I have mentioned, such contracts might well be incomplete or uncertain, with that implication in reserve they are neither incomplete nor uncertain.[21]

The preceding recognises a more co-operative approach to contracting that many would argue is now the accepted view of English contract law. It is now clear in English law that express obligations to negotiate in good faith change or variation orders that are included in complex and lengthy written contracts previously concluded between parties will be sufficiently certain to be enforceable if mechanisms are included within the agreements to resolve with sufficient certainty any differences between the parties.[22] In *Petromec Inc v. Petroleo Brasileiro S.A. Petrobas, Braspetro Oil Services Company* the matter expressly provided to be agreed in good faith was the actual and reasonable extra costs of upgrading a vessel in accordance with an amended specification. It was noted in the judgment that although the concept of bad faith was elusive, the parties had here entered into a completed agreement including an express obligation to agree in good faith. That obligation was contained within a complex agreement, and the parties clearly had the intent and reasonable expectation to be bound by its terms. Accordingly the court found such costs would be relatively easy to ascertain by a court in the absence of agreement by the parties by applying pricing principles set out in other clauses within the agreement, and as such the outcome of the good faith negotiations was sufficiently certain to be enforceable. In reaching the decision it is clear that the courts needed to be satisfied that sufficient criteria and mechanisms were available to it on the face

[20] *Ibid.*, at 503 to 504.

[21] *Ibid.*, at 504.

[22] See Petromec Inc v. Petroleo Brasileiro S.A. Petrobas, Braspetro Oil Services Company, Queens Bench Division, [2004] EWHC 127 (Comm) and in particular from paragraphs 86 to 92.

of the agreement for the courts to determine the good faith rather than rely on an abstract principle.[23]

However, subsequent decisions demonstrate that English courts are ambivalent in their attitude to the scope and extent of such duties of good faith. In support of upholding the restricted approach of *Petromec*[24] are the cases of *BBC Worldwide Ltd v. Bee Load Ltd (t/a Archangel Ltd)*[25] and *Tramtrack Croydon Ltd v. London Bus Services.*[26]

The *BBC Worldwide* case concerned the licensing of unreleased archive television recordings of various pop musicians and artists. A number of concluded contracts related to the arrangements. The court found that a clause in the first agreement that provided 'If at 31 December 1997 the Licensor has failed to deliver one hundred (100) cleared titles, the parties agree to discuss in good faith extending the time frame in which this number of titles can be cleared' had to be construed so far as possible to give effect to its intended purpose. It was found that clause therefore was to be construed so as to allow a proportionate reduction in the size of the advance previously paid for the release, manufacture and sale of such recordings and, 'if the parties were unable to agree such a figure, it could be determined by the court'.[27] However, the first agreement between the parties had been set aside by a subsequent agreement. That subsequent agreement provided that 'BBCW agrees to consider in good faith any request by Archangel to extend the scope of this Agreement'. It was held that clause was unenforceable for uncertainty as a matter of law under the principles of *Walford v. Miles.*[28] Having considered the case of *Petromec*[29] Lord Justice Toulson declared:

> In the present case clause 15 cannot be regarded as machinery for determining the amount of a contractual liability. The clause provides no criteria by which a court could determine whether 'in good faith' any particular request for any particular form of extension should be considered favourably.[30]

In the *Tramtrack* case[31] an express obligation to negotiate in good faith and acting reasonably was found to be enforceable because of the need to give effect to

23 See also for example the Privy Council decision in *The Queensland Electricity Generating Board v. New Hope Collieries* [1989] 1 Lloyd's Rep 205 where a long term coal supply agreement which provided that after the first five years the price was to be agreed and which contained an arbitration agreement was found sufficiently certain to be enforceable.

24 See *supra note*, at 22.

25 [2007] EWHC 134.

26 [2007] EWHC 107.

27 Lord Justice Toulson: See *supra note*, 25 at paragraph 50.

28 See *supra note*, at 12.

29 See *supra note*, at 22.

30 [2007] EWHC 134, at paragraph 95.

31 See *supra note*, 26.

the parties' intent to create legal relations. This case concerned an amended and restated concession agreement under which Tramlink Croydon Limited (TCL) held the concession to run the Croydon Tramlink for a period of ninety-nine years. An early PFI project several contracts were put in place between the parties. Under clause 3 of the original concession agreement TCL agreed to develop, finance, construct, operate and maintain the tramlink system at its own risk 'and save as expressly provided without recourse to London Regional Transport, governmental or other public funds or guarantees'. Under the terms of an amended and restated concession agreement TCL was obliged to accept such new transport tickets and passes as might be required by the regulator from time to time and clause 23.3 of the agreement provided 'the parties shall in good faith agree (acting reasonably) the financial arrangements to be put in place to compensate [TCL] for the introduction of such tickets and passes.' Alongside this provision complicated fare compensation provisions were put in place allowing compensation to be payable to TCL should a 'stored value ticket' (pre-paid ticket or pass) be introduced in such a way that it reduced TCLs anticipated revenues and a further agreement determined how TCL would be entitled to a share of monies raised on the sale of combined travel tickets and cards. A subsequent dispute arose as to the amount to be paid to TCL following the introduction of certain combined travel tickets. The question before the court was whether clause 23.3 of the amended and restated concession agreement had legal effect. Mr Justice Clarke held:

> Neither party has submitted that the decision in Walford v Miles means that Clause 23.3 is devoid of legal content and, in my opinion rightly so. The parties did not limit their agreement to an obligation of good faith. They agreed (a) to act reasonably in agreeing and (b) that any failure to agree should be referred to expert determination. In those circumstances the Court can, in my judgment, decide, in the case in dispute, at least what they, and the expert, acting reasonably are bound to take into account or ignore.[32]

A much more generous and potentially extensive approach by the courts can be seen in the Court of Appeal case of *Balfour Beatty Civil Engineers Ltd v. Dockland Light Railway*.[33] In that case a dispute arose as to the length of an extension permitted to a contractor for the carrying out of engineering works for the continuation of the London Docklands Light Railway. Under the agreement the contractor was entitled to such extension of time to complete the project as the employer determined. No express duty of good faith or honesty was imposed in the agreement upon the employer when exercising his discretion. Nevertheless, in order to give effect to the intent of the parties the court held the employer had a duty 'in all its judgments,

[32] *Ibid.*, at paragraph 90.
[33] [1996] CLC 1435.

decisions and certificates....to act honestly, fairly and reasonably.'[34] In particular the court was keen to point out that it rejected any suggestion the contractor be left with no means of challenging any partial, self-interested or unreasonable decision made by the employer:

> We would then have wished to consider whether an employer, invested (albeit by contract) with the power to rule on his own and a contractor's rights and obligations, was not subject to a duty of good faith substantially more demanding than that currently recognised in English contract law. [Counsel for the employer] has, however accepted ... that the employer was not only bound to act honestly but also bound by contract to act fairly and reasonably.... Even on a more expansive approach to good faith it may be that no more is required in the performance of a contract.[35]

However, this does not yet mean that English law is now ready to accept a wide interpretation of express or implied duties to negotiate changes in good faith. The courts have returned to a much more restrictive approach in the decision of *Gold Group Properties Ltd v. BDW Trading Ltd (formerly Barratt Homes Ltd).*[36] In a development agreement the defendants agreed to develop the land for residential and other mixed use purposes. The agreement provided any revenue raised from the sale and leasing of the premises built on the land would be shared between the parties and reference was made to a minimum price schedule. That term was defined in the agreement by reference to the fourth schedule to the agreement 'or any schedules substituted therefore from time to time by agreement by the parties'. A general clause 11 was included within the agreement that provided:

> Good Faith
>
> The parties mutually covenant and agree that
>
> 11.1 during the continuance of this Agreement all transactions entered into between the parties shall be conducted in good faith and on the basis set out in this Agreement or if not provided for herein on an arm's length basis;
>
> 11.2 each of them shall at all times act in good faith towards each other and use all reasonable endeavours to ensure the observance by themselves of the terms of this Agreement and the agreements referred to in, or contemplated by this Agreement; and
>
> 11.3 neither will seek to increase its profit or reduce its loss at the expense of the other.

34 Lord Justice Bingham: *Ibid.*, at p. 1441

35 *Ibid.*, at p. 1442.

36 [2010] EWHC 1632.

Planning and other reasons led to a delay in the start of the demolition and development on the site and in spring 2008 it also became apparent that there was a significant downturn in the property market following the economic crisis. Eventually relations between the parties broke down and by January 2009 both alleged the other was in breach of the agreement. The court found that in failing to commence the development Barratt was in repudiatory breach of the agreement. Barratt counterclaimed that the claimant was also in breach of the agreement for failing to negotiate or agree an adjustment to the revenue sharing provisions or the minimum price schedule as Barratt asserted the claimant was obliged to do under the agreement's general obligation of good faith. By reference to the case of *Berkeley Community Villages Ltd v. Pullen*[37] the court held that the reference to good faith in this context required the parties:

> to observe reasonable commercial standards of fair dealing in accordance with their actions which related to the Agreement and also requiring faithfulness to the agreed common purpose and consistency with the justified exceptions of the [claimant].[38]

Judge Furst went on to consider the Australian case of *Automasters Australia Pty Ltd v. Bruness Pty Ltd*,[39] which by referring to earlier case law, held:

> It must be accepted that the party subject to this obligation is not required to subordinate the party's own interests, so long as pursuit of those interests does not entail unreasonable interference with the enjoyment of a benefit conferred by the express contractual terms.... A party is precluded from cynical resort to the black letter. But no party is fixed with the duty to prefer the interests of the other contracting party. It is rather, a duty to recognise and to have due regard to the legitimate interests of both parties in the enjoyment of the fruits of the contract as delineated by its terms.[40]

Accordingly Judge Furst held:

> Thus good faith, whilst requiring the parties to act in a way that will allow both parties to enjoy the anticipated benefits of the contract, does not require either party to give up a freely negotiated financial advantage clearly embedded in the contract.[41]

This formalistic approach to the duty appears to revert to the classical view of contract as an adversarial and competitive process. It is reminiscent of the English courts' reluctance to interfere with the risk/reward bargain agreed upon between the

37 [2007] EWHC 1330 (Ch).

38 Mr Justice Morgan: *ibid.*, as quoted by Judge Furst at op. cit 36 paragraph 89.

39 [2002] WASC 286.

40 Hasluck J: ibid., as quoted by Judge Furst, *supra note, at* 36 paragraph 90.

41 *Ibid.*, at paragraph 91.

parties as seen in such cases as *Philips Electronique Grand Public SA and Another v British Sky Broadcasting Limited*.[42] From the previous discussion it is clear English law demonstrates a conflicting and ambivalent approach to the concept of good faith, being a discussion widely driven by a classical view of contracting as an individualistic process. Even when a more co-operative approach to contracting is adopted the courts are reluctant to allow an unrestricted construct of good faith.

IV. DOES THE RESTRICTED APPROACH TO GOOD FAITH ACCORD WITH PRACTICE?

This chapter contends that to adopt a predominantly formalistic, individualistic and competitive approach to express duties to negotiate in good faith changes to long-term outsourcing agreements is inappropriate. It is unsuited as it assumes a utility-maximising model.

Various empirical studies suggest that such individualistic behaviour does not in fact predominate when changes to long-term agreements take place in practice. Rather the parties to such complex and interdependent relationship agreements engage in long-term co-operative behaviour acting as joint maximisers prepared to forego short term individual gains for long term gain (or sophisticated self interest).[43] Parties do so to reinforce their 'mutual expectations that their relationship can and will be maintained in the future' – elements of immediate self interest, mutuality and reciprocity are apparent.[44] An empirical study of local governmental outsourcing arrangements has shown the parties use "specialised relational governance features drawing upon economic inter-dependence and the joint maximising potential of the relationship."[45]

[42] [1995] EMLR 472. Here the Court of Appeal refused to imply terms into agreement between Philips and British Sky Broadcasting (BSB) whereby Philips agreed to develop and manufacture 80,000 TV set-top satellite receivers and to thereafter maintain capacity to produce a minimum of 1,110,000 receivers over a further period of 31 months. Some 18 months into the agreement, and following BSBs failure to obtain a significant share of the UK satellite TV market and its subsequent merger with Sky, BSB announced its intention to switch to alternative set-top receivers in order for its UK customers to receive Sky satellite TV. Philips sought compensation by requesting a declaration that implied terms be imposed into the agreement. The court held that its power to imply terms was an extraordinary and intrusive power that should not be applied lightly. It was material that comprehensive agreement had been written that dealt with some risks but not the risk that the BSB operation would be a commercial flop. It was by no means clear how the parties would have dealt with that risk if they had contemplated it. Accordingly it was improper for the court to imply such a risk allocation in the absence of express provisions by the parties.

[43] David Campbell and Donald Harris, *Flexibility in Long-term Contractual Relationships: The Role of Co-operation*, 20 JOURNAL OF LAW AND SOCIETY 166, 166–191 (1993).

[44] Brendan Burchell and Frank Wilkinson, *Trust, Business Relationships and the Contractual Environment*, 21 CAMBRIDGE JOURNAL OF ECONOMICS 217, 219 (1997).

[45] See *supra note* 6, at p. 1.

In contrast, some studies suggest that although contracts may be entered into, many parties rely on non-contractual co-operative relations rather than contractual relations.[46] However, it is suggested the contracts in those studies often differed in nature from the complex interdependent outsourcing arrangements considered in this chapter. Long-term repeat supply arrangements for discrete off-the-shelf goods with the possibility of ready competition supply and purchase elsewhere will arguably adopt very different governance structures from heavily interdependent arrangements where complex services requiring multiple interfaces are provided; where limited competing service providers may be available; and/or where easy and low-cost migration to another service provider is not an option. Every outsourcing contract will have different contractual governance mechanisms given the nature of the contract and the relationships established under it. 'The complex inter-relation of contractual and extra-contractual practices revealed in the research cast doubt on the opposition sometimes drawn between contractual and non-contractual relations.'[47]

As has been seen earlier in this chapter, long-term and complex outsourcing agreements are, by their nature, thick with a web of complex relations and interfaces. Joint maximisation and enlightened self-interest behaviours prevail. As such it is suggested a less adversarial and more co-operative approach to the construct of good faith should apply to reflect the reasonable expectations of the parties to those relations more readily. In beginning to understand this contention, a relational contract law view may help.[48] Before considering how that view would shape such a duty, it is first necessary to consider relational contract theory briefly.

V. THEORY OF RELATIONAL CONTRACT

Ian Macneil's formulation of relational contract theory (or what he eventually called his 'essential contract theory') suggests that for contracts to be analysed and considered properly, they must always be viewed first in the context of the social relations surrounding them.[49] The theory identifies ten social norms or behaviours

[46] See for example Stewart Macaulay, Non-Contractual Relations in Business: A Preliminary Study, 45 AMERICAN SOCIOLOGICAL REVIEW, 55–69 (1963); Hugh Beale and Tony Dugdale, Contracts between Businessmen: Planning and the Use of Contractual Remedies, i 2 BRITISH JOURNAL OF LAW AND SOCIETY, 45–60 (1975).

[47] See *supra note* 6, at p. 12

[48] In doing so this chapter adopts a device used by others. For example Feinmann views relational contract law theory as an important prism which traditional contract law can use to ensure it is sensitive to context. See: Jay M Feinmann, Relational Contract Theory in Context, 94 NORTHWESTERN L. REVIEW. 737, 737–748 (1999).

[49] See his brief summary of his theory in: Ian R Macneil, *Reflections on Relational Contract theory after a Neo-classical Seminar*, in IMPLICIT DIMENSIONS OF CONTRACT, pp. 207–217, (D. Campbell, H. Collins and J. Wightman eds., Hart Publishing: Oxford and Portland, Oregon 2003).

that can, to a greater or lesser extent, be observed at play in all contracts, namely: role integrity; reciprocity; implementation of planning; effectuation of consent; flexibility; contractual solidarity; restitution, reliance and expectation; creation and restraint of power; propriety of means; and harmonisation with the particular social matrix. The theory contends that the relations behind all contracts (whether one-off spot contracts or complex, long-term and highly interdependent agreements) should be analysed to establish which of the ten behaviours predominate. It argues that this analysis 'makes it possible to determine what circumstances should or should not be taken into account in dealing with such transactions. In addition, a relational approach can yield a better understanding of the more discrete aspects of the transactions such as express terms.'[50] It therefore contends that 'a combined contextual analysis of relations and transactions is more efficient and produces a more complete and sure final analytical product than does commencing with a non-contextual analysis'.[51] It therefore asserts, 'Recognition and consideration of all significant relational elements becomes particularly essential where the subject of the examination is behavioural aspects, such as structuring of contractual relations in which transactions occur, including all questions of law pertinent to them.'[52]

Macneil observed that in heavily relational contracts – where interdependence is high – the contractual norms of role integrity, contractual solidarity, harmonisation of relational contracts, propriety of means and the role of other supra-contract norms predominate.[53] Role integrity (requiring consistency and involving internal conflict) becomes very complex to reflect the complex and multiple, formal and informal, social and customary, and expected and otherwise relations in existence. Equally this norm supports and expands the contractual solidarity norm requiring the preservation of certain individuals as members of certain relationships. To try to reduce conflict, harmonisation is required – encompassing precision and focus, adherence to planning and the need for flexibility in response to changed circumstances. Propriety of means – norms concerning the way ends may or may not be achieved – becomes complex and varied, and multiple principles and practices may need to be adopted. Underpinning these predominant norms, the contractual norms of flexibility, planning, restitution, reliance and expectation and creation and restraint of power also carry important roles.

50 *Ibid.*, at p. 217.

51 Ian Macneil, *Relational Contract Theory: Challenges and Theories*, in THE RELATIONAL THEORY OF CONTRACT: SELECTED WORKS OF IAN MACNEIL 368 (I. MacNeil & D. Campbell eds., Modern Legal Studies: London 2001).

52 *Ibid.*, at 373.

53 Ian Macneil, *Values in Contract: External and Internal*, in THE RELATIONAL THEORY OF CONTRACT: SELECTED WORKS OF IAN MACNEIL 163–165 (I. MacNeil & D. Campbell eds. Modern Legal Studies: London 2001).

It is submitted that the needs of the long-term relational outsourcing contracts described at the beginning of this chapter meet this view. A study of a particular local government outsourcing contract supports this observation:

> The tendering process was unusually thorough and the contract meticulously planned but in a highly relational manner with extensive negotiation and consultation between the parties even at the pre-tender stages.... The cooperative relationship that had already been established pre-award continued to develop post-award through joint collaboration in refining and implementing the contract. The relationship exhibited elements not just of previous hierarchical relations but of a form of solidarity that might be said to stem from the peculiar mutual dependencies of individuals under 'clan conditions'.[54]

This therefore raises the question that if the law is to be mindful of the interdependence and complex relationships underpinning long-term outsourcing agreements, what particular construct of good faith could the law adopt to reflect the mutuality and inter-dependence of such relationships?

VI. A CONSTRUCT OF GOOD FAITH AS SEEN THROUGH A RELATIONAL PRISM

Before setting out an alternative construct of good faith in this section, the limits of the construct proposed and the context within which this concept is to be used should be made clear. The construct is suggested as a good faith requirement rather than as a good faith regime[55] for use only in relation to the complex long-term outsourcing contracts. Its applicability in other situations and contexts is outside the scope of this chapter. It is suggested it applies only if an express duty to negotiate change in good faith is included within the contractual mechanisms to which the parties agreed. It is not intended to have a wider or more dynamic role suggesting a duty to negotiate all changes in good faith should always be implied or imposed upon such relations. Further empirical studies may be required before such a proposal can be made.

In adopting a relational contract law view it is not suggested that the parties should always reach agreement on the change whatever the cost to them – they may not and they must remain free ultimately to fail to agree. A lack of agreement may have varying consequences for their relationship with differing results – but relational contract law does not suggest co-operation to the complete exclusion of

[54] See *supra note* 6, at p. 9.

[55] Roger Brownsword, Positive, Negative, Neutral: *The Reception of Good Faith in English Contract Law*, in GOOD FAITH IN CONTRACT, 34–38 (R. Brownsword, N. J. Hird and G. Howells eds., Ashgate Publishing: Aldershot, 1999).

competition. Nor does it require the parties always to put the others' needs before their own. The joint maximisation or enlightened self-interest behaviour referred to previously does not require the parties to forsake their own interests in their entirety. In the spirit of joint maximisation, however, a balance between co-operation and competition is required.[56] Such balance is necessary to imbue the construct with a backcloth of the context within which it sits. In that sense the construct is suggested as an example of a developed concept of private autonomy.[57]

A. *The Extent of the Duty*

Given the mutuality and interdependence of the relationship, it is suggested that any express duty to negotiate in good faith changes to long-term outsourcing contracts could be shaped so as to require the following obligations:

- To commence negotiations.
- Not to enter dishonestly into negotiations never intending to reach an agreement.[58]
- To enter negotiations with an open mind – prepared to listen to suggestions proposed by the other side and to respond with suggestions to them.[59]
- Not to ignore the other's suggestions – to consider each of them before deciding whether or not to reach an agreement.
- To consider each suggestion in the spirit of co-operation and mutuality.
- To act consistently with the negotiation in other dealings under the outsourcing agreement with the other party.
- Not to act with fraud.
- Not to misrepresent.
- To disclose to the other side such information as may be required consistently with any benchmarking, audit or "most favoured customer status" obligations required by the outsourcing agreement.
- Not to withdraw from negotiations without giving the other party an opportunity to respond.[60]
- If withdrawing from the negotiations, to say why, giving truthful reasons.[61]

[56] See *supra note* 48, at p. 747.

[57] John Wightman, *Good Faith and Pluralism in the Law of Contract*, in GOOD FAITH IN CONTRACT 177 (R. Brownsword, N. J. Hird and G. Howells eds., Ashgate Publishing: Aldershot, 1999).

[58] Lord Justice Steyn, *Contract law: Fulfilling the Reasonable Expectations of Honest Men*, 113 LAW QUATERLY REVIEW 433, at p. 439 (2009).

[59] Alan Berg, *Promises to Negotiate in Good Faith*, 119 LAW QUARTERLY REVIEW, 357, at p. 363 (2003).

[60] *Ibid.*

[61] *Ibid.*

- If withdrawing from negotiations, not to do so knowing the reasons for withdrawal given are not something the other party could not reasonably accept.[62]

It is *not* suggested such a construct would go so far as to require the party to put the other party's interests always above his own during the course of the negotiations. However, ground could be given up during the negotiations if the disutility of the concession given were less than the disutility of failing to reach an agreement. Co-operative gestures could also be made in the course of such negotiations.[63] However, should negotiations fail, gaps in the continuing contract may arise. Failure to agree to a particular change would not prevent a party from taking up an opportunity previously offered to be forsaken by it during the negotiations in respect of that change.[64] However, such an action might nevertheless lead to tensions and conflicts elsewhere in the remaining relationship.

B. Criticisms of the Construct

It is anticipated some would object to such a construct of good faith, suggesting it would necessarily require the courts to enquire as to the subjective and actual intent of the parties during negotiations. However, to do so is to ignore the constraints placed upon the obligations by their wording and by the bounds imposed by the norms of the particular relationship. The obligations have been, so far as possible, limited to establishing dishonest and uncooperative behaviour. English courts have little trouble establishing dishonesty. [65] The question of non-cooperation is more illusory but Wightman's theory of contextual good faith in commercial dealings would help here. It would restrict the courts to considering closely the nature and context of the contractual and commercial relationship to allow both 'calculability' and 'normative accuracy'.[66] The usefulness of the construct "lies precisely in its relationship to concrete environment of practices and values."[67] Such constraints would ensure the duty is tightly bound and fetter the courts' discretion, thereby going a long way to avoid fears of visceral justice.[68] Such an approach would also ensure a level of normative transparency to the parties involved (and their advisers) by allowing a

[62] *Ibid.*

[63] See *supra note* 55, at p. 29

[64] Steven J. Burton, *Breach of Contract and the Common Law Duty to Perform in Good Faith*, 94 HARVARD L. REV. 369–403 (1980).

[65] See *supra note* 58, at p. 438.

[66] See *supra note* 57, at pp. 42–52.

[67] Thomas Wilhelmsson, *Good Faith and the Duty of Disclosure in Commercial Contracting – The Nordic Experience*, in GOOD FAITH IN CONTRACT 185 (R. Brownsword, N. J. Hird and G. Howells eds., Ashgate Publishing: Aldershot, 1999).

[68] Michael Bridge, *Good Faith in Commercial Contracts*, in GOOD FAITH IN CONTRACT 140 (R. Brownsword, N. J. Hird and G. Howells eds., Ashgate Publishing: Aldershot, 1999).

clear reference to the contextual expectations of the parties and the communities in which the relationship is founded. In doing so it allows them some probability in forecasting how the courts would view such a concept. Such a concept also has the added advantage of recognising only a system of internal morals prescribed by the relationship and the communities within which it is set. The construct thereby prevents the imposition of any of a number of differing external moral standards.

That such a context-specific approach will lead to different outcomes in different contexts is not in debate. After all, in a "contextual approach, every case is different",[69] but that would not by itself make the law uncertain. Instead, over time, patterns and working trends will appear and although all may differ in their substance they will all fulfil a common theme – that of being consistent with the recognition of the reasonable expectations of the parties in that context.[70] Some might argue that the need for certainty is still sacrosanct, but English law is accustomed to dealing with fractured rules and to developing rules in specific contexts to deal with otherwise vague concepts such as fairness and justice.

C. *Should Such a Construct Be Accepted?*

It is suggested there are many reasons why the proposed construct of good faith should be accepted. A limited construct imposed upon an express obligation to negotiate in good faith in a pre-existing and binding contract is not contrary to the parties' autonomy or their freedom to contract. Rather it confirms and extends the bargain they entered into at the time of their contract. Both freely agreed to it and both have a legitimate expectation to enter into negotiations in good faith to agree a change:

> Common human behaviour patterns are seldom if ever pointless, and this is no exception. In general parties probably use this technique because they are not yet prepared to agree on details which will require agreement, but they want to emphasise to each other that resolution will be required and to express a willingness to engage in the process of agreement at the appropriate time.[71]

This legitimate expectation also illustrates the expectations of trust and co-operation between the parties. Expectations which they implicitly agreed to by entering into an outsourcing contract include such governance mechanisms. For

69 Stewart Macaulay, *The Real and the Paper Deal: Empirical Pictures of Relationships, Complexity and the Urge for Transparent Simple Rules*, in IMPLICIT DIMENSIONS OF CONTRACT, 59 (D. Campbell, H. Collins and J. Wightman eds., Hart Publishing: Oxford and Portland, Oregon 2003).

70 See *supra note* 67.

71 Ian Macneil, *A Primer of Contract Planning*, in THE RELATIONAL THEORY OF CONTRACT: SELECTED WORKS OF IAN MACNEIL 223 (I. MacNeil & D. Campbell eds., Modern Legal Studies: London 2001).

those suspicious of good faith, it is a limited construct. It does not seek to allow good faith to be used generally or in a dynamic fashion. Rather it is a normative construct embedded in and bounded by the context of the particular relationship. Morals are imposed but only those internal to that relationship. The principle of legitimate expectations also reinforces the principle of loyalty to the relationship and makes the relationship central to a court's consideration of the duty.

It is argued that it is important that the courts not refuse to give meaningful effect to such an express duty; to do so would be to deny the reasonable expectations of the reasonable man. Such an approach is in danger of bringing the law into disrepute. The very nature of the complex long-term contracts that are the subject of this chapter is that their future cannot be predicted in its entirety. Variations can and will happen: some will be foreseen; some will not; some may be certain; some may not; but the parties cannot include all possibilities in an exhaustive contract and provide for all eventualities at the time of signing it. All the parties can do is plan for changes and put in place various mechanisms to try to deal with them. What is the point of including such express governance mechanisms in such contracts if they are to be ignored by the courts?

Courts should, so far as possible and in line with their doctrines and general principles, support the autonomy of the contracting parties by upholding the contracts they have entered into freely. It is inappropriate for courts to fail to recognise expressly agreed and cooperatively based provisions in relationship contracts of this sort. It is erroneous for the courts to determine disputes that arise in contracts including co-operative constructs using purely adversarial constructs.[72]

VII. CONCLUSION

This chapter has identified the nature of long-term relational contracts that form its subject, the complex web of relations and interfaces that underpin some of them, and has speculated as to some of the changes that may occur to them during the course of their contract term. It has also considered some of the co-operative governance mechanisms that the parties may include in their contracts to deal with uncertain change. Some such devices include an express obligation to negotiate variations in good faith.

This poses a dilemma for English contract law: English law has traditionally been suspicious of the concept of good faith. An examination by this chapter of the case law considering the doctrine of good faith in negotiation of change has illustrated that English law is ambivalent to such a duty and has generally permitted only a limited recognition of a duty of good faith. That recognition is founded on a

[72] See *supra note* 55, at pp. 31 to 32.

classical and individualistic view of contracting. However, this does not reflect the co-operative model that empirical studies have found in the practices of parties to such long-term relational contracts. This chapter suggests that reconceptualising those change control devices to situate them in a relational contract theory view of law will more closely align the contracting relationships with the norms and behaviours observed in the practice of them. This chapter has gone on to use a relational contract prism to suggest a particular construct of good faith that may apply to an express obligation of good faith imposed in governance mechanisms concerning the agreement of change in contracts of this type.

This co-operative model is intended to be limited and specific in its application. However, it is suggested that in adopting such a concept it allows English contract law to be more faithful to the co-operation and enlightened self interest that occur in such relations. It does not require the parties to subjugate entirely their own interests but it does allow English law to recognise a system of contract that is not totally adversarial in its approach. In doing so, it is suggested, it is more faithful to the practices and expectations of the contracting parties. Most importantly, it is truthful to English contract law's need to fulfil the reasonable and legitimate expectations of reasonable men.

PART IV

Implied Terms and Interpretation

This part examines the key area of contract interpretation. All contracts, no matter how highly specified, are incomplete in some way. Classical contract law would see severe contractual incompleteness as uncorrectable and proclaim that any such agreement is unenforceable. Modern contract law recognizes the variety and complexity of the contractual landscape and sees incompleteness as endemic in contractual transactions. Thus, modern contract law, especially as formulated in the American Uniform Commercial Code and as applied by analogy in American common law, is much more aggressive in overcoming contractual incompleteness in cases where contractual intent is clear. The need to interpret contracts and to fill in gaps by the implication of terms covers numerous scenarios including, contractual ambiguity, strategic or intentional incompleteness, and the occurrence of unintended events. The English and American common law of contracts respond in similar ways, but not to the same degree.

Chapter 10 explores the implication of terms from the England and Wales' common law perspectives. It asserts that because of the limited recognition of good faith in these jurisdictions, the implication of terms acts as a surrogate for good faith. It further argues that the implication of terms must work within a framework similar to a rules-based system – terms can be or must not be implied in certain contexts. In this way, the neutrality of implied term is maintained.

Chapter 11 reviews the different methods or approaches to contractual interpretation including, contextualism, purposivism, consequentialism, formalism, and literalism. It then focuses on the implication of terms and contract interpretation through a consequentialist interpretive methodology. It uses a law and economics approach that asks: "Given the words the parties used, what is the best (surplus maximizing) interpretation of the bargain?" Despite the law and economics approach forwarded in the chapter, it argues that a more expansive rule of interpretation is needed that is not captured by textualism or formalism. In the end, the chapter answers a multitude of questions relating to the different interpretative methodologies reviewed, and the role, if any, of contractual intent in the interpretation of contracts.

10

Implied Terms in English Contract Law

Richard Austen-Baker

The law of England and Wales, in respect of contracts, recognizes no general doctrine of good faith, such as exists in other jurisdictions. Nevertheless, various doctrines and techniques in the law, for instance misrepresentation, mistake, duress, and implied terms, are frequently seen as playing specialized roles in securing at least a minimum level of good faith. This chapter considers implied terms from this perspective and argues that they certainly have been used in this way but that, as a technique, implication of terms is neutral, in no small part because of the double-edged nature of the rules (term can be/must not be implied in given circumstances). Decisions which decline to imply a term are as telling about the technique's tendency to secure good faith outcomes as those in which a term is actually implied.

I. INTRODUCTION

This chapter will consider the development and role of the implied term in English law. This topic raises questions that are historical, theoretical and practical in scope.

The implied term has a long history in English contract law. So long, in fact, that it is not feasible to establish when or in what area of law it made its first appearance: the frequent tendency of the old judges (or perhaps just the old reporters) to omit any reference to authority when stating the law[1] is very unhelpful for the would-be historian attempting to trace from case to case. The best we can do, really, is to look for the earliest incidences we can find. We can also, with some hesitation, speculate

[1] Indeed, also unhelpful is the tendency of old reporters simply to make up the judge's reasoning to make the case support and illustrate a particular principle (in much the same way a modern textbook writer offers hypothetical scenarios supported by a reference to a real case on very different facts), hence, we believe, the notorious differences in reasoning reported in the Campbell and the Espinasse reports of *Stilk* v. *Myrick*.

based on the language employed by judges when speaking of particular implied terms and combine this with what we know about the social importance of particular areas of law at different times.

The theoretical basis is problematic in that the phenomenon of the implied term can be justified in different ways according to one's preferred standpoint. Some, but not all, of these can be reconciled with the history we know or can reasonably confidently construct. The degree to which different justifications can be reconciled with history does not necessarily make any difference to their respective validity, depending upon the purpose of the theory: a theory as to how they came to be must necessarily depend for its validity upon being thus reconcilable; a theory as to why we ought to have them or ought to continue to use them need not be the least bit reconcilable with history.

The current state of affairs in respect of implied terms is also a practical issue in the sense of an issue upon which practitioners might have definite opinions driven by their professional experience. This relates both to defining the 'rules' on implied terms and to the desirability of widespread or frequent recourse to implication and to how one ought to draught contracts (as completely as possible or as loosely as feasible?). The author has attempted elsewhere to state the 'rules',[2] and in any event it would be hopeless to discuss such a detailed question in a chapter of this nature.

II. THE HISTORICAL DEVELOPMENT OF THE IMPLIED TERM

The author tried recently to trace the origins of the implied term. It was a rather hubristic enterprise, since Brian Simpson had already tried and failed. The author failed, too. The reason for this, as already alluded to in the introduction to this chapter, is the broad unsupported judicial statements that the implication in question was well established. It is not doubted that in fact the implication in such cases was well established, but judicial accuracy in this respect was nevertheless unhelpful in our quest. That said, the author believes it is possible to make some meaningful and perhaps useful hypotheses from such evidence as we do have coupled with general historical context.

A. *Historical Context*

In this chapter, we intend to ground the discussion in a historical context, which would be characterized as having undergone a series of transformations in terms of the centre of social-economic-political gravity. For a very long time the principal

[2] Richard Austen-Baker, IMPLIED TERMS IN ENGLISH CONTRACT LAW (Edward Elgar: Cheltenham and Northampton Mass., 2011).

social, political and economic underpinning was land. Land brought wealth (and wealth got in other ways was quickly put into land), power and social position (really all the same thing at the time). Trades were highly regulated and bound in custom, which only slowly evolved. Markets were likewise highly regulated and bound in custom. Neither trades nor trade was really central to the English economy (though they were central concerns in the cities, of course, which, excepting London, were all quite small until relatively recently). Even where manufacture, especially of cloth and clothing, was a significant part of local economies, land remained the dominant signifier and conferrer of social and political authority.

In 1696 Gregory King estimated that in 1688 merchants and traders, shopkeepers and tradesmen and artisans and handicraftsmen amounted to 110,000 households totalling 484,000 persons (including their servants), with income totalling £6.6 millions. Those whose income was based on land, however, accounted for 346,586 households (excluding cottagers, paupers, etc.), totalling (including their servants) 1,935,520 with an income totalling £23,725,800.[3] King estimated that 50 percent of all income was from agriculture alone, which is close to modern estimates for that time of 43 percent.[4] Somewhat more than half the population consisted of 'common seamen, labouring people and out-servants, cottagers and paupers, common soldiers and vagrants' meaning that of an estimated population of 5.5 millions, the poor (excluding in-servants) amounted to 2,795,000, leaving 2,675,500 'productive' (as King saw it) people, of whom 1,935,520 drew their income from the land. It becomes starker if we bear in mind that merchants and shopkeepers, and so on, would have had most of their workmen counted in with their households, so that the 1,275,000 labouring people and out-servants would have mostly been labourers on land and out-servants to the landed (e.g., gamekeepers, gardeners) and the 1,300,000 cottagers and paupers would mostly be tied into rural communities and economies, giving a rural and landed economy accounting for probably 4 millions of a population of 5.5 millions. If that were the case today, I suspect Parliament would have been readier to ban football than to ban hunting in 2005.

Later, trade and manufacturing became more concentrated and significant and began to take over from the agricultural economy as the main economic drivers. By 1803, shopkeepers and tradesmen had increased from 40,000 to some 74,500 households (totalling 372,500 persons), and artisans and handicraftsmen and their employees had risen from 60,000 to some 445,726 households (2,005,767 persons

[3] Gregory King's Estimate 'Calculated for the Year 1688' reproduced in Dorothy George, ENGLAND IN TRANSITION (Pelican: London, 1953). The author has included Bishops and Clergymen in with landed interests because their incomes were primarily derived from glebe lands, land taxes and the granting of interests in land in the form of rectories (greater tithes) and vicarages (lesser tithes).

[4] Asa Briggs, A SOCIAL HISTORY OF ENGLAND (BCA: London, 1984) at 200.

in all).[5] Later still, trade and manufacturing required ever-larger staffs of employees in each individual enterprise. To facilitate the growth of enterprises, legislation was passed in 1856 and again in 1862 consolidating rules on joint stock companies but, none the less, Briggs has observed that 'as late as the 1880s there were, for example, only four limited liability companies in Birmingham' and 'as late as 1882, the paid-up capital of all the companies quoted on the London Stock Exchange was only £64 million out of a total of £5,800 million'.[6] All the same, trade, commerce and industry had taken over from agriculture and landholding as the main economic drivers and in due course the effects were to tell. 'In 1873 four-fifths of the land [in England] was held by 7,000 individuals, peers prominent among them'.[7] But the 1880s were to see the beginning of the end for the dominance of the landed interest, as David Cannadine explained at length in his *Decline and Fall of the British Aristocracy*.[8] One could go into this in considerable detail, but the trend was for the rise of a business plutocracy, the retrenchment of landed holdings, and the shift of property-based fortunes either into other assets or else at least away from rural land.[9]

B. *Creation of Implied Terms*

One might, then, expect that the first implied terms related to the ownership and tenancy of land, followed by terms related to buying and selling trade goods and terms related to shipping and insurance, then an access of terms touching the relationship of master and servant. Is this, then, what one does one find?

The answer is, I think, only partially. Implied terms relating to land-based transactions or relations seem to be relatively thin on the ground and not of any ancient date. There is a minor flurry of activity in the early nineteenth century. In *Baker v. Holtpzaffel*[10] a tenant tried to persuade the court that he should not be liable for continuing rent when the premises had burned down but was unsuccessful (the court, Lord Mansfield C.J. and Heath J., holding that the land was still there and the tenant had not yielded it up to the landlord for rebuilding). In *Edwards v. Hetherington*[11] Lord Abbott C.J. allowed a tenant the right to throw up a tenancy in mid period without proper notice where the state of the premises was sufficiently problematic

5 Colquhoun's Estimate based on 1801 census returns and the Pauper Returns of 1803. See Dorothy Gregory, *supra* note 3.

6 Asa Briggs, *supra* note 4 at 271. He does not, however, say how the £5,800 million was computed.

7 *Id.*, at 315.

8 David Cannadine, DECLINE AND FALL OF THE BRITISH ARISTOCRACY (Yale UP: New Haven, Conn., 1990).

9 Those particularly interested should see Cannadine's book, see especially chapter 3 and appendices A and H.

10 (1811) 4 Taunt. 45; 128 ER 244.

11 (1825) 7 Dow. & Ry KB 117; Ry & M. 268; 171 ER 1016.

and the tenant was not under an obligation to repair. But *Edwards v. Hetherington* was overruled in *Hart v. Windsor*[12] in which a clear distinction was drawn between furnished and unfurnished lettings: in the former but not the latter case a term of habitability could be implied as in *Smith v. Marrable*.[13] None of these seems to be rooted in long-standing authority.

The case seems to be otherwise with sales. According to Brian Simpson, 'in sale of goods the original position was *caveat emptor*' and that 'on an *express* warranty if one had been given, it was possible to sue in tort for deceit'.[14] The *caveat emptor* rule applied as much to title as to quality or conformity with description. The earliest reported case identified by Simpson where an action was brought on the contract for breach of an express warranty as to title was *Stuart v. Wilkins*,[15] as late as 1778, but Simpson states that the practice began around 1750. However, he also dates the beginning of the gradual erosion of the insistence on an express warranty to the case of *Medina v. Stoughton* (1700)[16] and opines that 'by the time of the decision in *Eichholz v. Bannister* (1864)[17] the exception had for all practical purposes eaten up the rule'.[18]

The implied terms in the Sale of Goods Act have their origins in the common law. The original position appears to have been caveat emptor,[19] but this was clearly not considered particularly satisfactory as markets became more sophisticated. Simpson dated the erosion of the requirement of express warranty as to title to *Medina v. Stoughton* in 1770 but as early as 1688, in the case of *Crosse v. Gardner*[20] it was held that a warranty of title was to be inferred from mere affirmation and the surrounding circumstances. *Crosse v. Gardner* concerned a sale of oxen. There was no express warranty of title, but the court held that mere affirmation amounted to a warranty that the defendant was entitled to sell, since the oxen were in his possession and the plaintiff had no way of knowing of the rights of another, the true owner, who in fact recovered the oxen from the plaintiff. It is, however, all made much clearer in *Medina v. Stoughton* itself, some twelve years later. In this case, the defendant sold

12 (1843) 12 M. & W. 68; 152 ER 1114.

13 (1843) 11 M. & W. 5; 152 ER 693.

14 Brian Simpson, *Historical Introduction* in Michael Furmston, CHESHIRE, FIFOOT AND FURMSTON'S LAW OF CONTRACT *Cheshire*, 15th ed. (OUP: Oxford, 2007), 17.

15 (1778) 6 Doug. KB 18; 99 ER 15. The case concerned a mare sold at Hatfield, Hertfordshire for £31 10s and warranted sound, but in fact suffering from windgalls and therefore unsound.

16 1 Salk. 210; 1 Ld Raym. 593; 91 ER 1297. This concerned the sale of a lottery ticket represented as belonging to the seller but in fact belonging to another. This early national lottery was for a prize of £1 million, with tickets at £10 each (well over £600 at today's prices).

17 17 CBNS 708; 144 ER 284. Sale of printed cloth pieces displayed in a warehouse. Display of goods in a shop or warehouse was held to imply a warranty that the seller is the owner of the goods.

18 Simpson, *supra* note 14, at 17.

19 See, for example, *Deering v. Farrington* (1675) 3 Keble 303; 84 ER 734.

20 (1688) Carthew 90; 90 ER 656.

what he claimed to be his lottery ticket to the plaintiff but actually it belonged to a third party. The court dismissed the defendant's argument that he bought it bona fide then sold it to the plaintiff, Holt C.J. holding that 'where one having the possession of any personal chattel sells it, the bare affirming it to be his amounts to a warranty, and an action lies on the affirmation, for his having the possession is a colour of title, and perhaps no other title can be made out'.[21] Here it is not the content of the term, which is implied, but the nature of the statement: what would be a bare affirmation becomes, by a process of implication, a warranty.

We only really begin to see implication of terms in employment contracts from about the middle of the nineteenth century, an early example being *Harmer v. Cornelius* (1858)[22] which implied a warranty on the employee's part that he possesses the necessary skills for the job. The cases begin to come more thickly in the late nineteenth century and early twentieth century but really thick and fast in about the past thirty years. The late development of implication in employment contracts can doubtless be put down to a complex of factors, for instance the perception of master and servant as a status relationship, the large proportion of working people who were in apprenticeship which was seen, officially at least, as a master-pupil rather than master-servant arrangement (though the reality was often quite different, as will be seen below). The essential feature, at any rate, seems likely to be relative rarity of employment contracts of the sort we might broadly recognize today until after the middle of the nineteenth century.

To understand why this is, one must understand a little of the processes of what is apt to be called 'the industrial revolution'. The picture typically presented to the popular reader or viewer, or to the schoolchild, is of a romantic rural idyll in which each person plied his (or her) trade on his own account and got a fair price for his work. Then came big ugly factories owned by wicked capitalists who built around them hellish townscapes and imprisoned the poor as wage slaves. This picture is not entirely an accurate representation. Certainly some villagers did pursue a trade on their own account: every little town and every village of noticeable size would have its tailor and its shoemaker, its alewife and its blacksmith, and so on. But these cottagers were mostly very poor. A cottage became legally defined, in effect, as a dwelling with less than four acres of land. Many had much less and many none at all but merely a right (or pretended right) to graze a cow or a horse on the manorial waste. Many cottages were illegally erected: effectively shanty settlements.[23] A moment's thought will tell us that the tailor and the shoemaker did not grow rich and fat from satisfying the demand for high-fashion from other poor villagers (and the Lord

21 (1770) 1 Salk. 210, 210; 91 ER 188.

22 5 CBNS 236 (CP); [1843–60] All ER Rep. 624.

23 See, generally, ASA BRIGGS, *supra* note 4, chapter 6 and Edward P. Thompson, WHIGS AND HUNTERS: THE ORIGIN OF THE BLACK ACT (Allen Lane: London, 1975), chapters 1 and 2.

would undoubtedly patronize the tailors of London or some other great town). The charge for beer could not be much, because the customers had not the money to pay very much. At best, incomes of about twelve shillings a week would come to the industrious cottager. The spinners and weavers and knitters and dyers were not cottage industrialists. They did not work on their own account and sell their output into the market. They were out-workers to capitalists of the various cloth trades (which dominated English industry for centuries). The work would arrive (or, quite often, not) and they would work long into the night (if they were lucky enough to have sufficient work), ruining their eyesight for inadequate piece-rates, until they had to throw themselves on the parish, being too decrepit or blind to work. Often there was some machinery involved (e.g., stocking frames) which it was customary for them to rent from the clothier, rent which was payable whether or not any work was supplied.

It was workers in these types of trades, not the independent tradesmen and craftsmen who gradually concentrated into factories (the first of which actually date to long before the traditional start date of the 'industrial revolution', namely, 1760: there was a famous silk mill in Derby from the late seventeenth century, and it is recorded that Thomas Bell, a Gloucester clothier, made a factory out of a Dominican priory which he obtained in the dissolution of the monasteries, in the 1540s).[24] This home-based piece-work economy actually survived to a very large extent well into the nineteenth century: the boom in demand for English cloth and other wares allowing for a vast growth in factories and towns without eliminating the scope for out-workers based in the countryside. Whilst the percentage of the population living in rural areas (according to census returns) declined from 76.2 percent in 1801 to 22 percent in 1901, actual numbers were fairly static over the long term, actually growing very slightly: 6.78 millions in 1801, 8.22 millions in 1841, 7.69 millions in 1871 and 7.81 millions in 1901 (though out-working doubtless did decline during this period whilst domestic service in rural houses increased, with ever more elaborate staffs being demanded at the big houses).

Therefore, it remained the case that a lot of work *for* the factory owners and other 'industrialists' was done out-of-house by what we should call 'independent contractors'. Again, much employment was of apprentices. Apprentices' indentures made some of them; children of better-off parents, entered into a desirable and profitable trade under a master in receipt of a considerable premium – Dorothy George cites £1,000 for a City merchant, £100 for a surgeon or apothecary – genuinely pupils.

[24] Asa Briggs, *supra* note 4 at164. Edward Thompson, writing of the period before the 'industrial revolution' refers to the '…complex society of manufacturing industry and of capitalist agricultural improvement which scholars persist in calling a "pre-industrial" society' (Edward P. Thompson, *The Crime of Anonymity* in D. Hay et al. (eds.), ALBION'S FATAL TREE (Peregrine Books, London: 1977), at 304).

Others, while theoretically pupils, were effectively slave labour: the same source cites the indenture of a poor girl to a family of street hawkers, living in a one-room slum, to be instructed 'in the art of housewifery'. Again, no employment contract as such, as the apprentice was to become, officially at least, the live-in pupil of the master; though there were legal rules governing apprenticeship, such as not to beat or starve the apprentice to death (anything short of that seems pretty much to have been regarded as lawful 'due correction').[25]

The earlier implications into employment contracts, by the way, appear largely to have been duties owed by the employee to the employer. The recent flood of implication has been largely of employers' duties to employees.[26]

Much earlier than any of these implied terms is the implication of assumpsit: that is to say, the implication of a whole contract, where before none had existed. This was done in cases where a plaintiff sought to recover a debt. He could, of course, sue in an action of debt; but this would mean trial by compurgation. Since the burden of proof lies on the plaintiff, the defendant had merely to recruit the necessary number of compurgators (oath-helpers) to swear that he was not indebted to defeat the action. Such oath-helpers were available for hire at the royal courts. An action of assumpsit, however, was tried by jury and therefore much to be preferred. The implication was that, the debt being owed, the defendant had promised to pay it: the separate promise to pay creating an assumpsit. We have implied contracts today, of course, notably in the maritime field, but I suggest that the implication of assumpsit might well be the father of the implied term, though in a reversal of the usual arrangement, the identity of the mother might remain shrouded in mystery.

We have seen that although implied terms tend to appear as particular economic activities come to prominence, this is by no means a linear or necessary process. Land was the most important economic factor long before trade came to its modern dominance, yet land-related contracts do not yield many implied terms nor yet early examples of implied terms. It is also worth noting that whilst land was, outside London anyway, the dominant organizing factor of the English economy, the modern dominant organizing factor of the economy is the corporation and here, too, we see remarkably little implication: it is generally regarded as illegitimate to imply any term whatsoever into articles of association.[27] Our hypothesis, then, is that an increase in the volume or frequency of transactions of a given sort tends to lead to

25 Dorothy George, *supra* note 3, at117ff.

26 See generally Richard Austen-Baker, *supra* note 2 above, chapter 4.

27 The traditional reasoning for this is that investors buy shares on the basis of the published constitution of the company; but this is clearly nonsense and modern judges upholding the rule cannot have thought that it was true, so this was merely a traditional pretext. Recently, Lord Hoffmann has signalled a more flexible approach at least in respect of private companies, but the rule remains nonetheless fairly rigid.

the generation of implied terms, but greater value and significance (in overall economic terms) of individual transactions forming any given class of transactions leads to greater insistence on completeness and formality. This seems to be borne out by the history and seems also to be a common-sense tendency. Accepting this hypothesis has implications for the way we view implication of terms when theorising about contract and potentially for the approach we take to draughting of contracts (and should also affect judicial attitudes to implication as a tool of dispute resolution in court).

III. THEORETICAL CONTEXT

Implication of terms is often spoken of as a method or technique of contractual interpretation or construction.[28] We submit that there is a distinction to be drawn between these two terms: 'interpretation' should be reserved for the process of properly understanding what is there in the contract; 'construction', we venture to suggest, conjures the wider process of understanding the contract as a whole, including its context and the important question of what is not there and why not. Implication of terms is, then, a technique of construction rather than interpretation.

The *Shorter Oxford English Dictionary* carries the following definitions of 'construction', among others.

I. 1. The action of framing, devising, or forming, by the putting together of parts; erection, building …

II. 1. *Gram.* The action of syntactically arranging words in a sentence … **2.** The action of construing; translation … **3.** The construing, explaining or interpreting of a text, statement, action, words, etc…

Of course, when lawyers or jurists speak of the construction of a contract they mean it, as it has already implied, in sense II. 3, but it seems clear that we could very well consciously use it in sense I. We do not do so because, in common law countries certainly, we are wedded to notions of freedom and sanctity of contract. It is for the parties to make their contract and for the courts to enforce it and not, in any circumstances, for the court to make a contract for the parties.

The difference between these two meanings is fundamental to the question of the nature of the process of implication and for what implication of terms says about freedom and sanctity of contract. Is implication of terms merely an exercise in discerning the true intentions of the parties as to the contents of contractual obligations freely entered into, respecting both freedom and sanctity at once? Or is a court, which

[28] This section is in part adapted from Chapter 2 of the author's book IMPLIED TERMS IN ENGLISH CONTRACT LAW, *supra* note 2, which see for a more thorough treatment.

implies a term into a contract engaged in making a contract for the parties? It has often been said that implication of terms is rooted in the intention of the parties. Bowen LJ said as much in *The Moorcock*: 'Now, an implied warranty, or, as it is called, a covenant in law, as distinguished from an express contract or express warranty, really is in all cases founded on the presumed intention of the parties, and upon reason'.[29]

However, this is not an unchallenged position. Elizabeth Peden, writing about terms implied in law states that they are so 'because of the nature of the contract, rather than the supposed intentions of the parties'.[30] But Bowen LJ does not seem to have been speaking only of terms implied in fact. His words do not bear that construction and although *The Moorcock* is today seen primarily as a case about implication in fact, it was also relied upon as importing a term implied in law into contracts of the wharfage and mooring types.[31] The difference is important but may arise from an examination of the issue at two quite different levels and even from using words in different senses. If one says 'this implied term is designed to give effect to the parties' intentions' when speaking of a term implied in law, the statement is true and untrue in a number of different ways. It is untrue if by it we mean 'the court has concluded that in order to give effect to the subjective intentions of these two parties before it, as judged by objective evidence, an implied term must be inserted to this particular effect'. This would be a direct misrepresentation of the process by which the term has been arrived at, for one thing. If, however, we say 'these parties intended to enter into a perfectly normal contract for employing a legal secretary', for instance, then go on to say 'surely, therefore, they must have intended all the usual unspoken terms that you get in such contracts, particularly ones which courts in the past have held to be a necessary incident of contracts of this particular type', then this is quite likely true to some extent at least. The employer, who might well know of such terms, would be expected, in what is normally a contract of adhesion, to have sought to exclude any such normally implied terms that were not wanted. The employee probably would not know of such terms, but equally is likely to want to have all the usual incidents of such contracts and expect the usual burdens as well as benefits. We could also say, with some truth, that 'this term is one which parties *in general* intend to operate within their contractual relation', as opposed to the particular parties involved in the particular contract before the court.

What one sees from an examination of the judgments in such cases is that the judiciary certainly appear to place the strongest emphasis on the intentions of the parties.

[29] (1889) 14 PD 64, 68.

[30] Elizabeth Peden, *Policy Concerns behind Implication of Terms in Law* 117 Law Quarterly Review 459 (2001), at 459.

[31] See further Richard Austen-Baker, *supra* note 2 above, chapter 7.

But judicial rationales are, of course, not always the same as actual reasons. With a theory of contracts, which emphasises party autonomy it is natural to rationalize rules relating to implication of terms in the language of ascertaining the true intentions of the parties.

The underlying viewpoint of English contract law is objectivism. Giving effect to the intention of the parties does not involve an exercise in ascertaining the subjective intentions. The endeavour is always to ascertain objectively what the intentions of the parties were. That is to say, that it is outward appearances that matter. Whether one adopts offeror, offeree or third party objectivity, it must necessarily be assumed that the objective viewer is a reasonable person, since it would clearly be perverse to assume otherwise.

But what where the court is clearly not construing the parties' words but is building a contract from the ground up? This is an extreme case but not without precedent. For instance, the leading case of *Liverpool City Council v. Irwin*,[32] involved a tenancy in writing wherein the only terms concerned the tenant's obligations. The court was not obliged to construct the entirety of the landlord's obligations, no mention of which appeared in the tenancy 'agreement', only to decide whether one of these involved keeping lifts in operation and stairways lit, since this was the substance of the principal complaint. The process is nonetheless a creative one: what the court did was to discover a term implied by law into all tenancies of multiple-occupancy, multiple-storey local authority owned apartment blocks that the landlord had to take reasonable care to ensure the operation of the means of access falling within the common parts of the building.

That of course does not really answer the question in relation to terms implied from custom or trade usage. Where, however, such customs are, as they must be to result in an implied term, notorious, it may be taken that if the parties have not excluded the operation of the term, the implication simply reflects the intention of the parties: there is no need to state expressly what is regarded as automatically part of the deal. Similarly, where a term is implied from a prior course of dealing between the parties, if they have not taken the trouble specifically to indicate that such a term is no longer to be considered part of their deal, it seems probable that they intended to carry on with the same terms. In these cases, then, they are part of the armoury of construction of contracts in the sense of construing the proper meaning of the parties' words and actions.

On the other hand, terms implied by statute are evidently an attempt at imposing either a mandatory or a default solution on the parties to particular types of contracts, but these are a parliamentary rather than a judicial construction of a contract for the parties.

[32] [1977] AC 239.

So, the technique of implication of terms into contracts is both a technique of construction in the sense of construing a contract and a technique of construction in the sense of making a contract for the parties.

The present author has argued elsewhere that implication of terms is one means by which contract law gives effect to various of the relational norms proposed by Macneil.[33]

Viewed through the useful lens of relational contract theory, then, what is the role or position of implication of terms? It is submitted that implied terms are supportive of the norm of implementation of planning, in the sense of enabling effective planning. It is impossible for any party to imagine every possible permutation of circumstances which may arise in the course of the performance of a contract, particularly where the contractual relationship is likely to be complex, involve whole-person relations, or of extended duration. Implication of terms as a gap-filling device enables the implementation of plans according to their broad intention without burdening the planners with the need for omniscience and perfect precognition. The technique can thereby also be said to effectuate the parties' consent.

Implied terms, whether default or mandatory also serve the norm of mutuality or reciprocity by ensuring certain minimum standards (or, if the term is sought to be excluded by an express term, highlighting the want of an acceptable level of reciprocity). The implied terms in the Sale of Goods Act 1979 certainly perform this function to a large extent, and particularly in relation to consumers, since, by virtue of the Unfair Contract Terms Act 1977, they cannot be excluded. By insisting that as good a title as claimed is passed, that the goods conform to description or the bulk corresponds with the sample and that goods are of satisfactory quality, a minimum level of reciprocity is exacted from the seller willy-nilly. Even when there is scope for exclusion of the term by express provision, the attempt to do this clearly puts the buyer on notice to take particular care in proceeding and to demand a lower price, thus normalizing the reciprocation.

In terms of the present author's own version[34] of Macneil's norm-based theory of contractual relations,[35] implied terms serve to support the norms of 'substantial fairness' and 'satisfying performance expectations'.[36] To the extent that there is a norm of substantial fairness (that is to say, rough and approximate fairness, or reasonable reciprocity) in contract, a measure which will always vary according to bargaining

33 Richard Austen-Baker, *A Relational Law of Contract?* 20 Journal of Contract Law (2004) 125.

34 Which he calls "comprehensive contract theory." Ian R. Macneil, *Contracting Worlds and Essential Contract Theory* 9 Social and Legal Studies (2000) 431

35 Which Macneil called "essential contract theory." *Id.*

36 For further explanation see Richard Austen-Baker, *Comprehensive Contract Theory: A Four-Norm Model of Contract Relations* 25 Journal of Contract Law (2009) 216.

position of the parties, and insofar as the technique of implication in one or more of its forms, this chimes in with Peden's argument, alluded to previously, that implied terms serve in England to supply the need met in other jurisdictions by generalized doctrines of good faith in contract.

The argument for the technique of implication of terms rooted in the need to serve norms of contractual relations – in essence, that something needs to be supplied by the law if there are to be as few broken contractual relations as reasonably feasible, be it a doctrine of good faith or implication of terms – only explains them to an extent. The way in which they achieve the ends of helping to ensure substantial fairness and the fulfilment of contractual expectations, thus helping to hold contracts together, are obvious enough to pass without further explanation, but why are the aims desirable (or, why are such norms norms at all?), and why is this a desirable way of achieving them? And can various theories sit together at the same table?

A number of arguments might be posited. One is that really what is being achieved by many implied terms, particularly those implied at common law and by statute, is a species of good faith, but one which sits more easily with the common law's assumption of adversarial bargaining than civilian-type good faith doctrines. This does not answer why good faith needs to be supplied in some way. It is submitted that it is equally sufficient to say that good faith (using the term in a general way) is a good in itself, morally right and therefore ought to be enforced against bad people. Or one could say that insisting on some degree of good faith results in a more efficient distribution of resources, because parties know better what the subject matter of the contract is in fact and can value it more accurately. Or else that if parties are encouraged to act broadly in good faith fewer contracts will break down, particularly litigiously, saving transaction costs. None of these can be proven to be the one true explanation.

Alternatively, one might argue that implied terms have nothing to do with good faith. They give effect to the will theory of contract by allowing the court to use objective methods of ascertaining the joint will of the parties to the extent that implied terms typically identify what would likely have been agreed had the matter been discussed.

Can these sit at the same table? The present author thinks they can. First, such theories are enduring features of the landscape of contract theory. If someone or other were demonstrably at fault in being unable to explain some significant aspect of contract law, then it would fall away. All these explanations are capable of being right and all might be right in their different ways. What is surely beyond doubt is that parties enter into contractual relations with the intention that they should not break down in acrimony and litigation but rather should be seen through in the manner anticipated. This is the will of the parties to every contract. That being the case, a technique which ascribes some detail to the intentions of the parties, even though they had not addressed their minds to it so far as objective evidence can tell us, implements the will of the parties to have a workable contract. (Of course, one party might want a demonstrably unfair contract, but if he is not prepared to be open about this and suggest positive unfair terms then his will cannot be judged objectively.) Contracting itself is a more or less universal phenomenon, presumably because it has been found efficient. It would be the task of a moral philosopher to ask whether good faith for good faith's sake is the result of innate human morality, divine will, or an instinctive tendency to economically efficient solutions. All the present author can say is that insofar as such requirements exist in our law, contracting parties can be considered to have willed them as part of their contract and implied terms can all, therefore, be imputed to the will of the parties.

A final word on the role of implied terms as the present author sees it. At a recent excellent dinner at Inner Temple, he suggested to a Queen's Counsel, regularly engaged in contract disputes, that, by and large, contracts were probably best left fairly incomplete; implication could take care of most gaps. The important point was to know which gaps could be left to be so filled and how they would be filled. This could save a good deal of management time in negotiation and, indeed, might well secure a better outcome to negotiations, since each attempt to secure a contractual term suggested by party A will typically mean some concession in terms or price to party B. The QC was aghast and told the author that incomplete contracts just leave a lot of work for her and other counsel to do in litigation. (Quite why she would see this as a bad thing, I cannot imagine.)

It is believed that the QC missed the point, however. Only a tiny minority of contracts end in a dispute; still smaller is the minority which end in litigation; smaller yet those which reach a courtroom. The vast majority of contracts never go wrong and recourse is never had to their terms. The phenomenon of implication of terms allows us to trust to this fact, play the numbers game, but still deal with the occasional breakdown. This is a good practical tool in the courts' armoury and allows the courts to avoid taking an over-strict approach to certainty. By not being too strict on this front, the courts enable parties to leave an awful lot unsaid, which, we submit, is a highly efficient solution.

IV. CONCLUDING REMARKS

In this chapter, the author has sought to shew that implied terms are really an organic part of English contract law. Just as we can trace the development of contract law against economic and social history (not to mention the history of the judicial system), so implication as a technique has been applied in different ways to different areas of law at different times, broadly in keeping with trends in society and the economy.

Even the areas where there has been little tendency, generally or at particular times, to use implication (and perhaps a clear antipathy to it), mirror social and economic patterns. This is interesting in itself; we can think of no other doctrine which has been so persistently in tune with its times over a period of centuries. Moreover, it seems to us indicative of the sheer importance of implication as a technique in contract law; an importance which seems, on the face of it, at odds with both judicial expressions of reluctance and more casual attitudes of bar and bench, such as alluded to previously. But perhaps those very expressions of judicial distaste protect the technique's existence and flexibility, by serving to deflect to active a criticism of this activist phenomenon.

11

Contract Interpretation

Judicial Role Not Parties' Choice

Juliet P. Kostritsky

Employing an economics-based consequentialist approach to contract interpretation (focusing on the prospective effect and the factors that might justify intervention) this chapter attempts to identify the precise parameters of an optimal framework for contract interpretation. Such a framework would seek to maximize gains from trade. The issue in such cases is always, given the words the parties used, what is the best (surplus maximizing) interpretation of the bargain. Courts can achieve that interpretation by, in part, minimizing the interpretive risk that parties face when they draft an express contract but do not completely resolve all possible issues. Contracts often fail to reach the level of particularity needed to resolve a later disputed matter. This chapter uses a framework in which cost considerations predominate to identify realistic models of how parties bargain and plan for disputes in drafting their contracts. The model will use the probabilistic thinking of the parties, with respect to both the meaning of words and the parties' likely goals for contracting. These goals include the minimization of opportunism and other similar risks that might chill future contracting and the parties' views on an expected judicial role in interpretation. On the basis of conclusions from these cost-conscious models, this chapter argues for a more expansive interpretive rule than textualism or formalism.

The author argues that the new formalists require the contractin parties to make ex ante choices over factors that they are unlikely to consider at the time of contracting. As a result, formalistic interpretation – the implication that parties prefer the courts

Thanks to Professors Shawn Bayern, Ronald J. Coffey, Lee A. Fennell, Peter M. Gerhart, Robert W. Gordon, Saul Levmore, Kevin C. McMunigal, David P. Porter, Robert E. Scott, Liza Vertinsky, and William C. Whitford, the Florida State University faculty workshop participants, and my fellow participants at the September 2011 University of Sheffield conference upon which this book is based, for their valuable comments; to Lauren Ackerman, Glenn Kimball, Shane Lawson, Benjamin Ristau, George Skupski, and Julia Weissman for their superb research assistance; and to the Case Western Reserve University School of Law Dean's Summer Research Fund for financial support. Finally, Robert R. Myers's library and research assistance was of a caliber every scholar would wish for and more.

to rely solely on the words of the contract – will work to constrain the role of courts severely in contract interpretation. By contrast, purposivism, contextualism, and consequentialism all challenge the idea that words can or should be interpreted without consulting either the overall purpose of the parties, the extrinsic circumstances, or the consequences of adopting a particular interpretation. The explanatory theory offered here is based on minimizing the costs to parties when there is residual uncertainty in a contract. The decision about crafting a particular interpretive rule should depend on which approach best reduces costs and would be most preferred by parties ex ante. The chapter will argue that new formalism decreases surplus by requiring the parties to bargain over a term (whether to allow ex post interpretation) that raises transaction costs in a way that will preclude many bargains.

I. INTRODUCTION: CHALLENGING PARTY CHOICE THEORY

Contract interpretation presents some of the most vexing and litigious issues in contract law.[1] Narrow approaches to interpretation – textualism and formalism – vie for academic and judicial legitimacy with more contextual approaches.[2]

A new strain of formalism – party choice theory – argues that parties must expressly opt into contextual interpretation or live with the consequences of a narrow, off-the-shelf default rule. This chapter rejects that approach in favor of courts' retaining the power to control opportunistic behavior at the expense of parties likely to assume that courts have such power as a matter of course. In any given case, a court should apply the interpretive rule that best reduces costs and best approximates the rule the parties would have preferred *ex ante*.[3]

Because parties seek to maximize the gains from trade, the issue in interpretation is always, given the words the parties used, how to maximize the surplus the parties' bargain creates. Requiring express delegation, as party choice theory does, increases

1 *See* Richard Posner, *The Law and Economics of Contract Interpretation*, 83 TEX. L. REV. 1581 (2005). Courts face the daunting task of "giv[ing] meaning to the symbols of expression used by another person." Margaret N. Kniffin, CORBIN ON CONTRACTS 5 (Joseph M. Perillo ed., rev. ed. 1998).

2 Other scholars questioning the formalist/textualist approach to contract interpretation include Shawn J. Bayern, *Rational Ignorance, Rational Closed-Mindedness, and Modern Economic Formalism in Contract Law*, 97 CAL. L. REV. 943 (2009), and James W. Bowers, *Contract Interpretation for Clairvoyant Firms Without Histories* (unpublished manuscript on file with author).

3 A recent article seeks to provide new content to the hypothetical bargain standard used by courts. Professor Yair Listokin argues that courts dealing with language that fails to clarify which of two meanings was intended should consider not only the written contract but also a Bayesian analysis of the "background knowledge of the prior likelihood (the base rate) that any pair of contracting parties has one possible intent relative to the other possible intent." Yair Listokin, *Bayesian Contractual Interpretation*, 39 J. LEGAL STUD. 359 (2010). Such knowledge, Listokin argues, allows a judicial decision-maker evaluating disputed contractual language to come closer to the parties' actual *ex ante* meaning.

contracting risk by displacing common law courts and taking away a judicial safety valve[4] that enhances exchange by reducing the risks of trusting the other party.

This chapter employs an economics-based, consequentialist[5] approach to contract interpretation, focusing on an interpretive method's prospective effects to evaluate whether it is optimal to require parties to opt in or be foreclosed from having a court consider the parties' overall goals, a wide range of extrinsic circumstances,[6] and the economic consequences of adopting a particular interpretation.

Minimizing the interpretive risk[7] that parties face when they draft a contract but do not completely resolve a later disputed issue should resolve the opt-in question. To determine whether the lowest cost approach requires an express opt in, courts need to ascertain the parties' most likely view[8] of what interpretive powers courts would retain absent an express opt in,[9] taking into account the parties' likely contracting goals (including minimizing opportunism and other similar risks that might chill future contracting).

4 See Henry E. Smith, *The Equitable Dimension of Contract*, 45 Suffolk U. L. Rev. 897 (2012) (discussing the "equity as a structured safety valve ...." *Id.*

5 Consequentialism is "[t]he view that the value of an action derives entirely from the value of its consequences." Simon Blackburn, *Consequentialism*, THE OXFORD DICTIONARY OF PHILOSOPHY 77 (1994). Consequentialist common law adjudication, at least in difficult cases, decides the better rule by analyzing the "prospective effects" of a legal decision. Consequentialists include the law and economics scholars who put a premium on the *ex ante* incentive effects of legal rules, including the efficiency consequences. This approach differs from the deontics who put a premium on deciding the case in light of the "pre-existing rights and duties" created by the agreement. Jody S. Kraus, *Philosophy of Contract Law*, *in* THE OXFORD HANDBOOK OF JURISPRUDENCE AND PHILOSOPHY OF LAW 701 (Jules Coleman & Scott Shapiro eds. 2002). Deontics regard the focus on *ex ante* consequences as violating Kant's injunction to "treat persons as ends in themselves and not as means to an end." *Id.*

6 Contextualists and intentionalists argue that "text can only be properly understood when taken in context." Jonathan R. Siegel, *Textualism and Contextualism in Administrative Law*, 78 B.U. L. REV. 1023, 1028 (1998). Thus, even though Professor Scott says that under conditions of ambiguity, "the divide between formalist and antiformalist positions essentially disappears," Alan Schwartz & Robert E. Scott, *Contract Interpretation Redux*, 119 YALE. L.J. 926, 963 (2010), there is still a divide in the type of context evidence to be admitted. Formalists would exclude course of performance and trade usage evidence. *Id.*, at 931, 933. Also there is no indication that they would be willing to interpret contracts in a way that minimizes the interpretive risk for the parties and reduces the danger of opportunism as a means of improving welfare.

7 For a discussion of the importance that minimizing interpretive risk should play as a source of welfare improvement, see Juliet P. Kostritsky, *Interpretive Risk and Contract Interpretation: A Suggested Approach for Maximizing Value*, 2 ELON L. REV. 109 (2011). This chapter builds on the insights of that article, but (1) expands the focus to address the connections between formalism and textualism in contract interpretation and legal realism, common law adjudication, and statutory interpretation, (2) seeks to carefully delineate the different strands of thinking in textualist and formalist approaches to contract interpretation, (3) identifies precisely and critiques the assumptions underlying textualist and formalist approaches and offers a competing set of more realistic assumptions, and (4) examines the impact of capturing the probabilistic thinking of the parties on contract interpretation.

8 *See* Listokin, *supra* note 3 (emphasizing probabilistic analysis of the meaning the parties attached to words when they expressed them).

9 *See* Avery Wiener Katz, *The Economics of Form and Substance in Contract Law Interpretation*, 104 COLUM. L. REV. 496 (2004).

A contract begins with express terms. If all contracts were complete and precise, and the exact way in which the express terms were meant to settle any later-arising controversies were obvious, a court's role would be limited.[10] However, because even carefully drafted contracts involving commercial firms fail to address all possible contingencies or the language may be intractable,[11] questions arise about a possible role for courts.[12]

Suppose, for example, that a contract designates an agent to use a trademark to sell products and to receive a designated percentage of any sales. Is that agent entitled to that percentage for licensing when the company enters into a joint venture and sells the entire business to another entity?[13] Such a contract does not cover the matter despite seeming to address the trademark issue with particularity.[14] Or, suppose

[10] *See* George M. Cohen, *Interpretation and Implied Terms in Contract Law, in* CONTRACT LAW AND ECONOMICS 125 (Gerrit De Geest ed., Edward Elgar 2011) (noting that generally if a contract is complete "there is no *efficiency*-enhancing role for a court other than to enforce the contract according to its terms").

[11] Intractability may arise because the express terms, while clear when considered individually, lack clarity when read together. *See United Rentals, Inc. v. Ram Holdings, Inc.*, 937 A.2d 810, 815–19 (Del. Ch. 2007) (holding that a contract clause stating that the seller's exclusive remedy in the event that the buyer did not close the deal was a walk away/termination fee superseded a conflicting clause entitling the seller to specific performance); *see also* Gregory M. Duhl, *Conscious Ambiguity: Slaying Cerberus in the Interpretation of Contractual Inconsistencies*, 71 U. PITT. L. REV. 71 (2009) (discussing *United Rentals*). Questions may also arise when parties draft carefully to deal with some risks but fail to contemplate other risks, which later arise. *See* Kostritsky, *supra* note 6. Analogous difficulties of intractable meaning may arise in the interpretation of statutes. To address such difficulties, some have embraced a uniform interpretive method. A recent article details the efforts of some state courts to adopt an interpretive methodology with the force of *stare decisis*. *See* Abbe R. Gluck, *Laboratories of Statutory Interpretation: Methodological Consensus and the New Modified Textualism*, 119 YALE L.J. 1750 (2010); *see also* Jonathan T. Molot, *The Rise and Fall of Textualism*, 106 COLUM. L. REV. 1, (2006) (discussing the "convergence" between textualism and purposivism and urging textualists to recognize the "consensus"). *But see* Ethan J. Leib & Michael Serota, *The Costs of Consensus in Statutory Construction*, 120 YALE L.J. ONLINE 47 (2010) (advocating a more variegated approach).

[12] *See* Cohen, *supra* note 9, at 127 (observing that "no real-world contracts are fully complete" because no contract actually describes all possible contingencies and explicitly provides a response for each contingency).

[13] *Beanstalk Group, Inc. v. AM General Corp.*, 283 F.3d 856 (7th Cir. 2002), addressed precisely that issue. *See infra* notes 50–62 and accompanying text.

[14] When should a court, confronted with interpreting a particular word or phrase, invoke another seemingly unrelated interpretive principle? Often a court faces a "choice ... between two different norms." Frederick Schauer, *Formalism*, 97 YALE L.J. 509, 516 (1988). Schauer discusses an unreported case involving a statute requiring that nominating petitions be filed by 5:00 p.m. and a clerk who misled a petitioner into missing the filing deadline by three minutes. In determining that the petitioner had timely filed, notwithstanding the statute's plain language, the court looked to another case in which equity refused to enforce a similar deadline because "reliance on erroneous actions on behalf of the State has put ... its citizens in conflict with the literal terms of the time requirements instituted by that same sovereignty." *See id.* at 515–16 (discussing *Hunter v. Norman*, No. S197–86-WrC [Vt. July 28, 1986]). The *Hunter* court chose between reading the statute literally and applying an equitable principle derived from case law; but even a court lacking another case directly on point to lead it to apply a

that a contract addresses an issue explicitly: no three-wheeled ATVs allowed. The contract specifies precisely what type of vehicle is banned. If the future contingency of the development of new four-wheeled ATVs is unaccounted for, however, the express terms seem incomplete.[15]

When such interpretive issues arise, courts often state that they must ascertain the parties' actual intent.[16] If the parties have formed no actual intent on the disputed matter, a language-based interpretive approach is likely to be unproductive.[17] Even if the parties formed an actual intent, the contract's language may not reveal that intent to a court; the language may be unclear or fail to resolve whether a precise term was meant to apply in all circumstances (are there any exceptions?).

An express opt-in requirement may leave a party requesting relief without a remedy. If a contract pegs the price at the "delivery date" but does not specify whether that date means "scheduled" or "actual" delivery date,[18] the party whose case depends on persuading a court of a particular meaning may lose if the court adopts an interpretive rule which excludes many matters beyond the text.[19] The text itself is inconclusive: there is no literal or formalist meaning of "delivery date."[20]

norm in a different context must confront whether there are any other principles (such as an equitable principle limiting the reach of a strict rule when the party seeking to enforce it has contributed to its violation) that might alter the result of a seemingly rigid statute.

Courts face the same choice – to apply principles, which might call for a different result than the one the language read in isolation would suggest is inevitable – when interpreting express contract language. The court in *Jacob & Youngs, Inc. v. Kent*, 129 NE 889 (NY 1921), discussed *infra* Part VII.A, had to choose between interpreting the contract's language as an express condition excusing the buyer from performing and declining to give effect to the language in order to prevent forfeiture. As such, a formalistic insistence on interpreting just the language masks the underlying inescapable choices that judges have to make routinely, as when they decide that what appears to be a simple case is really more complex because of some other principle that the judge himself must identify. *See* Schauer, *supra*, note 13, at 517.

15 *See infra* Part VII.B (discussing the interpretive issue involved in the ATV case). For another example in which a contract has express terms that *seem* to address the controversy but leave certain matters on which the dispute turns unresolved, see *TKO Equip. Co. v. C&G Coal Co.*, 863 F.2d 541 (7th Cir. 1988) (discussed *infra* note 37). Broad interpretation means using a justificational framework that invokes the pursuit of chosen consequences, such as minimizing the *ex ante* risk (costs) facing parties who use express terms – the consequence sought being to encourage exchanges and the gains they bring.

16 Ascertaining the parties' intent remains the "central objective of contract law." *See* Jody S. Kraus & Robert E. Scott, *Contract Design and the Structure of Contractual Intent*, 84 N.Y.U. L. REV. 1023, 1025 (2009).

17 Steven Shavell, *On Writing and the Interpretation of Contracts*, 22 J.L. ECON. & ORG. 289 (2006).

18 *See infra* notes 63–71 and accompanying text. Where the text "delivery date" is inconclusive for either side, textualism does not provide a solution.

19 Textualists would admit the parties' pleadings and briefs, a dictionary, and the judge's life experience, so they would contend that textualism should not be confused with literalism. *See* Schwartz & Scott, *supra* note 5, at 933 (admitting that "literalism is impossible" since courts "necessarily see the pleadings" and briefs).

20 Once the text is found to be inconclusive, one option would be to treat the text as containing a gap. The fact that an interpretive question has arisen suggests the "written contract contains some gap."

Choosing the correct interpretive method has proved extremely controversial even among scholars who agree that the goal of contract rules should be to maximize gains from trade and to minimize transaction costs.[21] Party choice proponents argue that courts concerned with costs and the economic goal of adding value should employ only formalism (or textualism) when they interpret contracts, ignore parties' unexpressed objectives,[22] and exclude most contextual evidence in the interpretive process *unless* parties have signaled to a court that they are choosing such methods.[23]

Party choice proponents justify that approach on the basis of assumptions regarding parties' preferences as they are expressed in the contract or hypothesized to

Bayern, *supra* note 2, at 958. Formalists, however, suggest that if the contextual evidence consisting of the life experience of the judge, the text, and the context of the transaction (as for example reflected in the company's business plan), *see* Schwartz & Scott, *supra* note 5, at 952, does not resolve the matter, the court is faced with a choice "to dismiss on the ground that the contract is too indefinite to enforce, or to read the contract to reach a reasonable result." Schwartz & Scott, *Contract Theory and the Limits of Contract Law*, 113 YALE L.J. 541, 609 (2003). Schwartz and Scott write that courts refuse to enforce contracts on grounds of indefiniteness more often than conventional wisdom holds. *Id.* at 609 n. 145. Refusing to enforce a contract can pick a winner just as easily as using a gap-filler.

21 Oliver E. Williamson, THE ECONOMIC INSTITUTIONS OF CAPITALISM: FIRMS, MARKETS, RELATIONAL CONTRACTING 17 (1985) (advancing the "proposition that the economic institutions of capitalism have the main purpose of economizing on transaction costs").

22 Professors Kraus and Scott use the ALCOA/Essex contract to illustrate that courts interpreting contract language should ignore the parties' objectives. *See* Kraus & Scott, *supra* note 15. In *Aluminum Co. of America v. Essex Group, Inc.*, 499 F. Supp. 53 (W.D. Pa. 1980), the parties drafted a clause that pegged the seller's price to an amount that was 3% above a particular industry index, but the index failed to function as planned due to unforeseen economic variables. Formalists would want courts to ignore such objectives in contract interpretation even if the contract, as written, fails to achieve the parties' objectives. However, the notion that there are specific contractual goals shared by both parties is misguided. Instead, each party has a different project in mind with a projected payoff in the form of a future return stream, *individual to that party*. However, the absence of shared objectives for a particular project does not negate shared goals that cut across all contracting parties, including a desire to maximize wealth and minimize transaction costs.

23 Evidence that the formalist/textualist approach would be excluded includes trade usage and contextualized evidence that is currently permitted by the *Restatement (Second) of Contracts* and the Uniform Commercial Code. *See* RESTATEMENT (SECOND) OF CONTRACTS (1979) §§ 222 & 223; UCC §§ 1–303 & 2–202 (2002). Those taking a narrow approach to context evidence would exclude trade usage unless the parties have specifically indicated that they want trade usage (non-ordinary meaning) to govern their contract. The textualist/formalists would change the current default rule by setting the linguistic default at ordinary meaning. *See* Schwartz & Scott, *supra* note 19, at 585. Excluding the parties' objectives, and focusing solely on the express terms, also seem to rule out judicial consideration of the various interpretive rules and, thus, to reject consequentialism as an interpretive methodology. Although Kraus and Scott do not specifically negate consideration of the consequences of interpretation, because they do rule out considering the parties' contractual objectives and forbid a court looking beyond the express terms without specific delegation, one can surmise that the authors also intend courts to refrain from weighing presumed jointly shared economic goals in contractual interpretation. This Article suggests that courts must consider what is "more or less common and durable … in the behavior of individuals, acting alone or collectively" in contract interpretation. *See* Ronald J. Coffey, Methodologies 14 (Aug. 12, 2002) (unpublished manuscript) (on file with the author).

be based on a rational choice analysis. Formalists argue commercial parties would usually prefer a minimum evidentiary base.[24] Party choice advocates argue that we must honor the parties' terms, as well as their interpretive choices, out of fidelity to the parties' intent and for maximizing the gains from trade. Intervention costs (the cost of broad interpretation without party delegation) are presumed to outweigh the benefits.

The formalists' key assumption is that parties wanting broad interpretation will write that choice into their contracts. Bargaining costs, however, often make that assumption unreasonable. Parties often use words believing that they have identified the object of contracting with enough particularity that they never anticipate that a term will require interpretation and often see no need for party choice.

Requiring parties to bargain over a term (whether to allow *ex post* interpretation) increases transaction costs in a way that may make bargains more costly or even preclude them. The express opt-in rule would require that parties undertake costly protective measures to preclude unreasonable results that courts could easily reject if they retained discretion in interpretive approaches, without specific party delegation. This chapter challenges the assumptions underlying the rule requiring express party choice as the default rule for contract interpretation. Under more realistic assumptions of bargaining, parties would assume that current broad rules on interpretation would apply as part of a default rule.[25]

The default rule should be that courts can use broad contextual evidence of prior negotiations, trade usages, course of dealing, and course of performance.[26] Courts should also be free to use consequentialist analysis that models likely incentive effects on the parties to see whether the contract makes sense from a business perspective[27] and probabilistic models about parties' likely expectations about judicial interpretive powers and engage in traditional jurisprudence in which courts consider equity and invoke other legal principles, even without an express party opt in.

[24] *See* Schwartz & Scott, *supra* note 19, at 569 ("Typical firms prefer courts to make interpretations on a narrow evidentiary base whose most significant component is the written contract.").

[25] *Id.*, at 609–10. Schwartz and Scott posit that current default rules are mandatory and paternalistic because they overlook party choice. However, because the test for party choice sets a high bar for expressly opting into expansive interpretation with silence plus the use of specific terms amounting to an opt out, there may be no meaningful party choice to begin with. Thus, a court supplied interpretive default rule may not be mandatory at all and may not paternalistically override party choice if such a choice does not in fact exist.

[26] *Id.*, at 572 (detailing components of broader evidentiary base).

[27] Although Schwartz and Scott assert that the "life experience of the judge" would enable a court to use its business sense in deciding contract interpretation issues, Schwartz & Scott, *supra* note 5, at 952–53, the usefulness of such life experience may be limited. It might allow a judge to decide that a structure to be built for a chemical company to store dangerous materials would not be satisfied by a construction of a gazebo, *id.*, but it might not enable the judge to make more sophisticated decisions, especially if the judge's life experience is not specifically conceptualized to include consideration of the wealth effects of a particular interpretation.

The approach offered here would promote welfare gains[28] and explain the disparate doctrines of the contract law governing interpretation,[29] including the doctrine avoiding unreasonable results, gap filling[30] and certain doctrines of construction.[31]

Because party choice proponents require a specific opt in to allow courts to consider reasonableness or other matters requiring court discretion, the dominant approach fails to explain how and why courts regularly depart from textualism to avoid negative welfare effects even without an express invitation from the parties.[32] These judicial departures from an express opt-in "grand theory"[33] demonstrate the

[28] *See* Frank I. Michelman, *Norms and Normativity in the Economic Theory of Law*, 62 MINN. L. REV. 1015, 1035 (1978).

[29] *See* Keith A. Rowley, *Contract Construction and Interpretation: From the "Four Corners" to Parol Evidence (and Everything in Between)*, 69 MISS. L.J. 73, 113–163 (1999) (updating and expanding upon Edwin W. Patterson, *The Interpretation and Construction of Contracts*, 64 COLUM. L. REV. 833 (1964)).

[30] On the other hand, if the express terms do not even seem to address the matter, a court has to decide whether to imply a term into the contract. It may be difficult to determine whether the court is "interpreting" a term or "filling a gap." As Professor Cohen explains:

> Interpretation and implied terms are closely related concepts. For example, if the question is whether to read in an exception to an express term, such as a price or quantity term, that could be viewed either as an act of *interpreting* the express term or of *implying* an additional term (the exception).

Cohen, *supra* note 9, at 125 (emphasis added).

[31] Construction and interpretation of contracts refer to distinct concepts. As Professor Kniffin notes, "Through 'interpretation' of a contract, a court determines what meanings the parties, when contracting, gave to the language used. Through 'construction' of a contract, a court determines the legal operation of the contract – its effect upon the rights and duties of the parties." Kniffin, *supra* note 1, at § 24.3. The most common example given to distinguish the concepts arises in satisfaction clauses in express conditions. Where the court must decide whether to apply an objective or subjective standard, it is engaging in construction rather than contract interpretation. *Id.* However far apart the concepts may seem, when courts interpret incomplete or ambiguous language, they are utilizing the same tools that they resort to in the construction of a contract.

[32] For an extended argument against a unitary textualist approach to interpretive issues in favor of a wealth effects approach, see Juliet P. Kostritsky, *Plain Meaning vs. Broad Interpretation: How the Risk of Opportunism Defeats a Unitary Rule for Interpretation*, 96 KY. L.J. 43 (2007–2008). In the same vein, Professor Adam Badawi suggests a departure from a unitary approach to selecting an interpretive approach and argues that that court should consider the frequency of the transaction as a relevant factor in deciding whether contextualism or formalism should govern. *See* Adam Badawi, *Interpretive Preferences and the Limits of New Formalism*, 6 BERKELEY BUS. L.J. 1 (2009). Badawi argues where transactions are frequent and in standard goods, formalism may be more appropriate since the parties can easily draft complete contracts; where transactions are infrequent, drafting obstacles may be greater and contextualism a more appropriate method of interpretation.

Frequency may be a relevant but not dispositive factor. In many goods cases, the frequency and repetition of a transaction can lead parties to rely on usages and customs without seeing any need to incorporate them into the formal contract. Parties assume those practices will be automatically incorporated without the need for formal language, making a contextualized incorporationist strategy appropriate. Thus, the determinative factor should be the wealth effects of a formal versus contextualist interpretive method.

[33] Skepticism for grand interpretive theories is evident in statutory interpretation scholarship. *See, e.g.*, William N. Eskridge, Jr. & Phillip P. Frickey, *Statutory Interpretation as Practical Reasoning*, 42 STAN.

superiority of a judicial approach that assesses the wealth consequences of a particular decision on a case-by-case basis.[34]

Looking at the actual results of cases is consistent with the "law in action" method.[35] Courts depart from textualism or formalism if such an approach would lead to catastrophic or deadweight losses for both parties,[36] promote opportunistic behavior,[37] result in an interpretation at odds with good business sense,[38] or lead to

L. Rev. 321 (1990). Using diverse, even opposing, interpretive techniques can help courts reach better results. Different techniques produce different arguments, which can help courts "generate productive, useful, and important dialogue about the difficult issues before them." Leib & Serota, *supra* note 10, at 51.

34 Professor Cohen notes that one advantage of this judicial approach is that it may "provide the necessary flexibility – efficient adjustments to contingencies – that an incomplete contract otherwise lacks." Cohen, *supra* note 9, at 130; *see also* Leib & Serota, *supra* note 10, at 48 (citing the "underappreciated benefits that ... methodological diversity" provides in statutory interpretation).

35 The law in action method is associated with Stewart Macaulay, Marc Galanter, and William C. Whitford, and with the Wisconsin Law School. Macaulay's path breaking article on the way in which businessmen often ignored the governing contract and avoided litigation in favor of working disputes out with one's contractual partner caused people to rethink the importance of how contract law actually affected the operations of businesses. *See* Stewart Macaulay, *Non-Contractual Relations in Business: A Preliminary Study*, 28 Am. Soc. Rev. 55 (1963). For an extended treatment of law in action, see 1 & 2 Stewart Macaulay et al., Contracts: Law in Action (3d ed. 2010 & 2011).

36 A recent case illustrating a court justifiably departing from a contract's express terms involves Dow Chemical's acquisition of Rohm and Haas. A case could have been made that, on a projected basis, forcing the combination would have sunk both firms, resulting in a rather clear economic waste in a broadly social sense. Of course, the merger was completed and Dow seems to be handling the fusion well. But that was not the expectation when things went awry at Dow just before the deal was to be consummated. *See* Answer of Defendants at 25, *Rohm & Haas Co. v. Dow Chem. Co.*, No. 4309-CC (Del. Ch. Feb. 3, 2009), available at 2009 WL 286591 (alleging that the acquisition would threaten "the very existence of both companies"). The case settled before the Delaware Court of Chancery resolved the issue of whether the court should depart from the express terms of the contract calling for specific performance. However, equity would be justified in refusing to enforce specific performance if doing so would have led to catastrophic losses for both firms.

Because textualism put a premium on the parties' choice *ex ante* to select language that indicates whether or not they wish to invoke equitable principles, textualists would conclude that a court should stay its hand and enforce the clause requiring specific performance when the parties have not expressly delegated equitable decision-making to a court.

37 *See* Kostritsky, *supra* note 31, at 85–86 (opportunistic behavior from adherence to formal term). As Professors Schwartz and Scott have explained, their preference is for a different rule than exists in U.C.C. §2–202. "A plain meaning default rule that presumes the parties have written in the standard language." Schwartz & Scott, *supra* note 5, at 932. Thus, unless specifically invoked by the parties, the ordinary plain meaning would govern. Parties would have to opt out by specifically invoking non-ordinary trade usages. *But see* Jeffrey M. Lipshaw, *The Bewitchment of Intelligence: Language and Ex Post Illusions of Intention*, 78 Temp. L. Rev. 99 (2005) (denying "that opportunism is a problem of any import to be addressed").

38 *See, e.g.*, *TKO Equip. Co. v. C&G Coal Co.*, 863 F.2d 541 (7th Cir. 1988) (construing a contract that expressly provided it was a lease with an option to purchase, and also expressly provided that the parties did not intend to create a security interest, as a lease if the option to purchase was exercised, because to construe it otherwise would allow opportunistic behavior by the parties to interpret the contract in whichever way best suited their interests at any particular moment).

other consequences that act as a drag on gains from exchange. Because the approach to interpretive risk outlined here explains the current case law and the doctrines better than the express opt-in rule or party choice, it constitutes a more comprehensive explanatory theory.[39]

If parties omit any express provision on delegation, courts must make assumptions based on probabilities. Since most parties would want courts to avoid unreasonable results or results that would likely (again on the basis of probabilities) add to transaction costs or chill exchange, even if the parties do not clearly signal their desire for broad judicial interpretive powers, such an approach would match their *ex ante* intent and should be implemented.

II. THE IMPORTANCE OF A JUDICIAL INTERPRETATION RULE

In many cases, parties do not select an interpretive method expressly, so a workable solution to interpretive problems therefore requires courts to retain discretion and broad interpretive powers in a judicially formulated rule. A discussion of hypotheticals and cases shows why leaving interpretation to party choice will not solve real problems.

The party choice solution fails to devise "a workable solution to complex questions."[40] It says that absent party choice, the default rules of formalism will govern. If the parties use express terms and do not delegate interpretive authority to a court through the use of vague terms such as "good faith" or "reasonableness," courts should uniformly refuse to go beyond the text.[41] This announced party choice rule

This chapter suggests that courts should interpret contracts in order to constrain opportunistic behavior or reduce deadweight losses, which would include interpreting contracts to excuse an express condition if it would lead to forfeiture. That is a result that Professors Kraus and Scott would clearly disapprove. *See* Kraus & Scott, *supra* note 15, at 1095–97. Yet, under the approach suggested here, courts should feel empowered to excuse a condition in order to reduce the potential drag on gains from trade that would result from a literal enforcement of the express condition.

39 The ability of an underlying contract theory to explain the case outcomes constitutes a hallmark of an economic approach to law. Jody Kraus explains that "economic theories tend to treat the outcomes of cases as the principal legal data for contract theory to explain and justify, accord primacy to the explanatory task of contract theory, and aspire to explain away, rather than explain, the conceptual distinctiveness of contract law." Jody S. Kraus, *Philosophy of Contract Law*, *in* THE OXFORD HANDBOOK OF JURISPRUDENCE AND PHILOSOPHY OF LAW 689 (Jules Coleman & Scott Shapiro eds. 2002). The ability of a theory to explain actual case outcomes does not constitute a relevant indicator of a theory's success in deontic theories. In contrast, deontological theories "tend to treat the doctrinal statements as the principal legal data for contract theory to explain and justify, accord primacy to the normative task of contract theory, and require that contract theory explain and justify the conceptual distinctiveness of contract law." *Id.*

40 *See* Eskridge & Frickey, *supra* note 32, at 324 (suggesting deficiencies of grand theories in statutory interpretations and embracing approach that can yield "workable resolution").

41 Kraus & Scott, *supra* note 15, at 1030.

provides that whenever a party uses precise words, and the party's lawsuit depends on the court's going beyond the text, invoking equity, or using an economics-based consequentialist approach to deciding on which interpretive rule should govern the controversy,[42] that party will lose unless it had the foresight to add a clause specifically delegating broad interpretive authority to a court. Such an approach would necessarily lead to a lack of resolution on issues not determined by the express language.[43]

If a party's interpretation depends on matters extrinsic to the contract, the court will refuse to consider such evidence unless the express terms are ambiguous.[44] This anti-contextualist default would preclude trade usage evidence to interpret contracts unless the parties specifically agreed to incorporate such terms.[45] Party choice advocates would essentially say to parties that they must opt out of textualist default rules or risk a court's excluding extrinsic evidence unless the court finds the term to be ambiguous on its face. Even with ambiguity, the evidence would be limited to a minimum evidentiary base. A party whose success depends on a broad array of extrinsic evidence or on an analysis of economic incentives will likely lose.

Under the contrary approach suggested here, courts would retain their powers of interpretation without the need for any express delegation. Courts would be able to reference goals beyond the contract in determining a delivery date or the number of wheeled ATVs that were banned. A broader interpretive rule would allow the court to reference overall goals of maximizing joint surplus and go beyond the express terms if necessary.

The parties in the delivery date scenario[46] could have drafted their contract with a greater degree of specificity but failed to do so. They may have assumed that the delivery date term would raise no interpretive issues or that the law would supply a standard of reasonableness by which to measure performance. Such an implied standard would permit the court to determine that the price should be pegged at the scheduled delivery date even if the contrary meaning meets the literal meaning of the express terms.

Denying a court the discretion to make such determinations absent an express opt in would increase costs for all future transactors, who would incur additional drafting costs to prevent courts from insisting on a literal interpretation. If most

42 *Id.*

43 Professor Scott would, if the court cannot resolve the matter after looking at unclear language and then looking at context evidence and default rules on mistake and excuse, "prefer courts to find the contract insufficiently definite to enforce against either party rather than ask the court to devise a novel solution." E-mail from Professor Robert E. Scott, Columbia School of Law (Feb. 6, 2011) (on file with author). In contrast, I suggest that courts can devise solutions that are welfare maximizing and preferred by both parties.

44 Schwartz & Scott, *supra* note 5, at 963 (indicating that context evidence may be admissible where term ambiguous).

45 Schwartz & Scott, *supra* note 19, at 586.

46 *See supra* note 17 and associated text.

parties would assume, probabilistically, that an express opt in would not be needed to rule out an unreasonable interpretation,[47] then ignoring reasonableness concerns in interpretation absent an express opt in would deter future transactors from contracting. Future transactors might worry that parties would have to draft exceedingly carefully to eliminate any residual uncertainty totally in order to avoid unreasonable interpretations of language by courts. Similarly, if a court could only admit context evidence in the form of the contract text, information about the basic business of the parties, and the life experience of the judge,[48] a court might ignore its mission to interpret contracts to deter opportunistic behavior as a means of maximizing wealth.

The problem of express terms' leaving residual uncertainty can have other negative effects. In many cases, if a court adhered to a rule requiring an express opt in, it would potentially promote opportunism. Even under formalist analysis in which courts can refer to context to interpret ambiguous terms, it is not clear that a judge could consider anything beyond the restricted sphere of evidence consisting of the contract itself, the judge's life experience, and a dictionary.[49] External evidence supplied from course of dealing, trade usage, and other sources, the consideration of which could clarify the admitted ambiguities and reduce interpretive risk, would be excluded absent an express opt in.[50]

A rule in which the interpretive powers of a court depend entirely on party choice would add to transaction costs and fail to solve many interpretation problems. In the two cases that follow, since the parties used precise terms and did not opt into a judicial rule, the default rule of formalism would govern. Yet, the courts managed more sensible results.

In *Beanstalk Group, Inc. v. AM General Corp.*,[51] Beanstalk contracted with AM General to negotiate license agreements for AM General's "HUMMER" trademark. The contract provided that Beanstalk was AM General's "sole and exclusive non-employee representative" and was entitled to 35 percent of the "gross receipts ... received on Owner's [AM General's] behalf under any License Agreements" for the Hummer trademark.[52] During the period governed by the representation agreement,

47 An analogous doctrine in statutory interpretation permits courts to rule out interpretations that would promote "unreasonable interpretations." William N. Eskridge *Public Values in Statutory Interpretation*, 137 U. Penn. L. Rev. 1807, 1011 (1989). Similarly, if a court could only admit context evidence in the form of the contract text, information about the basic business of the parties, and the life experience of the judge, a court might think that its central mission of contract interpretation would not extend to deterring opportunistic behavior as a means of maximizing wealth by lessening transaction costs.

48 *See* Schwartz & Scott, *supra* note 6, at 952.

49 *See id.*

50 Schwartz & Scott, *supra* note 19, at 572–74.

51 *Beanstalk Group v. Am General Corp.*, 283 F.3d 856 (7th Cir. 2002).

52 *Id.*, at 858 (internal quotation marks omitted). The agreement defined "License Agreement" as "'any agreement or arrangement, whether in the form of a license agreement or otherwise, granting merchandising or other rights to the Property,' which in turn is defined to mean trademarks and related rights." *Id.*

AM General and General Motors entered into a joint-venture agreement.[53] Under the agreement, GM would design and engineer a new Hummer vehicle, loan money to AM General to build the new Hummer, obtain an option to buy 40 percent of AM General, and "*would acquire the Hummer trademark*."[54] Beanstalk argued that the agreement between AM General and GM was a license agreement, a strong argument under the literal terms of the Beanstalk agreement because the transaction transferred rights to the Hummer trademark.[55] Therefore, Beanstalk claimed it was entitled to 35 percent of the value of the Hummer trademark.[56]

Although the court accepted the presumption that contracts should ordinarily be enforced "in accordance with the ordinary meaning of the language used and without recourse to evidence, beyond the contract itself,"[57] the court ultimately decided the case by interpreting the contract to promote future business exchanges best and discourage opportunistic behavior. The court noted that since Beanstalk was in the business of merchandising trademarks, it could, for example, have licensed the Hummer brand to a toy company seeking to make toy Hummers.[58] The agreement between AM General and GM, however, differed from such an agreement. Instead, it was a joint venture, where AM General "essentially transferred the Hummer business, including ... all its trademarks" to GM.[59] Since "Beanstalk [was] not a business broker,"[60] the court noted that it would make little sense to pay an agent, such as Beanstalk, for work that AM General did itself, an observation supported not only by common sense, but by implication from the agreement's terms.[61]

In reaching the result that makes the most economic sense, Judge Easterbrook spelled out the court's logic:

> In the case of a commercial contract, one must have a general acquaintance with commercial practices. This doesn't mean that judges should have an M.B.A. or

53 *Id.*, at 859.

54 *Id.*, (emphasis added).

55 The joint venture agreement, through its grant of the trademark to GM, was technically an "agreement or arrangement ... granting merchandising or other rights" in the Hummer trademark – a License Agreement under the Beanstalk contract. *See id.* at 858.

56 *Id.*, at 859.

57 *Id.*

58 *Id.*, at 860.

59 *Id.*, at 861.

60 *Id.*

61 *See id.*, at 862 (AM General appointed Beanstalk its "'sole and exclusive *non-employee* representative,' implying that AM General's employees can negotiate license agreements without going through Beanstalk.... No reason is given why AM General would compensate Beanstalk for services rendered wholly by AM General's own employees."); *id.*, (citing provisions "keying Beanstalk's commissions to gross receipts" received by Beanstalk on AM General's behalf and requiring Beanstalk to "account to AM General periodically for the gross receipts of the license agreements" as implying that Beanstalk would receive compensation only for those licenses it negotiated).

> have practiced corporate or commercial law, but merely that they be alert citizens of a market-oriented society so that they can recognize absurdity in a business context. A blinkered literalism, a closing of one's eyes to the obvious, can produce nonsensical results, as this case illustrates.[62]

The court did not interpret the contract literally; in refusing to do so, it promoted future transactions between AM General and other companies seeking to represent their brands – a consequentialist interpretation. A literal interpretation of the licensing agreement would have required a party selling its business to give up a huge percentage of its overall assets to a licensee who had nothing to do with brokering the sale or building the assets of the company. That windfall might provide a future disincentive for parties entering licensing agreements or selling assets. The prospect of an unearned windfall would act as a drag on all gains from trade across transactions. In refusing to require an express opt in, the court discouraged opportunistic behavior and an unearned windfall. This willingness to depart from a literal-minded interpretation helps to increase the surplus by reducing the prospect of future litigation. Parties hoping to gain windfalls from literalistic interpretation of contracts will be discouraged from bringing lawsuits in the future.

A court employing a formalistic interpretation may not have reached such an obviously reasonable solution. In adhering only to the terms of the contract, and not referring to external business knowledge or incentives in exchange, the essential issue – that Beanstalk contributed nothing to the deal between AM General and GM – would be lost. The *Beanstalk* court recognized that "blinkered literalism"[63] would provide only a flawed and "nonsensical" interpretation.

Though certain iterations of formalism might allow the judge's life experience to resolve cases of ambiguity, the court itself recognized that a judge may not (and should not necessarily) have an MBA or business knowledge. Thus, the pool of evidence a court may draw from will vary significantly with the appointed judge. To avoid such disparate results and to ensure that courts have the discretionary powers to maximize wealth in interpretive disputes, courts should be specifically directed to consider the incentive effects when crafting a rule of interpretation.

Literal interpretations of certain contracts can also lead to opportunistic results that hinder fair and efficient transactions. Adherence to a rule of party choice requiring express opt in would be detrimental to incentives to exchange. In *Deloro Smelting and Refining Co. v. United States*,[64] the parties disagreed on how price terms in a supply contract were to operate. The United States contracted with a Canadian smelting company, Deloro, to purchase cobalt metal in 1950. If Deloro

[62] *Id.*, at 860.

[63] *Id.*

[64] 317 F.2d 382 (Ct. Cl. 1963).

delivered the cobalt after a certain date, an escalation clause enabled the United States to pay Deloro a price based on a fixed percentage of the domestic U.S. market price for cobalt, found in the *Engineering and Mining Journal* "as of the date of delivery of the cobalt metal."[65] Deloro failed to deliver the cobalt according to the contract's delivery schedule, but the United States did not terminate the contract. Once the escalation clause became operative, the accounting and financial personnel working for the United States paid Deloro on the basis of the price quotation on the actual date of delivery, not the scheduled date. In 1954, the United States insisted it had been overpaying Deloro because its payments were based on a higher cobalt price at the later actual delivery date. The United States began paying Deloro on the basis of the scheduled date of delivery and subtracted sums equal to its prior over-payment. After this change, Deloro refused to continue its contractual performance until the United States paid it the amounts taken out of its payments and signed a binding agreement to base future prices on the actual date of delivery.

The United States Court of Claims addressed the interpretation issue: whether the phrase "as of (or at) the date of delivery of the cobalt metal" in the price escalation clause referred to the actual date of delivery or the scheduled date of delivery.[66] The court's analysis focused on a reading of the contract that would have been "understood by reasonable men standing in the parties' shoes."[67] First, the court noted that prompt delivery of cobalt was expected because the U.S. government's statutory authority to receive cobalt had an expiration date.[68] The parties must have assumed that Deloro would be able to make timely delivery. The court also pointed out that parties must have anticipated the rise in cobalt prices because they included an escalation price adjustment clause.[69] The combination of these two factors led the court to reason that the "price-change provisions were plainly meant to be intertwined with the due dates for delivery – expected by both sides to be the actual dates of delivery."[70] Second, the court pointed out that if Deloro's interpretation were accepted, then "there would be a malevolent incentive ... for the contractor deliberately to postpone performance in order to increase its recovery."[71] From a business standpoint, it would make little sense for the United States to pay higher prices for shipments of cobalt that were late. Therefore, the court construed the contract with "business sense, as [it] would be understood by intelligent men of affairs" to determine that date of delivery meant the scheduled date of delivery.[72]

65 *Id.*, at 384 (internal quotation marks omitted).

66 *Id.* at 385.

67 *Id.* at 386.

68 *Id.*

69 *Id.* The court attributed this price-rise anticipation to the parties' awareness of Korean hostilities.

70 *Id.* at 386–87.

71 *Id.* at 387.

72 *Id.* (quoting *The Kronprinzessin Cecilie*, 244 US 12, 24 [1917]) (internal quotation marks omitted).

This case illustrates how a seemingly precise term can turn out not to be so precise. Even if a formalist admits that a term is ambiguous, the dominant theory of party choice does not lay out a plan for resolving the ambiguity to minimize transaction costs. Without the security that a seemingly unambiguous term will be interpreted reasonably in light of the parties' ultimate contractual intent, transacting may chill, or become prohibitively complicated and expensive, because of concern that a contract cannot be drafted to protect party interests. If a party cannot anticipate that a term will become ambiguous, it cannot draft a safe contract because a formalist interpretation will exclude that party's intent and contractual ends in interpreting meaning. However, recourse to a court interpretive rule that takes into account party intent in the sense of maximizing joint surplus will promote transacting. When courts interpret contracts with a sensible, business-oriented reading, parties can be more confident that they will not be victims of opportunistic behavior.

III. FAULTY ASSUMPTIONS UNDERLIE THE NEW FORMALISTS' OPT-IN RULE

Under party choice theory, parties would be able to opt out of the narrow approach, for example, by expressly "signal[ling] *ex ante* their preference for more aggressive modes of interpretation of the contract terms."[73] However, if parties fail to make that choice, a number of consequences follow. These consequences constitute the different strands of formalism. A court should not incorporate trade usages in the interpretation of a contract; unless expressly included, they would be excluded.[74] If parties fail to delegate broad discretion to a court, as by invoking standards of reasonableness, then the court should decline to exercise discretion.[75] Similarly, if the parties do not indicate *ex ante* that they want courts to depart from "formal contract doctrine," then courts should decline to do so.[76] Current formalists shun both *ex ante* defaults[77] and *ex post* adjustments.[78] Formalists also reject the resort to equitable principles, such as an anti-forfeiture principle, as a misguided use of

[73] Robert E. Scott, *The Case for Formalism in Relational* Contract, 94 Nw. L. Rev. 847, 851 (2000).

[74] Schwartz and Scott advocate overturning of the current "contextualist linguistic default" embodied in the U.C.C. in favor of a linguistic default of ordinary meaning. Schwartz & Scott, *supra* note 19, at 584–85.

[75] Kraus & Scott, *supra* note 15, at 1030.

[76] *Id.* at 1032.

[77] Formalists argue that party heterogeneity makes *ex ante* default rules inefficient. *See* Schwartz & Scott, *supra* note 19, at 594–601.

[78] Schwartz and Scott argue that the current approach to interpretation misguidedly sets the rule as a mandatory rule of contextualism. They view the rule as a mandatory one that paternalistically refuses to recognize party choice for a narrow approach excluding evidence. Schwartz & Scott, *supra* note 19, at 609–10. They view the failure of courts to respect merger clauses as an overturning of the parties' choice for a non-contextualized approach.

doctrine.[79] Yet another iteration of formalism excludes the parties' contractual goals from the determination of contractual intent and gives primacy to the contractual language even if it undermines the parties' goals.[80] At other times, the narrow approach rejects certain "interpretive rules" in contract such as that favoring promises over conditions.[81] Formalists also reject courts' adopting interpretive rules that invoke other norms.[82] Before party choice theory became dominant, a variety of interpretive approaches prevailed. Early formalism proponents embraced literalism.[83]

All of the formalist arguments favoring limits on courts tie back to party choice. In each instance parties can opt into a whole array of broader approaches to interpretation. However, if they fail to do so, party choice theory dictates a narrow approach. Party choice theory relies on a number of assumptions, some articulated and some implicit, which are open to question.[84] The logic of the party choice proponents' opt-in approach would seem to foreclose courts from using a consequentialist[85]

However, Schwartz and Scott fail to recognize several points, which undermine the assertion that a contextualized approach to interpretation is a mandatory one imposed by paternalistic courts, which contravenes party choice and undermines party welfare. First, to apply the parol evidence rule, courts must first decide how to interpret the meaning of the terms. Without that initial determination, a court cannot decide if the extrinsic evidence contradicts or adds to the terms. To settle on a meaning of the term, courts do and "should, as part of the process of interpretation, welcome testimony concerning antecedent agreements communications, and other factors that may assist in indicating the parties' original intentions." Kniffin, *supra* note 1 § 24.11. Second, the rejection of *ex ante* defaults is premised on a series of assumptions about presumed party preferences for a non-contextualized approach, which are open to question.

Finally, the rejection of *ex post* adjustments by courts policing to bring about fairness too broadly rejects all *ex post* adjustments by assuming that all *ex post* judicial adjustments would be inefficient interventions by courts. For an example of an *ex post* adjustment that would be efficient, see the discussion of Jacob & Youngs, *infra* Part VII.A, in which the court applied an anti-forfeiture principle to reject a literal reading of an express condition in a way that actually minimized an interpretive risk for parties.

79 Kraus & Scott, *supra* note 15, at 1047–48.

80 *Id.* at 1027.

81 *Id.* at 1078.

82 One example suggesting that a court should interpret a term as a promise rather than a condition invokes norms against forfeiture. *See* RESTATEMENT (SECOND) OF CONTRACTS § 227 ("In resolving doubts as to whether an event is made a condition of an obligor's duty … an interpretation is preferred that will reduce the obligee's risk of forfeiture …."). Moreover, the inclusion of a precise term and the failure to opt in indicate party choice to courts to limit interpretation to "the formal obligations that the parties have explicitly specified in advance." Kraus & Scott, *supra* note 15, at 1030.

83 Scott, *supra* note 72, at 847.

84 *See* Part V. For a recent article challenging some of the assumptions underlying the textualists' arguments in contract interpretation, *see* Bayern, *supra* note 2. For a comparable critique of the assumptions underlying a textualist approach to statutory interpretation, *see* Eskridge & Frickey, *supra* note 32, at 340 (documenting indeterminacy in textualism).

85 *See supra* note 4.

analysis to supply default rules, to decide whether ambiguity exists,[86] or to resolve ambiguous, vague,[87] or incomplete contracts. The party choice rule provides that a party whose interpretation depends on extra-contractual considerations, whether those considerations involve trade usages, equity, parties' goals, or the use of norms, *will always lose*, unless that party has expressly delegated interpretive authority to a court by using broad, open-ended language or unless the text is clearly ambiguous.[88] Even when the text is ambiguous, the formalists (and textualists) would severely

[86] Ambiguity refers to a situation in which the precise meaning of express terms is unclear. Judge Posner refers to the process of deciphering meaning as one of "disambiguating" contracts. Posner, *supra* note 1, at 1589.

[87] *See* Schwartz & Scott, *supra* note 5 (noting failure of courts to distinguish vague from ambiguous terms).

[88] *See* Kraus & Scott, *supra* note 15, at 1030 (arguing that the use of "precise" terms demonstrates a choice by parties to "withdraw authority from courts" and to "direct them to enforce the formal obligations that the parties have explicitly specified in advance"). It is not clear what good that directive would do when the meaning is unclear. Textualism operates differently when express terms appear to cover the situation but the parties offer differing meanings to the express terms. Textualism would lead courts to literally interpret the terms of a contract or to leave the matter unresolved if the terms are express but their meaning is unclear. Professor Scott has indicated that "when the disputed contract language is ambiguous, the differences between textualists and contextualists essentially disappears" since in those cases, courts can look to contextual evidence. Schwartz & Scott, *supra* note 5, at 963 n. 94. The rule, moreover, would only apply if the parties had an integrated agreement, which was clear and plain on its face. Scott E-mail, *supra* note 42.

However, there are still differences between textualists and contextualists with how readily they are to resort to contextual evidence. First, as Corbin indicated, you really can't know whether a text is unambiguous until you look at the context. Corbin, *supra* note 2 at § 24.7 Meanings may look "plain," but if you know more about the trade, party negotiations, or other background information, words can suddenly take on a lot of different meanings. Thus, the willingness to look beyond the contract depends on an initial finding that the contract has no plain meaning and is ambiguous. That initial determination seems to foreclose more contextual evidence than would be the case under a Corbinian approach or a Restatement approach that finds that context evidence should be readily admissible without a prior finding of ambiguity. *See* RESTATEMENT (SECOND) OF CONTRACTS, § 212 comment b.

The remaining differences with the textualists can also be seen by reading the NYU article authored by Professors Kraus and Scott. In that article, the authors suggest that the selection of precise terms instead of vague terms means that the parties have chosen not to delegate discretion to the courts to fill in those terms, and the choice of a precise term should therefore cause the court to "enforce the formal obligations that the parties have explicitly specified in advance." Kraus & Scott, *supra* note 15 at 1030.

The view is that if a term is ambiguous, both textualists and contextualists would reach similar results on the decisions about admitting context evidence. However, it is important to note that the textualists would significantly restrict that context evidence and admit only the contract, the experience of the judge, a dictionary, the pleadings, and some business information. Thus, even though Scott says that under conditions of ambiguity, "the divide between formalist and antiformalist positions essentially disappears," Schwartz & Scott, *supra* note 5, at 963, there is still a divide in the type of context evidence being admitted. Formalists would still exclude course of performance and trade usage evidence, Schwartz & Scott, *supra* note 19, at 592, and there is no indication that they would be willing to allow courts to interpret contracts in a way that minimizes the interpretive risk for the parties and reduces the danger of opportunism as a means of achieving the presumed goal of improving welfare.

limit the type of context evidence that can be included.[89] Therefore, it is not clear that courts could directly consult a cost/benefit analysis of consequentialism under the umbrella of the "life experience of the judge," the broadest type of context evidence allowed by formalists.[90]

The preference for party choice depends on a number of assumptions that mask the substantive choices being made. The assumption is that parties will choose their interpretive method when they draft their contracts, and the courts' role should be limited to enforcing or deciphering that choice. The parties, however, often do not make *ex ante* choices over the proper role for courts since parties would not even see the need to choose an interpretive method; the need is simply not on the parties' radar screen.

Even if the parties might choose an interpretive method, the formalists suggest unusual tests for identifying party choice. The test, therefore, may fail to correspond with the parties' likely intent. A different approach to discerning interpretive choice should be adopted. The test suggested here is that courts should retain discretion to craft interpretation rules without any party choice.

The party choice theory depends on the notion that the use of a precise term and the avoidance of broad or vague terms represent a deliberate decision by parties to avoid the back end costs associated with vague terms.[91] Parties may use a precise term, however, for a variety of reasons that do not signal a desire to foreclose a court from any later interpretive role. Courts must decide what significance to attribute to the use of a precise term in a contract and ascertain whether it indicates a choice by the parties as to the preferred interpretive method. It may reflect the parties' certainty that the term is self-evident, obviating any need for any later interpretation by a court.[92]

89 *Id.*

90 The contextualized evidence permitted by the formalist/textualist would consist of a "minimum evidentiary basis" consisting of "the pleadings and supporting briefs, evidence as to what the seller delivered, the contract, a recent 10-K SEC filing by the buyer (if any), and the life experience of the judge." Schwartz & Scott, *supra* note 5, at 952.

91 Kraus & Scott, *supra* note 15, at 1030.

92 The modern party choice advocate attributes great significance to the use of a precise term. The background to the debate regarding the importance of a precise term is traceable to a distinction drawn between observable and verifiable matters. The classic instance is the problem of a shirking worker whose behavior, while observable by an employer, may not be verifiable to a court. Alan Schwartz analyzed this distinction when he explained why parties might settle on a precise term rather than an open-ended one. Parties might, for example, choose a contract in which the manufacturer's price for an item was set at a certain fixed price per unit in order to avoid "the strategic-behavior risk" that accompanied a contract in which the price fluctuated with demand since that matter might not be observable to the seller and certainly not verifiable to a court. *See* Alan Schwartz, *Relational Contracts in the Courts: An Analysis of Incomplete Agreements and Judicial Strategies*, 21 J. LEGAL STUD. 271 (1992). This chapter differs from these types of analyses in surmising that the use of a precise term may be due to bounded rationality constraints; parties simply settle on a precise term without being aware of the need to draft further or they settle on such

Under this assumption, the use of a precise term should not be interpreted as a disavowal of interpretive authority by the court.

Second, the use of a precise term may reflect a failure to anticipate how a future event might affect the term in a way which might benefit from or require *ex post* interpretation. For example, if the parties "specify that material A should be used in construction but that they would really prefer substituting B if an unusual problem arises with A,"[93] the use of the precise term should not necessarily be read as a rejection of *ex post* interpretation, but, rather, as a drafting choice that arose because of the unforeseeability of the future.

If one assumes that a matter like the advent of four-wheeled ATVs was unanticipated, the use of a precise term might reflect an unthinking, unreflective choice of a word. The question of whether the parties intended to foreclose all future interpretation should therefore not depend solely on the presence or absence of a precise term. Instead, the court should ask whether it is likely that parties intended to foreclose courts from having discretion to interpret contracts to achieve the parties' likely goals, like the minimization of transaction costs and the curbing of opportunistic behavior. If such intent were improbable, then express opt in should not be required and the court can and should use the interpretive method that will best promote welfare improvement. The use of a precise term, such as "a fixed quantity of material at a fixed price," might sometimes foreclose a court from intervening to incorporate trade usage if using the term would encourage opportunistic behavior by a party advantaged by price changes. However, in other cases, where a precise term such as one banning a three-wheeled ATV fails to anticipate a change in technology, courts should expand the term to include four-wheeled ATVs, even without discretion, if doing so would achieve the parties' original goals, regardless of the number of wheels.

Just as courts must decide what parties likely intended when they used precise terms, courts also have to deal with contracts lacking a clause phrased in broad or open-ended terms expressly to allow *ex post* interpretation. If a contract fails to use terms like "reasonable" or "good faith," what implications can and should a court draw from that failure to delegate *ex post* interpretive authority? The party choice proponents' assumption requires that if parties want *ex post* interpretation, they must draft for and anticipate the need for such interpretation *ex ante*. They are forcing parties to make choices about *ex post* interpretation that may not be an appropriate subject of bargaining. Thus, if parties are bargaining over the sale of a tractor, for example, they also have to anticipate the need for *ex post* interpretation, or they will

a term to save on transaction costs on the assumption that a court will be able to interpret the term to maximize gains from trade.

93 Shavell, *supra* note 16, at 289.

be subjected to a narrow approach to interpretation. If they fail to anticipate the need for opting into *ex post* interpretation by the court, they will be foreclosed from accessing courts' broad interpretive powers.

That assumption seems counterintuitive, especially when one considers the drafting costs for contracts and the parties' reasonable assumption that courts will supply reasonable terms using a variety of broadly used interpretive techniques. Why would parties want courts, because of their failure to opt in, to abandon all routinely used interpretive techniques? And would it be safe for courts to assume that parties had intended to foreclose such techniques simply on the basis of the failure to adopt a specific phraseology such as "good faith" or "reasonable"? Parties would likely want to avoid giving courts the power to infer that the absence of an open-ended phrase or vague term meant that the parties intended to exclude the application of good faith and reasonableness standards.

Whether the parties intend to foreclose all future interpretation should therefore depend not solely on the presence or absence of a precise term. Because the absence of an open-ended term itself requires interpretation, the court is intervening, but it is doing so on the basis of a questionable assumption about party choice. Instead, the court should ask whether it is likely that parties' use of a precise term evidences an intention to foreclose courts from using discretion to interpret contracts to achieve the parties' likely goals, such as the minimization of transaction costs and the curbing of opportunistic behavior. If express opt in is not required, then the court can promote welfare improvement.

Another significant assumption underlying party choice theory is that if the parties fail to invoke broad interpretive authority expressly, they intend to rely exclusively on informal mechanisms of enforcement to deal with the residual uncertainty problem in contracts.[94] They assume that if parties do not use vague terms, which would directly invoke a court role, they have chosen to remove discretion from the court and have also subscribed exclusively to informal enforcement mechanisms to deal with unexpected events or disputes.[95] If the parties do not address a matter with a sufficient degree of precision in the contract and no express delegation exists, then the parties have knowingly chosen to exclude it from legal enforcement.[96] Yet, it is far from clear that when the parties stop short in drafting, they are deliberately opting out of all legal enforcement for matters not explicitly addressed.

A number of problematic assumptions undermine this party choice argument for exclusive and deliberate reliance on informal mechanisms. These assumptions include the propositions (1) that parties mentally choose to partition between

94 *See* Schwartz & Scott, *supra* note 19, at 557.

95 *See id.*

96 Kraus & Scott, *supra* note 15, at 1048.

informal and legally enforceable parts of the overall agreement, (2) that all firms are risk-neutral in all of their decision making, (3) that parties would opt for exclusive reliance on informal mechanisms regardless of how robust those mechanisms were in a particular setting, (4) that formal enforcement will crowd out the informal enforcement and (5) that accuracy rather than minimization of interpretive risk lies at the heart of the interpretive task.

The argument erroneously assumes that parties deliberately and rationally partition between legally enforceable and legally unenforceable aspects of their contracts. The assumption is that if parties fail to use vague terms, they have chosen to remove interpretive powers from courts and to rely exclusively on private strategies to resolve disputed matters as the least costly alternative. Often, however, because parties believe that the precise term covers every possible circumstance, they cannot envision any need for a court to intervene. Accordingly, they likely neither partition between legally enforceable and legally unenforceable aspects nor invoke the authority of a court. Such oversight should not be determinative of the interpretive approach taken.

If most parties are generally happy with the principal terms of their deal, such as what is being bought or sold, price or value return, timing, duration, and so forth, and a party is satisfied with the big picture (the so-called business points) and reluctant to expend time and resources to niggle smaller items ("lawyer points"), then the parties may fail to opt into a broad interpretive rule or plan out what parts of the contract will be subject to formal or informal sanctions for reasons that do not signal a deliberate choice to remove the court. Parties' failure expressly to opt into a broad rule could be based on the view that (1) reputational and informal mechanisms will be the sole means to solve any later arising interpretive dispute or (2), on the contrary assumption, that a neutral party, such as a court, will be available to interpret the contract in such a way as to maximize the surplus. Investments in bargaining and drafting, trust in a neutral court, and re-bargaining in the shadow of the law are all possible means of achieving the benefits of bargains.

The proposition that parties intend to rely exclusively on informal mechanisms and to foreclose judicial *ex post* interpretation rests on a particular assumption about the role of the judiciary in contract litigation that is not likely to be held universally. In fact, a common assumption would be that the court would have broad authority to interpret contracts and to decide on the best interpretive rule or any other rule in contracts without an express delegation by the parties.[97]

97 Of course, the parties could bargain for a court to rely exclusively on a literal interpretation of the contract. If they did so, the court would be likely to respect such a term, although as Professor Charny has pointed out, that clause itself would require interpretation. David Charny, *Hypothetical Bargains: The Normative Structure of Contract Interpretation*, 89 MICH. L. REV. 1815, 1819 (1991).

The dominant party choice assumption seems contrary to what most parties would assume. Under the guise of protecting party choice built on the empirically questionable assumption that every party who wants expansive interpretation will include the appropriate language and those who do not do so wish to reject such interpretation, courts would be disabled from engaging in the kind of interpretation of contracts that they have routinely engaged in and that most parties would assume they have the discretion to continue to engage in.

Another problematic assumption of the party choice proponents is that the level and degree of informal enforcement will be workable. In many instances, the conditions for such enforcement are not present, as where there is no effective means for transmitting information about possible shirking behavior by contracting parties, the group is too large or lacks homogeneity, or there is no agreement on what behavior would warrant reputational sanctions. In such instances, it may be unwise to assume universally that the parties intend to rely exclusively on informal enforcement if they stop short of drafting with a sufficient level of precision to resolve all issues yet also fail to invoke discretion. It would not make sense for parties to give up court interpretive authority where the conditions are not conducive to informal sanctions. In such cases, one would assume that even if the parties fail to opt in expressly, they would prefer courts to retain interpretive powers over the contract.

The party choice argument also seems to be based on a particular (though largely unacknowledged) behavioral assumption about dispute resolution. The argument suggests that if a court lends legal enforcement to a matter that either does not demand judicial resolution via an express delegation or does not clearly resolve the matter in question through a relevant contractual clause, then the legal enforcement will have negative welfare effects. It will "crowd out informal enforcement."[98] While there is some experimental data supporting this crowding out thesis,[99] the author remains skeptical for two reasons. First, other experimental data suggests that there

[98] Kraus & Scott, *supra* note 15, at 1058. Professors Scott, Gilson, and Sabel argue that "sophisticated parties know better than courts how best to mix" informal and formal enforcement. Ronald J. Gilson, Charles F. Sabel & Robert E. Scott, *Braiding: The Interaction of Formal and Informal Contracting in Theory, Practice, and Doctrine*, 110 COLUM. L. REV. 1377 (2010). This interesting article makes the case that parties themselves are engaged in allocating enforcement between informal and formal enforcement when they arrange their affairs in pharmaceutical contracts between the investor and pharmaceutical company. In those contracts, the parties agree to share information, and they would be liable for the breach of the agreements. But as the parties learn more about the counterparty and start to work together on a project or a new drug, the formal enforcement is displaced by informal enforcement. As the entities become more entwined, the costs of switching increase, which in itself acts as a kind of informal enforcement mechanism. Scott, Gilson, and Sabel have uncovered a real life example in which parties have allocated enforcement strategies between informal and formal sanctions.

[99] Kraus & Scott, *supra* note 15, at 1058 at n. 140.

can be complementarities between legal and non-legal enforcement.[100] Second, if one accounts for the high cost of litigation, a logical objection to the crowding out phenomenon undermines the thesis.[101] Litigation is so expensive that parties would rarely prefer litigation to informal sanctions. In the rare case of litigation, it is usually because there are large dollar amounts at stake and those dollars have prompted one party to act in an opportunistic fashion. This is precisely the type of case where litigation could helpfully supplement informal sanctions, which are likely to be ineffective because the benefits of opportunism outweigh the reputational costs.[102]

IV. REDUCING PARTY COSTS AND RISKS

The prior section illuminated flaws in the assumptions of party choice theory. Since most parties will fail to see the need to opt in to broad judicial interpretation and will assume courts will retain such powers, the presence or absence of express opt in language should not be determinative of whether a court should intervene with interpretive rules of its own.

If party choice is problematic, then the question for courts is what interpretive approach would match party preferences and what cost/benefit approach should be used in any contract requiring interpretation. This section suggests that a cost/benefit analysis with realistic assumptions favors a judicial rule of interpretation in which courts retain broad powers without an express opt-in requirement.

The party choice version of cost/benefit analysis makes two errors. First, it assumes that if parties draft express terms, they have invested large front-end costs to avoid *ex post* enforcement costs and the exclusive job for courts is one of reaching an accurate interpretation. The second error they make is to assume that parties are risk-neutral.

The first assumption is that if a term is important to the parties, the parties themselves will devise an answer in the contract, but that it will sometimes be costly for a court to figure out the right answer (the accuracy problem). The party choice proponents view the costs and benefits in terms of a tradeoff between weighing the *greater* accuracy that can be achieved by taking in more evidence and the *sufficient degree of accuracy* that can be achieved by looking at the contract's terms alone or as supplemented by a minimum evidentiary base. If courts depart from the text and

100 *See* Sergio Lazzarini, Gary J. Miller & Todd Zenger, *Order with Some Law: Complementarity vs. Substitution of Formal and Informal Arrangements*, 20 J.L. ECON. & ORG. 261 (2004).

101 William C. Whitford also independently contributed this insight. Email from Professor William C. Whitford, Professor Emeritus University of Wisconsin Law School to Juliet P. Kostritsky, Professor of Law Case Western Reserve law School dated February 11, 2009.

102 *See* Karen Eggleston, Eric A. Posner & Richard Zeckhauser, *The Design and Interpretation of Contracts: Why Complexity Matters*, 95 NW. U. L. REV. 91 (2000); *see also* Robert E. Scott, *Conflict and Cooperation in Long Term Contracts*, 75 CAL. L. REV. 2005, 2044 (1987) (discussing when "the short term gains from defection exceed the present discounted value of future cooperation").

evaluate more evidence, they would have a greater probability of reaching the accurate result. Firms are willing to give up some degree of accuracy (*i.e.*, some wrong judicial determinations of terms) to save costs since the greater accuracy is not worth the costs of achieving it.

The problem with looking at the costs and benefits as a trade-off between greater accuracy and the costs of achieving that greater accuracy is that there may be no correct or accurate answer *at all* to the disputed matter. The failure to recognize that leads to a misspecification of the problem. If each party admits that it did not know the other party's meaning, then the "accuracy" at the center of a contract is mythical.[103]

Even when parties employ express terms, there may be no "accurate interpretation" if the parties' *own strategy* is to leave some matters to less, rather than more, elaborate specification. When matters remain unresolved for cost reasons, courts should reduce the interpretive risk stemming from that residual uncertainty because the parties will deduct the interpretive risk from their gains from exchange and will stop drafting when the interpretive risk becomes less than the costs of drafting further. If the court stays its hand because of the absence of an express opt in, the court will add to interpretive risk since the parties likely assumed a court would be available to solve the problem if informal mechanisms do not work.

To resolve interpretive problems given the lack of resolution at the center, courts should frame an interpretive rule that reduces the interpretive risk for all classes of transactors as a way of achieving the parties' presumed goal of lowering transaction costs and maximizing surplus. Since accuracy does not exist in many cases, courts should feel free to adopt the optimal method that lowers interpretive risk for the parties and overall costs.

In making those determinations, courts should assume that parties are not risk-neutral.[104] Although the party choice proponents argue the contrary,[105] in fact most actors, including commercial firms, are not risk-neutral when evaluating projects in which they might *initially* invest. The sense in which firms are thought to be

[103] *See* Cohen, *supra* note 9, at 130 ("Economists and courts start from the presumption that courts should follow the intention of the parties. To admit incompleteness, however, is to admit that the intention of the parties is uncertain, or at least disputed.").

[104] The formalists argue the contrary, suggesting that parties are risk neutral and only care about a court getting the correct answer on average. *See* Schwartz & Scott, *supra* note 19, at 575. For that reason formalists believe that a firm "is unwilling to incur additional costs in order to increase the accuracy of any particular finding." Schwartz & Scott, *supra* note 5, at 931.

There is only one sense in which firms are risk neutral, and that refers to parties who, "in arriving at the present value of a future income stream of possible values do not discount the *ex ante* expected value in light of their uncertainty, risk." Second, if firms are not risk neutral, then they would indeed care about achieving greater accuracy in interpretation.

[105] *See supra* note 103.

risk-neutral is "with reference to selecting from among risky projects after valuation of a future income stream of risky values has been correctly established in light of risk."[106] "At this second stage, if managers can, without incurring any cost, shift from one risky project to another, then as amongst those differing and risky projects, firms are risk-neutral."[107] This is the sense in which economists mean to refer to firms' being risk-neutral. But at the initial stage in evaluating among projects (or contracts) to invest in, parties, including commercial firms, do care about risk. The purchaser of a project with a payoff will care about variance in interpretation and will view it as a cost. The purchaser will expend resources to reduce variance and minimize interpretive risks. Just as contractors attempt to structure transactions to lessen moral hazard or opportunism, so too would parties subscribe to courts adopting a judicial rule to lower interpretive risk unless the offsetting costs of judicial errors were greater than the expected increase in surplus.

Since parties care about risk, courts should focus on whether the interpretation adopted pursuant to a judicial rule or party choice will increase or decrease risks (and costs) over time to different classes of transactors.[108] Parties want to increase the payoff from entering transactions by reducing *all costs, including the cost of interpretive risk affecting contracts.*[109] Parties want courts to use an interpretive rule that maximizes payoffs by reducing the drag of interpretive risk. Parties who exchange do so to minimize the costs of exchange.[110] They want to reduce the risk of transacting as a way of minimizing costs, including the interpretive risk from leaving a contract with residual uncertainty given a particular interpretation rule. These costs and risks are viewed by the parties to any transaction *ex ante* and probabilistically.

[106] E-mail from Professor Ronald J. Coffey, Case Western Reserve University School of Law (Dec. 15, 2006) (on file with author).

[107] *Id.*

[108] Courts must defend their intervention choice in terms of cost because parties themselves want to minimize the costs of transacting.

[109] Moreover, parties care about more than achieving a mean or average payoff; they care about courts minimizing interpretive risk. Courts should not focus on the costs and benefits of achieving greater "accuracy" in interpretation. Since the parties themselves stopped drafting in a way that left the central problem unresolved, courts cannot realistically access an accurate answer but party choice advocates assume that the purchaser of a project covered by a contract and subject to interpretive risk would be indifferent to variance or be risk neutral. *See* Bowers, *supra* note 2; Bayern, *supra* note 2, at 946.

The tradeoff is between admitting more evidence to increase accuracy and the costs of doing so, which includes greater uncertainty from the admissibility of such evidence. Two problems undermine this trade-off analysis. Risk neutrality has two meanings. In one of its two distinct meanings, risk neutral parties comprise those who "in arriving at the present value of a future income stream of possible values, do not discount the *ex ante* expected value in light of their uncertainty, risk." Second, if firms are *not* risk neutral, then they would indeed care about achieving greater accuracy in interpretation. *See* Coffey E-mail, *supra* note 105; Cohen, *supra* note 9, at 144 ("Contracting parties do not demand enforceable coin flips to resolve their disputes.").

[110] *See* Williamson, *supra* note 20, at 46.

Before using a cost/benefit analysis to assess the best interpretive strategy for courts to take in cases in which the parties have adopted express terms but failed to delegate broad interpretive authority to a court, one must model how parties bargain, why they enter into exchanges and how a particular interpretive rule would affect the achievement of the parties' goals.

The parties may adopt an express term that is meant to settle a controversy in some way. But the parties may fail to draft with the level of particularity and detail needed to resolve all possible questions, given uncertainty and the unforeseeability of the future. Each party has to decide how many resources to put into bargaining and drafting. Each will invest when the costs of doing so are outweighed by the benefits. The costs include the haggling time necessary to develop a mutual understanding, investment in information, and the thinking cost of anticipating future states of the world and the proclivities of the other party for opportunistic behavior. The benefits of investing in bargaining and drafting include the reduction of opportunism and similar actions that would reduce gains from trade. Contract interpretation is necessary and important because parties cannot devote infinite resources to articulating their bargain. If drafting and, even more importantly, thinking costs were free, interpretive problems would never arise. Thus, the use of express terms including the cost of expressly delegating interpretive powers of a court is beset by the same cost of drafting issues as where parties decide to use no express terms or leave gaps in contracts.[111]

The interpretive rule analysis suggested here generally asks whether the "costs of specifying" are either (1) more than the costs of risking non-specification or (2) more than the surplus achievable by the exchange. The first prong of the cost analysis is important although sometimes overlooked. One would *not* want to continue to draft if the drafting costs outweigh the risk of non-specification. And, under the second prong, one would not undertake drafting costs if such costs outweigh any possible gains from trade. Thus, parties may compare the residual cost of an interpretation risk[112] against the cost of drafting further. The interpretive risks include (1) inaccuracies in interpretation which occur when courts depart from a meaning of express terms that both parties agreed on[113]; (2) the risk that courts will invest the contract

[111] For that reason, this chapter will treat these two issues together and use examples from both interpretive and gap-filling disputes.

[112] In evaluating the cost of interpretive risk to the parties *ex ante* in any contract setting, one must factor in the interpretive rule that a court would use and would announce in the future to interpret that contract. One would expect courts to attempt to minimize *ex ante* interpretation risks to classes of transactors represented by each party to a contract and thereby decrease the overall costs of contracting, at least in cases where the court can intervene at a lower cost than whatever other mechanisms exist to lower the interpretive risk (including reputational and informal sanctioning mechanisms). Such a rule would presumably affect the resources parties devote to drafting.

[113] The difficulty of proving that the parties jointly agreed on a particular meaning to be attached to given words is well known in both contractual and statutory interpretation contexts. *See* Kniffin, *supra*

with a meaning that fails to maximize gains and minimize costs;[114] and (3) the risk that courts will interpret the contract to facilitate opportunism.[115]

In evaluating the cost of interpretive risk to the parties *ex ante* in any contract setting, one must factor in the interpretive rule that a court would use and would announce in the future to interpret that contract. One would expect courts to attempt to minimize *ex ante* interpretation risks to classes of transactors represented by each party to a contract and thereby decrease the overall costs of contracting, at least in cases where the court can intervene at a lower cost than whatever other mechanisms exist to lower the interpretive risk (including reputational and informal sanctioning mechanisms).[116] Such a rule would presumably affect the resources parties devote to drafting.

When parties have not invested enough resources to eliminate all interpretive risks, courts must determine whether and when to engage in *ex post* interpretation. The benefits to be achieved from bargains could be obtained through more specific and complete drafting, but courts should recognize that these benefits could alternatively be achieved by trusting in one's ability to work out any interpretive problems with the counterparty or by trusting a *neutral* to interpret the contract in a way that maximizes gains from trade. It is important to recognize that interpretive approach is built on assumptions about the parties' expectations and drafting choices.[117]

Once the benefits to the parties of a judicial role in minimizing interpretive risk are fully realized and the likelihood that parties would assume they could invoke informal or formal sanctions is established, it becomes possible to understand why it would not make sense to follow the strand of party choice outlawing the use of equity in deciding ordinary contract disputes unless parties opt into it. There is often nothing in the parties' contract that forecloses such resort to equity so the question is whether retaining such judicial powers to invoke equity would be optimal and why.

note 1, at § 24.2 (detailing difficulty that "tension between the parties' respective interests "presents for contract interpretation"); *see also* Eskridge & Frickey, *supra* note 32, at 325–32 (discussing problems of discerning legislative intent including indeterminacy and lack of access to actual intent in statutory words).

114 The risk could materialize in several other ways. A court could adhere to a literal interpretation that it increases the costs of contracting. Alternatively, a court could add to interpretive risk by "incorrectly refus[ing] to enforce 'express terms' in favor of some implied term or contextualist interpretation." Cohen, *supra* note 9, at 134.

115 Several scholars have explored the connections between interpretation methodologies and opportunism. *See, e.g.*, Juliet P. Kostritsky, *Judicial Incorporation of Trade Usages: A Functional Solution to the Opportunism Problem*, 39 Conn. L. Rev. 451 (2006); James W. Bowers, *Murphy's Law and the Elementary Theory of Contract Interpretation: A Response to Schwartz & Scott*, 57 Rutgers L. Rev. 587 (2005) (explaining preference of some firms for broader interpretive approach as a means of curbing opportunism).

116 For a discussion of reputational sanctioning mechanisms, see Kostritsky, *infra* note 114 at 477–80.

117 It may be that ultimately the choice of an interpretive method depends on empirical data not readily available.

Formalists object when courts "apply[] the formal doctrines in a nonstandard fashion"[118] by which they mean a resort to equitable principles. For example, party choice advocates believe that courts err if they permit parol evidence of an oral condition despite an integrated agreement. In their view, the introduction of such evidence undermines formal doctrines, such as the parol evidence rule. They believe that the foundational premise for such judicial action – one that surmises that the intervention is necessary to facilitate rational ends of the parties – is flawed and undermines party choice.[119] Formalists would also rule out the invocation of equitable considerations when the court is charged with interpreting a term, such as the wording of an express condition, unless the parties expressly authorize such equitable intervention.

The total ban on the consideration of equity in the interpretation of contracts *absent authorization* should be rejected in favor of an approach in which the invocation of equity depends on a court rule, not party choice. This permits courts to implement an equitable dimension in contract law in a way that furthers the parties' overall goals of maximizing gains from trade and minimizing interpretation risks.

V. THE OPT-IN RULE SHOULD BE JUSTIFIED LIKE ANY OTHER COMMON LAW DOCTRINE

Whether the rule requiring parties to opt into the courts' broad interpretive powers should be the preferred default rule for contract interpretation can best be understood in the context of common law adjudication. In particular, the role that formalism has played in the distinct arena of common law decision making and the reasons why scholars and some courts later rejected it[120] should play an important part in deciding on the default rule of interpretation *as the rule is itself a common law rule*. The insights of legal realists into the deficiencies of formalism[121] in common law decision making can resolve whether parties should be required to opt in to escape a narrow approach dictated by party choice or whether court rules on interpretation should prevail and be available even without party choice.

Early adherents to formalism argued that goal achievement should play no role in legal decision making. Instead, courts were to use a purely deductive process

[118] Kraus & Scott, *supra* note 15, at 1031.

[119] *Id.*

[120] Later scholars rejected and, in fact, developed "an aversion to formalism" rejecting the idea that "the language of rules either can or should constrict choice in this way." Schauer, *supra* note 13, at 509.

[121] These deficiencies have been well documented. *See* Matthew Stephenson, *Legal Realism for Economists*, 23 J. ECON. PERSP. 191, 197–8 (2009) (describing the inability of formal legal reasoning to accurately predict judicial decisions and claiming that there "may be relatively consistent, stable patterns in judicial decisions ... that are captured neither by the formal rules nor by crude ideological measures").

in which judges could work from the generality of law in the form of an expressly stated doctrinal rule to their application (or non-application) to a set of facts.[122] David Hume demolished this notion by demonstrating that it was impossible for a generality to tell which special cases were contained within it.[123] A noun cannot tell you what categories are included within the noun. The idea that pure deduction can be used to work from a doctrine to its application (or non-application) to facts that vary from those stated in the generality of the doctrine has thus been rejected as impossible. It was therefore no longer possible "to believe that every legal question has a right answer that a properly trained lawyer or judge can deduce by correctly applying the canonical legal materials to the facts."[124]

The legal realists relentlessly pursued the insights of Hume and suggested that since doctrine alone would not predict what case outcome should prevail, cases should be resolved by uncovering the policy considerations that were operating in the cases at a *sub rosa* level.[125]

The view that *cases* cannot be decided without considering the projected consequences of a legal rule prevailed, and we are all now consequentialists, or at least were until the recent resurgence of formalism.[126] Courts cannot decide what the legal test for an offer should be or whether silence should operate as assent without considering the consequences on the costs of transacting.[127] In confronting whether an objective or subjective theory should govern the determination of an offer, courts consider the costs of a subjective approach – the consequences, given the difficulty of ascertaining a party's unmanifested subjective intent.[128] Because courts do

[122] Mechanical legal formalism holds "that the 'law' consists of a collection of rules contained in a well-defined set of source materials – principally statutes, regulations, contracts, and prior judicial decisions – along with a relatively small number of fundamental legal concepts. At least according to the pure version of formalism, every legal question has a right answer that a properly trained lawyer or judge can deduce by correctly applying the canonical legal materials to the facts of the case." *Id.* at 193.

[123] *See* David Hume, A TREATISE OF HUMAN NATURE 378 (2003).

[124] Stephenson, *supra* note 120, at 193.

[125] *See, e.g.*, John P. Dawson, *Duress through Civil Litigation*, 45 MICH. L. REV. 571 (1945); *see also* Robert W. Gordon, *Unfreezing Legal Reality: A Critical Approach to Contract Law*, 15 FLA. ST. U. L. REV. 195 (1987).

[126] *See* Charny, *supra* note 96; Schwartz & Scott, *supra* note 19; Kraus & Scott, *supra* note 15; Schwartz & Scott, *supra* note 5. *But see* Henry E. Smith, *The Equitable Dimension in Contract*, 45 SUFFOLK L. REV. 897 (2012). The new formalists and the consequentialists share welfare improvement as a goal, but the new formalists argue that courts should pursue that end by honoring party choice on interpretive method rather than consulting consequentialism to interpret ambiguous language.

[127] *See* Avery Katz, *Strategic Structure of Offer and Acceptance: Game Theory and the Law of Contract Formation*, 89 MICH. L. REV. 215 (1990) (looking at "implementation costs" of offer and acceptance rules).

[128] The role of the objective test was "to create and maintain a framework of reasonably well defined and assured expectations as to the likely official and nonofficial consequences of private venture and decision." Ian Ayres & Richard E. Speidel, STUDIES IN CONTRACT LAW 235 (7th ed. 2008) (citing J. W. Hurst, LAW: THE CONDITIONS OF FREEDOM IN NINETEENTH CENTURY AMERICA 21–2 (1956)).

consider consequences in contract law when they choose what doctrine to apply, and thus craft a common law rule of contract formation, they should take the same approach in determining whether a legal rule should govern contract interpretation or whether the matter should be left entirely to party choice.

However, when law and economics scholars consider how courts should interpret contested contracts, they curiously depart from the economics-based consequentialist method they advocate for common law adjudication. They instead embrace formalism and suggest that the parties' goals or objectives should play no role in deciding cases.[129] They posit that, if the parties fail to adopt expressly a rule delegating broad interpretive authority to courts[130] or use precise terms, the parties intend to foreclose courts' consideration of goals or anything else beyond the parties' express language and a minimum evidentiary base when interpreting contracts.[131] They justify their approach on the basis of party choice; the postulated choice is that parties prefer a narrow approach to interpretation on minimum evidentiary base of evidence without any consideration of equity.

What remains hidden from the formalist scholarship is that in postulating a rule for how parties must express their choice if they desire a broader interpretive rule, the formalists appear to be merely implementing parties' choices with a seemingly "linguistic inexorability."[132] Yet, by imposing the duty on parties to opt in and devising an interpretive rule to determine what suffices as an opt in, the formalists have set a high bar for opting in, relying on their own substantive choices. The decision about what rule to adopt in interpreting the parties' language is itself a choice. There is always a choice about whether and when to apply the rule and there is often an "escape route" that a court may advert to avoid the application of a rule.[133]

Party choice theorists project negative welfare consequences if courts go beyond the parties' express terms absent express delegation.[134] Following Hayek, who

[129] *See* Kraus & Scott, *supra* note 15, at 1026.

[130] Professors Kraus and Scott explain, "Sophisticated commercial parties ... might prefer their future contracts to be adjudicated under a regime that applied formal doctrine exclusively unless the parties indicate otherwise at the time they form the contract." *Id.* at 1032.

[131] *Id.*

[132] Schauer, *supra* note 13, at 512. The party choice theorists would like to eliminate such escape routes.

[133] *Id.* at 516.

[134] They project a party preference for an interpretive strategy of plain meaning or formalism or textualism since it would "(a) reduce contracting costs; (b) expand the set of efficient contracts parties could write." Schwartz & Scott, *supra* note 5, at 962 n. 92 (citing Schwartz & Scott, *supra* note 19, at 584–94). By inference, a contrary approach would increase costs, increase errors by courts, increase opportunistic behavior and decrease efficient contracting. *But see* Posner, *supra* note 1, at 1587 (positing that in certain cases rigid adherence to textualism might, by "creating pressure for recognizing exceptions ... reduce clarity"). The formalist view, moreover, is premised on a number of assumptions including that of "competent parties and incompetent courts." Scott, *supra* note 72, at 875. Other assumptions underlying the choice of a narrow preferred interpretive approach include the

projected obstacles to outsiders attempting to make improvements by intervening in a private exchange beyond implementing the spontaneous order,[135] the party choice advocates have offered an instrumental defense of formalism.

Even when an express term addresses the circumstance at issue, the court must also identify *the way in which the express term is meant to settle the question*. Party choice theorists have formulated a legal rule focused exclusively on party choice. The problem of interpretation and the choice of an interpretive rule will not go away unless the court lets the party asking for relief fail whenever the express terms do not settle the application because the term is unambiguous and has unquestioned meaning, or the party expressly, or by using vague language, indicated it wanted the court to decide matters *ex post* or indicated it wanted the court to advert to trade usage or other extrinsic matters.[136] Interpretive rules ultimately must be crafted by courts as even the decision to opt for party choice and to set the rules for such choice constitutes a legal rule.

view adopted by Schwartz and Scott that parties are indifferent to risk and care only about courts getting the correct result on average. Schwartz & Scott, *supra* note 20, at 550 n. 16, 577. That assumption has been questioned on a number of grounds. *See supra* note 103 (discussing the competing idea that parties are only indifferent to risk in one limited setting); Bowers, *supra* note 114 (challenging the idea that courts are likely to get the right result on average if the language is muddled). If the assumptions are not incontrovertible, then the decision to use them reflects a choice by the formalists to use those assumptions and exclude others. That deliberate choice then makes the resultant choice of formalism less assuredly correct.

135 Hayek maintained that judicial decision making is restricted by the spontaneous order in society and legal intervention outside such order will be ineffective. *See* Friedrich A. Hayek, Law, Legislation & Liberty 118–22 (1973) ("The judge … serves, or tries to maintain and improve, a going order which nobody has designed, an order that has formed itself without the knowledge and often against the will of authority, that extends beyond the range of deliberate organization on the part of anybody.… But even when … he creates new rules, he is not a creator of a new order but a servant endeavoring to maintain and improve the functioning of an existing order.").

136 A recent example involves the meaning of the term "subsidiary" in a cross-license agreement between Advanced Micro Devices (AMD) and Intel. Per a 2001 agreement between the companies, AMD and its subsidiaries were allowed to use Intel patents to manufacture chips. AMD spun off its manufacturing operations and formed a new company, Globalfoundries. The parties disagreed as to whether Globalfoundries met the subsidiary requirements as set forth in the cross-license agreement and was therefore eligible to use the Intel patent. Although the parties resolved the dispute on their own and executed a new cross-license agreement allowing AMD to outsource its manufacturing to third parties, if the dispute had gone to court, it could have been resolved using the interpretive rules suggested in this chapter. There is no indication in the 2001 agreement that the language describing the meaning of "subsidiary" would specifically address this particular situation. The court would therefore have to determine the way in which the express subsidiary requirements were meant to settle the question of whether a third-party like Globalfoundries is a real subsidiary that is eligible to use Intel's proprietary information. *See* generally *Advanced Micro Devices Inc.*, Current Report (Form 8-K) (Nov. 17, 2009) (see exhibit 10.2 for the new cross-license agreement between Intel and AMD); Don Clark, *Intel Threatens Fight over AMD Spinoff*, Wall St. J., Mar. 17, 2009, at B6 (describing the dispute over the proper interpretation of the term "subsidiary"); *Patent Cross License Agreement* (Jan. 1, 2001), http://contracts.corporate.findlaw.com/operations/ip/ 802.html (original cross-license agreement between Intel and AMD).

VI. RAWLSIAN THEORY, CONTEXTUAL EVIDENCE, CONSEQUENTIALIST ANALYSIS, EQUITY, AND PROBABILISTIC MODELS SUPPORT A JUDICIAL INTERPRETATION RULE

Once a lack of resolution in contracting and the inevitability of court decisions as to party choice are accounted for, the question becomes whether the parties would prefer courts to resolve the lack of resolution with an announced interpretive rule or decline to interpret contracts broadly absent party opt in. The choice should depend on which approach will enhance the willingness of parties to exchange. Courts should interpret contracts in order to maximize the gains from trade, minimize transaction costs, and control hazards of contracting, including opportunism.[137] Doing so mimics the legitimate goals of the parties in making the bargain and therefore reflects the intention of the parties, which courts should honor. To accomplish that, courts must determine the obligations of the parties under the contract as written, given the context in which the deal was made, and the intentions of the parties that reflect the goal of maximizing gains from trade, minimizing transaction costs, and controlling hazards and the likelihood that the parties will not see the need to opt in. If one assumes that the parties did not resolve a matter, the court still has to interpret the language that supposedly encapsulated that meaning. Interpretive rules are needed to guide the process of identifying the agreed upon meaning. Thus, whether one assumes that the parties reached consensus on an agreed meaning or failed to do so, leaving residual uncertainty, a court must decide what to do.

If parties could perfectly craft a complete contract, it might be self-enforcing, and courts would never have to interpret the contract because there would never be a breach or a need for interpretation. But because the parties have bounded rationality, they may not be able to foresee a future dispute prompting the need for judicial intervention or reputational sanction. They may not even see the need for judicial intervention to deal with behavioral uncertainty, which includes the proclivities for opportunistic behavior by a counterparty. It may not be efficient to invest in addressing future contingencies or future opportunism, the exact nature of which may not be anticipated, especially in light of the other ways of addressing the contingencies, such as relying on trust or judicial intervention. Bargaining requires the parties to determine how much effort to put into forecasting relevant circumstances that might change and the terms of their performance under those circumstances. Parties can rationally decide not to invest in investigating changed circumstances or

[137] Thus, while adverting to overall goals of maximizing surplus and minimizing transaction costs, courts should, on the other hand, not use specific contractual goals that were not enacted into the contract precisely because they were avoiding use of a contract term that might remain unverifiable to courts.

to deal with changed circumstances by relying on trust (new good faith negotiations in the face of the law) or judicial intervention.

Because the court's function is to achieve the legitimate goals of the parties (wealth maximization, minimization of transactions costs, and reduction of opportunism), it must put itself in the role of the parties and interpret the contract in light of what they must have intended in order to reach those goals.[138] One point parties negotiate over is the interpretive methodologies for the bargain. But if the parties do not select an interpretive methodology, courts should start with a default interpretation that maximizes the gains from trade, minimizes transaction costs, and controls hazards of contracting. A default rule that says that language will be interpreted narrowly or literally unless the parties expressly provide for a different scope and expressly delegate authority to the courts would raise transaction costs in a way that will preclude many bargains.

Realistic assumptions about how parties bargain should help courts select an appropriate rule. Courts should not decline to exercise interpretive authority merely because the parties have used a precise term or failed to grant broad interpretive authority. There are many reasons why they would use a precise term without intending to foreclose later judicial intervention by a court. They may also settle on a precise term thinking that it completely resolves all future issues. Parties normally negotiate in reliance on trust and renegotiation in the shadow of the law, and that means that judicial intervention – the shadow of the law – is the default rule. There are so many reasons why parties might use precise terms and fail to delegate on the basis of transaction costs and limits on rationality[139] that the optimal approach should proceed by considering how likely it is that parties would have wanted to limit judicial restraint of opportunism whenever parties failed to opt in, given the context of the bargaining process and the costs of drafting to eliminate all residual uncertainty. And if only one of the parties would have wanted to forbid judicial intervention to police opportunistic behavior, how likely is it that such party compensated the other party for giving up that means?

Courts should consider, on a probabilistic basis, parties' assumptions. Most parties would assume that courts are not indifferent to the goals of parties in contracting and that parties, at least behind a Rawlsian veil of ignorance,[140] would want judges to make decisions that realize those joint goals. Thus, parties may assume that there is no need to adopt a specific phrase inviting courts to exercise broad interpretive authority.

138 If one of the parties intended some other goal, and that intent is itself a form of self-dealing and opportunism, a court need not recognize that goal.

139 WILLIAMSON, *supra* note 20, at 45 (distinguishing bounded rationality from non rationality).

140 E-mail from Professor Robert W. Gordon, Yale University School of Law (to author Feb. 1, 2011) (on file with author).

Given the parties' likely assumptions, the default should be a judicial rule that allows courts to use broad contextual evidence, consequentialist analysis that models likely incentive effects on the parties, probabilistic models about likely assigned meaning,[141] to avoid unreasonable interpretations and engage in traditional jurisprudence in which they consider equity and can invoke other legal principles.[142] Retaining such power helps courts to police opportunism. Interpretive doctrines should not unduly restrict the role of the court in ways that parties would not have anticipated or wanted. At the same time, courts should refrain from *ex post* adjustment of contracts to achieve fairness if the negative incentive effects on parties would make the intervention inefficient.[143]

Courts should be able to invoke reasonableness to prevent absurd results and to provide "escape routes" for parties,[144] to imply terms of good faith even when not expressly agreed to, and to invoke norms or rules of law outside the particular field without parties' needing to have the foresight to invoke such principles. For example, in deciding how to interpret an express condition, or to decide on whether several words constitute an express condition or a promise, the court should be able to invoke legal principles that the parties have not expressly invoked. The burden should not be on parties to select methods of contract interpretation to which courts have regularly subscribed. Because there is a strong bias against a change in the common law standard,[145] courts should not lightly decide that the parties have chosen to forgo many traditional interpretive tools without an express and knowing renunciation of such tools.

An interpretive rule should be crafted as an intervention choice, recognizing that there is an interpretive risk inherent in all contracts and that parties would willingly subscribe to a rule *ex ante* if it would enhance the willingness of both parties to engage in exchange. Concerns that a broad interpretive rule will inevitably lead to

[141] Courts should feel free to invoke models of probability in inquiring into the probability that parties drafting a contract were concerned with or assigned a certain meaning to a particular term. They should use Bayesian analysis to assign meaning to a written term given realistic assessments of the parties' drafting skills and to calibrate the interpretation according to such estimates.

[142] *See* discussion of *Jacob & Youngs*, *infra* Section VII.A.

[143] Otherwise, parties will draft around it, adding to transaction costs. Thus, *ex post* judicial revision of contracts of the kind seen in the ALCOA case would not be permissible unless it is clear that both parties *ex ante* would have agreed to such revision as part of an interpretive rule that would maximize surplus and minimize cost across contracts for all classes of transactors going forward.

[144] Schauer, *supra* note 13, at 516.

[145] *See, e.g.*, *Monell v. Department of Social Services*, 436 U.S. 658, 708 (1978) (Powell, J., concurring) (recognizing a general hesitance to overrule prior interpretations of common law rules); The Common Law and the Environment: Rethinking the Statutory Basis for Modern Environmental Law 130, 142–3 (Roger E. Meiners & Andrew P. Morriss eds. 2000) (noting that the common law is "not simply a series of unconstrained choices"; rather, courts are constrained from making policy judgments by the specific facts of their cases, their limited geographic jurisdiction, and the law itself, the rule of *stare decisis* and a strong bias against overruling prior decisions).

uncertainty and greater costs in litigation and enforcement can be mitigated – at least if that rule is one that interprets terms by resorting to a justificational framework that invokes the pursuit of chosen consequences, such as minimizing the *ex ante* risks (costs) facing parties who use express terms.

VII. COURTS, RESTATEMENTS, AND EMPIRICAL EVIDENCE CHALLENGE PARTY CHOICE THEORY

Many doctrines and cases in contract law cannot be explained by party choice theory. The illustrations in the next section from current doctrine and case law demonstrate instances in which courts broadly interpret text with extrinsic evidence or interpret text with reference to the parties' objectives even if the parties have not specifically delegated interpretive authority to a court. In other cases, courts add terms to contracts even if not expressly agreed on. Any theory of contracts must explain the results in these cases or offer an explanation as to why courts persist in approaches that the party choice advocates argue should be rejected.

Judges (with certain exceptions in outlier cases)[146] are doing an excellent job of handling interpretive issues in a way that enhances value for the parties by controlling opportunism and diminishing interpretive risk. They do so by interpreting contracts to incorporate trade usages that directly control such opportunism, by interpreting express terms using an economic-based consequentialist technique invoking norms using equitable powers, and by directly supplying terms if doing so will curb opportunism and lower overall transaction costs.[147] Courts refuse to adhere to strict textualism or formalism even when the parties have not opted in to broader approaches, thus undermining party choice theory.

A. Jacob & Youngs: *Should Goals Affect Interpretation?*

If courts should ignore objectives or goals in contract adjudication and give exclusive effect to the parties' chosen means,[148] then the court reached the wrong result in the famous case of *Jacob & Youngs, Inc. v. Kent.*[149] The court decided what effect, if any, to give to the express conditions in terms of an anti-forfeiture objective. Under the party choice approaches, since the parties did not invoke the broad interpretive authority of the judiciary, the court should have totally ignored forfeiture concerns

[146] Kostritsky, *supra* note 6, at 137–43 (discussing ALCOA case as an outlier case).

[147] One such example is the law-supplied term in Restatement (Second) of Contracts § 45 option contracts limiting the power of an offeror to revoke an offer once part-performance has occurred.

[148] *See* Kraus & Scott, *supra* note 15, at 1046.

[149] 230 N.Y. 239 (1921).

and strictly enforced the condition. Despite the formalist criticism for the court's invoking the anti-forfeiture principle, doing so may improve welfare.

In *Jacob & Youngs*, the parties' chosen language created several express conditions, including a condition on the installation of a particular brand of pipe (Reading). Formalists assume that commercially sophisticated firms deliberately choose language and terms that effectuate their goals. When the parties choose to delineate the pipe brand as a condition, they are choosing strict enforcement of the condition if they do not simultaneously opt into broad judicial discretion. Had the parties not wanted to opt for strict enforcement, they could have avoided express condition language or delegated interpretive authority to a court through the use of a term like "Reading quality pipe."

In the opinion, Justice Cardozo chose to forgo strict enforcement largely on the ground that doing so would lead to forfeiture since it would deprive the contractor of the final payment.[150] The precise doctrine tells courts that when interpreting language that might be either a promise or a condition courts should take account of possible forfeiture. Using that approach, the court construed the language as creating a duty to use Reading pipe. The failure to use the correct brand of pipe would therefore result in a breach of contract action for damages but not in forfeiture since the owner would not be discharged from payment.

Formalists criticize the result as one that will add to parties' costs of contracting.[151] They argue that if the court simply enforces the language denominating the brand of pipe, the owner will avoid the costs of proving that the pipe installed is inferior since any departure results in an automatic discharge. Textualists and formalists claim that if the court fails to adhere to this approach of strict textualism, even when parties have not expressly opted in broad interpretive powers for a court in the treatment of the condition in the contract, costs will necessarily rise.[152]

[150] *Id.* at 243–44 ("This is merely to say that the law will be slow to impute the purpose, in the silence of the parties, where the significance of the default is grievously out of proportion to the oppression of the forfeiture.").

[151] Kraus & Scott, *supra* note 15, at 1096 (suggesting that because "commercially sophisticated parties such as" the contractor in *Jacob & Youngs* deliberately chose an express condition with knowledge of its consequences (including the doctrine strictly enforcing express conditions), a court should enforce the condition. Scott and Kraus are worried that the Restatement and case law evince "a deep seated policy against the enforcement of conditions that create forfeiture ex post"). Kraus and Scott argue that the courts overlook the sound commercial reasons for express conditions based on the difficulty of the verification costs that would be involved if one party, the owner, had to demonstrate the non-comparability quality of a specific pipe to a court *ex post*. What Kraus and Scott ignore is that the parties both would have wanted to control opportunistic behavior in order to mitigate a contractual hazard. Thus, there would be a sound basis for the parties' wanting courts to be able to invoke another doctrine, such as the anti-forfeiture doctrine, if doing so would curb clearly evident opportunistic behavior. The mere fact that it might be theoretically difficult for the owner to demonstrate the quality differences to a court when the differences are slight does not mean that the court should refuse to excuse the condition when there are apparently no differences in quality.

[152] *See id.* at 1094–6.

The cost analysis is based in part on determining who would bear the burden of proof. If the parties adopt an express condition and the court enforces the condition as it was written, it would "set out a precise rule that allows B [the owner] to verify performance or non-performance at relatively low cost."[153] Reaching a contrary result would saddle the owner with costs since he would have the burden of proving that the substitute pipe did not conform, a relatively high burden that would increase "back-end verification or enforcement costs."[154]

However, the analysis of costs in *Jacob & Youngs* is more complicated than it initially appears. First, the party choice approach would ignore certain costs, which, if accounted for, might change the conclusion as to whether a party choice approach would foster net improvements in welfare. The party choice analysis of costs ignores that there might be some residual uncertainty about whether the parties would want the clause of the express condition enforced under all circumstances,[155] even in cases where it would lead to economic waste and forfeiture for one party. Since the contract contains a condition but does not specify whether it would apply in every case regardless of the circumstances, there is an interpretive issue that requires judicial resolution. Would the party choice theorists want that ambiguity resolved in favor of a forfeiture outcome? Would the textualists want to deny any restitutionary recovery to the builder?[156] What would the parties themselves want?

To decide whether there are any circumstances that might justify the outcome in *Jacob & Youngs* and similar cases, all of the costs of an announced interpretive rule that denied any recovery should be considered. If a court denied any recovery solely on the basis of whether there was a clause containing an express condition, that approach would allow one party to engage in opportunistic behavior and seize upon insignificant defects to gain a large windfall at the other party's expense.

One could argue that when such costs are accounted for, both parties *ex ante* would not have wanted the court to deny *any* recovery. Such a result would have allowed the owner to avoid making payment despite having received substantially what he bargained for. If the interpretation of enforcement despite minor deviation were adopted whenever parties have not exercised an express opt in, it would constitute an interpretive risk for all future transactors. Potential contractors might demand higher payment up front to deal with the interpretive risk of a court strictly enforcing conditions despite their trivial departure. That result is something that

[153] *Id.* at 1097.

[154] *Id.*

[155] *See* Shavell, *supra* note 16, at 289 (explaining that parties "often employ broad terms that do not reflect their wishes in particular circumstances (suppose that they specify that material A should be used in construction but that they would really prefer substituting material B if an unusual problem arises with A)").

[156] Thanks to Bill Whitford for this suggestion.

most owners would presumably want to avoid *ex ante* since it would unnecessarily add to their cost of contracting, especially if one could shift the burden of proving equivalence to the contractor.

The counterargument rests on concerns with verifiability[157] issues. To preclude courts' having to grapple with such complex equivalence issues, the parties may choose to adopt an express condition so that there is no inquiry into the magnitude of the departure.[158] One way to deal with the owner's reluctance to shoulder the cost of proving to a court that an item is not equivalent would be to reassign the burden of proof. One could shift the burden to the contractor to prove that the pipes were substantially equivalent.

Rearranging the burden of proof[159] could thereby achieve the owner's goal of avoiding costly back end enforcement costs and simultaneously diminish the opportunity for opportunistic behavior. This result could presumably maximize the gains from trade.

The analysis suggested here is consistent with the idea that parties would balance the costs of drafting with greater particularity against the interpretive risk of not explicitly specifying whether the court should give effect to the condition no matter how insignificant the deviation or great the forfeiture. Part of the answer to resolving such balancing of costs lies in analyzing how most parties in the population would resolve that question. That projection should then be used to interpret a contract using Bayes's theorem. As Professor Yair Listokin explains:

> Suppose that there are many more parties in the population who prefer pipe of Reading quality rather than Reading brand pipe. This means that when confronted with a contract that specifically calls for Reading pipe, it may be more likely that the contract stemmed from parties who wanted pipe of Reading quality (high prior) and drafted their contract poorly rather than from parties who wanted Reading brand pipe (low prior) and drafted their contract well. If this is the case, then the most likely bargain between the parties is pipe of Reading quality, in spite of the fact that the contract calls for Reading brand pipe.[160]

157 *See* Eggleston et al., *supra* note 101, at 100 (2000) (discussing verifiability in the context of contractual incompleteness).

158 Kraus & Scott, *supra* note 15, at 1097.

159 *See* Kostritsky, *supra* note 6, at 158 (suggesting such a rearranged burden of proof).

160 Listokin, *supra* note 3, at 361. Professor Listokin's discussion of the probability of one meaning attaching rather than another pertains to a particular term (pipe quality), which leads him to suggest that in some cases, the courts should veer away from the "natural reading" of the language toward an interpretation which takes the likely meaning attached by the general population. *Id.* at 365. The same analysis could be applied to the likely probability that parties would want the forfeiture term in a contract strictly enforced under all circumstances. One could surmise that the contract was drafted with a certain set of implicit assumptions about various states of the world. If all of those assumptions proved accurate, forfeiture under a natural reading of the contract result as the parties accepted that forfeiture would result under those assumptions. However, if those assumptions change and new

A similar application of Bayes's theorem could be applied to population preferences regarding large forfeiture in the context of an express condition. If most parties would want to avoid such a result, then in interpreting the language of an express condition, the court should depart from a literal interpretation, adjusting the meaning of the contract according to the "high prior."[161] The court should presumably announce an interpretive rule for dealing with express conditions, which also involves a potential forfeiture based on a similar projection of party preferences. The announced rule can then take account of the concern regarding high *ex post* costs when matters are highly unverifiable (as when the stipulated event that is the subject of a condition is a matter of personal taste). The rule should determine whether those costs should be evaluated differently in cases with matters that are more susceptible to objective measurement (such as the difference in two brands of pipe) and which also involve a large forfeiture potential, based in part on what most parties probabilistically would prefer. The rule could also take account of cost concerns by shifting the burden of proof on the quality issue to the party seeking payment. The interpretive rule, as crafted, would take account of the danger of forfeiture and the potential for opportunistic behavior while remaining sensitive to the burden of proof issues for matters that are unverifiable by a court.

The actual case law in the area of conditions takes account of precisely these factors in a nuanced analysis. The courts consider the avoidance of forfeiture as a goal when deciding whether to enforce the conditions of the contract literally. Doing so in cases where there is large potential forfeiture and a readily verifiable minor deviation arguably results in a net improvement in overall welfare by deterring opportunistic behavior, but pure party choice theory would not achieve such welfare improvement because it would require courts to ignore such concerns, absent an express opt in.

B. *Residual Uncertainty: Overall Objectives and Prospective Consequences*

The express terms of any contract may also leave residual uncertainty and require interpretation by the court. For example, an easement prohibited use of three-wheeled ATVs but failed to cover or prohibit the use of four-wheeled ATVs, which did not exist at the time of the contract. When the grantor of the easement sought to restrict

information is provided, for example, that the pipes are equivalent and a large forfeiture would result, the law would need to deal with that new information. "Although the intent of the parties is still to maximize wealth, we revise our hypothesis about what is a wealth maximizing strategy in light of this new information. With the passage of time, the role of forfeiture as a wealth maximizing strategy ought to change." E-mail from Professor Peter M. Gerhart, Case Western Reserve University School of Law (Aug. 9, 2011) (on file with author).

[161] Listokin, *supra* note 3, at 361.

the holder of the easement from using four-wheeled ATVs, the easement holder argued that the express terms did not expressly rule out four-wheeled ATVs and that they should therefore be permitted.[162]

This case raises the question of what the intervention choice should be. If it followed as party choice dictates, the court should refuse to intervene beyond the express terms and should refuse to consider the parties' objectives to interpret the contract unless the parties authorized such authority to a court. At the time that the easement was drafted, four-wheeled ATVs were not in existence; that explains why there was no express term covering the contingency or the later arising condition of four-wheeled ATVs. The lack of such vehicles may explain why the parties failed to adopt a clause forbidding similar vehicles which might be developed in the future.

This is a case where the express term is meant to settle the controversy in some way but one must still ask: in what way does the express term settle the question? Using the party choice approach, one would posit that the absence of a broad or open-ended term would foreclose interpretation that looked to goals or ends beyond the contractually chosen means. Yet, deciding that there is no interpretive issue itself requires interpretation that cannot be settled by the express terms. Therefore, if the court refuses to intervene in that way, then it is nonetheless a choice, which must be justified.

One could argue that this residual uncertainty should be resolved by consequentialist decisions about how much the four-wheeled vehicle adds to dust/smoke/noise. That is what the court did by admitting extrinsic evidence.[163] Such an approach seems to make sense. Whether it can be justified as an interpretive rule that will minimize the costs and risks of contracting requires further analysis.

The parties could have decided that there was some interpretive risk of not further specifying the kinds of vehicles that would be prohibited on the easement, and not drafting the clause in such a way that it took account of vehicles that were later developed. Since the parties were not aware of four-wheeled vehicles at the time of contract execution, they may not have realized that the clause in question would later require interpretation beyond the express terms.

The question for the collective (judiciary, agency, and legislature) is whether intervention using the parties' objectives – a broad interpretive rule admitting evidence beyond the "minimum evidentiary base" – would minimize costs for the parties more than a literalistic interpretation that excluded such objectives *absent an express opt in*. In deciding what a court should do, one must consider why the parties may have failed to try to eliminate all interpretive risk. One could argue that the

[162] *See* Steven J. Burton, Elements of Contract Interpretation 168 (2009).

[163] *Gillmor v. Macey*, 121 P.3d 57, 72 (Utah Ct. App. 2005).

parties may have decided that leaving the term unresolved as to the matter of later developed vehicles would present little danger to the parties since courts could readily expand the class of covered vehicles to achieve the objective of reducing noise and dust. Literalism, on the other hand, would promote a kind of opportunistic behavior by the holder of the easement, yet another case where literal interpretation would act as a drag on gains from trade.

The rule should mimic what the parties would want in hypothetical bargain terms. The decision about intervention should depend on which approach best reduces costs for the parties and is most preferred by parties *ex ante*. *Ex ante*, the parties will prefer an interpretive rule that will minimize the costs of transacting. In cases where the risk of an event's occurring (such as the development of a four-wheeled ATV) is not foreseeable, the parties might decide that pursuing further drafting is not worth the cost. This may be due to the interpretive risk that they face and because they can safely cease drafting, since a court could readily resolve such a straightforward issue at a low cost and determine what vehicles should be included within the parameters of a clause covering three-wheeled vehicles.

The literalistic approach will increase costs for all parties in the form of an unremedied opportunism. Parties will have to exert defensive costs to constrain such opportunism. Instead of being able to rely on a court to interpret three-wheeled vehicles broadly to cover four-wheeled vehicles, they may undertake the extra drafting costs to cover unforeseeable developments even if they would prefer to rely on a court to resolve such residual uncertainties. The question for the court is whether intervention beyond the express terms will minimize costs for the parties *more than a decision not to intervene under the literalist approach*. Intervention would be justified in cases (1) where the objectives are readily ascertainable and self-evident from inquiring into the purpose of the clause (why were any all-wheeled vehicles prohibited in the first place?); (2) where the contract is not subject to ready manipulation by a party, as would be the case in which a party would profit at the expense of the other by falsely inflating a term such as seller's costs[164]; and (3) where the court is convinced that intervention will minimize costs by preventing defensive expenditures.[165]

For commercially sophisticated parties, courts in the Seventh Circuit and elsewhere look beyond a literal interpretation of contracts when doing so would maximize gain from trade and minimize transaction costs, even when they announce their intention of following a textualist interpretation. In *Abbott Laboratories v. Unilever United States, Inc.*,[166] Abbott purchased Sequoia Turner Corporation, a medical research and manufacturing company, from Unilever because it was

[164] *See* Schwartz *supra* note 91.

[165] *See* Todd D. Rakoff, *Good Faith in Contract Performance: Market Street Associates Partnership v. Frey*, 120 HARV. L. REV. 1187 (2007).

[166] *Abbott Labs. v. Unilever U.S., Inc.*, 45 F.3d 187 (7th Cir. 1994).

in a better position to distribute Sequoia's products than DuPont, Sequoia's long-time distributor.[167] Foreseeing that DuPont would retaliate, Abbott and Unilever contracted to share all losses from the expected DuPont suit jointly. Section 9.3 of their agreement stated that Abbott would "direct and manage any and all litigation related to … DuPont" notwithstanding anything to the contrary in Section 9.5.[168] Section 9.5 provided that Abbott could not settle any lawsuits without approval from Unilever, and if Unilever disproved of the settlement, it assumed the defense of the action. DuPont sought an injunction against the change of distributor and filed suit. After Abbott settled with DuPont, Unilever refused to share the losses, claiming that Section 9.5 required their approval of the settlement.

Although the court employed New York law and announced its intention to "ask[] what the words in the contract" would have meant at the time of contracting, the court's decision in fact seemed to turn on its desire to remedy the situation to promote trade and increase gains.[169] The court's analysis focused on the negative consequences of allowing a literal, non-contextual interpretation to govern the outcome, including the problem of moral hazard that would result if one party could take actions that would favor itself at great cost to the other party and defeat the overall purpose of sharing losses. If Unilever's version of the contract were accepted, then Abbott would be "at Unilever's mercy" because Unilever could have rejected the settlement and then unilaterally allowed DuPont's injunction. Such a result would "have protected Unilever's treasury at a great cost to Abbott" and would have the potential of defeating the purpose of the initial sale of Sequoia.[170] Instead, the court found that Unilever was liable for joint losses with Abbott; thus reaching the result that made the most commercial sense.

C. *When Should Trade Usage Govern Meaning?*

Another contentious issue for the interpretation of contracts is whether parties need to specifically opt in for trade usages to govern meaning. The party choice approach would deprive the court of any interpretive authority to go beyond ordinary meaning

[167] *Id.* at 188.
[168] *Id.* at 189.
[169] *Id.* at 190.
[170] *Id.* Unilever counter-argued that Section 9.5 should apply because it constrained the reciprocal moral hazard risked by Section 9.3, which it contested, permitted Abbott to "spend[] Unilever's money too freely." *Id.* The court dismissed this argument, stressing that the caps on Unilever's liability and its ability to approve Abbott's law firm provided in Section 9.3 adequately restricted opportunistic behavior by Abbott by aligning the parties' interests in minimizing litigation costs. *Id.* In effect, the court found that the magnitude of the risk that Unilever could completely frustrate the purpose the deal if its interpretation of Section 9.3 were applied outweighed the risk that Abbott would unreasonably use its settlement discretion under the accepted interpretation of Section 9.3. In addition there was no evidence that Abbott's failure to consult caused any harm. *Id.*

without an explicit authorization by the parties to do so. Current law is to the contrary and provides that unless specifically negated by the parties, trade meaning may be admitted to interpret or supplement parties' agreements.[171]

The requirement of explicit party choice proposed by the formalists to govern trade usage in contract interpretation seems to mask the idea of judicial intervention. It makes the interpretive approach depend on party choice. The court, however, is choosing whether and on what basis it will go beyond the express terms of the contract and consider trade usages in ascertaining meaning. The court is announcing an interpretive rule regarding the degree of explicit choice required for parties wanting courts to consider trade usages in contract interpretation.

What interpretive rule should be adopted to govern trade usage and contract interpretation should not depend on whether a party expressly authorizes a court to go beyond the text, but rather on a consideration of which rule or opt out would minimize all costs of exchange for all future parties and promote growth.

The costs of requiring parties to opt in to trade usages expressly include the transaction cost of knowing that the meanings that parties in the trade attach to words are different from the ordinary meanings that parties not in the trade attach to those same words. Because parties in the trade are likely to assume that the trade meaning *is* the ordinary meaning, they may see no need to expressly opt in to a trade usage term in the contract.[172] Requiring such express opt-in provisions poses large transaction costs for parties in the trade. Courts should design a default rule on incorporation based on the likelihood that parties in the trade would want trade usage to prevail when the trade usage can be verified by objective evidence.

Requiring parties to opt in may allow parties to strategically and opportunistically rely on ordinary meaning to escape from the trade meaning whenever it turns out to be a bad deal.[173] While there may be contrary cases in which the parties opportunistically rely on trade meaning, the cases most emblematic of this kind of strategic behavior seem to be "outlier" cases in which the evidence of the trade usage is so vague that it invites opportunistic behavior, such as when a fixed quantity is deemed to be merely an estimate under trade usage.[174] The courts can easily police such opportunistic behavior when the party seeking to rely on a vague trade usage also takes advantage of a low fixed price and a market shift suddenly to sell more products. However, there are many cases in which courts usefully invoke trade usage in a way that seems to deter rather than promote opportunistic behavior.

Often a party relying on plain meaning seems to be trying to escape from a trade usage that was definite and applicable for no other reason than that it is advantageous

[171] U.C.C. § 2–202 cmt. 2.

[172] Kostritsky, *supra* note 114, at 516.

[173] *Id.* at 517.

[174] *See S. Concrete Servs. v. Mableton Contractors*, 407 F. Supp. 581 (N.D. Ga. 1975).

to do so.[175] The potential costs of this and other opportunistic behavior must be weighed in determining which interpretive rule, opt in or opt out, would minimize the costs of transacting. Certainly, if a default rule of ordinary meaning will promote opportunistic behavior, and the court could constrain that behavior with an opt out rule, then the parties would probabilistically be inclined to prefer the opt out rule.

In considering the costs and the reduction in costs that might occur with a particular version of an interpretive rule (either opt in or opt out), one would also have to consider the effect that requiring an opt in rule would have in a class of cases where the trade usage at issue is specifically designed to control a specific form of opportunistic behavior. Absent express opt in, the trade usage would not govern the outcome of those cases. That failure would generate costs in the form of uncontrolled opportunistic behavior unless the parties could effectively control it by other private strategies such as informal enforcement.

The decision to exclude valid trade usages that are universally adhered to and are designed to curb opportunism would generate costs that might deter future transactions and should be considered a cost of the exchange. Those costs could be mitigated by parties resorting to informal mechanisms. However, the informal mechanisms themselves have a cost, which might outweigh the costs associated with a court announcing in advance an interpretive rule that would incorporate trade usages into contracts as part of interpretation. Moreover, to the extent that the informal mechanisms are not pervasive and robust in a certain factual setting, the cost to parties of denying effect to trade usages designed to deter opportunism might be that opportunism itself would remain unchecked. For that reason, courts should be able to incorporate trade usages because viewed *ex ante* parties would want courts to be able to do so in order to police opportunistic behavior and maximize surplus.

VIII. CONCLUSION

When contracts remain ambiguous or incomplete, courts and scholars must confront the inevitable question of when intervention in private contracts is justified. To deal with the residual uncertainty, party choice theory suggests that any intervention would be a fool's errand. Their position amounts to an unvarying posture that any party asking for an additional term or a broad interpretation will always lose unless the parties delegated authority to a court.

Recognizing that there is an interpretive risk in all contracts, courts should adopt an interpretive methodology that would enhance the willingness of both parties to engage in exchanges. To achieve that goal, courts should focus on how the interpretation adopted would increase or decrease interpretation risks (costs) over time

[175] *Id.* at 517.

to different classes of transactors. By tailoring and applying interpretive rules, courts can (and do) promote increases in net welfare in a range of cases and contexts examined in this article. If the prospect of adding a term or even overriding a term would prevent opportunistic behavior or catastrophic consequences to both parties, then courts can intervene in a way that maximizes surplus and would be preferred by both parties. An effective model of contract interpretation should use the probabilistic thinking of the parties with respect to (1) implicit assumptions about underlying meaning that might affect the choice of certain words or phrases, (2) the parties' likely goals for contracting, and (3) the set of implicit assumptions about various states of the world (including the future). These probabilistic mechanisms are crucial in interpreting contracting because our brains are hard wired to use these tools and it is the only way courts can form a basis for deciding on meaning in a contract. The court must weigh all of these in deciding what meaning would best achieve the parties' intended meaning and overall goals. Thus, a consequentialist framework must be part of any attempt to decide on an optimal interpretive strategy. The alternative party choice approach suggesting a test requiring parties to delegate broad interpretive authority expressly in order for the court to use it will result in the radical result of parties' being foreclosed from having courts acting as ordinary courts customarily do in adjudicating cases, a result that is contrary to the likely expectations of the parties.

Parties often acquiesce in this approach since there are few instances in which parties expressly adopt a textualism rule in their contractual agreements. The failure to employ such terms regularly provides further evidence that parties do *not* prefer textualism. Courts are therefore correct not to insist on a unitary method of contract interpretation.[176]

[176] Parties occasionally draft express contract language providing for strict textualism in interpretation. The inclusion of such explicit provisions in some contracts indicates that parties do not expect courts to adhere to strict textualism absent such express language. Given the rarity with which such provisions are included in contract language, most parties do not desire such strict textualism when a court is interpreting a contract. For an example of a contract that contains a rule providing for strict textualism, see Alliance Agreement, E. I. du Pont de Nemours and Company – EarthShell Corp., July 25, 2002, *available at* http://contracts.onecle.com/earthshell/ dupont.collab.2002.07.25.shtml ("The Parties' legal obligations under this Alliance Agreement are to be determined from the precise and literal language of this Alliance Agreement and not from the imposition of state laws attempting to impose additional duties of good faith, fair dealing or fiduciary obligations that were not the express basis of the bargain at the time this Agreement was made.").

PART V

Policing Contracting Behavior

This part examines the regulatory role of contract by examining both narrow and broad examples of contract law's policing function. The European experience with the implementation of the Directive to protect self-employed commercial agents is taken up in Chapter 12. The American perspective on standard form contracting and the doctrine of unconscionability is covered in Chapters 13. Finally, Chapter 14 provides a comparative analysis of unfair terms in standard forms in the age of digital, mass-market contracting.

Chapter 12 reviews a distinctly European contract law development – the European Directive on Commercial Agency. Much like the need for regulatory control or judicial intervention to protect consumers in standard form contracting, the Directive and related Regulations, single out self-employed commercial agents as needing additional legal protections. Chapter 12 also looks at how English law responded to concepts foreign to the common law – the use of indemnity and compensatory payments at the termination of agency contracts. Unlike other countries, the English implementation of the Directive did not choose between the payment of compensatory damages and indemnity payments. The chapter analyzes how the Directive has been applied differently in United Kingdom, France, and Germany. The chapter advances a reverse unjust enrichment-restitution model for calculating damage-payments in order to reconcile the differences among the national implementations of the Directive.

In 1917, Nathan Isaacs in the law review article *The Standardizing of Contracts* first coined the term standard form. He also recognized that standard form contracting posed a challenge to classical contract law's intent-based framework of contract enforcement. Chapter 13 revisits this issue and suggests the proper regulatory framework that balances the intent-based core of contract law and the problems posed by the non-intent basis for the enforcement of fine print terms in form contracts. Chapter 13 reviews the history of the unconscionability doctrine in the United States and examines the modern unconscionability doctrine through the issue of the enforcement of arbitration clauses in consumer form contracts. The chapter concludes by analyzing the possibile future developments and applications of the doctrine.

Chapter 14 analyzes standard terms contracting by focusing on digital, mass-market contracts. It rejects the illusion of mutual assent advanced through techniques like education, disclosure, and market discipline. The author notes that unlike relational contracting, where reputational effects and deal-preserving incentives help police the use of such terms, "it is particularly difficult to do so in anonymous, technologically-mediated relationships such as those involving digital products." The chapter examines the weaknesses of the American *Principles of the Law of Software Contracts* and the European Union's *Directive on Unfair Contract Terms.* In the end, both fail to adequately police the use of abusive, unfair standard terms.

Chapter 15 analyzes the Draft Common Frame of Reference (DCFR) and its rules relating to standard terms. The chapter exposes the contradictions between the DCFR and the Common Frame of Reference (CFR) with the Consumer Rights Directive and the "optional instrument" developed under the auspices of the "Expert Group," currently known as the Proposed Common European Sales Law (CESL). It analyzes the reasons for such disharmony and suggests a more modest, incremental approach to European Union private law consolidation.

12

The Paradox of the French Method for Calculating the Compensation of Commercial Agents and the Importance of Conceptualising the Remedial Scheme under Directive 86/653

Séverine Saintier

In 1986, the Council of Ministers of the European Union enacted Directive 86/653 on self-employed commercial agents. The Directive was implemented in English law by the Commercial Agents (Council Directive) Regulations 1993 (thereafter the Agency Regulations) which came into effect on 1 January 1994. The Directive and the Agency Regulations have been held to be in the nature of mandatory law so that they apply where a commercial agent acted in the UK for a Californian principal under a contract governed by Californian law (Ingmar GB Ltd v. Eaton Leonard Inc.).

The Directive is based on the civil law assumption that commercial agents are in need of protection (France and Germany), which is in direct contrast with the traditional English common law position that principals are the ones who deserve protection. When the Agency Regulations came into force, confusion arose because they introduced a level of protection for commercial agents on termination, by way of the civil law concepts of "compensation" and "indemnity", which are alien to traditional English common law. In implementing the Directive, the UK, alone amongst EU Member States, chose not to opt for one remedy – either "compensation" or "indemnity" – but provided for both to be available and the choice between the two to be made by the parties. When applying the "compensation" option, the UK courts have shown a remarkably methodological approach emphasising the need to conceptualise the notion of "loss" before quantifying it (Lonsdale v. Howard and Hallam Ltd). This is in contrast with France, where the implementation and interpretation of the Directive is consistent with the French legal tradition. The result has been an implementation that appears inconsistent and (perhaps) unduly harsh on the principal.

The aim of this chapter is to study the impact of the differences in implementation among France, Germany and the UK and propose a solution to reconcile such differences. This chapter will first consider the nature and rationale of such remedies to see how they differ from common law concepts. The chapter then critically considers the French system and compare it with the common law courts which appear to have applied such concepts with a, perhaps, unexpected ease. The author offers a solution to unify the damage-related nature of "compensation" and the restitutionary nature of "indemnity" – by viewing the principal-agent relationship as a quasi-joint venture. Using a "reverse un-equitable enrichment approach," it is possible to argue that the aim of both termination payments under the Directive is to compensate or indemnify the commercial agent for his loss.

I. INTRODUCTION

Directive 86/653[1] was enacted with the dual aim of reinforcing the protection of commercial agents as well as harmonising the laws of the various Member States. The Directive, inspired by French[2] and German law,[3] is based on a civil law rationale that commercial agents are, economically, the weaker party within the relationship and as such deserve protection.[4] This is in sharp contrast with the position in common law countries such as the UK where the assumption is that the principal is in need of protection. Among the Directive's most important provisions for the commercial agent's reinforced protection is the right, on termination of the relationship, to receive payment of, either "compensation" or "indemnity", the two concepts drawing on French and German law, respectively. Yet, this part of the text has also proved to be one of the most difficult aspects to apply since it has two major flaws, that of leaving the choice to Member States between "compensation" and "indemnity", and remaining silent on the meaning of such concepts as well as how "compensation" or "indemnity" should be calculated. Unsurprisingly, France and Germany have implemented the text so as to follow their legal tradition. In the United Kingdom, where no such legal tradition existed, the implementing

1 Directive on the Co-ordination of the Laws of the Member States Relating to Self-Employed Commercial Agents, OJ of 31–12–1986, No L 382/17.

2 France has protected commercial agents since 1958 through a decree enacted on 23 December 1958, decree 58–1345, D 1959, L, p. 132. France implemented the Directive in 1991 through a statute, which has since been inserted *verbatim* in articles L 134–1 to L 134–16 of the French commercial code.

3 Germany has protected commercial agents since 6 August 1953. The relationship between commercial agents and their principals is now regulated by §§ 84–92 of the German commercial code. For more detail on the German system, see Serge Mégnin, LE CONTRAT D'AGENCE COMMERCIALE EN DROIT FRANCAIS ET ALLEMAND, (Litec, Paris, 2003).

4 See the preamble of the first proposal of the EU Commission in 1976, Doc Com 76/60 submitted on 17 December 1976 and published in OJ C13/2, 18 January 1977.

legislation,[5] almost copying the Directive *verbatim*, provides for both to be available (regulation 17[1]), leaving the ultimate decision to the parties, albeit with the default in favour of compensation (regulation 17[2]). In the light of the lack of details in the Directive as to the meaning of "compensation" and the poor effort of the European Commission to provide guidance over its application in its 1996 report,[6] differing levels of interpretation on the calculation of the compensation option have emerged in France and in the United Kingdom, creating discordance between these two Member States as well as with Germany and all the other Member States which have opted for the indemnity option.

Although the aforementioned flaws of the Directive were highlighted by the European Commission as a prime exemplar of the need to improve the quality of European legislation in its Action Plan in 2001,[7] the institutional response as to a potential solution has been less than adequate.[8] Whereas the draft Common Framework Reference (hereafter DCFR) did contain specific rules for commercial agency contracts, it only provided for the indemnity option and failed to explain the legal nature of the concept of termination payments.[9] The latest proposal for a Common European Sales Law[10] does not even cover such contracts, representation being seen as a less litigious area of law[11] and consequently not requiring intervention. The silence is regrettable since the differences in the calculation of the two termination payments that exist between France, Germany and the UK in this field not only create differing levels of protection for commercial agents[12] but also potentially disrupt intra community trade, hereby undermining at once the aims of Directive itself as well as the goals at the heart of the harmonisation of private law project[13].

5 Commercial Agents (Council Directive) Regulations 1993, SI 1993/3053 as amended by SI 1993/3173 and SI 1998/2868.

6 European Commission 1996 report on the application of Council Directive on the coordination of the laws of the Member States relating to self-employed commercial agents (Com (1996) 364 final).

7 European Commission Communication on European Contract Law, COM (European Commission Documents) 2001, p. 398, 11 Jul. 2001, at p. 18.

8 Interestingly, in this matter, the Court of Justice of the European Union has played a far more proactive role as an enforcer of European law. For details, see Séverine Saintier, *France, Germany and the United Kingdom's Divergent Interpretations of Directives 86/563 and 93/13's Exclusionary Provisions: An Overlooked Threat to Coherence?* EUROPEAN REV. OF PRIVATE LAW, 511–44, at 540–4 (2011).

9 Christian Von Bar & Eric Clive, PRINCIPLES, DEFINITIONS AND MODEL RULES OF EUROPEAN PRIVATE LAW: DRAFT COMMON FRAME OF REFERENCE (Oxford University Press, 2010).

10 Proposal for a regulation of the EP and of the Council on a Common European Sales Law (Com 2011/635/final).

11 *Ibid.* at p. 10.

12 Given the mandatory nature of termination payments, (case C-381/98 *Ingmar Ltd v Leonard Technologies Inc*, [2001] 1 CMLR 9), the Directive is not of mere parochial interest.

13 The European Commission reiterated the need to make it less costly for traders to conclude contracts with partners of other Member States: See the proposal for a Common European Sales Law, supra note 10.

Given the unwavering commitment of the European institutions for such a project, the silence of the recent proposal for a Common European Sales Law on this issue is therefore all the more surprising.[14] The need to rationalise in broad terms the legal nature of the concepts of "compensation" and "indemnity" in order to inform calculation is consequently still pressing[15] and is the aim of this chapter. In a first part, we will critically consider the impact of the differences in implementation between France and the UK. It will show how following the failure of the French implementing text to define compensation as a concept, the method for calculating the compensation used by the French courts consequently appears inconsistent and unduly harsh on the principal.[16] The approach of the English courts, although more methodical, appears less protective of commercial agents and is more closely aligned to the German system of indemnity.[17] Such differences reiterate the need to rationalise the legal nature of the concepts of termination payments before being able to devise a method for its calculation. In a second part, we will therefore consider how although "compensation" and "indemnity" appear radically different, French and German law nevertheless share the same rationale that commercial agent are, economically, the weaker party and in need of protection on termination. Moreover, given the manner in which the Directive deals with the two termination payments, their differences may not be that profound. This part will therefore seek to consider whether "compensation" and "indemnity" can be reconciled[18] in order to help provide a common method for their calculation.

[14] Although commercial agents are intermediaries since they do not act for themselves but for their principal, given the specific nature of the profession, most Member States had specific rules applying to them even before the Directive was enacted. Not to include such agreements in the proposal therefore not only denies the specific nature of the profession but also negates the important economic role that the profession plays in the distribution sector.

[15] As Saintier argued, *'only by understanding the nature and rationale behind the two termination payments can the courts define criteria upon which to calculate the amount of compensation that commercial agents can claim'* (Séverine Saintier, *New Developments in Agency Law*, JOURNAL OF BUSINESS LAW, 77–81 at 90 [1997]). Such an approach has been closely followed by the English courts, as will be seen later on with the case of *Lonsdale (t/a Lonsdale Agencies) v. Howard and Hallam Ltd* [2007] UKHL 32, [2007] 1 WLR 2055, see footnotes 66–76 and associated text.

[16] For the most recent critics, see Serge Mégnin, *supra note* 3, para 321, at 250, FREDERIC FOURNIER, L'AGENCE COMMERCIALE, 10 ANS APRES (2nd ed., Litec, 2005), 277–95 and VALERIE WAGNER, LE NOUVEAU STATUT DE L'AGENT COMMERCIAL (These, Université Paris I, 1996, Presses Universitaires du Septentrion, 1996).

[17] Séverine Saintier, *Final Guidelines on Compensation of Commercial Agents*, 124 L. QUARTERLY REV. 31–7, at 36 (2008).

[18] This part will expand on the idea that "compensation" and "indemnity", as concepts, may not be different as first published in Robert Bradgate and Séverine Saintier, *'Compensation' and 'Indemnity' under the Agency Regulations: How the Common Law System Copes with the Invasion of Civilian Concepts* in ANGLO-CANADIAN PERSPECTIVES ON CONTRACT LAW 311–37, 336 (P Giliker [ed.] Martinus Nihoff, 2007).

II. THE DIFFERENT INTERPRETATIONS ON THE CALCULATION OF "COMPENSATION" BETWEEN FRANCE AND UK

The main weakness of the French system is to have implemented this part of the Directive so as to ensure legal continuity with pre-existing legislation.[19] By simply stipulating that commercial agents have a right to claim compensation for the loss suffered when the contract ends (Article L 134–15 C Com), the French commercial code fails to define the legal basis of such compensation hereby failing to conceptualise the notion of compensation or provide guidelines for calculation.[20] Instead and in line with the previous text, the commercial code simply defines the relationship as a common interest mandate (Article L 134–4 C Com).[21] Although the notion helps to explain the economic weakness of the commercial agent and its consequent underlying need for protection on termination, it nevertheless fails to explain the type of loss suffered or the legal basis of the ensuing compensation. Following on from this deliberate silence of the implementing text compared to the Directive,[22] the French courts have continued to use different methods to justify the compensatory award, which creates inconsistency and two years worth of gross commission remains the rule of thumb for the calculation of the loss suffered.

The right for French commercial agents to claim compensation on termination goes back to 1958,[23] when the first text that formally recognised the need for commercial agent to be protected by giving statutory value to the notion of "common interest mandate" was enacted.[24] The economic weakness of commercial agents lies in their primary function, which is to create and/or develop a customer base, that is, goodwill for the principal's goods (or services). This creation or development of the

[19] The 1958 decree, see *supra note* 2. The fact that France follows its legal tradition rather than the Directive chimes rather well with a point made by Dr Kenny on the difference between the interpretation and the application of European texts. See Mel Kenny, *The (D)CFR Initiative and Consumer Unfair Terms:* in CONTRACT LAW, TRANSATLANTIC PERSPECTIVES (L. DiMatteo, K. Rowley, S. Saintier and Q. Zhou [eds.], CUP, 2012).

[20] Serge Mégnin, *supra note* 3, para 320, at 250. This is in sharp contrast with the considerable discussion over the legal basis of the *indemnité de clientèle* for employed sales representatives, which is that they bring customers to the principal. Employed sales representatives were formally recognised as a separate profession in 1937. The statute is now incorporated in the employment code: article L 7313–13 requires the personal role of the employed sales rep in bringing/creating or developing a customer base for his employer before he can claim the *indemnité*.

[21] *Mandat d'intérêt commun.*

[22] Where the Directive gives examples of deemed damage, i.e., loss (article 17[3]), the French implementing text deliberately remains silent, as to follow the Directive was felt to risk undermining the French legal tradition. See Debates in the National Assembly, report of Bouquet, National Assembly, Official Journal of 23 May 1991, at 2244.

[23] Decree 1958, see *supra note* 2.

[24] The notion of common interest mandate is of judicial origin. For more details see Séverine Saintier & Jeremy Scholes, COMMERCIAL AGENTS AND THE LAW 175–7 (LLP, 2005).

customer base is also the primary reason for the principal and the commercial agent to enter into the relationship and is therefore the "common interest". Both parties contribute to the relationship with a view of attaining the "common interest", the principal by selling his goods and the commercial agent by using his marketing skills to attract more customers. As such the relationship is seen as a *quasi partnership*. Indeed, during the life of the relationship, there is a perfect balance; both parties equally benefiting from the "common interest", that is, the customer base; the principal by selling more of his goods and the commercial agent by receiving the commissions on the sales he has generated. The weakness of the commercial agent lies in his status as representative. Since he does not act for himself but for the principal, the mandate is the instrument by which he can benefit from his share of the "common interest". When the contract ends, he loses his link to the "common interest" since he cannot claim commissions anymore; the principal alone continues to benefit from the "common interest". In other words, termination destroys the balance between the parties. Compensation is consequently due, as the commercial agent's right, as an attempt to re-establish the lost balance and to compensate him for the loss he suffers, the loss of his share of the common interest, the commission on sales.

From the preceding, it seems clear that the *fondement* for the commercial agent's right to claim compensation is the creation or development, *in common*, of a customer base and that the compensation recognises the patrimonial nature of the commercial agency. Yet, there is a discrepancy between the rationale for the need to award compensation and the actual calculation of the award by the French courts. Indeed, in order to claim compensation, the commercial agent does not have to establish that he has increased the customer base of the principal[25]; nor does he have to establish that the principal continues to benefit from the customer base after termination (as the loss crystallises at the moment of termination, what happens afterward is irrelevant) and the French courts have tended to award two years worth of gross commission as compensation.[26] Given that the sole rationale for both parties to enter into a relationship is the creation, *in common*, of a customer base, not linking the loss of the agent to the principal's gains appears paradoxical,[27] at best.

[25] Consistent case law (*jurisprudence constante*), *Cass Com* 3–4–1990 case No 497 lexilaser, *Cass* 4–1–2000, No pourvoi 96–22.372, case no 37; *Cass Com* 25–6–2002, CCC 2002, p. 12. See also *Paris* 3–10–2001 Lettre de la distribution Novembre 2001 where the Court of Appeal of Paris clearly emphasised the difference between commercial agents and employed sales representatives when it stated, "*contrary to the indemnité de clientèle of VRP (sales representatives), the indemnity of termination due to the commercial agent does not require him to have created or brought clients*". For earlier cases, see Cass 14–10–1974, RTD Com 1975, 590, Gaz Pal 1974, II, Som Comm 285; D 1974, Som Com 141.

[26] *Cass Com* 26–2–1958, D 1958, 541, note Vidal.

[27] Serge Mégnin, *supra note* 3, para 321 at 250.

The legal basis for not linking the loss of the commercial agent to the gains of the principal, a practice, which started shortly after the 1958 decree was enacted, is not entirely clear, especially given the aforementioned rationale behind the creation of the notion of common interest.[28] It has been said that the need to distinguish commercial agents from employed sales representatives whose statutory right to a lump sum termination payment, the *indemnité de clientele*, which *is* based on an increase of the customer base, may have played a part.[29] Yet, this does not seem to be a sufficient legal explanation.[30] Some argue that not to take the principal's financial gains in the form of the customer base is perfectly logical since the customer base was never of the commercial agent in the first place.[31] As a result, the commercial agent's loss is not the loss of the clientèle itself but the loss of the benefits of the clientèle, that is, the loss of commissions he would have expected had the contract been performed.[32] Given that the commissions derive precisely from the customer base which the commercial agent has helped to create, this argument appears circular and therefore unconvincing.[33] In the same vein, others add that the financial gains of the principal are irrelevant because the commercial agent can continue to use the clients lost by selling them different goods than the ones under the agency he has just lost. This however does not tally with case law where the compensation is based on the loss of the resources the agent would get from the clientèle[34] or the commissions he would expect had the contract continued.[35] A better legal basis for the loss of the commercial agent is to compensate the commercial agent for his inability to amortise his investments. Yet, its impact is limited since this will only apply when

[28] See early comments that the basis for the need to protect the commercial agent for his loss of his share of the common interest is that the principal can still enjoy the commercial relations with the customer base created through the collaboration with the commercial agent. This loss is the transfer of his share of the common interest to the principal, who alone benefits from it: Jean-Marie Leloup, Les Agents Commerciaux, Statuts Juridiques, Strategies Professionnelles, para 238 at 35 (6th ed., Delmas, 2003).

[29] Serge Mégnin, *supra note* 3, 250.

[30] As Professor Hémard himself stipulates, it is difficult to say with certainty why the courts took such a stance given the absence of discussion over the legal basis of the loss during the debates over the drafting of the 1958 decree. Jacques Hémard, *Les agents commerciaux*, Revue Trimestrielle De Droit Commercial 1959, 573 at 613.

[31] In fact, Professor Leloup says that one should not even mention the word "clientèle" as it is confusing. Jean-Marie Leloup, supra note 28, para 1237, at 232.

[32] JM Mousseron, *Lisons dans le marc de café: a propos de l'indemnité due, demain, aux agents commerciaux*, JCP ed E, Cahiers Du Droit De L'entreprise 1992, suppl, N 5. The formula is accepted by the courts: *Cass Com 19–3–2002, case No 648, pourvoi 99–21–439*, where the court held that he was entitled to the loss of commissions due had the contract been performed.

[33] In fact, according to a constant jurisprudence, the courts have made clear that the loss suffered by the commercial agent is the loss of commission he would have made had the contract continued. *Cass Com 19–03–2002*, pourvoi No 99–21.439, case No 648.

[34] T Com Paris, 15–10–2001, Lettre de la Distribution, December 2001.

[35] *Cass Com 19–03–2002*, pourvoi No 99–21.439, case No 648.

the commercial agency is terminated a reasonably short time after it was started. The courts have sometimes explained the nature of the loss suffered as the loss of the right to assign the agency.[36] This explanation has the advantage of recognising the patrimonial nature of the relationship, the fact that the right of the commercial agent to represent the principal (or the *carte* as it is sometimes referred to) has a financial value. Yet, to some, this is not satisfactory either since it allows the commercial agent not to establish the reality of the loss.[37] Indeed, since what the commercial agent is selling is the right to exploit, *in common*, the existing clientèle for the future; the fact that the courts base their calculation on the commissions gained since the loss is evaluated at the moment of termination and what happens afterwards is irrelevant, this is perhaps the area where the fact that the loss of the commercial agent is not being linked to the gains of the principal seems most problematic.

This, together with the practice of the French courts to value the loss suffered as two year worth of gross commissions has led some to state that "*the situation of the commercial agent whose contract ends is abusively lucrative and enviable*"[38] as it does not reflect the true nature of the loss. In addition, the paradox creates inconsistency in the case law since the French courts appear to use different reasons when awarding compensation. Indeed, although the increase of clientèle or the benefits to the principal are not taken into consideration, some troublesome cases nevertheless seem to point to the contrary. For instance, if the commercial agent increases the clientèle, more compensation will be due.[39] If, on the contrary, the commercial agent has caused, through his inability to get customers, the clientèle to fall, this failure is treated as a fault serious enough to terminate the agency without having to give compensation.[40] Furthermore, the fact that the trademark of the principal is so powerful that the commercial agent is not regarded as having brought any clients is a relevant factor to lower the amount of compensation.[41] All this seems to point to the fact that although not openly acknowledged, whether the principal gains financially from the clientèle is nevertheless important. This has led several academics to claim that the fact that the loss is linked to the principal's gains is an unwritten condition[42] and should consequently be acknowledged openly.[43] This

[36] CA Paris 5eme, ch Sect A, 8–9–2004, RG No 2002/3068 unreported, as cited by Frédéric Fournier, L'Agence Commerciale, 10 Ans Apres (2nd ed., Litec, 2005), 287.
[37] Frédéric Fournier, supra note 36, para 508 at 286.
[38] *Ibid.*, at 271.
[39] *Cass Com* 6–2–1996, RJDA 4/96, NO 492; *CA Lyon* 28–2–2002 jurisdata No 174712 and *CA Versailles* 15–9–2000 BRDA 21/00, No 10.
[40] CA Versailles 15–9–2000, BRDA 21/00, No 10.
[41] TC Paris, 15–10–2001, jurisdata 180161.
[42] C. Klein, Der Ausgleichsansoruch des Handelvertreters nach franzosischem Recht, as cited by Serge Mégnin, *supra note* 3, footnote 1143.
[43] For the most recent critics, see details in fn 16. For earlier critics, see Lambert's note under *Cass Com* 20–5–1969, JCP ed G 1970, II, 16189 bis.

would not only solve the inconsistency but would also solve another problem, that of the courts, more recently, taking into consideration the faults of either party to either increase or decrease the compensation due.[44] For instance, to consider whether the termination was abrupt for the commercial agent.[45] In this instance, the court awarded two years worth of commission for a relationship, which had only lasted nine months. It seems that the court awarded such an amount so as to punish the principal for terminating the relationship so abruptly. To do so is entirely wrong since it not only denies the mandatory nature of the award[46] but also the fact that it is a non-fault-based award.[47] A third problem with the method used by the French courts is the fact that as the loss crystallises at the moment of termination, what happens afterwards is irrelevant. Since the loss is not linked to the gains of the principal, there is no obligation for the commercial agent to mitigate his loss. And yet, in some instances, it was held that if the principal gives the commercial agent a longer notice of termination, the latter has extra time to find other principals, which therefore limits the loss he has suffered and less compensation should consequently be due.[48]

The final, and perhaps more serious problem with the manner in which the French courts actually calculate the loss, is the fact that the rule of thumb of awarding two years worth of gross commissions still applies, giving the impression of a tariff.[49] Although the practice was criticised when it first appeared,[50] it nevertheless flourished.[51] It is precisely because it is so entrenched that, following a political compromise, the compensation option was included in the Directive.[52] Moreover, it is clear from debates in the French parliament that the intention was that such a practice should continue after the implementation of the Directive.[53] Over the

44 Serge Mégnin, *supra note* 3, para 349.

45 CA *Nancy* 22–9–1999 *Groh v. Borowski*, les petites affiches 2000, 16.

46 Case C-381/98, [2001] 1 CMLR 9.

47 It is clear that it is termination that triggers the right to claim compensation regardless of the manner of termination since the commercial agent can claim compensation when the termination is due to age, illness and retirement: article 18(b) of the Directive.

48 CA Paris, 12–3–2003, Lettre de la distribution, Mai 2003; CA Paris 8–10–2003, 5eme Ch, Section A, RG 2002/01449.

49 FREDERIC FOURNIER, supra note 36., para 510 at 288.

50 Jean Catoni, LA RUPTURE DU CONTRAT D'AGENT COMMERCIAL ET LE DECRET DE 1958, These Paris, 1969, para 162 at p. 153. For early examples, see *Cass Com 26–2–1958*, D 1958, 541 note Vidal; *Cass Com 20–5–1969*, JCP ed G 1970, II, 16189bis, note by P. Lambert

51 Although the decree of 1958 was the first text to be officially enacted, a previous attempt, which failed, was the arrête of 1946, which expressly stipulated that two years worth of commission was regarded as an equitable amount (art. 39[3]). For details of case law where it was used over the years, see Séverine Saintier & Jeremy Scholes, *supra note* 24, fn 126–7 at 186.

52 The first proposal of the European Commission only provided for the indemnity option. Doc Com 76/60 submitted on 17 December 1976 and published in OJ C13/2, 18 January 1977.

53 Debates in the National Assembly, report of Bouquet, National Assembly, Official Journal of 23 May 1991, p. 2244. As highlighted earlier at fn 23, where the Directive talks of a deemed damage, the French

years, the courts have used two main reasons for evaluating the loss suffered to two years of gross commissions; (a) two years is the time that it will take the commercial agent to rebuild a customer base similar to the one lost[54] and (b) two years is the price that one would expect an incoming agent to pay for the outgoing agent's interest in the common interest mandate.[55] Interestingly, the practice came under more criticisms following the implementation of the Directive,[56] requiring the French Supreme Court to defend the manner in which the lower courts assess the loss and calculate the compensatory award to prove that it is not applied as a tariff.[57] In spite of this, nothing has changed.[58]

As seems now clear, the main weakness of the method used by the French courts when assessing compensation is that it appears too protective of the commercial agent. The recognised practice[59] of valuing the loss at two years worth of gross commission has led some principals to require a potential commercial agent to pay him a pre-estimated two years worth of commissions for the right to represent him, a *droit d'entrée*. Although this practice does exist, it is not widely publicised[60] and has never been used in the courts as the justification for the two years worth of commissions for the compensation. This is undoubtedly regrettable since when this *droit d'entrée* is paid by the commercial agent, it seems fair that he should receive back some

implementing text remains silent and simply stipulates that the commercial agent is entitled to compensation for the loss he suffers when the contract ends.

54 Hereby contradicting the earlier argument that not linking the loss of the commercial agent to the gains of the principal is logical since the clientèle is not that of the commercial agent.

55 See Séverine Saintier & Jeremy Scholes, *supra note* 24, footnotes 124 and 125 at 186.

56 For Dr Mégnin, the practice fails to represent the true nature of the loss suffered and penalises the principal too much: Serge Mégnin, *supra note* 3, para 345 at 262. In the same vein, Dr Wagner argues that it is unjust on the principals as it leaves some of them with no other alternative than to keep the commercial agent on simply so as to avoid having to pay compensation, thereby allowing the commercial agent to be unjustly enriched: Valérie Wagner, *Agent commercial: le pari communautaire (l'indemnite de cessation de contrat après la directive du 18 decembre 1986)*, CONTRATS, CONCURRENCE, CONSOMMATION 1998, Chron. 9, No 8. The most virulent criticism is from Fournier, who thinks that it marginalises the requirement for the commercial agent to show that he has suffered a loss (FREDERIC FOURNIER, L'AGENCE COMMERCIALE, Litec, 1998, para 498, at 271).

57 For the various ways in which the Supreme Court did so, see Séverine Saintier & Jeremy Scholes, *supra note* 24, 187–8.

58 The criticisms from the UK are particularly virulent. Again, see Séverine Saintier & Jeremy Scholes, *supra note* 24, ch 6, 195–8.

59 It was such that some courts referred to the "custom" of awarding 2 years worth of gross commission to award just that regardless of the reality of the loss suffered. However, as mentioned in *Ingmar Ltd v. Eaton Leonard Technologies Inc* [2002] ECC 5, Professor Ferrier was very cautious about not calling it a custom but merely a practice. Others, however, disagree; see the reference in Rep Dalloz, (1996) at para 87, to the fact that the compensation due on termination is customarily calculated to (…).

60 Pierre Crahay, LES CONTRATS INTERNATIONAUX D'AGENTS ET DE CONCESSIONS DE VENTE para 200, 116 (1991). See also Yves Guyon, DROIT DES AFFAIRES, Tome I, DROIT COMMERCIAL ET DES SOCIETES, para 813 at 870 (11th ed., Economica, 2001).

similar sum when the relationship ends. It certainly explains why, when assessing the loss of the commercial agent, the financial gains of the principal do not come into it or why the loss crystallises at the moment of termination and what happens afterward is irrelevant. The practice of the French courts to award two years worth of gross commission too appears logical and also seems to clarify why, during parliamentary debates of the implementing text, the intention was that the practice of two years worth of commission should remain. However, as this *droit d'entrée* is not widely publicised, it is difficult to verify how often the payment occurs. Yet, if it does occur,[61] this means that France may have implemented the Directive not only to suit its legal needs but also to suit its commercial needs. If this is indeed the case, this therefore raises different problems for harmonisation than the one highlighted in the Action Plan.[62] Whether it does or not, the fact remains that the French approach to compensation is problematic as perhaps unduly harsh to principal and as such very different from the English approach, to which we now turn.

As previously mentioned, prior to the implementation of the Directive, the English law rationale was that the principal was the party in need of protection. This part of the Directive was therefore always going to be one of the most difficult to apply. Following the near verbatim implementation of the Directive; much depended on the English and Scottish courts to clarify the scope of application of this part of the Agency Regulations. The English courts have approached the question of the compensation and its calculation in a much more methodical manner than their French counterparts. After an uncertain start, the English and Scottish courts rapidly accepted that the right for the commercial agent to claim compensation for the loss suffered on termination, in spite of being "*redolent of the language of breach of duty*"[63] was not damages for breach of contract. Following the criticism of the French rule of thumb to award two years worth of commission as an "*excessive windfall*" for the commercial agent,[64] the English courts quickly called for the need to evaluate the compensation by using criteria, which are "*sufficiently UK-based and developed*".[65] In 2007, in *Lonsdale (t/a Lonsdale Agencies) v. Howard & Hallam Ltd*,[66] the House of Lords finally answered that call. In this case, Mr Lonsdale was representing the defendant for the sale of shoes within a given territory. Following

[61] Dr Saintier is currently undertaking some empirical research in order to find out whether the practice does occur.

[62] On this, see Séverine Saintier, *The Interpretation of Directive to Suit Commercial Needs, a Further Threat to Coherence*, Journal of Business Law, 165–80, at 177–8 (2012).

[63] Moore-Bick in *Lonsdale* in CA [2006] EWCA Civ 63, [2006] 1 WLR 1281, at [24].

[64] *Ingmar GB Ltd v. Eaton Leonard Inc* [2002] ECC 5, per Morland, at para 52.

[65] *Barrett McKenzie v. Escada (UK) Ltd* [2001] EuLR 567, per Bowers J, at para 21.

[66] [2007] UKHL 32, [2007] 1 WLR 2055. This is so in spite of an earlier decision indicating the courts would follow what the French courts were doing; see Séverine Saintier & Jeremy Scholes, *supra note* 24, ch 6, 191–3.

the decline of sales within the area, the defendant terminated the contract. Mr Lonsdale sued for compensation. The issue at the core of this case was therefore to determine how much compensation Mr Lonsdale was entitled to claim. Given the uncertainty surrounding the application of this part of the Directive principally because of a lack of consensus between the Scottish and English courts over the principles behind the assessment of the compensation due,[67] the question was of considerable importance.[68]

Lord Hoffmann delivered the leading speech (with which their Lordships Bingham, Rodger, Carswell and Neuberger agreed). Adopting a very methodical approach, and thus in contrast to the French position, Lord Hoffmann stated that before deciding how compensation should be determined, he first had '*to decide exactly what the agent should be compensated for*'.[69] Although accepting the French origin of the notion, his Lordship nevertheless rejected the French approach to its calculation and instead, emphasised the need for a precise method for calculating the loss. After recognising the specific nature of the loss suffered by the commercial agent,[70] Lord Hoffmann held that the level of compensation was to be assessed by reference to the market value of the agency. Lord Hoffmann then insisted on the need for the valuation to be done by reference to what is happening in the '*real world*'[71] by considering what a '*hypothetical purchaser*'[72] '*would have been willing to pay for similar businesses at the time*'.[73] In clear contrast to the French approach to compensation and relying on the text of the Directive, Lord Hoffmann then stated that since what had to be valued was '*the agent's expectation that "proper performance of the contract" will provide him with a future income stream*',[74] it was therefore necessary to assume that the agency would have continued.[75] The fact that the agency was in decline could therefore not be overlooked. This is where the fundamental difference with the French approach lies; his Lordship took into

67 Compare and contrast the Scottish position in *King v. Tunnock* [2000] Eu LR 531 with the English position in *Lonsdale* [2006] EWCACIV 63, [2006] 1 WLR 1281 in the Court of Appeal. In Scotland, in *King v. Tunnock*, the fact that the relationship is terminated following the closing down of the part of the business that the commercial agent was in charge of was of no relevance to the amount of compensation he could claim. For the Court of Appeal in *Lonsdale*, this was of great importance (see Robert Bradgate & Séverine Saintier, *supra note* 18, 329–32). *King v. Tunnock* is discussed in Severine Saintier & Jeremy Scholes, *supra note* 24, 191–2.

68 For details of the evolution of the case law on this, see Severine Saintier & Jeremy Scholes, *supra note* 24, ch 6, pp. 190–8.

69 [2007] UKHL 32, [2007] 1 WLR 2055, at [7].

70 His Lordship stated that the loss that the Directive requires commercial agents to be compensated for is the loss they suffered by being deprived of the benefit of the agency relationship (at [11]).

71 [2007] UKHL 32, [2007] 1 WLR 2055, at [13].

72 *Ibid.*, at [12].

73 *Ibid.*, at [28].

74 *Ibid.*, at [11].

75 *Ibid.*, at [21].

consideration the financial gains of the principal, or in this case, the absence of, to decide that although some compensation was due, the amount was, by necessity, very little. The fact that the House of Lords did not follow the French method is not a problem *per* se, yet, the fact remains that the calculation method used by the courts of the UK is now very different from that of the French courts. The English method is less protective of commercial agents since to take into account the financial gains of the principal is beneficiary to him when business is good, but bad when business is down, which, one could argue, is precisely the time where commercial agents need protection since, when business is good, the relationship is unlikely to be terminated.

The difference in the French and English courts' approach to calculating the compensation represents a serious threat to European coherence. Indeed, given that the French method is too protective and the English one, perhaps, not sufficiently protective of the commercial agent, both cannot be correct. In spite of such a threat, it is not clear whether a European-based intervention is possible. Indeed, as the Directive is a minimum protection measure, France, by being more protective than the Directive itself, is not at fault. Moreover, as previously highlighted, it is possible that the French method of calculation may simply reflect commercial considerations, that is, the practice of the *droit d'entrée*, as Lord Hoffmann seems to have emphasised when he commented that the manner in which the French courts calculate compensation conforms with "commercial practice".[76] Even though the practice is not officially recognised, the fact remains that the French approach to compensation appears over advantageous to commercial agents, which could be a problem in relation to the underlying aim of the Directive to facilitate trade. Indeed, the high level of protection might prevent some principals from outside France appointing commercial agents in France for fear of having to pay too much compensation on termination. Given the unwavering commitment of the European institutions to facilitating trade between consumers and business alike,[77] if France does infringe cross-border trade, intervention is necessary. However, whether that is indeed the case remains to be proven.[78] Until that is, a stronger argument for a European-based intervention might be that even though the Directive was inspired by the French system, there is nevertheless an obligation on France to have a purposive interpretation of the Directive as recently reiterated in *Turgay Semen v. Deutsche*

[76] *Ibid.*, at [18].

[77] See the Proposal for a regulation of the EP and of the Council on a Common European Sales Law (Com 2011/635/final).

[78] If one judges from the amount of cases reaching the courts in France, in the United Kingdom and at European level, very few cases actually involve commercial agents and principals who are in different Member States. Because of this, there seems to be very little cross-border trade. However, given the unscientific basis of this comment, empirical research is necessary. Dr Saintier is currently undertaking such research in order to find out whether this is indeed the case or not.

Tamoil GmbH.[79] As the Directive does stipulate that a loss is deemed to exist when termination deprives the commercial agent of his commissions "*whilst providing the principal with substantial benefits*" (Article 17[3]), the fact that France does not, may well be a problem, not only as it is a threat to coherence,[80] but also because of the complexities that this creates in France as well.

Although a European-based solution appears necessary, what precisely can be done is however not entirely clear. As stated by Lord Hoffmann in *Lonsdale,* in the case of *Honyvem Informazioni Commerciali Srl v. Mariella De Zotti,*[81] the then–European Court of Justice (ECJ) gave discretion to Member States in relation to the calculation of indemnity and compensation. Yet, more recently, in the case of *Turgay Semen*, the European Court emphasised that, in the light of the mandatory nature of the termination payments,[82] this discretion was not absolute and could be controlled. In this case, the ECJ did precisely that, by, in effect, censuring the German courts for being too strict in their calculation of the indemnity option. Following such a ruling, the German code has been changed so as to reflect the new method of calculation. This highlights the crucial role that the European Court could play in ensuring proper coherence[83]. However, as Saintier remarked elsewhere,[84] given the lack of guidelines within the Directive on the compensation option, the same control by the European court appears difficult. Moreover, although the House of Lords' approach to calculating the compensation due is clearly less advantageous to commercial agents compared to their French counterparts, it is not clear whether this is too a restrictive approach, which was the basis for referral to the European Court in the *Turgay Semen* case. Indeed, as previously highlighted, the French courts can be criticised for not linking the loss of the commercial agent to the gains of the principal since this does not reflect the reality of the loss suffered. The House of Lords, in its clear intent to calculate the compensation precisely so as to reflect the true nature of the loss suffered, should perhaps be praised. Given that France is overprotective of commercial agents and the UK perhaps not enough, the two interpretations cannot both be correct. A solution must consequently be found to settle the matter.

79 Case C 348/07, [2009] ECR I 2341.

80 Interestingly, the ICC model contracts only consider the indemnity option. See ICC MODEL COMMERCIAL AGENCY CONTRACTS, 2nd ed., 2002, article 21.1A.

81 Case 465/04 [2006] ECR I 2879.

82 Case C-381/09 *Ingmar Ltd v Eaton Leonard Technologies Inc*, [2001] 1 CMLR 9.

83 The idea of the proactive role of the (then) ECJ as an enforcer is not new; see Peter Rott, *What Is the Role of the ECJ in Private Law?* HANSE L. REV., 6–17, (2005). For an in-depth discussion over the question whether the ECJ's proactive role could help coherence in the consumer and the business context see Severine Saintier, *France, Germany and the United Kingdom's Divergent Interpretations of Directives 86/563 and 93/13's Exclusionary Provisions: An Overlooked Threat to Coherence?* EUROPEAN REV. OF PRIVATE LAW, 511–544, 539 (2011).

84 Séverine Saintier, *The Interpretation of Directive to Suit Commercial Needs, A Further Threat to Coherence*, JOURNAL OF BUSINESS LAW, 165–180, at 178 (2012).

An obvious solution would be for the Court of Justice of the European Union (CJEU) to monitor the application by Member States since it already does so, as seen previously, in the case of *Turgay Semen*. However, as this relies on the preliminary reference procedure, this is unlikely to be effective since either Member State referring the matter to the CJEU is very unlikely.[85] The need for an effective referral process referred to previously, although still pressing, has not been answered and considering the latest step in the European development on this front, is unlikely to happen in the near future.[86] Since the source of the various problems highlighted in this part emanate from the failure of the Directive to define the termination payments as concepts, the need to rationalise, purposively and in broad terms their legal nature in order to see whether this helps inform their calculation appears to be a possible solution, to which we now turn.

III. RECONCILING COMPENSATION AND INDEMNITY?

As just mentioned, following the silence of the Directive on the meaning of "compensation" and "indemnity" as concepts as well as how they should be calculated has led to drastically different interpretations of the calculation of the compensation option in France and the UK. Whereas the French courts do not link the loss of the commercial agent to the financial gains of the principal and assess the compensation at the date of termination, the English courts, by taking into account post-termination events that affect the financial gains of the principal, do so. As such, the method adopted by the House of Lords when calculating "compensation" appears more closely aligned to the German-based "indemnity".[87] Yet, given the aforementioned weaknesses of the French system for not doing so, together with the similarity between the French and German rationales and the treatment that "compensation" and "indemnity" receive in the Directive, the two notions are perhaps not that different as we will attempt to establish.

Given that the Directive is inspired by the French and German law rationale that commercial agents are, economically, the weaker party within the relationship and

85 In *Lonsdale*, Lord Hoffmann stated that there was no need to refer the matter to the ECJ since it was acte clair, [2007] UKHL 32, [2007] 1 WLR 2055 (at [40]). This chimes well with the idea of Dr Kenny that there is a distinction between the interpretation and the application of European law. See Mel Kenny, *The (D)CFR Initiative and Consumer Unfair Terms* in CONTRACT LAW, TRANSATLANTIC PERSPECTIVES (L. Di Matteo, K. Rowley, S. Saintier and Q. Zhou (eds.), CUP, 2012).

86 See Séverine Saintier, *France, Germany and the United Kingdom's Divergent Interpretations of Directives 86/563 and 93/13's Exclusionary Provisions: An Overlooked Threat to Coherence?* EUROPEAN REV. OF PRIVATE LAW, 511–544, at 540 (2011).

87 Séverine Saintier, *Final Guidelines on Compensation of Commercial Agents*, LAW QUARTERLY REV. 31–37, at 36 (2008).

as such deserve protection, there is considerable common ground between the two systems. Similarly to France, German law too accepts that the sole reason for entering into a commercial agency relationship is the creation and/or development of a customer base for the principal's goods. In consequence, German law too considers that the commercial agent has a quasi-patrimonial interest in the agency, which entitles him, on termination, to the right to claim a lump sum payment.[88] Yet here the similarities end since the two systems differ over the theoretical justification and calculation of that lump sum payment.[89] For France, it is to repair the loss caused by the termination; for Germany, it is to indemnify the commercial agent who has created or developed the customer base for the principal.[90] French-based "compensation" therefore appears to be a compensatory remedy, akin to damages, which compensates the agent's expectation interest, whilst German-based "indemnity" would appear to be restitutionary, concerned with protecting the agent's reliance and restitutionary interests, yet, the reality may not be as straightforward.

German law recognises the imbalance that termination creates between the parties since the commercial agent cannot claim commissions anymore and the principal alone continues to benefit from the commercial agent's efforts after the relationship has ended. As highlighted by the European Commission report, this results in an inequitable distribution of gains from the commercial agent's activities from which the principal disproportionally benefits since "*the commercial agent will only have received commissions during the duration of the contract, which will not typically reflect the value of the goodwill generated by the principal. It is for this reason that the payment of a goodwill indemnity is commercially justified*".[91] German law makes it clear that after termination the principal continues to benefit from the customer base in two main ways, the transactions that he can continue to conclude with the customers as well as the fact that he does not have to pay commissions to the commercial agent on such transactions.[92] The financial gains of the principal are therefore closely linked to the loss of the commercial agent. By doing so, the German system appears very logical. The same cannot be said about the French text, which, in theory, focuses solely on the loss of the commercial agent. Yet, as previously explained, the financial gains of the principal are nevertheless important, hereby blurring the distinction between "compensation" and "indemnity".

88 As previously mentioned, this is formally recognized under French law under the notion of *common interest mandate*. Although no similar notion exists in German law, the rationale that commercial agents need protection on termination is nevertheless clear.

89 Serge Mégnin, *supra note* 3, para 318 at 249.

90 *Ibid.*

91 European Commission 1996 report on the application of Council Directive on the coordination of the laws of the Member States relating to self-employed commercial agents (Com [1996] 364 final), at p. 1.

92 See Séverine Saintier &Jeremy Scholes, *supra note* 24, p. 203.

This blurring of the distinction gives us, it seems, a basis upon which to reconcile the French-based "compensation" with the German-based "indemnity". Both French and German law give commercial agents the right to claim a lump sum payment on termination because of his inability to claim commissions anymore. Both systems therefore accept that on termination commercial agents suffer a loss of some sort for which they must be compensated or indemnified. On that basis, it seems possible to say that indemnity seeks to compensate the commercial agent for the loss of the chance to share in the continuing benefits from the agency, and compensation represents the loss to the commercial agent of a valuable asset in the form of the agency itself[93]. In other words, both systems consider the commercial agency in quasi-proprietary terms viewing the commercial agent's interest in the agency as an asset. The Directive clearly recognises and accepts this analysis since commercial agents have the right, with the consent of the principal, to assign the agency, in which case, they cannot claim compensation or indemnity.[94] Given the need for a purposive solution, let us now see whether the aforementioned similarities between the German and the French system are replicated in the Directive. It is worth quoting the relevant part of the Directive *verbatim*.

> Under article 17(3) of the Directive, the commercial agent can claim indemnity if and to the extent that:
>
> (a) He has brought the principal new customers or has significantly increased the volume of business with existing customers and the principal continues to benefit from it and
> (b) Payment of indemnity is equitable.
>
> Under article 17(6) the commercial agent is entitled to receive compensation for the damage he suffers, (…) such damage is deemed to occur particularly when the termination takes place in circumstances:
>
> (a) Depriving the commercial agent of the commission which proper performance would have procured him whilst procuring the principal with substantial benefits linked to the commercial agent's activities
> (b) Has not enabled the commercial agent to amortise costs and expenses incurred on the advice of the principal.

The Directive clearly highlights the aforementioned similarities between "compensation" and "indemnity" in France and Germany since both articles take the loss of the commercial agent and the gain of the principal into account in some way, although the latter does so more. As the Directive accepts that the commercial

[93] Robert Bradgate & Séverine Saintier, *supra note* 18, at 322.

[94] Article 18(b) of the Directive. In that case, the commercial agent receives the value of the agency from the assignee. This proprietary analysis is further reinforced by the fact that when the commercial agent dies, the right to claim compensation or indemnity passes onto his heir (article 18(c) of the Directive).

agent's interest in the agency is a quasi-proprietary interest in an asset, we can therefore rationalise the right to a termination payment as a right to be compensated or indemnified for the expropriation of that asset or the legal response to the unjust enrichment of the principal which results from that expropriation.[95] For both "compensation" and "indemnity", the basis for the payment could be said to be the reversal of an "unjust", that is, inequitable enrichment[96] that would occur if the principal were allowed to keep for himself the whole value of the agency. Let us consider whether this analysis can help resolve the problem of the calculation of the loss under the French-based compensation.

By adopting the preceding quasi-proprietary analysis of the right for the commercial agent to claim compensation on termination for the expropriation of the asset by the principal, one inevitably links the loss of the commercial agent to the gains of the principal. Although in most cases the loss of the commercial agent and the gains of the principal will coincide, the central issue for the calculation is what to do when they do not and, more importantly for our purpose, when, after the relationship has ended, the principal does not continue to benefit. Can/should this post-termination factor be taken into consideration when assessing the loss the commercial agent suffers or should the loss be assessed at the date of termination? This question, which arose in the United Kingdom in the case of *Lonsdale*, is of crucial importance since it is precisely the issue upon which the French and the English courts differ. Following our argument that the basis for the compensation is the inequitable enrichment that would occur if the principal were allowed to keep for himself the whole value of the agency, in such a situation the principal does not benefit at all since there are very few remaining customers. The low number of customers inevitably affects the value of the agency, hereby reinforcing the symmetry between the loss of the commercial agent and the financial gains to the principal. It therefore seems that the House of Lords was correct in taking such a factor into account. Following such an analysis seems possible in the light of the Directive since Article 17(6) does not provide a clear method for calculating the loss, but only guidelines, as to when a loss is deemed to exist as the word "particularly" attests. In consequence, this allows some flexibility as was adeptly argued by Moore-Bick LJ in the Court of Appeal in *Lonsdale*,[97] a too rigid application of the valuation at the date of termination can be detrimental to the commercial agent.[98]

95 Robert Bradgate & Séverine Saintier, *supra note* 18, at 325.

96 It is clear that the basis is not unjust enrichment in the legal sense of the word attached to this expression in the United Kingdom since the necessary requirements are not met. The matter was nevertheless discussed in early cases by the English courts; for detail, see Severine Saintier & Jeremy Scholes, *supra note* 24, at 199–200.

97 [2006] EWCACIV 63, [2006] 1 WLR 1281.

98 He offered as an example the case where an agency entered into for a fixed period expired in accordance with its own terms. Moore-Bick LJ remarked that a rigid application of the 'valuation

The approach to calculating compensation adopted by the House of Lords in *Lonsdale* appears correct in the light of our analysis of the rationale of the two termination payments. This approach has the advantage of solving the paradox of the French method previously highlighted as well as furthering the broader objective of harmonisation by unifying the compensatory regime of the Directive.[99] In spite of this, as the method is detrimental to the commercial agent, this factor cannot be ignored. Although Member States do have some discretion in the method they use when calculating the loss, the discrepancy between the two methods is nevertheless a problem. Given the protective stance of the Directive together with the mandatory nature of termination payments and the lack of guidance of the Directive on this, it is not clear whether which of the two interpretations was intended. The matter is therefore not '*acte clair*'[100] and the question should consequently have been referred to the Court of Justice of the European Union. It has not and is unlikely to be. Considering that in its 1996 report the European Commission predicted that some problems with regard to the interpretation of this part of the Directive would arise,[101] the lack of action represents another wasted opportunity to settle the matter once and for all.

IV. CONCLUSION

The lack of guidance within the Directive over the meaning or the calculation of the two termination payments of "compensation" and "indemnity" illustrates rather

at the date of termination' approach would mean that the commercial agent would be left with no compensation. Indeed, as the agency had expired, it has no sale value. Since it is clear from the terms of the Directive that it is intended that the commercial agent should receive compensation in such a case, Moore-Bick LJ conceded that it was therefore appropriate to depart from such a rigid approach. Moore-Bick's remarks are very perspicacious since in France, the commercial agent would too be entitled to compensation. See Cass Com 23–4–2003, pourvoi No 01–15.639, case No 643.

99 Article 17(6) of the Directive required the Commission to submit a report on the implementation of the two termination payments by the Member States and gave the Commission the possibility, if necessary to submit proposals for amendments. For some, this proves that the aim of the Council of Ministers was that the report would establish the need for reform to unify the regime. Serge Mégnin,*supra note* 3., para 314, at 247. We disagree with this view.

100 Although Lord Hoffmann agreed that the lack of consensus between the Scottish and the English courts created uncertainty, he added that what was uncertain was not the meaning of the Directive, but the method by which domestic courts calculate the damage. Since domestic courts have some discretion in this matter, his Lordship concluded that the task of resolving this uncertainty therefore fell on the House of Lords and not on the ECJ. [2007] UKHL 32, [2007] 1 WLR 2055 (at [40]).

101 It was feared that the courts in the United Kingdom would interpret the notion of loss by applying common law principles. European Commission 1996 report on the application of Council Directive on the coordination of the laws of the Member States relating to self-employed commercial agents (Com [1996] 364 final), p. 20.

nicely the forces that led to the Action Plan and the draft CFR.[102] In this chapter, we have attempted to show that although "compensation" and "indemnity" appear radically different, by conceptualising the legal nature of these two payments and by relying on the fact that France and Germany share a similar rationale of protection for the commercial agents, there is a way of unifying "compensation" and "indemnity" under the Directive. Both France and Germany consider that the commercial agent and the principal are engaged in a quasi joint-venture which results in the commercial agent enjoying a quasi-property interest in the agency. As termination deprives the commercial agent of benefit of that interest whilst enriching the principal, using a reverse inequitable enrichment basis, it is possible to argue that the aim of both termination payments under the Directive is therefore to compensate or indemnify the commercial agent for his loss. Although this analysis is more easily recognisable in the German-based indemnity, considering the paradox of the French method of calculation and the text of the Directive, a similar analysis nevertheless seems possible for the French-based compensation scheme. Yet, as this method inevitably leads to reducing the amount of compensation the commercial agent can claim when the principal does not benefit after termination, this interpretation, although possible in the light of the text of the Directive, is nevertheless controversial with regard to the protective stance of the Directive as well as the mandatory nature of the termination payments. Following the lack of referral to the Court of Justice of the European Union and the silence of the proposal for a common European sales law on the matter, uncertainty appears set to continue.

[102] In spite of the repeated commitment to the harmonisation of private law project by the representatives of the various European institutions, the latest proposal for a common European sales law appears to show a shift in the aim of the project. Whether this is a good or bad thing remains to be seen.

13

Unconscionability in American Contract Law

A Twenty-First-Century Survey

Charles L. Knapp

The notion that a court tasked with enforcing a private agreement should be allowed – even, in some cases, required – to withhold enforcement because of the unfairness of the agreement is not a new one; scholars have traced it back well beyond the earliest days of the Anglo-American legal system. In the United States, the current formulation of that idea can be found principally in the doctrine of unconscionability, which has enjoyed since its incorporation into the Uniform Commercial Code a place in the menu of contract law's policing doctrines, even if a somewhat insecure and sometimes disputed one.

The chapter summarizes with a few broad strokes the earlier story of modern unconscionability law in the United States. This chapter will then focus on the history of that doctrine in American courts over the last two decades, identifying those situations in which it has been most frequently advanced, and those where it has been most likely to succeed. This also entails exploring the interaction of that doctrine with the federal law favoring the enforcement of private contractual agreements to submit future disputes to arbitration. Finally, the chapter considers the possible future development of unconscionability law, with particular regard to the continued utility of the "procedural-substantive" dichotomy, and the employment of unconscionability as a tool for policing contracts of adhesion.

I. INTRODUCTION

The American law of contract, although fed by – and circumscribed by – a host of statutes, has been and remains at its heart a common-law system. At least since the mid-twentieth century, one of the doctrines commonly said to form a part of that system has been the principle that a court has the inherent power to decline to enforce a contract (wholly or in part) if it deems the contract (or some term(s) thereof) to be "unconscionable." This chapter will briefly survey the American court decisions and academic commentaries that have invoked this doctrine, particularly over the past two decades (the 1990s and the 2000s), with an eye toward making some observations about its present importance and future development.

II. MID-TWENTIETH-CENTURY DEVELOPMENT – THE 1950S AND 1960S

Although the employment by courts of an unconscionability-type principle has been traced back at least to Roman days,[1] the story of modern unconscionability law in the United States can be said to begin with the incorporation of that principle in the Uniform Commercial Code in the mid-twentieth century. The Uniform Commercial Code (or UCC) is styled a "uniform" law rather than being "federal" law (adopted by the Congress and in force throughout the nation in a single form), because the UCC in its official version is not actually "law" in any American jurisdiction. Like other "Uniform Laws" in American jurisprudence, it is rather an ideal, promulgated as a model for state legislatures to adopt, in the hope that it will by virtue of nearly universal adoption become in that sense a uniform law throughout the American federal union. The UCC contains a collection of "articles," each devoted to a different kind of commercial law. Article 2, dealing with sales of goods, is attributed principally to Professor Karl Llewellyn, who is generally regarded as one of the handful of people most influential in shaping American contract law during the twentieth century.[2] It was he who drafted and argued for the inclusion in Article 2 of §2–302, which provides as follows:

> § 2–302. Unconscionable Contract or Clause.
>
> (1) If the court as a matter of law finds the contract or any clause of the contract to have been unconscionable at the time it was made the court may refuse to enforce the contract, or it may enforce the remainder of the contract without the unconscionable clause, or it may so limit the application of any unconscionable clause as to avoid any unconscionable result.
>
> (2) When it is claimed or appears to the court that the contract or any clause thereof may be unconscionable the parties shall be afforded a reasonable opportunity to present evidence as to its commercial setting, purpose and effect to aid the court in making the determination.

As its drafters and proponents hoped it would, much of the UCC and particularly of Article 2 has indeed been adopted throughout the United States in substantially its "official" form. This has been true of §2–302; although initially regarded as one of

[1] Dando B. Cellini & Barry L. Wertz, *Unconscionable Contract Provisions: A History of Unconscionability from Roman Law to the U.C.C.*, 42 TULANE L. REV. 193 (1967). See also Allen R. Kamp, *Uptown Act: A History of the Uniform Commercial Code: 1940–49*, 51 SMU LAW REVIEW 275, 308–313 (1998).

[2] E. Allan Farnsworth, CONTRACTS 298 (4th ed., Aspen Publishers: New York, N.Y. 2004).

the more controversial sections of a somewhat controversial codification, it has been adopted even by states which originally resisted it.[3]

Because UCC Article 2 is limited in its scope to contracts for the sale of goods, §2–302 might have remained of minor importance to American contract law in general, except for a number of factors: one was that Article 2 when first promulgated was seen by many in the legal community (and the academic legal community in particular) as representing the best in "modern" thinking about contract law, much of which was widely regarded by that time in academic/legal circles as being unduly doctrinaire and out of touch with commercial reality. As a result, courts began to cite and apply parts of Article 2 "by analogy" in contract disputes not involving sales of goods.[4] Not all sections of Article 2 had any practical application apart from sales of goods, of course, but many of them did; among those was §2–302.

Another factor contributing to the influence of §2–302 was the growth of a body of case law discussing and applying the notion of unconscionability in the context of contractual disputes. Many of these were applications of §2–302, of course. In some cases, however, courts asserted the power to employ the notion of unconscionability as a matter of general common law, not dependent on Article 2 or any other statute for authority. Probably the most important of these was *Williams v. Walker-Thomas Furniture Co.*,[5] in which a federal appeals court held that, apart from the UCC, courts had the inherent power to refuse enforcement to contracts or contractual terms which they found to be "unconscionable." *Williams* involved consumers who had purchased furniture and other household items from the plaintiff store on an installment-payment plan, pursuant to contracts which provided that as long as any item remained unpaid for, in whole or part, all items purchased from the seller would be subject to repossession as security. The trial court had held that although that clause might affect the buyers unfairly and even harshly, the court had no power to withhold enforcement of it, and the plaintiff should be permitted to replevy the goods in question.[6] The appellate court ruled, however, that in fact the trial court did have power to find a contract or term "unconscionable" and thus unenforceable. While suggesting strongly that the clause in question might fall into that category, the appellate court did not actually resolve that issue, but sent the case back to the lower court for rehearing.[7] Since cited and quoted innumerable times, by courts and commentators, the majority opinion in *Williams* contributed a set of analytical

[3] California, for example, did not adopt §2–302 until 1979. The history of 2–302 in California is recounted in Harry G. Prince, *Unconscionability in California: A Need for Restraint and Consistency*, 46 Hastings. L.J. 459, 490–493 (1995).

[4] E. Allan Farnsworth, Contracts 40 (4th ed., Aspen Publishers: New York, N.Y. 2004).

[5] 350 F.2d 445 (D.C. Cir. 1965).

[6] *Williams v. Walker-Thomas Furniture Co.*, 198 A.2d 914 (D.C. Ct. App. 1964).

[7] *Williams v. Walker-Thomas Furniture Co.*, 350 F.2d at 450.

tools – "absence of meaningful consent" and "terms unduly favorable to one party" – that courts in later cases, both under the UCC and otherwise, have found useful in addressing the issue of unconscionability.[8]

Beginning in the 1960s, courts applied the principle of unconscionability to a variety of situations involving consumer contracts, where imbalance of economic and other types of power were seen as fostering oppressive practices. These cases involved parties who in one or more senses were at a bargaining disadvantage in the transactions at issue. Some were persons of limited education and/or economic means;[9] some were members of minority groups often subject to invidious discrimination in American society;[10] some were immigrants or first-generation Americans who could read or perhaps even speak English only with difficulty or not at all.[11] In many cases the court's finding of unconscionability involved a particular term in a standardized-form "boilerplate" contract that the consumer perhaps could not have read and understood and in any event was unlikely to have actually read and understood at the time of contracting.[12] The offending terms were often, like the one in *Williams*, part of the seller's remedial provisions, but they could also be disclaimers of warranty, limitations of liability, or restrictions on the assertion of claims.[13] Although not seen originally as being applicable to a contract's price term, §2–302 was in time also applied in cases where courts found the contract price for goods or services to be unconscionably high.[14]

Also contributing to the growing prominence of the notion of unconscionability during this early period was an unusually influential 1967 law review article by Professor Arthur Leff, examining at length both the drafting history of UCC §2–302 and the decision in the *Williams* case. Entitled "Unconscionability and the Code – the Emperor's New Clause,"[15] Leff's article was in many respects severely critical of both the statutory provision, which he regarded as amorphous and unfocused, and the *Williams* decision, which he found unclear in its justification for a finding of (potential) unconscionability. Nevertheless, the article did present a lengthy,

8 *Id.*, at 449.

9 *Weaver v. American Oil Co.*, 276 N.E.2d 144 (Ind. 1972).

10 *Kugler v. Romain*, 279 A.2d 640 (N.J. 1971).

11 *Frostifresh Corp. v. Reynoso*, 274 N.Y.S.2d 757 (N.Y. Dist Ct. 1966).

12 The clause in the *Williams* case read as follows: "The amount of each periodical installment payment to be made by (purchaser) to the Company under this present lease shall be inclusive of and not in addition to the amount of each installment payment to be made by (purchaser) under such prior leases, bills or accounts; and all payments now and hereafter made by (purchaser) shall be credited pro rata on all outstanding leases, bills and accounts due the Company by (purchaser) at the time each such payment is made."

Williams v. Walker-Thomas Furniture Co., 350 F.2d at 447. Judge Wright dryly observed that the clause was "rather obscure." *Id.*

13 *A & M Produce Co. v. FMC Corp.*, 186 Cal. Rptr. 114 (Ct. App. 1982).

14 *American Home Improvement, Inc. v. MacIver*, 201 A.2d 886 (N.H. 1964).

15 Arthur Allen Leff, *Unconscionability and the Code: The Emperor's New Clause*, 115 U. Pa. L. Rev. 485 (1967).

substantial and serious examination of both, and it also contributed to this area the dual analytic framework of "procedural" and "substantive" unconscionability, which, like the *Williams* factors (to which it roughly corresponded), quickly became and remained standard in judicial discussions of the unconscionability principle. Many commentators followed Leff in examining and critiquing the code and the common-law applications of unconscionability,[16] and for a decade or so it continued to generate vigorous discussion, pro and con.

III. FURTHER DEVELOPMENT – THE 1970S AND 1980S

As court decisions identified and reacted to various perceived abuses in the area of consumer transactions, other institutions of government began to play a more active role in attempting to provide remedies to those affected. At both the federal and state levels, statutory provisions and agencies dealt in a more organized and effective way with practices that courts had been able to deal with only on a case-by-case basis. Some required disclosure of various terms that were typically obscured or hidden entirely[17]; some imposed substantive regulation of practices that had hitherto been freely employed.[18] Statutes in this area sometimes invoked the concept of unconscionability, perhaps defining it in more elaborate or detailed ways than the case law had previously done.[19] By 1980, however, court decisions in this area appeared to be declining in numbers and in importance, and public interest in furthering (and funding) consumer protection generally seemed to be waning, as America's national mood shifted away from faith in governmental regulation of business and toward "free market" principles, as proclaimed by newly elected President Ronald Reagan.

Despite this shift in societal priorities, one development during this period did play a positive role in solidifying the doctrine of unconscionability as a principle of American common law. This was the promulgation by the American Law Institute in 1979 of the Restatement (Second) of Contract Law. The original Restatement of Contract Law, which was officially adopted in 1932, purported to be an authoritative compilation and formulation of America's common law of contract. As the first of its kind, the first Restatement of Contracts established a pattern for its successors in various other areas of law, and it had a tremendous influence on courts. It reflected the earlier, "classical" contract law of the 1900s, however, and fifty years later was seen

[16] M. P. Ellinghaus, *In Defense of Unconscionability*, 78 YALE L.J. 757 (1969); John E. Murray, Jr., *Unconscionability: Unconscionability*, 31 U. PITT. L. REV. 1 (1969); John A. Spanogle, Jr., *Analyzing Unconscionability Problems*, 117 U. PA. L. REV. 931 (1969).

[17] E.g., the Truth In Lending Act, 15 USCA §§ 1601–65 (West), requiring disclosure of interest rates and other charges in consumer credit contracts.

[18] The Uniform Consumer Credit Code (UCCC) is one example. Among other things it prohibits the type of "cross-collateralization" clause found in the contract in *Williams v. Walker-Thomas*, 198 A.2d 914. UCCC § 3.303.

[19] E.g., UCCC § 5.108.

as ripe for updating. Its successor, Restatement (Second), attempted to do this in part by incorporating and adopting many of the innovations that had been included in Llewellyn's Article 2 of the UCC. Among the provisions new to the Restatement (Second) of Contracts was the following:

> §208. Unconscionability
>
> If a contract or term thereof is unconscionable at the time the contract is made a court may refuse to enforce the contract, or may enforce the remainder of the contract without the unconscionable term, or may so limit the application of any unconscionable term as to avoid any unconscionable result.

Accompanying commentary made it clear that the drafters saw §208 as a complement to UCC §2–302, extending its principle to areas outside the sale of goods and approving of the efforts of courts that had previously applied §2–302 "by analogy" in other types of cases.[20]

During this period, legal academics continued to devote significant energy to the general topic of unconscionability. In the wake of Leff's "Emperor's New Clause" article, discussed previously, many commentators had attempted to suggest ways to give shape and structure to a concept that he had criticized as essentially formless and unhelpful.[21] In the 1980s and 1990s, however, prominent writers, some reflecting the growing influence of "law and economics," tended to minimize the importance of unconscionability, and to advocate restraint in its application, as unduly interfering with the operation of "freedom of contract" and the "free market."[22] Most commentators appeared to regard enforcement of standardized contracts as appropriate and necessary for the functioning of a capitalist economy, and to be skeptical of judicial efforts to restrain them.[23]

IV. UNCONSCIONABILITY AT THE DAWN OF THE TWENTY-FIRST CENTURY

By the last decade of the twentieth century, therefore, it was common to view the doctrine of unconscionability as being of marginal importance to American contract law generally. Rarely applied to contracts between business enterprises, and

[20] *See* Restatement (Second) of Contracts § 208, cmt a, reporter's note (1981).

[21] Richard E. Speidel, *Unconscionability, Assent and Consumer Protection*, 31 U. Pitt. L. Rev. 359 (1970); articles cited in n. 16, *supra*.

[22] Richard A. Epstein, *Unconscionability: A Critical Reappraisal*, 18 J.L. & Economics 293 (1975); Robert A. Hillman, *Debunking Some Myths about Unconscionability: A New Framework for U.C.C. Section 2–302*, 67 Cornell L. Rev. 1 (1981; Allan Schwartz, A *Re-Assessment of Non-Substantive Unconscionability*, 63 Virginia L. Rev. 1053 (1977).

[23] *See* Jeffrey W. Stempel, *Arbitration, Unconscionability, and Equilibrium: The Return of Unconscionability Analysis as a Counterweight to Arbitration Formalism*, 19 Ohio State J. on Dispute Resolution 757, 822–825 (2004).

used sparingly even where consumer contracts were at issue, it seemed destined to play at best a distinctly minor role in the further development of American contract law.[24] But in the early 1990s, development in an entirely different area of law had the somewhat surprising side effect of reviving interest in the doctrine of unconscionability. This was the United States Supreme Court's expansive construction of the Federal Arbitration Act,[25] in ways that made it difficult or even impossible for parties to adhesion contracts to preserve and pursue what would otherwise have been their right of access to the American judicial system – state or federal – for the resolution of contract disputes.

A. *Unconscionability as Applied to Mandatory Arbitration Clauses*

In the early twentieth century, American courts had been generally hostile to the notion that parties could by contract bind themselves to submit future disputes to private arbitration, rather than resolving them through litigation in the public courts. Judges saw such arrangements as improper encroachments on judicial power and often declined to enforce contractual arbitration clauses. But contracting parties, particularly commercial enterprises, were increasingly drawn to arbitration as a mechanism for dispute resolution, for a combination of reasons: arbitration was seen as faster than litigation; it was thought to be often less expensive; and arbitrators selected by the parties were potentially better able to grasp the commercial realities of the business world than judges with possibly little or no real-world experience in commercial affairs might be. Arbitrators were also generally freer than courts to reach a commercially reasonable resolution of a business dispute without being bound by rigid and possibly "unrealistic" rules of law. Eventually, at both the state and federal levels, American legislatures adopted Arbitration Acts: laws requiring courts to respect and enforce contractual provisions by which parties bound themselves to arbitrate disputes that might in the future arise between them.[26] Such agreements for "mandatory" (or "compulsory") arbitration – so called because they were designed to be binding even against a party that might in the meantime have changed its mind about using the arbitration process – could thereafter no longer be ignored or overridden by courts on the ground that they somehow usurped the courts' prerogatives.

[24] E.g., *The Uncertainty of U.C.C. Section 2–302: Why Unconscionability Has Become a Relic*, 105 Commercial L.J. 287 (2000); *see* E. Allan Farnsworth, *Developments in Contract Law during the 1980's: The Top Ten*, 41 Case Western L. Rev. 203, 222 (1990) (during the 1980s, unconscionability was an area of "arrested development").

[25] 9 USC §§ 1–16.

[26] *See generally* Thomas E. Carbonneau, *The Reception of Arbitration in United States Law*, 40 Maine L. Rev. 263, 263–6 (1988) (describing historical development).

By the latter part of the twentieth century, the tables had rather completely turned. American courts, led by the federal Supreme Court (the highest court in the land, at least with respect to issues of "federal" constitutional or statutory law), interpreted and applied the Federal Arbitration Act (FAA) so vigorously – some would say aggressively – that lower courts and state legislatures found it difficult or impossible to impose any sort of regulatory procedures or decisional process that might in any way prevent disputes from being shunted out of the court system and into arbitration whenever a contract so provided, even if that contract was a "contract of adhesion" or otherwise of dubious validity.[27] And where the enthusiasm for arbitration clauses had earlier been mostly confined to contracts between commercial enterprises, large-scale businesses began to insert them into contracts with their customers on a massive scale. Banks, credit-card lenders, telecommunications companies, sellers of goods, insurance companies, even health-care providers turned to mandatory arbitration, as did employers.[28] Proponents of this development saw in consumer arbitration the same virtues that an earlier generation had seen in its use in commercial disputes[29]; others were less sanguine.[30] Consumer advocates in particular saw this development as problematic.[31] By drafting their contracts so as to require arbitration of future disputes, business enterprises with the economic power to impose terms on their customers or employees could obtain a variety of practical advantages, a situation to which the Supreme Court and many lower courts as well seemed oblivious or indifferent in their zeal to relieve the strain on court dockets by furthering arbitration whenever possible.[32]

Despite its breadth of application, the FAA does have some limitations on its scope: it expressly provides that a written agreement to arbitrate "shall be valid, irrevocable,

[27] Jeffrey W. Stempel, *Bootstrapping and Slouching toward Gomorrah: Arbitral Infatuation and the Decline of Consent*, 62 Brooklyn L. Rev. 1335 (1996)

[28] David S. Schwartz, *Enforcing Small Print to Protect Big Business: Employee and Consumer Rights Claims in an Age of Compelled Arbitration*, 1997 Wisconsin L. Rev. 33.

[29] Michael Z. Green, *Debunking the Myth of Employer Advantage from Using Mandatory Arbitration for Discrimination Claims*, 31 Rutgers L.J. 399 (2000); Stephen J. Ware, *Paying the Price of Process: Judicial Regulation of Consumer Arbitration Agreements*, 2001 J. Dispute Resolution 89.

[30] Richard E. Speidel, *Consumer Arbitration of Statutory Claims: Has Pre-dispute [Mandatory] Arbitration Outlived Its Welcome?* 40 Arizona L. Rev. 1069 (1998).

[31] Richard M. Alderman, *Pre-Dispute Mandatory Arbitration in Consumer Contracts: A Call for Reform*, 38 Houston L. Rev. 1237 (2001); Frederick L. Miller, *Arbitration Clauses in Consumer Contracts: Building Barriers to Consumer Protection*, 78 Michigan Bar J. 302 (1999).

[32] Jean R. Sternlight, *Rethinking the Constitutionality of the Supreme Court's Preference for Binding Arbitration: A Fresh Assessment of Jury Trial, Separation of Powers, and Due Process Concerns*, 72 Tulane L. Rev. 1 (1997); William J. Woodward, Jr., *Constraining Opt-Outs: Shielding Local Law and Those It Protects from Adhesive Choice of Law Clauses*, 40 Loyola of Los Angeles L. Rev. 9 (2006).

and enforceable, save upon such grounds as exist at law or in equity for the revocation of any contract."[33] As we have seen, one of the doctrines that American courts have applied to invalidate contracts, for half a century at least, is the doctrine of unconscionability – if the court finds a contractual clause to be unconscionable, then as a matter of law that clause ought not to be enforceable. As applied to a clause that would require arbitration as the means of resolving future disputes arising between the contracting parties, the doctrine of unconscionability might thus permit a holding that the clause was unconscionable and therefore should not be enforced, leaving the dispute to be resolved in the court system. For this reason, the burgeoning application of the FAA triggered a corresponding expansion in the attention paid by state courts (and lower federal courts as well) to the doctrine of unconscionability. Unable to challenge directly the Supreme Court's insistence on a strong preference for arbitration, parties desiring to avoid being forced to submit to arbitration increasingly mounted unconscionability attacks on arbitration clauses, and with increasing success.[34]

As a result of these developments, the number of court decisions in which the unconscionability doctrine was applied increased substantially after 1990. In a recent study, published in 2009, researchers sought to gather the reported court decisions (state and federal) from 1990 on in which the claim that a contract should be deemed (wholly or partly) unconscionable was presented to a court and either accepted or at least seriously discussed by that court in the course of resolving the case. The cases so identified included many in which arbitration clauses were at issue, but also other situations as well. Results of this study indicated that the number of unconscionability decisions increased rather dramatically over the period between 1990 and 2010, with much (but not all) of that increase being attributable to disputes over contractual provisions calling for mandatory arbitration.[35]

Despite assertions by many observers that the Supreme Court was applying the FAA in ways not intended or even contemplated by Congress, it became clear early on that the US Supreme Court, in its zeal to effectuate a strong "presumption" in favor of arbitration, would insist that both federal and state courts toe the line in

[33] FAA, 9 USC § 2 (West). The Supreme Court has stated, citing this provision, that "generally applicable contract defenses, such as fraud, duress, or unconscionability, may be applied to invalidate arbitration agreements." *Doctor's Associates, Inc., v. Casarotto*, 517 US 681, 687 (1996).

[34] *See generally* Jeffrey W. Stempel, *Arbitration, Unconscionability, and Equilibrium: The Return of Unconscionability Analysis as Counterweight to Arbitration Formalism*, 19 Ohio State J. on Dispute Resolution 757 (2004) (approving expansive use of unconscionability doctrine in arbitration context); Susan Randall, *Judicial Attitudes toward Arbitration and the Resurgence of Unconscionability*, 52 Buffalo L. Rev. 185 (2004) (critical of this development).

[35] Charles L. Knapp, *Blowing the Whistle on Mandatory Arbitration: Unconscionability as a Signaling Device*, 46 San Diego L. Rev. 609, 619–626 (2009).

enforcing arbitration clauses.[36] As part of that process, the Supreme Court refused to countenance the argument that arbitration as a process might disfavor any particular party or class of parties, "unconscionably" or otherwise. Arbitration, the Court insisted, is merely an alternate form of dispute-resolution process, socially desirable in general, and surely not unfair to either side as a general proposition.[37] But courts both state and federal, in California and elsewhere, over time developed criteria for testing the conscionability of particular arbitration clauses. Where the clause (or the process it provided for) would deprive a party of legal procedures such as discovery that might be crucial to their ability to establish a factual case,[38] where the arbitration clause imposed on one party costs that she could not reasonably be expected to bear,[39] where procedures for selecting arbitrators seemed unfairly slanted to favor one side,[40] where an arbitration clause would deprive one side but not the other of its right to go to court,[41] where the clause operated to prevent plaintiffs with similar claims from joining them in a class-action proceeding[42]: all these factors could be and were, in the eyes of some courts, unconscionable components of an arbitration clause.[43] Having so ruled, a court could still go on to sever the offending portion(s) of the clause and send the case on to arbitration with the unconscionability presumably remedied, and courts often did so.[44] However, courts were also willing in many cases to go farther and simply rule the clause as a whole to be unenforceable, on the ground that it was too permeated by unconscionability to be allowed to stand.[45]

36 *Southland Corp. v. Keating*, 465 US 1, 10–16 (1984) (holding that FAA binds state courts and preempts state statute restricting arbitration); *Allied-Bruce Terminix Cos., Inc. v. Dobson*, 513 US 265 (1995) (Congress intended FAA to extend to full reach of federal power over interstate commerce; *Southland* reaffirmed).

37 *Moses H. Cone Mem'l Hosp. v. Mercury Constr. Corp.*, 460 US 1, 24–5 (1983) (FAA establishes liberal policy favoring arbitration; any doubts should be resolved in favor of arbitration); *Gilmer v. Interstate/Johnson Lane Corp.*, 500 US 20 (1991) (federal statutory claim of age discrimination subject to arbitration).

38 *Kinney v. United Health Care Services, Inc.*, 70 Cal. App. 4th 1322, 1332 (1999); *Acorn v. Household Int'l, Inc.*, 211 F. Supp. 2d 1160 (N.D. Cal. 2002).

39 *Cole v. Burns Intern. Security Services*, 105 F.3d 1465 (D.C. 1997); *Brower v. Gateway 2000, Inc.*, 676 N.Y.S.2d 569, 573 (App. Div. 1998); Mark E. Budnitz, *The High Cost of Mandatory Arbitration*, 67 Law & Contemp. Probs. 133, 143–4 (2004).

40 *McMullen v. Meijer, Inc.*, 355 F.3d 485, 487–8 (6th Cir. 2004); *Burch v. Second Judicial Dist Ct.*, 49 P.3d 647 (Nev. 2002).

41 *Armendariz v. Found. Health Psychcare Servs. Inc.*, 6 P.3d 669 (Cal. 2000) (clause imposed arbitration on employees but left employer free to litigate).

42 *Discover Bank v. Superior Court*, 113 P.3d 1100 (Cal. 2005).

43 *Armendariz*, 6 P.3d 669, has been particularly influential in its discussion of the various features of an arbitration clause that might be deemed unconscionable.

44 *Saika v. Gold*, 49 Cal. App. 4th 1074, 1082 (1996); *Thicklin v. Fantasy Mobile Homes, Inc.*, 824 So.2d 723 (Ala. 2002) (clause negated possible award of punitive damages; that portion stricken and balance of clause enforced).

45 *Stirlen v. Supercuts, Inc.*, 60 Cal. Rptr.2d 138 (Cal. App. 1997).

From an early point in the development of this FAA jurisprudence, the arbitration-clause cases were shunted away from courts and into arbitration wherever the Supreme Court could force that result. So, for instance, claims that a contract had been procured by fraudulent misrepresentations would not form a basis for denying the defendant the power to enforce arbitration, even though such fraud would ordinarily provide a basis for avoiding the contract (including the arbitration clause) as a whole: the claim of fraud would simply be addressed, and decided, by the arbitrator(s).[46] In the theoretical world of the Supreme Court's imagining, this was not a cause for concern; since arbitration was intrinsically no less fair than litigation, it did not matter where the claim of fraud was heard, as long as it had a hearing *somewhere*. In fact, however, consumer advocates complained that private arbitrators – paid by the parties, and dependent on repeat business from the enterprises that used these clauses – had little incentive to bite the hand that was feeding them, by finding some defect in the contract-formation process.[47] For many years, however, claims of unconscionability were seen as an exception to this principle of leaving challenges to the contract to be decided by the arbitrator. Many trial courts (state and federal) were willing in appropriate cases to uphold in the first instance claims that an arbitration clause was unconscionable and thus unenforceable; many appellate courts (again, both state and federal) were approving of such rulings.[48] Over the past decade, however, the Supreme Court has continued to whittle away at the proposition that the courts might have the power to decide issues of unconscionability before the arbitrators take over.[49] So until there is either some change in the makeup of the Court or a willingness on the part of Congress to intervene, prospects for further development of the unconscionability principle in the context of challenges to arbitration clauses seem clouded, if not downright gloomy.[50]

46 *Prima Paint Corp. v. Flood & Conklin Mfg. Co.*, 388 US 395, 403–5 (1967).

47 For an extensive analysis of the possibility of arbitrator bias, see Lisa B. Bingham, *On Repeat Players, Adhesive Contracts, and the Use of Statistics in Judicial Review of Employment Arbitration Awards*, 29 McGeorge L. Rev. 223 (1998); Richard M. Alderman, *Pre-Dispute Mandatory Arbitration in Consumer Contracts: A Call for Reform*, 38 Hous. L. Rev. 1237 (2001–2).

48 *Alexander v. Anthony Int'l, L.P.*, 341 F.3d 256, 271 (3d Cir. 2003); *Murray v. United Food & Commercial Workers Int'l Union*, 289 F.3d 297, 305 (4th Cir. 2002); *Iberia Credit Bureau, Inc. v. Cingular Wireless LLC*, 379 F.3d 159, 176 (5th Cir. 2004); *Macias v. Excel Bldg. Services LLC*, 767 F. Supp. 2d 1002, 1012 (N.D. Cal. 2011); *Davis v. Global Client Solutions, LLC*, 765 F. Supp. 2d 937, 942 (W.D. Ky. 2011); *Ctr. of Hope Christian Fellowship, Local, Church of God in Christ v. Wells Fargo Bank Nevada, N.A.*, 781 F. Supp. 2d 1075, 1080 (D. Nev. 2011); *Gentry v. Superior Court*, 42 Cal. 4th 443, 452 (2007); *Chavarria v. Ralphs Grocer Co.*, 2011 WL 4104856 (C.D. Cal. Sept. 15, 2011). See Charles L. Knapp, *Blowing the Whistle on Mandatory Arbitration*, 46 San Diego L. Rev. 609, 621–6 (2009).

49 The most recent examples include *Rent-A-Center, West, Inc. v Jackson*, 130 S. Ct. 2772 (2010); *AT&T Mobility LLC v. Concepcion*, 31 S. Ct. 1740 (2011).

50 *See generally* Aaron-Andrew P. Bruhl, *The Unconscionability Game: Strategic Judging and the Evolution of Federal Arbitration Law*, 83 N.Y.U.L. Rev. 1420 (2008); David Horton, *Unconscionability Wars*, 106 Northwestern Univ. L. Rev. 13 (2011).

B. *Unconscionability in Non-Arbitration Cases – Doctrinal Developments*

Faced with the increasing prevalence and seeming inevitability of mandatory consumer arbitration, some commentators saw a potential silver lining in the possibility that the increased judicial attention to the doctrine of unconscionability thereby engendered would have the effect of strengthening courts' willingness to consider and apply that doctrine in areas outside of mandatory arbitration. While much of the arbitration jurisprudence has been addressed specifically to aspects of the arbitration process, such as the composition of arbitral panels or the high costs imposed on consumer plaintiffs, some strands of the arbitration-clause unconscionability analyses can be applied to other kinds of contractual provisions as well. These include at least the following: increased scrutiny of adhesion contracts; willingness to find unconscionability despite the presence of only a small amount – or even an absence – of one of the traditional components; and a heightened sensitivity to "lack of mutuality" as an indicium of unfairness.

1. Adhesion Contracts

Since early in the twentieth century, prominent contracts scholars have been grappling with the challenge to traditional contract law inherent in the ever-increasing use of standardized forms in contracting, particularly in situations where one party presents to the other a form for assent on a non-negotiable, "take-it-or-leave-it" basis.[51] Where the drafting party over time enters into a large number of essentially similar transactions, the employment of contract forms that can be used over and over with only a few changes from one transaction to the next has obvious efficiencies; indeed, for many decades it has been impossible to visualize commercial life without them. But when used in transactions where there is likely to be a distinct imbalance of bargaining power in many respects – economic power and other types as well – they carry the risk that parties will give their apparent assent to terms they have not read, terms they would not understand even if they had, and terms which are surprisingly harsh in their impact on the non-drafting party.

Such contracts have come to be known as "contracts of adhesion." As to their identifying characteristics, there is probably a general consensus: the presentation by one party to the other of a contract, the terms of which are not open to negotiation, in a situation where the other party simply "adheres" to the terms offered, often with little or no attempt to read or understand fully the offered terms.[52] There is

[51] Friedrich Kessler, *Contracts of Adhesion – Some Thoughts about Freedom of Contract*, 43 COLUMBIA L. REV. 629 (1943); Karl N. Llewellyn, *What Price Contract? – An Essay in Perspective*, 40 YALE L.J. 704 (1931); W. David Slawson, *Standard Form Contracts and Democratic Control of Law-Making Power*, 84 HARVARD L. REV. 529 (1971).

[52] Todd D. Rakoff, *Contracts of Adhesion: An Essay in Reconstruction*, 96 HARVARD L. REV. 1173, 1176–7 (1983).

disagreement, however, about the degree to which it must also have been difficult or impossible for the "adhering" party to obtain better terms from some other contracting party by "shopping around," or else for her to simply refrain from entering into the transaction at all. Ever since the *Williams* case and Professor Leff's analysis of it, courts and commentators have sparred over these questions. In *Williams*, the remedial clause at issue was hardly a model of transparency or clarity; law students for decades have generally been willing to admit that they found it difficult or impossible to decipher on a first reading (or even a second or third) the language in Walker-Thomas's contract.[53] In that respect at least, the defendants in *Williams* can be said not to have enjoyed a "meaningful choice," and to be victims of "procedural unconscionability." But the subject matter of Mrs. Williams's final purchase was a stereo system. Leff and others have suggested that because that sort of item is a luxury and not a necessity, she had the "meaningful choice" of simply doing without – abstaining from the transaction entirely.[54] Courts faced with claims of unconscionability have in many cases insisted on a showing that the terms in question were truly non-negotiable (established perhaps by the plaintiff's unsuccessful attempt to engage in bargaining), that better terms could not have been obtained elsewhere (as witnessed by plaintiff's fruitless search for a better deal from another party), and that the transaction was one which for some reason the plaintiff could not be expected simply to forgo.[55] The ultimate end of this process – the *extensio ad absurdum*, one might say – is the not-uncommon holding that an employee cannot protest an agreement she entered into with her employer (perhaps for arbitration; perhaps involving other matters) on grounds of unconscionability because, after all, she could have just refused to sign it, couldn't she? – even though she knew that this would cost her the job.[56]

In this respect, the recent wave of unconscionability litigation has helped to some degree to bring a perceptible shift in judicial attitudes. Although many courts continue to impose a high threshold for procedural unconscionability, others in recent years have evidenced a much more realistic attitude towards the "adhesion contract" characterization issue. When the adhering party is a consumer, dealing with a business organization, in a situation where the reality is that neither party expects any bargaining to take place (except perhaps over a few terms where consumer-choice is solicited), then the terms of the contract as a whole will be those in the form; no sensible consumer will take the time to read through the whole contract, nor indeed

53 *See* n. 12 *supra*.

54 Professor Leff characterized Ms. Williams' stereo as a "frill" – a luxury item. Leff, *supra* n. 15, 115 U PENNSYLVANIA L. REV. at 556.

55 *Am. Gen. Fin., Inc. v. Branch*, 793 So. 2d 738, 751 (Ala. 2000).

56 *E.g., D'Sa v. Playhut, Inc.*, 102 Cal. Rptr. 2d 495 (Cal. Ct. App. 2000) (employee fired for refusing to sign agreement containing illegal covenant not to compete). *See* Sara Lingafelter, *Lack of Meaningful Choice Defined: Your Job vs. Your Right to Sue in a Judicial Forum*, 28 SEATTLE U. L. REV. 803 (2005).

is she likely to be encouraged or even allowed to.[57] In such cases, where there is truly an "adhesion contract" in this sense, courts are increasingly willing to recognize that fact, and as a result to find the presence of "procedural unconscionability." This is by no means to say that all adhesion contracts should be per se unenforceable; clearly a huge proportion of everyday contracts fits this description, and nobody seriously argues that they should all be unenforceable simply for that reason. But a finding of *procedural* unconscionability permits the court to do what it would otherwise probably not feel free to do – test the contract for the presence of *substantive* unconscionability.[58]

2. Sliding Off the Scale

As we have seen, from early in the modern history of the unconscionability doctrine courts have for the most part employed some version of a two-prong test: the *Williams* duo of "absence of meaningful choice" and "unreasonably favorable terms" or Leff's procedural/substantive dichotomy. But in practice the strict application of these tests has been repeatedly tempered by the expressed willingness of courts to take what they often refer to as a "sliding scale" approach to finding unconscionability: where there is clearly an abundance of one of the unconscionability factors, the court will settle for a relatively smaller amount of the other.[59] This approach was well established long before the arbitration clauses became a major potential application of the unconscionability doctrine, so it is not surprising to see it in the arbitration jurisprudence as well.[60] Given the Supreme Court's insistence on a general presumption in favor of arbitration, one would assume that a court applying the unconscionability doctrine to an arbitration clause might be less likely to settle for just a little "substantive" unconscionability; the particular aspects of unfairness would need to be clearly spelled out. Conversely, the pervasiveness of the adhesion-contract form

[57] One author has written, "Anyone with the slightest knowledge of today's world knows that most mass-transaction contracting takes place in an environment in which it is clear that, except for a few 'dickered' terms, bargaining is neither expected nor permitted, and even reading the relevant documents is implicitly discouraged. Imposing a general 'duty to read' is one thing; imposing such a duty in circumstances where we know it cannot or will not be performed is Catch-22 with a vengeance." Charles L. Knapp, *Taking Contracts Private: The Quiet Revolution in Contract Law*, 71 Fordham L. Rev. 761, 770 (2002).

[58] Charles L. Knapp, *Opting Out or Copping Out? An Argument for Strict Scrutiny of Individual Contracts*, 40 Loyola of Los Angeles L. Rev. 95, 130–1 (2006).

[59] *Chalk v. T-Mobile USA, Inc.*, 560 F.3d 1087 n. 4 (2009); *Gonski v. Second Judicial Dist. Court of State ex rel. Washoe*, 245 P.3d 1164, 1170 (2010); *Hayes v. Oakridge Home*, 122 Ohio St.3d 63, 77 (2009); *State ex rel. Richmond American Homes of West Virginia*, 717 S.E.2d 909, 920 (2011); *Brown v. Genesis Healthcare Corp.*, 2011 WL 2611327 ¶20.

[60] *Geoffroy v. Washington Mut. Bank*, 484 F. Supp. 2d 1115 (S.D. Cal. 2007); *Armendariz v. Found. Health Psychcare Services, Inc.*, 24 Cal. 4th 83, 114 (2000); *Zobrist v. Verizon Wireless*, 354 Ill. App. 3d 1139, 1141 (2004); *Harper v. Ultimo*, 113 Cal. App. 4th 1402, 1405 (2003); *Lhotka v. Geographic Expeditions, Inc.*, 181 Cal. App. 4th 816 (2010), review denied (Apr. 14, 2010), cert. denied, 131 S. Ct. 288 (2010).

of transaction could mean that courts would be willing to spend less time and effort on explaining why procedural unconscionability could be found in a given case. So the sliding scale there might be tipped in favor of a less procedural/more substantive analysis. And indeed, this has often been the case; courts applying the two-prong test in arbitration cases typically place more emphasis on the reasons why the particular clause at issue operates unfairly, and less on the means by which the agreement was reached.[61] That is not always so, however; there are cases in which the procedural side has appeared so egregiously unbalanced that the court has not felt it necessary to laboriously parse the contemplated arbitration process for substantive fairness.[62]

So far, the application of unconscionability to arbitration clauses seems generally to mirror the traditional judicial approach to unconscionability generally. Both in the arbitration area and elsewhere, however, there are instances of a court's going even beyond the "sliding scale" approach, to find unconscionability of a contract or term based entirely on only one of the two prongs, with little or no attention paid to the other one. Sometimes this can be explained as a case where one of the prongs is so obviously present that it needs little or no discussion.[63] But there are cases in which the court explicitly declares that although only one of the two traditional prongs has been satisfied, this will nevertheless be sufficient.[64] Viewed from the perspective of the conventional applications of the doctrine, this may seem problematic: where there is no procedural insufficiency at all, why should any degree of seeming unfairness be a basis for finding overall unconscionability, in light of the strong preference in American law for "freedom of contract" – the power of contracting parties to make their own agreements, even if others might find them unreasonable or even unfair? Conversely, where there appears to be nothing unfair about the substance of the resulting bargain, what could there be in the transaction to merit judicial intervention, possible procedural shortcomings notwithstanding?

The answers to those questions can be found in the different nature of the two factors in question. Where procedural unconscionability is extreme, the facts may well bring the case close to satisfying the requirements of other, more analytically focused types of bargain defect. Some of those, such as fraud, duress, or undue influence, involve actual misconduct by one of the bargainers. Those common-law

[61] *Jay Cashman, Inc. v. Portland Pipe Line Corp.*, 559 F. Supp. 2d 85 (report and recommendation adopted sub nom. *Jay Cashman, Inc. v. Portland Pipe Line, Inc.*, 573 F. Supp. 2d 335 (D. Me. 2008)); *Gordon v. Branch Banking & Trust Co.*, 666 F. Supp. 2d 1347 (N.D. Ga. 2009); *Potts v. Potts*, 303 SW3d 177 (Mo. Ct. App. 2010); *Woodall v. Avalon Care Ctr.-Fed. Way, LLC*, 155 Wash. App. 919 (2010).

[62] 64 UCC Rep. Serv. 2d (Callaghan) 201.

[63] *In re Owens Corning*, 291 BR 329, 334 (Bankr. D. Del. 2003).

[64] *Monsanto v. DWW Partners, LLLP*, 2010 WL 1904274 (D. Ariz. May 10, 2010); *Gordon v. Branch Banking & Trust Co.*, 666 F. Supp. 2d 1347 (N.D. Ga. 2009); *Helstrom v. N. Slope Borough*, 797 P.2d 1192 (Alaska 1990).

doctrines can independently be bases for contract avoidance, but they are more precise in their elements, and may also have higher requirements of proof. When one of those defenses is applied, the law does not necessarily require for avoidance that the resulting contract be shown to be substantively unfair as well; it may be enough that the innocent party was wrongfully induced to enter into a bargain that she otherwise would not have been willing to make. Other "procedural" defenses to enforcement, such as lack of capacity or mistake, do not necessarily involve bargaining misconduct, but they do suggest reasons for relieving one party of her obligation which are based more on lack of true assent than on the substance of the resulting bargain. It therefore seems appropriate that the more a claim of unconscionability is based on bargaining that borders on actual misconduct, or at least on a failure of real assent based on mistake, the less insistent the law should be on proof that the resulting bargain is unfair. On the other hand, if procedural unconscionability is deemed to be present merely because fine print terms have been buried in a lot of "boilerplate" clauses, a court may well need to be convinced that there is something seriously unbalanced about the resulting bargain as well.

In the converse situation, where substantive unconscionability is clear, when if ever should a court be willing to dispense with a finding of procedural unconscionability? Here the key may be the nature of the substantive defect. There are some kinds of agreements that the law simply will not allow one to make, even with an apparently free will: a minor below the age of consent cannot effectively agree to sexual intercourse, even where his/her consent was apparently freely given; an employee cannot bargain away the right to a minimum wage under an effective regulatory statute; one cannot sell a child. A finding of unconscionability that is truly based entirely on the presence of substantive unconscionability, with no procedural unconscionability as a complement, is really a finding that the contract or term in question is one that for reasons of policy, statutory or otherwise, the law will simply not tolerate or enforce, even if it appears to have been freely consented to.

3. Mutuality

Particularly in the early phase of arbitration/unconscionability jurisprudence, it was common for arbitration clauses to provide that one side (the adhering party) was bound to arbitrate all disputes, while the other (the drafter) was free to resort to the litigation process either in all cases, or at least in certain specified situations. This lack of "mutuality" was frequently one of the aspects of an arbitration scheme that a court would find objectionable, and take into account in weighing its substantive unconscionability.[65] Some courts and commentators critical of judicial attempts to resist mandatory arbitration have found this emphasis on mutuality to

[65] *Armendariz v. Found. Health Psychcare Servs., Inc.*, 6 P.3d 669, 680 (Cal. 2000).

be inappropriate, arguing that since contract law in general has no requirement of "mutuality of obligation," to treat the absence of mutuality as a basis for a finding of unconscionability in arbitration cases is to impose a burden on arbitration clauses that other types of contracts would not have to bear, thus flouting the Supreme Court's version of the FAA.[66]

That argument has some plausibility, to be sure. In §71, the Restatement (Second) of Contracts reaffirms its commitment to the "bargained-for exchange" theory of consideration, as expounded by Holmes and Williston, and in §79 it announces as a corollary that if this requirement for consideration is met, there are no additional requirements such as "benefit" or "detriment" (the earlier common-law test), "equivalence in the values exchanged," or "mutuality of obligation."[67] So should lack of mutuality be potentially an ingredient of unconscionability? The answer appears to be yes, it should, whether or not the contract at issue is one providing for arbitration. The provisions of §79 are a part of the Restatement's explication of the consideration doctrine, and must be read in that context; indeed, Section 79 refers specifically to the consideration requirement. That section should therefore not be seen as limiting in any way the operation of §208, the Restatement (Second) rule of unconscionability. The comments to §208 make clear that an unbalanced bargain is nevertheless one symptom of potential unconscionability: "Gross disparity in the values exchanged may be an important factor in determining that a contract is unconscionable."[68] The same principle should apply to the issue of mutuality; the arbitration-clause cases that focus on lack of mutuality are merely identifying, appropriately, another way in which a contract may be substantively unfair.

C. *Unconscionability in Action: Recent Examples*

As we have seen, the frequency of unconscionability application in cases involving mandatory arbitration clauses is likely to decline substantially in the near future, as a result of restrictive court decisions in that area. Moreover, many courts and commentators – although by no means all – have regarded that development as being somewhat anomalous anyway, not really part of the mainstream of unconscionability doctrine. So, for both those reasons, this chapter will from this point on focus on courts' use of unconscionability in cases not involving challenges to arbitration. While the recent cases are not numerous, together they do indicate that unconscionability will at least continue to play its traditional role in consumer transactions involving goods and services. In the aftermath of the recent economic downtown,

66 Steven J. Burton, *The New Judicial Hostility to Arbitration: Federal Preemption, Contract Unconscionability, and Agreements to Arbitrate*, 2006 J. Dispute Resolution 469, 488 (2006).

67 *See* Restatement (Second) of Contracts § 79 cmt f.

68 Restatement (Second) of Contracts § 208 cmt c.

however, other decisions indicate a possibly wider and more significant role for the concept of unconscionability as the new century unfolds.

1. Sales and Leases of Goods

The doctrine of unconscionability gained prominence by its inclusion in Article 2 of the UCC, and it continues to play a role in the area of sales of goods. Two cases involved individual purchases of boats: In both *Muscioni v. Clemons Boat*[69] and *Pierce v. Catalina Yachts, Inc.*,[70] plaintiff buyers complained of defects in the boats they had purchased. In *Muscioni*, a contract provision that required the buyer to transport his boat from Ohio back to the manufacturer in Illinois in order to obtain needed repairs was held to be so "outrageous" – indeed, "ludicrous" – as to be unconscionable.[71] In *Pierce*, a limitation of consequential damages was deemed unconscionable when the seller's limited warranty failed, and the buyers were entitled to both consequential damages and attorney fees under the Magnuson-Moss Act. In a third case, *DJ Coleman, Inc., v. Nufarm Americas, Inc.*,[72] a federal court in North Dakota denied summary judgment to the defendant herbicide manufacturer where the operator of a commercial farming operation sued for injury to its crop assertedly caused by the defendant's herbicide. Although some of the plaintiff's claims were barred by the economic loss doctrine and by federal preemption, the language on seller's label attempting to bar consequential damages was held to be both procedurally and substantively unconscionable, permitting the buyer to claim damages for the loss of its crop, rather than just refund or replacement of the defendant's product:

> It is undisputed that DJ Coleman had no bargaining power to alter the language of the limitation of remedies provision. The limitation of remedies provision contained on the ... label was pre-printed and was not negotiated. There is a substantial inequality in bargaining power between DJ Coleman and Nufarm. DJ Coleman is a commercial farming operation located in North Dakota, and Nufarm is part of an enormous, highly diversified, and international conglomerate.... The evidence reveals that the parties had unequal bargaining power and there was no room for meaningful negotiation. The purchasers of herbicides, regardless of their experience, are not in a position to bargain for more favorable terms than those listed on the pre-printed label, nor are they in a position to test the effectiveness of a herbicide before purchasing it. The fact that Clark Coleman was an experienced farmer that had used [defendant's product] on sunflower crops for ten years should not control whether he is entitled to consequential damages for a breach of warranty.

[69] 2005 WL 2008021 (Ohio App.).
[70] 2 P.3d 618 (Alaska 2000).
[71] 2005 WL 2008021 at 3.
[72] 693 F. Supp.2d 1055 (D.N. Dak. 2010).

> Accordingly, the Court finds that the limitation of remedies provision was procedurally unconscionable....
>
> The clause at issue here would limit DJ Coleman's remedy for a breach of an express warranty to the purchase price.... Once the crop has failed, the farmer's only recourse is monetary compensation to cover his lost profit and expenditures; replacement and repair are not viable options.... It is clear that the allocation of risk for defective herbicides is better shouldered by the manufacturer of the herbicide, rather than the consumer. The consumer does not have the ability or resources to test its use, but the manufacturer does.[73]

Two cases involved consumer leases of storage space. In one, *Gonzalez v. A-1 Self Storage, Inc.*,[74] a New Jersey court permitted the lessee of storage space to recover for water damage to her belongings despite contract language which would have limited the lessor's liability to fifty dollars even for its own negligence; the court characterized the contract as a whole as "outrageous":

> The contract attempts to: (1) avoid liability for all of defendant's actions, including defendant's own negligence; (2) require plaintiff to obtain insurance while denying a potential third party insurance company its right to sue defendant; (3) require plaintiff to indemnify and defend defendant against all related claims if defendant is sued; (4) limit all liability of defendant to a sum of only $50; (5) deny the formation and obligations of a bailment; (6) require plaintiff to waive and release any rights of recovery; (7) require plaintiff to pay all attorney's fees and costs associated with any related action; and (8) exclude all warranties, whether express or implied.[75]

Similarly, in *Dubey v. Public Storage, Inc.*,[76] a damage limitation was held to be unconscionable and not effective to bar plaintiff's suit for the defendant's wrongful entry into the leased premises and disposition of plaintiff's household goods.

2. Service Contracts

Services rendered to individuals were the subject of three actions. In *Perry Homes v. Alwattari*,[77] a Texas court ruled there was legally sufficient evidence for a trial court to find that gross disparity between contract price and value received rendered the contractor's conduct "unconscionable" for purposes of applying the state's Deceptive Trade Practice Act. In *Repair Masters Construction, Inc., v. Gary*,[78] a contractor's claim for liquidated damages under the homeowner's contract for repairs

73 693 F. Supp.2d at 1073–74.
74 795 A.2d 885 (N.J. Super. Ct. 2000).
75 *Id.*, at 890.
76 918 NE 2d 265 (Ill. App. 2009).
77 33 SW 3d 376 (Tex. Ct. App. 2000).
78 277 SW 3d 854 (Mo. Ct. App. 2009).

was disallowed on a strong showing of both procedural and substantive unconscionability where the contract was signed the same night the owner's house was damaged by fire.

> Homeowner stated that she does not read well. The failure to read a document prior to signing it is not a defense, and does not make a contract voidable, absent fraud.... A party capable of reading and understanding a document is charged with the knowledge of its contents if he or she signs it, even if the party fails to review it.... The fact that Homeowner may not have read or fully understood the documents does not make the "contract" void or voidable, although we note that the liquidated damages provision was placed under a section titled "DELAYS, ETC." However, the circumstances surrounding the formation of the "contract," namely one of Contractor's salesmen encouraging Homeowner to sign binding agreements to repair her home only hours after it was extensively damaged by fire, lacking any definiteness as to scope of work or price, or at least making the contract contingent upon acceptance of Contractor's proposed scope of work and price estimate, is evidence of procedural unconscionability.[79]

And in *In re Kenneth Plaza*,[80] a federal bankruptcy court declined to permit a debtor's trustee in bankruptcy to pay an attorney's fee claimed to be due under a contingency fee agreement which, among other things, prohibited the client from settling his claim without the consent of the attorney. The bankruptcy court held that such an agreement was unconscionable, and void as against public policy under the Texas Rules for Professional Conduct.

Unconscionability is commonly viewed as being seldom applicable to disputes involving business-to-business transactions, but such cases do occasionally arise.[81] One such is *Spectrum Networks, Inc., v. Plus Realty, Inc.*,[82] where a telecommunications consulting firm sued its corporate client for compensation claimed to be due under their contract's liquidated damages clause. In the course of applying Ohio's rule distinguishing "penalties" from "liquidated damages," the court examined the clause in question and found it to be unconscionable both substantively and procedurally, with the result that the entire contract – not just the offending clause – was held to be unenforceable.[83]

3. Domestic Relations

Although perhaps not an area that comes immediately to mind when one thinks of claims of unconscionability, several recent cases involve interspousal transactions.

79 *Id.*, at 858.
80 363 BR 517 (S.D. Tex. 2007).
81 See, e.g., *DJ Coleman, Inc., v. NuFarm Americas, Inc., supra* n. 72.
82 878 N.E.2d 1122 (Ohio Com. Pl. 2007).
83 *Id.*, at. 1128.

Two involved the validity of prenuptial agreements. In *Potts v. Potts*,[84] the trial court was upheld in its determination that the agreement was both procedurally and substantively unconscionable, because of its late presentation to the wife (literally on the eve of their marriage), her failure to consult an attorney, and its substantive unfairness:

> The trial court also presumably recognized that the agreement contained elements of substantive unconscionability. Raymond came into the marriage as the only one with assets that would generate future assets. As already mentioned, the agreement allowed him to categorize all assets generated in the future as separate property.... The agreement, by its terms, allowed Raymond to generate a large estate of non-marital property while limiting the distribution to Susan (upon dissolution) exclusively to a formula to be in lieu of maintenance, even after a twenty year marriage in which Susan had devoted her efforts to raising the children and running the household and thereby supporting Raymond's business.[85]

In *In re Marriage of Rosendale*,[86] the trial court was instructed to reconsider the possible unconscionability of a premarital spousal support waiver in light of the circumstances at the time of enforcement, including the wife's serious auto accident and resulting health problems, and the husband's "vast separate property holdings."[87] Citing several statutory provisions relating to spousal support, the court declared:

> The rule ... that one spouse may be required to support an ill spouse in a manner contrary to the terms of an interspousal agreement, is consistent with public policy as expressed in several Family Code provisions.... These statutory provisions underscore the continued importance of spousal support in our modern society, under appropriate circumstances. In that way, they also support the continued application of the rule of unconscionability ... in the premarital agreement context. Courts cannot permit one spouse to discard his or her disabled spouse without providing spousal support, even when a spousal support waiver in a premarital agreement would permit the same, if it would be unconscionable to do so at the time enforcement of the waiver is sought.[88]

A more difficult question was presented to a Virginia court in *Sims v. Sims*,[89] testing the validity of a property settlement agreement reached in contemplation of divorce. In *Sims* the wife had serious health problems and limited education, and no assets or means of supporting herself. Nevertheless, a trial court upheld their agreement, finding that the husband had not engaged in any overreaching

[84] 303 SW 3d 177 (Mo. Ct. App. 2010).
[85] *Id.*, at 189–190.
[86] 15 Cal. Rptr. 3d 137 (Cal. Ct. App. 2004).
[87] *Id.*, at 146.
[88] *Id.*, at 145.
[89] 685 SE 2d 869 (Va. Ct. App. 2009).

or oppressive conduct, and that the wife had entered into it freely and knowingly. Citing the state's interest in not having the wife become a public charge, the appellate court held that unconscionability could be found in the extremely gross disparity in the division of assets, plus the wife's infirmity and pecuniary necessity:

> Although the evidence supported the trial court's finding that husband did not engage in any overt overreaching or oppressive conduct, his act of entering into a contract with wife in which she waived spousal support and relinquished to him almost 100% of the marital estate – including the marital residence, all retirement benefits and deferred compensation – literally left her penniless with no practical means for supporting herself.... The evidence established that wife had in fact already become a public charge, receiving food stamps, despite husband's retention of substantial marital assets. Thus, the evidence established not only a gross disparity in the division of assets but also infirmity and pecuniary necessities which, in combination, established unconscionability.[90]

A different type of domestic relations issue was raised by *Snell v. Snell*:[91] could an ex-husband accused by his former wife of domestic violence and improper conduct toward their daughter resist her request for issuance of a civil protection order on the ground that a post-nuptial agreement between the parties barred her from seeking such relief? An Ohio trial court characterized that argument as "ludicrous."[92] While asserting its power to give the issue de novo review, the appellate court essentially agreed with the court below, finding the provision to be unconscionable and in clear violation of public policy.

4. Real Estate Transactions

Along with bank lending and consumer credit, discussed in a later section of this chapter, the area of real estate transactions appears to show a noticeable increase in unconscionability applications over the past decade. Given the virtual collapse of the residential real estate market in many areas of the United States and the associated boom in mortgage foreclosures, causing many debtors to find themselves unable to keep up with payments on "underwater" mortgages, it is not surprising that claims of unconscionability are being made in that area, with some success. Of course, such one-by-one judicial interventions can hardly be a cure for what amounts to systemic dysfunction, but the cases do at least indicate that resourceful attorneys and responsive judges can provide relief to some of the most vulnerable actors in this area.

90 *Id.*, at 875.

91 *Snell v. Snell*, 2010-Ohio-2245.

92 *Id.*

A representative case is *Swayne v. Beebles Investments, Inc.*,[93] an Ohio case decided in 2008. Plaintiff Swayne, an elderly widow of limited means who needed funds to repair the home she had inherited from her late husband, was induced by the defendant's principal Farkas to enter into a mortgage loan agreement with a "balloon" payment at the end of a year, on the assurance that she would then be able to refinance at an affordable rate. When the loan matured she was not able to refinance (with this lender or any other) and instead was pressured into deeding her home to the defendant, on the assurance that she could eventually recover it through refinancing. Defendant rented the property to plaintiff for two years and then sold to a related entity managed by defendants' associates. Plaintiff sued the defendant and related parties to have both the balloon loan agreement and the subsequent sale and lease agreement declared to be unconscionable. The trial court granted plaintiff summary judgment on both claims, and also found defendant in violation of a state statute regulating mortgage brokers. Quoting *Williams v. Walker-Thomas Furniture Co.*, the court applied the two-prong test and held both procedural and substantive unconscionability had been amply demonstrated:

> Swayne was in her 70s when she engaged in this transaction. She had not worked outside the home since 1972. Her husband, who had managed the couple's finances, had died two years before. Swayne soon found herself in need of money to pay bills and to repair the roof, kitchen, and bathroom of her home of 20 years.... Beebles knew that with a monthly income of $1,206, Swayne would be unable to make the balloon payment when it became due. Thus, Beebles placed Swayne in a position in which Beebles knew or should have known that Swayne was certain to default. All of these factors demonstrate substantive unconscionability.
>
> With respect to procedural unconscionability, the relative bargaining positions of the parties could not be more disparate. Beebles and Farkas were in the business of brokering mortgages. Beebles took advantage of Swayne's lack of financial sophistication by having Swayne execute two sets of loan documents with differing terms. Swayne was unfamiliar with financial matters, as she was a recent widow whose husband had managed the couple's finances. Swayne did not consult a lawyer or even a financially sophisticated friend. Rather, she relied upon the representations of the loan officer, and then Farkas himself.
>
> Farkas, on the other hand, knew the poor state of Swayne's finances, knew of her bad credit, knew of her lack of resources, knew that no lenders were willing to lend her money, and knew that Swayne could not possibly pay back the balloon note. He also testified that even with the loan, there was "no way" that Swayne had enough money to do the necessary repairs to her house. Despite all of that knowledge, appellants entered into a loan agreement with terms that Swayne could not

93 891 NE 2d 1216 (Ohio Ct. App. 2008).

possibly meet. On these undisputed facts, Farkas and Beebles took advantage of the parties' unequal bargaining positions to create a one-sided agreement in their favor.[95]

Cases with facts similar to *Swayne*'s included *Cleveland v. O'Brien*[96] (defendants had committed fraud and were guilty of unconscionable conduct under New Jersey Consumer Fraud Act) and *In re Emery-Watson*[97] (bankrupt relieved of deed conveying property to her neighbor as part of an unconscionable scheme ostensibly to rescue bankrupt's home from foreclosure). Other cases where borrowers were given relief from unconscionable mortgage provisions involved less sophisticated borrowers, with little proficiency in English: *HSBC Bank USA v. Benevides*[98] and *Thelemaque v. Fremont Investment & Loan*.[99]

Not every real estate case in this area involved a mortgage loan transaction. In *Sitogum Holdings, Inc., v. Ropes*,[100] an elderly widow was maneuvered into signing an option contract to sell residential property in New Jersey for a price of roughly half of its true market value. The seller had essentially no effective legal counsel, and the case appears to have had at least borderline elements of undue influence, diminished capacity, and fraud. Carefully applying the traditional procedural/substantive test for unconscionability, the court concludes that although the seller did not fit the common pattern in such cases – she was "not financially vulnerable, … illiterate or of limited education" – the transaction as a whole was procedurally unconscionable, and the gross inadequacy of the sale price justified the court in granting summary judgment to the seller and declaring the contract void.[101] A very different application of the unconscionability principle was at stake in In *re Union Square Associates, LLC.*, [102] a bankruptcy proceeding. Here the plaintiff seeking relief had mistakenly made a bid on property sold in foreclosure proceedings at some $70,000 more than it intended to, because of a mistake in computing certain escrow deposits previously made. The mistake was characterized by the court as a unilateral one, which meant that in order to be relieved of its purchase obligation the plaintiff had to show the existence of a non-negligent, material mistake, resulting in a bargain which would be unconscionable if enforced. Nothing in the facts suggests overreaching on the part of the seller, but the court found both prongs of the unconscionability test to be satisfied: the factual circumstances were indeed confusing, conducive to mistake

95 891 NE 2d at 1222–3 (D. N.J. 2010).

96 2010 WL 4703781 (D.N.J. 2010).

97 412 BR 670 (D.Del. 2009).

98 2011 WL 262431 (Conn. Super. Ct.).

99 2011 WL 2734490 (Mass. Super. Ct.)

100 800 A.2d 915 (N.J. Super. 2002).

101 *Id.*, at 923.

102 392 BR 474 (D. Utah 2008).

(hence a kind of procedural unconscionability), and the resulting bargain would have been "lopsided, unfair and unconscionable" if enforced against the buyer.[103]

5. Consumer Lending and Credit

Perhaps the most adventurous applications of the unconscionability principle in the past few years have been in the area of bank lending and credit cards. Although none of the cases discussed in this section has yet been reviewed by the highest court of its jurisdiction, collectively they represent a somewhat bolder assertion of judicial regulatory power over this area of consumer transactions.

In *Johnson v. The Cash Store*,[104] a Wisconsin debtor had entered into a series of transactions with a "payday" lender, by the end of which she had paid more than double the amount of an original $500 loan, lost her trailer residence to foreclosure, and still owed $20,000 to her mortgage lender. She sued the defendant lender for unconscionability and violation of the state's Consumer Protection Act. Bungling on the part of the defendant's agent allowed the plaintiff to obtain a deficiency judgment of treble damages for the full amount she had paid to the defendant, plus $15,000 for emotional distress. Eventually the defendant moved to vacate the judgment and the award of damages, but the trial court denied the motion and the Washington Court of Appeals affirmed. On appeal, the defendant argued that because its operations had been approved by the state's Department of Financial Institutions, they could not possibly be unconscionable or otherwise actionable. The court held otherwise, however, pointing out that the defendant's operations appeared to violate the state's statute regulating small loans to consumers at higher rates:

> In Washington, [state law] prohibits the classic form of roll over for … small loans: "No loan made under this act shall be repaid by proceeds of another loan made under [this act] by the same lender or affiliate. The proceeds from any loan made under this act shall not be applied to any other loan from the same lender or affiliate." In an attempt to comply with this regulation, Cash Store requires its customers to "pay off" each loan with cash that is promptly returned to the customer when he or she pays the finance fee for the original loan, signs a new consumer loan agreement, and writes out a new postdated check.… Labeling roll overs as new loans is common in the payday loan industry.… By paying back the loan and immediately taking out a new loan for the same amount, the consumer enters a debt treadmill, where the loan is nonamortizing and payment of a finance fee every two weeks is necessary to prevent a default.… The payday loan industry maintains that the risk of default is high and justifies exorbitant finance fees. However, "because the rollover practice is part of its business model, the risk of losing capital decreases over time."[105]

[103] *Id.*, at 480.

[104] 68 P.3d 1099 (Wash Ct. App. 2003).

[105] *Id.*, at 1106.

Except for the award of attorney's fees, the judgment below was affirmed. Emotional distress damages were allowed because plaintiff had successfully demonstrated emotional distress sufficient to constitute a tort cause of action, and the defendant had not effectively appealed that award. A similar lending operation was challenged in *O'Donovan v. CashCall, Inc.*,[106] by plaintiffs who claimed excessive interest rates, oppressive collection procedures and a host of other improper and illegal practices on the part of the lender and sought to have their claims certified as a class action. A California federal district court held that at least some of the claims were appropriate for class certification, including their claims of procedural and substantial unconscionability, and allowed the case to go forward.

Another payday loan operation was challenged in *Payday Loan Store of Wis., Inc. v Mount.*[107] Plaintiff invoked the Wisconsin Consumer Act, which provides that a court may limit or refuse to enforce any consumer credit transaction that it finds to be unconscionable, and argued that an effective annual interest rate of over a thousand percent should be deemed substantively unconscionable. Defendant argued that because state statute law imposed no cap on interest charges by lenders such as plaintiff, the court was precluded from doing do on grounds of unconscionability. The Wisconsin Court of Appeals reviewed the arguments pro and con, and referred the matter to the state's Supreme Court, which granted certiorari in August of 2011.[108]

Major banks engaged in credit-card lending may not appear to be quite as "predatory" as the "payday" lending industry is often said to be, but their practices are not above challenge. Interest rates in excess of 18 percent on a credit card – and going up as high as 55 percent in this case – were held by a Massachusetts Superior Court to be unconscionable, in the case of *Citibank v. DeCristoforo.*[109] The defendant bank argued that under state statute it could charge whatever interest rate it chose, with no interference from the courts. In an opinion remarkable as much for its breadth as for its succinctness, the court reviewed the history of national regulation of banking practices going back to the founding of the federal banking system, and traced the gradual erosion of legal controls over usury capped by a "race to the bottom" in states that effectively give the banks carte blanche to do as they pleased. In this case, however, the court held that defendant was not under Massachusetts law free to charge unconscionable rates. It continued:

> Although the facts pertaining to the formation of [plaintiff's] credit card agreements are not set forth in the record, the court can fully grasp the one-sided nature of those

[106] 2011 WL 5573845 (N.D. Cal.).
[107] 2011 WL 2577365 (Wis. Ct. App.).
[108] 804 NW 2d 82 (Wis. 2011).
[109] 2011 WL 1020497 (Mass. Super. Ct.).

> proceedings. Nevertheless, even putting procedural unconscionability aside, the court concludes this is an instance where unconscionability can be based on the substantive component alone.... The court acknowledges that Citibank's interest rate charges are not always unreasonable. For example, at times, Citibank charged ... as little at 10.65%. As time went by, however, Citibank continually increased its rate, especially as [plaintiff] began to fall behind with her payments, until it reached rates as high as 54.7333%. Substantial interest rate hikes such as this have greatly contributed to the consumer credit crisis in America.
>
> With interest rates as high as forty and fifty percent, a significant portion of the debtor's monthly payment goes toward paying interest without touching the underlying debt. At these rates, individuals must make monthly payments for years before putting a dent in their debt, especially when one owes credit balances in excess of $25,000, as is the case [here]. Interest charges at these rates drain needed resources and slow economic growth. Citibank's charges, in excess of eighteen percent, "drives too hard a bargain for a court of conscience to assist."... The court concludes interest rate charges above eighteen percent are unconscionable and "so outrageous as to warrant holding [them] ... unenforceable."[110]

Although its full story has yet to be told, a class action in a federal district court in Florida appears to have already yielded perhaps the most dramatic outcome in the cases surveyed for this report. In an action captioned *In re Checking Account Overdraft Litigation*,[111] multiple account holders sued multiple banks on a number of claims, including procedural and substantive unconscionability, arising out of the banks' actions with respect to overdraft charges. Plaintiffs alleged that the defendants followed a practice with respect to their debit card customers of debiting large-amount overdraft before ones of smaller amounts (even when the latter were received earlier), so as to maximize the amount of overdraft fees chargeable to their customers. Plaintiffs asserted that this practice was both procedurally and substantively unconscionable. They also alleged a variety of other improper practices by defendants. The defendant asserted, among other defenses, federal preemption; with respect to the plaintiffs' claims of unconscionability, they also asserted that common law unconscionability could not be used as an affirmative cause of action, only as a defense against some claim by another party. In a long and careful opinion, the court granted some of defendants' motions to dismiss and denied others. Of particular interest here is the court's treatment of the issue of unconscionability as a cause of action:

> Defendants make two arguments attacking Plaintiffs' unconscionability count in this Motion. First, Defendants argue that unconscionability is not an affirmative

[110] *Id.* at 5.
[111] 694 F. Supp. 2d 1302 (S.D. Fla.2010).

> cause of action, but merely a defense to the enforcement of a contract.... Plaintiffs respond by asserting that the Court can utilize its equitable powers to issue a declaratory decree that the contractual terms and practices are unconscionable.... Moreover, Plaintiffs argue that, if the Court finds the terms or practices to be unconscionable, the Court has the power to award damages for the banks' past enforcement of the terms....
>
> The Court finds Plaintiffs' argument more persuasive. If the overdraft fee provisions are found to be unconscionable, the Court retains the authority and discretion to fashion appropriate equitable relief. Moreover, a declaration of unconscionability may affect the legal status of the contractual terms that Defendants seek to enforce, which may, in turn, affect the analysis of the other causes of action that Plaintiffs assert. Finally, Defendants appear to be correct in their assertion that, ordinarily, unconscionability is properly asserted as a defense to a contract rather than an affirmative cause of action. But this is not the ordinary case. An ordinary case in this factual context would be one in which the customer allegedly overdraws his or her account, the bank provides the overdraft service, and then the bank demands payment of the overdraft fee from the customer. Then, when the customer refuses to pay, the bank sues the customer for breach of contract, and the customer at that time can raise an unconscionability defense to the enforcement of the contract. In the instant case, however, the bank is never required to file suit because it is already in possession of the customer's money, and simply collects the fee by debiting the customer's account. Thus, the customer never has the opportunity to raise unconscionability as a defense for nonpayment. The only opportunity to do so is through a lawsuit filed by the customer, after payment has been made. Hence, the facts of the instant case weigh in favor of permitting Plaintiffs to pursue an unconscionability claim.[112]

The court went on to rule that the plaintiffs had sufficiently pled procedural unconscionability, noting the "disparity in sophistication and bargaining power" between the parties, the "voluminous boilerplate language" in the bank's forms, the lack of any "meaningful opportunity to negotiate," and the lack of notice to customers that they could decline the overdraft fee arrangement.[113] With respect to substantive unconscionability, the court rejected defendants' argument that the practice must be acceptable because it is standard trade practice, and noted that electronic posting makes the practical arguments for it untenable.[114]

The court's opinion in this case left many issues to be resolved in future proceedings, and perhaps a higher court will yet reject some or all of the court's reasoning with respect to unconscionability. But in November of 2011, the same court (and

[112] *Id.*, at 1318–19.
[113] *Id.*, at 1319–20.
[114] *Id.*, at 1320–1.

judge) approved a settlement between plaintiffs and one of the defendants, Bank of America, in a lengthy opinion reviewing the terms of the settlement and the attorneys fee provided thereby. The amount of the settlement was $410 million.[115] Noting that the case "involves millions of Settlement Class Members and alleged wrongful overdraft fees in the billions of dollars," and that recovery by any means other than settlement would require additional years of litigation, the court upheld not only the total settlement but specific awards to class representatives as well as legal fees to counsel of 30 percent of the settlement. Indeed, the court declared:

> Class Counsel achieved an extraordinary result and overcame numerous procedural and substantive hurdles to obtain the Settlement for the Class. As Plaintiffs' several experts have noted, Class Counsel took on a great deal of risk in bringing this case, and turned a potentially empty well into a significant judgment. That kind of initiative and skill must be adequately compensated to insure that counsel of this caliber is available to undertake these kinds of risky but important cases in the future.[116]

V. CONCLUSION

Looking back over the last half-century or so of modern unconscionability law in America, it would take a brave observer indeed to venture with any certainty a prediction of what the next half-century will bring in this regard. Two decades ago, the doctrine of unconscionability seemed relegated to a sort of legal backwater – it had become, as one observer put it, "a disfavored stepchild of contract law."[117] A decade later, however, events had taken an unexpected turn, and unconscionability was being pulled back into the mainstream of American jurisprudence, as a possible counterweight – perhaps the only one available – to the pressure from the United States Supreme Court for ever-greater abdication of judicial power and responsibility to the corporate drafters of adhesion contracts. As this chapter is being written, well into the second decade of the new century, it seems apparent that the Supreme Court is determined to keep up the pressure for arbitration, in a way that only the United States Congress could (it if chose to do so) ameliorate.[118] It thus may be that unconscionability has had its brief day in the sun and will fade again into the shadows of legal marginality.

[115] In re Checking Account Overdraft Litigation, 2011 WL 5873389 (S.D. Fla. 2011).

[116] *Id.*, at 22.

[117] Jeffrey W. Stempel, *Arbitration, Unconscionability, and Equilibrium: The Return of Unconscionability Analysis as a Counterweight to Arbitration Formalism*, 19 OHIO STATE J. ON DISPUTE RESOLUTION 757, 840 (2004).

[118] The FAA is federal law, and the US Supreme Court is the supreme interpreter of federal law, so no state legislature or court can override that statute or the Court's interpretation of it. However, it is not a constitutional provision, so Congress could alter it at will. (If Congress had the will, that is.)

This need not be the case, however. As the doctrine assumed greater importance in the area of mandatory arbitration, some observers saw in that development the possible seeds of a greater judicial appreciation for the expanded role that unconscionability could play in contract law generally.[119] Professor Jeffrey Stempel expressed it this way:

> The answer of many courts to the new twenty-first century problem of arbitrability has been the rediscovery and reinvigoration of a venerable doctrine that deserves greater respect and more frequent use across the board. Continued use of the unconscionability norm would serve contract law well generally.... The rediscovery of unconscionability has softened the rougher edges of the Supreme Court's arbitration formalism and made both the judicial and arbitration systems more effective. The arbitration-unconscionability experience suggests that a relatively less constrained version of the unconscionability norm should continue to play a role in contract construction, both for arbitration terms and other contract provisions.[120]

Whether the doctrine will indeed continue to play a role in the area of arbitration law is unclear; this is something that the lower federal and state courts can influence, but not control. As for its importance to contract generally, however, the signs are promising. As the preceding sampling of recent decisions demonstrates, the concept of unconscionability has far outgrown its place as UCC §2–302, an aspect of sale-of-goods law, to being recognized as a concept that both predates and transcends the UCC, with a role to play both in the common law generally and as a concept increasingly employed in the statutory regulation of commercial activity, particular where consumers are concerned.[121] Perhaps a new generation of attorneys and judges will once again find in the concept of unconscionability a means of tempering economic efficiency with social justice, and moral decency as well.

[119] See n. 34, *supra*.

[120] Jeffrey W. Stempel, *Arbitration, Unconscionability, and Equilibrium: The Return of Unconscionability Analysis as a Counterweight to Arbitration Formalism*, 19 Ohio State J. on Dispute Resolution 757, 860 n. 23 (2004).

[121] *See generally* Amy J. Schmitz, *Embracing Unconscionability's Safety Net Function*, 58 Alabama L. Rev. 73 (2006).

14

Unfair Terms in Comparative Perspective

Software Contracts

Jean Braucher

The phenomenon of unfair terms in mass-market contracts is widely acknowledged, as is the fictional nature of "assent" or "consent" to all but a few obvious terms, such as price and key product features. Although some still argue for facilitating choice through better disclosure and education of customers, most policymakers, regulators, and scholars concede that there often can be no real assent to mass-market standard terms, but then balk at meaningful solutions to address market failure. The problem of nasty standard terms is seen as intractable.

A good example of recognition of the problem of unfair terms but reluctance to provide effective remedies is the recent project of the American Law Institute – the Principles of the Law of Software Contracts. The Principles address every issue raised by the coalition of software customers concerning unfair terms and practices, but they rely too heavily on after-the-fact judicial policing using broad standards and do not call for administrative prevention or enforcement. The Principles thus are mostly symbolic, although in several places they propose meaningful commands and in others they use illustrations to target specific suspect terms. Overall, they suggest some important ways to make software contracts fairer and succeed in making the point that policing of terms is more tractable if done industry by industry, with attention to particularities, but they stop short of a workable implementation strategy.

An alternative regulatory model is presented by the EU Unfair Contract Terms in Consumer Contracts Directive. The Directive has its own limitations, such as a scope limited to natural persons acting outside their trade or business. However, its greatest strength is an explicit recognition that unfair terms not only should be unenforceable, but also have to be kept out of contracts in the first place. Prevention of unfair drafting requires responsive regulation designed to curb and channel corporate culture. The United Kingdom's Office of Fair Trading (scheduled for elimination in 2014 by the Coalition Government by being merged into a new Competition and Markets

Authority) has made use of such an approach in its implementation of the Directive in UK law.

The quest for effective implementation of constraints on unfairness should continue. From a comparative perspective, the US and Europe each have something to learn from the other, and an amalgam of their approaches to unfair terms may provide better oversight than what either has devised so far.

I. INTRODUCTION

Overreaching in the drafting of standard-form terms is a central problem in contract law, one for which there is no thoroughly convincing theory or easy and practical remedy. Ridiculous standard-form contracts (SFKs) have long been the butt of comedy, going back at least to the hilarity of the Marx Brothers' *Night at the Opera* contract scene.[1] The richness of the material has only grown in the twenty-first century. Digital technology has made it possible for SFK terms to become even longer, at little cost to drafters. The American actor Richard Dreyfuss recently performed a dramatic reading of selected terms from Apple's I-Tunes software license.[2] He showed

[1] A *Night at the Opera* (Metro Goldwin Meyer 1935), *Contract Scene, available at* http://www.searchlores.org/contract.html, with dialogue such as this:

FIORELLO: Can *you* read?

DRIFTWOOD *(struggling to read the fine print)*: I can read but I can't see it. I don't seem to have it in focus here. If my arms were a little longer, I could read it. You haven't got a baboon in your pocket, have ya? Here, here, here we are. Now I've got it. Now pay particular attention to this first clause because it's most important. It says the, uh, "The party of the first part shall be known in this contract as the party of the first part." How do you like that? That's pretty neat, eh?

FIORELLO: No, it's no good....

DRIFTWOOD: ... – look, why should we quarrel about a thing like this? We'll take it right out, eh?

FIORELLO: Yeah, it's a too long, anyhow. *(They both tear off the tops of their contracts.)* Now, what do we got left?

(... The two then proceed to tear off everything they don't like or don't understand until there is practically nothing left.)

DRIFTWOOD: We got a contract...

FIORELLO: You bet.

DRIFTWOOD: No matter how small it is...

FIORELLO: Hey, wait, wait. What does this say here? This thing here.

DRIFTWOOD: Oh, that? Oh, that's the usual clause. That's in every contract. That just says uh, it says uh, "If any of the parties participating in this contract is shown not to be in their right mind, the entire agreement is automatically nullified."

FIORELLO: Well, I don't know...

DRIFTWOOD: It's all right, that's, that's in every contract. That's, that's what they call a "sanity clause."

FIORELLO: Ha ha ha ha ha! You can't fool me! There ain't no Sanity Clause!

[2] Rafe Needleman, *Richard Dreyfuss reads the I-Tunes EULA*, CNET (June 8, 2011), *available at* http://www.cnet.com/8301–30976_1–20068778–10348864.html.

by turns a Shakespearian world weariness, more in sorrow than in anger, about a direction to read the license or otherwise not use the software; a devilish enjoyment of the disclaimer of any responsibility for quality; a screeching near-hysteria about the possibility of death, personal injury, or severe physical or environmental damage from use of the software in connection with nuclear, air traffic control, or life support systems; and a clipped, chilling Waffen-SS efficiency when declaring the licensor's right to "terminate" all rights without notice.[3]

This chapter examines the current state of theory and practice about SFK terms through a comparative lens and using the example of software contracts. While addressing overreaching in SFKs is difficult, advanced legal systems tend to take on the challenge. The European Union's Unfair Contract Terms Directive is limited in scope to contracts made between sellers or suppliers and natural persons acting outside their trade or business and thus is predominantly a consumer protection measure.[4] The problem of contractual unfairness is, unfortunately, much broader, extending at least to mass-market transactions with business customers under SFKs with unreasonable terms buried in the fine print.[5] Although the scope is limited, the EU Directive's greatest strength is its explicit recognition that unfair terms not only should be unenforceable, but also have to be kept out of form contracts in the first place, and that administrative oversight is a good way to do that.[6] The Directive seeks ex ante prevention, not merely ex post refusal to enforce (in the unlikely event litigation ensues). It also provides an annex of "grey-listed" terms that are presumptively unenforceable.[7] In Europe, there is a recognition that prevention of unfair drafting requires responsive regulation designed to curb and channel corporate culture.[8] The Directive requires each EU country to implement it.[9] Meanwhile, the US depends too much on case-by-case policing of standard forms in litigation after

3 *Id.* (with links to each of the readings referred to in the text).

4 Council Directive 93/13/EEC of 5 April 1993 on unfair terms in consumer contracts, *available at* http://eur-lex.europa.eu/LexUriServ/LexUriServ.do?uri=CELEX:31993L0013:en:NOT. [hereinafter, EU Directive] at Articles 2, 6, and 7. Furthermore, a lesser degree of policing of unfair terms in business-to-business contracts has been proposed as part of a draft for a possible optional additional instrument on European contract law produced by a European Commission expert group. *See* Martijn Hesselink, *Unfair Terms in Contracts between Businesses* (2011), Amsterdam Law School Legal Studies Research Paper No. 2011–11, *available at* http://ssrn.com/abstract=1871130.

5 Jean Braucher, *The Failed Promise of the UCITA Mass-Market Concept and Its Lessons for Policing of Standard-From Contracts*, 7 J. SMALL & EMERGING BUS. L. 393 (2003) [*hereinafter*, Braucher, *Mass-Market Concept*].

6 EU Directive, *supra* note 4, Articles 6 and 7.

7 *Id.* at Article 3(3) and Annex. See *infra* notes 123–5 and accompanying text.

8 Ian Ayres & John Braithwaite, RESPONSIVE REGULATION: TRANSCENDING THE DEREGULATION DEBATE (Oxford University Press: Oxford 1992).

9 EU Directive, *supra* note 4, Article 10.

the fact, using broad standards such as unconscionability[10] or consumer deception, although the latter standard is also enforced administratively.[11]

The American Law Institute's PRINCIPLES OF THE LAW OF SOFTWARE CONTRACTS frequently use weak common law methodology in their blackletter, but not always, and the Principles' commentary and illustrations target a number of specific types of unfair terms.[12] The ALI project claims to reject the European approach to unfair terms,[13] yet as we will see, its approach is actually more similar to than different from the EU Directive's methodology.[14] Furthermore, the ALI project is promising in another way: the ALI addressed every troubling issue raised by the coalition of software customers concerning unfair terms and practices,[15] thus succeeding in demonstrating that policing can be more tractable if done industry by industry. Software is an economically important industry, worthy of detailed attention and probably ultimately needing specific statutory and administrative social control, with a residual power to address new forms of unfairness. From a comparative perspective, then, the US and Europe may each have something to learn from the other, a point the ALI Principles acknowledge by saying the EU's list of suspect terms can serve as a guide to what terms are unconscionable.[16] An amalgam of EU and ALI approaches to unfair terms could provide better oversight than what either has devised so far.

This chapter will proceed as follows: Part II provides an overview of the challenge that SFK terms present to contract theory and to design of constraints, also known as social control to balance freedom of contract. Part III analyzes an important

[10] Unconscionability is a contract law concept; *see* American Law Institute, RESTATEMENT (SECOND) OF CONTRACTS) (1981), Section 208 on Unconscionable Contract of Term, [*hereinafter*, ALI, RESTATEMENT (SECOND)], and it has also been incorporated into the Uniform Commercial Code, Article 2, Section 2–302. *See also* American Law Institute, PRINCIPLES OF THE LAW OF SOFTWARE CONTRACTS (2010), Section 1.11 on Unconscionability, [hereinafter, ALI PRINCIPLES]. The ALI is a private non-profit law reform organization. *See* http://www.ali.org/index.cfm?fuseaction=about.overview.

[11] State consumer protection statutes usually provide consumers a private right of action using a consumer deception standard. *See* Jonathan Sheldon & Carolyn L. Carter, UNFAIR AND DECEPTIVE ACTS AND PRACTICES (7th ed. National Consumer Law Center: Boston 2008) & Supplement (2011) (describing consumer protection statutes in effect in every state and their relation to the Federal Trade Commission Act, which does not include a private right of action, and discussing the administrative powers of the FTC as well as state agencies to implement consumer protection).

[12] ALI PRINCIPLES, *supra* note 10. *See also infra* Part IIID (concerning use of broad standards in the blackletter of the ALI PRINCIPLES dealing with terms that upset the balance of federal intellectual property law between the rights of producers and users of software but also use of examples to address specific problems of this type) and Part IIIB-C (concerning recommended rules).

[13] ALI PRINCIPLES, *supra* note 10, at Section 1.11 on Unconscionability, cmt. c. *See also infra* note 105 and accompanying text.

[14] *See infra* notes 106–8, 122–30, 138–42, and accompanying text.

[15] *See infra* Part III.

[16] ALI PRINCIPLES, *supra* note 10, at Section 1.11 on Unconscionability, cmt. c. *See also infra* note 105 and accompanying text.

illustration, unfair terms in software contracts, showing how the US law reform process has identified the issues but addressed them only weakly in places but with surprising strength in others. Part IV compares US and European approaches. The conclusion, Part V, proposes a combination of the two approaches to unfairness in SFKs.

II. THE CHALLENGE TO CONTRACT THEORY PRESENTED BY SFKS

Private ordering achieved through mutual assent is widely agreed to be the central purpose of contract law.[17] Furthermore, a contract is the most basic unit in making up a market; thus contract law facilitates the operation of markets.[18] Efficient markets require rationality, information and competition, yet achieving these ideal conditions is the exception rather than the rule.[19] As a result, contract law has always included a great deal of social control, provided by such doctrines as incapacity, illegality and other public-policy grounds for denying enforcement, duress and undue influence, misrepresentation, implied obligations of good faith and fair dealing, and unconscionability, among others such as warranties implied in law.[20] These doctrines set public limits on private ordering or use default terms to promote norms of substantive fairness. The public dimension of the institution of contract is even more basic in two important ways. Background social order is essential to enable contracting, for example, by containing usurpations by force and channeling parties into voluntary exchange. Furthermore, by supplying judicial enforcement, state power at a fundamental level constitutes the institution of contract, leading to a demand that contracts be used for purposes that are not antithetical to social norms.[21] A baseline norm is that transactions generally should be experienced as win-win propositions rather than as exploitation.[22]

[17] ALI Principles, *supra* note 10, at Section 1.10 on Public Policy, cmt. a (noting that a public policy should be fundamental to override freedom of contract, because "freedom of contract is itself an important public policy because it allows private parties to govern themselves and, in the absence of market failure, to move goods and services to their highest-valued uses.")

[18] *See* Lon L. Fuller and William R. Perdue Jr., *The Reliance Interest in Contracts Damages*, 46 Yale. L. J. 52, 64–65 (1936) (noting that exchanges "form the very mechanism by which production is organized in a capitalistic society.").

[19] *See* Russell Korobkin, *Bounded Rationality, Standard Form Contracts, and Unconscionability*, 70 U. Chi. L. Rev. 1203 (2003).

[20] *See* ALI, Restatement (Second), *supra* note 10, Sections 12–15 (capacity doctrines), 178–96 (unenforceability on grounds of public policy), 174–6 (duress and undue influence), 159–73 (misrepresentation), 205 (duty of good faith and fair dealing), 208 (unconscionable contract or term), and Uniform Commercial Code Sections 2–314 and 2–315 (implied warranties of merchantability and fitness for a particular purpose).

[21] Morris R. Cohen, *The Basis of Contract*, 46 Harv. L. Rev. 553 (1933).

[22] Ian R. Macneil, The New Social Contract: An Inquiry into Modern Contractual Relations 102–3 (Yale U. Press: New Haven 1981) (discussing how the psychology of exchange can rapidly shift from "trading in goods to that of harms").

Contract is supposed to be about voluntary exchange, which requires mutual assent. Yet the mutuality of contracts, particularly SFKs, is often fictional. The non-drafter of a SFK usually will not read the terms, and, indeed, the contract document is not meant to be read.[23] Thus there is a huge potential for unnoticed and thus unknown bad terms to appear in forms, and even with good disclosure, many customers do not understand and appreciate of significance of SFK terms. Despite widespread recognition of the problem, it is much harder for the law to produce a workable response, and thus it is easier to cling to a fiction of assent than to design effective interventions to contain and prevent use of unfair terms. An alternative to pretending that there is assent, one with more realism and descriptive power but less appeal, is to explain SFK enforcement as a means to facilitate low prices based on liability containment.[24] The problem with this theory, however, is that it means that the unlucky or those with idiosyncratic needs or wants can suffer large losses without recourse; they are sacrificed so that others can pay less. Policing of unfair terms thus can be seen as a form of insurance, with all customers paying a small amount to spread the burden of risks.

The American legal realist Karl Llewellyn developed the most widely accepted analysis of SFKs among American legal scholars, offering a "blanket assent" theory.[25] He acknowledged that there is typically no specific assent to SFK terms, other than a few that may have been "dickered," meaning negotiated, or that are salient, such as price and basic transaction type.[26] In addition, he posited that there is "blanket assent (not a specific assent) to any not unreasonable or indecent terms the seller may have on his form, which do not alter or eviscerate the reasonable meaning of the dickered terms."[27] Broadening this analysis, he also said that blanket assent extends to the form "en bloc," but only to the extent "that its terms are neither in the

[23] Stewart Macaulay, *Private Legislation and the Duty to Read – Business Run by IBM Machine, the Law of Contracts and Credit Cards*, 19 VAND. L. REV. 1051 (1966).

[24] See James J. White, *Autistic Contracts*, 45 WAYNE L. REV. 1693 (2000) (arguing that contract rituals involving an opportunity for the offeree to learn of the terms should still be observed despite the cost).

[25] Karl N. Lewellyn, THE COMMON LAW TRADITION: DECIDING APPEALS 370 (Little, Brown and Co.: Boston 1960) [*hereinafter*, Llewellyn, THE COMMON LAW TRADITION]. *See also* ALI PRINCIPLES, *supra* note 10, at Section 2.02 on Standard Form Transfers of Generally Available Software; Enforcement of the Standard Form, cmt. e (discussing Karl Llewellyn's blanket assent theory as a basis to enforce unread terms).

[26] Llewellyn, THE COMMON LAW TRADITION, *supra* note 25, at 370. In the case of software transactions, even the transaction type may not be understood by customers. Producers often label their transactions as "licenses," but what that means may be obscure. See Jean Braucher, *New Basics: 12 Principles for Fair Commerce in Mass-Market Software and Other Digital Products* [*hereinafter* Braucher, *New Basics*], in CONSUMER PROTECTION IN THE AGE OF THE 'INFORMATION ECONOMY' 191 (Jane K. Winn, ed., Ashgate Publishing Ltd.: Aldershot, Hampshire 2006). *Also available at* SSRN: http://ssrn.com/abstract=730907 or doi:10.2139/ssrn.730907 (noting customer lack of understanding of what it means to "license" a software product as an end user).

[27] Llewellyn, THE COMMON LAW TRADITION, *supra* note 25, at 370.

particular nor in the net manifestly unreasonable and unfair."[28] No US legal scholar has done any better than the blanket assent theory, but that does not mean that the theory is fully satisfying.

Llewellyn sought to explain SFKs in terms of assent while also saying that "dickered terms ... constitute the dominant and only real expression of agreement."[29] At the core of his theory, then, is a legal fiction of assent: SFK terms defeated the leading American legal realist's attempt to explain them in a realist way. Llewellyn discussed SFKs early in his career[30] and then again later.[31] The grand late work, THE COMMON LAW TRADITION – DECIDING APPEALS,[32] is a celebration of common law judging. As a result, Llewellyn's discussion of "blanket assent" in the late work is in the context of an invitation to common law judges to police SFKs case by case. He wanted their work to "cumulate,"[33] but he also wanted their policing of unfair terms to be discretionary and attuned to the nuances of context.[34] This is a very tall order, perhaps a contradiction in terms.

Stewart Macaulay's early work examined the implementation strategies of contract law. To the complex dualism of mutual assent and social control, discussed previously, he added another dualism: the question of how the law assures each of them, whether by rules or instead by case-by-case evaluation.[35] As Arthur Leff[36] and William Whitford[37] later elaborated, common law methodology is not a very effective means of assuring fairness in SFKs. Leff criticized the "cute litigation game" involved in using unconscionability to police "mass problems in mass contracts" and argued that administrative enforcement can be much more effective.[38] Whitford noted that very specific prohibitions of overreaching terms often produce voluntary compliance,[39] although of course residual standards are needed to address later innovations in unfairness. While Llewellyn acknowledged in his early work that statutes are more

28 *Id.* at 371.
29 *Id.* at 370.
30 Karl N. Llewellyn, THE CASE LAW SYSTEM IN AMERICA (with an Introduction by Paul Gewirtz, ed., U. Chicago Press: Chicago 1989) at ix–x (noting that the book was originally published in German in 1933 and was based on lectures given in 1928–9 in Germany) at 67 (arguing that with some case law and experience, statutes can become the more efficient and direct way to address a problem and that consumer protection is a problem that calls out for statutory solutions).
31 Llewellyn, THE COMMON LAW TRADITION, *supra* note 25.
32 *Id.*
33 *Id.* at 365.
34 *Id.* at 362–71.
35 Macaulay, *supra* note 23, at 1057.
36 Arthur Allen Leff, *Unconscionability and the Crowd – Consumers and the Common Law Tradition*, 31 U. PITT. L. REV. 349 (1970).
37 William C. Whitford, *Structuring Consumer Protection Legislation to Maximize Effectiveness*, 1981 WIS. L. REV. 1018.
38 Leff, *supra* note 36, at 357–8.
39 Whitford, *supra* note 37, at 1022.

direct and thus efficient as a way to reach a goal and that consumer protection is an enormous problem not suited to case-by-case methodology,[40] unfortunately – as mentioned previously – his late statement of the "blanket assent" theory was tied to case-by-case common law development of policing doctrines.[41] Thus, the weakness of Llewellyn's great fiction was compounded by his recommendation of ineffective implementation. The point can be made this way: even if one accepts the attenuated premise that parties who adhere to SFKs are giving blanket assent to all the terms unless they are unfair or unreasonable, it is pure fantasy that these parties are also assenting to the unpredictability and variability of having to pursue common law-style litigation to persuade a judge that a given unknown term is unfair in a particular case. Assent, even "blanket assent," cannot be stretched that far. More realistically, adhering parties are either looking to the reputation of the drafting party, expecting adjustment in a fair way,[42] or crossing their fingers and hoping for the best. Parties can and often do informally maintain reciprocity, the substantive goal of contracts, but sometimes this norm breaks down. This may be particularly likely in anonymous, technologically mediated relationships such as those involving digital products.

The consumer protection movement that began in the United States in the 1960s was not content with contract law doctrine and its implementation case by case in court as the means to address unfairness, leading to an explosion of federal and state statutes to address both particular types of deals and unfairness in general through administrative rules and enforcement. Much of the resulting law required disclosure,[43] but substantive policing has been employed as well.[44] In consumer contracts, the general law of contract became only a backup theory, with less powerful remedies than those provided by statute.[45] Some types of consumer contracts were subjected to detailed statutory regimes.[46] Particularization has its own difficulties,

[40] Llewellyn, The Case Law System in America, *supra* note 30, at 67 (arguing that statutes can be more efficient and are needed to achieve consumer protection).

[41] Llewellyn, The Common Law Tradition, *supra* note 25.

[42] This is the perspective added by the law in action approach to contracts, which emphasizes that norms and reputation are often the most important "law" applicable to transactions, particularly small ones. *See* Stewart Macaulay et al., Contracts: Law in Action, Vol. I (3d ed. LexisNexis: 2010) and Vol. II (3d ed. LexisNexis: 2011) (casebook developing this perspective on contract law).

[43] *See* the Truth in Lending Act, 15 USC §§ 1601–67e.

[44] *See* Jean Braucher, *Defining Unfairness: Empathy and Economic Analysis at the Federal Trade Commission*, 68 BUL Rev. 349 (1988) (discussing the Federal Trade Commission's Credit Practices Rule, promulgated under its power to address unfairness in consumer contracts and banning particular practices; the FTC did not just make certain terms unenforceable but rather made it an unfair practice under the FTC Act to use the terms at all). For a discussion of recent attention to substance in consumer credit regulation, see Jean Braucher, Form and Substance in Consumer Financial Protection, 7 Brooklyn J. of Corp., Fin. & Com. L. __ (forthcoming 2012), *available at* http://ssrn.com/abstract=2126859.

[45] Stewart Macaulay, *Bambi Meets Godzilla: Reflection on Contracts Scholarship and Teaching v. State Unfair and Deceptive Trade Practices and Consumer Protection Statutes*, 26 Hous. L. Rev. 575 (1989).

[46] *See, e.g.*, Truth in Lending Act, *supra* note 43.

however, in that legislatures and even administrative agencies are never going to reach every type of deal with specific rules and also because human creativity is infinite when it comes to designing evasions of mandates. Administrative consumer protection agencies need and generally have residual general powers to police unfairness and thus deal with new evasions. The common law also has a residual role to play to deal with inevitable gaps in statutory and administrative policing of SFKs. Furthermore, contract law standards such as unconscionability and good faith and fair dealing are often the only vehicle for policing of unfair terms beyond the realm of consumer transactions.[47]

III. US LAW REFORM AND SOFTWARE CONTRACTS

Attempts by US law reform organizations to address recurrent issues in software contracts with a successful uniform state statute proved unavailing by about 2003.[48] The American Law Institute stepped into the breach and produced its PRINCIPLES OF THE LAW OF SOFTWARE CONTRACTS, published in 2010.[49] Rather than offering a proposed statute, this principles project is primarily addressed to courts, providing them with a guide to common law adjudication of software contract disputes, as well as gloss on how to apply Article 2 of the Uniform Commercial Code, on sales of goods, to software transactions.[50] Parts of the Principles would also make good statutory provisions and could be adopted as such by legislatures.

The ALI Principles were drafted in reaction to the Uniform Computer Information Transactions Act (UCITA), which was enacted in only two states, Maryland and Virginia, in somewhat different versions, prompting five other states to enact "bomb-shelter" statutes to prevent application of UCITA to their residents by means of

[47] Uniform Commercial Code (UCC) Article 2 incorporates both unconscionability and good faith and fair dealing. UCC Sections 2–302 and 1–104, applicable generally in the UCC to B2B as well as B2C contracts.

[48] Braucher, *New Basics*, *supra* note 26, at 179–83 (recounting the failure of attempts to promulgate an Article 2B as part of the UCC, covering licenses, as well as the inability to enact a free-standing uniform state law, the Uniform Computer Information Transactions Act (UCITA), in more than two states after successful mobilization by a coalition of software customers).

[49] ALI PRINCIPLES, *supra* note 10.

[50] *Id.*, Introduction, at 2 (noting that the principles are not the law until adopted by a court but can serve as gloss on application of the common law, Article 2, and other statutes). UCC Article 2 applies to transactions in goods, and courts have frequently applied it to software as well as to hard goods. See *Metro Data Base Systems, Inc. v. Dharma Systems, Inc.*, 148 F. 3d 649, 651–4 (7th Cir. 1998) (in an opinion by Judge Richard Posner, applying Article 2 to a transaction in customized software under an agreement involving a "license fee" and reasoning "we can think of no reason why the UCC is not suitable to govern disputes arising from the sale of custom software"). *See also* Jean Braucher, *Contracting Out of Article 2 Using a "License" Label: A Strategy That Should Not Work for Software Products*, 40 LOY. L.A. L. REV. 261 (2006).

choice of law or choice of forum clauses.[51] The software industry had dominated the UCITA drafting process, and UCITA's overreaching had the unusual effect of galvanizing software customers into an effective coalition made up of business customers such as insurance companies and manufacturers, as well as libraries and consumers.[52] This coalition, Americans for Fair Electronic Commerce Transactions (AFFECT), first worked to defeat UCITA and then decided to promulgate a set of principles, thus providing an outline of what positive law reform concerning software and other digital products should address to provide basic protections to customers.[53] AFFECT began its principles project in 2003 and completed it in early 2005.[54]

The 12 AFFECT Principles for Fair Commerce in Software and Other Digital Products are as follows:

I. Customers are entitled to readily find, review, and understand proposed terms when they shop.
II. Customers are entitled to actively accept proposed terms before they make the deal.
III. Customers are entitled to information about all known nontrivial defects in a product before committing to the deal.
IV. Customers are entitled to a refund when the product is not of reasonable quality.
V. Customers are entitled to have their disputes settled in a local convenient venue.
VI. Customers are entitled to control their own computer systems.
VII. Customers are entitled to control their own data.
VIII. Customers are entitled to fair use, including library or classroom use, of digital products to the extent permitted by federal copyright law.
IX. Customers are entitled to study how a product works.
X. Customers are entitled to express opinions about products and report their experiences with them.
XI. Customers are entitled to the free use of public domain information.
XII. Customers are entitled to transfer products as long as they do not retain access to them.[55]

[51] Braucher, *New Basics*, *supra* note 26, at 181 and 200 & n. 35 (concerning enactment of bomb shelter laws by Iowa, North Carolina, Vermont, and West Virginia). *See also* Idaho Code § 29–116 (enactment by fifth state of bomb shelter law in 2007).

[52] Braucher, *New Basics*, *supra* note 26, at 178, 181–2.

[53] *Id.* at 181–83 (discussing the drafting of the AFFECT Principles for Fair Commerce in Software and Other Digital Products [*hereinafter*, AFFECT Principles]). *See also* Jean Braucher, *US Influence with a Twist: Lessons about Unfair Contract Terms from US Software Customers*, 15 AUSTRALIAN COMPET. & CONS. L. J. 7 (2007), *available at* http://ssrn.com/abstract=976439.

[54] Braucher, *New Basics*, *supra* note 26, at 182–3.

[55] *Id.* at 183.

These principles address both form and substance of digital product transactions. They can be categorized as based on four concerns: (1) the need for meaningful disclosure, so that terms are available when customers shop for products, and for an active sign of assent as part of the process of entering a transaction (Principles I and II); (2) reducing the impact of product defects by requiring disclosure of known flaws, in particular to foster security of systems and privacy of data (Principle III and also Principles VI and VII in part); (3) providing a minimum remedy and accessible dispute resolution to customers and policing against unfair remedies of producers (Principles IV and V, and Principles VI and VII in part); and (4) protection of information policy reflected in intellectual property law (Principles VIII through XII).

Like the AFFECT Principles, the ALI Principles address form and substance, or mutual assent and social control. Strikingly, the ALI project gave some force to all of the AFFECT principles, validating the coalition's diagnosis of the problems in software transactions and providing means of relief in each of the four problem areas identified by AFFECT, as discussed in the following.

A. *Advance Disclosure and a Step for Active Assent*

Assent to SFKs was an issue that plagued the UCITA process, with producers insisting on a right to withhold terms until after customers paid for and received delivery of products. Two decisions of the U.S. Court of Appeals for the Seventh Circuit had given the industry a sense of entitlement to continue this dubious practice.[56] Although dealing with digital products, the two decisions, both written by Judge Frank Easterbrook, who had been a University of Chicago law professor, seem quaintly old-fashioned a decade and a half after they were written in the mid-1990s. At the time, the Internet was just beginning to gain general usage. Neither decision took account of this technological revolution and its ability to solve the problem of advance disclosure. Notably, both decisions – one dealing with an in-store purchase of a product that included telephone numbers and software to navigate them, and the other dealing with a telephone order of a computer loaded with software – did not consider the impact that e-commerce could have. They did not discuss the possibility of pre-transaction disclosure of terms by posting them on the Internet, making Judge Easterbrook's analysis dated.

Advance disclosure is a cornerstone of meaningful assent. It provides sunshine to allow customers to avoid bad deals and to engage in negative word of mouth,

[56] *Pro-CD, Inc. v. Zeidenberg*, 86 F. 3d 1447 (7th Cir. 1996) (finding assent to terms in the box and not available in the store when the customer paid at the counter) and *Hill v. Gateway 2000, Inc.*, 105 F. 3d 1147 (7th Cir. 1997) (finding that a contract was formed not on the telephone by the making of and acceptance of an order, or even by shipment, as provided in UCC § 2–206, but only by non-return of the product within 30 days of receipt of a box containing the product and terms).

particularly easy in the age of blogs.[57] Advance disclosure is a necessary part of unfair terms regulation, although it is not sufficient in itself and must be supplemented with substantive checks. The key point is that policing should use both disclosure and substantive oversight.

Unlike the Seventh Circuit decisions, the ALI Principles were written after the Internet had become a leading means of shopping for and ordering products. The ALI Principles embrace the use of the Internet to facilitate advance disclosure as well as an active step for assent. Furthermore, the ALI Principles use rule-like provisions, not standards, to address both advance disclosure and active assent. Section 2.02(c), applicable to standard-form transfers of generally available software, calls for terms to be accessible *prior to* as well as at the time of initiation of a transaction.[58] This means that terms should be available on a Web site before a customer begins to order, not just during or after the order process. This provision applies whether or not the order is made on the Internet. The ALI Principles also call for active assent in electronic orders,[59] which can be achieved by clicking at the end of or adjacent to terms displayed on an Internet site.[60]

The text of the ALI Principles' provision on disclosure and active assent is as follows:

> (c) A transferee will be deemed to have adopted a standard form as a contract if
>
> (1) the standard form is reasonably accessible electronically prior to initiation of the transfer at issue;
>
> (2) upon initiating the transfer, the transferee has reasonable notice of and access to the standard form before payment or, if there is no payment, before completion of the transfer;
>
> (3) in the case of an electronic transfer of software, the transferee signifies agreement at the end of or adjacent to the electronic standard form, or in the case of a standard form printed on or attached to packaged software or separately wrapped from the software, the transferee does not exercise the opportunity to return the software unopened for a full refund within a reasonable time after the transfer; and
>
> (4) the transferee can store and reproduce the standard form if presented electronically.[61]

57 ALI Principles, *supra* note 10, at Section 2.02 on Standard-Form Transfers of Generally Available Software; Enforcement of the Standard Form, cmt. e (discussing the Principles' adoption of Web site disclosure and the possibility that watchdog groups can spread the word about "unsavory terms").

58 *Id.* at Section 2.02(a) and (c)(1). Concerning the definition of "standard-form transfer of generally available software," *see infra* note 114.

59 *Id.* at Section 2.02(c)(3). An exception to active assent is made for non-electronic transactions.

60 *Id.* and cmt. c.

61 *Id.* at Section 2.02(c).

Subsection (d) adds a provision calling for standard terms to be "reasonably comprehensible."[62]

The disclosure and assent provisions are stated as safe harbors or best practices, but they certainly call into question a conclusion of enforceability if the producer uses delayed disclosure, passive assent to terms on a Web order form, or obscure, difficult language. On the other hand, the ALI Principles' use of safe harbors may make some producers willing to adopt less robust disclosure and assent protocols and try to defend their practices after the fact if challenged in litigation. Thus, ALI stopped short of actually promulgating rules. Given the nature of the project, which is primarily persuasive authority addressed to courts called upon to apply either the common law or the open-textured provisions of UCC Article 2,[63] this is not surprising. Interestingly, however, as we shall see, in other areas the ALI Principles did announce mandatory rules, albeit ones that only go into effect if a court or legislature adopts them.

B. *Reducing the Impact of Product Flaws*

A major concern for software customers, particularly business customers, is security vulnerabilities in mass-market digital products that allow hackers to access their systems and data. When producers reveal such flaws, businesses and some consumers find it easier to guard against their risks. The ALI Principles responded to this concern with a non-disclaimable warranty against known material hidden defects, another rule-like customer protection. Furthermore, this provision is presented in statute-like form as a command, showing that ALI felt it could go beyond promulgating best practices, the approach it used for disclosure and assent. The warranty against known hidden defects, applicable to any software transaction, even a negotiated one between businesses, is stated in Section 3.05(b) as follows:

> A transferor that receives money or a right to payment of a monetary obligation in exchange for the software warrants to any party in the normal chain of distribution that the software contains no material hidden defects of which the transferor was aware at the time of the transfer. This warranty may not be excluded. In addition, this warranty does not displace an action for misrepresentation or its remedies. [Emphasis added.][64]

[62] *Id.* at Section 2.02(d).

[63] *See supra* note 50 and accompanying text.

[64] ALI PRINCIPLES, *supra note* 10, at Section 3.05(b) on Other Implied Quality Warranties. See also Reporters' Notes to cmt. b (crediting Cem Kaner, both a lawyer and a computer scientist as well as a participant in drafting the AFFECT Principles, for identifying the need for a rule of disclosure of known defects).

A comment to this section discusses the policy reasons for the warranty, that it allocates risk to the party best able to address it and creates incentives for disclosure to minimize costs to customers.[65] Externalization of the costs of product flaws has been a major problem in the software industry. Security vulnerabilities in particular make customers' systems and data subject to hacking and planting of spyware, and businesses spend vast resources trying to guard against attacks. Having information about flaws allows customers to take steps to address them at lower cost. To put teeth in the warranty, the ALI Principles make an exclusion of liability for consequential damages for its breach unenforceable.[66]

The same comment also discusses web posting as a means of disclosure, indicating that this may not be sufficient and that direct communication with customers is the best means of disclosure. Although the provision by its terms does not require disclosure of defects found after transfer of software, as applied to mass-market products, the warranty effectively requires producers to make public disclosure because future customers will constantly be coming along and making purchases. Public disclosure means existing customers benefit from the warranty as well, despite the stated limitation to transfers made after the producer obtained knowledge of the defect.

C. *Remedies and Dispute Resolution*

Customers of digital products have been concerned both about overreaching remedies of producers and about having usable remedies themselves. Perhaps the single biggest remedial concern of customers is use of electronic self-help against them, which UCITA ultimately banned in response to an outcry from customers.[67] The problem with self-help is that producer threats to shut down customers' systems for alleged contract breaches would have *in terrorem* effect, particularly on business customers. Furthermore, customers do not want the products they acquire to have undisclosed security backdoors, installed as the mechanism for self-help but also making their systems subject to hacking.

The ALI Principles take a strong stand against electronic self-help. There is a prohibition, not variable by agreement, on "automated disablement"[68] as a remedy in transactions involving a standard-form transfer of generally available software and in

[65] *Id.* at Section 3.05(b), cmt. b.

[66] *Id.* at Section 4.01(c) on Contractual Modification or Limitation of Remedy.

[67] Concerning the failure of UCITA to win wide enactment, *see supra* notes 48–52 and accompanying text. Concerning the ban on self-help in UCITA, *see* UCITA § 816(b) ("Electronic self-help is prohibited.").

[68] "Automated disablement" is defined as "the use of electronic means to disable or materially impair the functionality of software." ALI Principles, *supra* note 10, at Section 4.03(a) on Use of Automated Disablement to Impair Use.

consumer transactions.[69] Even in negotiated transactions, electronic self-help is not allowed; a court order must be obtained to use automated disablement.[70] Violations of these prohibitions subject the transferor to liability for consequential damages caused by use of electronic disablement, notwithstanding any agreement to the contrary.[71] Once again, the ALI Principles use a mandatory rule, not variable by agreement even in negotiated transactions. Not only is self-help barred, but so is limitation of consequential damages in the event of violation of this rule.

Comment a to Section 4.03 of the ALI Principles recognizes that when a software producer includes code in its product to allow the producer to disable software electronically in the event of a perceived threat to contract rights, innocent customers can be harmed because even "the existence of the disabling code itself on the transferee's computer may make it vulnerable to security breaches."[72] As a result, including such code without disclosure should violate the warranty of no material hidden defect discussed previously.[73]

The ALI Principles have also addressed the AFFECT Principles' concern that customers deserve at least minimum remedies. The AFFECT Principles proposed a concession to producers of digital products – that consequential damages no longer be the default rule for ordinary contract breaches, absent personal injury. This was intended to allow producers to routinely use background terms supplied by law and remove the premium on getting effective terms agreed to by customers.[74] ALI, however, stuck with a background rule of consequential liability absent exclusion, while also allowing exclusion except for breach of the warranty against known hidden material defects, unauthorized automated disablement, or personal injury from consumer software.[75]

AFFECT advocated a minimum remedy of refund for non-performing digital products.[76] The ALI Principles so provide, allowing both for cancellation for material breach and return of the price plus expectation damages.[77] Furthermore, the

69 *Id.* at Section 4.03(c). A "standard-form transfer of generally available software" is a defined term that goes beyond consumer transactions in the sense of transactions for personal, family or household purposes. *Id.* at Section 1.01 (l) on Definitions and *see infra* note 114.

70 ALI Principles, *supra* note 10, at Section 4.03(d)(3). Furthermore, there must be a conspicuous term in the agreement authorizing automated disablement, and there must be notice and an opportunity to cure. *Id.* at Section 4.03(d)(1) and (2).

71 *Id.* at Section 4.03(e).

72 *Id.* at Section 4.03, cmt. a.

73 *See supra* Part IIIB.

74 Braucher, *New Basics*, *supra* note 26, at 187, 202 & n. 61.

75 ALI Principles, *supra* note 10, at Section 4.01(c).

76 Braucher, New Basics, *supra* note 26, at 187.

77 ALI Principles, *supra* note 10, at Sections 4.04(a) on Cancellation and 4.05 on Expectation Damages and its cmt. d ("When an injured transferee has not received or has rightfully cancelled and returned the software, it is entitled to a refund of what it has paid plus damages.").

ALI Principles pick up from Uniform Commercial Code Article 2 the idea of failure of essential purpose of a limited remedy.[78]

Choice of law and choice of forum were also addressed by both projects. The AFFECT Principles reject many of the approaches adopted by UCITA and thus implicitly reject as a matter of public policy its application by means of a choice of law clause. AFFECT also called for use of a local convenient forum in disputes over mass-market digital products.[79] For standard-form software transactions, the ALI Principles adopt the choice of law approach of the UCC, which is to require a "reasonable relationship" between the transaction and the jurisdiction chosen.[80] Choice of forum under the ALI Principles is constrained by principles of convenience, unconscionability, and public policy.[81] In sum, the ALI Principles allow for results consistent with what AFFECT sought as far as choice of law and forum selection.

D. *Protecting Intellectual Property Rights*

Probably the number one concern of software customers when it comes to SFKs for digital products is that their terms not take away customer rights that are part of the delicate balance in intellectual property law. Producers have attempted to write themselves more expansive intellectual property rights using form terms, thus trying to cut back on customers' rights as users.[82] Customers want social control to stop this practice. Five of the AFFECT Principles are aimed at preserving customers' intellectual property rights, including fair use, transferability of copies, and access to public domain materials.[83] Fair use includes rights of comment, testing, and study.[84]

The ALI Principles address intellectual property rights in three sections, concerning federal preemption of state law, contracts against public policy, and unconscionability.[85] This gives customers three theories to pursue: that a given term is

[78] *Id.* at Section 4.01(b), using the concept of UCC Section 2–719(2). However, section 4.01(c) allows an exclusion of consequential damages to be upheld notwithstanding failure of essential purpose of a limited remedy, absent unconscionability.

[79] Principle V of the AFFECT Principles. *See supra* notes 53–5 and accompanying text.

[80] Section 1.13(a) on Choice of Law in Standard Form Transfers of Generally Available Software and its cmt. 1.

[81] Section 1.14 (a), (b), and (d) on Forum-Selection Clauses.

[82] Charles R. McManis, *The Privatization (or "Shrink-Wrapping") of American Copyright Law*, 87 Cal. L. Rev. 173 (1999).

[83] Principles VIII–XII of the AFFECT Principles. *See supra* notes 53–5 and accompanying text. *See also* Braucher, *New Basics*, *supra* note 26, at 188–90.

[84] Principles VIII–X of the AFFECT Principles. *See supra* notes 53–5 and accompanying text.

[85] ALI Principles, *supra* note 10, at Sections 1.09 on Enforcement of Terms under Federal Intellectual Property Law, Section 1.10 on Public Policy, and Section 1.11 on Unconscionability.

explicitly preempted by federal intellectual property law or conflicts impermissibly with the purposes and policies of that body of law; that the term is against public policy; and that it is unconscionable. Only one of these theories needs to work for a customer to prevail, and a problem in making out one theory may be solved by switching to one of the other two theories. The subsection on conflict with federal purposes and policies serves as a reminder that contract law as applied to software transactions operates in conjunction with a well-developed set of federal rights for intellectual property owners and users.[86] The other two provisions, inviting policing based on public policy or unconscionability, are general common law doctrines under state law, also set forth in the RESTATEMENT (SECOND) OF CONTRACTS.[87]

The policing theories based on preemption policy, other public policy, and unconscionability are stated as standards and thus do not promise the customer protection of some other aspects of the ALI Principles, such as the warranty against known hidden defects or the bar on self-help use of automated disablement discussed previously. A long comment explains reluctance to be more definitive as resulting from the unsettled nature of federal preemption law and the fact-sensitive nature of the two state-law doctrines.[88] Yet the ALI Principles' commentary and illustrations address with specificity the most common types of terms that attempt to cut back on customers' intellectual property rights, making the Principles a powerful form of guidance, assuming the courts pay attention. Singled out as problematic, particularly in SFKs, are terms that purport to

(1) preclude the transferee generally from making fair uses of the work;
(2) ban or limit reverse engineering;
(3) restrict copying or dissemination of factual information; or
(4) forbid transfer of the software.[89]

Commentary stresses policy reasons for disfavoring such terms, including negative impact on innovation and competition.[90] Some examples follow of the ALI analysis favoring customers' intellectual property rights in very specific ways.

Fair use. The ALI Principles discuss the importance of fair use, an intellectual property concept that includes comment about software products as well as study (reverse engineering) and testing. An illustration questions enforceability of a SFK

86 *Id.* at Section 1.09(b) (making a term unenforceable if it "conflicts impermissibly with the purposes and policies of federal intellectual property law").

87 RESTATEMENT (SECOND), *supra* note 10, at Sections 178–96 (concerning unenforceability of grounds of public policy) and 208 (concerning unconscionable contracts or terms).

88 ALI PRINCIPLES, *supra* note 10, at Section 1.09, cmt. c (discussion purposes and policies preemption). Preemption is a doctrine based on the Supremacy Clause of the US Constitution, Article VI, Clause 2, making federal law supreme over that of the states in the event of conflict.

89 ALI PRINCIPLES, *supra* note 10, at Section 1.09, cmt. c.

90 *Id.*

term that prohibits criticism of the performance of software, saying that the term may be unenforceable on public-policy grounds.[91] Restrictions on reverse engineering get extended discussion in commentary, with the point made that these threaten both competition and innovation and may be against state public policy even if not preempted.[92]

Fair use testing is given strong support in this illustration:

> A makes its software generally available to the public. A's standard-form contract prohibits transferees from benchmarking the software and distributing the information so obtained. (Benchmarking involves testing the product against others as well as establishing facts about its performance. Such a term implicates copyright law because benchmarking normally requires running the software, which in turn requires loading the software into RAM. Loading the software into RAM creates a copy according to some courts and the Copyright Office.) Because there is a strong public interest in permitting customers to evaluate the software's performance and in disseminating the information obtained in part to encourage the production of other innovative, competitive software modules, the term may be unenforceable because preempted by copyright law. It may also be unenforceable on grounds of state public policy.[93]

This analysis stops short of saying that anti-benchmarking terms are always unenforceable, but it encourages courts to consider non-enforcement on the basis of either federal or state policy when such a term is included in a SFK for a product made generally available to the public.

Transferability. The ALI Principles explain that restrictions on transfer in SFKs may be problematic either under federal law, based on the concept of exhaustion of producers' rights in copyright and patent law, or under state law public policy disfavoring restraints on alienation.[94] As with restrictions on certain fair uses, the analysis encourages considering both grounds for declining to enforce, particularly in SFK transactions:

> B, a consumer, buys a package containing A's word-processing software. A term accompanying the package bars all transfers of the software. B gives her copy of the software to C, a neighbor, after deleting the program from B's computer.

91 *Id.* at Section 1.10, Ill. 2. (also contrasting a general restriction on comment in SFK terms for a product made available to the public to a contract restriction applicable only to an early version of a product distributed to only a few customers for testing, where a prohibition on comment is unlikely to be viewed as contrary to public policy).

92 *Id.* at Section 1.09, cmt. c, and at Section 1.10, cmt. c and cmt. d.

93 *Id.* at Section 1.09, Ill. 7; Section 1.10, Ill. 3 (indicating that if preemption on conflict grounds does not work, public policy is an alternative basis for non-enforcement).

94 *Id.* at Section 1.09, cmt. c.

> Preemption is likely but uncertain (see § 1.09). A state may refuse to enforce the restriction on transfer on public-policy grounds. Public policy disfavors restraints on alienation. The copyright law's first-sale doctrine reflects that policy. In the case of software, however, transfers between parties such as B and C are problematic because the transferor may retain a copy of the software that it also provides to the transferee. Thus, preemption is uncertain, and a public-policy analysis that considers the circumstances – B has deleted the software – may be preferable.[95]

As in the AFFECT Principles, the ALI analysis is that a customer cannot both keep a product and transfer a copy of it, but that a customer who does not keep a copy should be able to transfer the customer's copy or copies to another user for the same type of use.[96] Another illustration disfavors restrictions on transfer of software that unreasonably impede the marketability of a business, making the point that unreasonable restraints on alienation can also be problematic for business customers, not just customers acquiring for personal or household use.[97]

The scope of the ALI Principles is narrower than the AFFECT Principles in that the ALI project does not cover digital content products.[98] Thus the ALI project does not cover, for example, e-books, although these may include incidental software to navigate digital content. On the other hand, the ALI Principles invite their extension by analogy where appropriate.[99] A very big concern for the AFFECT project was protecting the mission of libraries. Restrictions on transfer of digital content that would impair the ability of libraries to lend e-books should be suspect on both

95 *Id.* at Section 1.10, Ill. 4.

96 Enforceable restrictions on types of use are necessary to allow price differentiation, for example, to charge one price for business use and another for household use, which should generally be permissible. *See id.* at Section 1.09, cmt. c. *See also* Principle XII of the AFFECT Principles, *supra* notes 53–5 and accompanying text.

97 ALI PRINCIPLES, *supra* note 10, at Section 1.10, Ill. 5

98 *Id.* at Section 1.06, cmt. f (excluding digital databases and digitized expression, such as movies and music). An unfortunate choice of the ALI project was to focus in detail not only on positive scope of the project but also on exclusions from scope and on mixed software and other elements, such as hardware or data that is not copyrightable, using a predominant purpose of the transaction test. *Id.* at Sections 106–108 (on various aspects of scope, that is, to which sorts of transactions the project is applicable). This detailed elaboration of scope seems neurotic given that the project also notes that it can be applied by analogy. *Id.* at 15 ("nothing in the scope provisions precludes a court from applying these Principles by analogy if deemed appropriate."). *See also supra* note 50 and accompanying text (concerning use of the ALI PRINCIPLES to develop the common law or as gloss on application of Article 2 to software). It would have made more sense to define the scope of the ALI PRINCIPLES positively, as covering software, but not negatively. The treatment of scope is a legacy of the troubled uniform law projects that preceded the ALI project. See supra notes 48–52 and accompanying text.

99 ALI PRINCIPLES, *supra* note 10, at 15. *See supra* note 98 (quoting the relevant language concerning application by analogy).

preemption policy and public-policy grounds, extending the approach of the ALI project by analogy.[100]

Access to public domain information. Given the ALI Principles' scope excluding digital content products,[101] there is limited treatment of the issue of attempts to use SFK terms to limit access to information not copyrightable under US law or that has become part of the public domain. One illustration addresses this issue in the context of a software contract with a term attempting to control non-copyrightable data; it involves software that arranges raw data, with the producer using a SFK term to attempt to restrict the customer from disseminating its non-copyrightable data.[102] Consistent with the ALI's overall concern about conflict with federal intellectual property policy and protecting a balance of producer and user rights, the analysis of the illustration questions enforcement of the term both on federal preemption policy and state public-policy grounds.[103] Another illustration, concerning a digital product that is comprised predominantly of data rather than software, ventures beyond the scope of the project, which is odd given all the detail on scope; furthermore, the illustration is not sensitive to user rights to disseminate data that is neither copyrightable nor kept confidential as a trade secret but rather non-original and widely distributed to the public.[104] While the ALI Principles are generally supportive of a balance of producer and user rights, where the project draws that line is sometimes overly producer-oriented.

Overall, the ALI Principles are attuned to the need for social control of producers' attempts to write themselves broader intellectual property rights using SFKs. While the black letter provisions use broad standards (conflict with federal intellectual property policy or state public policy as well as unconscionability), commentary and illustrations get more specific and show courts where policing of SFKs is

[100] Braucher, *New Basics*, *supra* note 26, at 188–90 (concerning the need for a digital first-sale doctrine that permits libraries to lend digital content products notwithstanding SFK terms to the contrary; public policy should support the mission of libraries, and furthermore, libraries cannot possibly keep track of the restrictions in long SFKs that come with digital content products, so that producers should have to negotiate with libraries if they want restrictions to apply).

[101] *Supra* note 98.

[102] ALI Principles, *supra* note 10, at Section 1.09, Ill. 4.

[103] *Id.*

[104] *Id.* at Section 1.09, Ill. 6. The illustration adopts a "sweat of the brow" policy, that it took a lot of effort to produce a vast electronic database of telephone numbers, as a basis to enforce a SFK term restricting use of the database to household use, even though the U.S. Supreme Court rejected an argument that telephone numbers could be copyrighted in *Feist Publ'ns, Inc. v. Rural Tel Serv. Co.*, 499 U.S. 340 (1991). In the controversial case *Pro-CD v. Zeidenberg*, *supra* note 56, the U.S. Court of Appeals for the Seventh Circuit distinguished *Feist* because Pro-CD had included a contract term against use of the data for other than household purposes. But the case involved a SFK term in a mass-market product, essentially creating an intellectual property right by contract, which could be seen as a public policy ground to deny enforcement. *See also supra* note 98 concerning the detail on scope in the ALI project; Ill. 6 is beyond the scope of the project, which makes including it a questionable choice.

needed to preserve the balance of producer and user rights provided by intellectual property law.

IV. UNFAIR TERMS IN COMPARATIVE PERSPECTIVE

The ALI Principles include an explicit discussion of the European Union's Unfair Contract Terms Directive and purport to reject the EU approach of grey-listing terms. Here is what the ALI Principles say on this subject in a comment to the section on unconscionability:

> The European Union in its 1993 Directive on Unfair Contract Terms took the approach of enumerating a nonexclusive list of terms that may be considered unfair when not individually negotiated. The relevant question is similar to that of a substantive unconscionability inquiry, namely whether a term creates a significant imbalance in the bargain to the consumer's detriment. The European Union, however, takes a more pro-regulatory stance to consumer protection generally and contract terms specifically than U.S. law. Indeed, as a practical matter, firms doing business in Europe may find it less expensive to develop standard forms that comply with European law for use worldwide than to use different forms in the U.S. and Europe. Nevertheless, these Principles opt to rely on traditional unconscionability doctrine rather than defining which terms are enforceable and which are not. A court may, however, find the Directive's list useful in evaluating unconscionability claims. Generally, terms that authorize the transferor to add spyware to a transferee's computer, allow the transferor to modify the contract without notice or an opportunity to object or consent, extend obligations automatically and without notice, allow the transferor to change the nature of the software unilaterally, or authorize cancellation without notice are suspect under these Principles.[105]

While it is refreshing to see American law reform take comparative analysis into account, something that is expected in Europe but often not done in the US,[106] this statement in the commentary should not be accepted at face value. As will be discussed later, the ALI Principles' illustrations are very similar to grey-listing under the EU Directive, which involves flagging certain sorts of terms as probably unenforceable.[107] Furthermore, the statement about the EU approach is part of the commentary on the unconscionability provision, but some of the most effective "regulatory" provisions in the ALI Principles are placed elsewhere in the project.[108]

[105] ALI Principles, *supra* note 10, Section 1.11 on Unconscionability, cmt. c.

[106] James R. Maxeiner, *Standard-Terms Contracting in the Global Electronic Age: European Alternatives*, 28 Yale J. Int'l L. 109, 129–30 (2003) (discussing the lack of comparative analysis of the approaches to standard terms used in Europe as part of the Uniform Commercial Code drafting process in the 1990s, in contrast to the European expectation that law reformers will engage in comparative study).

[107] *See infra* notes 122–30 and accompanying text.

[108] *See infra* notes 116, 142, and accompanying text.

The ALI Principles propose quite a bit of regulation in the form of mandates not variable by agreement. This part of the chapter analyzes the differences and similarities between the ALI Principles and the EU Directive.[109]

A. ALI Principles and the EU Unfair Contract Terms Directive: Differences

Scope. The EU Unfair Contract Terms Directive is limited to natural persons acting for purposes outside their trade, business, or profession in contracts that are not "individually negotiated," a phrase defined to exclude "pre-formulated standard contracts."[110] This scope thus extends somewhat beyond consumer contracts in the sense of the common US definition of "consumer" as a person entering a transaction for personal, family or household purposes.[111] The EU Directive covers contracts with individual business persons and professionals acting outside the scope of their work.[112] Nonetheless, a limitation to consumers, somewhat broadly defined, is part of the Directive's approach. On the other hand, the EU Directive is not limited to a particular type of contract such as software; it covers unfair terms of any seller or supplier,[113] while the ALI Principles are limited to software contracts. In other ways, however, the ALI Principles are broader in their reach. They generally cover contracts involving business customers as well as individuals, and they also have several provisions that are applicable to "a standard-form transfer of generally available software,"[114] a term that includes some business-to-business (B2B) transactions in recognition of the fact that problems with overreaching in SFKs are not limited consumers or natural persons acting outside their business or profession. The ALI Principles thus recognize a category of mass-market transaction not limited to

[109] EU Directive, *supra* note 4. See also generally Maxeiner, *supra* note 106.

[110] EU Directive, *supra* note 4, at Articles 1–3.

[111] *See e.g.*, Uniform Commercial Code, Article 9, Section 9–102(a)(25) (defining a "consumer obligor" as an individual who incurred an obligation "primarily for personal, family, or household purposes").

[112] An interesting contrast is to another European legal document, the UNIDROIT Principles of International Commercial Contracts (1994), which provides in Section 2.20(1) that "no term contained in standard terms which is of such a character that the other party could not reasonably have expected it, is effective unless it has been expressly accepted by that party." This provision is not limited to natural persons and thus extends generally to business-to-business (B2B) contexts. See also Hesselink, *supra* note 4 (concerning discussions in Europe of the possibility of including a provision on unfair terms, albeit with a more forgiving test than for unfair terms in consumer contracts, in a possible optional instrument on European contract law and arguing that policy justifications such as information asymmetry and market failure apply to B2B as well as B2C contracts and thus support having one standard for unfair terms).

[113] EU Directive, *supra* note 4, at Articles 2(c), 6, and 7.

[114] ALI PRINCIPLES, supra note 10, at Section 1.01(l) on Definitions (setting some fuzzy limitations, such as to a "small number of copies" or to "a small number of end-users" on the definition of standard-form transfer of generally available software). See also *supra* notes 58–61 (discussing the special disclosure and assent provision applicable to this type of transaction).

consumers or even to natural persons but including some transactions with business customers and in that way encourage more expansive policing of SFKs.[115] In addition, some of its policing, such as promoting disclosure of unknown hidden flaws and prohibition of self-help automated disablement, extend to B2B transactions generally, even in negotiated contracts.[116]

Prevention. The EU Directive does not merely invalidate unfair terms by denying their enforcement;[117] it seeks to keep them from being used in the first place. The directive commands that, "Member States shall ensure that adequate and effective means exist to prevent the continued use of unfair terms."[118] This is important because unenforceable terms, particularly when an arguable standard is the basis of denying enforcement, can still have *in terrorem* effect on unsophisticated parties or on those not willing or able to spend resources to mount a litigation challenge. Although not necessarily required by the Directive, administrative enforcement is obviously a good method of prevention, and it has been adopted in some EU countries, for example by the United Kingdom through its Office of Fair Trading, although that agency is slated to be merged into a Competition and Markets Authority and to have its consumer protection powers reassigned.[119] The Directive requires that there be a means for persons or organizations to go "before the courts or before competent administrative bodies" for relief to prevent continued use of unfair terms.[120] Thus, European law is highly attuned to the difficulties of after-the-fact litigation as a means of enforcement. The ALI Principles, in contrast, rely on common law adjudication, including non-enforcement according to various standards including unconscionability, and they do not pick up the administrative law tools used in US consumer law

[115] For a discussion of the advantages of a mass-market category, see Jean Braucher, *Mass-Market Concept*, *supra* note 5.

[116] *See supra* notes 64–6, 68–71, 108, and accompanying text.

[117] EU Directive, *supra* note 4, at Article 6(1) (making unfair terms non-binding on consumers).

[118] *Id.* at Article 7(1).

[119] Unfair Terms in Consumer Contracts Regulations 1994, S.I. 1994/3159 (U.K.), *available at* http://www.opsi.gov.uk/si/si1994/Uksi_19943159_en_1.htm, as subsequently amended by the 1999 Regulations of the same name (S.I. 1999/2083) [hereinafter "the Regulations"], *available at* http://www.opsi.gov.uk/si/si1999/19992083.htm and also by the Unfair Terms in Consumer Contracts (Amendment) and Water Act (Transitional Provision) (2003) Regulations 2006, *available at* http://www.legislation.gov.uk/uksi/2006/523/introduction/made. *See also* Christian Twigg-Flesner, *The implementation of the Unfair Contract Terms Directive in the United Kingdom*, CONTEMPORARY ISSUES IN LAW 2006/2007, *available at* http://ssrn.com/abstract=1399631. The UK Office of Fair Trading, however, is slated to be merged into a new Competition and Markets Authority in 2014 and its consumer protection powers are to be reassigned to local council trading standard officers and the Citizens Advice Bureau, which may lack authority and resources to be effective. See Caroline Binham, *New watchdog to monitor competition law*, Financial Times (March 15, 2012), *available at* http://www.ft.com/cms/s/0/66c987e6–6ec9–11-e1-afb8–00144feab49a.html#axzz24tQrsj6k and Sean Poulter, *Shoppers will pay the price of scrapping the Office of Fair Trading, consumer group warns*, Mail Online (March 9, 2011) *available at* http://www.dailymail.co.uk/news/article-1364380/Shoppers-pay-price-scrapping-Office-Fair-Trading.html

[120] EU Directive, *supra* note 4, at Article 7(2).

by both federal and state consumer protection officials, which include rule-making, prevention, and agency enforcement actions.[121]

B. ALI Principles and the EU Unfair Contract Terms Directive: Similarities

Grey-listing. The EU Directive begins with a general standard that contract terms not individually negotiated are unfair if they create "a significant imbalance in the parties' rights and obligations arising under the contract, to the consumer's detriment."[122] The Directive also provides for an annex that is "an indicative and non-exhaustive list of the terms which may be regarded as unfair,"[123] and the Annex lists 17 types of terms or practices of this type.[124] The fact that the list is "indicative" means that the terms are not absolutely deemed unfair but rather are subject to suspicion in any judicial review; they are grey-listed.[125]

Despite the ALI Principles' stated disapproval of having a list of terms that are under suspicion of being unfair, as in the EU Directive,[126] the Principles effectively do the same thing. As discussed previously, the Principles often suggest that certain types of terms should not be enforced, often on multiple grounds, for example, in commentary and illustrations concerning terms that would bar criticism of software products,[127] study and testing,[128] transfer of copies,[129] and access to public domain content.[130] These terms are put under suspicion, subject to particular scrutiny; they are effectively grey-listed.

Attention to procedure as well as substance. The ALI Principles' comment on unconscionability quoted at the outset of this part refers to the approach of the EU Directive on Unfair Contract Terms as being like inquiry into substantive unconscionability.[131] However, the EU Directive includes in its Annex list of grey-listed terms and practices a focus on the procedure used to enter into the contract. The relevant Annex provision makes suspect the practice of "binding the consumer to terms with which he had no real opportunity of becoming acquainted before the

[121] See *supra* notes 11, 43–7, and accompanying text.

[122] EU Directive, *supra* note 4, at Article 3(1).

[123] *Id.* at Article 3(3).

[124] *Id.* at Annex (1)(a)–(q).

[125] *See* Jane K. Winn and Mark Webber, *The Impact of EU Unfair Contract Terms Law on US Business-to-Consumer Internet Merchants*, 62 Bus. Law. 209 (2006) at notes 75–80 and accompanying text (discussing implementation of the EU Directive and its use of grey-listing).

[126] *Supra* notes 105, 123–5, and accompanying text.

[127] *Supra* note 91 and accompanying text.

[128] *Supra* notes 92–3 and accompanying text.

[129] *Supra* notes 94–7 and accompanying text.

[130] *Supra* notes 102–3 and accompanying text; *but see supra* note 104 and accompanying text.

[131] *Supra* note 105 and accompanying text.

conclusion of the contract."[132] This is similar to the approach of the ALI in its provision concerning advance disclosure (as well as active assent).[133] The EU Directive also requires "plain, intelligible language,"[134] which is similar to the ALI's call for "reasonably comprehensible" disclosure.[135]

Both the EU Directive and the ALI Principles pay attention to procedure and substance. Procedural protocols that make terms available and understandable during shopping make it possible for at least the most sophisticated and interested customers to avoid bad deals; they also permit discussion among customers – for example, on blogs – of harsh terms.[136] Advance disclosure should be required, but it is not sufficient to police unfair terms, so attention to substance of terms is also necessary, and both the EU and ALI embrace that point.[137]

Option for mandates. Beyond grey-listing, both the EU Directive and the ALI Principles permit courts and legislatures to be more protective of customers. The EU Directive is a minimum harmonization piece of legislation, one that requires Member States to comply and that also prohibits a contract drafter from using a choice of law clause to escape its provisions when the contract has a close connection with the territory of the Member States.[138] The Directive explicitly permits Member States to adopt provisions to ensure maximum protection for consumers, more stringent than its provisions.[139] EU members can, for example, adopt any of the encouraged or discouraged terms and practices on the Annex list as mandates. Furthermore, the Directive is not intended as a complete system of contract policing; it takes into account that Member States have numerous mandatory statutory or administrative regulatory provisions, which are unaffected by the Directive's provisions.[140]

The ALI Principles pick up many doctrines and statutory provisions from existing law, and in that sense they are mandatory to the extent the law in question does not permit variation by agreement. When they go beyond current law, the ALI Principles

[132] Annex at (1)(i). Furthermore, in assessing the unfairness of terms, the EU Directive calls for attention to context, by looking at "the nature of the goods or services for which the contract was concluded" and "all the circumstances attending the conclusion of the contract and to all the other terms of the contract." *Id.* at Article 4. This hardly seems to be equivalent to pure substantive unconscionability, as the ALI PRINCIPLES suggest. *See supra* note 105 and accompanying text.

[133] *Supra* Part IIIA.

[134] EU Directive, *supra* note 4, at Article 5.

[135] See *supra* note 62 and accompanying text.

[136] *See supra* notes 57–62 and accompanying text.

[137] *Supra* Part IIIB-D and notes 117–18, 122–5, and accompanying text, and *infra* notes 138–42 and accompanying text.

[138] EU Directive, *supra* note 4, at Article 6(2). In this, the Directive is similar to the ALI PRINCIPLES, supra note 10, as discussed *supra* notes 80–1 and accompanying text.

[139] EU Directive, *supra* note 4, Article 8.

[140] *Id.* at Article 1(2).

are persuasive authority.[141] When a term is grey-listed by an ALI illustration, a court or a legislature could choose to turn the analysis into a rule applicable to a particular class of cases, such as all SFKs, and in that way black list it. Furthermore, the Principles contain several sections that set forth proposed mandatory rules, inviting courts or legislatures to adopt them as such. Examples are the ban on self-help use of automated disablement even in negotiated B2B deals and the mandatory warranty against known hidden material defects in all software contracts, both of which are stated in the ALI Principles as provisions not subject to variation by agreement, with even consequential damages for violating these provisions not subject to contractual limitation.[142] Thus, the ALI Principles and the EU Directive both contemplate mandates as one means of policing SFKs.

V. CONCLUSION

The ALI Principles and the EU Directive have different strengths, which is not surprising given their different characters. The ALI Principles are conceived of as part of general contract law, although directly applicable to only one type of contract (software transactions), while the EU Directive is a consumer protection measure, but applicable broadly across different types of consumer transactions. An amalgam of the two approaches requires contemplating a merger of these two perspectives on contracts.

The Directive's emphasis on prevention of use of unfair terms in SFKs is a consumer protection technique, as is its invitation to accomplish prevention using administrative agencies. Prevention and use of administrative enforcement and rule-making are strengths of its approach. Both of these techniques exist in US consumer protection law, too, but they are not imported into the ALI Principles.

The ALI Principles, with their focus on software transactions, can comprehensively address problem areas in one type of contract. It is notable that the ALI Principles have recognized as legitimate concerns all of the problem areas identified by a coalition of the US software customers: the need for advance disclosure of and active assent to standard terms; the importance of disclosure of known hidden flaws in software products to protect security of customers' systems and data; fair remedies, particularly no electronic self-help; and maintaining the balance of rights between producers and users provided by federal intellectual property law. The ALI Principles apply to business and consumer transactions and thus call for legal mandates to disclose known hidden defects and to refrain from self-help automated disablement in the B2B context generally. They also identify mass-market, SFK transactions, which include some B2B transactions, as requiring particular attention to police for unfairness.

[141] *See supra* note 50 and accompanying text.

[142] *See supra* notes 64–6, 68–71, 108, 116, and accompanying text.

Both projects engage in grey-listing of certain terms and practices. The ALI project may have the advantage here, in that by focusing on one type of transaction, it can be very specific and comprehensive. Furthermore, both projects call for advance disclosure of terms in addition to attention to substantive unfairness.

If we put the two approaches together, the result would be to include prevention and administrative enforcement in policing of B2B as well as B2C SFKs, particularly mass-market transactions. We would also see examination of SFK unfairness proceed contract type by contract type, with administrative agencies or law reformers using expertise to identify particular problems before setting specific rules about what fairness demands. Furthermore, we would see attention both to the process of contracting and to the substance of deals. Imagining such an approach to SFKs is, if nothing more, an interesting thought experiment. Some will find it too "regulatory" and insufficiently deferential to the flexibility of markets. On the other hand, this approach has promise to correct for unfairness imposed by SFK drafters, which involves one-sided private governance rather than private ordering by mutual assent.

15

(D)CFR Initiative and Consumer Unfair Terms

Mel Kenny

This chapter will examine the development, current state and coherence of initiatives aimed at advancing the harmonisation of European private law, initiatives which are traced back to the European Union Commission's 2001 Communication on Contract Law. In this regard the broadly cast 'academic' Draft Common Frame of Reference (DCFR) initiative, the emergent, more focused Common Frame of Reference (CFR) and the 'optional instrument' developed under the auspices of the 'Expert Group,' as well as the evolution of proposals for the Consumer Rights Directive are initiatives which are, at times, contradictory. The chapter focuses on the contradictions among these different initiatives, as well as inconsistencies within the initiatives.

Given the fragmentation of private law that has always accompanied the process of Europeanisation, and the underlying controversy surrounding EU competence to launch a programme of private law consolidation, the chapter considers more modest and more imaginative initiatives. In particular, issues in consumer protection are analysed by examining the adequacy of traditional standards and mechanisms of protection. The chapter argues that the dissonance within harmonisation discourse is significant and that greater circumspection is called for in terms of the EU's competence to legislate in this area. It concludes by offering recommendations as to which areas of private law can be realistically consolidated.

I. INTRODUCTION

This chapter analyses the (Draft) Common Frame of Reference (D)CFR initiative as it affects, in particular, the elaboration of unfair terms in consumer contracts and asks whether, in the development of Europeanised private law, we risk taking the *legislative* coherence of EU law too seriously and destabilising consumer and commercial law as a result. The chapter argues that, rather than further recourse to legislative measures, more could be done at the administrative level to ensure the effectiveness of Europeanised standards. Analysis begins by tracking the evolution of the initiative from DCFR to CFR (Section II) and then explores the rationale for the initiative (Section III). Attention then turns to the emergence of a cross-border concept of unfairness. This process, it is argued, is reliant on a number of non-legislative factors, *inter alia,* judicially activist case-law contributions (Section IV, Part A) and the operation of a robust reference procedure from the national courts to the Court of Justice of the European Union (CJEU (ex ECJ)) (Section IV, Part B). Beyond these factors the keys to Europeanisation are also to be found in a mixture of substantive and procedural factors: the impact of national background rules (Section IV, Part C), the need for a multi-dimensional perspective (Section IV, Part D) and the availability of collective proceedings (Section IV, Part E) in the fleshing out of our conceptualisation of Europeanised Unfairness.

II. EVOLUTION OF THE (D)CFR INITIATIVE

The (D)CFR initiative centres, under the auspices of the Study Group on an European Civil Code,[1] on the elaboration of '*Principles, Definitions and Model Rules of European Private Law: Draft Common Frame of Reference*',[2] a framework published in the UK by Oxford University Press in 2010 and embracing six volumes and divided into ten books dealing, respectively, with general contract (Books II and III), non-contractual obligations (Book VI), unjust enrichment (Book VII), trusts (Book X), sales contracts (Book IV, Part A), and personal security (Book IV, Part G). Subsequently, in April 2010, an *Expert Group on a Common Frame of Reference in the area of European Contract Law* was assigned the task of assisting the commission: 'in the preparation of a proposal for a CFR in European Contract law, including consumer and business contract law.'[3] This was followed, in July 2010, with the 2010 Green Paper on Policy Options for Progress towards a European Contract Law, which set out the following range of options:

1. Publication of the results of the Expert Group;
2. An official 'toolbox' for the legislator;
3. Recommendation on European Contract Law;
4. Regulation setting up an optional instrument;

1 Study Group on a European Civil Code (SGECC): http://www.sgecc.net/.

2 Christian Von Bar & Eric Clive, Principles, Definitions and Model Rules of European Private Law: Draft Common Frame of Reference (Oxford University Press, 2010). By this author: *The 2004 Communication on European Contract Law: Those Magnificent Men in Their Unifying Machines,* 30 European Law Rev. 724 (2005); *The Commission's 2007 Green Paper on the Consumer Acquis: Deliberate Deliberation?* 32 European Law Rev 740 (2007) (With B. Heiderhoff).

3 Commission Decision 2010/233/EU; (2010) OJ L 105/109.

5. Directive on European Contract Law;
6. Regulation on European Contract Law;
7. Regulation establishing a European Civil Code.[4]

More recently, on 11 October 2011, the fourth option was given further substantiation with the formulation of an Optional Instrument aimed at the promotion of a 'Common European Sales Law'.[5] From a commercial law perspective a number of points can be made on this move: first, the general importance of the proposals for EU consumer law in general, though the breadth of the consumer definition remains contentious. Second, that the scope of the CFR is arguably likely to be narrower than that originally conceived in the DCFR.[6] Third, that there is an alternative proposal to the CFR for a cross-border regulation for Consumer Law.[7] Finally, that there is support for a CFR in the form of an 'Optional Instrument', though even in the formulation of the 'Common European Sales Law' the boundary between Sales Law and General Contract Law is transgressed in a number of significant areas.[8]

The (D)CFR initiative thus presents a range of options from the minimalistic publication of the results of the expert group, the adoption of a European Sales Law, to the establishment of a European Civil Code. Yet these proposals also beg further questions, *inter alia*, are these proposals merely a listing of individual pragmatic options, or is wider codification being promoted? Axiomatically, how is the new circumspection within the proposals, seen in the optionality of the instrument in Sales Law, to be interpreted: as recognition of the limits of consolidation, or, given the overlaps with general contract law, the catalyst for codification?

III. RATIONALE FOR EU PRIVATE LAW CONSOLIDATION

The rationale for the (D)CFR initiative has always been connected with ensuring the wider coherence of EU law. As Twigg-Flesner observes: "The impact of ... harmonisation ... has not been the creation of a single, consistent and coherent body of consumer law ... instead there are now 27 national rules on doorstep selling,

4 Green Paper on Policy Options for Progress towards a European Contract Law for Consumers and Businesses, Brussels 1.7.2010, COM(2010) 348 final.

5 Introduction of the Optional Instrument, The Common European Sales Law: 11 October 2011: http://ec.europa.eu/justice/newsroom/news/20111011_en.htm.

6 Stefan Vogenauer, *Common Frame of Reference and UNIDROIT Principles of International Commercial Contracts: Coexistence, Competition or Overkill of Soft Law*, 6 European Review of Contract Law. 143 (2010) at 147.

7 Christian Twigg-Flesner, *Time to Do the Job Properly – the Case for a New Approach to EU Consumer Legislation*, 33 Journal of Consumer Policy 355 (2010).

8 http://ec.europa.eu/justice/policies/consumer/policies_consumer_intro_en.htm.

distance selling"[9] Yet while we may acknowledge the importance of this leitmotif, the full implications of chasing an ellusive idea of 'coherence' remain to be developed. Private lawyers are thus inevitably drawn into a critical examination of the paradigm of effective enforcement of EU law. This paradigm relies, on the one hand, on the forms of action: direct actions against Member States for failure to fulfil their obligations (Articles 258 & 259 TFEU), judicial review on the legality of EU legislative acts (Article 263 TFEU), preliminary references to the Court of Justice of the European Union (ex ECJ) (Article 267 TFEU), actions for non-contractual institutional liability (Art. 340 TFEU). Yet, on the other hand, the tangible effects of EU law also need to be taken into account in ensuring effectiveness: the doctrines of Direct Effect and Supremacy, the more specific effects of Directives (direct, indirect, incidental),[10] and the doctrine of State Liability. In theory, the forms of action coupled with these effects of EU law offer a comprehensive regime for ensuring the coherence of EU law, as famously asserted in *UPA*:

> The Treaty has established a complete system of legal remedies and procedures designed to ensure judicial review of the legality of acts of the institutions, and has entrusted such review to the Community courts.... Where natural or legal persons cannot ... directly challenge (EU) measures ... they are able ... either indirectly to plead the invalidity of such acts ... or to ... ask (national courts)[...] to make a reference.[11]

Within the 'completeness' of this enforcement paradigm the CJEU's role is to ensure the uniform application of EU law, and the national courts' reciprocate in a spirit of 'sincere cooperation'.[12] But effectiveness and coherence, beyond their substantive or procedural dimensions, have to be appreciated as part of a broader concept involving implementation and compliance.[13] This uncovers a perennial governance problem, especially acute in the EU because it operates via a system of indirect administration, a model in which EU policies are implemented non-centrally, by national executive and judicial authorities, which enjoy a margin of discretion in implementation and procedural autonomy in deciding whether to refer under Article 267 TFEU.[14] Within this paradigm, lawyers have traditionally been less

9 Christian Twigg-Flesner, *Good-Bye Harmonisation by Directives, Hello Cross-Border only Regulation? A Way Forward for EU Consumer Contract Law*, 7 European Review of Contract Law 235 (2011) at 241.

10 Paul Craig & Gráinne De Búrca, EU Law (4th ed., Oxford University Press: 2008), 'vertical', 'indirect' and 'incidental' effects, discussed, respectively, at 279–87, 287–96 and 296–300.

11 Case C-50/00 P *Unión de Pequeños Agricultores v Council (UPA)* [2002] ECR I-6677; para 40.

12 Francisco Mancini, *The Making of a Constitution for Europe*, 26 Common Market Law Review 595 (1989) at 606: the national legal order reliant on the ECJ's 'unlimited patience'.

13 Francis Snyder, *The Effectiveness of European Community Law: Institutions, Processes and Techniques*, 56(1) Modern Law Review 19 (1993) at 19–20.

14 *Id.*, at 22.

concerned with the importance of transposition or the commission's compliance role; the main focus has been placed on the doctrine of State Liability and the Article 267 TFEU reference. A wider understanding of the effectiveness of EU law is therefore required: effectiveness as a judicial and administrative concept, involving substantive, procedural and non-legislative dimensions.

Inevitably, the importance attached to judicial coherence and effectiveness means that broader effectiveness is compromised on two levels: by reliance on litigation which is necessarily ad hoc in nature and the variation in the legal remedies between Member States. As Snyder observes, judicial effectiveness is therefore

> less normatively coherent and less comprehensive than a legislative scheme.... [Furthermore] differences in national remedies affect the extent to which individuals can rely ... on rights derived from Community law.... Achieving a harmonisation of national remedies sufficient to ensure effective enforcement ... while ... respecting the legitimate differences among Member States is a difficult task.[15]

Moreover, the 'incompleteness' of EU law is buttressed by the basic characteristics of EU law: subsidiarity, national margins of discretion in implementation and procedural autonomy, the attributed competences of the EU,[16] the margins of direct and individual concern under 263 TFEU, the margins of State Liability for failure to refer under Article 267 TFEU,[17] the European Commission's discretion to take action under Article 258 TFEU.

Effectiveness discourse thus emerges in a crucible of pressures.[18] Historically, in 'exchange' for market integration, the ECJ has had to integrate national concerns into its articulation of economic freedoms. Furthermore, the integration effects of EU law have always been partly artificial.[19] Regulations, for example, frequently fail to produce uniformity because of compromise in the law-making process.[20] Similarly, directives operate, in the main, to address sectoral issues, disrupting the remaining patterns of national laws. Where directives, such as the Unfair Terms in Consumer Contracts Directive (Directive 93/13/EEC),[21] have had a more 'horizontal' ambit

[15] *Id.*, at 51.

[16] Articles 2(5), 169 & 114 TFEU.

[17] Case C-224/01 *Köbler v Austria* [2003] ECR I-10239; Case C-173/03 *Traghetti del Mediterraneo v Italy* [2006] ECR I-5177.

[18] James Devenney & Mel Kenny, *Unfair Terms, Surety Transactions and European Harmonisation: A Crucible of Europeanised Private Law?* 73 CONVEYANCER 295 (2009).

[19] M. Amstutz, *Zwischenwelten: Zur Emergenz einer interlegalen Rechtsmethodik im europäischen Privatrecht* in RECHTSVERFASSUNGSRECHT (C. Joerges & G. Teubner eds., Nomos: Baden-Baden 2003) at 237.

[20] Peter K. Burbidge, *Cross-Border Insolvency within the EU: Dawn of a New Era*, 27 EUROPEAN LAW REVIEW 589 (2002).

[21] Directive 93/13/EEC, (1993) O.J. L95/221.

across different contract types, their fragmentary effects in the national legal orders can be even greater.[22] Finally, as previously alluded to, procedural autonomy leads to uneven judicial protection among the national legal orders.[23] The suspicion which emerges is that there may be an unhelpful fixation on the legislative effectiveness of EU law.

IV. (D)CFR INITIATIVE AND THE EFFECTIVE POLICING OF UNFAIR TERMS IN CONSUMER CONTRACTS

In the policing of Unfair Terms in consumer contracts we look to Chapter 9, Book II, of the DCFR, specifically to provision 9:403, which states: 'In a contract between a business and a consumer, a term [which has not been individually negotiated] is unfair … if it is supplied by the business and if it significantly disadvantages the consumer, contrary to good faith and fair dealing.' This test is supplemented by II. – 9:407 and a 'grey list' of unfair terms.[24] The effect of a finding that a term is unfair is specified in II. – 9:408: '(1) A term which is unfair … is not binding on the party who did not supply it.' And: '(2) If the contract can reasonably be maintained without the unfair term, the other terms remain binding on the parties.'

A resonance thus emerges between the (D)CFR and the pre-existing Article 3, of the Unfair Terms Directive, which sought 'to fix in a general way the criteria for assessing the unfair character of contract terms.'[25] Both provision 9:403 and Article 3, Directive 93/13/EEC, can be seen as building on national social, economic and behavioural norms, representing core provisions which are shaped by the diverse nature of legal institutions, protective mechanisms and doctrine across Europe.

The law on Unfairness, and, necessarily, the Unfair Terms Directive, transgresses the boundaries of many different types of contracts and, if we are to elaborate a cross-border conceptualisation of unfairness, we need to draw together the different strands of unfairness case law. In the brief survey that follows we critically contrast the interpretations of consumer unfairness in the fields of bank charges, suretyship transactions and social housing tenancy agreements. Just in these three areas there is

[22] Mel Kenny, *The 2003 Action Plan on European Contract Law: Is the Commission Running Wild?* 28 European Law Review 538 (2003) at 540.

[23] Case C-321/95P *Stichting Greenpeace v. Commission* [1998] ECR I-1651, appeal from Case T-585/93 *Greenpeace and others v. Commission* [1995] ECR II-2205.

[24] DCFR *supra* note 2, II. – 9:410.

[25] Recital 15 (emphasis added).

a striking diversity in the unfairness conceptualisation, a conceptualisation ordained by the same Directive. The diversity of approach can be mapped out|:

- Bank Charges litigation: juxtaposition of *First National*[26] and *Abbey National*[27] case aw on the issue of whether a contract clause is unfair or whether the relevant provision is a core term, and therefore exempt from the unfairness test, under Directive. Similar contractual provision were held an unfair default term in *First National*, but as a core, exempt term in *Abbey National*.
- Suretyships: on whether the atypical category of surety transactions was or was not subject to the Directive. According to *Bank of Scotland v. Singh*,[28] *Manches LLP*,[29] *Williamson*[30] surety agreements were not subject to the unfairness test, while in *Kufner*[31] suretyships were held within the test.
- Social Housing Tenancy Agreements: *Khatun*[32] is authority for the proposition that there is a need to apply the unfairness test broadly to all types of consumer transaction under the Directive.

Given this diverse case law we recall, in *First National*, Lord Bingham's view in the context of bank charges that 'good faith in this context is not an artificial or technical concept; nor ... is it a concept wholly unfamiliar to British lawyers. It looks to good standards of commercial morality and practice.'[33] Yet unfairness tests are evidently built on varying social, economic and behavioural norms and, across the EU, there are differences in such norms. Moreover, as Schulte-Nölke elaborates, Member States deploy

> different benchmarks ... when reviewing contractual terms.... Accordingly, traders cannot use a contractual clause which is valid across the EU, but must instead formulate different clauses for each member state. Hence, considerable obstacles to the functioning of the internal market exist. Providers can only perform pre-formulated contracts across borders with considerable transaction costs.[34]

[26] *Director General of Fair Trading v. First National Bank plc* [2001] UKHL 52, [2002] 1 AC 481 (HL), clause 8, para. 2, contrast with *DGFT v. First National Bank plc* [2000] 1 WLR 98 (HC), *DGFT v. First National Bank plc* [2000] QB 672 (CA); Elizabeth Macdonald, *Scope and Fairness of the Unfair Terms in Consumer Contracts*, 65 Modern Law Review 763, (2002).

[27] *The OFT v Abbey National plc* [2009] UKSC 6.

[28] QBD, unreported, 17 June 2005.

[29] *Manches LLP v. Carl Freer* [2006] EWHC 991.

[30] *Williamson v. Governor of the Bank of Scotland* [2006] EWHC 1289.

[31] *Barclays Bank plc Kufner* [2008] EWHC 2319 (Comm).

[32] *R. (Khatun) v. Newham LBC* [2004] EWCA Civ 55.

[33] Lord Bingham [2002] UKHL 52 at [17].

[34] Hans Schulte-Nölke, *EC Consumer Law Compendium – Comparative Analysis* (2008) at 348, at: http://ec.europa.eu/consumers/cons_int/safe_shop/acquis/comp_analysis_en.pdf.

Yet equally, such divergence questions any exclusively legislative response to Europeanisation[35]; non-legislative harmonisation and, in particular, the role of judicial convergence require greater attention.[36] The extent to which EU concepts of 'good faith' can be developed in the case law crucially depends on active judicial participation in the elaboration of Europeanised unfairness standards and the robust initiation of the reference mechanism under Article 267 TFEU. Moreover, beyond these factors, background rules, a multi-dimensional perspective and the procedural framework within which conceptualisations of unfairness operate play important roles. This chapter proceeds with an analysis of these factors as they have shaped the English experience of Europeanisation.

A. *National Judges' Elaboration of Europeanised Unfairness Standards*

Given the importance of the judicial role in elaborating Europeanised unfairness standards, the domestic record in England and Wales on the application of the UTCCR, transposing the Unfair Terms Directive, is not encouraging. As seen previously, while the English courts have, sporadically, taken a 'Europeanised' approach to UTCCR interpretation, for example, in *Khatun*,[37] the approach is mixed, as seen in the context of non-professional suretyships.[38] This is part of the wider debate on

[35] Mel Kenny, James Devenney & Lorna Fox O'Mahony, *Conceptualising Unconscionability in Europe: in the Kaleidoscope of Private and Public Law*, in UNCONSCIONABILITY IN EUROPEAN PRIVATE FINANCIAL TRANSACTIONS: PROTECTING THE VULNERABLE (M. Kenny, J. Devenney & L. Fox O'Mahony (eds.), Cambridge University Press: 2010) 377. Further critique: Basil Markesinis, *Why a Code Is Not the Best Way to Advance the Cause of European Legal Unity*, 5 EUROPEAN REVIEW OF PRIVATE LAW 519–24 (1997); Pierre Legrand, *European Legal Systems Are Not Converging*, 45 INTERNATIONAL COMPARATIVE LAW QUARTERLY 52 (1997); Pierre Legrand, *Against a European Civil Code*, 60 MODERN LAW REVIEW 44 (1997); Pierre Legrand, *The Impossibility of Legal Transplants*, 4 M.J. 111 (2003), Pierre Legrand, *'Antivonbar'*, 1 JOURNAL OF CONTRACT LAW 1 (2006); Martin W. Hesselink, *The Politics of European Contract Law: Who Has an Interest in What Kind of Contract Law for Europe?* 2 GLOBAL JURIST FRONTIERS (2002); generally: Gunter Teubner, *The Two Faces of Janus: Rethinking Legal Pluralism* 13 CARDOZO LAW REVIEW 1443 (1992) at 1445–8.

[36] Aurelia Colombi Ciacchi, *Non-Legislative Harmonisation of Private Law under the European Constitution: The Case of Unfair Suretyships*, 13 EUROPEAN REVIEW OF PRIVATE LAW 285 (2005). Cf. Hans. M. van Erp, *European Private Law: Post-modern Dilemmas and Choices*, (1999) 3 EUROPEAN JOURNAL OF CONTRACT LAW at http://www.ejcl.org/31/abs31–1.html; Anthony I. Ogus, *Competition between National Legal systems: A Contribution of Economic Analysis to Comparative Law* 48 INTERNATIONAL COMPARATIVE LAW QUARTERLY 405 (1999).

[37] James Devenney, *Gordian Knots in Europeanised Private Law: Unfair Terms, Bank Charges and Political Compromises*, 62 NORTHERN IRELAND LEGAL QUARTERLY 33 (2011) at 40. *See R. (Khatun) v. Newham LBC* [2004] EWCA Civ 55.

[38] Gerard McCormack, *Protection of Surety Guarantors in England – Prophylactics and Procedure, in* PROTECTION OF NON-PROFESSIONAL SURETIES IN EUROPE: FORMAL AND SUBSTANTIVE DISPARITY (A. Colombi Ciacchi ed., Nomos, Baden-Baden, 2007) at 172–3.

whether, under the UTCCR, the consumer must be the *recipient* of goods/services[39]; one of the difficulties here is that, in the atypical context of surety transactions, it is the non-professional surety who supplies the service whereas the creditor, as beneficiary, will be acting in the course of business.[40] *Dietzinger*[41] supports the proposition that the UTCCR should apply to suretyship agreements: the ECJ, determining the applicability of Directive 85/577/EEC, on doorstep sales, to situations in which "a trader supplies goods or services to a consumer", held

> It is apparent that the directive (Directive 85/577) covers only a guarantee ancillary to a contract whereby, in the context of "doorstep selling", a consumer assumes obligations towards the trader with a view to obtaining goods or services from him. Furthermore, since the directive is designed to protect only consumers, a guarantee comes within the scope of the directive only where, in accordance with the first indent of Article 2, the guarantor has entered into a commitment for a purpose which can be regarded as unconnected with his trade or profession.[42]

The case allows us to see how the CJEU (ex ECJ) might approach this issue under the Unfair Terms Directive,[43] and, as previously alluded to, in *Kufner*[44] Field J., relying on *Dietzinger*, held that suretyships were not excluded from the scope of the UTCCR.[45] By contrast, in *Singh*,[46] Judge Kershaw QC held that the UTCCR did not apply to surety agreements; this view was subsequently held "compelling" in *Manches LLP*[47] and "convincing" in *Williamson*.[48] As these cases make clear, national judges have an important role to play in minimising legal fragmentation.[49] Yet sensitivity to the importance of this judicial role is barely acknowledged; Moore-Bick LJ's dicta in *RÖHLIG (UK) Ltd v. Rock Unique Ltd*, denying the value of any cross-referencing of UTCCR and the Unfair Contract Terms Act 1977, are emblematic of

[39] *Cf.* Chitty on Contracts (H. G. Beale [ed.], 30th ed., Sweet & Maxwell: 2008) para 15–32.

[40] James O'donovan & John Phillips, The Modern Contract of Guarantee, (Sweet & Maxwell, London: 2003) at 223.

[41] Case C-45/96 *Bayerische Hypotheken und Wechselbank v. Dietzinger* [1998] ECR I-1199.

[42] *Kufner, supra* note 31 at [20]. Although *cf.* Case C-208/98 *Berliner Kindl Brauerei AG v. Andreas Siepert* [2000] ECR 1–1741 at [25]-[26] where the ECJ, in considering the Consumer Credit Directive (Directive 87/102/EEC), noted: 'the scope of the Directive cannot be widened to cover contracts of guarantee solely on the ground that such agreements are ancillary to the principal agreement whose performance they underwrite, since there is no support for such an interpretation in the wording of the Directive … or in its scheme and aims.'

[43] Chitty on Contracts, *supra* note 39 at para 44–139.

[44] [2008] EWHC 2319 (Comm).

[45] *Id.* Field J., at [28].

[46] QBD, unreported, 17 June 2005.

[47] *Manches LLP, supra* note 29 at [25] *per* Judge Philip Price QC.

[48] *Williamson, supra* note 30 at [46] *per* George Bompas QC.

[49] Mel Kenny, *Orchestrating Sub-Prime Consumer Protection in Retail Banking: Abbey National in the Context of Europeanised Private Law*, European Review of Private Law 43 (2011) at 68–9.

the general approach: "The principles that are to be applied (UTCCR and Unfair Terms Act 1977) are broadly the same.… In my view no assistance is to be gained in the present case from the (UTCCR)."[50]

B. Judicial Approach to Article 267 TFEU References

In much the same way, the robustness of approach to the Article 267 TFEU reference procedure leaves much to be desired.[51] Famously, in *CILFIT*, the ECJ defined the two cases in which national courts need not refer under Article 267 TFEU: first, where a matter has previously been clearly decided (*acte éclairé*)[52]; second, *acte clair* determinations where the Court need not refer where 'the correct application of EU law may be so obvious as to leave no scope for any reasonable doubt'.[53] National courts can thus only decline referral where they are 'convinced that the matter is equally obvious to the courts of the other Member States and to the Court of Justice'. Furthermore, the national court must take the 'state of evolution' of EU law into account,[54] such that it is 'completely confident' that it can resolve the matter at hand.[55]

In England and Wales, there has been a notable reluctance to engage Article 267 TFEU in reviewing unfair contract terms. For example, in *Abbey National*, the Supreme Court refused referral of an interpretation of Article 4(2) of the Unfair Terms Directive in the context of bank charges, holding that 'if … the Court is unanimous that the appeal should be allowed, then … we should treat the point as *acte clair*, and decide against making a reference …'.[56] In *Abbey National* the Supreme Court was faced with an important 'compromise' provision balancing consumer protection with freedom of contract, a provision which the ECJ had not previously considered. Moreover, the provision had been transposed divergently

[50] [2011] EWCA Civ 18. More-Bick LJ at [24]–[25]: expanding "I doubt very much whether the extended list of terms that may be regarded as unfair which is set out in schedule 2 to the Regulations adds much of substance to schedule 2 to the 1977 Act."

[51] *Cf.* Christopher Turner & Rodolphe Munoz, *Revisiting the Judicial Architecture of the European Union*, 19 YBEL 1 (1999/2000).

[52] Case 283/81 *CILFIT* [1982] ECR 3415, para.14 derived from Cases 28–30/62 *Da Costa* [1963] ECR 31.

[53] *Id.*, para 16.

[54] *Id.*, para 20: 'Every provision of Community law must be placed in its context and interpreted in the light of the provisions of Community law as a whole, regard being had to the objectives thereof and to its state of evolution' Case C-461/03 *Gaston Schul* [2005] ECR I-10523, A. G. Colomer at 58: '[T]he Court must … amend … *Cilfit* … to adapt … to the demands of the times, since only a less stringent interpretation … (satisfies) the requirements of the principle of judicial cooperation.'

[55] *R v. International Stock Exchange of the UK and the Republic of Ireland Ex p. Else* [1993] 1 All ER 420.

[56] [2009] UKSC 6. Lord Walker at [49].

in different Member States.[57] In these circumstances, recalling the *CILFIT* criteria, it can be argued that a reference should have been made[58]

- First, following a juxtaposition of *Abbey National* with the domestic case law of *First National, Singh, Kufner* and *Khatun* there were reasonable domestic doubts as to the resolution of the matter.
- Second, in the light of ECJ case law, notably *Mostaza Claro*[59] on the duty of the national court to assess unfairness of its own motion and *Honyvem*[60] and *Turgay*[61] on the limits of national judicial discretion, it is doubtful that the matter would have been equally clear to ECJ.
- Finally, given the determinations of other national courts, notably the German bank charges cases, it is doubtful whether the Supreme Court determination would have been equally clear to other national courts.[62]

However, the Supreme Court in *Abbey National* felt a reference was unnecessary. Lord Walker's view,[63] supported by Lord Mance[64] and Lady Hale,[65] was that the issue was *acte clair* and this view prevailed. Nevertheless, as Lord Walker implicitly acknowledged,[66] this was fragile given the very different views of experienced judges in the lower courts, as well as the dissenting judgments of Lords Phillips and Neuberger[67] in the Supreme Court itself.[68]

Alternative grounds, suggested by Lords Walker and Mance, for not referring concerned national procedural autonomy: that while the *construction* of Article 4(2) was a matter for EU Law, its *application* was a matter for domestic law.[69] On these lines it was argued that, even if the Court of Appeal's construction of Article 4(2) was correct, it was incorrect in its *application* of the law. Clearly, while such reasoning is not without merit, even though it simultaneously rendered the Court's

57 Hans Schulte-Nölke, *supra* note 34.

58 *Cf.* Paul Davies, *Bank Charges in the Supreme Court*, 69 CAMBRIDGE LAW JOURNAL 21 (2010) at 23.

59 Case C-168/05 *Elisa Maria Mostaza Claro v. Cento Móvil Milenium* [2004] ECR I-10421.

60 Case C-465/04 *Honyvem Informazioni Commerciali Srl v. Mariella De Zotti* [2006] ECR I-2879.

61 Case C-348/07 *Turgay Semen v Deutsche Tamoil GmbH* [2009] ECR I-2341.

62 BGH, judgment 7 May 1996 [cash machines]; BGH, judgment 14 October 1997 [credit cards]; BVerfGE, judgment 6 July 2010, EuZW, 2010, 828.

63 *Abbey National supra* note 27 [48]–[50].

64 *Id.*, at [115]–[117].

65 *Id.*, at [92].

66 *Id.*, at [49].

67 *Id.*, at [120].

68 *Id.*, at [91].

69 *Abbey National, supra*, note 27: [50] and [116]. *Cf* Case C-237/02 *Freiburger Kommunalbauten* [2004] ECR-I 3403 at [22] (the ECJ) 'may interpret general criteria used by the Community legislation in order to define the concept of unfair terms. However, it should not rule on the application of these general criteria to a particular term.'

comments on the *acte clair* determination *obiter*, it is not clear that this argument entirely separates questions of law from those of fact. Finally, the conclusion that the Court of Appeal wrongly applied their interpretation of Article 4(2) is dependent, as Devenney observes, on a *particular view* of the core/ancillary terms dichotomy, which is in itself, in part, a question of law.[70]

Whatever the formal reasons for refusing to refer, wider factors were evidently at play: on the one hand, the Court was concerned at the delay which a reference might entail.[71] Additionally, the Court was also rendering judgment in the shadow of the banking crisis.[72] Furthermore, the rules on limitation in the wake of *Kleinwort Benson*[73] for mistakes of law clearly had an impact. Finally, the ruling was rendered in the context of the pre-existing and long-standing domestic model of bank charges: the 'free-if-in-credit' model of UK banking, a model upon which a range of expectations had been based. Clearly, the court had to take the weight of these expectations and implications of even a modest change into account in rendering its judgment.

C. *(Non-harmonised) National Background Rules*

Yet beyond ensuring the necessary active participation of national judiciaries in the Europeanisation process, there are further reservations as far as the effective elaboration of Europeanised contractual fairness is concerned. Primarily, these reservations concern the effect of national background rules. As the European Commission itself has noted: 'The application of the same general criterion in two Member States may give rise to very different decisions, as a result of the divergences between the rules of substantive law.... Hence harmonisation ... is more apparent than real.'[74] Thus in *First National* the House of Lords, in considering the relevant contract term on the accrual of interest on default, held that the term was not unfair in part because the problem related to the relevant national background legislation. In contrast, in *UK Housing Alliance (North West) Ltd v. Francis*[75] the procedural protection available in possession proceedings led to a finding that a term in a sale and leaseback arrangement was not unfair because of a different constellation of background rules. As Longmore LJ noted: 'Mr Francis necessarily

[70] James Devenney, *supra* note 37 at 51.

[71] For example, at [50] *per* Lord Walker (Lady Hale and Lord Neuberger agreeing).

[72] Mel Kenny, James Devenney & Lorna Fox O'Mahony, *supra* note 35 at 378. As Lord Walker noted, in 2006 the banks had made ca. £2.56 billion from these charges (one-third of the current account revenue; see Judgment, Lord Walker at [36] and [47]).

[73] Limitation Act 1980, s. 32(1) and *Kleinwort Benson Ltd v. Lincoln CC* [1999] 2 AC 349. Recalling Lord Browne-Wilkinson in *Kleinwort Benson Ltd v. Lincoln CC* [1999] 2 AC 349 at 363.

[74] European Commission, *Report from the Commission on the Implementation of Directive 93/13 EEC of 5th April 1993 on Unfair Terms in Consumer Contracts*, Com (2000) 248 final, at 30.

[75] [2010] EWCA Civ 117.

had the protection of a solicitor at the time … the protection of the court if and when a possession order was sought.… I cannot see here any failure to conform with good standards of commercial morality and practice'.[76] Juxtaposing the different impact of national background rules in *First National* and *Housing Alliance*, a need to elaborate yet deeper coherence emerges. This is not to say that the background rules should be harmonised, but that there is a need to find agreement on the characteristics of 'background' rules which contribute to a determination that a particular term is fair or not.

D. Towards a Multi-Dimensional Perspective

Similarly, if greater coherence in standard terms is required, it is necessary to reflect on both those substantive provisions aimed directly at policing such terms as well as those which may indirectly police such terms. Again, this is clearly demonstrated in the case of suretyship.[77] A surety typically assumes a secondary and accessory liability. Moreover, he or she may be discharged from liability in certain situations, for example, when the creditor is under an equitable duty not to release any security held in respect of the principal debt[78]; here the surety will normally be discharged if the creditor does so.[79] As a result, it is common to find terms in surety agreements purporting to allow creditors to release such securities.[80]

However, as we have seen, whether such terms are subject to the UTCCR controls is disputed. Even setting the UTCCR to one side, it is clear that standard terms in surety agreements may be controlled through other mechanisms, and the substantive provisions indirectly policing unfairness may involve a cocktail of disclosure requirements,[81] interpretive techniques,[82] formalities,[83] and undue influence

[76] *Id.*, at [29].

[77] James Devenney, Lorna Fox-O'Mahony & Mel Kenny, *Standing Surety in England and Wales: The Sphinx of Procedural Protection*, LLOYDS MARITIME COMPARATIVE LAW QUARTERLY 527 (2008).

[78] For example, *Skipton Building Society Ltd v. Stott* [2001] QB 261.

[79] *Re Darwen & Pearce* [1927] 1 Ch. 176, but *cf. Carter v. White* (1883) 25 ChD 666.

[80] *Kufner, supra* note 31 at [16]. *See* Gerard McCormack, *supra* note 38 at 172–3.

[81] For example, *London General Omnibus Co Ltd v. Holloway* [1912] 2 KB 72, *Levett v Barclays Bank plc* [1995] 1 WLR 1260, *Crédit Lyonnais Bank Nederland v. Export Credit Guarantee Department* [1996] 1 Lloyd's Rep 200, and *Royal Bank of Scotland v. Etridge (no. 2)* [2001] UKHL 44.

[82] English courts traditionally interpreted terms which sought to exclude a surety's right to be discharged strictly: *Trafalgar House Construction (Regions) Ltd v. General Surety & Guarantee Co Ltd* [1996] 1 AC 199. Yet the courts now need to consider more 'modern' approaches, for example, in *Investors Compensation Scheme Ltd v. West Bromwich Building Society* [1998] 1 WLR 896.

[83] In *J. Pereira Fernandes SA v. Mehta* [2006] EWHC 813 (Ch) at [16] Judge Pelling QC noted that the purpose: 'is to protect people from being held liable on informal communications because they may be made without sufficient consideration or expressed ambiguously or because such communication might be fraudulently alleged against the party to be charged.'

considerations.[84] Indeed insolvency provisions may also affect the reach and effectiveness of standard term regulation.[85] Crucially, the substantive control of standard contract terms may be multi-dimensional, and it is therefore necessary to study the effect of the (D)CFR initiative on the control of such terms.

Indeed closer analysis of surety agreements illustrates a broader point: the protection of the surety across Europe is *polycontextual* in nature, transcending traditional legal boundaries and protecting non-professional sureties from one State to the next in different fields of law. Indeed, whilst most States have sought to enhance the protection of non-professional sureties, there is a significant amount of diversity in the nature of that protection.[86] The protection available in individual legal orders often involves context-specific orchestrations of various legal fields, concepts and mechanisms including contract law, consumer law, family, property and even constitutional law.[87] To focus on and harmonise specific aspects of those orchestrations may have profound and unforeseeable fragmentary effects in the different legal orders and lead, with significant implications for access to credit, financial institutions to withdraw from the market.[88] Incremental, judicially facilitated harmonisation will therefore continue to play an important role notwithstanding any measures of legislative harmonisation that are adopted; again the emphasis will be on the non-legislative contribution of national judges to minimising fragmentation.

E. Procedural Dimension: Collective Proceedings

Yet substantive provisions, whether part of the polycentric infrastructure or the relevant background rules, constitute only part of the picture; *procedural* provisions also affect the effectiveness of standard terms. For example, the extent to which *collective proceedings* are available may affect the substantive regulation of standard terms, especially as many consumers may not have the information, resources or inclination to challenge 'unfair' standard terms.[89] Moreover, the seller or supplier may seek to settle out of court before a relevant precedent is established.[90] Such

[84] *Dunbar Bank plc v. Nadeem* [1998] 3 All ER 876 discussed in James Devenney, Mel Kenny and Lorna Fox-O'Mahony, *supra* note 35 at 156–7.

[85] Mel Kenny & James Devenney, *The Fallacy of the Common Core: Polycontextualism in Surety Protection – a Hard Case in Harmonisation Discourse*, in THE THEORY AND PRACTICE OF HARMONISATION (M. Andenæs & C. Andersen [eds.], forthcoming, Edward Elgar, 2012).

[86] Generally: Aurelia Colombi Ciacchi, *supra* note 36.

[87] Mel Kenny & James Devenney, *supra* note 85.

[88] Mel Kenny, *Standing Surety in Europe: Common Core or Tower of Babel* 70 MODERN LAW REVIEW 175 (2007) at 195–196. *Royal Bank of Scotland v. Etridge (no.2)* [2001] UKHL 44, see Lord Nicholls' reflections on the importance of such arrangements [34]–[35].

[89] *Supra* note 74.

[90] Arthur A. Leff, *Unconscionability and the Crowd: Consumers and the Common Law Tradition*, 31 UNIVERSITY OF PITTSBURGH LAW REVIEW 349 (1970) at 356–7.

concerns were reflected in Article 7 of the Unfair Terms Directive, which specified that Member States ensure, in the interests of consumers, that

> adequate and effective means exist to prevent the continued use of unfair terms in contracts concluded with consumers by sellers or suppliers.... The means ... shall include provisions whereby persons or organizations, having a legitimate interest under national law in protecting consumers, may take action according to the national law concerned before the courts or before competent administrative bodies for a decision as to whether contractual terms drawn up for general use are unfair, so that they can apply appropriate and effective means to prevent the continued use of such terms.[91]

Yet the (D)CFR makes no provision for collective proceedings in respect of 'unfair' terms. This is cause for concern as the effective substantive regulation of 'unfair' terms may be undermined by an inadequate procedural framework. This, in turn, could weaken support for the (D)CFR/CFR in important constituencies such as consumer interest groups. Indeed, Book II. – 9:401 DCFR, specifying that 'the parties may not exclude the application of the provisions in this Section or derogate from or vary their effects' might be interpreted as excluding collective proceedings altogether. On the other hand, there are signs that such an exclusion was not intended by the drafters. First, the commentary to II 9:408, states: 'A consumer has to be protected, even if he ... fails to raise the unfair nature of the term, either because unaware of available rights or because deterred from enforcing them'. This seems to accept the proposition that the effectiveness of the provisions may be undermined if too much emphasis is placed on the consumer challenging the term(s) in question. Second, the comment on II.–9:406 explicitly refers to collective proceedings: 'In the case of terms which are insufficiently transparent, an informed market decision has not been made so that it is appropriate to apply judicial control. Furthermore, there is an interest to eliminate terms lacking transparency in collective proceedings'. By extension it can be argued that II.–9:401 does not exclude the possibility of collective proceedings in accordance with the Commission's broader strategy[92]; therefore the (D)CFR/CFR provisions should be read alongside existing EU provision on collective proceedings.

However, the existing EU collective proceedings regime is not unproblematic. Three points arise in particular: first, while collective proceedings may indeed

[91] In C-240–244/98 *Océano Group Editorial SA v. Murciano Quintero* [2000] ECR I-4941, at paras. 26–28: 'the court's power to determine of its own motion whether a term is unfair must be regarded as constituting a proper means both of achieving the result sought by Article 6 of the Directive, namely, preventing an individual consumer from being bound by an unfair term, and of contributing to achieving the aim of Article 7, since ... that may act as a deterrent and contribute to preventing unfair terms in contracts concluded between consumers and sellers or suppliers.'

[92] Seen, *inter alia*, Article 38 of the (original) proposed Consumer Rights Directive.

become the main battleground on 'unfair' terms,[93] this presents risks for any legislative harmonisation agenda, and a further examination and consolidation of the collective proceedings regime(s) would be necessary to support the Directive's objectives.[94] Second, collective proceedings often require an abstract review of the relevant term(s).[95] This would require, *inter alia*, a conceptualisation of a 'typical consumer',[96] and such conceptualisations vary between legal orders[97]; the Directive provides little guidance.[98] Finally, there is a risk of differences between the enforcement practices of bodies empowered to bring collective proceedings, and this again may lead to an unevenness of judicial protection.[99]

V. CONCLUSION

The (D)CFR initiative is a significant contribution to comparative private law research and an indicator on the future direction of Europeanised Private Law in general and consumer law in particular.[100] Yet, as even the editors of the (D)CFR note, the precise direction of development remains unclear.[101] While there is at least some support for a CFR in the form of an optional instrument, any such instrument would be much narrower than the (D)CFR. The particular focus of this chapter has been to examine some of the obstacles for a legislative CFR through the lens of unfair terms. As this chapter has argued, there is a real risk of taking the effectiveness of EU law too seriously, of placing too much emphasis on legislative harmonisation. Commercial and consumer lawyers need to appreciate that the EU legal order requires flexibility and an understanding of the administrative dimension of effective implementation and compliance. Legislative harmonisation on its own threatens further legal fragmentation and a destabilisation of consumer and commercial law and policy. By extension, it has been argued that the extent and success of future Europeanisation will be shaped by two key factors: the supporting role played by non-legislative harmonisation and judicial convergence as advanced by the national

93 Chris Willett, Fairness in Consumer Contracts: The Case of Unfair Terms (Ashgate: 2007), 173–4.
94 *Cf.* Hans Schulte-Nölke, *supra* note 34.
95 Iain Ramsay, Consumer Law and Policy, (2nd ed., Hart, Oxford, 2007) at p. 195.
96 For example, *Office of Fair Trading v. Foxtons, Ltd* [2009] EWCA Civ 288.
97 Mel Kenny et al., *supra* note 35 at 377.
98 *Cf.* Consumer Protection from Unfair Trading Regulations 2008, Regulation 2(2)–(6).
99 James Devenney, *supra* note 37.
100 Green paper, *supra* note 4.
101 Von Bar & Clive, *supra* note 2 at 23: 'whether or not the CFR, or parts of it, might at a later stage be used as the basis for one or more optional instruments, i.e. as the basis for an additional set of legal rules which parties might choose to govern their mutual rights and obligations. In the view of the two Groups such an optional instrument would open attractive perspectives, not least for consumer transactions.'

judiciaries, on the one hand, and the broader substantive and procedural environment, and explicitly the impact of national background rules, an appreciation of the polycentricity of legal institutions and doctrine and the procedural issue of collective redress, on the other. These factors describe the framework within which a CFR, whether in the form of an Optional Instrument or not, might operate. It is to be hoped that these factors will be taken into account before further steps towards what would otherwise become a self-defeating process of codification are undertaken.

PART VI

Misrepresentation, Breach, and Remedies

This part provides original ideas for the re-setting of the legal premises behind common law damages. Chapter 16 argues that the dual remedies for misrepresentation – rescission and damages – should not be seen as alternatives, but as binary in nature. It rejects the premise that rescission can be singularly used as a "holistic remedy." The chapter compares the U.K. Misrepresentation Act of 1967 with the law of misrepresentation found in the United States and Australia. It concludes that the U.K. Misrepresentation Act should be repealed. Chapter 17 continues the theme of Chapter 16 by looking at recent cases in England and Wales that show an "over-zealous" use of damages in cases of fraudulent misrepresentation.

Chapter 18 analyzes the interplay between governing law, performance, and the remedies regimes of English law and the Convention on Contracts for the International Sale of Goods (CISG) in the area of documentary transactions. It examines the strengths and shortfalls of both laws, and makes suggestions as to which law or combination of laws is best suited to the regulation of documentary transactions.

Chapter 19 analyzes the critique that the common law of remedies (payment of damages) does not adequately protect the performance interests of contracting parties. It dismisses the vehicle of restitutionary damages as a better way to protect the performance interest. Instead, the chapter focuses on the English courts' favoritism of defendants in determining whether a specific performance order is justified. The chapter examines a series of English and Scottish cases that frame different views as to whether specific performance should be considered a normal or an extraordinary remedy. The term that provides the grist for the analysis is the "keep open covenant" found in commercial leases.

16

Remedies for Misrepresentation

An Integrated System

David Capper

This chapter endeavours to integrate the two principal remedies for misrepresentation, namely rescission and damages. Its principal thesis is that legal certainty requires a reasonably clear delineation of the losses to be remedied by rescission and those by damages. Discretionary remedialism is to be deplored as is any tendency to treat rescission as a holistic remedy for misrepresentation. A contract is rescinded for misrepresentation because it would not have been entered into but for the misrepresentation. This justifies only the cutting away of the contract itself and the restoration of the parties to the position they were in before contract so far as the contract is concerned.

Consequential losses should be remedied by damages, but under contract law that requires an independent justification. That justification may be found in the law of torts through the actions of deceit and negligent misstatement. The chapter contends that the Misrepresentation Act 1967 does not provide a sound basis for the award of damages for misrepresentation and should in the main be repealed. The power to declare a contract subsisting under section 2(2) where rescission would be excessive should be retained but there should be no damages awarded in lieu. The treatment of misrepresentation in other common law jurisdictions, particularly in the United States, will be considered, especially in the context of remedies for losses lying beyond rescission.

A coherent system of remedies should clearly delineate the job each remedy is to do. So rescission should be confined to 'cutting away' the vitiated contract and should not be fashioned into a holistic remedy for misrepresentation. Rescission should thus be combined with damages by allowing it in cases where the claimant wants specific (as opposed to monetary) relief. Damages should only be awarded in a case of misrepresentation where there has been a tort, i.e. where the defendant has been dishonest (the tort of deceit) or is in breach of a duty of care (the tort of negligent misstatement). This is broadly the position in the United States and in Australia. The Misrepresentation Act 1967 and the Misrepresentation Act (NI) 1967 should be repealed so far as they provide for a damages remedy beyond the torts of deceit and negligent misstatement. These more extensive damages remedies lack moral and policy based justification and provide for more extensive relief than is available for breach of contract.

I. INTRODUCTION

Misrepresentation is one of several vitiating factors in the Law of Contract. To say that a contract is vitiated means that an apparently valid contract has been formed but that something went wrong in the formation. Although English law treats one of the vitiating factors, common mistake, as making the contract void or producing a nullity,[1] other vitiating factors like misrepresentation, duress, undue influence and unconscionable bargain make the contract voidable at the instance of the innocent party. This means that in a misrepresentation case the misrepresentee may seek to rescind the contract *ab initio*. This involves the cancellation of future obligations under the contract and the reversal of transfers of value between the parties with a view to effecting *restitutio in integrum*. The implications of this will be explained in more detail later; in brief, rescission attempts to restore the parties to the position they were in before the contract was made, so far as the contract is concerned. There may be other losses consequent upon entering into the contract, but these are not proper matters for rescission. If the innocent party wishes to recover for these losses a further remedy, damages, must be sought. To recover damages it is generally necessary to establish that either the torts of deceit[2] or negligent misstatement[3] have been committed or that the claimant has a right to damages under section 2(1) of the Misrepresentation Act 1967.[4]

This chapter offers a critique of the principles applicable to rescission and damages awards for misrepresentation with a view to the construction of an integrated system of remedies for this vitiating factor. English law is its principal focus although other common law materials will be sourced where this is thought to be helpful. An integrated system is important for coherent development of the law and legal certainty. This in turn will facilitate fairness and justice. The central argument is that there needs to be a reasonably clear delineation of the respective jobs that rescission and damages are supposed to do. Rescission should not attempt to remedy those

1 *Bell* v. *Lever Brothers Ltd* [1932] AC 161 (HL); *Great Peace Shipping Ltd* v. *Tsavliris Shipping Salvage (International) Ltd (The Great Peace)* [2002] EWCA Civ 1407, [2003] QB 679. For an argument that common mistake should preferably make a contract voidable see David Capper, *Common Mistake in Contract Law*, SINGAPORE J. LEGAL STUDIES 457 (2009).

2 *Derry* v *Peek* (1889) 14 App Cas 337 (HL).

3 *Hedley Byrne & Co* v *Heller & Partners* [1964] AC 465 (HL).

4 Damages may be awarded in lieu of rescission under section 2(2) of the Misrepresentation Act 1967, but these are on a different basis than the present context.

losses which are proper matters for damages only. However, no attempt will be made to study the entire law of rescission,[5] the focus instead being on those areas where rescission requires greater integration with itself and with damages. Rescission will be examined first as it is the remedy available for all kinds of misrepresentation. When the chapter turns its attention to damages, the focus will be twofold – the integration of this remedy with rescission and the identification of the appropriate circumstances for the award of damages for misrepresentation. But first it is necessary to state a few important points about misrepresentation.

II. MISREPRESENTATION

As Cartwright has pointed out, there is no all-embracing definition of misrepresentation.[6] A condensed definition of misrepresentation – a false statement of material fact[7] inducing the misrepresentee to enter the contract[8] – truly only explains rescission. The torts of deceit and negligent misstatement, together with the statutory action for damages under section 2(1) of the Misrepresentation Act 1967, share much in common with this definition but have additional requirements that reflect particular features of these actions. As rescission is concerned with the reversal of transactions which ought not to have been entered into it is unnecessary to demonstrate that the misrepresentor was guilty of any tortious conduct. There being no satisfactory basis for the retention of benefits transferred under the contract by either party to the other all that needs to happen is the restitution of benefits received by the misrepresentor and accompanying counter restitution from the misrepresentee.[9]

A clear judicial statement of the policy reasons for rescinding a contract for misrepresentation was provided by Jessel MR in *Redgrave v. Hurd*:[10]

> A man is not to be allowed to get a benefit from a statement which he now admits to be false. He is not to be allowed to say, for the purpose of civil jurisdiction, that

[5] An excellent study is Dominic O'Sullivan, Steven Elliott & Rafael Zakrzewski, THE LAW OF RESCISSION (Oxford University Press: Oxford 2008), to which this chapter is indebted.

[6] John Cartwright, MISREPRESENTATION, MISTAKE & NON-DISCLOSURE 2.02 (2nd ed., Sweet & Maxwell: London 2007), citing the speech of Lord Herschell in *Derry* v. *Peek* (1889) 14 App. Cas. 337 (HL), 359–60.

[7] This probably includes statements of law. See *Brennan* v *Bolt Burden* [2004] EWCA Civ 1017, [2005] QB 303.

[8] Mindy Chen-Wishart, CONTRACT LAW, ch. 5 (2nd ed., Oxford University Press: Oxford 2008).

[9] It should be noted, however, that rescission also takes account of changes to the position of both misrepresentor and misrepresentee that occur after the vitiated contract has been entered into, with a view to restoring the *status quo ante*. See Elise Bant, *Restitutio in Integrum and the Change of Position Defence*, RESTITUTION LAW REV 13 (2007). As will be seen later (see ns 46–60 and text) this is where rescission intersects with damages and particular care needs to be taken to ensure that rescission relief does not trespass on damages' territory.

[10] (1881) 20 Ch.D 1 (CA), 12.

> when he made it he did not know it to be false; he ought to have found that out before he made it.

Later Jessel MR said[11]:

> Even assuming that moral fraud must be shown in order to set aside a contract, you have it where a man, having obtained a beneficial contract by a statement which he now knows to be false, insists upon keeping that contract. To do so is a moral delinquency: no man ought to seek to take advantage of his own false statements.

To similar effect were statements by Turner LJ in *Rawlins v. Wickham*,[12] Fry J in *Hart v. Swaine*,[13] Lord Blackburn in *Brownlie v. Campbell*,[14] and Lord Shaw of Dunfermline in *Mair v. Rio Grande Rubber Estates Ltd*.[15] These dicta are all concerned with situations where the misrepresentor made an inaccurate non-tortious pre-contractual statement, which the courts regarded as making it unconscionable for that party to retain the benefits received under the contract. Without going so far as to accept the wider theory that relief against a vitiated contract is concerned with the claimant's defective consent as opposed to the defendant's wrongdoing, it is considered that Professor Birks was right to contend that in rescinding a contract for misrepresentation all that needs to be asked is whether the defendant received any enrichment which must be reversed, with the claimant giving counter restitution of any enrichment it has received.[16] The question whether the claimant has suffered any loss which should be compensated requires proof of tortious conduct.[17] These are the respective roles for rescission and damages in an integrated system of remedies for misrepresentation.

One last preliminary is an acknowledgement of Professor Bridge's very powerful critique of the law of innocent (non-fraudulent) misrepresentation.[18] He argues that rescission should not be allowed for non-fraudulent misrepresentation and that serious criticism can be levelled at the damages remedies provided by the Misrepresentation Act 1967. In relation to rescission Professor Bridge argues that the law is unbalanced when a contracting party has to demonstrate serious breach to terminate a contract *de futuro* but can rescind a contract *ab initio* for comparatively minor misstatements. In this chapter the position taken is that rescission is

11 *Id.*, 12–13.
12 (1858) 3 De G & J 316, 317.
13 (1877) 7 Ch.D 44 (Ch.D), 46–7.
14 (1880) 5 App Cas (HL) 925, 950.
15 [1913] AC 853 (HL), 870.
16 Subject to the caveat about change of position, n. 9.
17 Peter Birks, *Undue Influence as Wrongful Exploitation*, 120 Law Quarterly Rev 34 (2004); Peter Birks, Unjust Enrichment 176–8 (2nd ed., Oxford University Press: Oxford 2005).
18 Michael Bridge, *Innocent Misrepresentation in Contract*, 57 Current Legal Problems 277 (2004).

appropriate for all kinds of misrepresentation because the contract ought never to have been made. Professor Bridge's arguments carry more weight when it comes to damages, particularly under the Misrepresentation Act 1967.

III. RESCISSION

As O'Sullivan, Elliott and Zakrzewski have pointed out, rescission restores the contracting parties to their pre-contractual positions, not in all respects, but "as regards the rights and obligations which have been created by the contract."[19] The parties are released from obligations created by the contract, have returned to them advantages transferred under the contract, and are indemnified for any detriments incurred pursuant to the contract.[20] As Dr Bant has pointed out, account may have to be taken of any changes in position by the parties after the contract was entered into.[21] If the rescinding party has suffered additional losses, such as expenses incurred in connection with the contract but not under it,[22] or seeks to recover profits that would have been made had some other contract been entered into,[23] damages are the appropriate remedy. This could be either in addition to or instead of rescission, in the latter case damages compensating for those losses made good by rescission as well as the additional losses.

A. *Rescission as a Self-Help Remedy?*

There is no consensus among the authorities[24] or commentators[25] as to whether rescission is effected by the election of the innocent party or whether the court must determine that the contract should be rescinded. O'Sullivan, Elliott and Zakrzewski[26] regard rescission at common law for fraud, duress and the avoidance of insurance contracts as the self-executing act of the innocent party; and all other cases as rescission in equity requiring the decision of the court. It is asserted that cases of rescission at common law tend to be wholly executory contracts requiring only the release of parties from contractual obligations. Rescission in equity has to

[19] O'Sullivan, Elliott & Zakrzewski, *supra note* 5, at 13.01–02, citing *Newbigging* v. *Adam* (1886) 34 ChD 582, (CA) 592–4.

[20] *Id.*

[21] *Supra note* 9.

[22] O'Sullivan, Elliott & Zakrzewski, *supra note* 5, at 13.04.

[23] *East* v *Maurer* [1991] 1 WLR 461 (CA).

[24] *Abram Steamship Co Ltd* v. *Westville Shipping Co Ltd* [1923] AC 773 (HL Sc) and *Alati* v *Kruger* (1955) 94 CLR 216 (HCA) favour self-help, whereas *Spence* v. *Crawford* [1939] 3 All ER 271 (HL) assumed differently.

[25] For a thorough discussion of this issue see Janet O'Sullivan, *Rescission as a Self-Help Remedy: A Critical Analysis*, CAMBRIDGE L. J. 509 (2000).

[26] *Supra note* 5, ch. 11.

be via court decree because orders for restitution and counter restitution are necessary in executed contracts. Even if it is correct that self-executing rescission in practice occurs in executory contracts only, it is hardly helpful to the development of an integrated remedy of rescission to preserve a distinction based only on historical antecedent. Rescission should in all cases be either a self-help remedy or the decision of the court. Janet O'Sullivan has argued that it should be the decision of the court because of the need in many cases to make orders for restitution and counter restitution and in that context to protect innocent third parties.[27] She points out that rescission is different from termination *de futuro* which involves release from future obligations and remedying breach. But even if rescission is self-executing, the court may have to determine whether a party was entitled to rescind and to make restitution and counter restitution orders to effect rescission. The innocent party should be entitled to take whatever remedial action it can before this point.

B. Practical Justice

In giving effect to rescission, the court seeks to do what is "practically just"[28] and tends to lean a little in the claimant's favour in fraud cases.[29] The quest for practical justice increasingly takes the form of orders for pecuniary restitution instead of requiring a party to transfer assets specifically.[30] As damages are capable of meeting all the claimant's pecuniary losses, including those otherwise remedied by rescission, the question arises whether rescission should be reserved for those cases where specific transfers of assets are required. However, it should be recognised that some cases of rescission may involve a mixture of orders for specific and pecuniary relief so this additional flexibility is useful.[31] Ultimately this concern for practical justice comes to no more than unwillingness to conclude that rescission should be barred because *restitutio in integrum* cannot be effected.[32]

C. Rescission as of Right

Before examining the orders that may be made to effect *restitutio in integrum*, it may be helpful to differentiate rescission from other equitable remedies like specific performance and injunction. The latter are discretionary remedies in the sense that

[27] *supra note* 25.

[28] *Erlanger* v *The New Sombrero Phosphate Company* (1878) 3 App Cas 1218 (HL), at 1278–9 (Lord Blackburn).

[29] *Spence* v *Crawford* [1939] 3 ALL ER 271 (HL).

[30] This was strongly advocated by N. Y. Nayan in *Rescission: A Case for Rejecting the Classical Model?* 27 UNIV OF WESTERN AUSTRALIA L. REV 66 (1997).

[31] See also n. 81 and text later.

[32] *Mahoney* v *Purnell* [1996] 3 All ER 61 (ChD); *Smith New Court Securities Ltd* v. *Citibank NA* [1997] AC 254 (HL); and O'Sullivan *supra note* 25, at 510–11.

the discretion is at large. A claimant never has a right to specific performance or an injunction, although the former is granted as of course in contracts for the sale of land[33] and the latter is similarly granted in cases of continuing interference with property rights.[34] Since damages would most often be available as of right where specific performance or injunction is sought the refusal of equitable relief rarely leaves the claimant without a remedy. By contrast, rescission is as of right and probably needs to be since damages would only be available as an alternative in cases where a tort is committed. This will be so for fraudulent misrepresentation, negligent misstatement, and the statutory claim under section 2(1) of the Misrepresentation Act 1967. But it is not generally so for duress, undue influence, or unconscionable bargain.[35]

There are, it is true, various bars to rescission, such as affirmation, delay, impossibility of making *restitutio in integrum*, and the intervention of third party rights. While the decision that one of these bars applies does in a sense involve the court exercising discretion, these are not conceptually discretionary grounds for withholding relief, as the discretionary grounds for withholding specific performance and injunction are. If one of these bars is made out, then the claimant is not entitled to rescission. If none is made out and the claimant has established grounds for rescission, the claimant is entitled to it. There is judicial discretion in settling the terms of rescission, but this is a far cry from whether there should be rescission.[36]

This discussion of bars to rescission raises serious questions about the soundness of recent judicial recognition of a discretionary bar to rescission, where this remedy is considered to be disproportionate. In *Johnson v. EBS Pensioner Trustees Ltd*[37] a loan was made by solicitors to a client, a £100 company effectively owned by another client, Mr Johnson. Mr Johnson guaranteed the loan and as security for it executed a charge over a property which the company held on a twenty-one year lease. This transaction was challenged as a breach of fiduciary duty on the part of the solicitors. In refusing rescission, Mummery LJ based himself on the principal's (Mr Johnson) inability to make counter restitution of the benefits he received under the loan.[38] Dyson LJ also relied upon this ground but went further when he said:[39]

> When exercising its equitable jurisdiction, the court considers what fairness requires not only when addressing the question of the precise form of relief, but also when considering whether the remedy should be granted at all.

[33] J. E. Martin, HANBURY & MARTIN MODERN EQUITY, 24–014 (18th ed., Sweet & Maxwell 2009).
[34] *Redland Bricks* v. *Morris* [1970] AC 652 (HL).
[35] An award of equitable compensation was made in *Mahoney* v. *Purnell* [1996] 3 ALL ER 61 (Ch.D), an undue influence case, but this may be better regarded as pecuniary rescission. See Peter Birks, *Unjust Factors and Wrongs: Pecuniary Rescission for Undue Influence* RESTITUTION L. REV. 72 (1997).
[36] O'Sullivan, Elliott & Zakrzewski, *supra note* 5, 13.09.
[37] [2002] EWCA Civ 164, [2002] Lloyd's PN 309 (CA).
[38] *Id.*, [58].
[39] *Id.*, [79].

Douglas Brown J agreed to dismiss the appeal, but it is not clear where he stood on the rescission question. O'Sullivan, Elliott and Zakrzewski prefer to see this case as an unconventional application of the inability to make *restitutio in integrum* bar[40] rather than a new discretionary bar. Further support for this discretionary bar comes from *Wilson* v *Hurstanger Ltd*,[41] a case where the lender in a regulated consumer credit agreement failed to provide adequate disclosure to the borrower of a £240 commission paid to the broker who was the borrower's agent.[42] Instead of rescission of the entire contract, the Court of Appeal confirmed the trial judge's award of £240 equitable compensation for the borrower. The earlier passage from Dyson LJ's judgment in *Johnson* was quoted with approval,[43] but the case may be better viewed as one of pecuniary rescission. Traditional rescission of the credit agreement would have released the borrower from the obligation to repay in accordance with the contractual terms, but it would have been unsatisfactory to allow the borrower to keep the loan without any repayment obligation. However, the following passage from the judgment of Tuckey LJ[44] suggests that rescission was refused because it was considered to be disproportionate[45]:

> To rescind the transaction altogether would be unfair and disproportionate. This is my view irrespective of whether the defendants would be able to make counter restitution.

These cases are best seen as intuitively correct results better rationalised in more conventional ways. A discretionary ground for refusing rescission is also inconsistent with the statutory discretion under section 2(2) of the Misrepresentation Act 1967 to declare a contract subsisting notwithstanding a non-fraudulent misrepresentation, as this provision would be unnecessary if discretion to refuse rescission already existed.

D. *Indemnity*

As Bowen LJ explained in *Newbigging v. Adam*[46] rescission involves not just the taking and giving back of benefits arising under the contract but also of obligations. A misrepresentor must reassume a burden which the innocent party has taken on. So in *Newbigging*, where the innocent party was induced to become a partner in a firm,

[40] It is certainly this because the loan was made to the company and no attempt was made to justify piercing the corporate veil.

[41] [2007] EWCA Civ 299.

[42] The broker was in breach of fiduciary duty and the lender subject to accessory liability.

[43] *Id.*, [48].

[44] Waller and Jacob LJJ agreeing.

[45] *Id.*, [51].

[46] (1886) 34 Ch.D 582 (CA), at 595.

he was indemnified against all current and future liabilities of the partnership.[47] But an indemnity will not cover consequential losses and expenses caused by entering into the contract but not required by it. So in *Whittington v. Seale-Hayne*[48] the claimant entered into a lease of a poultry farm as a result of an innocent misrepresentation as to its sanitary condition when the water supply was actually poisoned. He obtained an indemnity against rates and repairs required by the contract but not for any costs of running the farm, including the loss of poultry and medical costs necessitated by the poisoning of the manager. These could only be recovered through damages and the claimant had no cause of action at that time. If this decision seems harsh it should be remembered that today the claimant may well have had a cause of action under negligent misstatement or the statutory action under section 2(1) of the Misrepresentation Act 1967.[49]

E. Compensation

Rescission may be barred where an asset passing under the contract has been altered in a way which changes its nature but if change is less fundamental compensation may be ordered for any improvements or deterioration to the asset.[50] Compensation for repairs or improvements is only appropriate where the party in possession of an asset has carried out those repairs or improvements at their own instance. If this is something required by the contract the indemnity principle applies.[51] Compensation should be made where repairs and improvements are made in good faith and the court must be careful about the party in possession speculating at the other's expense.[52] A difficult case on repairs and improvements is *Brown v. Smitt*.[53]

In *Brown v. Smitt* the purchaser of a sheep farm was entitled to rescind it on the ground of the vendor's fraudulent misrepresentation. The issue before the High Court of Australia was whether as part of the rescission decree he was entitled to compensation for improvements he made to the land by way of clearing it and providing a permanent water supply. The majority (Knox CJ, Gavan Duffy and Starke JJ) held that he was on the apparent basis that a rescinding vendor would be required to compensate the purchaser so the same rule should apply to rescinding purchasers. The minority (Isaacs and Rich JJ) considered that the position was different where the

47 O'Sullivan, Elliott & Zakrzewski, *supra note* 5, 17.21–22. The text also discusses *Forum Developments Pte Ltd* v *Global Accent Trading Pte Ltd* [1995] 1 SLR 474 (CA) where a rescinding tenant obtained an indemnity for sums he had expended renovating premises as required under the lease.

48 (1900) 82 LT 49 (ChD).

49 O'Sullivan, Elliott & Zakrzewski, *supra note* 5, 17.23.

50 *Id.*, 17.30–31, citing *Lagunas Nitrate Company* v. *Lagunas Syndicate* 2 Ch 392 (CA).

51 *Id.*, 17.34.

52 *Id.*, 17.36–52.

53 (1924) 34 CLR 160 (HCA).

purchaser sought to rescind and give back a property he had improved. The vendor in this sort of case did not ask for the improvements, which were not required by the contract. Requiring the vendor to pay compensation is really an award of damages, not the restitution of benefits transferred under the contract. The minority suggested that the majority might have been driven by the fraudulent nature of the misrepresentation, implying that the better way to compensate for this would have been an action in deceit. One point which makes the position of the minority seem attractive is the proposition that rescission involves the restoration of the parties to the position they occupied before the contract so far as the contract is concerned. The repairs and improvements here were not required by the contract and could be compensated by an award of damages for deceit. However, this would surely have applied to the rescinding vendor as well. The majority judgment is preferable because otherwise the vendor would have received as counter restitution a farm demonstrably more valuable than the one he sold. To reverse this unjust enrichment by requiring the purchaser to bring an action in deceit is needlessly increasing causes of action. *Whittington v. Seale-Hayne* was a different case because the claimant was only seeking compensation for loss.

In principle it seems right that where an asset has been used as contemplated by the contract and has deteriorated otherwise than through ordinary wear and tear the party returning it should pay compensation for that deterioration. This is orthodox *restitutio in integrum*.[54] It is also correct that compensation in this context does not include detriments suffered as a consequence of the contract but not pursuant to it. So the rescinding party in *Redgrave v. Hurd*[55] was properly denied the expenses of travelling to Birmingham to take up the practice, and the order in *Newbigging v. Adam*[56] rightly did not include anything for opportunities forgone to take up this one. These losses are the subject of damages claims only.[57]

F. *When* Restitutio in Integrum *Is Impossible*

Rescission will be barred whenever *restitutio in integrum* for both parties is impossible. This is commonly thought to be concerned with ensuring that the claimant is not unjustly enriched by keeping benefits acquired under the contract as well as recovering benefits transferred to the other party. However, it is not entirely concerned with this because if the claimant has lost the enrichment received without being at fault the defendant is still entitled to be restored to its pre-contractual

54 O'Sullivan, Elliott & Zakrzewski, *supra note* 5, 17.53–58.

55 (1881) 20 Ch.D 1 (CA).

56 (1886) 34 Ch.D 582 (CA).

57 O'Sullivan, Elliott & Zakrzewski, *supra note* 5, 17.59–64.

position as regards the contract so far as practically just.[58] *Restitutio in integrum* is concerned with ensuring that the defendant is not left in an unjustifiably worse position. So if the claimant can take back what was transferred under the contract but this is actually less than the value transferred there is no problem. In *Spence v. Crawford*[59] Spence was defrauded of his 50 percent shareholding in a company by Crawford, the holder of the other 50 percent. After the fraud the share capital of the company was increased and another shareholder (Richardson) was taken on board. The fact that Spence's shares were no longer the 50 percent shareholding they were before the fraud was no obstacle to rescission because it did not leave Crawford in an unjustifiably worse position. There was a further twist in the tail in that Richardson, who had previously been Crawford's accomplice, fell out with Crawford and went over to Spence's side, with the result that the two together controlled the company. This was left out of account when fashioning the relief following on from rescission, ostensibly on the basis that Crawford was a fraudster and the court leaned against such persons when fashioning relief. Today Crawford might have tried to rely on the defence of change of position but he would almost certainly have failed as it is recognised as a fairly narrow defence.[60]

G. *Partial Rescission*

If rescission is the 'undoing', 'unravelling' or 'cutting away' of a contract,[61] partial rescission refers to cutting away only part of a contract and leaving the remainder intact. It is not the same as severance which is the sub-division of a contract into two or more contracts with integral mutual obligations.[62] It is discussed here because it goes to the very nature of the remedy that is rescission. Discussion begins with an outline of the three main cases where this remedy was considered in a misrepresentation context.[63]

58 *Id.*, 18.06, citing Phillip Hellwege, *Unwinding Mutual Contracts:* Restitutio in Integrum *v. the Defence of Change of Position*, in UNJUSTIFIED ENRICHMENT: KEY ISSUES IN COMPARATIVE PERSPECTIVE 243 (D. Johnston & R. Zimmermann eds., Cambridge University Press: Cambridge 2002). The claimant might be able to assert a change of position defence.

59 [1939] 3 All ER 271 (HL).

60 *Lipkin Gorman* v *Karpnale Ltd* [1991] 2 AC 548 (HL), 580 (Lord Goff); Bant, *supra* note 9, 35.

61 These are three of the descriptions of the process used in Nyuk Yin Nayan, *Rescission: A Case for Rejecting the Classical Model?* 27 UNIV OF WESTERN AUSTRALIA L. REV. 66, 69 (1997).

62 Jill Poole, TEXTBOOK ON CONTRACT (10th ed., Oxford University Press: Oxford 2010), 320–321.

63 Partial rescission has been the subject of a voluminous amount of literature. See Louis Proksch, *Rescission on Terms* RESTITUTION LAW REV. 71 (1996); John W. Carter and Greg Tolhurst, *Rescission, Equitable Adjustment and Restitution* 10 J. CONTRACT LAW 167 (1996); Dominic O'Sullivan, *Partial Rescission for Misrepresentation in Australia* 113 LAW QUARTERLY REV. 16 (1997); Mindy Chen-Wishart, *Unjust Factors and the Restitutionary Response* 20 OXFORD J. OF LEGAL STUDIES 557 (2000); Andrew Robertson, *Partial Rescission, Causation and Benefit* 17

In *Vadasz v. Pioneer Concrete (SA) Pty Ltd*[64] the High Court of Australia, confirming the decisions of the courts in South Australia, ordered the partial rescission of a guarantee misrepresented as being for just future supplies of concrete to the guarantor's company instead of the past and future supplies it truly covered. It appears that the misrepresentation may have been fraudulent but the High Court did not come to a conclusion on this. As the guarantor had all along been willing to guarantee future supplies of concrete to his company, had no other practicable means of obtaining concrete, and as his company had received the concrete, the High Court made a partial rescission order that 'cut away' only the obligation to pay for past supplies. As the discussion later will demonstrate, it may be possible to rationalise this case as one where ordering the guarantor to pay for the future supplies that had now been received was an exercise in *restitutio in integrum* although this does not seem to have been the way that the High Court conceived of its order.[65]

In *TSB Bank plc v. Camfield*[66] the English Court of Appeal decisively rejected partial rescission. In this case a wife stood surety for a loan to her husband and his business partner. The guarantee was vitiated by the husband's non-fraudulent misrepresentation that it was limited in amount to £15,000 when it covered all of the business' indebtedness which stood at £30,000 at the time of proceedings. The wife was held to be entitled to rescind the guarantee against the bank because the latter had constructive notice of the husband's 'wrongdoing' under the principle in *Barclays Bank plc v. O'Brien*.[67] Different bases were provided for rejecting the bank's plea that rescission should leave the wife answerable for the £15,000 she was prepared to guarantee. Roch LJ thought that as rescission was the self-executing act of the party the court had no means of ensuring that the wife only rescinded the guarantee in part. Nourse LJ thought that rescission was an 'all or nothing' process and could not be ordered in part. To the argument that the wife should be required to pay £15,000 to the bank as a pecuniary form of *restitutio in integrum* he replied

J. CONTRACT LAW 163 (2001); Peter Watts, *Rescission of Guarantees for Misrepresentation and Actionable Non-Disclosure* CAMBRIDGE L. J. 301 (2002); Daniel Meikle, *Partial Rescission – Removing the Restitution from a Contractual Doctrine* 19 J. CONTRACT LAW 40 (2003); Jill Poole and Andrew Keyser, *Justifying Partial Rescission in English Law* 121 LAW QUARTERLY REV 273 (2005); Peter Watts, *Partial rescission: disentangling the seedlings, but not transplanting them* in EXPLORING PRIVATE LAW 427 (E. Bant & M. Harding eds., Cambridge University Press: Cambridge 2010).

[64] (1995) 184 CLR 102 (HCA).

[65] The High Court said, (1995) 184 CLR 102, 115: the "concern of equity, in moulding relief between the parties, is to prevent, nullify, or provide compensation for, wrongful injury. If it appears that the other party would not have entered into the contract at all if the true position were known, the contract will be set aside in its entirety."

[66] [1995] 1 WLR 430 (CA).

[67] [1994] 1 AC 180 (HL). The principle has since been restated in *Royal Bank of Scotland plc* v *Etridge (No 2)* [2001] UKHL 44, [2002] AC 773.

that she had received nothing under the guarantee of which she could be required to make restitution. This argument will be revisited later; it is clear that the ascertainment of a benefit for Mrs Camfield to make restitution of is more difficult than any similar exercise on the facts of *Vadasz*.[68]

Partial rescission was accepted by the New Zealand Court of Appeal in *Scales Trading Ltd v. Far Eastern Shipping Co Public Ltd*.[69] Scales supplied apples to ACFES and payment was guaranteed by FES, which was a minority shareholder in ACFES and earned freight from carrying cargo on its behalf. Both ACFES and FES were Russian companies and the guarantee document deliberately overstated the amount of the debt in order to evade Russian exchange control laws. FES was unaware of this and when the case went on appeal to the Privy Council it held that the guarantee should be rescinded in its entirety because had FES been aware of the truth it would not have entered into the guarantee at all.[70] But in the Court of Appeal this view of the facts was not taken and FES was required to honour the guarantee to the extent of the true price of the apples.

In all of the literature on the subject of partial rescission, only two sound bases for the kind of court orders made by the High Court of Australia in *Vadasz* and the New Zealand Court of Appeal in *Scales* have been identified. These are an order requiring the claimant to make counter restitution to the defendant in the form of a pecuniary substitute for strict *restitutio in integrum* and an order in effect rectifying the contract in the defendant's favour so that the claimant is obliged to meet a guarantee in the sum and form represented. There is more support for the former than for the latter. No support can be found for any kind of cutting away of part only of the contract because this is simply incompatible with the fundamental nature of rescission. If a contract is vitiated by misrepresentation or anything else rescission cuts away the whole of that contract because it should never have been made. The desire to cut away only part of the contract comes from a wish not to punish a defendant whose misrepresentation may only be innocent[71] and to present the claimant with a windfall. But these rough edges to rescission can be avoided via the application of existing principles and do not require alterations to rescission that would produce uncertainty and possibly incoherence in the application of the law.

[68] Partial rescission was also rejected in England by Colman J in *De Molestina* v. *Ponton* [2002] 1 Lloyd's Rep 271.

[69] [1999] 3 NZLR 26.

[70] [2001] 1 All ER (Comm) 319, [2001] 1 NZLR 513. The High Court of Australia had expressed a similar opinion in *Vadasz* n. 64 above, referring to its earlier guarantee case of *Commercial Bank of Australia* v. *Amadio* (1983) 151 CLR 447 where there was rescission of a guarantee that would not have been entered into at all had the truth been known.

[71] It is highly unlikely that anything resembling partial rescission would be undertaken for fraudulent misrepresentation or any other vitiating factor because these would all likely be cases where the innocent party would not, absent the vitiating factor, have entered into the contract at all.

Where it is sought to avoid injustice through the requirement of counter restitution by the claimant guarantee cases require some creativity in recognising the benefit the claimant is required to make counter restitution of. The Court of Appeal in *Camfield* dismissed the notion of benefit to the claimant quite summarily by pointing out that the loan was made to the borrower. In *Vadasz* it is easier to see benefit to the guarantor because the company was the claimant's business vehicle and almost entirely owned by him. Mindy Chen-Wishart has presented a powerful argument to the effect that if someone offers to pay for something to be received by another with whom they have a relationship benefit to the payer should be assumed because it arises out of that person's personal choice.[72] On that basis even Mrs Camfield should be treated as having benefited from the loan. In her case the difficulty then becomes one of measuring the benefit she should be required to make counter restitution of. Detailed examination of this question is beyond the scope of this chapter. All that needs to be said here is that a little creativity in the making of counter restitution to the defendant is compatible with an integrated system of remedies for misrepresentation.

Daniel Meikle has advocated allowing the defendant to seek rectification of the guarantee so that it places the guarantor under the obligation (s)he believed was being accepted.[73] Presumably the defendant would file a counterclaim to the claimant's claim for rescission and rectification would only be allowed in cases where the defendant innocently (*i.e.*, non-fraudulently) induced the contract. Partial rescission in this way would operate by analogy with rectification for unilateral mistake. As Professor McLauchlan has pointed out,[74] both common and unilateral mistake rectification assume a continuing common intention by both parties to the contract that the contract shall be in certain terms and a transcription error when it comes to reducing the contract to writing. In the case of unilateral mistake relief against the defendant is justified because of that party's sharp practice or unconscionable conduct in allowing the other party to sign in ignorance of the transcription error.[75] It is submitted that to allow rectification to the defendant, even one guilty of nothing worse than non-fraudulent misrepresentation, would not be in keeping with the fundamental principles on which this relief is granted.

72 Chen-Wishart, *supra note* 63.

73 Meikle *supra note* 63. This argument receives a large measure of support from Professor Poole and Mr Keyser *supra note* 63.

74 David McLauchlan., *The "Drastic" Remedy of Rectification for Unilateral Mistake* 124 LAW QUARTERLY REV. 608 (2008).

75 A *Roberts and Co Ltd* v. *Leicestershire County Council* [1961] Ch 555 (ChD); *Riverlate Properties Ltd* v. *Paul* [1975] Ch 133 (CA); *Thomas Bates and Son Ltd* v *Wyndham's (Lingerie) Ltd* [1981] 1 WLR 505 (CA); *Taylor* v *Johnson* (1983) 151 CLR 422 (HCA); *George Wimpey (UK) Ltd* v. *VI Construction Ltd* [2005] EWCA Civ 77, [2005] BLR 135 (CA).

All of the cases discussed previously concerned defendants seeking to limit court orders for rescission to only part of the contract. Before leaving partial rescission it is worth pointing out that Professor Watts has canvassed the possibility that the victim of a misrepresentation or other vitiating factor may prefer a partial rescission order to damages.[76] The argument essentially is that sometimes damages are very difficult to assess so why not allow the claimant to keep some part of the impugned transaction as damages equivalent and allow a refund for the rest? The difficulty with this is that it is partial rescission pure and simple and runs the risk of causing that uncertainty and incoherence in the law which was the previous argument against partial rescission.[77] For this reason the position taken here is in accord with Professor Watts' observation that "its absence from the remedial menu is hardly a source of serious injustice, or shame for the common law."[78]

H. Summary of Rescission

Rescission terminates a contract prospectively and retrospectively. The parties are released from future performance obligations and are restored to their pre-contractual position so far as rights and obligations incurred under the contract are concerned. This means that each party has restored to it any benefits it transferred under the contract to the other party and is indemnified against or compensated for other losses directly arising under it. But the rescinding party is not entitled to recover as part of rescission any consequential losses that flowed from the contract. This is a proper matter only for a damages award. The process of *restitutio in integrum* here described does not appear to be as exact as it used to be, with pecuniary payments being ordered in place of specific restitution. The latter may not fully reflect the purist form of integrated remedial regime but can be justified on the basis that difficulty in effecting *restitutio in integrum* should not too readily serve as an excuse to bar rescission.

Rescission is an 'as of right' remedy and does not depend on the discretion of the court as do specific performance and injunctions. Judicial assertions of discretion to refuse rescission are not strictly in keeping with this principle and may be indicative of the sort of unease Professor Bridge expressed that rescission should not be too easily available for innocent misrepresentation.[79] That unease may be tempered by remembering that contracts are rescinded because they should not have been entered into and this remains the case even for non-tortious misrepresentation. Section 2(2) of the Misrepresentation Act 1967 further reduces any drastic consequences

[76] Watts, in Bant and Harding (eds.), *supra note* 63.

[77] *Supra note* 71.

[78] Watts, in Bant and Harding (eds.), *supra note* 63, at 445.

[79] *supra note* 18.

of rescission in these situations. The law is uncertain as to whether rescission is a self-help remedy or requires a decree from the court. The view expressed previously is that self-help would make for a more integrated remedy. Rescission is an 'all or nothing' remedy which cannot be partial, although a partial rescission effect can be produced by creative application of the *restitutio in integrum* principle.

IV. DAMAGES

At this point the study of remedies for misrepresentation crosses the boundary between contract and tort. Rescission is a contract remedy because it cuts away a contract that should not have been made. Damages are awarded essentially for the different torts that different kinds of misrepresentation can be, although in the case of a wholly innocent misrepresentation where damages are awarded in lieu of rescission there is no tort committed but damages are probably best assessed on tort principles. In line with the argument presented in this charpter the quest is two-fold – damages awards which integrate with rescission, and damages awards for the different kinds of misrepresentation which integrate with one another.

A damages award which integrates with rescission must allow for rescission and damages to discharge separate but coherent functions in remedying the problems caused by the misrepresentation. The study so far has shown that rescission should be confined to restoring the parties to their pre-contractual positions "as regards the rights and obligations which have been created by the contract."[80] Further and consequential losses should be left to damages. Damages are capable of compensating for losses that can be remedied through rescission and to this extent damages can provide something close to the holistic remedy which this chapter argues rescission should not be. In this connection the tendency to award pecuniary rescission is interesting but it should not be thought that this leaves no role for traditional rescission. Remedying the problems caused by misrepresentation is not always just about money. The claimant may prefer specific rescission so far as this is possible, settling for pecuniary rescission where specific is impracticable, and suing for damages for consequential losses. In this way the integrity of the two remedies may be preserved and a specific role for one (rescission) sufficiently clearly delineated that rescission and damages integrate satisfactorily with one another.[81] The remainder of this chapter will concentrate on how the different damages awards for different misrepresentations integrate with one another. But first it may be useful to discuss one case on damages for misrepresentation to indicate the specific kind of loss that only damages can remedy.

[80] O'Sullivan, Elliott & Zakrzewski, *supra note* 19.

[81] *supra note* 31.

The case is the decision of the English Court of Appeal in *East v. Maurer*.[82] The claimants purchased one of the defendant's two hair dressing salons in Bournemouth substantially in reliance on his fraudulent misrepresentation that he did not intend to work regularly in the one he retained. The claimants sustained losses on the salon they purchased because its clientele migrated to the defendant's other salon where he continued to work regularly despite his representation that he would not. The claimants sold the salon they purchased at a loss and sued the defendant in the tort of deceit for all losses they argued were sustained as a result of the misrepresentation. These included the difference between the price paid for the salon (£20,000) and the price realised on resale (£7,500), trading losses sustained before they were able to sell the salon, and a further sum calculated to represent the profits they would have made had the misrepresentation not been made. The lost profits were the issue before the Court of Appeal, which decided that they were a proper matter for damages for misrepresentation because absent this false statement the claimants would have bought another, probably profitable salon, in the same town. The claimants also recovered the other losses claimed and to this extent it can be seen that damages can be a holistic remedy for misrepresentation. But if the claimants had been able to and preferred to rescind the contract for the purchase of the salon an order of rescission should only cover these other losses and not the lost profits. *Restitutio in integrum* would demand that the claimants get their money back minus credit for the value they received, plus compensation for trading losses that were an incidental part of the purchase they made, at least until the duty to mitigate demanded they accept a suitable opportunity to sell. It was because the claimants had mitigated their losses by selling the salon that rescission was no longer an option. The lost profits were consequential losses and could only be remedied via a damages award.

A. *Tort Damages*

Damages claims for misrepresentation are for tort. Tort damages aim to place the innocent party so far as money can in the position (s)he would have been in if the wrong had not been done. As the House of Lords recognised in *Smith New Court Securities Ltd v. Citibank* NA[83] the conventional starting point for tort damages is the 'out of pocket' measure, comparing the claimant's financial position before and after the wrong was done. Where it can be shown that the claimant would have earned profit from other business transactions had (s)he not made the contract induced by misrepresentation, then these profits are recoverable too because this

[82] [1991] 1 WLR 461 (C.A).

[83] [1997] AC 254 (HL).

is putting the claimant into the position (s)he would have been in if the wrong had not been done.[84]

B. Fraudulent Misrepresentation (Deceit)

The classic definition of deceit comes from the speech of Lord Herschell in *Derry v. Peek*.[85] It must be shown that a false statement was made "(1) knowingly, or (2) without belief in its truth, or (3) recklessly, careless whether it be true or false." This definition must not be applied mechanically and the need for clear and convincing proof of dishonesty must always be kept in mind.

Damages awards for deceit tend to be heavier than at least some other forms of misrepresentation in three respects. First, the 'out of pocket' measure is not limited by remoteness. All losses directly flowing from the deceit are recoverable even if they could not reasonably have been foreseen at the time of the tort.[86] Secondly, emphatic statements were made in the House of Lords in *Pearson and Son Ltd v. Lord Mayor of Dublin*,[87] many years before the Unfair Contract Terms Act 1977, squashing any argument to the effect that a contract clause might exclude liability for fraud. Thirdly, the House of Lords has also ruled out any defence of contributory negligence in cases of fraudulent misrepresentation.[88]

84 *East* v. *Maurer*, *supra* note 81; *Clef Acquitaine SARL* v. *Laporte Minerals (Barrow) Ltd* [2001] QB 488 (CA). In *4 Eng Ltd* v. *Harper* [2008] EWHC 915 (Ch), [2009] Ch 91 (ChD) David Richards J calculated these damages on a loss of chance basis. See Paul Mitchell, *Loss of Chance in Deceit* 125 Law Quarterly Rev. 12 (2009). See also *Parabola Investments Ltd* v. *Browallia Cal Ltd* [2010] EWCA Civ 486, [2011] QB 477, where the claimant's investment fund was drastically reduced by the fraud of the defendant. He recovered damages first to replenish the fund and second to compensate for the profits he would have made down to the date of the trial on the footing that the fund had been replenished.

85 (1889) 14 AC 337 (H.L), 374.

86 *Doyle* v. *Olby (Ironmongers) Ltd* [1969] 2 QB 158 (CA), applied in *Smith New Court Securities Ltd* v. *Citibank NA* [1997] AC 254 (HL). However, losses must still be caused by the misrepresentation, and subsequent falls in the market price of an asset sold after a misrepresentation are not likely to be recoverable. In *Downs* v. *Chappell* [1997] 1 WLR 426 (CA) the claimants failed to recover for a fall in the value of a bookshop that occurred after they refused reasonable offers to buy it. Note, however, that elsewhere in this volume Professor Devenney has drawn attention to some bewildering signs that causation is not always required in compensating losses for deceit. See James Devenney, *Re-examining Damages for Fraudulent Misrepresentation: Towards a More Measured Response to Compensation and Deterrence*. Note also that Professors Poole and Devenney have challenged a tendency to award high levels of damages against fraudulent misrepresentors on a speculative assessment of the misrepresentee's loss. This does not, however, challenge heavier damages awards for fraud so long as the losses are truly evidenced. See Jill Poole & James Devenney, *Reforming Damages for Misrepresentation: The Case for Coherent Aims and Principles*, Journal of Business Law 269 (2007).

87 [1907] AC 351 (H.L), 353–4 (Lord Loreburn LC), 356 (Earl of Halsbury), 360 (Lord Ashbourne), 362 (Lord James), and 365 (Lord Atkinson).

88 *Standard Chartered Bank* v. *Pakistan National Shipping Corporation* [2002] UKHL 43, [2003] 1 AC 959.

Moral rather than economic considerations explain why the courts have come down so heavily on fraudulent misrepresentation.[89] This is an eminently satisfactory reason for offering more extensive relief and presents no problems in terms of integrating damages awards for this kind of misrepresentation with other kinds. Although as noted previously[90] there is a tendency to lean in the claimant's favour in rescinding a contract for fraudulent misrepresentation this is only around the margins. The right place for penalising fraud or compensating it more extensively is in addressing its tortious consequences.

C. *Negligent Misstatement*

This tort is committed where in breach of a duty of care a defendant negligently makes a false statement either directly to the claimant or with knowledge that the statement will be passed on to the claimant.[91] The courts are very circumspect about the recognition of a duty of care to a large extent because a very large number of persons could be affected by a negligent misstatement. Hence there must be a very clear indication of the claimant's justifiable reliance on the defendant's statement.[92] As the relationship between contracting parties is to a greater extent adversarial,[93] a duty of care would be relatively rare in this context. One case where it was found was *Esso Petroleum Co Ltd v. Mardon*[94] but in that case the defendant (Esso) clearly had special knowledge about the likely throughput of the garage leased and also took it upon itself to advise the claimant about this. Furthermore as the statutory action for damages under section 2(1) of the Misrepresentation Act 1967 is so much easier for claimants and apparently offers the same measure of damages as for deceit the only value of a negligent misstatement action between contracting parties seems to be where a false statement other than a misrepresentation is made.[95] However as the argument later questions the appropriateness and utility value of the section 2(1) action and the power of the court to award damages in lieu of rescission under

89 See the speeches of Lord Browne-Wilkinson (263) and Lord Steyn (279–80) in *Smith New Court Securities Ltd* v. *Citibank NA* [1997] AC 254; I. Brown and A. Chandler, *Deceit, Damages and the Misrepresentation Act 1967, s. 2(1)* LLOYD'S MARITIME & COMMERCIAL L.QUARTERLY 40, 41–9 (1992).

90 N. 29 and text.

91 The first case to recognise a duty of care in these circumstances was *Hedley Byrne & Co Ltd* v *Heller & Partners* [1964] AC 265 (HL). Other important cases on this subject include *Smith* v *Eric S Bush* [1990] 1 AC 831 (HL), and *Caparo Industries Plc* v *Dickman* [1990] 2 AC 605 (HL).

92 See John Cartwright, MISREPRESENTATION, MISTAKE AND NON-DISCLOSURE 6.17 (2nd ed., Sweet & Maxwell: London 2007).

93 *Id.*, 6.28 citing *Walford* v. *Miles* [1992] 2 AC 128 (HL), 138 (Lord Ackner).

94 [1976] QB 801 (CA).

95 *E.g.*, an opinion.

section 2(2) of the 1967 Act an expanded role for negligent misstatement would be expected if sections 2(1) and 2(2) were to be repealed.

Reflecting the much less egregious nature of negligent misstatement this tort differs from deceit in all three of the areas mentioned previously. Damages awards are subject to remoteness,[96] and in principle may be reduced because of the claimant's contributory negligence.[97] Although no judicial decision appears to confirm this there seems no reason to doubt that an exclusion clause could eliminate or at least reduce the extent of liability for negligent misstatement.[98]

The damages remedy for negligent misstatement satisfactorily integrates with deceit and, as the argument later in relation to sections 2(1) and 2(2) of the Misrepresentation Act 1967 will try to show, should in future be the damages remedy for all non-dishonest misrepresentations.

D. Negligent Misrepresentation

The damages remedy for negligent misrepresentation contained in section 2(1) of the Misrepresentation Act 1967 was introduced following the recommendations of the Law Reform Committee.[99] The Committee believed that a misrepresentor who was at fault should be liable in damages. When it reported the only circumstances in which someone could obtain compensation for non-fraudulent misrepresentation was under an earlier incarnation of section 90 of the Financial Services and Markets Act 2000, which deals with false statements in company prospectuses soliciting offers for the purchase of shares.[100] *Hedley Byrne & Co Ltd v. Heller & Partners*[101] had not been decided and the Committee did not have the benefit of the House of Lords' cautionary words about overly extensive liability for negligent words. This decision

96 *South Australia Asset Management Corporation* v. *York Montague Ltd* [1997] AC 191 (HL).

97 *Platform Home Loans Ltd* v. *Oyston Shipways Ltd* [2000] 2 AC 190 (HL). However, as Sir Donald Nicholls V-C observed in *Gran Gelato Ltd* v. *Richcliff (Group) Ltd* [1992] Ch 560 (ChD), a contributory negligence argument which rested upon the claimant's reliance upon the defendant's words, as opposed to something else, is not likely to get very far, as if it were not reasonable to rely on the defendant's words, no duty of care would be owed.

98 The relevant statutory provision governing this is section 2 of the Unfair Contract Terms Act 1977. Section 3 of the Misrepresentation Act 1967, inserted by section 8 of the 1977 Act, deals with exclusions of liability for negligent misrepresentation and will be discussed later. Section 2 deals with exclusions of liability for negligence in general and provides that business liability for negligently caused personal injury or death cannot ever be excluded and that liability for other loss and damage is subject to the Act's reasonableness criteria.

99 Law Reform Committee Tenth Report, *Innocent Misrepresentation* (1962, Cmnd 1782).

100 The original statute was the Directors Liability Act 1890 passed in the aftermath of *Derry* v. *Peek*, which had insisted on proof of fraud before damages could be awarded. Whatever the merits of providing compensation in this discrete case these provisions do not support a general right to damages for non-fraudulent misrepresentation.

101 [1964] AC 265 (HL).

calls seriously into question whether there was any gap in the law of remedies for misrepresentation by the time of the Misrepresentation Act 1967.[102]

There are several specific problems with section 2(1) of the Misrepresentation Act 1967 which should be considered before returning to the overriding question of whether it should be repealed. To analyse these problems fully the provision should be set out in full:

> Where a person has entered into a contract after a misrepresentation has been made to him by another party thereto and as a result thereof he has suffered loss, then, if the person making the misrepresentation would be liable in damages in respect thereof had the misrepresentation been made fraudulently, that person shall be so liable notwithstanding that the misrepresentation was not made fraudulently, unless he proves that he had reasonable ground to believe and did believe up to the time the contract was made that the facts represented were true.

The analysis following will attempt to bring out the problems with section 2(1) by comparison with negligent misstatement.

Negligent misrepresentation is narrower than negligent misstatement in two respects. First, it only applies between parties to a contract and not in the additional non-contractual circumstances that negligent misstatement is mostly used in. Secondly, the closing words of section 2(1) – "the facts represented were true" – strongly suggest that only factual statements or statements falling within the brief description of misrepresentation earlier[103] are included in it. But it is considerably broader in three other respects, all of which are incompatible with an integrated system of remedies for misrepresentation. The first of these, that liability arises in the absence of a duty of care, will be considered later. The other incompatibilities will now be explained.

Secondly, all a misrepresentee needs to do in a case of negligent misrepresentation is prove that a false statement was made. Then the burden of proof shifts to the misrepresentor to show both reasonable grounds for believing the statement to be true and actual belief in its truth. The Law Reform Committee offered no justification for this recommendation other than the underlying assumption that there should be a right to damages for false statements accompanied by fault. It is undeniable that misrepresentations often cause loss over and above what is made good by rescission but this does not even begin to justify making the defendant liable for it. Even less does it justify making defendants liable unless they can prove their innocence.

Thirdly, it seems tolerably clear that the measure of damages for negligent misrepresentation is the same as for deceit: that is, it is not limited by remoteness. This

[102] John Cartwright, *supra note* 92, 7.17.

[103] *supra notes* 7 and 8. Statements of opinion, for example, would be excluded.

was what the Law Reform Committee recommended, justifying its position in the following terms:

> If the statement has in fact been fraudulent, no doubt the victim's right to be compensated is even clearer, but it is not in general the function of the civil law to grade the damages which an injured person may recover in accordance with the moral guilt of the defendant. The tort of deceit will still be needed for those cases where a fraudulent statement has induced a person to act to his detriment otherwise than by entering into a contract. There may also be some cases where the victim, for special reasons of his own, wishes publicly to brand the defendant as dishonest and therefore voluntarily takes upon himself the heavy burden of proof needed to establish fraud.[104]

There should be some pause for thought before the conclusion is reached that Parliament simply enacted the Law Reform Committee's recommendations in the Misrepresentation Act 1967 because negligent misstatement was born in between the Report and the 1967 Act. Indeed it has been stated that the view was originally held that negligent misstatement did not apply to pre-contractual statements.[105] However this view cannot be accepted now after *Esso Petroleum Ltd v. Mardon*[106] and so the task of synchronising negligent misrepresentation with the other damages remedies becomes even more difficult.

The most extensive judicial consideration of the damages measure for negligent misrepresentation came in *Royscot Trust Ltd v. Rogerson*[107] where a two judge Court of Appeal said *obiter* that the plain meaning of the statute[108] rendered remoteness irrelevant to the recoverability of damages.[109] This view has been doubted by several commentators. McGregor has written: "All that section 2(1) is purporting to say is this: before the Act the person induced by misrepresentation not forming part of the contract had only an action for fraudulent misrepresentation, now he has one

[104] *supra note* 99, at para 22. To the same effect see Patrick S. Atiyah and Guenter Treitel, *Misrepresentation Act 1967* 30 MODERN LAW REV. 369, 373 (1967) – "The measure of damages in the statutory action will apparently be that in an action of deceit."

[105] Richard Hooley, *Damages and the Misrepresentation Act 1967* 107 LAW QUARTERLY REV. 547, 549 (1991).

[106] [1976] QB 801 (CA).

[107] [1991] 2 QB 297 (CA). The earlier decision of Waller J in *Naughton* v *O'Callaghan* [1990] 3 All ER 191 also lends some support to this view. The judge (at 197) equated damages for fraud with section 2(1), but the question was not argued.

[108] *Id.*, 305–6 (Balcombe LJ), and 309 (Ralph Gibson LJ).

[109] Reliance was also placed on a number of *obiter* statements in other cases. See *F & B Entertainments Ltd* v. *Leisure Enterprises Ltd* (1976) 240 EG 455, at 461 (Walton J); *McNally* v. *Welltrade International Ltd* [1978] IRLR 497 (Sir Douglas Frank QC); *Chesneau* v. *Interhome Ltd* (1983) 134 *NLJ* 341 (Eveleigh LJ); *Andre & Cie* v. *Ets Michel Blanc et Fils* [1977] 2 Lloyd's Rep 166, 181 (Ackner J); *Cemp Properties (UK) Ltd* v. *Dentsply Research and Development Corporation (No 2)* [1989] 36 EG 90, 97–8 (Morritt J).

also for negligent misrepresentation."[110] Subsequent judicial pronouncements present no unanimous view. In *South Australia Asset Management Corporation v. York Montague Ltd* Lord Hoffmann, with whose speech the other Law Lords agreed, essentially equated section 2(1) with fraud.[111] In *Smith New Court Securities Ltd v. Citibank NA* Lord Steyn made clear that he was expressing no concluded opinion of the correctness of *Royscot Trust v. Rogerson* but put the question in terms of "whether the rather loose wording of the statute compels the court to treat a person who was morally innocent as if he was guilty of fraud when it comes to the measure of damages."[112] The basic problem with all these contrary views is that they attach insufficient weight to the express views of the Law Reform Committee and look for symmetry in the law which the Committee's recommendations never intended.

The 'fiction of fraud' underlying the argument that damages for negligent misrepresentation should be calculated on the same basis as for deceit also raises the question of whether the claimant's contributory negligence should result in a reduction of damages under section 2(1). If the words *so liable* in section 2(1) mean the same measure of damages as for fraud does it not follow that contributory negligence is similarly disregarded here as it is for fraud?[113] In *Gran Gelato Ltd v. Richcliff (Group) Ltd*,[114] Sir Donald Nicholls V-C treated contributory negligence as a defence to a section 2(1) claim where there was a concurrent claim for negligent misstatement. He founded himself on the decision of the Court of Appeal in *Forsikringsaktieselskapet Vesta v. Butcher*,[115] which decided that contributory negligence was a defence to concurrent claims in negligence and breach of a contractual duty of care. However, the Vice-Chancellor's reasoning strongly suggests that contributory negligence would still be a defence to a claim based entirely on section 2(1). This follows from his Lordship's analysis of sections 1(1) and 4 of the Law Reform (Contributory Negligence) Act 1945 in the context of section 2(1) of the 1967 Act. Section 1(1) of the 1945 Act provides for contributory negligence to apply "where any person suffers

[110] Harvey McGregor, McGregor on Damages 41–046 (17th ed., Sweet & Maxwell: London 2003). See also R. Hooley, *supra note* 105, and Ian Brown and Adrian Chandler, *Deceit, Damages and the Misrepresentation Act 1967, s.(1)* Lloyd's Maritime & Commercial Law Quarterly 40, 50 (1992) where it is argued "that the draftsman's intrusion of deceit was intended to be purely by way of explanation and analogy – the fraud of *Derry* v *Peek* being the only available source of damages for misrepresentation at the date of the Law Reform Committee's recommendations." The authors cite *Garden Neptune Shipping Ltd* v *Occidental Worldwide Investment Corp* [1990] 1 Lloyd's Rep 330 (CA), at 332, where Dillon LJ apparently read section 2(1) this way. Professor Bridge states that the reference to fraud in section 2(1) was merely to spare the draftsman the job of defining misrepresentation for the purposes of that subsection; see M. Bridge, *supra note* 18, 300.

[111] [1997] AC 191 (HL), 216.

[112] [1997] AC 254 (HL), 283.

[113] *Supra note* 87.

[114] [1992] Ch 560 (ChD).

[115] [1989] AC 852.

damage as the result partly of his own fault and partly of the fault of any other person." Section 4 defines 'fault' as "negligence, breach of statutory duty or other act or omission which gives rise to a liability in tort or would, apart from this Act, give rise to the defence of contributory negligence." The Vice-Chancellor reasoned that *liability* under section 2(1) of the 1967 Act is essentially founded on negligence, on the footing that the defendant had to show reasonable grounds for believing that the statement made was true. It is submitted that the distinction drawn here between a negligence theory for the purpose of determining liability and a fiction of fraud for the assessment of damages is an accurate reading of the statutory language.[116] Notwithstanding the theoretical availability of contributory negligence as a defence under section 2(1) it failed in *Gran Gelato*, and seems likely to fail in other cases, because of the obvious difficulty in the defendant contending that the claimant was careless in relying upon a statement that was intended to be relied upon.

In light of these problems there are two options for the future of section 2(1) – amendment or repeal. Amendment would require that the claimant prove negligence on the part of the defendant and would substitute a negligence based quantification of damages for the current fiction of fraud. This would be more integrated and fairer as it would not penalise the non-fraudulent misrepresentor excessively and effectively remove deceit actions from the law of misrepresentation. Negligent misstatement could co-exist with this reformed negligent misrepresentation action if confined to statements of opinion for which there is no remedy in misrepresentation. However, the better option, it is submitted, would be repeal. The justification for rescission for non-fraudulent misrepresentation is that the contract should not have been made. Rescission is a less extensive remedy than damages to reflect this. Damages require further justification and this exists only where the defendant is in breach of a duty of care. For this it is insufficient that the parties subsequently enter into a contract. Their relationship is insufficiently close at this stage to make that duty other than exceptional but in an appropriate case an assumption of responsibility can be found. The Law Reform Committee's reasons for recommending the statutory right to damages for negligent misrepresentation possessed some merit[117] so long as there was no right to any damages for negligent misrepresentation. But when the House of Lords decided *Hedley Byrne & Co v. Heller & Partners*[118] this recommendation should have become history.[119]

116 The Northern Ireland Court of Appeal found it unnecessary to decide whether contributory negligence was a defence to a claim under section 2(1) of the Misrepresentation Act (NI) 1967 in *Odyssey Cinemas Ltd* v *Village 3 Theatres Ltd* [2010] NICA 25 as there was a breach of contractual warranty claim in that case and contributory negligence is not a defence there.

117 Albeit not as to measure or burden of proof.

118 [1964] AC 465.

119 In passing acknowledgement should be afforded to the work of the Law Commission, whose consultation paper, *Consumer Insurance Law: Pre-Contract Disclosure and Misrepresentation* (2009, Law Com

E. *Innocent Misrepresentation*

Before the advent of the tort of negligent misstatement and the statutory right to damages under section 2(1) of the Misrepresentation Act 1967 'innocent misrepresentation' referred to all non-fraudulent misrepresentations. Now it refers to misrepresentations which do not ground any action for damages, either at common law or statute. Rescission is thus the primary remedial response to this kind of misrepresentation but the Law Reform Committee considered that there would be occasions when rescission for misrepresentations shorn of any kind of fault would be oppressive to the defendant. Hence the Committee recommended that the court should be empowered to award damages in lieu of rescission.[120] Section 2(2) of the Misrepresentation Act 1967 essentially implements this recommendation:

> Where a person has entered into a contract after a misrepresentation has been made to him otherwise than fraudulently, and he would be entitled, by reason of the misrepresentation, to rescind the contract, then, if it is claimed, in any proceedings arising out of the contract, that the contract ought to be or has been rescinded, the court or arbitrator may declare the contract subsisting and award damages in lieu of rescission, if of opinion that it would be equitable to do so, having regard to the nature of the misrepresentation and the loss that would be caused by it if the contract were upheld, as well as to the loss that rescission would cause to the other party.

Although damages in lieu of rescission in cases where there is no common law or statutory right to damages appear to be those cases the Committee most had in mind it should be noted that section 2(2) applies to all non-fraudulent misrepresentations. Thus the power to withhold rescission is not likely to arise in a case of negligent misstatement as that tort has little utility value in misrepresentation due to the more generous provision of section 2(1). But the court could decide that rescission should be denied in a case of negligent misrepresentation under section 2(1) and that damages in lieu be awarded instead. Where it does so, it is directed by section 2(3) to take account of any damages awarded under section 2(1) in making an award under

319), has resulted in the introduction of the Consumer Insurance (Disclosure and Representations) Bill (HL Bill 68) to the British Parliament in May 2011. This would make extensive amendment to insured persons' obligations of disclosure in making insurance contracts, but it would not fundamentally reform the law on misrepresentation generally. Also in passing reference may again be made to Jill Poole & James Devenney, *supra note* 86, where the authors attack the tendency to award fraud damages for negligent misrepresentation. While this article does not call for the repeal of section 2(1) it offers very little defence of it either.

120 Law Reform Committee (Tenth Report), *Innocent Misrepresentation* (1962, Cmnd 1782), paras 11–13. Although this report pre-dated the creation of rights to damages for negligent misrepresentations and the like, this recommendation should be seen in the context of the Committee's recommendation for a statutory right to damages for negligent misrepresentation.

section 2(2). Where the misrepresentee claims both rescission and damages under section 2(1) it is likely that any damages award would be reduced to avoid double compensation, and where rescission is refused the damages award increased to serve as a full substitute for rescission. Some misrepresentees may prefer the monetary remedy as it is capable of offering pecuniary rescission and compensation for consequential loss.

In the probably more usual context of rescission and wholly innocent misrepresentation the following three questions require some analysis:

1. Is the discretion to award damages in lieu of rescission dependent on the claimant retaining the right to rescind the contract?
2. On what basis should the discretion be exercised?
3. What are the proper principles applicable to the assessment of damages?

In relation to the first question the issue is whether the court can award damages in lieu of rescission where the right to rescind has been lost because of one of the bars to rescission discussed previously.[121] The words "if it is claimed … that the contract ought to be or has been rescinded" seem to suggest that the discretion would not be available in this case.[122] However, in *Thomas Witter Ltd v. TBP Industries Ltd*[123] Jacob J said *obiter* that this argument was "unattractive" because the unavailability of rescission at trial might have nothing to do with the behaviour of either party.[124] This view to some extent reflects the views discussed previously that rescission is a discretionary remedy,[125] but the latter is out of line with long-standing principle. A different view of section 2(2) was expressed by Judge Raymond Jack QC in *Government of Zanzibar v. British Aerospace (Lancaster House) Ltd.*[126] This view is a more natural reading of section 2(2) and seems to be widely accepted as correct.[127]

Assuming that the contract has been validly rescinded or that it is still possible to do so the court or arbitrator may declare the contract subsisting and award damages

121 *Supra notes* 33–45 and text.
122 This was the view of Atiyah and Treitel in Patrick S. Atiyah and Guenter Treitel, *Misrepresentation Act 1967* 30 MODERN LAW REV. 369, 377 (1967). It probably reflects the view of the Law Reform Committee (Cmnd 1782), para 27 (recommendation 3).
123 [1996] 2 All ER 573.
124 The judgment relied upon some *ex tempore* remarks of the Solicitor General made after 3 a.m. in the course of Parliamentary debate. See HC Official Report (5th series) cols 1388–9, 20 February 1967.
125 *Supra notes* 33–45.
126 [2000] 1 WLR 2333. This was part of the *ratio* of the judge's decision so carries more weight than Jacob J's *obiter dictum*. To similar effect see *Alton House Garages (Bromley) Ltd* v. *Monk* (unreported, Cantley J, 31 July 1981); *Atlantic Lines and Navigation Co Inc* v. *Hallam Ltd, The Lucy* [1983] 1 Lloyd's Rep 188, 201–2 (Mustill J).
127 Hugh Beale, *Damages in Lieu of Rescission for Misrepresentation* 111 LAW QUARTERLY REV 60 (1995).

in lieu of rescission if of opinion that it would be equitable to do so in light of the following factors:

(a) the nature of the misrepresentation;
(b) the loss that would be suffered by the misrepresentee if the contract were upheld;
(c) the loss that rescission would cause to the other party.[128]

The exercise of this discretion is illustrated by *William Sindall Plc v. Cambridgeshire County Council*.[129] There was no actionable misrepresentation in that case because the alleged misrepresentation (the existence of a private water fowl sewer on development land discovered nearly two years after the contract was entered into) was held to be a risk allocated to the claimants by the contract. Any actionable misrepresentation would have been wholly innocent, but the Court of Appeal went on to consider the section 2(2) discretion in case the matter proceeded to the House of Lords. Essentially the Court of Appeal would have awarded damages in lieu of rescission because the latter would have been excessive and disproportionate in the circumstances. The misrepresentation was of minor significance and would not have affected the value of the land for development purposes. The cost of removing the sewer would have been £18,000 in the context of a land development contract for some £5m. The reason the claimant buyers wanted to rescind was the considerable fall in land values in the late 1980s, which had rendered their investment loss making. Had the fall in land values been attributable to misrepresentation, the decision would probably have been different. The power to prevent rescission can be seen to be valuable in a case like this as otherwise this would have been a wholly disproportionate remedial response to any misrepresentation. The previous discussion[130] has indicated that some courts have apparently recognised disproportionality as a bar to rescission independently of section 2(2) but the legitimacy of this is doubtful to say the least. Whether the power to award damages instead of rescission is similarly valuable is another matter.

The most difficult issue concerning section 2(2) is how to quantify any damages award in lieu of rescission. The Law Reform Committee recommended that damages should be something similar to those that would be awarded for breach of a minor contractual warranty.[131] The Committee reasoned from the incongruity between rescinding a contract for a minor misrepresentation and having to settle

[128] In *William Sindall Plc* v. *Cambridgeshire County Council* [1994] 1 WLR 1016 (CA), 1042–3 Evans LJ suggested there might be additional relevant factors in individual cases, but the factors specifically mentioned in section 2(2) would be those to which most weight would be attached.

[129] *Id.*

[130] *Supra notes* 33–45.

[131] Law Reform Committee (Tenth Report), *Innocent Misrepresentation* (1962, Cmnd 1782), paras 11–13.

for a small sum in damages were the statement to become a term of the contract. In *William Sindall Plc v. Cambridgeshire County Council*[132] Hoffmann LJ would have awarded £18,000 (the cost of removing the sewer) on this basis. Evans LJ suggested a different contractual measure based on the difference between the value of the land the misrepresentee was misled into believing it was acquiring and the value it did acquire.[133] Russell LJ agreed with both judgments, which leaves the precise contractual measure unclear but at least is unanimous that these damages are not tortious. Another attempt to rationalise damages under section 2(2) was made by Jacob J in *Thomas Witter Ltd v. TBP Industries Ltd*[134] where it was suggested that a tort measure excluding consequential losses might be appropriate as damages *in lieu of* rescission.

In an integrated system of remedies for misrepresentation neither the tort nor the contract measure of damages is satisfactory. The tort measure is unsatisfactory because it either compensates for losses not made good by rescission or for all the claimant's losses. If rescission is to be withheld essentially because it is excessive, then damages would be equally excessive even if consequential losses are omitted. As Professor Beale has pointed out, the contract measure (which attempts to place the innocent party where it would have been if the contract had been performed) is a very uneasy fit into a remedial regime which generally seeks to place the innocent party in the position it would have been in if the contract had not been entered into.[135] It may produce a remedy that is not as extensive as rescission in particular cases but it requires the fiction of a warranty in a contract whose very existence is the problem an integrated system of remedies should be trying to solve.

If the problem here is, as Professor Bridge has argued,[136] that the remedies for innocent misrepresentation are not in harmony with those for breach of contract, would the solution not lie in abolition of the power to award damages in lieu of rescission for wholly innocent misrepresentation? Where a defendant has committed no tort and no breach of contract, what is the justification for awarding damages? Why should it be thought that because there has been a misrepresentation the misrepresentee must get something? Professor Bridge would argue that there should be no rescission and no damages in these cases. The alternative approach supported in this article accepts that sometimes rescission is appropriate for wholly innocent misrepresentation because misrepresentors should not generally be allowed to retain

132 [1994] 1 WLR 1016 (CA), 1037–8.

133 The two measures, cost of cure and difference in value, featured prominently in the decision of the House of Lords in *Ruxley Electronics and Construction Ltd* v *Forsyth* [1996] 1 AC 344.

134 [1996] 2 All ER 573 (ChD).

135 Hugh Beale, *Damages in Lieu of Rescission for Misrepresentation* 111 LAW QUARTERLY REV 60 (1995).

136 Michael Bridge, *Innocent Misrepresentation in Contract* 57 CURRENT LEGAL PROBLEMS 277, 298–302 (2004).

the benefit of a contract that would not have been entered into if no false statement had been made. But sometimes rescission would be excessive so the court should have discretion to refuse it. The preferred solution to this problem is an amendment to the section 2(2) power so that the court can bar rescission essentially on the current disproportionality grounds of that provision without awarding any damages in lieu.

F. *Comparative Perspectives*

The view presented in this chapter that damages should only be awarded where a tort has been committed seems to be the position for the most part in the United States and Australia. There seems to be no equivalent to the Misrepresentation Act 1967 in the federal systems of those countries. Rescission is the contract remedy in both countries.[137] In the United States damages are available for deceit and for two forms of non-fraudulent misrepresentation worth brief examination. Section 552 of the *Restatement of Torts (Second)* 1977 provides that "one who, in the course of his business, profession or employment, or in any other transaction in which he has a pecuniary interest, supplies false information for the guidance of others in their business transactions, is subject to liability for pecuniary loss caused to them by their justifiable reliance upon the information, if he fails to exercise reasonable care or competence in obtaining or communicating the information." This seems to be essentially similar to negligent misstatement in that it requires a special relationship importing a duty of care and proof of negligence. Section 552C provides that "[o]ne who, in a sale, rental or exchange transaction with another, makes a misrepresentation of a material fact for the purpose of inducing the other to act or to refrain from acting in reliance upon it, is subject to liability to the other for pecuniary loss caused to him by his justifiable reliance upon the misrepresentation, even though it is not made fraudulently or negligently." First impression of this is that it goes further even than section 2(2) of the Misrepresentation Act 1967 but section 552C(2) confirms that this is not so, as it provides that "[d]amages recoverable under [this] rule are limited to the difference between the value of what the other has parted with and the value of what he has received in the transaction." As the commentary following the rule makes clear damages under section 552C are essentially similar to pecuniary restitution following rescission. Before leaving this matter entirely it should be observed[138] that *Uniform Commercial Code* Article 2–313 usually makes

[137] For the USA see Allan Farnsworth, CONTRACTS 4.9–15 (3rd ed., Aspen: New York 1999). For Australia see O'Sullivan, Elliott & Zakrzewski, *supra note* 5.

[138] The author acknowledges the comments made to this effect by American delegates at the Current Issues in Commercial Contracts: Transatlantic Perspectives conference at the University of Sheffield on 10 September 2011.

it unnecessary in a sale of goods contract ever to rely on these principles of the *Restatement of Torts*. Article 2–313(2)(a) states that "any affirmation of fact or promise made by the seller which relates to the goods and becomes part of the basis of the bargain creates an express warranty that the goods shall conform to the affirmation or promise." In Article 2–313(3) it is stated that "it is not necessary to the creation of an express warranty … that the seller have a specific intention to make a warranty." This would make it comparatively easy to treat pre-contractual statements as contractual warranties as opposed to misrepresentations. The Northern Ireland Court of Appeal found an express warranty in *Odyssey Cinemas Ltd v. Village 3 Theatres Ltd*[139] and thus avoided difficult misrepresentation issues, applying English law principles which would require an intention to create a warranty. It is in no way suggested that the Court reasoned backwards from the conclusion that the claimant should win to an express warranty to enable it to do so, but any tendency to do this should be deprecated.

In Australia damages for misrepresentation at common law depend on establishing either the tort of deceit or negligent misstatement. In the ACT and South Australia the Civil Law (Wrongs) Act 2002 (ACT) section 174 and the Misrepresentation Act 1971 (SA) section 7(1) and (2) are modelled on the Misrepresentation Act 1967 section 2(1). But by far the most important protection against misleading statements in Australia is section 52 of the Trade Practices Act (Cwth) 1974 and the state provisions modelled on it.[140] The reach of the latter appears to be enormous and certainly much wider than misrepresentation. It thus does not detract much from the general observation that in Australia damages for misrepresentation usually require a tort to have been committed. The general view in the comparative systems discussed here essentially supports the argument advanced in this article that damages should only be awarded for misrepresentation where a tortious basis is established.

V. CONCLUSION – INTEGRATING DAMAGES WITH RESCISSION

A fully integrated system of remedies for misrepresentation, where damages integrated with rescission, would recognise that rescission avoids a contract that should not have been entered into and thus effects restitution and counter restitution of benefits and detriments directly arising under the contract. The justification for this is that the contract should not have been made so it is unnecessary to demonstrate that the misrepresentor was guilty of any tortious conduct. Since damages go further and compensate for consequential losses tortious conduct on the defendant's part

139 [2010] NICA 25.

140 For the position in Australia see generally Francis Trindade, Peter Cane & Mark Lunny, THE LAW OF TORTS IN AUSTRALIA 513–516 (4th ed., Oxford University Press: Oxford 2006).

is required to justify this remedy. Justification is demonstrated where the defendant has committed either of the torts of deceit or negligent misstatement. The more extensive damages remedy for deceit is justified by the more egregious nature of the conduct involved. It is understandable that the Law Reform Committee thought that there should be a damages remedy for negligent misrepresentation because there was no relief for consequential losses at the time it reported except for the special context of company prospectuses. Damages for misrepresentations shown to be negligent and limited to the measure of damages for negligent misstatement would not be wholly without merit. But here it should be remembered that the claimant can still rescind and is only being denied damages because the additional justification for the more extensive relief is not present. There is no justification whatever for awarding damages for purely innocent misrepresentation. The claimant can rescind unless this would be disproportionate within the meaning of section 2(2) of the Misrepresentation Act 1967.

17

Re-Examining Damages for Fraudulent Misrepresentation

Towards a More Measured Response to Compensation and Deterrence

James Devenney

This chapter will examine the assessment of damages for fraudulent misrepresentation in England and Wales. In so doing it will explore the nature of the damages awarded in such cases, highlighting the punitive and deterrent objectives inherent in such awards. The aim of the chapter is not to argue whether or not private law is the correct forum for punishing individuals. Rather the aim is to argue that, at times, judicial attitudes toward damages for fraudulent misrepresentation are "over-zealous"; and that, if punishment is appropriate in this arena, a much more measured approach needs to be adopted. The chapter will argue that the current law can grossly over-compensate the claimant whilst punishing the defendant in a disproportionate manner. The chapter will also make suggestions for the reform of this area of law.

> A policy of imposing more stringent remedies on an intentional wrongdoer serves two purposes. First it serves a deterrent purpose in discouraging fraud.... Secondly, as between the fraudster and the innocent party, moral considerations militate in favour of requiring the fraudster to bear the risk of misfortunes directly caused by his fraud. I make no apology for referring to moral considerations. The law and morality are inextricably interwoven. To a large extent the law is simply formulated and declared morality. And, as Oliver Wendell Holmes, The Common Law (ed. M. De W. Howe), p. 106, observed, the very notion of deceit with its overtones of wickedness is drawn from the moral world.
>
> *Smith New Court Securities v. Scrimgeour Vickers* (1997) A.C. 254 at 282 per Lord Steyn

I am grateful to Professor Mel Kenny (De Montfort University), Professor Bob Lee (Cardiff University), Professor David Campbell (Leeds University), Professor Allan Beever (University of South Australia), Professor Adrian Chandler (UWE), Dr. Paul Wragg (Leeds University), Dr. David Capper (QUB), Claire Devenney and Professor Jill Poole (Aston University) for their help in the preparation of this chapter. I am also indebted to the ESRC Centre for Business Relationships, Accountability, Sustainability and Society, Cardiff University, for its hospitality during my time there as a visiting scholar. I also wish to acknowledge my gratitude to the participants of the Current Issues in Commercial Contracts: Transatlantic Perspectives conference in Sheffield (September 2011), where an earlier version of this chapter was delivered.

I. INTRODUCTION

Etched into the law of contract in England and Wales is the dichotomy between terms and representations.[1] This distinction – broadly the distinction between those pre-contractual statements which become terms of the contract and those which do not[2] – is, of course, less significant than in previous times given the development of (wider) remedies for misrepresentation.[3] Nevertheless, the distinction remains important, as, although there is now a suite of remedies for misrepresentation, these remedies are different to those for breach of a contractual term. In particular, an action for damages for misrepresentation is largely an action in tort.[4] One oddity of this position is that damages for pre-contractual statements which were, in a general sense, not important enough to form part of the contract can sometimes, depending on the precise facts, exceed in quantum the damages which would have been payable had the statement in question been a contractual term. Of course, the shape of an award of damages for misrepresentation is linked to whether the misrepresentation is fraudulent, negligent or wholly innocent; and this chapter focuses on the measure and the overall approach to assessing damages for fraudulent misrepresentation. More specifically it is argued that the current approach to assessing damages for fraudulent misrepresentation, with its punitive flavour, needs to be revisited, not necessarily on the ground that punishment should be beyond the remit of civil courts, but as the current approach to the amount of punishment is unprincipled and depends on, for example, the extent of an unconnected fall in the market.

II. THE CRUCIBLE OF MISREPRESENTATION

In some ways, the law of contractual misrepresentation is law at an interface: the interface of the common law, equity and statute; and (more importantly for present purposes) the interface between tort and contract law. More specifically damages for fraudulent contractual misrepresentation are, of course, available through the

1 See, for example, Edwin Peel, TREITEL ON THE LAW OF CONTRACT, 13th ed., (Sweet & Maxwell: London, 2011) ch. 9.

2 On the possibility that a particular statement is both a representation and a contractual term see Misrepresentation Act 1967, s.1, *Esso v. Mardon* [1976] QB 801, and *Pritchard v. Cook* (unreported, 4 June 1998). An uncomfortable aspect of this possibility is that if the distinction between terms and representations is based on intention, this seems to mean that the statement in question was intended to be a term of the contract *and* not intended to be a term of the contract!

3 See Steven A. Smith, ATIYAH'S INTRODUCTION TO THE LAW OF CONTRACT (Clarendon, Oxford, 2006) Ch.5.

4 *Cf.* Misrepresentation Act 1967, s.2(2), which is discussed later at XI. 'Wider Considerations'.

tort of deceit, and, unsurprisingly, such damages adopt the tortious measure of damages:

> that sum of money which will put the party who has been injured, or who has suffered, in the same position as he would have been in if he had not sustained the wrong for which he is now getting his compensation or reparation.[5]

Yet the application of this measure to cases of fraudulent contractual misrepresentation raises a number of key issues. In particular, how does this measure of damages impact on the risk allocation inherent in the contract, and how should the courts deal with situations where the fraudulent misrepresentation is not the sole reason why the misrepresentee entered the contract.

III. FRAUDULENT MISREPRESENTATION AND CAUSATION

The relevant case law is replete with statements, often emanating (directly or indirectly) from cases on rescission, that the misrepresentation only needs to be 'a' reason why the misrepresentee entered the contract[6] or that the misrepresentation only needs to be a "real and substantial" inducement.[7] Indeed in *UCB Corporate Services Limited v Christine Ann Williams*[8] Jonathan Parker LJ stated:

> Expressed purely in terms of misrepresentation, the issue in the instant case is whether Mrs Williams was induced by the misrepresentation to execute the UCB Charge. In that context it matters not, in my judgment, whether, had she not been so induced, she would nevertheless have done so.[9]

Yet, as the Court of Appeal in this case also noted, there is a difference between (i) establishing an actionable (fraudulent) misrepresentation and (ii) determining the loss suffered as a result of the fraudulent misrepresentation (and hence the damages available). The difficulty for (ii) is, of course, the view that damages for fraudulent misrepresentation should be assessed on the basis that the misrepresentee would not have entered *into the transaction* but for the misrepresentation and that it is not open to the misrepresentor to advance evidence that the misrepresentee would have

5 *Livingstone v. Rawyards Coal Co.* (1880) 5 App. Cas 25 at 39 *per* Lord Blackburn.
6 See, for example, *Edgington v. Fitzmaurice* (1885) 24 Ch.D 459.
7 See, for example, *JEB Fasteners Ltd v. Marks, Bloom & Co* [1983] 1 All ER 583.
8 [2002] EWCA Civ 555.
9 *Id.* at [89].

entered into the, or at least a similar, transaction anyway.[10] Thus in *Doyle v. Olby (Ironmongers) Ltd*[11] Lord Denning MR stated:

> The defendant is bound to make reparation for all the actual damages directly flowing from the fraudulent inducement. The person who has been defrauded is entitled to say:
>
> "I would not have entered into this bargain at all but for your representation. Owing to your fraud, I have not only lost all the money I paid you, but, what is more, I have been put to a large amount of extra expense as well and suffered this and that extra damages."
>
> All such damages can be recovered.[12]

More recently in *Smith New Court Securities Ltd. v. Citibank* N.A.[13] Lord Steyn stated:

> The context is the rule that in an action for deceit the plaintiff is entitled to recover all his loss directly flowing from the fraudulently induced transaction.... In my view the orthodox and settled rule that the plaintiff is entitled to all losses directly flowing from the transaction caused by the deceit does not require a revision. In other words, it is not necessary in an action for deceit for the judge, after he had ascertained the loss directly flowing from the victim having entered into the transaction, to embark on a hypothetical reconstruction of what the parties would have agreed had the deceit not occurred. The rule in deceit is justified by the grounds already discussed.[14]

One problem with such a position is that where the misrepresentee would have in fact entered into the transaction (albeit, perhaps, on slightly different terms), the 'no-transaction' rule potentially allows the misrepresentee to recover for loss which he/she would have suffered even if the fraudulent misrepresentation had not been made, and the position is exacerbated by the willingness in the present context to move away from the date of transaction rule.[15] Of course there may be difficulty in

10 See, for example, *Smith v. Kay* (1859) 7 H.L. Cas. 750 at 759 *per* Lord Chelmsford LC; *Re Imperial Mercantile Credit Association* (1869) L.R. 9 Eq. 225 at 226 *per* James VC.

11 [1969] 2 QB 158.

12 *Id.* at 167.

13 [1997] A.C. 254. See generally Roger Halson, *Damages for the Tort of Deceit*, LLOYDS MARITIME AND COMPARATIVE LAW QUARTERLY 423 (1997).

14 *Id.* at 283 (emphasis added). *Cf.* the position at first instance where Chadwick J. seemed open to this possibility: [1992] BCLC 1104 at 1131–5.

15 In *Smith New Court Securities Ltd. v. Citibank* N.A. [1997] A.C. 254 at 282 Lord Steyn stated: "Significantly in the present context ... [damages are] ... not tied to any process of valuation at the date of the transaction. It is squarely based on the overriding compensatory principle, widened in view of the fraud to cover all direct consequences. The legal measure is to compare the position of the

establishing as a matter of evidence what the misrepresentee would have done if he/she had not been misled.[16] Thus in *United Motor Finance Co v Addison & Co Ltd*[17] the Privy Council stated:

> Nor can they modify the resulting damages on the footing that though in the absence of misrepresentation the plaintiff firm would not have made the contract with the defendants or with the hirer which it did in fact make, nevertheless even if it had known the facts it would have entered into some other contract and thus lost money in any event. It is not known, for example, whether any of the hirers could or would have paid a deposit of one-third of the real price, or what effect such payment might have had upon his subsequent action. It cannot be assumed that the plaintiff firm would have been willing to depart from its well considered terms – at all events without making special inquiry as to the hirer or asking for the defendants' guarantee.[18]

Yet it is one thing to give the misrepresentee the benefit of doubt where it is difficult to determine what he or she would have done if he or she had not been induced by the fraudulent misrepresentation in question; this might be done, as in some allied areas of law,[19] by reversing the burden of proof so that it is for the misrepresentor

plaintiff as it was before the fraudulent statement was made to him with his position as it became as a result of his reliance on the fraudulent statement."

16 In *Drincqbier v. Wood* [1899] 1 Ch. 393 at 403 Byrne J. noted: "Auguste Drincqbier was an honest and truthful witness. There is a passage I should like to refer to in the judgment of the Lord Chancellor (Lord Halsbury) in *Arnison v. Smith*, where he says: 'It is an old expedient, and seldom successful, to cross-examine a person who has read a prospectus, and ask him as to each particular statement what influence it had on his mind, and how far it determined him to enter into the contract. This is quite fallacious, it assumes that a person who reads a prospectus and determines to take shares on the faith of it can appropriate among the different parts of it the effect produced by the whole. This can rarely be done even at the time, and for a shareholder thus to analyse his mental impressions after an interval of several years, so as to say which representation in particular induced him to take shares, is a thing all but impossible. A person reading the prospectus looks at it as a whole, he thinks the undertaking is a fine commercial speculation, he sees good names attached to it, he observes other points, which he thinks favourable, and, on the whole, he forms his conclusion. You cannot weigh the elements by ounces.' To my mind, it is very frequently an extremely difficult thing for a man who has taken shares or debentures upon the faith of a prospectus, on being asked, 'Would you have taken the shares if something had been left out and something else put in?' to give a satisfactory answer, and probably in many cases his true answer would be, 'I can hardly answer that question, as I never saw a prospectus with the statement you mention in it.' In fact, Auguste Drincqbier took debentures on the faith of the prospectus and notice as he stated, and in my judgment he was influenced by statements contained in them, which I have held to be untrue. I think his answers on cross-examination meant that he placed more reliance on statements in the documents than on anything stated by H. Wood; and I have come to the conclusion that he is entitled to succeed."

17 [1937] 1 All ER 425.

18 *Id.* at 429.

19 See, for example, *CCC Films (London) Ltd v. Impact Quadrant Films Ltd* [1985] QB 16 at 40, where, in the context of a claim for breach of contract, Hutchinson J. stated, "I am impressed by, and respectfully adopt, the reasoning of Learned Hand C.J. in L. *Albert & Son v. Armstrong Rubber*

to prove that the misrepresentee would have entered the transaction in any event (there was no evidence to the effect in *United Motor Finance Co v Addison & Co Ltd*). Indeed *East v. Maurer*,[20] which will be discussed further later,[21] demonstrates a willingness of the courts to overcome evidential difficulties which cut the other way. However, it is entirely another matter to have a *conclusive* presumption, based on some vague policy notion that the misrepresentor must not qualify his or her wrong,[22] that the misrepresentee would not have entered the contract 'but for' the misrepresentation in question. Such a position was of concern to Hobhouse LJ in *Downs v. Chappell*,[23] who stated:

> In my judgment, having determined what the plaintiffs have lost as a result of entering into the transaction – their contract with Mr. Chappell – it is still appropriate to ask the question whether that loss can properly be treated as having been caused by the defendants' torts, notwithstanding that the torts caused the plaintiffs to enter into the transaction. If one does not ask this additional question there is a risk that the plaintiffs will be overcompensated or enjoy a windfall gain by avoiding a loss which they would probably have suffered even if no tort had been committed. This would offend the principle upon which damages are awarded.[24]

As a solution Hobhouse LJ proposed a cross-check:

> I consider that the appropriate way to give effect to these legitimate concerns is to compare the loss consequent upon entering into the transaction with what

Co. (1949) 178 F. 2d 182 and I do so the more readily because, as I have already mentioned, that case and *Bowlay Logging Ltd. v. Domtar Ltd* [1978] 4 W.W.R. 105 were relied upon by Ackner L.J. in *C. & P. Haulage v. Middleton* [1983] 1 W.L.R. 1461 in a different context without eliciting from Ackner L.J. any adverse comment on this point. Even without the assistance of such authorities, I should have held on principle that the onus was on the defendant. It seems to me that at least in those cases where the plaintiff's decision to base his claim on abortive expenditure was dictated by the practical impossibility of proving loss of profit rather than by unfettered choice, any other rule would largely, if not entirely, defeat the object of allowing this alternative method of formulating the claim. This is because, notwithstanding the distinction to which I have drawn attention between proving a loss of net profit and proving in general terms the probability of sufficient returns to cover expenditure, in the majority of contested cases impossibility of proof of the first would probably involve like impossibility in the case of the second. It appears to me to be eminently fair that in such cases where the plaintiff has by the defendant's breach been prevented from exploiting the chattel or the right contracted for and, therefore, putting to the test the question of whether he would have recouped his expenditure, the general rule as to the onus of proof of damage should be modified in this manner."

20 [1991] 2 All ER 733.

21 At VI 'Accentuating the Punishment'.

22 See *Livingstone v. Rawyards Coal Co.* (1880) 5 App. Cas 25 at 39 *per* Lord Blackburn.

23 [1997] 1 WLR 426.

24 *Id.* at 443.

would have been the position had the represented, or supposed, state of affairs actually existed.[25]

In *Smith New Court Securities Ltd. v. Citibank* N.A. the House of Lords disapproved of this cross-check. Whilst it is disappointing that the House of Lords failed to deal with the problem of potential overcompensation in that case, Hobhouse LJ's precise cross-check is difficult to support in so far as it appears, to some extent, to conflate the tortious and contractual measures of damages.

IV. IMPACT ON RISK ALLOCATION

As noted earlier, the law of contractual misrepresentation is at the interface between tort and contract law and an issue related to the potential for the measure of damages to result in overcompensation is the potential for it to undermine the risk allocation inherent in the contract. This can be illustrated by an example based, loosely, on *Smith New Court Securities v. Scrimgeour Vickers*. X and Y are negotiating for the sale and purchase of some shares in company Z; the relevant shares are trading at 78p per share and X (the seller) makes a fraudulent misrepresentation that others are interested in the shares. Accordingly, Y purchases 28 million shares at 82.25p per share. It later transpires that company Z has been subjected to a major, although unrelated, fraud and Y can only dispose of the shares at 40–30p each (resulting in a £11 million loss for Y). If Y would have purchased the shares at 78p per share if X would not have made the fraudulent misrepresentation, what loss can Y claim from X? 82.25p minus 78p per share? Or 82.25p minus 40–30p per share? In *Smith New Court Securities v. Scrimgeour Vickers*, of course, the House of Lords opted for the latter measure, thus meaning that the misrepresentee was able to recover loss which they would have suffered even if the fraudulent misrepresentation had not been made; and, to a certain extent, was indemnified for loss arising from a risk which was both inherent in the transaction (that the price of the shares might fall)[26] and unconnected to X's fraudulent misrepresentation.

[25] *Id.* at 444.

[26] *Cf. Henderson v Merrett Syndicates Ltd (No.1)* [1995] 2 A.C. 145 at 193–4, where Lord Goff stated: "the common law is not antipathetic to concurrent liability, and that there is no sound basis for a rule which automatically restricts the claimant to either a tortious or a contractual remedy. The result may be untidy; but, given that the tortious duty is imposed by the general law, and the contractual duty is attributable to the will of the parties, I do not find it objectionable that the claimant may be entitled to take advantage of the remedy which is most advantageous to him, subject only to ascertaining whether the tortious duty is so inconsistent with the applicable contract that, in accordance with ordinary principle, the parties must be taken to have agreed that the tortious remedy is to be limited or excluded."

V. NEGLIGENT CONTRACTUAL MISREPRESENTATION

A more restrained approach to damages for negligent misrepresentation is evident at least at common law.[27] For example, in *South Australia Asset Management v. York Montague*[28] Lord Hoffmann stated:

> normally the law limits liability to those consequences which are attributable to that which made the act wrongful. In the case of liability in negligence for providing inaccurate information, this would mean liability for the consequences of the information being inaccurate. [29]

In the passage quoted at the beginning of this chapter from *Smith New Court Securities v. Scrimgeour Vickers*, Lord Steyn suggests that the desire to punish the fraudulent misrepresentee is behind the different measures of damages for fraudulent and negligent (at common law) misrepresentation, a position acknowledged by Lord Hoffmann in *South Australia Asset Management v. York Montague*:

> There is no reason in principle why the law should not penalise wrongful conduct by shifting on to the wrongdoer the whole risk of consequences which would not have happened but for the wrongful act.[30]

[27] *Cf.* S.2(1) Misrepresentation Act 1967, which states: "Where a person has entered into a contract after a misrepresentation has been made to him by another party thereto and as a result thereof he has suffered loss, then, *if the person making the representation would be liable to damages in respect thereof had the misrepresentation been made fraudulently, that person shall be so liable notwithstanding that the misrepresentation was not made fraudulently*, unless he proves that he had reasonable grounds to believe and did believe up to the time the contract was made that the facts represented were true" (emphasis added). See generally Patrick S. Atiyah & Gunter Treitel, *Misrepresentation Act 1967*, 30 Modern Law Review 369 (1967). In *Royscot Trust v. Rogerson* [1991] 2 QB 297, s.2(1) was essentially interpreted as requiring the same measure of damages as in cases of fraudulent misrepresentation (although see Richard Hooley, *Damages and the Misrepresentation Act 1967* 107 Law Quarterly Review 547 (1991)). *Cf. Pankhania v. Hackney LB* [2004] EWHC 323 and *Avon Insurance v. Swine Fraser* [2000] CLC 665.

[28] [1996] 3 All ER 365.

[29] *Id.* at 371. Lord Hoffmann also noted (at 365): "The distinction between the 'no-transaction' and 'successful transaction' cases is of course quite irrelevant to the scope of the duty of care. In either case, the valuer is responsible for the loss suffered by the lender in consequence of having lent upon an inaccurate valuation. When it comes to calculating the lender's loss, however, the distinction has a certain pragmatic truth. I say this only because in practice the alternative transaction, which a defendant is most likely to be able to establish is that the lender would have lent a lesser amount to the same borrower on the same security. If this was not the case, it will not ordinarily be easy for the valuer to prove what else the lender would have done with his money. But in principle there is no reason why the valuer should not be entitled to prove that the lender has suffered no loss because he would have used his money in some altogether different but equally disastrous venture."

[30] *Id.* at 374.

Yet surely, in these circumstances, this is tantamount to awarding a head of indirect exemplary damages?[31] Moreover, whatever justification there might be for such a measure in cases of fraud, there is even less justification for such a measure in cases under s.2(1) Misrepresentation Act 1967, where the courts are dealing, in broad terms,[32] with negligence.[33]

VI. ACCENTUATING THE PUNISHMENT

The penal element of the measure of damages in cases of fraudulent, and to some extent 'negligent' under s.2(1) Misrepresentation Act 1967,[34] misrepresentation is also accentuated by a number of factors, some of which are discussed in this section of the chapter. The aim of this section is not necessarily to criticise these individual factors (although critical comment will be offered in relation to some of them); it is to highlight the cumulative effect of the inflexible no-transaction rule and these factors on the resultant calculation of damages in cases of fraudulent misrepresentation. Thus, first, damages for fraudulent misrepresentation are not really constrained by a remoteness test:

> (4) Concentrating on the tort measure, the remoteness test whether the loss was reasonably foreseeable had been authoritatively laid down in The Wagon Mound in respect of the tort of negligence a few years before *Doyle v. Olby (Ironmongers) Ltd.* was decided … *Doyle v. Olby (Ironmongers) Ltd.* settled that a wider test

[31] One is reminded of the words of Lord Reid in *Broome v. Cassell* [1972] AC 1027 at 1086: "That meant that the plaintiff, by being given more than on any view could be justified as compensation, was being given a pure and undeserved windfall at the expense of the defendant, and that in so far as the defendant was being required to pay more than could possibly be regarded as compensation he was being subjected to pure punishment."

[32] *Cf. Howard Marine v. Ogden* [1978] QB 574.

[33] In *Smith New Court Securities v. Scrimgeour Vickers* [1997] AC 254 at 282 Lord Steyn stated: "In *Royscot Trust Ltd. v. Rogerson* [1991] 2 QB 297 the Court of Appeal held that under section 2(1) of the Misrepresentation Act 1967 damages in respect of an honest but careless representation are to be calculated as if the representation had been made fraudulently. The question is whether the rather loose wording of the statute compels the court to treat a person who was morally innocent as if he was guilty of fraud when it comes to the measure of damages." There has been trenchant academic criticism of the Royscot case: see Richard Hooley, *Damages and the Misrepresentation Act 1967* (1991) 107 LQR 547. Since this point does not directly arise in the present case, I express no concluded view on the correctness of the decision in the Royscot case. See generally Ian Brown & Adrian Chandler, *Deceit, Damages and the Misrepresentation Act 1967, s.2(1)*, LLOYDS MARITIME AND COMMERCIAL LAW QUARTERLY 40 (1992).

[34] Although the 'fiction of fraud' under s.2(1) Misrepresentation Act 1967 has not been followed to its logical conclusion: see *Gran Gelato Ltd v Richcliff (Group) Ltd* [1992] Ch. 560 (contributory negligence) and Adrian Chandler & Steven Higgins, *Contributory Negligence and the Misrepresentation Act 1967, s.2(1)*, LLOYDS MARITIME AND COMMERCIAL LAW QUARTERLY 326, (1994).

> applies in an action for deceit. (5) The dicta in all three judgments, as well as the actual calculation of damages in *Doyle v. Olby (Ironmongers) Ltd.*, make clear that the victim of the fraud is entitled to compensation for all the actual loss directly flowing from the transaction induced by the wrongdoer. That includes heads of consequential loss.[35]

Second, damages for fraudulent misrepresentation are not reduced on account of any contributory negligence on the part of the misrepresentee.[36] Nor, it seems, are damages for fraudulent misrepresentation reduced on account of deceitful conduct by the *misrepresentee* (despite the fact that it might be thought that this would act as a counter-balance to any policy of making an intentional wrongdoing liable for all of the loses resulting from the transaction[37]). Third, this penal element may be supplemented by the availability of aggravated damages.[38] Fourth, such an award may be accentuated by the availability of damages for mental distress[39] and the possible exemplary dimension to such damages.[40] Fifth, it is at least very difficult, some might argue even impossible,[41] to limit liability for loss, even consequential loss, resulting from fraud.[42] Finally, whilst fraud is a serious allegation which must be distinctly proven,[43] once fraud is established, a court may be prepared to accept

35 *Smith New Court Securities v. Scrimgeour Vickers* [1997] AC 254 at 282 *per* Lord Steyn.

36 See *Alliance & Leicester v. Edgestop* [1994] 2 All ER 38, *Corporacion Nacional del Cobre de Chile v.. Sogemin Metals* [1997] 2 All ER 917 and *Nationwide Building Society v. Thimbleby* (1999) EGCS 34.

37 *Cf.* HLA Hart & Tony Honore, CAUSATION IN THE LAW (2nd ed., Oxford University Press: 1985) at 304; See *Standard Chartered Bank v. Pakistan National Shipping Co.* [1998] 1 Lloyd's Rep 684 (Cresswell J); [2000] 1 Lloyd's Rep 218 (CA, Evans LJ, Aldous LJ & Ward LJ asking for more argument); [2000] 2 WLR 1692 (CA, Evans LJ, Aldous LJ & Ward LJ); [2002] UKHL 43 (HL).

38 See, for example, *Archer v. Brown* [1985] QB 401.

39 See, for example, *East v. Maurer* [1991] 2 All ER 733.

40 See *Addis v. Gramophone Co Ltd* [1909] AC 488, particularly at 493 *per* Lord Atkinson, and 497, where Lord Collins stated: "the question which at the close of the argument I desired time to consider was whether in an action for wrongful dismissal the jury, in assessing the damages, are debarred from taking into their consideration circumstances of harshness and oppression accompanying the dismissal and any loss sustained by the plaintiff from the discredit thus thrown upon him. The jury in this case obviously did take these circumstances into consideration, for they assessed the damages at 600l. The contention of the defendants is that the damages must be limited to the salary to which the plaintiff was entitled for the six months between October, 1905, and April, 1906, together with the commission which the jury should think he would have earned had he been allowed to manage the business himself; that the manner of the dismissal itself has never been allowed and ought not to be allowed to influence damages in this kind of case. This contention goes the length of affirming that in cases of wrongful dismissal it is beyond the competence of a jury to give what are called exemplary or vindictive damages, and it was this point that I desired to consider further."

41 Edwin Peel, TREITEL ON THE LAW OF CONTRACT (13th ed., Sweet and Maxwell: 2011) at 261.

42 See, for example, *HIH Casualty & General Insurance v. Chase Manhattan Bank* [2003] UKHL 6.

43 See, for example, *Rafsanjan Pistachio Co-operative v. Bank Leumi Plc* [1992] 1 Lloyd's Rep 513 at 525.

certain losses on fairly flimsy evidence as, for example, in *East v. Maurer*,[44] where damages were awarded for the hypothetical profits the misrepresentee would have made if they had not bought the hair-dressing saloon in question but had instead bought another hair-dressing saloon in the Bournemouth area; and this was done despite the apparent paucity of evidence in front of the court on the availability of such an alternative![45]

VII. EXEMPLARY DAMAGES

One of the most striking features about the foregoing is that the courts appear to be doing indirectly that which would be highly controversial if it were done directly, namely, awarding exemplary damages in civil cases.[46] As Lord Reid noted in *Broome v. Cassell*:

> On the other hand when we came to examine the old cases we found a number which could not be explained in that way. The sums awarded as damages were more – sometimes much more – than could on any view be justified as compensatory, and courts, perhaps without fully realising what they were doing, appeared to have permitted damages to be measured not by what the plaintiff was fairly entitled to receive but by what the defendant ought to be made to pay as punishment for his outrageous conduct.... I thought and still think that that is highly anomalous. It is confusing the function of the civil law which is to compensate with the function of the criminal law which is to inflict deterrent and punitive penalties.[47]

The purpose of this chapter is not to reopen that debate into the desirability of exemplary damages in the civil law; the purpose is to argue that *if* exemplary damages are to be available for fraudulent misrepresentation, they should be awarded on a more principled basis: "...their availability (and assessment) must be placed on a clear, principled basis".[48] Yet, it has to be questioned whether an approach where the punishment depends on (a) the misrepresentee having suffered a loss as

[44] [1991] 2 All ER 733, noted Jonathan Marks, *Loss of Profits in Damages for Deceit* (1992) 108 Law Quarterly Review 386–389.

[45] See, generally, Jill Poole & James Devenney, *Reforming Damages for Misrepresentation: The Case for Coherent Aims and Principles*, Journal of Business Law 269 (2007). See also *Davis v. Churchward* (unreported, 6 May 1993), noted Adrian Chandler, *Fraud, Damages and Opportunity Costs*, 100 Law Quarterly Review 35 (1994).

[46] See generally Allan Beever, *The Structure of Aggravated and Exemplary Damages*, 23 Oxford Journal of Legal Studies 87–110 (2003).

[47] [1972] AC 1027 at 1086.

[48] Law Commission Report on Aggravated, Exemplary and Restitutionary Damages, (LC247), para. 1.16.

a result of entering *into the transaction* (allied to the fact that the misrepresentee would have suffered some (or all) of that loss notwithstanding the misrepresentation given, for example, the fact that he or she would have entered into the transaction anyway) and (b) where the amount of punishment essentially depends on how bad a bargain turns out to be for the misrepresentee (which, for example, may depend on whether or not the market has *happened to fall*), can accurately be described as "principled".

VIII. PROPORTIONALITY

Related to this is the question of proportionality and linking the punishment to the 'crime'. Fraud in this context was, as is well known, defined in fairly tight terms by Lord Herschell in *Derry v. Peek*[49]:

> I think the authorities establish the following propositions: First, in order to sustain an action of deceit, there must be proof of fraud, and nothing short of that will suffice. Secondly, fraud is proved when it is shewn that a false representation has been made (1) knowingly, or (2) without belief in its truth, or (3) recklessly, careless whether it be true or false. Although I have treated the second and third as distinct cases, I think the third is but an instance of the second, for one who makes a statement under such circumstances can have no real belief in the truth of what he states.[50]

The essence of fraud is, of course, dishonesty.[51] Yet, even within this framework, there may be different degrees of culpability.[52] Here one can draw an analogy with the approach to sentencing for fraud in criminal cases where the *Sentencing Council* ('Sentencing for Fraud – Statutory Offences', October 2009) has stated:

> the court must consider the offender's culpability in committing the offence and any harm that the offence caused, was intended to cause, or might foreseeably have caused. Key considerations are the degree of planning, the determination with which the offender carried out the offence and the value of the money or property involved … culpability will vary according to the offender's motivation, whether the offence was planned or spontaneous and whether the offender was in a position of trust.

[49] (1889) 14 App. Cas. 337.

[50] *Id.*, at 374.

[51] See *Thomas Witter Ltd v TBP Industries Ltd* [1996] 2 All ER 573. See also *Reese River Silver Mining Co. Ltd v. Smith* (1869) 14 App. Cas. 337 at 374 *per* Lord Cairns.

[52] *Cf. Rookes v. Barnard* [1964] AC 1129 at 1228 *per* Lord Devlin: "Everything which aggravates or mitigates the defendant's conduct is relevant."

A number of factors are listed as relevant to sentencing for fraud in this context including the difference between loss intended and resulting (para. 20), any aggravating factors such as whether or not there are multiple victims (para. 22), any mitigating factors such as the fact that the behaviour was not fraudulent from the outset (para. 32), and any personal mitigation factors such as a voluntary restitution (para. 44). By contrast in civil law, the current method of (indirectly) punishing the fraudulent misrepresentor through the measure of damages is much more blunt, and, accordingly, much less able to deal with differing degrees of culpability in relation to fraudulent misrepresentation. Thus, for example, the current approach does not take account of whether or not the misrepresentor intended to confer a benefit on himself,[53] any 'good faith' on the part of the misrepresentor,[54] and whether or not the misrepresentor was trying to help the misrepresentee.[55] Nor does the current civil law approach provide much scope for consideration of factors such as previous instances of fraud.

IX. FURTHER DANGERS OF THE COMPENSATION MYTH

The foregoing also suggests a further problem with the current approach: the myth that damages for fraudulent misrepresentation are purely compensatory risks the misrepresentor being punished twice when criminal sanctions[56] are also available. Indeed the myth that damages for fraudulent misrepresentation are purely compensatory risks triple punishment where a direct award of exemplary damages is also awarded[57] and criminal and/or professional[58] sanctions are also available.[59] The

53 See, for example, *Arnison v. Smith* (1889) 14 App. Cas. 337 at 374.

54 See, for example, *Polhill v. Walter* (1832) 3 B & Ad. 114 (where an agent who represented that he had authority, knowing that he did not have such authority but believing his actions would be ratified, was found guilty of deceit); see Edwin Peel, TREITEL ON THE LAW OF CONTRACT, *supra* note 42, at 375.

55 See, for example, *Smith v. Chadwick* (1884) 9 App. Cas 187 at 201, where Lord Blackburn stated: "I may say, though it is not necessary for the decision of the case, that I think, as a matter of law, the motive of the person saying that which he knows not to be true to another with the intention to lead him to act on the faith of the statement is immaterial. The defendants might honestly believe that the shares were a capital investment, and that they were doing the plaintiff a kindness by tricking him into buying them. I do not say this is proved, but if it were, if they did trick him into doing so, they are civilly responsible as for a deceit."

56 For example, under the Fraud Act 2006 or under the Consumer Protection from Unfair Trading Regulations 2008 (SI 2008/1277). Note also the s.130, Powers of Criminal Courts (Sentencing) Act 2000, on compensation orders in relation to certain criminal offences (and *cf.* s.134 on double recovery).

57 On which see later at X. 'Availability of Exemplary Damages for Fraudulent Misrepresentation'.

58 See, for example, *Levy v. General Medical Council* [2011] EWHC 2351 (Admin).

59 Of course, the courts should take into account any other punishment received by the misrepresentee but the circumstances, and timing, of the case(s) may make this difficult to achieve. See,

converse problem is where the misrepresentee has suffered no loss (or would not, in fact, have entered the transaction were it not for the misrepresentation and so the loss *does* represent their *actual* loss) and, so, the scope for punishing the fraudulent misrepresentor, through an expansive damages award, is much more limited.[60] This, worryingly for those who would argue that a fraudulent misrepresentor should be punished through the civil law, may result in a fraudulent misrepresentor going unpunished (subject now, it seems, to a direct award of exemplary damages, which tend, at present, to be subject to a glass ceiling).[61] This appeared to prompt the Court of Appeal in *Clef Aquitaine SARL v Laporte Materials (Barrow) Ltd*[62] to adopt a creative approach to finding loss; essentially the Court of Appeal awarded damages on the basis that although the misrepresentee was induced to enter into a profitable

for example, *Archer v. Brown* [1985] QB 401, where the misrepresentee was already in prison but had an appeal pending, Peter Pain J stating (at 423): "It seems to me, therefore, that the door, on the authorities, is open but there are other considerations which make it unnecessary for me to decide whether to plunge through it. I do not think that the argument that the defendant could not make a profit here defeats the plaintiff's claim. It seems to follow from what Lord Diplock said in *Broome v. Cassell & Co. Ltd.* [1972] A.C. 1027, 1130, that the wrongdoer may be caught if he weighs the risk of loss against the chance of getting away with it. In this case, as one sees from the course of proceedings, the defendant could well have got away with it against a less determined plaintiff. But what seems to put the claim under this head out of court is the fact that exemplary damages are meant to punish and the defendant has been punished. Even if he wins his appeal he will have spent a considerable time in gaol. It is not surprising that there is no authority as to whether this provides a defence, since there is no direct authority as to whether exemplary damages can be given in deceit. I rest my decision on the basic principle that a man should not be punished twice for the same offence. Since he has undoubtedly been punished, I should not enrich the plaintiff by punishing the defendant again." *Cf.* also *McNally v. Welltrade International Ltd* [1978] IRLR 497.

60 A glimpse into the problems of relying solely on criminal sanctions can be gleaned from the Law Commission's Consultation Paper *Consumer Redress for Misleading and Aggressive Practices*, (No. 199) which noted at 1.9–1.11: "In 2009, Consumer Focus said to us that the existing private law is overly complex, too difficult to use and leaves many gaps. They called for a new right to provide compensation for all consumers who have suffered loss through a breach of the Regulations. . . .In 2009/10, TSS brought 173 prosecutions under the Regulations. Consumer Focus suggests that the level of enforcement 'pales into insignificance' compared with the extent of the problem. Enforcement would be more effective if public authorities and consumers 'worked in tandem', using both private and public enforcement sanctions against misleading and aggressive practices. These calls have been echoed at European level. In January 2009, the European Parliament passed a resolution calling upon member states 'to consider the necessity of giving consumers a direct right of redress in order to ensure that they are sufficiently protected against unfair commercial practices'. In July 2010, the European Parliament's Internal Market and Consumer Protection committee identified a private right of redress as one of the options for improving the enforcement of the Directive."

61 See later at X. 'Availability of Exemplary Damages for Fraudulent Misrepresentation'. *Cf. 4 Eng Ltd v. Harper* [2008] EWHC 915 (noted Paul Mitchell *Loss of Chance in Deceit*, 125 Law Quarterly Review 12–16 [2009]).

62 [2001] Q.B. 488.

transaction, it would have entered into an even more profitable transaction if the misrepresentation had not been made! Sedley LJ stated:

> The choice presented by the appeal was therefore to award Mr Gwyer's companies the damages calculated by the judge or to let them go empty-handed having decided that they had been cheated by being overcharged. Only a lawyer could begin to understand a form of reasoning which led to the second of these results, and it is agreeable to be able to concur in different reasoning which produces a result corresponding far better with justice in this particular case.

If the civil courts are to be able to punish a fraudulent misrepresentor, a more appropriate way of so doing is through a direct award of exemplary damages rather than indirectly through the general measure of damages (and a reliance on, for example, a fall in the market). Such an approach would obviously require appropriate principles to be developed.[63] This would allow a more nuanced approach to punishment.

X. AVAILABILITY OF EXEMPLARY DAMAGES FOR FRAUDULENT MISREPRESENTATION

One difficulty, of course, is the view that exemplary damages are not available for fraudulent misrepresentation.[64] Yet *Kuddus v. Chief Constable of Leicester*[65] raised the possibility that exemplary damages may be available for deceit,[66] and in *Banks v. Cox*[67] Lawrence Collins J stated:

> The relationship between aggravated and exemplary damages, and their application in cases of deceit, has not been fully worked through, but I accept that in principle they may be awarded: see *Archer v Brown* [1985] QB 401; *Kuddus v. Chief Constable of Leicester* [2001] 2 WLR 1789, 1821.[68]

Moreover in *Parabola Investments Ltd v. Browallia Cal Ltd*[69] Flaux J. stated:

> my own researches and enquiries have revealed, exemplary damages have been awarded in cases of deceit, primarily in the case of fraudulent insurance claims by insureds dealt with in the county courts.[70]

63 Cf. Sentencing Council, 'Sentencing for Fraud – Statutory Offences', October 2009.

64 See, for example, *Broome v. Cassell* [1972] A.C. 1027 at 1076 *per* Lord Hailsham LC, *cf. Mafo v. Adams* [1970] 1 QB 548 at 558 *per* Widgery LJ.

65 [2001] 2 WLR 1789.

66 See, in particular, Lord Scott at [122].

67 [2002] EWHC 2166.

68 *Id.*, at [13].

69 [2009] EWHC 901 (Comm). See also *Parabola Investments Ltd v. Browallia Cal Ltd* [2010] EWCA Civ 486.

70 *Id.*, at [205].

A further difficultly is that awards of exemplary damages tend to be subject to a glass ceiling.[71] This practice would need to be examined if such awards are always to act as a deterrent[72] to fraud.[73]

XI. WIDER CONSIDERATIONS

So far it has been argued that the measure of damages adopted in cases of fraudulent misrepresentation has the potential to overcompensate the misrepresentee where, for example, the misrepresentee would have entered into the transaction, or a similar transaction, anyway and so would have suffered some or all of the loss anyway. It has also been argued that such an approach may alter the risk allocation in the contract in relation to matters unconnected to X's fraudulent misrepresentation. The other main remedy, of course, for fraudulent misrepresentation is, subject to certain bars, rescission; and that remedy may have a *similar effect* to damages for fraudulent misrepresentation in so far as it may allow the misrepresentee to *avoid* loss which he or she would have incurred even if the misrepresentation had not been made; and, again, this impacts on the risk allocation inherent in contracts.[74] To some extent, of course, this is a reflection on the orthodox view that partial rescission is not available in the law of England and Wales.[75]

[71] In *Parabola Investments Ltd v. Browallia Cal Ltd* [2009] EWHC 901 (Comm). At [202] to [208] Flaux J. stated: "Finally, since the award of such damages is in the discretion of the court, he urges me not to make such an award, since in any event (as Mr Kitchener accepts) such awards are normally limited to £10,000 to £15,000, and in the context of a case where the claimant will recover millions of pounds in compensatory damages, a further award of exemplary damages will hardly have any disapproving or deterrent effect. … In general I have considerable sympathy with the view of Lord Scott in Kuddus that exemplary damages are anomalous and that, since the common law has moved on since *Rookes v Barnard* in 1964 and now provides remedies which are much more appropriate (whether restitutionary damages or compound interest or indemnity costs), the time has come to abolish exemplary damages. However that was a minority view and the general principle was not argued in Kuddus, so the court has to proceed on the basis that such damages can still be awarded in an appropriate case. However, in my judgment this is not such a case. Quite apart from the inappropriateness of such an award against a defendant who is only liable vicariously, there seems to me something faintly absurd in the suggestion that, in this case where Tangent will recover substantial compensatory damages, the additional award of even £15,000 exemplary damages will express the court's outrage and displeasure at the fraud perpetrated on Tangent and Mr Gill. I decline to make any award of exemplary damages."

[72] On which see *Smith New Court Securities Ltd. v. Citibank N.A.* [1997] A.C. 254.

[73] *Cf.* Qi Zhou, *A Deterrence Perspective on Damages for Fraudulent Misrepresentation*, 19 JOURNAL OF INTERDISCIPLINARY ECONOMICS 83–96 (2008).

[74] See, for example, *F & H Entertainments v. Leisure Enterprises Ltd* (1976) 120 SJ 331.

[75] See, for example, *TSB Bank plc v. Camfield* [1995] 1 All ER 951. Although *cf. Bristol & West Building Society v. Henning* [1985] 1 WLR 778 and Jill Poole and Andrew Keyser, *Justifying Partial Rescission in English Law* (2005) 121 LAW QUARTERLY REVIEW 273–99.

In cases of non-fraudulent misrepresentation there is the potential for such an outcome to be side-stepped[76]; s.2(2) Misrepresentation Act 1967 provides:

> Where a person has entered into a contract after a misrepresentation has been made to him otherwise than fraudulently, and he would be entitled, by reason of the misrepresentation, to rescind the contract, then, if it is claimed, in any proceedings arising out of the contract, that the contract ought to be or has been rescinded, the court or arbitrator may declare the contract subsisting and award damages in lieu of rescission if of the opinion that it would be equitable to do so, having regard to the nature of the misrepresentation and the loss that would be caused by it if the contract were upheld, as well as to the loss that rescission would cause to the other party.

Thus thought needs to be given to whether or not s.2(2) needs to be amended so as to cover fraudulent misrepresentation.

XII. CONCLUSION

Oliver Wendell Holmes once wrote[77]:

> The law, so far as it depends on learning, is indeed, as it has been called, the government of the living by the dead. To a very considerable extent no doubt it is inevitable that the living should be so governed. The past gives us our vocabulary and fixes the limits of our imagination; we cannot get away from it. There is, too, a peculiar logical pleasure in making manifest the continuity between what we are doing and what has been done before. But the present has a right to govern itself so far as it can; and it ought always to be remembered that historic continuity with the past is not a duty, it is only a necessity.[78]

Such a statement finds resonance with the term-representation dichotomy in the law of England and Wales, where despite the oddity that a particular statement – which is, in general terms, deemed not important enough for inclusion in the contract – can, depending on the precise circumstances, give rise to greater liability than if the statement had been included in the contract. The time may have come, perhaps driven by developments at an EU level,[79] to re-examine the term-representation dichotomy in the law of England and Wales, with

[76] Although on the measure of damages under s.2(2) see *William Sindall v. Cambridgeshire CC* [1994] 1 WLR 1016.

[77] Joseph Harold Laski, (ed.) Collected Legal Papers: Oliver Wendell Holmes (Harcourt, Brace & Howe: 1920).

[78] *Id.*, at 138.

[79] Although *cf.* J. Cartwright & M. Hesselink (eds.), *Precontractual Liability in European Private Law* (Cambridge University Press: Cambridge, 2008).

particular emphasis on the expectations which may be generated by *contractual* misrepresentations.[80]

In the meantime, there is a need to reflect on the remedies for misrepresentation in general, and fraudulent misrepresentation in particular.[81] More specifically, *if* the law is going to punish the fraudulent misrepresentor, it must, of course, do so in a principled manner. Yet it has been argued earlier that the current approach to punishment in the civil law for fraudulent misrepresentation – where the punishment depends on (a) the misrepresentee having suffered a loss as a result of entering *into the transaction*, (b) the fact that the misrepresentee would have suffered some of that loss notwithstanding the misrepresentation given, for example, the fact that he or she would have entered into the transaction anyway) and (c) where the amount of punishment essentially depends on how bad a bargain turns out to be for the misrepresentee (which, for example, may depend on whether or not the market has *happened to fall*) – can hardly be described as principled. Of course there are some who would argue that punishment has no place in the civil law. This chapter has not sought to reopen that debate, save to note that the experience under the Consumer Protection from Unfair Trading Regulations 2008,[82] which of course implements the EU Unfair Commercial Practices Directive,[83] has shown that, from a practical point of view, the policing of misrepresentation through purely criminal sanctions may be inadequate.[84] By contrast this chapter has sought to argue that *if* the civil courts are to be able to punish a fraudulent misrepresentor, a more appropriate way of so doing is through a direct award of exemplary damages rather than indirectly through the general measure of damages (and a reliance on, for example, a fall in the market). This would allow a more nuanced approach to punishment although, as we have noted, it would require some development of existing practices in relation to exemplary damages.

80 *Cf.* the New Zealand Contractual Remedies Act 1979.

81 See generally Jill Poole and James Devenney, *supra* note 46.

82 SI 2008/1277.

83 Directive 2005/29, [2005] O.J. L.129/22.

84 See earlier at note 62.

18

Remedies for a Documentary Breach

English Law and the CISG

Djakhongir Saidov

While the UN Sales Convention (CISG) has gained importance, English law continues to play a leading role in the international commodities trading. There is a view that the CISG is not particularly well suited to highly volatile markets, such as commodities, where prices fluctuate heavily and traders are primarily concerned with speculation, rather than the use of the goods. Because of high price fluctuations, strings structures of many of the transactions, standardisation of goods and contracts, and the special significance of documents (with much of the trade being conducted by means of the transfer of documents which provide the buyers and/or banks with security), the legal regime appropriate for, and facilitative of, such a trading environment should be one which, among other things, is certain and predictable and contains a robust set of rules and principles governing documentary performance and consequences of documentary breaches. The CISG, on this view, is not an entirely satisfactory law since some of its crucial provisions are too open-ended, causing much uncertainty, while others, such as those allowing cure and the fixation of an additional time for performance, are inimical to the need for speedy decision making in volatile markets. As to documents, the CISG is, in the words of a proponent of this view, 'a blank page'. English law, in contrast, has a long history of governing commodities and documentary trade and is therefore much better suited to dealing with those trade sectors. In retort it can be argued that the CISG is no less capable of governing contracts in these trade sectors; its open-ended provisions together with its contextual rules of interpretation are, in fact, its strength because they enable the CISG to be adapted to the particular needs of businesses in a given trade sector.

This chapter seeks to engage with and to contribute to this discussion by focussing on remedies for documentary breaches under English law and the CISG, with the focus being placed on the remedies of termination, rejection, and damages. This chapter will identify some of the problems in English law, engage with the debates surrounding them and evaluate the claim that English law is better suited than the

CISG to governing documentary trade. As far as the CISG, the chapter will examine, in a detailed and focussed manner, the ways in which its remedies have been applied in connection with documentary breaches. The application of the CISG remedy provisions is then compared with that of English law. The chapter concludes with suggestions as to which of the laws are best suited for the needs of documentary and commodities trading.

I. INTRODUCTION

The more the UN Sales Convention (CISG) has featured on the international legal stage, having been ratified by seventy-eight states and applied in thousands of cases, the more intense the debate about what law is best for international sales has become. With English law playing a leading role in the international commodities and documentary trade, the debate often centres on the comparison of the CISG with English law. One view[1] is that the CISG is not particularly well suited to highly volatile markets, such as commodities, where traders are primarily concerned with speculation, rather than the use of the goods. Because of high price fluctuations, strings structures of many of the transactions, standardisation of goods and contracts, and the special significance of documents (with much of the trade conducted by means of the transfer of documents which provide the buyers and banks with security), the legal regime appropriate for, and facilitative of, such a trading environment should be one which, among other things, is certain and predictable and contains robust set of rules and principles governing documentary performance and consequences of documentary breaches.[2] The CISG, on this view, is not an entirely satisfactory law since some of its crucial provisions are too open-ended while some others, such as those allowing cure and the fixation of an additional time for performance, are inimical to the need for speedy decision making in volatile markets. As to documents, the CISG is, in the words of a proponent of this view, 'a blank page'.[3] English law, in contrast, has a long history of governing commodities and documentary trade and is therefore much better suited to dealing with those trade sectors. On another view,[4] the CISG is no less capable of governing contracts in these trade sectors. Its open-ended provisions together with its contextual rules of interpretation

1 See, e.g., Michael Bridge, A *Law for International Sales*, 37 HONG KONG L. J. 7 (2007).

2 See Michael Bridge, *Uniformity and Diversity in the Law of International Sale*, 15 PACE INTERNATIONAL L. REV. 55 (2003).

3 See *Id.*, 28.

4 See, e.g., Peter Schlechtriem, *Interpretation, Gap-Filling and Further Development of the U.N. Sales Convention*, 16 PACE INTERNATIONAL L. REV. 279 (2004); Ingeborg Schwenzer, *The Danger of Domestic Pre-Conceived Views with Respect to the Uniform Interpretation of the CISG: The Question of Avoidance in the Case of Non-Conforming Goods and Documents*, VICTORIA UNIVERSITY OF WELLINGTON L. Rev. 795 (2004–5).

are, in fact, its strength because they enable the CISG to be adapted to the particular needs of businesses in a given trade sector and to produce just outcomes in individual cases.[5] The Convention's purpose is to promote trade broadly, across various markets, and what is needed is a judge or an arbitrator who understands the needs of the surrounding commercial context and appreciates the Convention's flexibility.

This chapter seeks to take this debate further by examining the remedies of termination and damages for documentary breaches. Termination and damages are two of the most practically effective and widely used remedies whilst documentary obligations are an essential part of the seller's performance in the documentary and commodities trade. The conclusions reached in this chapter, albeit confined to its scope, will shed further light on the overall strengths and weaknesses of each of the two sales laws. Drawing comparison between them refines our understanding of what set of rules, together with their underlying considerations, is most appropriate for this trade sector. Taking the experiences of the two regimes cumulatively also equips a sales lawyer with an understanding of a broader range of factual settings that can arise in international trade and provides a more extensive insight into the needs and expectations of traders. Finally, this examination offers an opportunity to explore the remedies for a documentary breach in a more focussed and detailed way than it thus far has been done to highlight the areas where both English law and the CISG are in need of improvement and to make the relevant suggestions.

II. TERMINATION

A. *Duality of the Rights to Reject and Terminate*

There is a close link between the seller's obligations in relation to the goods (physical obligations) and in relation to the documents (documentary obligations) because the documents serve, amongst other things, as evidence of the extent to which the seller has complied with its physical obligations. For instance, a transport document, such as a bill of lading, is often used as evidence of: the shipment date; the quantity and description of the goods shipped; whether, for example, a CIF seller has made a proper carriage contract; or whether the goods have been loaded in a good order and condition. Where the seller is required to procure insurance, an insurance document is supplied to show that the seller has complied with those obligations. A contract may require the seller to supply quality, quantity, weight and

5 Koji Takahashi, *Right to Terminate (Avoid) International Sales of Commodities*, J. of BUSINESS L. 102, 105 (2003); Alastair Mullis, *Termination for Breach of Contract in C.I.F. Contracts under the Vienna Convention and English Law: Is There a Substantial Difference?* in CONTEMPORARY ISSUES IN COMMERCIAL LAW (ESSAYS IN HONOUR OF PROF. A. G. GUEST) 137 (E. Lomnicka & G. Morse eds., Sweet & Maxwell: London 1997).

other certificates as evidence of the compliance with the seller's obligations as to the conformity of the goods. But the documents may also perform other functions. A seller may be required to provide a negotiable bill of lading to enable the buyer to resell the goods in transit. Where the risk passes to the buyer on shipment, it is common to expect a transport document to be capable of transferring to the buyer the rights of suit against the carrier. In a CIF contract, an insurance document will be expected to enable the buyer to claim against the insurer.[6]

This multiplicity of functions that the documents perform is probably one reason why English law recognises that, although there is a close relationship between physical and documentary duties,[7] these are seller's separate duties, triggering separate sets of remedies. Another reason is that the commodities trade is often conducted by means of the delivery of documents passed down the chains of traders, with the goods being afloat. This prominence of documents has infamously led to the view that a CIF contract is a contract for the sale of documents, rather than goods.[8] Another related reason is that different business considerations enter the buyer's mind depending on whether the buyer is thinking about rejecting the documents or rejecting the goods. With the price often required to be paid upon the presentation of documents (cash against documents), the buyer will not have parted with the money at the time of the presentation of documents, whereas it may have parted with the price at the time of deciding whether to reject the goods and may have already had dealings with the goods by reselling them to a sub-buyer or pledging them to a bank.[9] Generally, therefore, the buyer under English law has separate rights of rejecting the documents and rejecting the goods and terminating the contract on each of these bases. This enables the buyer to terminate the contract solely on the basis of a documentary breach with no need to prove the impact of that breach on the physical obligations.[10] Although this position gives rise to more opportunities for committing a breach, hence creating greater room for the buyers to escape from a contract on a falling market, it seems sound and necessary if the law is to reflect the role played by documents fully and to facilitate documentary trade. Even in the context of the CISG, whose history and life have not been nearly

[6] See Djakhongir Saidov, *Documentary Performance and the CISG*, in I. Schwenzer and L. Spagnolo eds, State of Play: The 3rd Annual MAA Schlechtriem CISG Conference (The Hague, Eleven International Publishing 2012) p. 57.

[7] One further example of this close linkage relates to the rules on the loss of the right to reject. If the buyer accepts documents which on their face evidence a physical breach, which entitles the buyer to reject the goods (e.g., a late shipment), and nevertheless accepts the documents without reservation of its rights, the right to reject the goods on that basis will be lost (see BENJAMIN'S SALE OF GOODS, 19–156 (8th ed., M. Bridge ed., Sweet & Maxwell-Thomson Reuters: London 2010)).

[8] See *Arnold Karberg & Co v. Blythe, Green Jourdain & Co* [1915] 2 K.B. 379.

[9] *Kwei Tek Chao v. British Traders & Shippers Ltd* [1954] 2 Q.B. 459.

[10] See, e.g., *Procter & Gamble Philippine Manufacturing Corporation v. Kurt A Becher GmbH & Co KG* [1988] 2 Lloyd's Rep. 21.

as preoccupied with documentary trade, few doubt the duality of physical and documentary obligations in the light of the Convention allocating a specific provision to the seller's obligation to hand over documents relating to the goods.[11]

This duality means that the buyer should not be able to reject conforming documents if it knows that a pure physical breach has been committed.[12] For example, the buyer may become aware that the goods of non-contractual description have been shipped with the description not one which would appear on the face of the document (e.g., goods are of a different grade than that specified in the contract). This buyer will have to pay for the documents but will have the right to reject the goods and/or claim damages.[13]

One potential threat to the separation of documentary and physical obligations could emanate from the general contract law on repudiation. If a breach by the seller in relation to the goods evidences its intention or inability to perform the contract,[14] the buyer by accepting the repudiation can, in principle, terminate the contract, in which case the rejection of conforming documents is merely a part of the machinery of termination. This situation may arise in shipment contracts where, for example, a CIF buyer can prove at the time of documentary tender that the goods were non-conforming on shipment and there is no possibility of further appropriation or substitute tender.[15] Some have argued that such a position is justified by a sense of realism:[16] why should the buyer take the trouble of paying the price, knowing that soon afterwards it will have the right to reject the goods and reclaim the price?[17]

Another potential threat is the common law rule that the innocent party is entitled to terminate the contract despite having given no or a wrong reason for termination as long as at the time of termination a correct ground, giving rise to the right to terminate, existed.[18] The rule would mean that a CIF buyer, for example, who rejects conforming documents, alleging the termination of the contract without giving a reason, may subsequently be found to have been justified in doing so as long as, at the time of the rejection, the seller has already committed a repudiatory

[11] See Secretariat Commentary on Art. 32 of the 1978 Draft; Peter Huber & Alastair Mullis, THE CISG: A NEW TEXTBOOK FOR STUDENTS AND PRACTITIONERS 126–7 (Sellier European Law Publishers: München 2007). See also Arts. 30 and 34 of the CISG.

[12] See, generally, BENJAMIN'S, *supra note* 7, at 19–078, 19–164.

[13] The measure of damages will vary, depending on whether the goods have been rejected.

[14] See CHITTY ON CONTRACTS 24–018 (30th ed., H. Beale ed., Sweet & Maxwell: London 2010); BENJAMIN'S, *supra note* 7, at 12–019.

[15] Francis Reynolds, *Rejection of Documents*, LLOYD'S MARITIME & COMMERCIAL L. QUARTERLY 191, 192 (1984).

[16] See Paul Todd, CASES AND MATERIALS ON INTERNATIONAL TRADE LAW 7–027 (Thomson-Sweet & Maxwell: London 2003).

[17] GOODE ON COMMERCIAL LAW 1050 (4th ed., E. McKendrick ed., Penguin: London 2010).

[18] See, e.g., BENJAMIN'S, *supra note* 7, at 19–160.

(physical) breach.[19] This rule can induce the rejection of documents by those buyers who want to gamble on a falling market, hoping or suspecting that a repudiatory breach has already been committed.[20] This approach appears to have been taken in an Australian case, *Henry Dean & Sons (Sydney) Ltd v. P O'Day Proprietary Ltd.*[21] When the CIF seller drew on the buyer through a bank for the price, with the shipping documents attached to the draft, the buyer refused to take up the draft on the ground that the goods were not of contract description. By majority, the Australian High Court decided that the buyer was under no obligation to accept the documents issued in respect of the goods which, in fact, did not correspond to contract description.

It appears that English law has suppressed both threats in *Berger & Co Inc v. Gill & Duffus SA*,[22] which also concerned a CIF contract. In *Gill & Duffus*, the approach in *Henry Dean* was interpreted as based on the common law rule,[23] stated in the previous paragraph, and was strongly rejected as not being 'the law of England' since it 'would destroy the very roots of the system by which international trade, particularly in commodities, is enabled to be financed'.[24] Lord Diplock's statement of the principle was clear: a CIF buyer's refusal to pay against the documents which are conforming on their face constitutes a breach of condition, regardless of whether conforming goods have been shipped.[25]

The reasons are both practical and conceptual.[26] Firstly, for strings to be viable, the parties to it, who often do not know the condition of the goods, must be able to rely on the face of the documents. Secondly, such an approach is consistent with the documentary credit and 'cash against documents' arrangements, both of which infuse a sense of security to parties trading at a distance.[27] Thirdly, an allocation of risks in a CIF contract, the most widely used type of shipment contracts, is such that the buyer has to pay against conforming documents with no prior right to examine the goods.[28] This latter reason alone is sufficient to support the view that the traditional rule should not apply, at least, to CIF contracts with the additional rationalisations being that the seller's physical obligations are held in suspense before documentary

[19] This was the buyer's argument in *Braithwaite v. Foreign Hardwood Co* [1905] 2 K.B. 543.

[20] See Michael Bridge, The Sale of Goods 665 (2nd ed., Oxford University Press: Oxford 2009), posing a question of what *Braithwaite supra note* 19 has done to this common law rule.

[21] (1927) 39 C.L.R. 330.

[22] [1984] A.C. 382.

[23] *Id.*, 391–2.

[24] *Id.*

[25] *Id.*, 391.

[26] See Benjamin's, *supra note* 7, at 19–165.

[27] In that they enable the sellers to part with the goods before getting the price and the buyers to pay before getting the goods.

[28] See *E Clemens Horst Co v Biddel Bros* [1912] A.C. 18.

tender,[29] that parties to CIF contracts 'impliedly exclude rights of the buyer in respect of the seller's physical performance that would otherwise arise before the completion of the documentary exchange'[30] or that the CIF buyer's duty to pay against documents is an independent covenant which must be performed even if non-conforming goods were shipped.[31] These points reflect the view that a CIF contract and, arguably, other shipment contracts are *special* contracts whose structure, dual mode of performance and allocation of risks dictate the need to displace these traditional rules.[32] It is for these reasons that in *Gill & Duffus*, the CIF buyer's rights to reject the documents and the goods were held to be 'separate and successive rights'.[33]

Both potential threats to the duality of documentary and physical obligations seem equally present in the CISG context. Whilst the Convention does not rely upon the notion of a repudiation of contract, it allows the contract to be terminated where a fundamental breach has been committed.[34] Therefore, a buyer could terminate the contract relying on a fundamental *physical* breach and reject the documents as part of the machinery of termination. Similarly, under the CISG, the buyer can, in principle, be found to have validly terminated the contract, when conforming documents were tendered, on the wrong ground or by not specifying it at all, as long as a ground justifying termination existed at that time or where the buyer is able to prove a physical breach justifying termination. While the CISG requires a notice of avoidance to be given,[35] the prevailing view is that to be effective the notice does not have to specify a ground for avoidance.[36] If so, the absence of a valid ground will not render this notice ineffective as long as some valid ground did exist at the time. The Art 39 requirement that, in the case of non-conforming goods, the buyer must give a notice specifying the nature of a lack of conformity in order to be able to exercise its remedies reduces this risk for the seller to some extent since the buyer would

[29] Michael Bridge, THE INTERNATIONAL SALE OF GOODS: LAW AND PRACTICE 10–26 (2nd ed., Oxford University Press: Oxford 2007).

[30] Michael Bridge, *Documents and Contractual Congruence in International Trade*, COMMERCIAL LAW AND COMMERCIAL PRACTICE 220 (S. Worthington ed., Hart Publishing: Oxford 2003).

[31] Guenter Treitel, *Rights of Rejection under C.I.F. Sales*, LLOYD'S MARITIME & COMMERCIAL QUARTERLY 565, 570 (1984).

[32] It is rarely possible for a buyer to establish a physical breach at the time of the rejection of documents in CIF contracts since the seller can appropriate the goods afloat (see Todd, CASES, *supra note* 16, at 7–031). Any goods corresponding to the contractual description and specifications can be tendered unless the contract is for specific goods or the goods have been unconditionally appropriated (CIF contracts often require the seller to tender a notice of appropriation, in which case the seller is bound to perform the contract in a way specified in the notice).

[33] *Gill & Duffus* (n 22) 395.

[34] Art. 25.

[35] Art. 26.

[36] Christiana Fountoulakis in Schlechtriem & Schwenzer, COMMENTARY ON THE UN CONVENTION ON THE INTERNATIONAL SALE OF GOODS (CISG) 441 (4th ed., I. Schwenzer ed., Oxford University Press: Oxford 2010).

not be able to terminate the contract on the ground of non-conformity in the goods without giving such a notice. However, where the buyer gave such a notice or where a seller's breach is not subject to Art 39, it may be possible for the buyer to reject conforming documents by alleging the termination of the contract, unless the right to reject the documents and the goods are regarded as 'successive'. The reasons set out in the previous paragraph seem sufficiently strong to justify the CISG in taking a similar position to English law in relation to shipment contracts. Such an interpretation can be arrived at not from the CISG itself but from contractual payment provisions, such as 'cash against documents', the surrounding commercial context and such trade terms as CIF/CFR, which allow the sale of goods afloat.[37]

But there is a more real threat to the separation of documentary from physical obligations. In English law, certificates of quality have been said to be conforming even where they evidence a physical breach, because such certificates do what they were intended to do, that is, to verify the actual quality of the goods.[38] But in one case,[39] where a certificate showed an amount of fat in the goods higher than that permitted by the contract, the court accepted that the buyer could have rejected the documents. This position has been subsequently explained on the basis that where it is apparent on the face of a document that the goods are defective in a way which would justify the rejection of the goods, the buyer has the right to reject the documents, which are not in themselves defective.[40] If this is an accurate statement of English law, the principle of separate rejection rights encompasses only those cases where conforming documents do not reveal on their face non-conformity in the goods, which would justify the rejection of the goods.

At this juncture, English law is open to criticism. Firstly, it is not wholeheartedly committed to treating documentary duties as entirely autonomous since the buyer can reject *good* documents because they reveal a physical repudiatory breach. Secondly, this position is not in line with the division of commercial risks in documentary sales usually embodied in CIF terms and the 'cash against documents' arrangements. Another way of making these two points is to say that there is tension or even inconsistency between an often pronounced need for certainty and respect of autonomy of documentary duties, on the one hand, and this, with respect, ill-explained basis for rejecting *good* documents, on the other.[41] Thirdly, the problem of

37 See Arts. 8 and 9 of the CISG. See also Comments on CFR terms (A8) in Jan Ramberg, INCOTERMS 2010 in ICC GUIDE TO INCOTERMS 2010; UNDERSTANDING AND PRACTICAL USE 189 (ICC Publications Services: Paris 2011).

38 *Tradax Internacional SA v. Goldschmidt SA* [1977] 2 Lloyd's Rep. 604.

39 *Vargas Pena Apezteguia Y Cia SAIC v. Peter Cremer GmbH* [1987] 1 Lloyd's Rep. 394.

40 BENJAMIN'S, *supra note* 7, at 19–148.

41 If the basis for this position lies in the rules on repudiation – i.e., that a repudiatory physical breach shown in a document evidences the seller's inability to perform the contract – then such a basis would be inconsistent with the principle enunciated in *Gill & Duffus* (*supra note* 22).

consistency also arises if the English law's understanding of a conforming *certificate* is compared with the way English law defines a conforming *bill of lading*. As noted, even if the certificate evidences a physical breach it is still a good document. In contrast, a bill of lading which qualifies the goods' order, state, condition or packaging (unclean); shows a non-contractual quantity; or evidences shipment outside the shipment period is regarded as a defective bill, which can be rejected. Presumably, one way to justify this difference is to argue that a bill of lading is a more crucial document, because of its multi-functional nature, as opposed to a single-function orientation of a certificate: since it is usually a bill of lading that enables the goods to be traded while they are in transit, the requirements in relation to it ought to be more stringent.

This latter argument implies some kind of ranking of documents. Although this is not entirely alien to English law – *Gill & Duffus* itself stated that a certificate could not be regarded a *shipping* document,[42] the absence of which would justify the rejection of documents – it could be argued that the law should develop on a more principled and consistent basis by spreading the same standards of conformity to all documents. English law is arguably inconsistent in relation to both the grounds when the buyer is entitled to reject the documents, by generally not allowing the rejection of good documents except where a good certificate shows defects in the goods,[43] and the standards of conformity of documents. Adding the important considerations underlying the principle of separation of documentary duties from physical ones, the arguments in favour of reformulating the notion of conformity of a certificate along the lines of those applicable to a bill of lading seem strong. Accepting this position would mean that the buyer should be allowed to reject a certificate showing a physical breach, not because it shows a physical repudiatory breach, but because such a certificate is not a good certificate.[44] This also ensures that the autonomy of documentary duties is respected.

This problem is unlikely to arise under the Convention since the requirements of documentary conformity are to be derived solely from the contract itself. While certain provisions of the CISG can influence the contract interpretation in this respect,[45] there is no provision in it which has a direct impact on the question whether a certificate showing a physical breach is conforming or not. Nonetheless, a feature of the CISG cases has been not to take documents at their face value and the tribunals' willingness to challenge the evidentiary value of the certificates even where the

[42] 'The shipping documents are those which a seller is required to tender as a condition of obtaining payment' (BENJAMIN'S, *supra note* 7, at 19–024).

[43] See *Vargas Pena Apezteguia Y Cia SAIC v Peter Cremer GmbH* (n 39).

[44] For a similar view, see Charles Debattista, BILL OF LADING IN EXPORT TRADE 219 (Tottel Publishing: Haywards Heath 2009).

[45] See Arts. 32(2), 38, 58 and 68. See further Saidov (*supra note* 6), pp. 63–66.

contracts treated certificates as final.[46] Together with the demand for a contextual contract interpretation and regard for the particular facts,[47] the Convention can be seen as imbued in the spirit of idealism and perfectionism which may push a tribunal interpreting a contract, governed by the CISG, to hold that a certificate showing a physical breach cannot be conforming.

B. Rejection or Termination

The right of rejection is sometimes described as being solely a part of the machinery of termination,[48] but it must be borne in mind that rejection and termination are conceptually different remedies. Rejection will usually accompany termination, but a buyer may also decide to reject – that is, to refuse to accept or to nullify the delivery – without terminating the contract.[49] Where the seller presents documents at a point in time when, should the buyer reject them, there is still time for the seller to make a fresh presentation of documents, this (first) presentation will be generally regarded in English law as being merely a *tender* of performance[50] rather than the performance itself.[51] Rejection can be practically valuable to the buyer where it does not accept the tender of performance by the seller but still wants the contract to remain alive, expecting further conforming performance within the time set by the contract or implied by law. More importantly, if the price has not yet been paid, rejection enables the buyer to withhold the price since the payment usually has to be made against the documents, which means that the parties' obligations are concurrent; and it is a seller's breach of a condition that is concurrent with or precedent to the buyer's obligation that will entitle the buyer, through rejecting the seller's performance, to withhold its own performance.[52] In this sense, rejection provides the buyer with security and is an effective self-help remedy.[53]

[46] See Saidov, *supra note* 6, pp. 81–84.

[47] See Arts. 8 and 9.

[48] *Kwei Tek Chao*, *supra note* 9, at 480.

[49] See, e.g., Bridge, SALE, *supra note* 20, 620, 622. On the consequences of the rejection of documents for the rejection of the goods, and vice versa, see ibid, 662–3 ('The rejection of documents will entail the rejection of the goods, since the c.i.f. seller may not unilaterally alter the contract and tender the goods physically on shore. Likewise, the rejection of the goods will require the buyer to place any documents already received at the disposal of the seller.').

[50] *Albright & Wilson UK Ltd v. Biachem Ltd* [2001] EWCA Civ. 301, paras. [29] and [37] (reversed in part on different grounds in [2002] UKHL 37).

[51] But see the later discussion.

[52] Antonia Apps, *The Right to Cure Defective Performance*, LLOYD'S MARITIME & COMMERCIAL L. QUARTERLY 525, 528–9, 530–2 (1994); Robert Bradgate, COMMERCIAL LAW 310 (3rd ed., Butterworths-LexisNexis: London 2003).

[53] Bradgate, *id.*

One question that arises is whether the grounds for exercising this remedy are and should be the same as those applicable to termination. The position of English law is not easy to ascertain. S. 11(3), Sale of Goods Act 1979 (SGA), may be interpreted as indicating that it is only a breach of condition (a term a breach of which triggers the right to terminate) that constitutes the basis for the exercise of the right to reject.[54] At the same time, it may still be possible for the buyer to reject where a breach itself does not amount to a breach of condition or to repudiation of contract.[55] In *Mantovani v. Carapelli*,[56] the buyer argued that the seller had committed a breach by not supplying a weight certificate. The court doubted whether a weight certificate was a shipping document but held that even if the certificate were a shipping document, the buyer was not entitled to treat the breach as going to the root of the contract, unless 'this failure was persisted in and amounted to a refusal', adding that the 'buyers never asked for a weight certificate and one could and would have been provided by the sellers if the buyers had done so'.[57] Two points flow from these statements: first, even if the original breach does not amount to a breach of condition or to repudiation, the seller's persistent refusal to cure the breach can turn it into a ground for the buyer's right to reject the seller's non-conforming performance;[58] secondly, the buyer can demand cure by the seller, which either may be in itself a form of rejection (at least in part)[59] or, in any case, will put the seller in a position where the seller will have to react (or will fail to react) to the buyer's demand, thereby increasing the chances of the seller's conduct turning into repudiation.[60] Along with some other cases,[61] this decision also makes clear that for the buyer to be able to reject the documents on the ground of non-delivery of some document, the latter has to be, at the very least, a *shipping* document.[62]

Thus, there will be cases where answering the question of whether the buyer has the right to reject will require an assessment of the surrounding circumstances. The grounds for rejection in English law are, therefore, not always easily predictable. This point cannot be advanced too far in the context of documentary breaches because most such breaches are regarded as breaches of condition, which undoubtedly give rise to the right to reject.[63] However, some unpredictability remains in cases concerning non-shipping documents, as illustrated by *Mantovani v. Carapelli*.

54 *Id.*

55 See, e.g., BENJAMIN'S, *supra note* 7, at 12–019. See also *Hongkong Fir Shipping Co Ltd v Kawasaki Kisen Kaisha* [1962] 2 Q.B. 26, 56; Apps, *Right to Cure* (n 52) 533–4.

56 *Mantovani v. Carapelli SpA* [1978] 2 Lloyd's Rep. 63, 72.

57 *Id.*

58 See BENJAMIN'S, *supra note* 7, at 19–149.

59 See the discussion of this issue later.

60 See, generally, Apps, *Right to Cure, supra note* 52, at 533–4.

61 See, e.g., *Gill & Duffus, supra note* 22.

62 Apps, *Right to Cure* (n 52) 534.

63 See the discussion later.

More questions arise under the CISG, with the first one being whether the right to reject, independent of the right to avoid the contract, exists within its framework. The Convention does not expressly provide for such a right but allows for gaps to be filled, where a matter falls within its scope but is not expressly dealt with, by resorting to its general principles.[64] The potentially relevant provisions could be found in various parts of the CISG. In several specific instances, it refers to the buyer's right to refuse to accept 'performance'[65] or 'to take delivery'[66] and to 'reject' the goods,[67] and there may be room for arguing in favour of developing a general remedy of rejection by drawing on all these provisions. Further, if the legal character of the right to reject is described, as is often the case,[68] as a form of the right of retention/suspension, rather than of termination,[69] there are other provisions which can serve as the basis for the construction of the right to reject. First, a party is allowed to suspend the performance of its obligations if it anticipates the other party's non-performance of 'a substantial part of obligations'.[70] Secondly, the Convention's default position is that the buyer only has to pay against the handing over of the goods or documents controlling their disposition while the seller may make such handing over a condition for payment.[71] Similarly, in the case of carriage of goods, 'the seller may dispatch the goods on terms whereby the goods, or documents controlling their disposition, will not be handed over to the buyer except against payment of the price'.[72] The precise point of relevance of these provisions to the buyer's right to reject documents could be described thus: if the buyer does not receive a conforming documentary tender, it can suspend its own performance, which in the case of simultaneous/concurrent performance means that the seller's tender is not being accepted. The potential relevance of a provision on suspension in the case of anticipated non-performance (Art. 71) lies in showing that the Convention is, in principle, a 'suspension friendly' regime.[73] Finally, the buyer can demand performance from the seller,[74] which includes a demand for cure of a documentary breach. Such a demand, in turn, could be seen as implying the possibility of the buyer's non-acceptance (rejection) of a documentary tender.[75]

64 Art. 7(2).
65 Art. 50.
66 Art. 52(1), (2).
67 Art. 86(1), (2)
68 Vanessa Mak, *The Seller's Right to Cure Defective Performance – a Reappraisal*, Lloyd's Maritime & Commercial L. Quarterly 409, 414 (2007); Michael Bridge, *Avoidance for Fundamental Breach of Contract under the UN Convention on the International Sale of Goods*, 59 International & Comparative L. Quarterly 911, 937–8 (2010).
69 The rationale is that rejection is the suspension of an obligation to accept the tendered performance.
70 See Art. 71.
71 Art. 58(1).
72 Art. 58(2).
73 See further Bridge, *Avoidance, supra note* 68, at 938.
74 Art. 46(1).
75 But see the analysis of this issue later.

The buyer's right to reject the documents, particularly in the documentary and commodities trading, is increasingly recognised under the CISG, whether explicitly or indirectly as a form of the buyer's right to withhold its performance.[76] Apart from what has been said in the previous paragraph, this reflects the realisation that for the CISG to be capable of governing these trade sectors, it needs to be able to accommodate the practicalities of that environment. A sale in those trade sectors is often only possible by means of the transfer of documents. There may be little commercial sense in making the buyer accept non-conforming documents and in depriving the buyer of a useful remedy,[77] which may, after all, protect the interests of both parties, particularly where the buyer does not intend to terminate the contract and intends to give the seller a chance to cure, whilst enabling the buyer not to part with the price until the point of a conforming documentary tender. Rejection also accords well with a need for making speedy decisions.

If the reasons set out previously suffice to justify the existence of a right to reject documents under the CISG, the question arises as to what would constitute sufficient grounds for the exercise of this right. Will the same threshold, as the one required for the contract to be terminated, need to be established, that is, that the breach is fundamental?[78] It could be argued that once a right to reject (independent from termination) documents is recognised, the CISG can be interpreted as allowing the buyer to reject in *all* cases of documentary breach on the basis of Art 46(1) which allows it to 'require performance by the seller of his obligations unless the buyer has resorted to a remedy which is inconsistent with this requirement'. This provision clearly refers to *any* kind of obligation and the buyer's demand for performance, which includes a demand for curing documentary defects,[79] means that the buyer is not accepting the performance in the way it has been tendered; otherwise it would not and could not be demanding the performance. On this interpretation, there is an almost explicit support by the Convention of the position that any breach, no matter how minor, allows the buyer to demand cure which is another way of saying that the buyer is not accepting what it has received.

There are two objections to this position. One is that even English law which is perceived as more readily allowing contract termination, leaves room for trivial breaches which do not warrant legal response (the *de minimis* principle).[80] It is arguable that similar safeguards can be found in the Convention's general principles,

76 Schlechtriem, *Interpretation*, *supra note* 4, at 301–6; Bridge, *Avoidance*, *supra note* 68; CISG Advisory Council Opinion No. 5, *The Buyer's Right to Avoid the Contract in Case of Non-Conforming Goods or Documents* 4.18–4.20 <http://www.cisg.law.pace.edu/cisg/CISG-AC-op5.html>.

77 See also Bridge, *Avoidance*, *supra note* 68, at 937.

78 See Art. 25 CISG and the discussion later.

79 See by analogy Art. 46(3).

80 See later discussion.

such as good faith, reasonableness, proportionality and, possibly, abuse of rights.[81] A more serious objection concerns the meaning of 'rejection' and of its reverse side – 'acceptance'. The nature of the buyer's demand for performance is not the same as that of the right to reject since rejection takes place not only where the buyer wishes to keep the contract alive and demands cure, but also where rejection accompanies termination. Even if rejection could be viewed as the other side of the right to demand performance, the CISG could not be interpreted as allowing rejection for any breach: to draw an analogy with goods, under Art. 46(3) while the buyer may demand curing the defects in the goods, where a breach is not fundamental, such a demand cannot extend to cases where repair would be unreasonable. In this case, the buyer will have to keep non-conforming goods, which is the antithesis of the right to reject.

It seems that the question of whether a given documentary breach entitles the buyer to reject a documentary tender, without an intention to terminate, will rarely give much headache to the tribunal since this right on its own does not bring the contract to an end. It must be borne in mind though that if the right of rejection is recognised, a legal basis for its exercise will need to be defined. Since rejection in itself is not termination, then, using the Convention's logic in Arts. 71 and 72, a lower threshold will have to be adopted, and Art. 71 helpfully provides the relevant standard – a 'substantial' non-performance, which is a convenient middle ground between fundamental and trivial breaches.[82] Although this standard is inherently vague, it is submitted that in a commodities and documentary trading environment it should, as a rule, lead to the conclusion that the rejection of a documentary tender, which fails to comply with the contract, is justifiable.[83]

The earlier mentioned Art. 58(1) and (2) further adds some certainty to when the right of rejecting documents can be exercised. In the case of concurrent obligations, such as the 'cash against documents' arrangement, the buyer can refuse to accept a documentary tender, by withholding the payment, if 'documents controlling the disposition of the goods' are not presented. There is some uncertainty on the meaning of this provision, but at least it makes clear that rejection rights are available if such a document(s) is (are) not tendered.[84] Therefore, where obligations are concurrent, the uncertainty only exists in cases of discrepancies in the

81 See, e.g., Roberto M Paiva, *Fundamental Breach under the United Nations Convention on Contracts for the International Sale of Goods* (1980) <http://www.cisg.law.pace.edu/cisg/biblio/paiva.html'>; Lachmi Singh & Benjamin Leisinger, *A Law for International Sale of Goods: A Reply to Michael Bridge*, 20 Pace International L. Rev. 161, 184 (2008).

82 See Bridge, *Avoidance* (n 68) 937–8.

83 Similarly, see Schlechtriem, *Interpretation, supra note* 4, at 304–5; CISG-AC (n 76) 4.17. It goes without saying, however, that there can be no automaticity in the application of the Convention's remedies and the particular facts are ultimately decisive.

84 Supreme Court 3 April 1996 (Germany) <http://www.cisg.law.pace.edu/cases/960403g1.html>.

delivered documents, but not in cases of non-delivery of documents controlling the disposition of the goods.

C. *Rejection and Termination*

The starting point in English law is that documentary duties must be complied with strictly.[85] Documentary breaches will usually entitle the buyer to reject the documents and to terminate the contract, even if there was no physical breach[86] or only a breach in relation to the goods, evidenced in the document, which would not entitle the buyer to reject[87] the goods. The law here seeks to enable the buyer to ascertain its legal position, as far as it relates to the seller's documentary obligations, purely on the face of the documents. This is important because where payment is to be made against documents, documents are usually the only source of information concerning the seller's performance, with no opportunity to assess the consequences of a breach since there will often be no possibility to examine the goods at the stage of documentary tender.[88] Where strings are formed, documents need to be 'fit to pass current in commerce'[89] to enable the buyer to resell by transferring documents to its sub-buyer. Documents which do not comply strictly with the contract are likely to be refused by a sub-buyer[90] or by a bank, in the case of documentary credits. It is also arguable[91] that the grounds for the rejection in the 'cash against documents' sale need, in principle, to be aligned with those in letters of credit (strict compliance).[92] Therefore, documentary breaches would normally be regarded as breaches of condition entitling the buyer to terminate the contract.[93]

Nonetheless, English law may not always allow the buyer to reject the documents and to terminate the contract for any documentary breach. First, if the *de minimis*

85 See *Soules CAF v. PT Transcap of Indonesia* [1999] 1 Lloyd's Rep. 917, 919; *Cehave NV v. Bremer Handelgesellshaft mbH (Hansa Nord)* [1976] Q.B. 44, 70; *Soon Hua Seng Co Ltd v. Glencore Grain Ltd* [1996] C.L.C. 729, 734. See also BENJAMIN'S, *supra note* 7, at 19–018 and 19–148; Bridge, *Law*, *supra note* 1, at 27.

86 See *Procter & Gamble* (n 10) (a bill of lading was not genuine, by having been falsely dated, but goods shipped within the shipment period)

87 See *Cehave NV v. Bremer Handelgesellshaft mbH (Hansa Nord)* [1976] Q.B. 44 (a physical breach – goods not shipped in good condition as required by the contract – not entitling the buyer to terminate, but if a bill of lading had stated that the goods were not in good condition on shipment, the documents could have been rejected).

88 See cases in *supra note* 85; Takahashi, *Right*, *supra note* 5, at 115.

89 *Hansson v Hamel and Horley* [1922] 2 A.C. 36, 46.

90 On the basis that it did not contract to purchase litigation (see Mullis, *Termination* (n 5)).

91 Takahashi, *Right*, *supra note* 5, at 116.

92 See, e.g., BENJAMIN'S, *supra note* 7, at 23–097.

93 See, e.g., Debattista, BILL, *supra note* 44, at 212.

rule ('the law does not pay attention to trifles')[94] is applicable to documentary duties, even if a duty breached is classed as a condition,[95] the buyer will not be able to reject the documents if a discrepancy is too insignificant to carry legal consequences. Should this rule apply to documentary performance? If it should, which documentary discrepancies cross, and which do not, the *de minimis* margin?

De minimis is a rule of general application[96] and, in the absence of a pronouncement to the contrary, would appear to apply to documentary duties.[97] As a matter of policy, it has been argued[98] that this should not be so due to the considerations, already mentioned: strings trading is reliant on the confidence in the statements in the documents and a sub-buyer can only be expected to pay for a strictly complying tender, and; there needs to be an alignment of standards in the 'cash against documents' and documentary credits payment mechanisms for 'these contracts operated together and the business community is ill-served by commercial law if such answers were given to what is essentially the same question'.[99]

Accepting these arguments would carry the notion of strict compliance to its limit and create absolute certainty in the legal response to documentary breaches. At the same time, if termination for any documentary breach were allowed, English law would promote economic opportunism and manipulative behaviour even further than it already does, at the cost of utter disregard for the ideas of the sanctity of contracts and proportionality. While there is little scope for the *de minimis* rule, as

[94] See, e.g., CHITTY (n 14) 43–290; *Bremer Handelsgesellschaft Schaft MBH v Vanden Avenne Izegem PVBA* [1978] 2 Lloyd's Rep. 109. See recently Ji L. Yap, *No Trifling Matter: The De Minimis Principle in Relation to the Delivery of the Wrong Quantity of Goods under Hong Kong Law*, 1 INTERNATIONAL J. PRIVATE L. 222 (2008).

[95] See, e.g., *Arcos v. E A Ronaasen* [1933] A.C. 470, 477, 480.

[96] See *Margaronis Navigation Agency Ltd v Henry W Peabody & Co of London Ltd* [1965] 2 Q.B. 430, 444. In *Jydsk Andels Foderstofforretning v Grands Moulins de Paris* (1931) 39 LL. L. REP. 223, the buyer, who rejected the documents, was held not to have the right to terminate the contract for the sale of 400 tons of bran (±10%) due to the seller's delivery of 441.147 tonnes and tender of a weight certificate for that excess quantity because the excess was negligible. The decision does not make it clear whether the *de minimis* approach applied to a physical or to a documentary duty, and this has led to an argument that this case might not necessarily be regarded as supporting the application of the *de minimis* rule to documentary duties (Debattista, BILL, *supra note* 44, at 215). It is possible to go further and to argue that this case cannot be an authority for the latter proposition because, as shown previously, certificates evidencing a physical breach are in themselves good documents and there is no documentary breach to trigger the potential application of the *de minimis* rule.

[97] *SIAT di del Ferro v. Tradax Overseas SA* [1978] 2 Lloyd's Rep. 470, 493 seems to suggest that the buyer is not able to reject an altered bill of lading if an alteration is due to a 'minor clerical error' (see BENJAMIN'S, *supra note* 7, at 19–040, also restating the position in these terms). However, there may be a question of whether this constitutes a general position or whether it was formulated in the context of a Tradax documents clause not allowing the buyer to reject the documents in the case of a minor clerical error if the seller provided, at the buyer's request, a guarantee.

[98] Debattista, BILL, *supra note* 44, at 217–19.

[99] *Id.*

few documentary discrepancies would be trivial,[100] this rule at least leaves judges some room to curb an attempt of purely 'technical' termination, where justice so requires.[101] Its practical impact being small, its value arguably lies in signalling that the commercial law's function of facilitating commerce is not the same as promoting a naked self-interest. Further, this view isolates the documents too much from physical performance. Surely, a minor clerical error (e.g., a simple misspelling in the description of the goods on a bill of lading, which however leaves no doubt that the bill relates to the contract goods) should not allow the buyer to escape from what is, after all, a contract for the sale of *goods*.[102] As to the alignment of the documentary requirements with those under letters of credit, it can firstly be argued that, whilst desirable, the alignment is not vital since performing the contracts, such as those on CIF or FOB terms, is not the same as performing financial obligations in the context of a banking system where 'the autonomy principle is needed to facilitate the flow of payment in just the same way as a bill of exchange derives its character from being an unconditional order in writing divorced from the underlying transaction'.[103] But, more to the point, even 'strict compliance' in documentary credits has not been treated as meaning 'perfect tender', with some latitude given to cater for trivial discrepancies.[104] It is submitted that a similar function needs to be performed by *de minimis* in the cash against documents contract. While documentary duties are generally to be strictly complied with in sales contracts, strict compliance cannot mean perfection and *de minimis* should be there to identify tenders which are strictly complying but are imperfect.[105]

Secondly, a potential exception to the buyer's right to reject documents and terminate the contract for a documentary breach, which, as noted, would normally amount to a breach of condition, could flow from s. 15(A) SGA which restricts the buyer's right to reject the goods for a breach, which would otherwise be a breach of condition, if it 'is so slight that it would be unreasonable for [the buyer] to reject them'.[106] It is arguable that although this section refers to the goods, the same rule should, by analogy, apply to documents. However, this is unlikely since courts are

[100] See Bridge, *Documents, supra note* 30, at 224, stating, in the context of the requirement that a bill of lading must state the truth in all material respects, that most representations in a bill of lading would be material.

[101] See *Re Salomon & Co and Naudszus* (1899) 81 L.T. 325, 328. For criticism of the decision, see BENJAMIN'S, *supra note* 7, 19–040.

[102] For a detailed discussion, see BENJAMIN'S, *supra note* 7, at 19–008.

[103] Bridge, *Documents, supra note* 30, at 239. It can also be argued that if the buyer wants the level of documentary security as that afforded by the letter of credit mechanism, it should incorporate this mechanism into the contract, instead of agreeing to pay on the cash against documents terms.

[104] See, e.g., BENJAMIN'S, *supra note* 7, 23–097, 23–100–101 with references to the relevant case law.

[105] See *Re Salomon & Co and Naudszus* (n 101) 328.

[106] S. 15(A)(1)(b) SGA 1979.

conscious of the need to preserve legal certainty in documentary trade and would be able to derogate from this provision, by implying an intention to this effect from the contract, as allowed by s. 15(A)(2).[107] Section 15(A) can, however, creep into the documentary world from another direction. If the position that a buyer is entitled to reject the documents and to terminate the contract because a certificate, albeit a good certificate, evidences a repudiatory physical breach[108] is maintained, s. 15(A) may not allow such rejection and termination where what is initially a breach of condition 'is so slight' as to make 'unreasonable' for the goods to be rejected.[109]

Subject to the *de minimis* rule, s. 15(A) and the seller's right to cure, discussed in the next section, the scope of the buyer's right to reject the documents and to terminate the contract can be set out as follows. In the case of *defects* in shipping documents, the buyer is usually entitled to reject them and to terminate the contract. This will be so, for example, where a bill of lading is not genuine,[110] is unclean,[111] is dated outside the shipment period,[112] is not in a negotiable form, is not valid and effective, is not issued on shipment,[113] does not relate to contract goods or does not provide for contractual quantity,[114] does not state the destination specified in CIF contracts,[115] does not provide for a continuous documentary cover,[116] does not evidence a carriage contract on contractual terms,[117] or, if the latter (CIF) is silent, on usual terms, refers to the freight payable as per charter party.[118] A discrepancy in the invoice also generally entitles the buyer to reject the documents. If, for instance, the quantity of the goods stated in the invoice does not correspond to that specified in the contract and the bill of lading, the buyer can reject.[119] However, on occasions the courts exercise a degree of flexibility when considering the consequences of non-compliance of the invoice with the contractual requirements. In *John Martin of London, Ltd v. A E Taylor & Co, Ltd*,[120] the CIF contract provided that the invoices

[107] There is much support for this restrictive role of s. 15(A) in documentary matters in legal literature. See, e.g., Debattista, BILL, *supra note* 44, at 215; Takahashi, *Right*, *supra note* 5, at 111; BENJAMIN'S, *supra note* 7, at 19–182.

[108] See earlier for the explanation and assessment of this position.

[109] See Mullis, Termination, *supra note* 5.

[110] *James Finlay and Co Ltd v. NV Kwik Hoo Tong Handel Maatschappij* [1929] 1 K.B. 400, 408.

[111] *M Golodetz & Co Inc v. Czarnikow-Rionda Co Inc (The Galatia)* [1980] 1 W.L.R. 495; *Libau Wood v. H Smith & Sons* [1930] 37 Ll. L. Rep. 296.

[112] *Re General Trading Co and Van Stolk's Commissiehandel* (1911) 16 Com. Cas. 95; *Bowes v. Shand* (1876–77) L.R. 2 App. Cas. 455.

[113] *Hansson v. Hamel*, *supra note* 89.

[114] *Libau Wood*, *supra note* 111.

[115] *SIAT* (n 97); *Soules*, *supra note* 85.

[116] *Hansson v. Hamel*, *supra note* 89.

[117] *Soules* (n 85); *Shipton, Anderson v. John Weston* [1922] 10 Ll. L. Rep. 762.

[118] *Soules*, *supra note* 85.

[119] See *Tamvaco v Lucas* (1859) 1 Ellis & Ellis 581.

[120] [1953] 2 Lloyd's Rep. 589.

ought to state the lodgement of number of a certificate of origin whereas some of the tendered invoices merely stated that the forms had been lodged with the Customs Officer with the number 'to be advised'. Applying what the court called 'business sense', this contractual provision was held to be merely *directory*, and not *obligatory*, because the obtaining of the number was not within the seller's control as it was up to the Customs to issue the number and all that the seller could do was to send the forms to the Customs Office. The case reaffirms the point that justice and commercial realities, with their multitude of situational settings, demand some margin for latitude, even outside the boundaries of the *de minimis* rule and with the consideration of factors external to the document, in dealing with discrepancies in shipping documents.

The *non-delivery* of a shipping document should, generally, give rise to the rights to reject the documents and, subject to the possibility of cure, to terminate the contract. But the question of whether there are such rights if other documents (certificates of weight, quality, quantity or health) are not delivered, would appear to require the assessment of the relevant circumstances such as the commercial significance of the document.[121] As seen from *Mantovani v. Carapelli*,[122] a weight certificate was not regarded as vital whereas, in another case,[123] the seller's non-delivery of a sworn quantity certificate was treated as a breach of condition. The reasoning in both decisions is not sufficiently extensive to identify their distinguishing features, but a sense that English law simply leaves room for judicial discretion and flexibility is difficult to shake off.

Under the CISG, the buyer is able to terminate the contract for a documentary breach if it is fundamental, that is 'if it results in such detriment to the other party as substantially to deprive him of what he is entitled to expect under the contract' (Art. 25).[124] In relation to the goods, this provision has been interpreted as setting a very high bar. If the buyer is still able to resell the goods or to put them to a reasonable use, or if the seller offers to cure the defects, the breach is unlikely to be fundamental.[125] The CISG is widely viewed as treating termination as an exceptional remedy of last resort, with the central policies being respecting the binding nature of a contract, keeping it alive as long as possible and preventing costs and economic waste often resulting from termination.

[121] See BENJAMIN'S, *supra note* 7, at 19–149.

[122] See note 56 and the accompanying text.

[123] *Libau Wood* (n 111).

[124] Another route to termination under 49(1)(b) is not relevant in the case of documents.

[125] See, e.g., Supreme Court 28 October 1998 (Switzerland) <http://cisgw3.law.pace.edu/cases/981028s1.html>; Commercial Court of the Canton of Aargau (Switzerland) 5 November 2002 <http://cisgw3.law.pace.edu/cases/021105s1.html>. For further references, see Bridge, *Avoidance*, *supra note* 68, at 920–2.

However, the realisation that this approach is not well suited to the commodities and documentary trade, particularly in relation to timely and documentary obligations,[126] has led to the argument that a much lower standard of strict compliance applies to documentary duties. Such a position can be arrived at by implying the parties' intention to derogate from the fundamental breach test by virtue of Arts. 8 and 6[127] or by finding a usage to this effect, particularly where INCOTERMS or UCP are referred to in the contract.[128] It has even been suggested that strict compliance is an accepted custom in documentary sales,[129] to which the CISG would have to give effect.[130] A legal technique implied by those advocating this view is one of *derogation* from Art. 25. Another technique is not to derogate from Art. 25, but to focus on the standard of the 'deprivation of contractual expectation' and to argue that this notion of a 'detriment' refers not to the extent of the loss suffered, but to the '*importance of an interest*' created by the contract. This 'contractual interest' is again assumed to demand, on a notional application of Arts. 8 and 9, strictly conforming documents.[131]

It cannot be assumed that there will be sufficient grounds in every documentary trade case to warrant either derogation,[132] particularly considering the drafters' intention to discourage light departures from the Convention's express provisions, or the inference of a fundamentally important 'contractual interest' in strictly conforming documents.[133] With the Art. 25 test looking at the consequences of a breach and

[126] For example, termination in the commodities trading context is unlikely to give rise to the same level of costs as those often flowing from terminating, say, a contract for a heavy machinery, since there will normally be a readily available market in which the seller can dispose of the rejected goods (see, e.g., Bridge, *Avoidance, supra note* 68, at 915).

[127] See CISG-AC 5 (n 76) 4.17; Schwenzer, *Danger, supra note* 4, 803–6; Alistair Mullis, *Avoidance for Breach under the Vienna Convention; A Critical Analysis of Some of the Early Cases* in Anglo-Swedish Studies in Law 348–9 (M. Andreas & N. Jarborg eds., Lustus Forlag: Stockholm 1998); Maartje Bijl, *Fundamental Breach in Documentary Sales Contracts: The Doctrine of Strict Compliance with the Underlying Sales Contract*, 1 European J. Commercial Contract L. 19, 26 (2009).

[128] See CISG-AC 5 (n 76) 4.13; Singh & Leisinger, *Law, supra note* 81, at 182.

[129] Ulrich G. Schroeter in Schlechtriem & Schwenzer, Commentary, *supra note* 36 at 432.

[130] See Art. 9 CISG.

[131] Schroeter, *supra note* 129, at 433, taking this position in the context of CIF/FOB clauses which, in the commentator's view, necessitate the assumption that documentary duties are 'fundamentally important'. It must be borne in mind that while terms such as "CIF" and "FOB" are frequently used in the documentary and commodities trade, they are not necessarily confined to this context. It is not the CIF or FOB term itself which may dictate strict compliance with timely and/or documentary obligations, but rather a commercial context which is decisive.

[132] See, e.g., Schwenzer, *Danger, supra note* 4, at 805.

[133] See Bridge, *Avoidance, supra note* 68, at 935; Secretariat's Commentary on art. 5, 1978 Draft. In fact, there is a degree of inherent tension in this position. It seeks to draw on the surrounding context to derogate from Art. 25, which rightly implies that contract interpretation is a matter of individual case, and yet often advocates the assumption that Art 25. should *always* (or almost always) be derogated from.

'detriment' being a broad notion, the 'contractual interest' cannot be the only factor to be taken into account. This shows that a proper application of Art. 25 requires an overall assessment of the circumstances, including an innocent party's loss.[134] This also means that the test requires tribunals to look beyond the face of the documents to ascertain whether a breach is fundamental.

Unsurprisingly, therefore, the CISG decisions are far from adopting the strict compliance standard. In several cases, the tribunals assessed the consequences of discrepancies in a bill of lading and ruled that no fundamental breach had been committed.[135] What is more, in some of these cases,[136] the contracts provided for the payment under a letter of credit, with the documents having been rejected by the banks. The tribunals took the view that a letter of credit was only a conditional promise[137] by the buyer to pay, with the result that if the bank did not make a payment due to discrepancies in the documents, the seller had a right to claim the price directly from the buyer.[138] These decisions give rise to two points. Not only did the tribunals not think it necessary to interpret a fundamental breach as setting the same high standard as strict compliance in documentary credits, but also no attempt was made to explore whether an agreement on the letter of credit could lead to an inference of the parties' intention to apply the strict compliance standard to documentary duties under a sales contract. These decisions effectively deprive the buyer of the level of documentary security it sought to obtain when contracting for the payment by the letter of credit. While English law also presumptively regards such a payment mechanism as a conditional payment,[139] this condition is there to protect the seller from a default by a bank rather than to enable it to avoid the documentary security created by the letter of credit. The result is that the seller's non-compliance under a documentary credit is regarded as a repudiatory breach of the sales contract.[140] Tribunals applying the CISG are thus well advised to infer an intention to apply the same documentary standard to a sales contract as that under a documentary credit. This can be done as derogation from Art. 25 or by interpreting Art. 25 in the light of that intention.

Even where a documentary breach was treated as fundamental, the tribunals did not assume that *any* discrepancy would have entitled the buyer to reject. One

[134] See Secretariat Commentary on article 23 of the 1978 Draft; Bridge, *Avoidance*, supra note 68, at 918.

[135] CIETAC, 25 June 1997 <http://cisgw3.law.pace.edu/cases/970625c1.html>; CIETAC, 4 June 1999 <http://cisgw3.law.pace.edu/cases/990604c1.html>. See also Nantong Intermediate People's Court 29 September 2000 (China) <http://cisgw3.law.pace.edu/cases/000929c2.html>.

[136] CIETAC, 25 June 1997 (n 135); CIETAC, 4 June 1999 (n 135).

[137] See also CIETAC, 1 April 1997 <http://cisgw3.law.pace.edu/cases/970401c1.html>.

[138] See CIETAC, 25 June 1997 and 4 June 1999, *supra note* 135.

[139] See, e.g., *Ficom SA v. Sociedad Cadex Limitada* [1980] 2 Lloyd's Rep. 118.

[140] See BENJAMIN'S, *supra note* 7, at 23–216.

tribunal held that discrepancies in a bill of lading (different contract number to the one stated in the invoice, incomplete description of the goods, no date of issue) were sufficient to justify the avoidance of the contract,[141] but noted that the defects were not 'purely trivial'.

If tribunals make decisions on defects in a bill of lading on a case-by-case basis, a similar attitude can be expected in respect of other documents. In a well-known case (*Cobalt sulphate*),[142] a certificate of origin incorrectly stated the place of origin and only one correct copy of a certificate of analysis was received by the buyer whereas several copies were required. The certificate of origin was regarded as defective because the buyer could not be expected to resell the goods accompanied by such a certificate. Nevertheless, the court held that no fundamental breach had been committed because the buyer could have itself obtained a correct certificate to carry out a resale. No fundamental breach was likewise found in relation to the certificates of analysis. Having been given an opportunity of an expert examination, the buyer could be certain about the contractual compliance of the matters falling within the remit of such a certificate. Even if the buyer intended to resell several lots of the goods separately, requiring several copies of the certificates of analysis, it 'could have produced additional certificates itself by making photocopies'.

This case shows that reaching the fundamental breach threshold, even in documentary breach cases can be difficult. But, similar to English law on certificates, the stance in CISG cases is inconclusive as some other tribunals were willing to find a fundamental breach in not too dissimilar circumstances. In one case,[143] a certificate of origin, while referring to the contractually specified place of origin (Russia), was issued by a chamber of commerce in Texas, USA, presumably raising suspicions about the correctness of the certificate. The certificate also stated the incorrect quantity, referring to '950,71 tons' instead of '950,712 tons'. With no reasoning provided, the tribunal simply stated that the seller had committed a fundamental breach.[144] Finally, where it is clear that the defects in technical documentation accompanying the goods make it impossible to use the goods, it is clear that a fundamental breach has been committed. For example, where the regulations in the buyer's country require state agencies to inspect the equipment using its accompanying technical documentation, and where the documentation does not address the essential items, falling within the scope of such an inspection, the seller commits a fundamental

[141] ICC Arbitration Case No. 7645, March 1995 <http://www.cisg.law.pace.edu/cases/957645i1.html#cxiv> paras. [78]-[80].

[142] Supreme Court 3 April 1996 (Germany), *supra note* 84.

[143] CIETAC, 7 July 1997 <http://cisgw3.law.pace.edu/cases/970707c1.html>.

[144] What, however, these two cases share is how the notion of conformity of a certificate is understood – that is, an incorrect certificate is defective. This is similar to the position in English law, which defines a good certificate as the one which states the truth, even if it does not comply with the contractual requirements in relation to the goods.

breach since the state inspection cannot be carried out, resulting in the buyer's inability to use the goods.[145]

There is little doubt that because shipping documents perform a number of essential functions, non-delivery of at least one of them should, in principle, amount to a fundamental breach.[146] Outside the documentary trade or if a document is not a shipping document, the question of whether non-delivery of a document(s) constitutes a fundamental breach is to be answered by looking at the surrounding circumstances. The main factor is the extent to which such non-delivery affected the buyer's intention as to the use of the goods.[147] Here, documents are subordinate to the purpose for which the buyer purchased the goods or to the seller's obligations in respect of the goods. In one case,[148] the significance of non-delivery of the freight pre-paid airway bill, carrier's certificate, invoice and tax receipts was viewed in terms of the seller's failure to comply with its obligations to deliver the goods, to make a carriage contract and to pay export duties and taxes in respect of the goods. Similarly, non-delivery of a certificate of origin, where it is essential for the export of the goods, will be a fundamental breach since that breach will cause non-delivery of the goods.[149] In another case,[150] non-delivery of an insurance policy and of a quality certificate was found to constitute a fundamental breach since it made it impossible for the buyer to conduct import customs clearance and to take delivery of the goods. Where the contract requires the goods to be 'organic', non-delivery of a certificate confirming the goods' organic origin will constitute a fundamental breach, if the certificate is the only way to ascertain whether the goods are in fact organic.[151]

A major factor to reckon with in assessing whether and when the right to terminate is available is whether the seller has a right to cure non-conformity. A legal regime emphasising the binding nature of contracts and promises (thereby, condemning technical termination) and the prevention of economic waste would allow the seller to cure its breach. In contrast, the systems which have been shaped against the backdrop of trade sectors where legal certainty and speed are paramount, would be more hostile to the possibility of cure as it would prevent, or at least delay, the buyer's ability to terminate the contract at once, also creating uncertainty as to if and when the buyer will be able to do so.[152] Presumably, other policy reasons underlying

[145] CIETAC, 19 January 2000 <http://www.cisg.law.pace.edu/cases/000119c1.html>.

[146] This may be subject to the seller's right to cure (see later).

[147] See Arts. 8 and 9 CISG; Schwenzer, *Danger, supra note* 4, at 800.

[148] CIETAC, September 2006 <http://cisgw3.law.pace.edu/cases/060900c4.html>.

[149] Appellate Court Barcelona 12 February 2002 (Spain) <http://cisgw3.law.pace.edu/cases/020212s4.html>. See also ICAC, 2/1995, dated 11 May 1997 <http://cisgw3.law.pace.edu/cases/970511r1.html>.

[150] Arbitration proceeding 5 July 2005 (Ukraine) <http://cisgw3.law.pace.edu/cases/050705u5.html>.

[151] Appellate Court München 13 November 2002 (Germany) <http://cisgw3.law.pace.edu/cases/021113g1.html>.

[152] Another source of uncertainty emanating from the right to cure relates to the need to define the circumstances when this right can be exercised and to evaluate where these circumstances are present.

this approach in the context of the commodities trading are that in contrast with items such as machinery, often designed for the buyer's particular needs, there is a market at which the seller can dispose of the rejected commodities.[153] If so, it is arguable that easy termination should be allowed because the seller is in no worse position than the buyer to deal with the consequences of termination, particularly considering that many players in this sector are large corporations. All in all, easily available termination rights are, *in this context*, very much in line with the idea of maintaining a fair and reasonable allocation of commercial risks.

English law is often seen as being in this latter category. However, although there is no statutory right to cure, there are judicial pronouncements,[154] some relating specifically to documentary duties,[155] recognising the seller's right to re-tender after an original non-conforming tender has been rejected, provided the time for the seller's performance has not expired.[156] It has been argued that there should be no such right since the commodities trade conducted through strings heavily depends on a prompt tender of conforming documents and only a strict rule, allowing the seller one chance to perform, provides a real incentive to present conforming documents.[157] The courts are undoubtedly well aware of these considerations and the pronouncements supporting cure seem to reflect the reluctance to disregard entirely the idea that contracts are made to be performed, particularly where the time for performance has not yet expired: it is arguable that an express fixation of the time limit for performance evidences the parties' intention to allow the tender of the performance by that cut-off date.[158]

In any case, the scope of this right to cure is limited. First, if the original non-conforming tender evidences the seller's inability to perform – for example, an earlier notice of appropriation, accepted by the buyer, but referring, say, to a non-existent vessel, rendering it impossible for the seller to tender documents complying with that notice – the buyer may at once be entitled to terminate the contract on the ground of the seller's repudiation.[159] Secondly, where the contract does not set a precise time for a documentary tender, as is usually the case, a restrictive attitude to

[153] See Bridge, *Avoidance, supra note* 68, at 915.

[154] *Borrowman Phillips & Co v. Free & Hollis* (1878–79) L.R. 4 QBD 500; *Soon Hua Seng Co Ltd v. Glencore Grain Ltd* [1996] 1 Lloyd's Rep. 398, 403; *Motor Oil Hellas (Corinth) Refineries SA v. Shipping Corporation of India ('The Kanchenjunga')* [1990] 1 Lloyd's Rep. 391, 399.

[155] *SIAT* (n 97) 470; *EE Brian Smith Ltd v. Wheatsheaf Mills Ltd* [1939] 2 KB 302, 314–15; *Empresa Exportadora de Azucar v. Industria Azucarera Nacional SA (The 'Playa Larga' and 'Marble Islands')* [1983] 2 Lloyd's Rep. 171.

[156] Similarly, where the payment is by a letter of credit, the seller has the right to make a complying presentation, after the original presentation has been rejected for non-compliance, provided it does so before the final date for the presentation (see, e.g., BENJAMIN'S, *supra note* 7, at 23–194).

[157] Debattista, BILL, *supra note* 44, at 222.

[158] See *The Playa Larga, supra note* 155, at 171, 186.

[159] See further BENJAMIN'S (n 7) 12–032 and 19–072; Apps, *Right to Cure, supra note* 52, at 534.

the possibility of cure can be expected since the buyer cannot 'normally be expected to put with several attempted deliveries'.[160] Thirdly, just as the cure by substituting non-conforming goods is not possible where the contract calls for specific goods (assuming they cannot be repaired),[161] so may the re-tender of the documents not be an option: if a bill of lading is defective by evidencing a late shipment, the only way to cure is to tender a fresh bill relating to *another* consignment shipped on time, which is not possible if the contract required specific goods in respect of which the first bill was issued. In fact, there are suggestions that where the goods are specific, their delivery is not a *tender* but is the performance which cannot be cured.[162] It is only a tender of performance, and not the performance or delivery, which can be cured. This distinction is merely a conceptual formulation of what is a natural consequence of the unavailability of cure in the case of specific goods and hardly adds anything valuable, but if it is deemed to be valid, there is no reason why it should not apply to documentary duties.

The CISG confers more expansive rights of cure. The seller can cure any lack of conformity in its performance, including those in the documents,[163] up to the due time for performance provided that cure 'does not cause the buyer unreasonable inconvenience or unreasonable expense'.[164] At this stage, the CISG is not much different from English law. Even the factors limiting the right to cure, set out in the previous paragraph, will find their way into the Convention. If the original non-conforming tender evidences the seller's inability to perform in accordance with the contract, at least in an important respect (1), or if no precise time is set, with the documents having to be tendered within a reasonable time (2), it is arguable that cure in (1) and the possibility of repeated attempts to cure in (2) will cause the buyer 'unreasonable inconvenience'. If the parties' intention is to contract for specific goods, cure by means of tendering documents relating to some other consignment is impossible and the legal basis for this conclusion is either the 'unreasonable inconvenience' provision or, more pertinently, a finding that by contracting for specific goods, the parties implicitly derogated from the possibility of cure.[165]

Where the CISG goes much further than English law is in allowing cure after the due date for performance. Although Art. 48 subjects this right to the buyer's right to terminate, a number of courts brought cure through the 'back door' by treating it as

[160] BENJAMIN'S (n 7) 12–032; Filippo Lorenzon, *International Trade and Shipping Documents* in SOUTHAMPTON ON SHIPPING LAW 146 (Informa: London 2008) 146, more categorically asserting that where no time limit is set in the contract, the seller's tender is the performance of the contract, as opposed to a tender of performance which can be re-tendered.

[161] See *The Playa Larga*, *supra note* 155, at 186.

[162] Bridge, SALE, *supra note* 20, at 674.

[163] See Art. 34.

[164] See Arts. 34 and 37.

[165] See Art. 6 CISG.

a factor in deciding whether the breach is fundamental.[166] Cure after the due date can make the CISG ill-suited to the commodities trade, since such cure contravenes an expectation of a prompt tender of conforming documents and destroys the finality and certainty of the buyer's legal position at the due date of performance. It will be recalled that there have been calls to adopt a much lower threshold for a fundamental breach in the commodities trade. The argument is that since the CISG takes account of the peculiarities of the surrounding trading sectors, the seller should have no right to cure under Art. 48.[167]

Thus far, however, there is no indication that this approach has gained favour and, in fact, quite the opposite has, on occasions, taken place. In the earlier mentioned *Cobalt Sulphate* case,[168] the court suggested that there could be no fundamental breach if the innocent buyer itself could cure the defects in the certificate. In contrast with other cases, which merely treat the breaching *seller's* ability to cure as a relevant factor, this decision sets the fundamental breach threshold even higher by making the *buyer's* ability to cure a pre-requisite. This approach not only imposes an unjustifiable burden on,[169] and is repressive to, the buyer, but also amounts to the re-writing of the contract by turning the seller's obligation to procure a certificate into a buyer's obligation. Equally importantly, there is no support for this position in the Convention.[170]

The question that matters to both English law and the CISG relates to the extent to which cure is effective in relation to documentary obligations. The cure of goods can take the form of repair or replacement and the starting point is the same when it comes to documents, including a situation where a particular document is missing, in which case cure would mean the delivery of a missing document.[171] Remedying a defect in a document, however, is rarely possible. If a 'shipped' bill of lading is required and it is unclean, refers to a non-contractual quantity/weight, to non-contractual goods or is dated outside the shipment period, the breach cannot be remedied simply by altering the bill and inserting the contractually compliant information.[172] The bill, performing a 'receipt' function, evidences the non-compliance with physical obligations and the 'clock can never be turned

166 See *supra note* 125.

167 Schwenzer, *Danger*, supra note 4, at 805; Corinne Widmer in Schlechtriem & Schwenzer, COMMENTARY ON THE UN CONVENTION ON THE INTERNATIONAL SALE OF GOODS (CISG) 441 (4th ed., I. Schwenzer ed., Oxford University Press: Oxford 2010) at 564, arguing that this can also be possible under Art 9.

168 See *supra note* 142 and the accompanying main text.

169 See Mullis, *Avoidance*, *supra note* 127, 347.

170 *Id.*

171 See Widmer, *supra note* 167, at 565.

172 Similarly in relation to insurance documents and certificates, see Widmer, *supra note* 167, at 565; Supreme Court 3 April 1996 (Germany), *supra note* 84.

back'.[173] To cure such breaches, a new bill relating to another (conforming) consignment needs to be tendered.[174]

If a bill shows that a carriage contract was not concluded in accordance with the sales contract or, if it is silent, on ordinary and usual terms,[175] the only way for the seller to cure is to renegotiate a carriage contract and to ask the carrier to issue fresh bills reflecting a new compliant carriage contract.[176] But this is unlikely to be possible, particularly where a 'shipped' bill of lading was required, since by the time of the original documentary tender the vessel will have sailed away and the possibility of renegotiating a carriage contract even at a later stage is hardly conceivable.[177] If a mistake is made on a bill, such as where it is made out to a wrong party, it may be possible for a mistake to be corrected, but again fresh bills need to be issued.[178]

Cure by repair is probably only possible where alterations to a document are made to correct minor, clerical or typographical errors. However, considering that in such cases the buyer would generally not be entitled to reject such documents in the first place, these will only be cases where the seller does not object to the initial rejection and decides to correct and to re-tender the documents. Thus, whilst cure of documents may be feasible in certain settings, the scope for the exercise of this right is rather limited.

III. DAMAGES

In English law, the discussion of damages for documentary breaches centres around two scenarios. The first is where there is a physical breach, such as a late shipment, *and* a documentary breach, such as where a bill of lading is not genuine by being dated within the shipment period, thereby concealing a true shipment date. If the buyer pays against the apparently conforming documents and only learns the true facts later when the right to reject is lost, damages have been awarded for the loss of the right to reject on a falling market. In *James Finlay and Co Ltd v. NV Kwik*

[173] Bridge, *Avoidance* (n 68) 937; see further *Mendala III Transport v Total Transport Corporation (The 'Willomi Tanana')* [1993] 2 Lloyd's Rep. 41, 46.

[174] On the practice of issuing 'switch' bills of lading, see note 178.

[175] English law and Art. 32(2) CISG take a similar approach.

[176] See also *SIAT*, *supra note* 97.

[177] For example, if a bill of lading was defective in that it allowed the carrier to call at several ports, whereas the sales contract required the vessel to proceed directly to destination, the renegotiation of the carriage contract will be impossible if by the time where the seller wishes to do so, the carrier has already called at one or more ports.

[178] See *Toepfer v Lenersan-Poortman NV* [1980] 1 Lloyd's Rep. 143. Mention should be made of a common practice of the so-called switch bills whereby a carrier may issue new bills containing some alterations (e.g., of the identity or details of the shipper, origin of the goods, date of issue of the bills or of the port shipment) in exchange for the original set of bills of lading. This practice has been said to be dangerous, not least because it creates opportunities for fraud (see *Rudolf Oetker v. IFA Internationale Frachtagentur AG ('The Almak')* [1985] 1 Lloyd's Rep. 557).

Hoo Tong Handel Maatschappij,[179] the CIF buyer on these facts was awarded damages for the difference between the contract price and the market price at the time where the buyer resold the goods (market loss damages).[180] Since the risk of a market decline is thrown back to the seller, this is the same result as the one that would have been achieved had the buyer been able to reject the documents.

There has been some unease in connection with this and similar decisions.[181] It has been argued that the market loss damages 'make nonsense of the legal limitations on the right to reject'.[182] It made no difference to the buyer that the goods had been shipped a little late since they arrived at the same time as they would have arrived had the shipment been timely and it was felt that the buyer had taken advantage of the seller through a 'legal technicality'.[183] It has been suggested that the *Finlay* damages ought to be confined to cases where the seller is 'guilty of some degree of culpable complicity in the misdating of the bill of lading'.[184] If so, it has been argued that damages should be based on tort principles and, where fraud is involved, these damages would be particularly useful in terms of their deterrent effect.[185]

Ultimately, the decision in *Finlay* reflects not only a sense that the buyer suffered a real financial loss by being deprived of its right to reject, but also recognises a documentary breach as an independent ground for claiming damages since damages were based on what the buyer's position would have been had only a documentary obligation been performed, with no regard for what the position would have been had a physical obligation also been performed.[186] If so, a later decision appears to be more restrained, in the *second scenario* where there is no physical breach, with the

179 [1929] 1 K.B. 400.

180 See *Procter & Gamble* (n 10) 25; *Kwei Tek Chao* (n 9) 492. The question arises as to which date for determining the market price should, as a matter of principle, be taken. Since the rationale is that the buyer lost the right to reject, the relevant date should be that when the buyer would or ought to have rejected the documents had the bill of lading been correctly dated. This would be the date when the documents are tendered to the buyer since it is then that it becomes or ought to become aware of the late shipment, which would be apparent from the bill of lading (see BENJAMIN'S [n 7] 19–210).

181 *Kwei Tek Chao, supra note* 9.

182 Guenter Treitel, *Damages for Breach of a C.I.F. Contract*, LLOYD'S MARITIME & COMMERCIAL L. QUARTERLY 457, 461 (1988).

183 *Huilerie L'abeille v. Societe des Huileries du Niger ('The Kastellon')* [1978] 2 Lloyd's Rep. 203, 204.

184 BENJAMIN'S, *supra note* 7, at 19–206.

185 *Id.*

186 The counsel for the seller in *Finlay* argued that the court ought to have 'regard to the contract as a whole' and not just to 'a mere part of it' (*James Finlay, supra note* 179, at 404). If the *contract* had been performed, there would have been no late shipment and no reason for misdating a bill of lading. This approach would have resulted in the difference in value measure: a comparison between the situation in which the buyer found itself as a result of the (double) breach (with the goods and a false bill of lading on hand on a fallen market) and that in which it would have been had the shipment been made on time. But the traditional damages measure has not developed with the possibility of a double breach in mind and the buyer can choose a cause of action. Nonetheless, it may be worth considering whether damages need to take account of the duality of obligations, which are *inter-linked*, in order to have regard to the contract as a whole.

goods shipped on time, but there is a documentary breach where a bill of lading, although dated within the shipment period, does not state the true shipment date. In *Procter & Gamble Philippine Manufacturing Corp v. Kurt A Becher GMBH & Co KG*,[187] arising from these facts, the buyer was held not to be entitled to the *Finlay* damages because had the bill been correctly dated, it would have merely showed that the goods had been shipped on time and the buyer would not have been able to reject the documents. It was held that the loss of the right to reject had been caused not by the seller's failure to provide a genuine bill, but because the buyer did not know about the documentary breach when the documents had been tendered.[188]

Underlying this reasoning is also the reluctance to recognise a documentary breach as an independent ground triggering the market loss damages. The decision has been criticised on the basis that since documentary obligations are separate from physical obligations, a documentary breach in itself should give rise to the *Finlay* damages:

> If the breach complained of is documentary in nature, as it very clearly was both in Finlay and in Procter&Gamble, then it is not immediately clear why the same documentary breach was any more serious in the first case than it was in the second, simply because in the first, the seller was also in breach of his physical duty to ship goods within the contract period. If the seller owes the buyer two duties, one documentary and the other physical, and if both modes of performance provide the buyer with opportunities to sell goods on the market, then it should follow that a purely documentary breach should give the buyer substantive remedies.[189]

There is some force and logic in this view. If a documentary duty is to be a truly separate obligation, this should be duly recognised in the remedial responses. An example of this recognition is where the law allows the rejection of documents for revealing non-conformity in the goods, even if that non-conformity would not justify the rejection of the goods themselves. It could be argued that damages should be approached in the same vein and in the cases like *Procter* the buyer should be awarded substantial damages. This approach could facilitate documentary and commodities trade by, at the very least, deterring sellers from committing documentary breaches. Conceptually, this issue can also be linked to the debate surrounding the notion of the 'performance interest':[190] the innocent party has contracted for a right to receive, and a corresponding obligation by the seller to deliver, conforming documents and that right in itself has a value.

The bottom line, however, is that documents are, at the end of the day, a means of selling the goods, even if the transaction is described as a sale of documents or as

[187] *Supra note* 10.

[188] p. 32 (per Nicholls L.J.).

[189] Debattista, Bill, *supra note* 44, at 235.

[190] See Daniel Friedmann, *The Performance Interest in Contract Damages*, 111 L. Quarterly Rev. 628 (1995).

a 'trade in contracts for the shipment of goods'.[191] It is this function that should be central to whether substantial damages are due for a documentary breach, particularly considering that much protection is already afforded to the buyer by expansive rejection rights. As was held in *Procter*, if a bill of lading becomes 'unmerchantable' and the buyer is unable to sell the goods afloat, by being 'locked-in' on a falling market damages ought to be *prima facie* awarded for the difference between the market value for the goods when the buyer would have been able to deal with the goods, had there been no defect, and the market value of the goods at the time when the buyer was able to resell them.[192] If the buyer lost an opportunity to fulfil a previously concluded sub-sale as a result of a documentary defect,[193] a lost profit on that sub-sale may be recoverable if the sub-sale was within the parties' contemplation.

A similar approach, it is submitted, should be taken to defining and measuring the loss for a documentary breach under the CISG. The only difference is that the Convention's starting point is the 'concrete' calculation of damages. Therefore, where the buyer is unable to sell the goods afloat due to the unmerchantability of a bill of lading, damages will need to be *prima facie* calculated with reference to the buyer's actual conduct and circumstances, subject to the mitigation rule. If, on a falling market, after taking over the goods the buyer resold them as soon as an opportunity arose at the highest price reasonably possible, damages should be calculated as the difference between the price obtained in the resale and the price the buyer would have obtained had the documents been conforming. That latter price would normally be determined with reference to the market price, in which case the calculation becomes almost identical to that in English law. The only difference relates to the first reference point: English law still looks at the *market value* when the buyer would have been able to deal with the goods whereas under the CISG, it is suggested, it is the *price actually obtained* (assuming it is reasonable) that should be used. Practically, the difference is minor, since in assessing the reasonableness of the resale, tribunals tend to look to the market price.[194]

If, but for a breach, the buyer would have resold the goods under a specific sub-sale contract, the difference between the contract price and the price in that sub-sale can be awarded, subject to the 'duty to mitigate', which, as noted, would usually mean reselling at the highest price reasonably possible. Since benefits obtained as a consequence of the breach are to be taken into account to prevent over-compensation, the price obtained in a resale is to be set-off against the claimed profit margin under a sub-sale. The sub-sale measure may well be used in English law provided it

[191] *Procter & Gamble* (n 10) 22.

[192] *Id.*, 32.

[193] *Id.*, 31.

[194] Djakhongir Saidov, The Law of Damages in International Sales: The Cisg and Other Interational Instruments 179 (Hart Publishing: Oxford 2008).

was within the parties' contemplation.[195] In short, there is likely to be little practical difference in the damages awards under the two regimes.

The reported decisions take a similar approach to the one advocated here by awarding damages with references to the consequences arising from documentary breaches. Damages have been awarded for the amount of customs fees and taxes, which the buyer would have been exempt from paying had a contractually required certificate of origin been delivered,[196] or for the demurrage and other costs which the buyer had to incur as a result of the delay in delivering an export licence.[197] Where a failure to deliver an insurance policy and a quality certificate prevented the buyer from conducting customs clearance and taking over the goods, causing it to breach the currency regulations in its country and to pay a fine to state authorities, damages have been awarded for the amount of the fine.[198]

Finally, are the *Finlay* damages possible under the Convention's remedial scheme? The Convention does not expressly provide for the grounds for the loss of the right to reject or to terminate – such as waiver, acceptance, affirmation or estoppel – in the way English law does.[199] The right of termination will, however, be lost, if a declaration of avoidance is not given within a reasonable time.[200] Therefore, the buyer who had paid against the apparently conforming documents, which would have been rejected (and the contract would have been terminated) had they stated the truth, can, in principle, argue that it had lost the right to terminate if a period exceeding 'reasonable time' has passed. As shown, the loss of the right to terminate has real financial implications and may well constitute 'a loss' under Art. 74, which generally includes all types of financial loss.[201]

IV. CONCLUSION

The fact that English law has a much longer history of governing the documentary and commodities sales often leads to the view that it is a better sales law, than the CISG, for this purpose. However, the preceding analysis shows that the comparison between the two has to be much more nuanced. As there are now a number of reported cases

[195] The CISG, of course, also contains the foreseeability test, but it is primarily a test of *limiting* damages (see Art. 74), whereas, in this context, the parties' contemplation is used in English law for *defining* the loss and pre-determining a method of its calculation.

[196] See Foreign Trade Court of Arbitration, Serbian Chamber of Commerce, 23 January 2008 <http://cisgw3.law.pace.edu/cases/080123sb.html>.

[197] CIETAC, 15 December 1998 <http://cisgw3.law.pace.edu/cases/981215c1.html>.

[198] Arbitration proceeding 5 July 2005, *supra note* 150.

[199] There is scope for the development of similar grounds by drawing on the Convention's general principles (Art. 7[2]). For a similar view, see Bridge, *Law*, *supra note* 1, at 32.

[200] See Art. 49(2). See also Arts. 39 and 82 setting out the situations where the right to avoid may be lost.

[201] For concerns raised in this respect, see the paragraph, beginning with note 181, in the main text and note 186.

involving documentary matters, the CISG is no longer a 'blank page'. In fact, the tribunals thus far have approached the remedial consequences of documentary breaches in a broadly similar manner, curiously manifesting a fair degree of uniform treatment. One feature of the CISG cases is that the documents have not been taken at their face value, with the decisions on the availability of the right to terminate being made with reference to the surrounding factual circumstances. Since this introduces a degree of unpredictability and is inimical to the buyer's ability to make prompt decisions, English law, with its treatment of documentary obligations as conditions, may appear to be superior. But it is naïve to suppose that in a system, which has witnessed a great multitude of commercial scenarios for more than a century, would be predicated on so simple a position. The need to assess a surrounding factual background also arises in English law. Despite an often pronounced need for documents to be strictly complying with the contract, with some calls for treating that as nothing less than a perfect tender,[202] English law is not that stringent and inflexible.

All things considered, the two regimes are not as far apart as they are, at times, perceived to be. It is true that their starting points are at the opposite ends of the spectrum between certainty and flexibility. The pursuit of certainty in English law is evident in treating documentary breaches as breaches of condition while the CISG demands a factual analysis in order to ascertain whether a documentary breach amounts to a fundamental breach. As shown, however, this position of English law is subject to a number of qualifications which, taken together with some invasions into the separation of the rejection rights and the possibility of cure before the due date, show how English law has departed its end of the spectrum falling short of reaching the centre ground.

The CISG, with its half empty bag of imperfect case law, probably unsteadily occupies a symmetrical point on the other side. A demand for factual analysis can be a positive force even in the commodities trade by preventing excessively technical termination, particularly where buyers rely on minor discrepancies to escape from the contract. In other cases, the tribunals should interpret Art. 25 CISG in the light of the surrounding commercial context. This equally applies to the possibility of cure after the due date where, it is submitted, the tribunals should be particularly conscious of the need for predictability and prompt decisions. Arguably, there is greater support for this position in the CISG which provides that the seller's right to cure is subject to the right to avoid.[203] The real difficulties with some of the CISG decisions stem not from the Convention itself, but from the way it has been handled by the tribunals.

[202] See Debattista, Bill, *supra note* 44, at 218.

[203] See Art. 48(1).

19

The Irrelevance of the Performance Interest

A Comparative Analysis of "Keep-Open" Covenants in Scotland and England

David Campbell and Roger Halson

Much recent scholarship on the law of remedies for breach of contract has argued that greater protection should be afforded to a promisee's interest in the performance of the primary obligations it is owed under a contract. This chapter examines and rejects the desirability of expanding the availability of the remedy of specific performance. The argument is based upon a detailed comparison between the currently prevailing law of keep-open covenants in, on the one hand, England and Wales, and on the other hand, Scotland, represented, respectively, by Co-operative Insurance Society Ltd v Argyll (Holdings) Ltd and Highland and Universal Properties Ltd v Safeway Properties Ltd. The Scottish position over the specific implement of tenants' obligations to keep-open retail premises is the opposite to the position taken in England and Wales, and it is argued to be a superior position. The argument is that Scottish law reflects a greater respect for the performance interest and the position that this respect is derived from the civilian influences on Scottish law.

It has been argued that the Scottish position over specific implement of tenants' obligations to keep open retail premises is opposite and superior to the position in England and Wales. This chapter will show, however, that the two jurisdictions are not as different as many characterisations have suggested and, further, that the current Scots law, which indeed is likely to grant specific implement, is a recent and radical departure. More significantly, however, the chapter examines the impact of this wider availability of specific implement upon the contracting behaviour of parties contemplating a commercial lease containing a keep-open clause. The key finding is that there are different effects on contracting behaviour of default rules which either allocate the risk of an uncompensated loss to the tenant or favour the landlord with a presumptive entitlement

We are very much indebted to the members of the Edinburgh legal profession who were 'interviewed' in the course of researching this paper. In addition to the Sheffield conference, this paper was also presented to the School of Law, University of Edinburgh, February 2012; to the Department of Legal and Administrative Services, City of Edinburgh Council, March 2012 and to the Annual Conference of the Society of Legal Scholars, University of Bristol, September 2012. We are grateful for comments given at those presentations.

to a supra-compensatory remedy. The chapter argues in favour of the latter, English position, which was affirmed in Co-operative Insurance. It is emphasised, however, that it is not the default law, but rather the parties' actual response to it that is important. The analysis of this key issue presented here implies the argument that the law should more commonly enforce primary obligations is entirely irrelevant to the parties' behaviour.

I. INTRODUCTION

Over the last thirty-five years, a very great deal of academic literature[1] and a number of significant cases, of which A-G v *Blake (Jonathan Cape Ltd Third Party)* remains the most important,[2] have criticised the existing law of remedies for breach of contract for not sufficiently protecting the claimant's interest in the performance of primary obligations under the contract. It is certainly true that a law of remedies based on compensation of lost expectation cannot be understood as an attempt to prevent breach, for that law's extension to the defendant of the Holmesian choice of breaching if it is prepared to pay damages is singularly unfit for this purpose. It has therefore been sought to strengthen what has been called the 'performance interest', that is to say, an interest of the claimant in having the defendant literally perform its primary obligations under the contract.[3]

For various reasons, not all, or even principally, derived from the nature of the law of contract, the main device that has been used to strengthen the performance interest has been the award of 'restitutionary damages', which, because their quantum is in certain circumstances greater than the quantum of compensatory damages, are believed to provide a greater deterrent to breach and therefore a greater likelihood of performance.[4] At first blush, however, restitutionary damages are, from the perspective of the law of contract, a somewhat strangely indirect way of seeking to protect the performance interest.[5] The obvious devices for this are the equitable

1 Two interesting recent reviews of this literature, based on PhD theses written on the topic, are K Barnett, ACCOUNTING FOR PROFIT FOR BREACH OF CONTRACT, Oxford, Hart, 2012 and S Rowan, REMEDIES FOR BREACH OF CONTRACT, Oxford, Oxford University Press, 2012.

2 [2001] 1 AC 268 (HL).

3 D Friedmann, *The Performance Interest in Contract Damages* (1995) 111 LAW QUARTERLY REVIEW 628.

4 What may well transpire to be the apogee of this argument, though it itself involved a pronounced scaling back of Birks' ambitions, is J Edelman, GAIN-BASED DAMAGES, Oxford, Hart, ch 3. Like all apogees, it carried in itself the roots of the subsequent decline: D. Campbell, *The Defence of Breach and the Policy of Performance* (2006) 25 UNIVERSITY OF QUEENSLAND LAW JOURNAL 271, 274–8 and D Campbell, A *Relational Critique of the Third Restatement of Restitution sec* 39 (2011) 68 WASHINGTON AND LEE LAW REVIEW 1063, 1087–93.

5 In theory, from the claimant's perspective restitutionary damages should be a superior remedy to the equitable remedies in at least one respect. If restitutionary damages are damages, they avoid any equitable limitations on the claimant's remedies, and if the restitution is total, the defendant can have

remedies of specific performance or an injunction which indirectly amounts to specific performance,[6] but no attempt akin to *Blake*'s advocacy of restitutionary damages has been made to make these remedies more readily available to the claimant in the courts of England and Wales, though there is a US academic literature which has considered the issue at length.[7]

However, though it is essential to say that each decided case must be considered on its merits, it has been authoritatively argued that, broadly speaking, the courts have increasingly favoured the interests of the claimant when deciding whether to grant specific performance.[8] But to the extent that this is so, then the House of Lords' decision in the leading modern English case on specific performance, *Co-operative Insurance Society Ltd* v *Argyll Stores (Holdings) Ltd*,[9] certainly represents the 'bucking [of] this trend'.[10] The ultimate denial of specific performance in this case was met with a great deal of scandalised academic commentary from the perspective of the performance interest. Professor Tettenborn has said that it

> sits ill with the idea that it should be a function of the courts to make sure, as far as possible, that contracts are performed rather than broken, and that obligations can be carried out should not be able to be shrugged off with a mere offer to pay a sum of money to the other side.[11]

no rational incentive to breach at all as the claimant will be able to claim as of right the entirety of the defendant's gains from breach: D Campbell, *Hamlet Without the Prince: How Leng and Leong Use Restitution to Extinguish Equity* [2003] Journal of Business Law 131. We are unconcerned in this paper with how far the actual law of restitutionary damages has realised this theoretical potential.

6 D Friedmann, *Economic Aspects of Damages and Specific Performance Compared* in D Saidov and R Cunnington eds, Contract Damages, Oxford, Hart, 2008, 65.

7 The principal contribution, the influence of which on our argument will be clear, remains AT Kronman, *Specific Performance* (1978) 45 University of Chicago Law Review 351.

8 A Burrows, Remedies for Torts and Breach of Contract, 3rd edn, Oxford, Oxford University Press, 2004, 504. On background claims about the emergence of a 'non-hierarchical scheme of remedies', see R Halson, *Remedies for Breach of Contract*, in M Furmston, ed, The Law of Contract, 4th edn, London, LexisNexis, 2010, para 8.155.

9 [1998] AC 1 (HL); reversing [1996] Ch 286 (CA).

10 Burrows, n 8 above, 504.

11 AM Tettenborn, *Absolving the Undeserving: Shopping Centres, Specific Performance and the Law of Contract* [1998] Conveyancer and Property Lawyer 23, 38.

Those not formulating their, in substance not so different, views in terms derived from the explicit performance interest argument took a similar position. In particular, Dr Spry was so concerned to criticise Lord Hoffmann's failure to follow equitable principles that, at a late stage of the preparation of the fifth edition of his book, he included an appendix on *Co-operative Insurance* in order to do so: ICF Spry, Principles of Equitable Remedies, 5th edn, London, Sweet and Maxwell, 1997, appendix C; see now 8th edn, 2010, TLR Australia, 2009, appendix C.

Professor Jukier completed a recent comparison of *Co-operative Insurance* and an analogous case in Quebec, Construction Belcourt Lee v Golden Griddle Pancake House Ltd [1988] RJQ 716 (CS), by urging the abandonment of the Holmesian choice because 'the duty to keep a contract ought presumptively to mean a duty to perform it': R Jukier, 'Taking Specific Performance Seriously: Trumping Damages as the Presumptive Remedy for Breach of Contract' in R J Sharpe and K Roach

The particular obligation at issue in *Co-operative Insurance* was imposed by a commercial leasehold covenant to keep open a supermarket. It is against the background of arguments for the promotion of the performance interest that we should like to consider a set of Scots cases on such covenants, of which the decisions of the Inner House of the Court of Session in *Retail Parks Investments Ltd v The Royal Bank of Scotland plc (No 2)*[12] and *Highland and Universal Properties Ltd* v *Safeway Properties Ltd*[13] are the most important. These have been interpreted as taking a specifically Scottish line, derived from the civilian strand of the mixed Scots legal tradition, which is diametrically opposed to the law of specific performance set out in *Co-operative Insurance*. As a leading Scots commentator, Ms Macgregor, has put it: 'the Scottish and English courts were poles apart in their attitude to similar facts'.[14] If the House of Lords' decision in *Co-operative Insurance* showed a pronounced disinclination to grant specific performance of an obligation to continue to operate a supermarket over the long remaining period of the lease of the premises, *Highland and Universal* has been cited in subsequent Scots cases as authority for regarding specific implement as the 'normal remedy' for breach of a keep-open covenant in such a lease.[15]

Just as *Co-operative Insurance* was met with criticism by those writing from the perspective of the performance interest, it followed that, though *Retail Parks* and *Highland and Universal* have received much less attention throughout the UK than has *Co-operative Insurance*, they have been warmly praised from this perspective. In a paper which provoked our own interest in the Scots law and on which we have relied heavily, Dr Pearce has put the case for the superiority of the Scots law very strongly.[16] He is by no means alone. So superior is 'the more friendly environment for promisees under Scots law' believed to be that Dr Hogg has argued that it may be

eds, TAKING REMEDIES SERIOUSLY/RECOURS ET LES MESURES DE REDRESSEMENT: UNE AFFAIRE SÉRIEUSE, Montreal, Canadian Institute for the Administration of Justice, 2010, 85, 118.

12 [1996] SC 227 (IH Ex Div).

13 [2000] SC 297 (IH).

14 L Macgregor, *Specific Implement in Scots Law*, in J Smits *et al*, eds, SPECIFIC PERFORMANCE IN CONTRACT LAW, Antwerp, Intersentia, 2008, 67, 88. Dr Black was similarly of the opinion that 'the results could not have been more different': G Black, WOOLMAN ON CONTRACT, 4th edn, London, Thomson Reuters (trading as W Green), 2010, paras 10–14.

Jukier, n 11 above, 89, 104, 108 has described as 'diametrically opposed' the English and the civilian influenced Quebecois laws. See also R Jukier, *Where Law and Pedagogy Meet in the Trans-systemic Contracts Classroom* (2005) 50 MCGILL LAW JOURNAL 789, 801–8.

15 OAK MALL GREENOCK LTD v MCDONALD'S RESTAURANTS LTD [2003] ScotCS 135 (OH) para 5. The reporting of, or rather the failure to report, this significant case is a puzzle. It is not in the SESSION CASES, the SCOTS LAW TIMES, nor the SCOTTISH CIVIL LAW REPORTS. Lexis carries the versions in SCOTTISH CASE DIGESTS and SCOTTISH COURT OPINIONS. The neutral citation version used here, the SCOTTISH COURT OF SESSION DECISIONS, is the version found on BIALLI, which would seem to be the version on the Court of Session website, where, however, it has no neutral citation. The case appears to be unknown to *Westlaw*.

16 D Pearce, *Remedies for Breach of a Keep-open Covenant* (2008) 24 JOURNAL OF CONTRACT LAW 199.

'desirable for English landlords to consider whether they might wish to make Scots law the *lex contractus* if not the *lex fori* for their leases'.[17]

In this chapter, we will argue that examination of the decided cases shows the conflict of principle between a Scots civilian preference for specific implement and an English common law preference for compensatory damages to have been much overstated. In light of his Lordship's admission that he 'had made no investigation of civilian systems',[18] including, for these purposes, the Scottish, the weight that can be given to the *dicta* of Lord Hoffmann in *Co-operative Insurance* that 'there is less difference between common law and civilian systems than . . . general statements might lead one to suppose' has rightly been questioned.[19] Lord Hoffmann nevertheless was substantially right, certainly about the Scots law, at the time he spoke. However, although we will show that the position in the decided cases after *Highland and Universal* is equivocal, it would appear that keep-open clauses are indeed now far more likely to be enforced in Scotland by specific implement than they would, on similar facts, be likely to be enforced by a decree of specific performance in England and Wales. This does not, however, reflect a settled Scots position but rather that *Retail Parks* effected a marked change in the Scottish law, which was consolidated by *Highland and Universal*.

But discussion of the decided cases is merely preparatory to our main concern, which is with the impact of the law as set out in *Highland and Universal* on commercial leasing practice. This impact can be ascertained only obliquely and partially from the decided cases, for the law stated in those cases will be met with creative responses from those it is meant to regulate, and the implicit claim in the celebration of *Highland and Universal* as authority for recognition of the performance interest, that the law it sets out will lead to literal enforcement of keep-open covenants, is the merest speculation. What is fundamentally important to commercial practice in a system of freedom of contract is not the mandatory stipulation of outcomes by the law of contract but the clarity of that law's rules, around which commercial parties can plan and bargain, and any attempt to mandate that keep-open covenants will actually be literally enforced jeopardises that clarity. We will conclude that it is not so much that the pursuit of protection of a performance interest in keep-open cases is substantively bad, though, for reasons we shall set out, we suspect it is; it is that it is, to commercial parties, irrelevant.

This chapter greatly benefitted from discussions with nine eminent members of the Scots legal profession who were involved in the keep-open cases, including some of the leading counsel and instructing solicitors in *Retail Parks* and *Highland and Universal*, or who are otherwise prominently engaged in private and public sector commercial leasing in Scotland. When referring to these practitioners' views, we

[17] M Hogg, Promises and Contract Law, Cambridge, Cambridge University Press, 2011, 354.

[18] *Co-operative Insurance* (HL), n 9 above, 12G-H.

[19] Macgegor, n 14 above, 84.

shall, for want of a better word, call these gentlemen 'interviewees'. But to describe these discussions as interviews might imply a claim to rigour of qualitative method or to statistical significance, which we are anxious to disavow. The discussions were lightly structured meetings of between an hour and three hours conducted in as informal a way as possible at the practitioners' home, practice, or chambers or over lunch. The authors would like to thank these gentlemen for their generosity with their time. All of these gentlemen have had the opportunity to read this chapter in draft, but, of course, are not responsible for the views expressed here, with which, indeed, we fear they all may, at least in part, disagree.

After an examination of the Scots law of keep-open covenants (Section II), this chapter asks, and, we hope, answers, the question 'why do commercial parties ever seek literal enforcement?' (Section III) before turning to the meaning of a keep-open obligation in the law of England and Wales (Section IV). We then try to demonstrate the strengths of Millet LJ's dissenting judgment in *Co-operative Insurance* (Section V). There follows a critical evaluation of the significance accorded to supervisory problems in the Scots law as well as that of England and Wales (Section VI), before the following section asks 'what a competent claimant should do in commercial uniqueness cases' (Section VI). We then, by way of a synopsis of the preceding argument, offer advice to landlords contracting on the basis of the English law confronted with the problems we have described (Section VII) and consider the issues involved in changing the default law and the irrelevance of the performance interest to evaluation of these issues (Section IX). We then outline our conclusions (Section X).

II. SCOTS LAW OF KEEP-OPEN COVENANTS

Though in the interests of brevity we shall concentrate on the contrast between *Co-operative Insurance* and *Highland and Universal*, the facts of all the Scots cases we shall discuss may for our purposes be taken to be four square with *Co-operative Insurance*, involving the quitting in breach of a long-term lease by an anchor tenant operating a supermarket in a shopping centre. In *Co-operative Insurance*, nineteen years remained of a term of thirty-five years when, after sustaining a loss of £70,000 in the preceding year, the defendant quit the lease.[20] In *Highland and Universal*, the defender declared its intention to quit when fourteen years remained of a term of thirty years, having decided that, although no actual losses had been recorded, continued operation of the supermarket would not be consistent with a major reorganisation of its business it was undertaking at that time.[21] Given the similarity of their

[20] *Co-operative Insurance* (HL), n 9 above, 9H-10G.

[21] *Highland and Universal*, n 13 above, 304D-I, 306A-C. The commercial background to this reorganisation does not emerge from the report but lies in the fundamental disadvantage the Safeway chain of supermarkets, of which Argyll was part, suffered in the 1990s in competition with larger, then

facts, it is of great interest that Lord Hoffmann, who gave the single speech in the House of Lords decision in *Co-operative Insurance*, with which his brethren all concurred, refused to grant specific performance, but that the Inner House in *Highland and Universal* unanimously granted specific implement, the different results being attributed to the different laws.

It certainly is the case that the judgments of the Lord President, Lord Rodger and Lord Kingarth in *Highland and Universal*, with which Lord Kirkwood concurred, were anxious to identify a 'basic difference of approach between Scots and English law'[22] such that

> in appropriate cases it was plainly competent for the courts in Scotland to pronounce orders for specific implement ordaining a party to carry on business over a period of time. In Scotland, unlike in England, a party to a contract had a right to enforce it by specific implement … in England by contrast a decree of specific performance was a discretionary remedy, regarded traditionally as exceptional as opposed to common law damages to which a successful plaintiff was entitled as of right.… In Scotland, there is no doubt that – unlike the position in England – a party to a contractual obligation is, in general, entitled to enforce that obligation by decree for specific implement as a matter of right.[23]

Lord Rodger traced the Scots' approach back 'more than 300 years' to Stair's *Institutions*,[24] but both he[25] and Lord Kingarth[26] found particular assistance in the House of Lords' decision in *Stewart* v *Kennedy*, 1890, in which Lords Herschell, Macnaghten and Watson each gave classic expression to the necessity of seeing that, as Lord Watson put it,

> the laws of the two countries regard the right to specific performance from different standpoints. In England, the only legal right arising from a breach of contract is a claim of damages; specific performance is not a matter of legal right but a purely equitable remedy, which the court can withhold when there are sufficient reasons of conscience or expediency against it. But in Scotland the breach of a contract for the sale of a special subject such as a landed estate gives the party aggrieved the legal right to sue for implement, and although he may elect to do so, he cannot be compelled to resort to the alternative of an action of damages, unless implement is

market-leading rivals Tesco and Sainsbury, which, by 1999, had led to a situation in which 'City opinion … was that Safeway could no longer survive as an independent … and was in play for a predator': NF Piercy, MARKET-LED STRATEGIC CHANGE, 3rd edn, Oxford, Butterworth Heinemann, 2002, 725. In 2004, the Morrisons supermarket chain was able to acquire Safeway as its acquisition by any of the then market-leaders would have been opposed by the competition authorities.

22 *Highland and Universal*, n 13 above, 299I.

23 *Ibid*, 308F-G, 309D-E.

24 *Ibid*, 300E, 299B-E.

25 *Ibid*, 299E-H.

26 *Ibid*, 309E-310B.

shown to be impossible, in which case *loco facti imprestabilis subit damnum et interesse* [damages come in place of an act which was not performed]. Even where implement is possible, I do not doubt that the Court of Session has inherent power to refuse the legal remedy upon equitable grounds, although I know of no instance in which it has done so. It is quite conceivable that circumstances might occur which would make it inconvenient and unjust to enforce specific performance of contract of sale.[27]

An assessment of these cases from the perspective of the performance interest is bound to prefer *Highland and Universal* to *Co-operative Insurance*, but Lord Rodger's contrast between the two cases, whilst it partially captures a general truth,[28] involves an excessive simplification of the laws of both jurisdictions, one which amounts to real error in respect of keep-open covenants.[29] Three preliminary points must be made. First, though it is not discussed in *Highland and Universal*, for indeed the issue did not arise, it is important to see that, whilst it is in a sense right to say that specific implement is the 'primary' remedy for breach of contract in Scotland,[30] this does not mean that it is a common remedy.[31] When the subject matter of the contract is, as is typically the case, a generic good, the pursuer will typically find no advantage in an action for specific implement, and it may, at its election, seek a remedy in damages. Should the pursuer seek specific implement, the defender may raise it as a defence that 'the subject matter of the contract is of no particular significance and money compensation would be adequate', and, unless some special significance is shown, this defence will succeed.[32] In sum, in respect of the paradigm case of breach of contract for the sale of goods, 'in practice in the Scottish courts

27 *Stewart* v *Kennedy No 1* (1890) 15 App Cas 75, 102–3; see also 94–5 per Lord Herschell; 105 per Lord Macnaghten.

28 WW McBryde, The Law of Contract in Scotland, 3rd edn, Thomson (trading as W Green), 2007, para 23–09.

29 We do not, of course, wish to impugn the late Lord Rodger's learning on the history of the relationship between the commercial laws of England and Wales and Scotland, from which, indeed, we have learned a great deal: eg A Rodger, *The Codification of Commercial Law in Victorian Britain* (1992) 108 Law Quarterly Review 570.

30 Black, n 14 above, para 10.15; Hogg, n 17 above, 352 and HL MacQueen and L Macgregor, *Specific Implement, Interdict and Contractual Performance* (1999) 3 Edinburgh Law Review 239.

31 Macgregor, n 14, 70. It is entirely arguable that the approach taken by McBryde, n 28 above, para 23–08, which is to say that it is 'not true' 'that specific implement is the primary, or ordinary, remedy for enforcement of a contract in Scots law', is preferable.

As in England and Wales, the picture is muddled because by far the most common remedy furnished by the courts is judgment for debt, which can be regarded as a form of literal enforcement, but this can be put to one side for reasons which are set out in D Harris *et al*, Remedies in Contract and Tort, 2nd edn, London, Butterworths, 2002, ch 11.

32 A Gibb and A Gordon, Contract, 3rd edn, Thomson Reuters (trading as W Green), 2009, 71; MacQueen and Macgregor, n 30 above, 240; McBryde, n 28 above, para 32–21 and Scottish Law Commission, Discussion Paper on Remedies for Breach of Contract, Scot Law Com DP No 109 (1999) para 6.5.

implement is sought comparatively rarely, and has been even more rarely granted; and the reality therefore has been little different from the English situation'.[33] That this position is acknowledged by leading Scots commentators does not detract from, indeed it emphasises, the significance of the fact that no doctrinally coherent reason has ever been able to be advanced by the advocates of the performance interest for the exclusion of the paradigm case of the sale of goods from the argument for greater use of literal enforcement instead of compensatory damages.[34] It is unarguable that a flat inability to understand the positive law would emerge from an application of the perspective of the performance interest to the positive Scots law, even with its stronger formal commitment to specific implement, just as much as it does from the positive English law.

In essence, then, in the main class of cases the pursuer would obtain no advantage from specific implement and so does not seek it and would not be awarded it if it did seek it. But let us put the sale of goods aside and consider the Scots approach to keep-open covenants, which, as we shall show, are a subset of the class of cases which, adapting the term Sir Guenther Treitel coined in relation to sales of goods,[35]

[33] *ibid*, 239. See also TB Smith, Short Commentary on the Law of Scotland, Edinburgh, V Green and Son Ltd, 1962, 854. The position under the mixed Scots system reproduces the way the sale of goods is dealt with in the civilian systems: HD Lando and C Rose, *The Myth of Specific Performance in Civil Law Countries* [2004] American Law and Economics Association Annual Meetings paper 15, available at http://law.bepress.com/cgi/viewcontent.cgi?article=1014&context=alea; see further D Tallon, *Remedies: French Report*, in D Harris and D Tallon, eds, Contract Law Today: Anglo-French Comparisons, Oxford, Clarendon Press, 1989, 263, 267; GH Treitel, Remedies for Breach of Contract, Oxford, Clarendon Press, 1988, para 70 and K Zweigert and H Kotz, Introduction to Comparative Law, 3rd edn, Oxford, Oxford University Press, 1998, 484. The recent discussion by Dr Rowan, n 1, 37–56 above, is able to maintain the centrality of specific performance to French law by, most unwisely, not dealing with the sale of goods in any sustained way: *ibid*, 42–3. Her account of art 1142 of the Civil Code does not lead us to alter our agreement with Professor Nicholas' view that, 'subject to qualifications', 'this article might be thought to embody the common law approach, as expressed by Mr Justice Holmes': B Nicholas, The French Law of Contract, 2nd edn, Oxford, Clarendon Press, 1992, 217.

The position under the CISG also is informative: JM Catalano, *More Fiction than Fact: The Perceived Difference in the Application of Specific Performance under the United Nations Convention on Contracts for the International Sale of Goods* (1997) 71 Tulane Law Review 1807, 1832.

[34] D Campbell and P Wylie, 'Ain't No Telling (Which Circumstances are Exceptional)' [2003] Cambridge Law Journal 605, 615–7.

[35] GH Treitel, Law of Contract, 2nd edn, London, Stevens, 1966, 837; see now 13th edn, London, Sweet and Maxwell, 2011, para 21–023. See also GH Treitel, *Specific Performance in the Sale of Goods* [1966] Journal of Business Law 211, 213–6. In the second edition of his textbook, Sir Guenther seemed to distinguish, and in 3rd edn, 1970, 837 clearly did distinguish, commercial uniqueness cases from cases in which 'damages may be regarded as inadequate because of the difficulty of assessing them', which is what we are really driving at. We feel he in this way unduly limited the application of his very apt term, for in those cases he thought were cases concerning commercial goods, the ultimate problem is not that a substitute is unavailable on the market, it is that quantification of the consequential loss flowing from that unavailability will be difficult to assess. Consequential losses that can accurately be quantified should not give rise to a problem. We are trying to capture the commonality

we shall call 'commercial uniqueness' cases. In these cases, literal enforcement of a primary obligation would be of value to a pursuer, which, as we shall explain later, would be left uncompensated, in part or in whole, by compensatory damages. Even here, where the issues are entirely different from those raised by the sale of generic goods, the second important preliminary point arises that, prior to *Retail Parks*, the Scots law was, as leading counsel for the defendant put it in the Court of Appeal hearing of *Co-operative Insurance*, 'similar' to the English[36]; or, as we would put it, was, for practical purposes, indistinguishable from it.[37]

The position is so clear that it can be described briefly. Prior to *Retail Parks*, the Scots law of retail covenants was dominated by *Grosvenor Developments (Scotland) plc v Argyll Stores*,[38] in which the attempt by a landlord, cognisant of grave difficulties facing an attempt to obtain specific implement of a keep-open covenant, to avoid those difficulties by seeking interdict which would indirectly effect specific implement met with no success. The Outer House was particularly concerned to restrict or even to deny – no previous case had ever succeeded on this basis[39] – the possibility of effectively obtaining a decree of specific implement, denied on its own merits, by this side wind, in a way which is familiar in the English law as the principal issue raised by *Lumley v Wagner*.[40] Having decided *Grosvenor Developments* on this general point, Lord Jauncey's consideration of the merits of the application arguably was *obiter*, but, effectively affirming the decision of Sheriff Principal PI Caplan QC,[41] he said:

> As a general rule the law of Scotland requires that a party who has contracted for a particular object is entitled to secure that object by way of a decree [of specific implement] … to this general rule there are a number of exceptions, of which one is that a decree for specific implement will not be pronounced when it cannot be

indicated by commercial uniqueness and difficulty of assessment (and specific performance under the Sale of Goods Act) all appearing under the general heading 'Granted where damages inadequate' in Sir Guenther's initial treatment. Professor Peel now clearly separates these categories, and adds what we fear is the overlapping category of 'No satisfactory equivalent available': *ibid*, paras 21–019, 21–020, 21–022, 21–023.

36 *Co-operative Insurance* (CA), n 9 above, 290E. *Highland and Universal*, therefore, was 'contrary to earlier authority'.

37 E McKendrick, *Specific Implement and Specific Performance: A Comparison* (1986) SCOTS LAW TIMES (NEWS) 249 and A Smith, *Specific Implement*, in K Reid and R Zimmerman, eds, A HISTORY OF THE PRIVATE LAW OF SCOTLAND, vol 2, Oxford, Oxford University Press, 2000, 195, 213–8.

38 [1987] SLT 738 (OH).

39 *Ibid*, 743.

40 (1852) 1 De G M and G 604; 42 ER 687.

41 *Grosvenor Developments (Scotland) plc v Argyll Stores Ltd* [1987] SLT 134 (Sh Ct). The Sheriff Principal reversed the first instance decision of the Sheriff Court, though, after initially recalling the interim interdict that had been granted, he allowed it to continue pending the decision of the Court of Session.

> enforced ... the enforcement of any decree for the next 28 years would present formidable difficulties. What for the purposes of the order would constitute "use"? Would the defenders be bound to use the whole of the premises for the purposes stated or could they use a portion for other purposes or for no purpose at all? How is it to be determined at any particular time whether they are selling items which are "commonly sold in supermarkets and discount stores" or whether they are selling 'all hardware' so sold? In my view an action for specific implement of the contractual provisions referred to in the crave would fail ... because it would be impossible of enforcement. It follows that even if interdict were in general competent in circumstances such as the present it would not be granted in the present case.[42]

Three keep-open cases were heard by the Court of Session between the hearings of *Grosvenor Developments* in 1987 and *Retail Parks* in 1995. In *Church Commissioners for England v Abbey National plc*,[43] a case deemed of sufficient importance to merit being heard by a Full Bench of five judges of the Inner House, the relationship between specific performance and interdict was again explored and *Grosvenor Developments* explicitly and unambiguously followed. In the two other cases, *Postel Properties Ltd v Miller and Santhouse plc*[44] and *Overgate Centre Ltd v William Low Supermarkets Ltd*,[45] the pursuers directly sought specific implement and, if, in the interests of brevity, we may be allowed to avoid the complications involved in saying so, both of these also followed *Grosvenor Developments*.[46] *Retail Parks* itself is a difficult case. The pursuer's successes in interim proceedings[47] were reversed at the full hearing in the Outer House, which believed itself bound by *Grosvenor Developments*.[48] In sum, the decision of the Inner House in *Retail Parks* represented an effective reversal of the law, a point which may be readily grasped by comparing the very able arguments of counsel for the pursuers distinguishing *Grosvenor Developments* in *Retail Parks* from the equally able criticism of those arguments by the same leading counsel appearing for the defenders in *Highland and Universal*.[49]

The third preliminary point we wish to make is that the cases decided after *Retail Parks* by no means provide unambiguous support for the view of the Scots law taken

42 *Grosvenor Developments (Scotland) plc v Argyll Stores Ltd* (OH), n 38 above, 744–5.

43 [1994] SC 651 (IH).

44 [1993] SLT 323 (OH).

45 [1995] SLT 1181 (OH).

46 In 1999, the Scottish Law Commission decided that no reform of the relationship between implement and interdict set out in *Grosvenor Developments* was unnecessary: *Report on Remedies for Breach of Contract*, Scot Law Com No 174 (1999) paras 7.28–7.29.

47 *Retail Park Investments Ltd v The Royal Bank of Scotland plc* [1995] SLT 1156 (OH). This unusual reporting of interim proceedings seems to be have been the result of a decision by the Lord Ordinary, Lord Penrose, perhaps in light of the emerging significance of *Retail Parks*: *Retail Parks (No 2)* (IH), n 12 above, 230.

48 *Retail Park Investments Ltd v The Royal Bank of Scotland plc (No 2)* [1996] SC 52 (OH)

49 *Highland and Universal* (IH), n 13 above, 307D-308E.

in *Highland and Universal*. The Outer House granted a decree of specific implement in the first case which came before it for a full hearing after *Retail Parks*, *Co-operative Wholesale Society Ltd v Saxone Ltd*.[50] But in the next case, *Co-operative Insurance Society Ltd v Halfords Ltd*, specific implement of a keep-open clause was denied at interim proceedings,[51] and at the full hearing the interdict which had been granted, which the pursuer had sought in contemplation, not of obliging the defender to keep-open the premises, but of maintaining the value of the premises as security for unpaid rent, was allowed to continue only upon a joint motion of the parties which apparently led to the case being settled.[52] That interdict would otherwise have been lifted. Though generally sympathetic things were said of the possibility of granting specific implement in keep-open cases at the full hearing, this is, we submit, a case which on its facts does not support *Retail Parks*.[53]

We have been unable to identify any relevant cases which were determined in the Sheriff's Court and only three in the Court of Session, all in the Outer House, since *Highland and Universal*.[54] This could indicate that the new law of *Retail Parks* is considered to have been essentially settled by *Highland and Universal*, so that litigation which directly opposed a decree of specific implement for fundamental breach of a keep-open covenant would be fruitless, save in exceptional circumstances. With hesitation, we submit that this is indeed the case. Our interviewees are of this opinion, and the samples of professional literature some of them have kindly supplied us with, such as in-house briefings from solicitors' firms and articles in trade magazines available only by subscription, are all to this effect. As it was put by Lord Drummond Young in one of the Outer House cases, *Oak Mall Greenock Ltd v McDonald's Restaurants Ltd*:

> The proposition that specific implement is the normal remedy available to enforce a clause in a lease requiring the tenant to keep premises open for business and carry on business was established in *Highland and Universal Properties Ltd v Safeway Properties Ltd*.... I do not doubt that the court has an underlying equitable discretion to refuse specific implement. It is nevertheless quite clear that the discretionary power is exceptional in nature, and can only be granted in the presence of special circumstances which would render it unjust to grant decree of implement.[55]

50 [1997] SCLR 835 (OH).

51 *Co-operative Insurance Society Ltd v Halfords Ltd* [1998] SLT 90 (OH).

52 *Co-operative Insurance Society Ltd v Halfords Ltd (No 2)* [1999] SLT 697 (OH).

53 We cannot agree with the conclusion Professor Alastair Smith reaches, n 37 above, 216–8, that the full hearing concluded that 'for the moment it sufficed to follow the decision of the Extra Division in *Retail Parks*', though we are anxious to point out our differences are a question of emphasis.

54 We confine to a footnote, for we know nothing about the significance of this, that *Highland and Universal*, the decision in which was handed down on 1 February 2000, was itself on 2 May 2000 set down for appeal to the House of Lords, though it does, of course, lead to the suspicion that the case was settled: House of Lords Journal 233 (Session 1999–2000) 390: available at http://www.publications.parliament.uk/pa/ld199900/ldjournal/233/081.htm#1.

55 *Oak Mall*, n 15 above, paras [5], [14].

We agree with this statement of the Scots law even though, taken together, the three Outer House cases since *Highland and Universal* represent poor support for it. Although specific implement was granted in *Oak Mall*, which was the second of these cases, it had been denied in the first, *Britel Fund Trustees Ltd v Scottish and Southern Energy plc*,[56] and *Britel* had to be distinguished, in a way to which we shall return, in *Oak Mall*. In the third case, the remarkable *Douglas Shelf Seven Ltd v Co-operative Wholesale Society Ltd and Kwik Save Group plc (Third Party)*,[57] the pursuers did not even seek specific implement but confined themselves to a claim for compensatory damages,[58] the case proceeding on the basis of the defender's and the third party's judicial admissions that the keep-open covenant was enforceable but that breach sounded only in damages.[59] Despite its immense length,[60] as the matter was not before the court, the judgment does not allow one to explain why specific implement was not at issue.[61] But that it was not at issue is inconsistent with *Highland and Universal*.[62]

We do not wish to dwell on what we believe to be the case, that the view taken in *Highland and Universal* of the Scots law prior to *Retail Parks* was, with great respect, in important ways wrong, and that, if the law is as the Inner House in *Highland and Universal* claimed it left it, which we believe is indeed so, then this did not represent the continuity of the Scots legal tradition but a remarkable change in the law of keep-open covenants. We wish to emphasise that the situation must be more complex than *Highland and Universal* would lead one to believe, because, prior to *Retail Parks*, the Scots law had entertained quite the opposite position to the one

56 [2002] SLT 223 (OH).

57 [2007] CSOH 53 (OH).

58 *Ibid*, para [571].

59 *Ibid*, para [575]. See further the text accompanying n 133 below.

60 That this judgment has not been reported is perhaps explicable by its length of 625 paragraphs which, when printed single-spaced in 10 point font on A4 paper, take up 137 pages. The judgment invites obvious comparison with *Tito v Waddell (No 2)* [1977] Ch 106, which, taking up 221 pages of *The Law Reports*, was, we estimate, about the same length, although, of course, the immense difference in the significance of the causes shows just how much aspects of the Scots law of keep-open covenants are open to criticism. See further the text accompanying notes 67, 133 below.

61 One can speculate. The social conditions of the Whitfield area of Dundee in which the supermarket operated had been very poor and in some respects atrocious, and one would imagine that trading in such an area could amount to circumstances so exceptional as to justify the exercise of the equitable discretion. Or at least one would imagine this were it not the case that, as Lord Reed observed when rejecting the third party's argument that it breached the covenant *inter alia* because it could not guarantee the safety of its staff if the premises remained open, the third party had not closed premises which were beset by similar appalling problems, even one in which a 'store manager had been shot dead after he refused to reveal the code of the safe': *ibid*, para [89].

62 It is regrettable that Dr Hogg does not address this issue in his comment on the case: M Hogg, Damages for Breach of a Keep-open Clause: *Douglas Shelf Seven Lt v Co-operative Wholesale Society Ltd* (2007) 11 Edinburgh Law Review 416.

for which *Highland and Universal* has received such affirmation from the perspective of the performance interest; indeed, it had entertained the English position. In order to understand why it would ever do so, we must go back to the first principles of literal enforcement and answer the question why a commercial party would ever seek specific performance.

III. WHY WOULD COMMERCIAL PARTIES EVER SEEK LITERAL ENFORCEMENT?

That commercial parties ever seek specific performance is *prima facie* a puzzle. The ultimate expectation of a commercial party is always a money profit, and compensation of the loss of such a profit should always, by the nature of the case, be possible by payment of damages. As is now quite widely recognised but as Dr Austen-Baker has particularly clearly set out,[63] in what we are calling commercial uniqueness cases, it is not that damages would be inadequate in the doctrinal sense of being inappropriate to the nature of the loss; it is that the claimant fears that those damages will be inadequate in the sense that the claimant correctly believes that quantification will not encompass all its loss, and so the claimant will remain partially or wholly uncompensated.

The reason for this is that the default law of remedies for breach of contract which works perfectly well for simple contracts exemplified by the sale of generic goods may very well not work for complex contracts such as those we are discussing. The rules of causation, remoteness and mitigation (and other subsidiary doctrines) allow compensatory damages to work well in simple cases by ensuring that the quantification of loss is kept as simple and as low as is consistent with the protection of expectation. But, by the same token, these very same requirements that, in order to be compensated, loss must be certain, proximate and unavoidable (and satisfy other conditions) can themselves pose grave difficulties for the claimant in complex cases by making quantification of adequate damages impossible. A claimant which fears it will be unable to prove the full extent of its loss may seek to avoid the problem by seeking specific performance, which, of course does away with the necessity of proof of loss to the contractual standard.

In the cases we are examining, the proof problems arose from the particular importance of the tenants to the landlord. These were 'anchor' tenants whose operation of a supermarket was essential to the viability of the shopping centres of which they were part. When such tenants quit a long-term lease in breach, there will be

[63] R Austen-Baker, *Difficulties with Damages as a Ground of Specific Performance* (1999) 10 King's College Law Journal 1. Our own account of these problems as they inform the law of literal enforcement was written in ignorance of this paper: Harris *et al*, n 31 above, pt 3.

knock-on consequences for other tenants and for the shopping centre as a whole, the loss caused by which may well be difficult to quantify. The landlord's loss of basic rent from the anchor tenant is likely to be a liquidated sum, which can be quantified, though perhaps capped by the period of a notice provision in the lease. But any element of variable rent, usually provided for by periodic rent review, will be speculative, especially if the background business outlook is poor, as is highly likely to be the case, for, if it were not the case, the tenant would be unlikely to breach or a substitute tenant could be found, which would reduce or even eliminate the quantification problems. The landlord's losses from third party tenants demanding rent reductions or quitting their leases, perhaps after finding the landlord to be in breach of an obligation to secure an anchor tenant, would contain a highly uncertain element,[64] as would any reduction in the capital value of the shopping development in light of a bleak trading history.

These quantification problems played an important role in the majority decision in the Court of Appeal in *Co-operative Insurance*,[65] though they are quite briefly discussed there. In *Douglas Shelf Seven*, however, they are examined as exhaustively and as instructively as we have ever seen in the case law. But we nevertheless believe that the most unambiguous good to emerge from the recent litigation over keep-open clauses is the lesson that *Douglas Shelf Seven* teaches, that litigation to prove loss in a way which may be taken seriously, against the determined opposition of a competent commercial party, is of extremely questionable value.[66] We have said that *Douglas Shelf Seven* is an immense judgment, which examines quantification issues as thoroughly as we have ever seen them examined in the case law. But it is the product of a trial, entirely confined to quantum,[67] which occupied sixty-

[64] We do not wish to enter into that aspect of *Co-operative Insurance* which turns on the granting of specific performance to directly protect the interests of third parties, who were not, of course, privy to the contract. In the Court of Appeal, Roch LJ observed that 'those involved in the other businesses, who assumed obligations under their leases in reliance on there being a supermarket in the shopping centre and who will be adversely affected, have no remedy against the defendants': *Co-operative Insurance* (CA), n 9 above, 296. Indeed they did not, until the majority in the Court of Appeal, in the absence of any contract which might have been the basis of doing so (*Co-operative Insurance* (HL), n 9 above, 18F-G), tried effectively to give them one.

[65] *Co-operative Insurance* (CA), n 9 above, 295A, 298B. Lord Hoffmann paid almost no attention to these problems, accepting Judge Maddocks QC's conclusion that 'while the assessment of damages might be difficult, it was the kind of exercise which the courts had done in the past': *Co-operative Insurance* (HL), n 9 above, 11C. He is criticised for this by Dr Hogg, n 17 above, 351, but Dr Hogg himself does not consider the other side of the equation. These quantification problems were, of course, given weight in *Highland and Universal*, n 13 above, 306E-G.

[66] We hope it goes without saying that this is not intended to cast any disparagement on Lord Reed's judgment in the principal litigation, which, if one sets questions of the cost and the length of that judgment aside, as one must in the particular case, is excellent. See further the text accompanying n 135 below.

[67] See the text accompanying fn 59 above and 135 below.

three days between March 2005 and March 2006,[68] and which involved twenty-nine witnesses,[69] including four expert witnesses as to valuation, consideration of whose evidence takes up 166 paragraphs of the judgment.[70] Before interest, the damages awarded were slightly less than £600,000,[71] and it would be useful to know what relationship that figure bore to the defender's and the third party's costs. Such litigation, which the parties never originally contemplated,[72] appears to be neither in the longer-term interest of commercial leasing nor a justifiable use of the public resource of court time.

The current law of specific performance does not allow the direct pleading of inadequacy of damages in the sense of leaving uncompensated loss, and the commercial party seeking specific performance because it fears such inadequacy must frame its pleadings in terms derived from those cases in which the non-commercial interest which has usefully been called the 'consumer surplus' is at issue.[73] In essence, the claimant has to plead that the subject matter of the contract has some sort of unique, or at least unusual, value, even though that subject matter is not unique in the same way as an oil painting by Rembrandt and the claimant is not a consumer, and so has no ultimate interest in the use of the goods, which it wants only in order to carry out a commercial operation from which a money profit will flow. The resulting law is inextricably confused, as our adaptation of the term commercial uniqueness to describe these cases sufficiently indicates, for that term is, of course, an oxymoron. It is obviously arguable that a doctrine which allows parties only to obliquely address the fundamental issue of concern to them should be reformed, and one can conceive that reform which did directly address the inadequacy of damages in the sense we mean could very greatly strengthen the claimant's performance interest.

The obstacle to doing so is, of course, the position of the defendant who resists an order of specific performance. The other side of the coin of the claimant who seeks specific performance is a defendant who resists it because, from its perspective, specific performance is 'supra-compensatory', that is, more costly than compensatory damages, for, of course, were the costs of the two remedies the same, the commercial defendant would be indifferent about the claimant's choice between them. If specific performance is denied in England and Wales, the claimant will be left with inadequate damages and an uncompensated loss. But if specific implement is granted in Scotland, the defender will suffer hardship in the sense that it will be subject to a supra-compensatory remedy. This is a zero sum situation in the sense

68 *Douglas Shelf Seven*, n 57 above, para [2].

69 *Ibid*, paras [3]–[4].

70 *Ibid*, paras [356]–[522].

71 *Ibid*, paras [608]–[625].

72 *Ibid*, para [2].

73 D Harris *et al.*, *Contract Remedies and the Consumer Surplus* (1979) 95 Law Quarterly Review 581.

that, under either the English or the Scots laws as they are understood, both default laws create a situation in which the interests of the parties are completely opposed. Full compensation of the claimant or pursuer requires the imposition of a supra-comp remedy on the defendant or defender. Imposing only a compensatory remedy on the defendant or defender requires the inadequate compensation of the claimant or pursuer.

IV. ENFORCEMENT OF KEEP-OPEN OBLIGATIONS UNDER THE ENGLISH LAW

When deciding what to do in difficult specific performance cases, the English courts have made it known that they are aware that it cannot be right to focus only on the position of the claimant. Faced with the more expensive remedy of specific performance, the defendant will raise the defence of undue or severe hardship, and it is our argument that the English and Scots laws take different attitudes towards this defence and to the balance of convenience that lies behind it. But that this defence has any resonance at all surely shows the inadequacy of the common understanding of specific performance, for if, by agreeing to a primary obligation under the contract, the defendant was actually agreeing to give a strict undertaking literally to perform that obligation, then a defence of severe hardship should not normally carry weight. As Lord Prosser put it when dismissing arguments against the grant of interdict in a noted Scots case of an employer's failure to comply with agreed redundancy procedures, the defenders 'can hardly call it unfair to be held to their own bargain'.[74] If the defendant is merely being compelled to do what it agreed to do, then we are very firmly of the opinion that this is what the law of contract normally should do.[75] This chapter is written on the basis of the firm belief that, for competent commercial parties, liability should be strict.

[74] *Anderson v Pringle of Scotland Ltd* [1998] SLT 754, 756–7 (OH). These sentiments were echoed by the *Quebecois Golden Griddle* case, above n 11, para [78]. Enforcing a keep-open clause in the lease of a popular restaurant that was regarded as an anchor tenant in a new shopping centre development, the Court maintained that it would be 'specious to suggest that courts should refrain from enforcing contracts' merely because the defendant would '[u]ndoubtedly ... be obliged to expend considerable funds to re-open the restaurant and ... subsidise its operations'.

[75] Many of the limitations on competent commercial parties' choice of remedy, such as the penalty clause rule or the courts' reluctance to relinquish equitable jurisdiction over specific performance, are not, in our opinion, in principle defensible. The point has recently been ably argued in respect of the English law by Dr Rowan, n 1 above, ch 5, but the theoretical issues are perhaps best canvassed in P Rubin, *Unenforceable Contracts: Penalty Clauses and Specific Performance* (1981) 10 Journal of Legal Studies 237. These limitations are, however, to some degree currently justified by the current commercial practice, which misunderstands the nature of remedies for breach of contract.

But it is essential to see that in England and Wales the positive law to which the defendant should be strictly held is, by default, the Holmesian choice. It is in remote recognition of this that the defence of severe hardship is recognised in equity at all. The courts, typically but dimly, perceive that, though when it agreed its primary obligations under the contract the defendant was indeed agreeing to perform and, in the event of a breach, to provide a remedy, this remedy was by default compensatory damages, and only exceptionally specific performance. The question whether the exceptional remedy should be granted is one which involves a balancing of the opposed interests of the parties which is extremely difficult – why else is it litigated? – which the court reserves to its equitable discretion. We by no means entirely agree with this oblique approach to the fundamental issues, but the point is that treating the matter as one requiring the exercise of discretion is possible only because the court perceives that the defendant did not, *pace* the performance interest argument, ever agree to strictly guarantee literal performance of the primary obligation.

This is the background to English keep-open cases. The result that a claimant seeking specific performance of a keep-open covenant in an English court could expect prior to *Co-operative Insurance* could not have been clearer: save in circumstances so exceptional that they had never previously been found, that claimant would fail. No order of specific performance to carry on a business of any sort had ever been awarded, and there was 'no dispute' about the 'settled practice' of refusing such an order.[76] As even the majority of the Court of Appeal which granted specific performance acknowledged,[77] the law was as it was stated to be in an important 1979 judgment of Slade J in *Braddon Towers Ltd v International Stores Ltd*:

> Whether or not this may be properly described as a rule of law, I do not doubt that for many years practitioners have advised their clients that it is the settled and invariable practice of this court never to grant mandatory injunctions requiring persons to carry on business.[78]

A proper understanding of *Co-operative Insurance* must begin by recognising that, as Lord Hoffmann inferred at the beginning of his speech,[79] the remarkable point about the case is not its eventual result, but that the majority in the Court of Appeal ever questioned that result. The Court of Appeal decision was, as the immediate

[76] *Co-operative Insurance* (HL), n 9 above, 11D.

[77] *Co-operative Insurance* (CA), n 6 above, 291H,

[78] [1987] 1 EGLR 209, 213. Slade J's judgment was unreported when it was handed down. The learned editors of the ESTATES GAZETTE LAW REPORTS decided to publish it in 1987 because of the role it had played in subsequent cases.

[79] *Co-operative Insurance* (HL), n 9 above, 9A-B.

academic and professional reaction had it, a 'venture into uncharted waters',[80] which 'startled the business and legal world'[81] and 'caused consternation in the commercial property market'.[82] The significance of the House of Lords' decision was that

> [a] litigator's advice to his client *can again* be based on the usual English practice, where specific performance is an exceptional remedy. A party bound by a keep-open covenant can now make its choice about performance or non-performance in the knowledge that its non-performance almost certainly will not lead to an order for specific performance.[83]

As far as one is able to reconstruct it from the appeal court judgments, Judge Maddocks QC's refusal of specific performance at first instance appears not merely entirely correct, but to be the decision he was obliged to reach if the significance of precedent in determining the occasions for the exercise of equitable discretion is to be acknowledged. The judge had been 'not content … merely to follow authority',[84] but, after considering the equitable matters raised before him and not finding them to raise exceptional issues, handed down a decision in accord with settled practice.

In *Lumley v Wagner*, Lord St Leonards famously saw the role of the court as being, so far as possible, to bind defendants to 'a true and literal performance of their agreements, and … not suffer them to depart from their contracts at their pleasure, leaving the party with whom they have contracted to the mere chance of any damages which a jury might give'.[85] But, if the anachronism of applying this dictum to the contemporary law be allowed,[86] suffering defendants to depart if they pay damages is exactly what the positive common law, accurately analysed by Holmes, does do, and, as *The Common Law* was published in 1882, it is very disappointing to see Lord St Leonards' 1852 reasoning effectively repeated as the basis of the common understanding of *Co-operative Insurance*. Leggatt LJ reached his opinion about the case fundamentally because he thought that 'it would do the court no credit if',[87]

80 Anon, *Litigator's View* (17 June 1997) THE LAWYER 12.

81 G Jones, *Specific Performance: A Lessee's Covenant to Keep-open a Retail Store* [1997] CAMBRIDGE LAW JOURNAL 488. See also G Jones and W Goodhart, SPECIFIC PERFORMANCE, 2nd edn, London, Butterworths, 1996, 51: 'radical and controversial decision'.

82 P Luxton, *Are You Being Served? Enforcing Keep-open Covenants in Leases* [1998] CONVEYANCER AND PROPERTY LAWYER 396, 398.

83 Anon, n 80 above.

84 *Co-operative Insurance* (HL), n 9 above, 11A. See further A Phang, *Specific Performance: Exploring the Roots of "Settled Practice"* (1998) 61 MODERN LAW REVIEW 421.

85 *Lumley v Wagner*, n 40 above, 1 De G and M 619; 42 ER 693.

86 This involves giving no weight to the undoubted situational wisdom of Lord St Leonards' point about jury quantification of contractual damages.

87 *Co-operative Insurance* (CA), n 9 above, 294F.

in the case before him, it allowed the defendant to escape its obligation to 'keep an unambiguous promise',[88] with the further result 'that the common form of words of this covenant would hardly ever, if ever, be construed as meaning what they say'.[89]

But contract terms do not mean what they say as this is understood by those committed to the performance interest. Given that compensatory damages are the default remedy, when a party enters into a contract on default terms, it *never* gets a strict guarantee of literal performance. What it gets is a guarantee that the court will, behind the primary obligation, strictly impose on the defendant in breach a secondary obligation to provide a remedy. When, after breach, this secondary obligation crystallises into a remedy, that remedy will, by default, take the form of compensatory damages. There is a possibility of setting damages aside and getting some form of literal enforcement, but this is an exceptional possibility, and in keep-open cases the remedy is so exceptional that it has never been awarded. Having set out his understanding of the 'common form of words', Leggatt LJ went on to say that 'if the parties want to contract that a failure to keep-open will sound only in damages, they are quite at liberty to do so', without realising that that was exactly what they had already done.[90]

Professor Stephen Smith analyses this important argument as involving a conception of contract as a 'disjunctive obligation', the argument for which asserts

> that the debate about specific performance is based upon a misunderstanding [about] what it is that the contracting parties have promised to do. According to this justification, the obligations that contracting parties have agreed to are disjunctive obligations; specifically … to perform the primary obligation (eg to deliver goods, perform a service, make payment) *or* to provide compensation *in lieu* of such performance. [91]

Against this background, the award of specific performance after breach of a contract agreed on the basis of the English default law can be regarded as compelling the tenant to make a gift to the landlord because 'it forces the promisor to compensate for the

[88] *Ibid*, 295B.

[89] *Ibid*, 294F-G.

[90] *Ibid*, 294G. Dr Webb perforce concludes a paper which is notable for the cursoriness of its treatment of Holmesian choice (C Webb, *Performance and Compensation: An Analysis of Contract Damages and Contractual Obligation* (2006) 26 OXFORD JOURNAL OF LEGAL STUDIES 41, 49 n 24) on a note of puzzlement (*ibid*, 71): 'If we wish to continue the current prioritization of compensatory claims, an explanation is needed as to why the claimant is barred from enforcing his right to performance. It would be more honest to admit that, in such cases, the claimant acquired no such right upon contract formation'. Indeed it would, and it would then be better to give more weight to a theory which can show why we should because it has what one would have thought was the advantage of actually explaining the positive law. We do not mean to direct particular criticism of the views of Dr Webb, for the point is that his views are representative.

[91] S Smith, CONTRACT THEORY, Oxford, OUP, 2004, 400. The argument is ultimately rejected, *ibid*, 402.

non-fulfilment of a goal for which the promisor had never assumed responsibility.'[92] It is in this sense of amounting to a remedy that exceeds an objectively reasonable expectation of recovery under longstanding, settled principles that we have called specific performance in these circumstances supra-compensatory.

V. THE WISDOM OF LORD JUSTICE MILLET

Properly understood, *Co-operative Insurance* is actually a case in which, in the dissenting judgment in the Court of Appeal of one of the most distinguished of equity judges, Millett LJ (as he then was), the issues were made as clear as they have ever been made in the case law. The essential reason why Millett LJ's judgment is so wise is that, unlike the great preponderance of recent Commonwealth academic commentary on specific performance, and in stark contrast to the preoccupation with the position of the claimant in the performance interest argument,[93] that judgment *integrally* takes into account the interests of both parties: 'it is always necessary to consider the consequence to the defendant of granting such relief as well as the consequence to the plaintiff of leaving him to his remedy in damages'.[94] Limitations of space prevent us from fully tracing Millett LJ's wisdom back to the nineteenth-century equity jurisprudence so scorned in the 'restitution' or 'unjust enrichment' variant of the performance interest argument.[95] But it is essential to our argument to distinguish two different ways in which Millett LJ took the defendant's interests into account.

Warmly approving Judge Maddocks QC's decision, Millett LJ held that it was 'beyond dispute' that 'the settled practice of the court' was 'not to grant a final injunction or a decree of specific performance which would have the effect of compelling the defendant to carry on a business indefinitely'.[96] He noted that a reason given for this was difficulty of supervision, or the corollary difficulty of drafting a sufficiently clear order, but he placed 'little weight' on this and gave only little more weight to the particular supervision problems that arise in connection with the personal service elements of carrying on a business, which he regarded 'as only another way of putting the objection to the grant of an order which would require the defendant to carry on a commercial undertaking which he does not wish to carry on'.[97]

92 A Kramer, *An Agreement-Centred Approach to Remoteness and Damages* in N Cohen and E McKendrick eds COMPARATIVE REMEDIES FOR BREACH OF CONTRACT, Oxford, Hart 2005, 249, 284.

93 Barnett, n 1 above, 212.

94 *Co-operative Insurance* (CA), n 9 above, 304.

95 P Birks, *Equity, Conscience and Use* (1999) 23 MELBOURNE UNIVERSITY LAW REVIEW 1, 21–22.

96 *Co-operative Insurance* (CA), n 9 above, 303D, 302D.

97 *Ibid*, 303H. Lord Hoffmann did not agree with this part of Lord Millett's reasoning: *Co-operative Insurance* (HL), n 9 above, 16F.

The reason Millett LJ refused specific performance was that

> there is a fundamental objection to such an order. If granted for any length of time or for an indefinite period it is oppressive. To compel a defendant for an indefinite period to carry on a business which he considers is not viable, or which for his own commercial reasons he has decided to close down, is to expose him to potentially large, unquantifiable and unlimited losses which may be out of all proportion to the loss which his breach of contract has caused to the plaintiff.[98]

This is a conclusion reached on the balance of convenience. As such, then obviously the uncompensated loss of the claimant caused by confining it to compensatory damages could be pleaded against it. Millett LJ was perfectly well aware that such 'competing arguments' reflect a perennial ground of dispute; indeed, in a way which brings Lord Rodger's harking back to Stair to mind, he said that those arguments 'reflect a controversy which has persisted since the dispute between Sir Edward Coke and Lord Ellesmere LC'.[99] But, after giving his own arguments, which supported the conclusion quoted previously, he went on to give a 'secondary reason for refusing to depart from the practice which the courts have consistently followed for so long'.[100] It is this reason on which we wish to concentrate.

Millett LJ's secondary reason was:

> Over the years countless tenants with the benefit of legal advice have entered into commercial leases containing terms similar to those found in clause 4(19) of the present lease. If they had asked their legal advisers whether this meant that they could be compelled to keep the premises open for business regardless of the financial consequences, I have no doubt that they would have been told that it did not; they would have been advised that such a covenant sounds in damages only. If the courts were willing to compel performance, I do not see how any tenant properly advised could safely enter such an obligation. Yet the covenant is of great commercial value to developers, even if it does sound only in dam-ages. If the former practice is abandoned, developers may find it difficult to find anchor tenants willing to submit to such a covenant .... Consistent practice, no less than common error, makes the law. The equitable jurisdiction should not be exercised in a manner which would defeat the commercial expectations of the parties at the time when they entered into their contractual obligations.[101]

This is a very different argument from a balance of convenience argument. When determining that balance, the court weighs the merits of the positions of the parties and, ignoring the loss-splitting that effectively goes on in the drafting of many orders

[98] *Co-operative Insurance* (CA), n 9 above, 304A-B.

[99] *Ibid*, 304C.

[100] *Ibid*, 305G.

[101] *Ibid*, 305E-G.

for specific performance and injunction,[102] decides for one of them. The weighing is carried out according to standards of equitable jurisprudence which are exogenous to the parties' intentions expressed in the contract. But Millett LJ's secondary reason is quite the opposite of this. Here he is interpreting the meaning of the agreed terms – his second reason refers to the intentions of the parties. That this avoids the unsatisfactory feel inherent in all balance of convenience reasoning is less important than that it replaces exogenous decision making by the court with endogenous decision making by the parties negotiating on the basis of the decided law, which is, of course, the optimum way for the law of contract to proceed, if possible.

The reason the case law of specific performance has not usually proceeded in this way is that the parties' negotiations proceed on the basis of an error, exemplified by *Co-operative Insurance*, but typical of the common misunderstanding of the nature of contractual obligation expressed in the performance interest argument.[103] This error is at the heart of Lord St Leonard's thinking in *Lumley v Wagner*. It is a failure to recognise that, on the default terms, binding defendants to 'a true and literal performance of their agreements' is not to bind them to literal performance of their primary obligation. It is to bind them to furnishing a remedy, which will all but exceptionally be compensatory damages. We have shown that the claimant *never*, by merely agreeing a contract on default terms, gets a guarantee of literal enforcement of the defendant's primary obligations. But in an uncomplicated contract exemplified by the sale of generic goods, the claimant at least gets a guarantee of a remedy, which will adequately protect the claimant's expectation. This remedy will be market damages, which allow a buyer to purchase substitute goods at a market price higher than the contract price or a seller to sell goods at lower than the contract price. It is our view that, by promoting the real remedy of the claimant's procuring substitute goods or a substitute sale, taking what the Uniform Commercial Code Section 2-712 calls 'cover', the default law of compensatory damages, in a remarkable regulatory success story, constitutes the best conceivable remedial response to errors in the allocation of economic goods which are inevitable in any economic system.[104]

In certain consequential loss cases, complicating factors make the possibility that damages will be inadequate in the sense we have set out more likely, and in a complex contract such as that in *Co-operative Insurance*, that inadequacy should be in the contemplation of the parties when they negotiate. The default law creates an unavoidable risk of damages leaving the claimant with an uncompensated loss. It

[102] Harris *et al*, n 31 above, ch 25.

[103] D Campbell, *What Do We Mean By the Non-use of Contract?* in J Braucher *et al*, eds, REVISITING THE CONTRACTS SCHOLARSHIP OF STEWART MACAULAY: ON THE EMPIRICAL AND THE LYRICAL, Oxford, Hart, 2013, 159.

[104] D Campbell, *The Relational Constitution of Remedy: Co-operation as the Implicit Second Principle of Remedies for Breach of Contract* (2005) 11 TEXAS WESLEYAN LAW REVIEW 455.

is this risk that the claimant wishes to avoid by seeking specific performance in those commercial uniqueness cases in which the risk has become manifest after breach. But the claimant can do this after breach only by placing a burden of supra-compensatory loss on the defendant. What Millett LJ makes us see in *Co-operative Insurance* is that, in England and Wales, the claimant agrees to absorb this risk when it contracts on the basis of the default law of remedies for breach of contract.

The problem of risk allocation, which is the unavoidable background to commercial uniqueness cases, is made unmanageable because, in those cases, the claimant does not understand that it is exposed by breach to a subjectively unanticipated uncompensated loss to which it has objectively agreed. Believing itself to have a guarantee of literal enforcement of the primary obligation by agreeing the contract, the claimant fails to negotiate its position competently. This becomes manifest when it has to face up to quantification problems which, if they were to be fully canvassed, could lead to litigation like *Douglas Shelf Seven*. The commercial uniqueness pleadings are a desperate attempt by the claimant to extricate itself from the situation in which the claimant has placed itself. The real justification for refusing to allow the claimant to do this, to which Millett LJ leads us, is that the claimant has placed itself in the position it now finds so unsatisfactory when it contracted on the basis of Holmesian choice.

For though the performance interest argument insists the existing law is seriously deficient, in fact it is, in a most important sense, working perfectly well even in commercial uniqueness cases. But it is essential to grasp that its working well is the problem. The claimant's loss may be greater than that which it is able to prove, but the purpose of the causation rules is not to expose the defendant to all the claimant's loss but to expectation loss which is certain, proximate and unavoidable (and escapes other limitations). If the claimant does not recognise this at the stage of negotiation and take steps to deal with it, it then may well sustain an uncompensated loss, precisely because that loss cannot satisfy the causation tests which the default law works by imposing. If the claimant does not take these steps because it believes that, by incorporating a term stating a primary obligation into the contracts it gets a guarantee of the literal performance of that obligation, then contractual justice requires that its incompetence gets what it deserves from the contract, which is disappointment.

VI. SUPERVISORY PROBLEMS IN THE LAW OF KEEP-OPEN COVENANTS

It is one of our principal aims to show that neither the English nor the Scots law is sufficiently clearly focused on the reasons the parties adopt the strategies they do in cases like *Co-operative Insurance* and *Highland and Universal*. This has never been more clearly manifested than it has been in the way that the bulk of the discussion, following Lord Hoffmann's speech in *Co-operative Insurance*, is addressed to problems of court supervision of the performance of a long-term obligation which are, in our opinion, incidental.[105]

It is unarguable that the obligations to be compulsorily performed in *Co-operative Insurance* and *Highland and Universal* were, of their nature, in important respects indefinite. It is one thing to monitor, for example, hours of opening of a supermarket; it is another to monitor, for example, the effort made to make goods attractive to customers. But this does not mean that these problems are insurmountable. The Scots cases recognise, but have shown only limited sympathy with, claimed problems of devising a sufficiently precise decree of specific implement,[106] and the commercial conveyancing solicitors amongst our interviewees put as little weight on them as did Millet LJ. In particular, the view was expressed that obtaining expert testimony about the, as it were, quality of the defender's compliance would not raise difficulties which are not encountered in other disputes.

In order to advance our principal argument about the interpretation of the keep-open covenant, however, we feel obliged to state our beliefs that, first, the proposition that it was supervisory problems that the English law prior to *Co-operative Stores* regarded as the main bar to specific performance of keep-open covenants is wrong, and, secondly, that if it did so, the more robust Scots attitude towards those problems would be wholly preferable. If the matter is such that specific implement is the appropriate remedy, that is, if the parties contracted on this basis, then that the defendant can, in support of its own position, raise an implicit threat not to comply with, or at least to take an unco-operative attitude towards, a court order should not be condoned, and the court should be highly sceptical of claimed supervisory problems. In this we entirely agree with Professor Tettenborn, the vehemence of whose criticism of the eventual outcome in *Co-operative Stores* is based on the unacceptability of seeing the 'undeserving' escape their liabilities in this way.[107]

We do not deny that some cases do give rise to serious supervisory problems, which must be considered. The specification and supervision of a performance in personal service contract cases such as *Lumley v Gye* are a clear example, which has led to the very varied reception of that decision in subsequent cases. In these cases, the quality of the defendant's performance when given under compulsion may indeed be in a significant way out of the defendant's control. This is perhaps a worrying matter for

105 We put to one side the conduct of the defendant, deplored, as Lord Hoffmann noted, by all who heard the case, including Millett LJ, which obviously should have counted against it on equitable principles: *Co-operative Insurance* (HL), n 9 above, 18C.

106 Macgregor, n 14 above, 84–6 and Scottish Law Commission, n 32 above, para 6.2. See further the text accompanying n 128 below.

107 Tettenborn, n 7 above.

anyone flying to South Africa, where in a recent case the court ordered the specific enforcement of a commercial pilot's obligations under his contract of employment.[108] But these cases are not a helpful template for the analysis of commercial cases of a more ordinary sort, and their prominence in the discussion of commercial uniqueness is regrettable. As we have noted that Millett LJ observes,[109] the suspicion that is commonly raised by the judgment in these cases is that the court found supervisory problems insuperable because it was not persuaded of the underlying merit of the case for specific performance on the balance of convenience.

The appellate judgments in *Co-operative Insurance* are haunted by this issue, which, with respect, was handled badly by the majority in the Court of Appeal. Leggatt and Roch LJJs had to criticise Judge Maddocks QC's approach and did so in strong language. The judge had shown 'an unwarrantable reluctance to order specific performance' which had made it necessary for the Court of Appeal to 'intervene and exercise . . . discretion afresh unfettered by shibboleths which will otherwise continue to be unthinkingly applied'.[110] But this is a very unsatisfactory argument, for Leggatt and Roch LJJs nowhere argue that the situation in *Co-operative Insurance* actually had anything exceptional about it, and so the proper exercise of their equitable discretion should never have been an issue. Leggatt and Roch LJJs simply maintain that the court should consider each of the cases on its facts. We believe this would be a most unwise disruption of parties' settled expectations, for we repeat that clarity is paramount, and we believe that it was in partial recognition of this that the settled practice was not to consider covenants to carry on a business in this way, save as to ascertain whether they involved exceptional facts. If no such facts were present, the settled practice was not to reopen the issues, and certainly not after a Chancery hearing of the matter.

The majority's line obviously had the problem of dealing with the settled practice. Despite criticising it for lacking a thoroughgoing rationale in the case law,[111] Leggatt and Roch LJJs perforce acknowledged the settled practice and put forward the following argument to deal with it:

> Argyll may have been advised when they entered into their lease that if they found it unprofitable they could disregard their promise to keep the shop open upon payment of damages representing such loss as their dereliction could be proved to have caused. There is no evidence that any such advice was given. Even if it was, they

[108] *Nationwide Airlines (Pty) Ltd v Roediger* (2006) 27 ILJ 1469, following an earlier case involving a well-known football coach: *Santos Professional Club (Pty) Ltd v Igesund* (2002) 23 ILJ 2001, which to a common lawyer is equally striking but, to a frequent flyer, thankfully less unsettling.

[109] See text accompanying n 97 above.

[110] *Ibid*, 294E.

[111] *Ibid*, 292D. Roche LJ saw the case as an opportunity to supply the rationale for the opposite position to Judge Maddocks QC: *ibid*, 298B.

should have been advised also that the making of an order is discretionary, with the result that an order to keep-open might be made if the court considered that to be the appropriate remedy.[112]

This argument has two parts, and we are obliged to say that the second of them is misleading and that the first is unworthy. The second part, set out in the last sentence of the quoted passage, contains no overt error but nevertheless wrongly states the extant law, not as Slade J's settled practice, but as Leggatt and Roch LJJ would have it. The first part of their argument is flatly an attempt to avoid facing up to the consequences of deciding the matter before them on the basis of the law understood in this way. Leggatt and Roch LJJ effectively say that they are deciding the case on the basis of a legal position the opposite of that under which the lease was agreed, but that they do not allow that the tenant will be prejudiced by this as they have no evidence the tenant agreed the lease with the benefit of knowledge of that law.

This was met with a fair but sufficient response by Millett LJ,[113] and with a more than sufficient, indeed crushing, response by Lord Hoffmann, which must have given Leggatt LJ, to whom it was particularly directed, some understanding of the position in which he himself had left Judge Maddocks QC:

> the settled practice is based upon sound sense. Of course the grant or refusal of specific performance remains a matter for the judge's discretion. There are no binding rules, but this does not mean that there cannot be settled principles, founded upon practical considerations of the kind which I have discussed, which do not have to be re-examined in every case, but which the courts will apply in all but exceptional circumstances. As Slade J said … lawyers have no doubt for many years advised their clients on this basis. In the present case, Leggatt LJ … remarked that there was no evidence that such advice had been given. In my view, if the law or practice on a point is settled, it should be assumed that persons entering into legal transactions will have been advised accordingly. I am sure that Leggatt LJ would not wish to encourage litigants to adduce evidence of the particular advice which they received. Indeed, I doubt whether such evidence would be admissible.… Both landlord and tenant in this case are large sophisticated commercial organisations and I have no doubt that both were perfectly aware that the remedy for breach of the covenant was likely to be limited to an award of damages.[114]

On this basis, the conclusion Lord Hoffmann reached in *Co-operative Insurance* itself was entirely stated as follows:

> I think that no criticism can be made of the way in which Judge Maddocks exercised his discretion. All the reasons which he gave were proper matters for him to

[112] *Ibid*, 294A-B.
[113] *Ibid*, 305H-306A.
[114] *Co-operative Insurance* (HL), n 9 above, 16D, 18E.

> take into account. In my view the Court of Appeal should not have interfered and I would allow the appeal and restore the order which he made.[115]

Although Lord Hoffmann explicitly disagreed with Millett LJ's placing little weight on supervisory problems,[116] his doing so was not entirely consistent with this strongly expressed affirmation of Judge Maddocks QC's approach. If parties cannot be sure that when they enter into contracts such as that in *Co-operative Insurance* the issues will not be opened to the court's examination, save in exceptional circumstances which not even Leggatt and Roch LJJ actually maintained had arisen, they will not, as Millett LJ so penetratingly observed, enter into them.

In light of this, the judgment in *Highland and Universal*, with respect, misses the point. It is almost entirely preoccupied with distinguishing *Co-operative Insurance* on the point of supervisory difficulties. As we have said, we agree with the Scots position on this, but this should by no means have been the main point taken. That point should not have been the general nature of equitable discretion nor even the general discretion about supervisory issues, but rather the interpretation of keep-open covenants, and in particular the fact that, prior to *Retail Parks*, that covenant almost certainly would have been interpreted in the English way. The *Highland and Universal* lease was entered into in 1979,[117] and it is our opinion it should have been interpreted on the basis of the law which, if we can put it this way, was in force at that time. So, of course, should have been the lease in *Retail Parks*, which also was entered into in 1979.[118] We cannot account for the unsettling of the law which took place around 1995.[119] But, even allowing for the looming presence of *Co-operative Insurance*, it was, with the greatest of respect, unhelpful of Lord Rodger to focus almost entirely on supervision issues in *Highland and Universal*, even if his claim about a Scots tradition had been accurate. This misplaced focus prevented proper

115 *Ibid*, 19B.

116 *Ibid*, 16F.

117 *Highland and Universal*, n 13 above, 304D.

118 *Retail Parks*, n 12 above, 229.

119 The Outer House hearing of *Retail Parks* on 30 August 1995 was not cited to the *Court of Appeal* which heard *Co-operative Insurance* on 4 and 21 December 1995, but it was mentioned in skeleton arguments. Both it and the Inner House decision, following a hearing on 8 March 1996, were cited to the House of Lords, but Lord Hoffmann made no comment on the case. Interim proceedings in *Highland and Universal* which took place on 26 May 1995 were cited to the Court of Appeal but not to the House of Lords. (If the various law reports are not mistaken, these then unreported proceedings were incorrectly cited as '*Highway and Universal Ltd*'. The proceedings are now reported at [1996] SLT 559). The then unreported Court of Appeal decision in *Co-operative Insurance* was cited to the Inner House in *Retail Parks*. It would appear that, for some time just before 1995, there was, in the view of the (overlapping) Edinburgh and London commercial leasing Bars, something in the air that allowed the possibility of the settled practice being called into question.

consideration of the issue of interpretation of the covenant on which *Highland and Universal* should have turned.[120]

VII. COMMERCIAL UNIQUENESS CASES

As Millett LJ says, even if the covenant in *Co-operative Insurance* sounded only in damages, it was of great commercial value because in long-term contracts such as the one in *Co-operative Insurance*, the size of the claimant's investment is such that the claimant would be rash to undertake it without having secured a tenant on a lease which, because of the time needed to amortise an investment of this size, perforce was so long as obviously to invite risk of changed circumstances leading to breach. Natural resource exploitation contracts, distribution contracts of various types, supply chain contracts of various types, and a great many other contracts all take this form. What should a party do in this position?

The background risk the parties have to deal with cannot be eliminated. All the contract can do is allocate it. Both in England and Wales and in Scotland these cases turn on an underlying problem which is intractable given commercial parties' typical misunderstanding of the laws both of specific performance and of specific implement. A landlord which faces the possibility of its anchor tenant quitting and, under the law of England and Wales, of being left with an uncompensated loss, should do something about it, not at the stage of litigation, when the horse has bolted, but at the stage of negotiation, when the landlord should recognise that the default rule will favour the tenant by allocating the risk to landlords.[121] Providing for compulsory independent third party review and reallocation of the benefits and burdens when the tenant seeks to quit, or for liquidated damages, or for damages quantified on a gain-based rather than a compensatory basis, or for specific performance made as readily available as the court will allow,[122] are all possibilities, and no doubt there are others. In Scotland after *Highland and Universal*, the opposite position now obtains, placing the onus to do something about the default law on the tenant.

Which negotiating possibility is pursued should be no business of the law of contract.[123] But, of course, no such possibility will be pursued at all if the landlord

[120] Professor Alastair Smith, n 37 above, 214–5, keeps the issue of supervision alive by not confining himself to keep-open cases but by treating the keep-open cases as part of a general specific implement jurisprudence. But for the purposes of determining whether the equitable discretion should be exercised in keep-open cases, this, with respect, is a *petitio principii*.

[121] Luxton, n 82 above, 404–5.

[122] On this possibility in respect of *Co-operative Insurance* itself see Rowan, n 1 above, 210.

[123] In the only part of Millet LJ's judgment with which we disagree, he identifies the possibility of changing the basis of the quantification of damages, but sees it, not as a matter of the parties ousting the default, but as a matter of changing the mandatory rules of quantification, allowing what he reluctantly called 'restitutionary damages' 'in an appropriate case': *Co-operative Insurance*, n 9 above, 306C. With

believes that by agreeing the primary obligations it is obtaining a guarantee of literal performance. It does not, and the birth of contractual negotiating competence over the vital problem of the risk of uncompensated loss lies in the landlord, and all other potential claimants entering into a complex contract of this sort, recognising this and, if they believe it necessary, seeking to oust the default rule when negotiating the contract. The problems of these complex cases ultimately stem from their involving what the late Ian Macneil used to call relational contracts, and the solutions have been thoroughly well analysed by him in a very important paper which unfortunately has slipped into almost complete obscurity.[124]

VIII. ADVICE TO ENGLISH LANDLORDS

The dominant understanding of the nature of the obligations undertaken in keep-open cases is evidently so defective that we feel it helpful at this point to give a synopsis of the argument so far, presented in a fashion which is intended to be as clear as possible, even at the cost of inelegance and a degree of over-simplification. Let us assume a long-term lease of the *Co-operative Insurance* and *Highland and Universal* sort, agreed under the English law as stated by Slade J, by which the tenant covenants to keep open the premises for the term of the lease. Advice to the landlord conveying an accurate interpretation of this covenant will run as follows:

1. The tenant has an express primary obligation to keep open the premises for the term of the lease;
2. Assuming that this obligation is a term of an enforceable contract, the tenant has an implicit, latent secondary obligation to provide a remedy in the event of breach of the primary obligation;
3. As this lease has been agreed on the basis of the default law of England and Wales, it is almost certain that fundamental breach of the covenant will lead to a remedy of compensatory damages. These damages may be extremely difficult to prove under the default limitations on recovery, and their quantification on this basis is highly likely to leave the claimant with an uncompensated loss;
4. The chance of success in an attempt to get around this after breach, by seeking literal enforcement of the covenant by means of specific performance or

the greatest respect, Millet LJ did not appreciate the complete contradiction between his views over specific performance and the mandatory award of damages of a sort which, not merely could have the effect of specific performance, but would be an even more powerful weapon in the hands of the claimant as their award would not be subject to equitable discretion: Campbell, n 5 above.

124 IR Macneil, A *Primer of Contract Planning* (1975) 48 SOUTHERN CALIFORNIA LAW REVIEW 627. This paper is the framework for the part of Macneil's second casebook which deals with contract planning: IR Macneil and PJ Gudel, CONTRACTS: EXCHANGE TRANSACTIONS AND RELATIONS, 3rd edn, New York NY, Foundation Press, 2001, pt 2.

injunction, is vanishingly small, turning on circumstances so exceptional as never to have so far been established;

5. The default law of England and Wales therefore will not provide the landlord with full security of expectation in the event of fundamental breach of the covenant, and the landlord had best devise another strategy for obtaining such security, perhaps by obtaining the tenant's agreement to a bespoke remedy at the negotiating stage, or proceed in the knowledge that it does not have full security;
6. In summary, the keep-open covenant should be read as follows: 'the tenant will keep-open the premises for the term of the lease' (express primary obligation), 'but, if it fundamentally breaches, it will not literally have to keep the premises open but to pay compensatory damages, save in cases so exceptional as so far never to have been established' (implicit secondary obligation).

IX. CHANGING THE DEFAULT LAW, COMMERCIAL LEASING, AND THE IRRELEVANCE OF THE PERFORMANCE INTEREST

A party seeking to oust the default law must, of course, obtain the other party's agreement to do so. The default law of England and Wales, which turns on the Holmesian choice, conveys a negotiating advantage to the tenant as it allocates the risk of uncompensated loss to the landlord. It is, of course, possible to argue that this is a bad default law, and changing it so that an order of specific performance will normally be granted on the facts of *Co-operative Insurance* seems to be an obvious way of carrying forward the performance interest argument. The problem appears to be, and in a sense is, one of choice of default law. But it is essential to see that choice of the Scots law as the default will not necessarily lead to increased literal enforcement of keep-open obligations. We shall conclude this chapter by suggesting that, though we have no objection in principle to choice of the Scots law, the English default law is preferable. But this is merely incidental to our principal aim of showing how irrelevant the performance interest argument for mandating literal enforcement is to the real issues. We are now in a position to look at those issues with greater penetration.

Let us unambiguously allow that the Scots law after *Highland and Universal* is that keep-open covenants will be literally enforced save in exceptional circumstances. What would be the response of commercial parties to this? A properly competent party wishing to lease premises faced with this law will not, of course, automatically agree a clause which will place it in a situation which it is universally agreed could easily prove highly damaging and from which, especially as the clause places it in an oppressive bargaining situation, it will find it extremely costly to escape. As Professor Alastair Smith, writing from the performance interest perspective, insightfully observed in his commentary on *Highland and Universal*, 'tenants of Scottish premises … will now have to find a different way. … Chafing at the prospect of specific implement, they will try by other means to undermine' the Scots law.[125] Let us enumerate and briefly discuss the possibilities.

1. The most obvious result of the Scots law will be that tenants will not agree to enter into leases which contain a keep-open covenant or will agree only covenants expressed so flexibly, by, for example, the inclusion of 'break clauses' giving the tenant periodic options to quit the lease, as effectively to defeat the *Highland and Universal* law, with the result that commercial letting is possible only on the tenant's terms or may not be possible at all.[126] The public and private sector commercial leasing practitioners amongst our interviewees confirm this has commonly occurred, though they stress the importance of the current depression in strengthening the bargaining position of tenants. The landlords' bargaining position when agreeing the original rent and at periodic rent review is weakened in a corollary fashion because the keep-open covenant obviously reduces the value of the lease, and a landlord may perforce sacrifice the covenant in order to obtain the rent it wishes.
2. An almost equally obvious result is that the length of leases that tenants are prepared to agree will be considerably reduced. This certainly has occurred, though the effect of the depression should again be taken into account, for some reduction of lease length also has occurred elsewhere in the United Kingdom. It would, of course, be an absurd consequence, in utter contradiction of the performance interest argument, of the *Highland and Universal* law if it led to the underlying obligation disappearing, with serious economic consequences as, as we repeat that Millet LJ observed, that obligation, entered into on the basis of the English law, is of great value in commercial leasing.
3. When exogenous and unanticipated changes in circumstances have affected the viability of the tenant's business, confronted with a specifically enforceable keep-open clause, the tenant might seek to 'induce' a breach of contract by the landlord. If the tenant through a lack of co-operation which itself must

[125] A Smith, *Keep On Keeping Open* [2000] Edinburgh Law Review 336, 339.

[126] Discussing an earlier expression of our views, Dr Rowan, n 1 above, 234, argues that our concern that making specific performance the default remedy for breach will deter parties from entering into obligations they would enter into if the remedy for their breach was compensatory damages is 'largely unfounded'. But, with respect, we did not want to make a general, mandatory point, we wanted to make a point about specific obligations, all of which must be assessed on their merits, by parties who are able to negotiate their own remedies. We are perfectly aware that there are exchanges, which might best be served by providing a contractual remedy of specific performance. It is to the mandatory imposition of specific performance on exchanges to which it is inappropriate that we object, and we suspect that keep-open covenants are one of these.

crucially stop short of a breach of contract by the tenant causes the landlord himself to breach the contract, this might allow the tenant to terminate the lease legally. Leases like many long-term contracts anticipate a high degree of co-operation between parties over a protracted period which is difficult to specify *ex ante*. Such breach inducement serves no productive purpose but, faced with the prospect of continuing to operate a loss making business, such desperate action may be rational.[127]

4. Though it is impossible to challenge the enforceability of a valid keep-open covenant directly, it remains entirely possible to challenge the scope of the covenant as agreed in the terms of the lease. The challenge may be to what the parties initially agreed would be involved in keeping the premises open, the Scots law rightly being concerned not to 'innovate' on the parties' contract, by which is meant improve the pursuer's position by a decree of specific implement which imposes a burden greater than the actual performance stipulated. This argument is distinct from the argument about the difficulty of framing a decree sufficiently precise specifically to implement an agreed obligation in an equitable fashion.[128]

It may also be argued that the lease, and so burden of the covenant, may, on the lease terms, effectively be transferred to a third party by sub-lease, assignment, and so on, and that this would extinguish the tenant's own liability to the landlord. Such transfer may be particularly disturbing for the landlord, who likely does not know how substantial the third party may be.

Both of these lines were pursued in *Britel*, the first case decided by the Outer House after *Highland and Universal*, where Lord Macfadyen summarised the issue thus:

> As I understand the parties' positions in this case, there is no dispute that in light of the history of breach of the keep-open clause on the part of the defenders, and the fact that they accept that that clause is binding in general terms upon them and specifically enforceable against them, it is appropriate that a final order of specific implement should be pronounced. The only dispute is as to the proper scope of the order. I do not understand it to be disputed that the court cannot grant specific implement in terms more onerous than the underlying contractual obligation. The primary issue therefore comes to be whether the proposed final order in the form argued for by the pursuers purports to bind the defenders in circumstances in which they would not be bound by the contractual obligation.[129]

[127] The possibility and consequences of such behaviour when a party is confronted with a stipulated damages clause are discussed in KW Clarkson *et al*, *Liquidated Damages v Penalties: Sense or Nonsense?* [1978] Wisconsin Law Review 351.

[128] See n 106 above.

[129] *Britel*, n 56 above, para [18].

Lord Macfadyen concluded that the decree sought would innovate, and so refused it, making, as he rightly observed, the question of whether he should exercise the discretion left to him by *Highland Parks* irrelevant.[130]

Britel had to be distinguished in a way, which involved very close examination of the terms of the respective covenants in *Oak Mall* in order for the Outer House to grant specific implement.[131] *Britel* was also distinguished, *obiter*, in *Douglas Shelf Seven*, where arguments about innovation and the consequences of a purported transfer which flowed from the disputed wording of the lease had been advanced in protracted litigation some years prior to the case we have discussed,[132] which, as we have said, proceeded on the basis that the covenant was enforceable and that the sole issue was quantum. Nevertheless, although it involved the retraction of judicial admissions they had made,[133] the defender and the third party sought to raise the matter again on the ninth day of trial,[134] and this attempt, which would, of course, have made the continued hearing of the case on the agreed basis pointless, was quashed on procedural grounds by Lord Reed.[135] He nevertheless went on to say that, had the defender's and third party's argument been heard, it would have failed, and it was in the course of so doing that he distinguished *Britel*. All this did not stop the litigation, however, which has continued on a subsidiary point relating to the extent of the defender's obligation to maintain the condition of the premises at a certain standard.[136] Knowledge of these other proceedings in *Douglas Shelf Seven* merely emphasises the evaluation we have given of the principal litigation. If, as it appears, these remarkable proceedings are the result of the change in the law consolidated in *Highland and Universal*, it is not a happy result.

We do not wish to pretend to a competence in commercial conveyancing which we do not have when we say that it appears that the argument about transfer of burden seems to be in the process of being settled in the landlord's favour, but that the argument about innovation appears to be live and, indeed, we cannot see how this could be otherwise. That strengthening a remedy for breach of an obligation may push back the argument to determining to what degree the obligation has been breached, or to whether it has been breached at all, is an established lesson of equity.

We have seen that Millet LJ's 'fundamental objection' to granting an order of specific performance in *Co-operative Insurance* was that it would be oppressive. This

[130] *Ibid*, para [24].

[131] *Oak Mall*, n 55 above, paras 9–12.

[132] *Co-operative Wholesale Society Ltd v Ravenseft Properties Ltd and Douglas Shelf Seven Ltd* (2001) Scot (D) 9/7 (OH); (2002) SCLR 644 (OH); (2003) SCLR 509 (OH).

[133] *Douglas Shelf Seven*, n 57 above, paras [570], [575].

[134] *Ibid*, para [573].

[135] *Ibid*, para [575]. The entire handling by Lord Reed of this difficult submission appears to be exemplary: *ibid*, paras [559]–[575].

[136] *Douglas Shelf Seven Ltd v Co-operative Wholesale Society Ltd* (2009) CSOH 3 (OH).

objection, as Millett LJ went on to make clear,[137] is central to the equity jurisprudence of specific performance and injunction going back at least to the dictum of Lord Westbury LC in *Isenberg v East India House Estate Co Ltd*, that the court should not by its order 'deliver over the Defendants to the Plaintiff bound hand and foot, in order to be made subject to any extortionate demand that he may by possibility make'.[138] The superior wisdom of this core principle of equity over the crude commitment to the literal enforcement of primary obligations central to the performance interest argument cannot and should not be excluded from the law of keep-open covenants in particular and of primary obligations in general in either jurisdiction. The point is that the law should and will consider the interests of both parties.[139]

5. Landlords' understandable concern about the substance of a third party to which the burden of a keep-open covenant may be transferred leads one to consider whether tenants subject to that burden may resort to liquidation, or a company voluntary agreement under threat of liquidation, as a way of escaping their liability. Again, some of our interviewees and the professional literature confirm that this possibility is being actively explored, but, again, in the current trading conditions it is also being explored elsewhere in the UK. It is but a step from this for putative tenants to enter into leases via insubstantial shells they have created for this purpose, which would effectively render any keep-open obligation nugatory. Preliminary company law research conducted by Dr Richard Williams has led us to suspect that the all of these tactics are being employed to effectively deal with keep-open covenants, and, led by Dr Williams, we intend to publish a further paper on these matters.

We do not doubt that there are other possibilities we have not identified.[140] However, this list is surely enough to show the naïveté of the performance interest argument

[137] *Co-operative Insurance* (CA), n 9 above, 305.

[138] (1863) 3 De G, J and S 263, 273; 46 ER 637, 641.

[139] This balanced approach has received recent academic support in an important article by Professor Eisenberg: M Eisenberg *Actual and Virtual Specific Performance, the Theory of Efficient Breach, and the Indifference Principle in Contract Law* (2005) 93 CALIFORNIA LAW REVIEW 975.

[140] We are relegating to a footnote the possibility, argued before an Extra Division of the Inner House in *Co-operative Group Ltd v Propinvest Paisley LP* [2011] CSIH 41; [2012] SC 51, of obtaining statutory discharge of keep-open covenants as unreasonably burdensome. Under the Title Conditions (Scotland) Act 2003 s 90, the Lands Tribunal for Scotland may review and vary or discharge title conditions when it is reasonable to do so under s 90, on the basis of considerations which are identified in s 100. On the face of it, a typical keep-open covenant in a typical supermarket lease can be brought under s 100. The litigation so far has been procedural, and has cleared the way for the tenant's challenge under s 90 to go forward. *Propinvest*, which, in addition to the *Session Cases*, has been reported at [2011] SLT 987 and [2011] House LR 32, is viewed with very great concern by some of our interviewees. The opinion of the Lands Tribunal, Case ref LTS/TC/2009/09, is available via the Tribunal's website: http://www.lands-tribunal-scotland.org.uk/decisions/LTS.TC.2009.09.html

applied to keep-open clauses, for the belief that the *Highland and Universal* law will lead to more instance of actual performance of keep-open obligations is the merest speculation. In the US academic literature that is often referred to in discussions of these matters, the argument for, as it were, reversing the default priority of compensatory damages and specific performance was not assumed to increase the incidence of literal enforcement but was assessed in terms of its effect on 'pre' and 'post-breach' negotiations between the parties.[141] Whatever effect of this sort *Retail Parks* has had in Scotland, this is a very different thing than the 'more friendly environment for promises' that it is claimed that that case has created, and whatever has happened cannot be defended by the performance interest argument, which is a complete irrelevance to the assessment of the law in either jurisdiction. We repeat again that our aim is criticism of the performance interest argument and that we are, in principle, indifferent to whether the law of England and Wales or Scotland is adopted as the default law, but we conclude with some reflections on the choice between them.

X. CONCLUSION

Competent commercial parties who are aware that the security that may be gained by expressing their economic exchanges in contractual terms will, to varying degrees, have the possibility of negotiating around the default law, whether it be English or Scots. On no possible form of the law consistent with freedom of contract will the enforcement of these obligations be a question of choosing between mandatory compensatory damages or mandatory literal enforcement and the performance interest argument about this is an irrelevance. The real policy issue is the choice between default rules that will allocate the risk of an uncompensated loss to the claimant or of a supra-compensatory remedy to the defendant, which can be properly assessed only by analysing the practical response of the parties to the legislative choice that is made.

An evaluation of a default law usually will, in large part, turn on how often parties have to oust that law, a bad law being one that has to be continuously ousted.[142] But application of this criterion to keep-open clauses must not be thought to require a

[141] A Schwartz, *The Case for Specific Performance* (1979) 89 YALE LAW JOURNAL 271. See also the valuable comment: TJ Muris, *The Costs of Freely Granting Specific Performance* [1982] DUKE LAW JOURNAL 1035.

[142] See the concept of the penalty default rule in I Ayres and R Gertner, *Filling Gaps in Incomplete Contracts: An Economic Theory of Default Rules* (1989) 99 YALE LAW JOURNAL 87. It is, of course, implausible to suggest that law makers actually intentionally set such rules (EA Posner, *There Are No Penalty Default Rules in Contract Law* (2006) 33 FLORIDA STATE UNIVERSITY LAW REVIEW 563), but this is not to say that they do not exist.

choice between contracting on the basis of the English or the Scots default laws, as neither will really fit the bill in the difficult cases which give rise to real problems. Competent parties to contracts of sufficiently high value to justify the expense of doing so should negotiate a bespoke clause which splits potential loss on terms those parties agree. Working within the parameters of the existing law, the proper question is whether the English or the Scots default law would more properly lead the parties to negotiate superior bespoke terms to manage the ineradicable underlying risk. It our hesitant conclusion that the English position is better than the Scots because it places the burden of starting negotiations on the landlord who originates the retail investment, and so will provoke the more adequate planning of that investment. We also defer to the equitable wisdom that so influenced Lord Millett, for we believe that, should the parties proceed on the default basis, the English rule's avoidance of oppression makes it the best of the two rules, hopefully reducing the extent of the costly legal innovation that has taken place in Scotland since *Retail Parks*.

However, we again repeat that we have no objection in principle to the Scots law being chosen as the default law, have no objection of any sort whatsoever to the parties themselves choosing the Scots law, and have no very strong conviction about the choice of default law we have made. It is not our principal intention to argue for a particular law. The issues being clarified, the parties should make their own choice. It is our principal intention to argue against those who want a law that it is thought will mandate a desired outcome of literal enforcement of performance of the defendant's primary obligations. The performance interest argument, which seeks to do this, completely misunderstands the nature of the parties' agreement and the function of the law of remedies for breach of contract. The performance interest simply cannot come to terms with the positive law, which it therefore finds markedly deficient, markedly puzzling, or both, and substitutes its speculative supposition about the goal of the law for what the law is.

Were it possible, making literal enforcement of performance of a primary obligation the mandatory remedy for breach would be a drastic mistake. But the main shortcoming of the performance interest argument is that this goal is irrelevant so long as parties are free to enter or refuse to enter into contracts and to agree the terms, including the remedial terms, of those contracts. The proof of this which emerges from examination of the Scots law of keep-open covenants requires an assessment of the empirical effect of those covenants, for it is the merest speculation to maintain that their inclusion in leases conveys the guarantee of literal performance that the performance interest argument seeks.

PART VII

Harmonizing Contract Law

This part examines current trends in the harmonization of contract law in two major areas: general contract law in Europe and international sales law. Chapters 20 and 21 assess the current state and future of legal harmonization efforts in Europe. Chapter 22 analyzes the level of harmonization or lack of thereof brought about by the Convention on Contracts for the Sale of Goods (CISG). Chapter 20 makes the bold assertion that the harmonization of European contract law is doomed to fail. It asserts that the likely failure of harmonization of contract law in Europe is primarily due to the fact that current initiatives focus on the development of a regional set of default rules, while the real obstacles to European trade is found in divergences in the national mandatory rules of contract law and government regulation. The chapter further asserts that the adoption of regional default rules will likely cause more harm than benefit by increasing legal complexity through the insertion of another legal regime over existing national contract law regimes.

Chapter 21 concludes the coverage on the harmonisation of European contract law by examining the Europeanisation of contract law from a Scottish perspective. The Scottish mixed system of common and civil law is mined to build a framework or long-term strategy leading from convergence to the harmonisation of European contract law.

Chapter 22 assesses the current state of the CISG efforts to harmonize international sales law by asking the question: Has the CISG text and principles, and their application, set the foundation for a relative uniformity of application? It looks at current trends in the case law to determine if there has been a convergence of competing interpretations of CISG rules, if there has been a development of well-recognized default rules, and whether uniformity of application has been aided through the development of factors analyses to guide courts in applying CISG rules. The chapter concludes by pondering the following question: What are the possible "futures" of the CISG?

20

Harmonisation of European Contract Law

Default and Mandatory Rules

Qi Zhou

This chapter argues that the current harmonisation of European contract law will eventually fail. Supporters of the harmonisation suggest that the divergence in national contract laws not only generates unnecessary costs for cross-border trade, but also undermines fair competition in the European market. Thus, legal harmonisation is the necessary solution. Unfortunately, the harmonisation movement has failed to understand the crucial distinction between default and mandatory rules. The current and proposed harmonisation measures have focused on the development of sets of default rules. In fact, divergence in national contract laws is mainly due to differences in their mandatory rules.

This harmonisation effort suffers from two major defects. Firstly, it assumes that the national default rules are in need of harmonisation in order to facilitate trans-border transactions. In fact, there is no conclusive empirical evidence that differences in national default rules have retarded European trade. Conversely, several existing studies have indicated the opposite: that harmonisation of default rules at the regional level actually increases the complexity of contract law and trans-border trading. Secondly, even if a regional harmonised contract law were produced, it would not provide the certainty needed to warrant the effort due to problems of multi-jurisdictional interpretations. The chapter concludes that a European contract law regime, at this time and in its current form, will lead to an unnecessary layer of legal complexity to European trade.

I. INTRODUCTION

This chapter aims to answer two key questions in relation to the harmonisation of European contract law. Firstly, do the different national contract laws in the Member States give rise to problems for cross-border trade in the EU? Secondly, can the harmonisation of European contract law solve the problems effectively?

To answer the questions, we should consider the distinction between a default rule and a mandatory rule. On the one hand, most legal rules in contract law are default rules. The parties can freely replace them with their own contract terms. If the problems for cross-border trade are caused by the different default rules in the national contract laws, we should further investigate the question whether the harmonisation of European contract law can effectively solve them. On the other hand, mandatory rules exist in both contract law and regulatory law. The parties must comply with them as long as they make the contract. If the problems are caused by the different mandatory rules in the Member States, the harmonisation of European contract law will not solve the problem. The harmonisation of mandatory rules in both contract law and regulatory law is therefore necessary.

Two arguments are made in this chapter. Firstly, the justification for the harmonisation of European contract law, on the basis that different national contract laws generate high transaction costs for cross-border transactions, is both theoretically invalid and empirically unproved. Even if this proposition were true, the harmonisation of European contract law would still not be able to eliminate the transaction costs. Secondly, the problem for cross-border trade is largely caused by the differences in the mandatory rules, which distort competition in the European internal market. From a theoretical perspective, this problem can only be solved by the full harmonisation of mandatory rules in both contract law and regulatory law. Nonetheless, this is unachievable in practice. Therefore, the legal distortion of competition is inevitable in the EU.

The chapter proceeds as follows. Section II articulates the differences between a default rule and a mandatory rule. Section III critically evaluates the justifications for the harmonisation of European contract law. Sections IV and V examine the harmonisation of default rules and mandatory rules, respectively. Finally, Section VI concludes the discussion.

II. DEFAULT AND MANDATORY RULES: A COMPARISON

Although all contract lawyers know that contract law consists of both default rules and mandatory rules,[1] little academic literature has been produced to analyze the implications of their differences for the harmonisation of European contract

[1] For general discussion of default rules and mandatory rules in contract law, see Hugh Collins, REGULATING CONTRACTS (Oxford University Press: 1999), 31–93; Ian Ayres and Robert H. Gertner, *Filling Gaps in Incomplete Contracts: An Economic Theory of Default Rules*, 99(2) YALE LAW JOURNAL, 87–130 (1989); T. D. Rakoff, *Implied Terms: Of 'Default Rules' and 'Situation Sense,'* in GOOD FAITH AND FAULT IN CONTRACT LAW (Jack Beatson and Daniel Friedmann (eds.), Clarendon Press: 1995), 191–228; Attila Menyhard, Karoli Mike and Akos Szalai, 'Mandatory Rules in Contract Law', *German Working Papers in Law and Economics*, 18 (2007) at http://ssrn.com/abstract=1414110.

law.[2] A default rule is the legal rule, which can be replaced by the parties' express contract term. But if the parties do not opt out of the default rule, it will automatically become a contract term binding the parties. On the contrary, a mandatory rule is the legal rule, which the parties must obey as long as they make the contract.

Their differences can be exemplified by s.20 of the English Sale of Goods Act 1979, which governs the transfer of risk from the seller to the buyer.[3] It is provided that

> (1) Unless otherwise agreed, the goods remain at the seller's risk until the property in them is transferred to the buyer, but when the property in them is transferred to the buyer, the goods are at the buyer's risk whether delivery has been made or not.
> (2) But where delivery has been delayed through the fault of either buyer or seller the goods are at the risk of the party at fault as regards any loss which might not have occurred but for such fault.
> (3) Nothing in this section affects the duties or liabilities of either seller or buyer as a bailee or custodian of the goods of the other party.
> (4) In a case where the buyer deals as consumer or, in Scotland, where there is a consumer contract in which the buyer is a consumer, subsections (1) to (3) must be ignored and the goods remain at the seller's risk until they are delivered to the consumer.

S.20 contains three default rules and one mandatory rule. S.20(1), (2) and (3) are default rules; while s.20(4) is a mandatory rule. The phrase 'unless otherwise agreed' in s.20(1) indicates that s.20 (1) to (3) are default rules. If the parties do not write an express contract term to replace s.20 (1) to (3), they will apply. The risk transfers from the seller to the buyer when the property in goods passes from the seller to the buyer.[4] However, the sentence in s.20(4) that 'subsections (1) to (3) must be ignored.' shows that s.20(4) is a mandatory rule, which cannot be excluded by the parties. In a consumer contract, the risk passes from the seller to the buyer at the time of the delivery of the goods.[5]

This example demonstrates three differences between a default rule and a mandatory rule. Firstly, the parties can exclude a default rule, but they cannot exclude a mandatory rule. Secondly, if there is an express term which conflicts with a default

[2] Matthias Storme, 'Freedom of Contract: Mandatory and Non-Mandatory Rules in European Contract Law', 15 European Review of Private Law, 233–50 (2007).

[3] For general discussion of the legal rules governing the transfer of risk, see John Adams & Hector Mcqueen, Atiyah's Sale of Goods (12th ed., Longman Pearson: 2010) 342–8; Ewan McKendrick, Goode on Commercial Law, (14th ed., Penguin Books: 2010), 265–81.

[4] *Hansen v Craig & Rose* (1895) 21 d 432, 438 per Lord President Inglis, cited by Lord Normand in *Comptoir d'Achat et Vente SA v Luis de Ridder Limitada (The Julia)* [1949] AC 293, at 319.

[5] This mandatory rule is introduced by the Sale and Supply of Goods to Consumers Regulations 2002, SI 2002/3045, reg. 4(2).

rule, the express term prevails. The default rule becomes an implied contract term only when the parties do not stipulate explicitly the legal issue regulated by the default rule. On the contrary, if there is a conflict between an express term and a mandatory rule, the mandatory rule prevails.

Thirdly, if a party breaks a default rule, he is liable for the breach of the contract; the aggrieved party can claim the legal remedy available in contract law. However, if the party breaks a mandatory rule, there may be two possible consequences, depending on the nature of the mandatory rule. One consequence may be identical to the breach of the default rule. The breaching party is liable for the breach of the contract. For example, where the seller to a consumer contract breaks s.20(4) of the Sale of Goods Act 1979, he is liable for the breach of the contract, and the consumer buyer can claim the legal remedy provided by the Act. Yet, the other consequence may be that the breaching party is punished by public law. Not all of the mandatory rules, like s.20(4) of the Sale of Goods Act 1979, are characterized by contract law. In fact, most mandatory rules take the form of regulatory law. The contravention of regulatory law is subject to public law sanctions. Take the Consumer Protection from Unfair Trading Regulations 2008 as an example. It is provided that traders are prohibited from engaging in unfair commercial practices, such as providing false or misleading information to a consumer when making the contract.[6] The contravention of the Regulations by a trader may count as a criminal offense subject to a fine or imprisonment for a term not exceeding two years or both.[7] Compared to the breach of the default rule, the breach of the mandatory rule may result in a more serious legal sanction.

From a conventional perspective, contract law is part of the law of obligations, which is classified as a branch of private law, while regulatory law is part of administrative law, which is classified as a branch of public law.[8] So, regulatory law is not

[6] Article 9 of the Consumer Protection from Unfair Trading Regulations 2008 provides that a trader is guilty of an offense if he engages in a commercial practice which is a misleading action under regulation 5 otherwise than by reason of the commercial practice satisfying the condition in regulation 5(3)(b).

[7] Article 13 of the Consumer Protection from Unfair Trade Regulations 2008 provides that a person guilty of an offense under regulation 8, 9, 10, 11, or 12 shall be liable: (a) on summary conviction, to a fine not exceeding the statutory maximum; or (b) on conviction or indictment, to a fine or imprisonment for a term not exceeding two years or both.

[8] For discussion of the classification of public law and private law, see Michael Loughlin, PUBLIC LAW AND POLITICAL THEORY (Clarendon Press, 1992), 2–4; THE GOALS OF PRIVATE LAW (A. Robertson and Hang W. Tang (eds.), Hart Publishing, 2009); Peter Cane, ADMINISTRATIVE LAW (Clarendon Press, 2011), 69–246. For discussions of public law and contract law, see Jack Beatson, *Public Law Influences in Contract Law* in GOOD FAITH AND FAULT IN CONTRACT LAW (J. Beatons and D. Friedmann (eds.), Clarendon Press, 1995), 263–88; Sue Arrowsmith, *The Impact of Public law on the Private Law of Contract*, in EXPLORING THE BOUNDARIES OF CONTRACT, (R. Halson (ed.), Dartmouth, 1996), 3–22.

considered as contract law. This view is not adopted in this chapter, because, as will be discussed in the next section, mandatory rules in both contract law and regulatory law affect cross-border trade. More importantly, different regulatory laws in the Members States are the main problems for cross-border trade.[9] The harmonisation of European contract law would be in vain if different regulatory laws were not harmonised.

III. JUSTIFICATIONS FOR THE HARMONISATION OF EUROPEAN CONTRACT LAW

There are two key justifications for the harmonisation of European contract law, namely, that the different national contract laws in the Member States not only generate unnecessary transaction costs for cross-border trade, but also distort competition in the European internal market.[10]

According to the first justification, if the parties to a transaction are located in different states where their national contract laws are also different, they have to negotiate a national law as the applicable law to govern their transaction. Conversely, if the parties were in the same country or their national contract laws were the same, such negotiation would be unnecessary. Moreover, whichever national contract law is chosen as the applicable law, one of the parties may inevitably be unfamiliar with the foreign law and must study it, which is also costly. Therefore, the different national contract laws generate both unnecessary negotiation costs and learning costs for the parties to a cross-border transaction.

In addition, the different national contract laws also make consumers worse off. Unnecessary transaction costs caused by the legal differences discourage cross-border trade. Firms make less profit from a cross-border transaction, because the additional transaction cost has to be deducted from their return. Cross-border trade becomes

[9] Stefan Vogenauer and Steven Weatherill, *The European Community's Competence to Pursue the Harmonisation of Contract Law – an Empirical Contribution to the Debate*, in THE HARMONISATION OF EUROPEAN CONTRACT LAW, IMPLICATIONS FOR EUROPEAN PRIVATE LAWS, BUSINESS AND LEGAL PRACTICE (S. Vogenauer and S. Weatherill [eds.], Hart Publishing: 2006), 105–48.

[10] Ewan McKendrick, *Harmonisation of European Contract Law: The State We Are In*, in THE HARMONISATION OF EUROPEAN CONTRACT LAW, IMPLICATIONS FOR EUROPEAN PRIVATE LAWS, BUSINESS AND LEGAL PRACTICE, 5–30; Fernando Gómez, *The Harmonization of Contract Law through European Rules: A Law and Economics Perspective*, 4(2) EUROPEAN REVIEW OF CONTRACT LAW, 89–118, (2008); Ole Lando, *Optimal or Mandatory Europeanisation of Contract Law*, 8 EUROPEAN REVIEW OF PRIVATE LAW, 56–69 (2000); Roy Goode, *Insularity or Leadership? The Role of the United Kingdom in the Harmonisation of Commercial Law*, 50 INTERNATIONAL AND COMPARATIVE LAW QUARTERLY, 751–65 (2001); Hugh Collins, THE EUROPEAN CIVIL CODE, THE WAY FORWARD (Cambridge University Press, 2008).

less profitable and unattractive to firms. For consumers, their interests are impaired since they cannot enjoy the variety of options from cross-border shopping and lower prices resulting from the competition between domestic firms and foreign firms.

One recent study shows that businesses involved in cross-border trade face unnecessary transaction costs of close to one billion euros per year. The lost value in the forgone trade due to different national contract laws reaches nearly one hundred billion euros.[11] It is suggested that the harmonisation of European contract law could eliminate the differences in the national contract laws, thereby saving this huge amount of transaction cost for cross-border trade. If the contribution of removing differences in contract law were about one percentage point of this positive effect, the value of the increased trade would be around thirty billion euros.[12]

At first glance, the preceding argument seems to be sound. But a further scrutiny can reveal its flaws. In fact, this argument is invalid both theoretically and empirically. The argument is based on the assumption that neither do the parties to the cross-border transaction have sufficient knowledge of each other's national contract law, nor do they have a well-established set of legal rules to govern their transactions. In other words, the parties are new traders in the market. This is indeed an unrealistic assumption. In reality, every cross-border trade market comprises both established traders and new traders. More importantly, established traders play a leading role in shaping the legal rules governing their trade.[13] Through many years trading, they have developed a body of informal rules, norms and trade customs to govern their transactions. The majority of them may also have developed a shared preference for a national contract law as the applicable law. Differences in national contract laws are not a problem for them. They will not incur additional costs to negotiate the applicable law or learn the foreign law, because they have already used a given contract law to govern their trade for a very long time. For example, English contract law has been widely adopted by many international traders. Several leading international trade associations choose English law as the applicable law, such as the Grain and Feed Trade Association (GAFTA), Federation of Oils, Seeds, and Fats Association (FOSFA), Refined Sugar Association (RSA), and Shell and British Petroleum (BP).[14] They produce standard form contracts, which are used by most traders in the industry. For the established traders, differences in national contract laws incur no additional transaction cost. On the contrary, if a new uniform contract law were introduced,

[11] European Commission's Executive Summary of the Impact Assessment of Proposal for a Regulation of the European Parliament and of the Council on a Common European Sales Law, Brussels, 11.10.2011, SEC(2011) 1166 final, p. 1.

[12] *Id.*, at 2.

[13] Robert Bradgate, Commercial Law (3rd ed., Oxford University Press: 2005), 9–20.

[14] Michael Bridge, The International Sale of Goods Law and Practice (2nd ed. Oxford University Press: 2010), at 14.

they would have to learn the new rules. Rather than reducing their transaction costs, the uniform contract law would actually increase them. Surprisingly, this factor is not considered properly by the empirical studies in the current literature.[15]

Furthermore, these studies also did not address the question whether it is more costly for a new trader to learn the national law which is widely used in the industry or more expensive for him to learn a new uniform contract law. As far as new traders are concerned, both laws are unfamiliar. Learning costs are inevitable. It is obviously inappropriate to assume that the former is higher than the latter. The comparison of the two costs will have a significant impact on the result of the cost-benefit analysis of the harmonisation of European contract law. Unfortunately, this vital factor was not evaluated properly in the existing empirical studies. Thus, it is reasonable to say that the figure of the transaction cost cited previously, one billion euros per year, is highly unreliable and may be a great overestimation. More rigorous cost-benefit assessments are needed.

Apart from the flaw identified earlier, the first justification for the harmonisation of European contract law may also exaggerate the importance of contract law in cross-border trade. It draws on the assumption that contract law plays a crucial role in planning transactions and solving disputes. Differences in the national contract laws give rise to legal uncertainty, undermining the economic function of contract law and thereby generating unnecessary transaction costs for cross-border trade.

Nonetheless, this argument gains little support from empirical evidence; whereas a number of empirical studies have shown the opposite. Contract law actually plays a small role in commercial transactions; the parties rely more on informal norms and private institutions to regulate their contracts.[16] In 1951 Macaulay found that businessmen rarely rely on contract law to solve their disputes. In his seminal paper

[15] S Stefan Vogenauer and Steven Weatherill, *The European Community's Competence to Pursue the Harmonisation of Contract Law – an Empirical Contribution to the Debate* (cited, n 9), 105–48. European Commission's Executive Summary of the Impact Assessment of Proposal for a Regulation of the European Parliament and of the Council on a Common European Sales Law, Brussels, 11.10.2011, SEC(2011) 1166.

[16] Michael Trebilcock and Jing Leng, *The Role of Formal Contract and Enforcement in Economic Development*, 92 VIRGINIA LAW REVIEW, 1517–80 (2009); Stewart Macaulay, *The Real and the Paper Deal: Empirical Picture of Relationship Complexity and the Urge for Transparent Simple Rules*, 66 MODERN LAW REVIEW, 44–79 (2003); Stewart Macaulay, *Non-Contractual Relationship in Business: A Preliminary Study*, 28 AMERICAN SOCIOLOGICAL REVIEW, 1–19 (1963); Hugh Beale & Tony Dugdale, *Contracts between Businessmen: Planning and the Use of Contractual Remedies*, 2 BRITISH JOURNAL OF LAW AND SOCIETY, 45–60, (1975).; Lisa Bernstein, *Opting Out of the Legal System: Extralegal Contractual Relations in the Diamond Industry*, 21 JOURNAL OF LEGAL STUDIES, 115–57 (1992); Lisa Bernstein, *Merchant Law in Merchant Court: Rethinking the Code's Search for Immanent Business Norms*, 114 UNIVERSITY OF PENNSYLVANIA LAW REVIEW, 1765–821 (1996); Lisa Bernstein, *Private Commercial Law in the Cotton Industry: Creating Cooperation Through Rules, Norms and Institutions*, 99 MICHIGAN LAW REVIEW, 1924–90 (1999); Janet L. Landa, *A Theory of the Ethnically*

'Non-Contractual Relations in Business: A Preliminary Study', he showed that when a dispute occurs between businessmen, they often solve it informally without either referring to the contract which they signed or looking for solutions in contract law. Contract law actually plays a very minor role in their transactions. Often, they see contract law as causing a risk of terminating or undermining their business relationship.[17] Similar results were also found by Beale and Dugdate's empirical study of British business practice. Businessmen in the United Kingdom only use formal contract law or courts to solve their contractual disputes occasionally. Most of the contractual disputes are solved through negotiations or other informal means.[18] Recently, a number of empirical studies by Bernstein confirmed the preceding findings. More interestingly, Bernstein's studies reveal some new phenomena in commercial practice. In some industries, such as the diamond and cotton trades in the United States, traders deliberately opt out of formal legal institutions, creating their own private governing codes and internal organizations to solve disputes of their traders.[19] These empirical studies cast some serious doubts on the claim that there is a need for the harmonisation of European contract law, because different national contract laws generate unnecessary transaction costs for cross-border transactions. If contract law plays a very small role in commercial transactions, differences in the national contract laws will have a very limited impact on cross-border trade. The figure of the transaction cost, one billion euros per year, would therefore be an exaggeration.

Last, but not least, there is a vital question which the empirical studies have not answered, namely, whether the problem is caused by the default rule or the mandatory rule. If it is the difference in the mandatory rules which causes the problems, the harmonisation of European contract law cannot solve the problem, because most mandatory rules exist in regulatory law. This question must be answered before the official adoption of any version of European contract law produced by academic working groups. Otherwise, not only would the European contract law be unable to solve the old problems, but it would also give rise to many new ones.

In brief, the argument that different national contract laws generate unnecessary transaction costs for cross-border trade is highly unreliable, if not completely flawed.

Homogeneous Middleman Group: An Institutional Alternative to Contract Law, 10 JOURNAL OF LEGAL STUDIES, 349–62 (1981).

17 Stewart Macaulay, *Non-Contractual Relationship in Business: A Preliminary Study*, (cit. n 16).

18 Hugh Beale & Tony Dugdale, *Contracts between Businessmen: Planning and the Use of Contractual Remedies* (cit n 16).

19 Lisa Bernstein, *Opting Out of the Legal System: Extralegal Contractual Relations in the Diamond Industry* (cit n 16); Lisa Bernstein, *Merchant Law in Merchant Court: Rethinking the Code's Search for Immanent Business Norms*, 114 UNIVERSITY OF PENNSYLVANIA LAW REVIEW, 1765–821 (1996); Lisa Bernstein, *Private Commercial Law in the Cotton Industry: Creating Cooperation Through Rules, Norms and Institutions* (cit n 16).

It is far from sufficient to be a justification for the harmonisation of European contract law. A cost-and-benefit comparison of the current legal regime and any new European contract law is imperative. Without credible empirical evidence, the harmonisation of European contract law cannot be justified by a reduction of the transaction cost.

The second justification for the harmonisation of European contract law is that the different national contract laws distort competition in the European internal market.[20] According to this argument, national contract laws may differ in legal protection, which distorts the competition between domestic firms and foreign firms. Let us take the duty of good faith as an example. This legal principle has been a well-established contract law doctrine in most European jurisdictions, whereas, the general duty of good faith does not exist in English contract law except for a few special transactions, such as an insurance contract or a contract which creates a fiduciary relationship between the parties.[21] Under German contract law, the doctrine of good faith requires the contracting parties to disclose material information to each other.[22] On the contrary, the parties do not have this duty under English contract law. German contract law imposes a higher legal duty on the parties, thereby increasing their compliance costs. In comparison, the parties' compliance costs are lower under English contract law. This legal difference makes it easier for German firms to enter into the English market than English firms to enter into German market. So, German firms have an advantage in the competition with English firms. In addition, the weak legal protection in English contract law may drive domestic buyers into cross-border shopping in Germany, thereby making English sellers worse off. If German contract law and English contract law were the same, the problems would not exist. The harmonisation of European contract law, as suggested, is the effective solution.[23]

This example demonstrates vividly that the legal differences in the Member States may distort competition in the European internal market; more importantly, the distortion is largely attributable to different mandatory rules. If a default rule disfavors a contracting party, he can always exclude it through negotiation with the other party.

[20] Ewan McKendrick, *Harmonisation of European Contract Law: The State We Are in*, in THE HARMONISATION OF EUROPEAN CONTRACT LAW, IMPLICATIONS FOR EUROPEAN PRIVATE LAWS, BUSINESS AND LEGAL PRACTICE (cited n 9), 5–30.

[21] *Interfoto Picture Library Ltd v Stilletto Visual Programmes Ltd* [1988] 1 All ER 348, at 253, Bingham LJ; *Carter v Boehm* (1766) 3 Burr 1905; *Boardman v Phipps* [1967] 2 AC 46; also see Gunter Teubner, *Legal Irritants: Good Faith in British Law or How Unifying Law Ends Up in New Divergences*, 61 MODERN LAW REVIEW, 11–32 (1998).

[22] Section 242 of the German Civil Code (Bürgerliches Gesetzbuch) ("BGB").

[23] Jurgen Basedow, *A Common Contract Law for the Common Market*, 33 COMMON MARKET LAW REVIEW, 1169–95 (1996); Eve Truilhé-Marengo, *Towards a European Law of Contracts*, 10 EUROPEAN LAW JOURNAL, 463–78 (2004).

Although the negotiation incurs additional transaction costs, the party can circumvent the unfavorable rule. But if a mandatory rule disadvantages the party, he has to comply unless he forgoes the transaction.

This argument has been proved by some empirical studies. In the survey conducted by Vogenauer and Weatherill, the following findings are reported. When the participants were asked the question whether the existing divergences in national legal systems present an obstacle to cross-border trade at all, almost two-thirds said yes. When further asked about the most important obstacles, the first ranking obstacle mentioned was the need for compliance with different national regulations on commercial practices, advertising and other consumer protection regulations. However, when the question arises as to how best to solve the current problems, 38 percent opted for improvements on a more uniform implementation of regulatory laws and EU Directives, 28 percent preferred the option of having a European contract law in addition to the existing national contract laws, and 30 percent favored the idea of replacing national contract laws with a single uniform European contract law. Their research is based on the responses to the questionnaires from 2,899 companies in the EU.[24] So, the findings are a reasonable generalization of the views of the parties to cross-border trade.

Moreover, the European Commission recently conducted an evaluation of the impact of the proposal for a regulation on a common European sales law. This study is based on a survey of small or medium size enterprises. It is found that 61 percent of companies involved in commercial transactions and 55 percent in consumer transactions are adversely affected by different and inconsistent implementation of the EU Directives in national contract law. In addition, at least 23 percent of exporting European retailers refused orders by consumers from other Member States. Out of these, 5 percent refused sales to consumers in other Member States systematically and 18 percent did so occasionally.

The preceding empirical evidence shows that different mandatory rules, in particular, the different regulatory laws, in the Member States represent a real problem for cross-border trade in the EU. These findings provide us with a valuable insight that the harmonisation of European contract law is not an effective solution to the problem. As most mandatory rules do not exist in contract law, but in regulatory law, the problem can be rectified only through the harmonisation of regulatory law. The proposal for regulation of a common European sales law is such an attempt. But the key question is whether a uniform regulatory law is achievable. We will return to this issue in Section V.

[24] Stefan Vogenauer and Steven Weatherill, *The European Community's Competence to Pursue the Harmonisation of Contract Law – an Empirical Contribution to the Debate* in The Harmonisation of European Contract Law, Implications for European Private Laws, Business and Legal Practice 105–48 (cit n 9), at 125.

IV. HARMONISATION OF DEFAULT RULES

The harmonisation of European contract law is largely a harmonisation of default rules. As demonstrated in the previous section, there is still little empirical evidence to support the argument that the different default rules in the national contract laws generate high transaction costs for cross-border trade. So, the harmonisation of European contract law cannot be justified on these grounds. However, the lack of empirical evidence should not stop the theoretical investigation of the effect of the harmonisation. This section is based on the assumption that there is a need for the harmonisation of default rules and then examines whether the harmonisation of European contract law can provide an effective solution to the problem. It is argued that even though the different national contract laws do generate high transaction costs for cross-border trade, the harmonisation of European contract law would still be unable to solve the problem.

To reduce transaction costs for cross-border trade through the legal harmonisation, a European contract law ought to meet two conditions. Firstly, it must provide a set of default rules, which will be used by the majority of the contracting parties. If this goal is achieved, most parties will not incur costs to negotiate the issues governed by the default rules, and their transaction costs will be saved accordingly.[25] Secondly, legal interpretations of the European contract law in all of the Member States should be consistent. This condition ensures legal certainty, which is crucial for reducing the learning cost. If the European contract law is interpreted differently across jurisdictions, the parties have to learn different legal interpretations. The learning cost will not decline.[26] Only if the two conditions are met can the harmonisation of European contract law minimize transaction costs for cross-border trade. But, as this section shows, the European contract law can meet neither of the conditions. Let us consider them in turn.

To save the negotiation cost, the default rule must be a majoritarian default, which is the legal rule preferred by most contracting parties. But a further question should be asked. Does the majoritarian default rule exist? If it does not, the European contract law will not produce a set of default rules to save the negotiation cost.

The existence of majoritarian default is conditional upon the fact that most contracting parties have the same preference for the default rules in contract

[25] Ian Ayres and Robert Gertner, *Filling Gaps in Incomplete Contracts: An Economic Theory of Default Rules*, cit n 1.

[26] Robert. E. Scott, *The Uniformity Norm in Commercial Law: A Comparative Analysis of Common Law and Code Methodologies*, in THE JURISPRUDENTIAL FOUNDATIONS OF CORPORATE AND COMMERCIAL LAW (J. S. Kraus and S. D. Walt [eds.], Cambridge University Press: 2000), 149–93, at 158; Stewart Schwab, A *Coasean Experiment on Contract Presumptions*, 17 JOURNAL OF LEGAL STUDIES, 237–68 (1988).

law.[27] This condition requires that all of the parties to cross-border transactions prefer the same default rule, regardless of their differences in industry, transaction and personal expectation from the trade. Obviously, this condition can hardly be met in reality.[28] It is more likely that the parties' preferences are different. For example, a commercial buyer and a consumer buyer often have different views on the best legal remedy for breach of contract. The commercial buyer purchases goods for profit; the consumer buyer does so for personal use. When the seller breaches the contract, the former may prefer the legal remedy which can compensate for the loss of his expected profit, while the latter may prefer one which can provide him with the same goods he purchased. In choosing the default legal remedy, the commercial buyer may favor the remedy of expectation damages, but the consumer buyer may prefer the remedy of replacement. They have different preferences for the default rule. The gap in their preferences will become wider on other important default rules, such as the rules governing pre-contractual duties, passing risk and property.

Furthermore, the parties to a contract are usually in an adversarial position. Most of the legal rules distribute rights and duties between the parties, creating both winners and losers.[29] Often, the legal rule making one party better off inevitably makes the other worse off. It is impossible to produce a default rule which both parties would prefer. For example, in the sale of goods contract, both parties intend to minimize their personal risk in relation to the goods. The seller wants the risk to pass onto the buyer as soon as possible, but the buyer wants the opposite. The default rule which passes the risk at the time of the formation of the contract makes the seller better off and the buyer worse off. On the contrary, a default rule, which passes the risk on delivery of the goods makes the buyer better off, but the seller worse off. The parties have conflicting preferences for the default rule in relation to passing the risk.

If the parties to the same type of transaction do not even have the same preference for the default rule, it is more likely that the preferences of the parties for the different types of contracts are much more diverse. It is reasonable to assume that

[27] Charles. J. Goetz and Robert E. Scott, *The Limits of Expanded Choice: An Analysis of the Interactions between Express and Implied Contract Terms*, 73 California Law Review, 261–322 (1985); David Charny, *Hypothetical Bargains: The Normative Structure of Contract Interpretation*, 89 Michigan Law Review, 1815–79 (1991).

[28] Lisa Bernstein, *The Questionable Empirical Basis of Article 2's Incorporation Strategy: A Preliminary Study*, 66 University of Chicago Law Review, 710–80 (1999); Richard Craswell, *Do Trade Customs Exist?* in The Jurisprudential Foundations of Corporate and Commercial LAW, (J. S. Kraus and S. D. Walt [eds.], Cambridge University Press: 2000), 118–48.

[29] Richard Craswell, *Passing on the Costs of Legal Rules: Efficiency and Distribution in Buyer-Seller Relationships*, 43 Stanford Law Review, 361–98 (1991).

the more varied the transactions, the more disparate the parties' preferences for the default rule, and then it is more unlikely that the majoritarian default rule exists.

Yet, it is by no means the intent here to suggest that the majoritarian default rule never exists. In fact, it is more likely to be found where the parties are in the same industry and their private interests have more in common than in conflict. One of such examples is the Uniform Customs and Practice for Documentary Credits (UCP) produced by the International Chamber of Commerce. The latest version is UCP 600, which came into effect on 1st July 2007. The UCP is arguably the most successful harmonisation of commercial law to date.[30] The law of documentary credit needs to balance three sometimes conflicting interests, namely, the principal who opens the documentary credit, the bank which promises to undertake the payment, and the beneficiary who is assured to receive the payment by the bank. But the major players in drafting the UCP are banks. They have common interests – the codified customs and practice should ensure that banks are not exposed to excessive risks. This is reflected in the whole UCP from the general principle of the autonomy of the credit to specific duties of a bank to exercise due care to check the documents against payment. Unlike the parties to a sale of goods contract, the private interests of individual banks are aligned. This provides a solid foundation for the legal harmonisation, ensuring that the uniform law generates benefits for the whole banking community. Although UCP 600 is not a strictly 'hard law', it has been widely adopted by bankers and commercial parties in more than 175 countries, governing financial payments with the total value of more than one trillion US dollars each year.[31] The example of the UCP illustrates nicely that when the parties' private interests are in common, the majoritarian preference for the law is more likely to be found, and this is a prerequisite for the successful harmonisation of default rules.

The preceding discussion casts serious doubt on the harmonisation of European contract law, which is supposed to provide a one-for-all solution, namely, a single uniform contract law to govern all types of cross-border transactions. This is indeed too ambitious. Given the diversity in the nature and characteristics of the transactions, it is unlikely that the parties will have the same preference for the default rules.

Moreover, the condition that the majority of the contracting parties have the same preference for the default rules is only one prerequisite for the successful harmonisation of European contract law. Apart from this, the information factor is equally important.[32] Even though the majority of the parties have the same preference, the

[30] Roy Goode, Herbert Kronke, and Ewan McKendrick, TRANSACTIONAL COMMERCIAL LAW, TEXT, CASES AND MATERIALS (Oxford University Press: 2007), at 352.

[31] http://en.wikipedia.org/wiki/Uniform_Customs_and_Practice_for_Documentary_Credits

[32] Francesco Parisi & Vincy Fon, THE ECONOMICS OF LAWMAKING (Oxford University Press: 2009), 31–50.

majoritarian default rule still cannot be produced if the information about their preferences fails to be communicated to the lawmakers.

The amount of information required for the harmonisation is vast, in particular when the lawmakers intend to produce a single uniform contract law to govern all kinds of transactions. They not only need to find the preferences of the parties to all types of transaction, but also they should be able to generalize the majority preference. This undoubtedly represents a huge challenge for the lawmakers, if not an insurmountable task.

Legal harmonisation normally needs tremendous effort and a considerable amount of time. It took more than twenty-five years to produce the final version of the Draft of Common Framework Reference (hereafter (D)CFR).[33] This poses another challenge. By the time the harmonisation of European contract law is accomplished, those default rules may already be out of date and unable to meet the parties' new preferences. The market is dynamic, not static. It changes fast and forever. The changes in the market usually lead to changes in each individual transaction, thereby altering the parties' preferences for the default rules. It is reasonable to assume that the longer the harmonisation takes, the higher the likelihood that the uniform contract law will be outdated. Thus, there is a real risk that the European contract law may become obsolete when the harmonisation is eventually accomplished. If this happens, all of those valuable resources devoted to the harmonisation are wasted. From an economic perspective, it is certainly an inefficient outcome.

More involvement of stakeholders in the harmonisation can definitely mitigate this problem. They know better which default rules are suitable for their needs and how the default rules should be changed in accordance with the development in the market. A valuable lesson can be learnt from the International Chamber of Commerce in drafting the UCP. The UCP drafting group consisted of representatives nominated by banks, the main users of the UCP. When drafting the current version, UCP600, the drafting group and the Banking Commission distributed numerous drafts to banks around the world. More than five thousand comments had been received before the final draft was produced in October 2006.[34] The active contribution of banks to the drafting and the wide consultation process ensured that the UCP genuinely reflects the preferences of the stakeholders in the international banking industry.[35]

[33] Christian Von Bar & Eric Clive, PRINCIPLES, DEFINITIONS AND MODEL RULES OF EUROPEAN PRIVATE LAW: DRAFT COMMON FRAME OF REFERENCE (Oxford University Press, 2010), Vol. 1, at p. 25.

[34] Roy Goode, Herbert Kronke, and Ewan McKendrick, TRANSACTIONAL COMMERCIAL LAW, TEXT, CASES AND MATERIALS (cit n 30), *at* 352.

[35] UCP 600 is available at: ocw.usu.ac.id/course/download/…hukum…/hk_609_slide_ucp_600.pdf

However, this issue has not been sufficiently considered in the current harmonisation of European contract law. The (D)CFR was largely prepared by legal scholars. Each study group was led by a law professor; the whole document was drafted by law professors, and the members of the Study Group's Advisory Council are all law professors except Torgny Håstad, a Supreme Court judge in Stockholm.[36] Although stakeholders' voices were heard occasionally from numerous workshops on selected topics held by the European Commission, their input was minimal. Stakeholders did not play an active role in drafting the (D)CFR.[37] It is fair to say that most of the law professors have limited experience in legal practice and little knowledge of the commercial world. It is hardly convincing that the DCFR reflects the preferences of the traders in the market. It will not be a surprise that few parties will choose the DCFR as the applicable law to govern their transactions in the future.

Consistency in legal interpretation is another prerequisite for the successful harmonisation of European contract law. If legal interpretations are different in the Member States, the parties to a cross-border transaction have to learn different versions of legal interpretation and then bargain on the choice of the jurisdiction to solve their disputes. As a result, the harmonisation saves neither negotiation costs nor learning costs.

There are three key reasons for the divergences in legal interpretation across Europe. Firstly, the adoption of the European contract law into the domestic legal system is similar to the legal transplant, which directly imports one national law into another jurisdiction. The well-known problem of 'transplant effect' in comparative law literature can equally apply to the harmonisation of European contract law.[38] When a 'new rule' is imported into the domestic legal system, legal interpretations are still based on the national jurisprudence, which may vary significantly across different jurisdictions. This problem is even worse in the EU, where multiple legal traditions have co-existed. Not only are there common and civilian law traditions, but also ex-socialist legal systems. It gives rise to a real challenge to achieve a consistent legal interpretation of European contract law in the Member States.

Secondly, diverse interpretations may be caused by the fact that the default rule in European contract law conflicts with the mandatory rule in the Member State. Mandatory rules in national contract laws differ considerably. For example, the doctrine of consideration is a mandatory rule in English contract law,[39] but not in

[36] Christian Von Bar & Eric Clive, PRINCIPLES, DEFINITIONS AND MODEL RULES OF EUROPEAN PRIVATE LAW: DRAFT COMMON FRAME OF REFERENCE (cit n 33), Vol. 1, at 25–31.

[37] Id., at 16.

[38] TT Arvind, *The 'Transplant Effect' in Harmonisation*, 59 INTERNATIONAL AND COMPARATIVE LAW QUARTERLY 65–88 (2010); Esin Örücü, *Law as Transposition*, 51 INTERNATIONAL AND COMPARATIVE LAW QUARTERLY 205–23 (2002); Gunter Teubner, *Legal Irritants: Good Faith in British Law and How Unifying Law Ends Up in New Divergences* (cit n 21), 11–32.

[39] *Mark Currie v. Misa* (1875) LR 10 Ex 153.

German contract law. The rule governing liquidated damages is much stricter in common law jurisdictions than in civilian law jurisdictions.[40] There is a general duty to disclose material information in German contract law, but not in English contract law.[41] From a theoretical perspective, a default rule that conflicts with the mandatory rule is invalid. It is possible that a default rule in the European contract law may be valid in one state, but invalid in another. Consider the following scenario. The parties to a sale of goods contract choose the (D)CFR as the applicable law. According to the DCFR, the exchange of considerations is not necessary. Assume that after the contract is entered into but before the performance, the seller requests an increase in the contract price and the buyer agrees. In legal terms, this is a variation of the contract. The question is whether this variation is valid. The answer depends on the jurisdiction in which the (D)CFR is interpreted. If the dispute is solved in an English court, the variation is void for want of consideration. On the contrary, if it is solved in a civilian law jurisdiction such as in Germany, the variation is valid. So different mandatory rules in national contract laws can cause inconsistent interpretations of the default rule. Unless the European contract law completely replaces the national contract laws in all of the Member States, inconsistent legal interpretations are inevitable.

Thirdly, diverse legal interpretations may result from language differences in the Member States. The consistent interpretation of legal terms is dependent upon the precise understanding of the technical meaning of legal notion. Sometimes, the same legal term may be used differently across jurisdictions, and then confusion and uncertainty ensue. Take, for example, the notion of debtor. A debtor is defined in the (D)CFR as a person who has an obligation, whether monetary or non-monetary, to another person, the creditor.[42] However, the term "debtor" is used in a much narrower way in English law; it refers to a person who owes a financial obligation (a debt).[43] In English contract law, if the non-breaching party can also establish the action of debt against the breaching party, there are many more advantages for him than claiming damages for breach of contract. In the action of debt, the claimant does not owe the duty of mitigation to the defendant; he does not need to prove the fact that he suffered any loss as the result of the defendant's breach. However, these subtle differences do not exist in the (D)CFR.

Apparently, no solution has been proposed in the harmonisation of European contract law to overcome the problem of inconsistent legal interpretation. If the

40 Christian Von Bar & Eric Clive, Principles, Definitions and Model Rules of European Private Law: Draft Common Frame of Reference (cit n 33), at 961–7.

41 §§ 157, 242 of German Civil Code (BGB).

42 Christian Von Bar & Eric Clive, Principles, Definitions and Model Rules of European Private Law: Draft Common Frame of Reference, cit n 33, Vol. 1, at 68.

43 *White and Carter (councils) Ltd v McGregor* [1962] AC 413.

European contract law cannot be interpreted consistently in all of the Member States, the harmonisation can only achieve uniformity in form, but not in substance. Consequently, the European contract law can save neither negotiation costs nor learning costs for the parties to cross-border transactions.

To sum up, the analysis in this section is based upon the assumption that different default rules in national contract laws generate high transaction costs for cross-border trade, and that the harmonisation of European contract law is justified. To reduce transaction costs, the European contract law should meet two conditions. Firstly, it should produce a body of majoritarian default rules, namely, the default rules, which the majority of the contracting parties prefer. So, their negotiation costs can be saved. Secondly, the legal interpretation of the European contract law must be consistent in all of the Member States. Otherwise, the parties have to learn different legal interpretations and negotiate on the jurisdiction to solve their dispute. Inconsistent legal interpretations increase transaction costs for cross-border trade instead of reducing them. As this section shows, the European contract law cannot meet either of the conditions. In conclusion, even though the different default rules in the national contract laws incur unnecessary transaction costs for cross-border trade, the harmonisation of European contract law cannot solve the problem. Now let us turn to the issue of the harmonisation of mandatory rules.

V. HARMONISATION OF MANDATORY RULES

A mandatory rule can exist in either contract law or regulatory law. The parties to a cross-border transaction must comply with the mandatory rule as long as they enter into a contract. As discussed in Section III, different mandatory rules in the Member States may distort competition in the European internal market by creating the legal rule in favor of domestic firms. To solve this problem, the divergence in national mandatory legal rules must be eliminated. Four main suggestions have been made so far.[44] Firstly, no action should be taken. Convergence in the national mandatory laws can be achieved in the long term through legal competition among the Member States. Secondly, a minimum harmonisation should be undertaken through EU Directives, which set the minimum legal standards that the mandatory laws of every Member State ought to achieve. Thirdly, a full harmonisation should be achieved so

[44] European Commission, *Proposal for a Regulation of the European Parliament and of the Council on a Common European Sale Law, Brussels*, 11.10.2010, COM (2011) 635 final, 2011/0284; Christian Twigg-Flesner, THE EUROPEANISATION OF CONTRACT LAW (Routledge: 2008), 139–80; D. Irk Staudenmayer, *European Contract Law – What Does It Mean and What Does It Not Mean?* in THE HARMONISATION OF EUROPEAN CONTRACT LAW, IMPLICATIONS FOR EUROPEAN PRIVATE LAWS, BUSINESS AND LEGAL PRACTICE (Vogenauer and S. Weatherill [eds.], Hart Publishing: 2006), pp. 235–44.

as to eliminate all of the differences in the national mandatory laws. Finally, it was suggested recently that the optional instrument is the best way forward, as this would allow contracting parties to choose either a national law or the optional European law to govern their transactions. This section addresses the question whether any of the preceding harmonisation strategies can solve the problem of the distortion of competition due to the differences in the mandatory rules. It is argued that from a theoretical perspective, full harmonisation is the only effective solution, but it is unachievable in practice. Therefore, the legal distortion of competition is inevitable.

According to the first suggestion, no action should be taken. The current legal framework should be maintained without any policy change.[45] This suggestion is based on the economic theory of legal competition,[46] which argues that legal competition among the Member States can eventually lead to convergence in the national mandatory laws, so, there is no need for any 'top-down' harmonisation. Each State faces pressure from business and industry to adjust its mandatory laws to accommodate commercial and business requirements. If the compliance cost in one State is higher than in others, the industry will put pressure on the policymaker to change the law. Eventually, such forces can lead to convergence in the mandatory laws of all Member States.

Nonetheless, it seems to be that this predication is too optimistic to be true in reality.[47] The economic theory of legal competition draws on the assumption that the industry has the incentive to push through legal reforms. If the law in one State imposes high compliance costs on the given industry, firms in that industry are at a disadvantage when competing with firms from other States. So they will push the policymaker to change the law. But the firms have another option. Rather than pushing for legal reform, they can relocate their business to a more commerce-friendly State. They will choose the cheapest option between pushing for legal reform and relocating their business. It is often assumed that the latter is more effective and efficient than the former, because of not only the high lobbying cost but also the positive externality problem associated with legal reform. The firms that invest in lobbying for legal reform cannot realize all of the benefits. Once the law is changed, all of the firms in the industry can benefit. This poses the problem of the 'free-rider', thereby undermining firms' incentives for pushing for legal reform.

Secondly, even though the policymaker is under pressure to change the law, there is another vital question. Is the change socially desirable? There may be a

45 European Commission, *Commission Staff Working Paper, Executive Summary of the Impact Assessment*, Brussels, 11.10.2011, SEC (2011) 1166 final, at p. 3.

46 Frank Easterbrook, *Federalism and European Business Law*, 14 INTERNATIONAL REVIEW OF LAW AND ECONOMICS, 125–32 (1994).

47 Jeanne-May Sun and Jacques Pelkmans, *Regulatory Competition in the Single Market*, 33 JOURNAL OF COMMON MARKET LAW STUDIES, 67–89 (1995).

conflict between the private interests of the industry and the public interests of society. For example, if the industry forces the policymaker to lower the level of environmental law protection to reduce the compliance cost, the result is certainly unwelcome from the standpoint of society as a whole. Thus, the result of the legal competition is uncertain. The well-known problem of the 'race to bottom' is a realistic risk.[48]

Thirdly, even if legal competition could eventually lead to convergence in national mandatory laws, we still need to ask the question, How long will this endeavor take? From an economic perspective, the cost-benefit analysis must be made. It probably will take quite a long time to achieve legal convergence. Other considerations being equal, it is reasonable to assume that the longer it takes, the lower the benefit, and the higher the cost is. For the reasons noted previously, this strategy is not a viable policy option, even though it may eventually lead to legal convergence in national mandatory laws.

The second policy option is minimum harmonisation through EU Directives.[49] A Directive is a legislative instrument, which can be issued by the European Council or by the Council jointly with the European Parliament or the European Commission.[50] The Directive often deals with a specific issue in national laws. It sets out the results which the Member States should achieve by modifying their national laws, but it leaves the Member States to decide how the result should be achieved. This has two implications. Firstly, the Directive only specifies the minimum requirement which national laws should achieve. It is possible that the level of the existing legal protection in a national law is already higher than required by the Directive. If this is the case, the Member State does not need to modify its national law. However, if the national law of a Member State does not provide the minimum level of protection required by the Directive, the state is liable for loss and damages which an individual suffers as a result of not implementing the Directive.[51] Inevitably the Directive as a legal harmonisation strategy does not necessarily eliminate divergences in national laws.

Secondly, Each Member State has discretion to decide how the result required by the Directive is achieved. The Member States may choose different ways to implement the Directive. For example, one state may implement the Directive by amending the general law of contract such as the relevant articles in the Civil

[48] William L. Cary, *Federalism and Corporate Law: Reflections upon Delaware*, 83 YALE LAW JOURNAL 663–705 (1974); R. Winter, *State Law, Shareholder Protection, and the Theory of the Corporation*, 6 JOURNAL OF LEGAL STUDIES, 251–92, (1977).

[49] European Commission, *Commission Staff Working Paper, Executive Summary of the Impact Assessment*, Brussels, 11.10.2011, SEC (2011) 1166 final, at 3.

[50] Pierre S.R.F. Mathijsen, A GUIDE TO EUROPEAN UNION LAW (10th ed., Sweet & Maxwell: 2010), at 31.

[51] *Brasserie du Pecheur and Factortame* (Jointed Cases C 46/93 and C-48/93) [1996] E.C.R. I-1029 (31).

Code, and another state may decide to enact a piece of new legislation such as a regulatory law to implement the Directive. Consequently, rather than reducing divergences in the national laws, the Directive may lead to more legal differences in the Member States.[52]

The minimum harmonisation has an obvious advantage. As it allows each state to decide how the legislative goal is achieved, it is more likely to find unanimous agreement among the Member States. The more discretion the Member States have, the more likely they can reach the agreement. The minimum harmonisation could relatively reduce deadlocks in political negotiations and obstacles to the harmonisation of European contract law. Furthermore, it at least can ensure that the minimum legislative goal can be achieved in all of the Member States. This is also the reason why this approach was adopted in the harmonisation of European consumer law in the past.[53] Consumer law is a mix of both private laws and regulatory law. Because of differences in legal traditions and culture, each Member State has its own unique features in private law. None of them is prepared to revise its private law just for the sake of legal harmonisation. Minimum harmonisation could solve this problem. It just prescribes the minimum legal protection which each Member State should achieve, leaving each to decide how the Directive is implemented. The Directive not only enhances consumer protection in the EU, but also allows the Member States to retain their differences in consumer law.

It seems to be a very effective device for harmonisation. Yet, this approach has given rise to many problems. Instead of simplifying European consumer law and reducing legal differences and transaction costs for cross-border consumer sales, minimum harmonisation has led to considerable legal differences among the Member States. Rather than achieving a single European consumer law, there are now twenty-seven consumer laws, which increase the transaction costs considerably and undermine both businesses' incentive for cross-border trade and consumer confidence in cross-border shopping.[54]

The experience in the harmonisation of European consumer law vividly shows that minimum harmonisation cannot produce a uniform law which eliminates legal differences in the Member States. It may guarantee that minimum legal protection can be achieved by the national laws of the Member States, but it cannot effectively overcome the problem of the legal distortion of competition, because it allows differences in the national laws to remain.

[52] Christian Twigg-Flesner, THE EUROPEANISATION OF CONTRACT LAW, cit n 44, 119–33.

[53] Angus Johnston and Hannes Unberath, *European Private Law by Directives: Approach and Challenges*, in EUROPEAN UNION PRIVATE LAW (Christian Twigg-Flesner [ed.], Cambridge University Press: 2010), 85–100.

[54] European Commission, *Proposal for a Regulation of the European Parliament and of the Council on a Common European Sale Law, Brussels*, 11.10.2010, COM (2011) 635 final, 2011/0284.

The third policy option is full harmonisation. This is the most ambitious proposal, which aims to produce a uniform body of mandatory rules to replace the national laws in all of the Member States.[55] To achieve this goal, both the regulatory laws and the mandatory rules in the national contract laws need to be harmonised. If the full harmonisation were successful, there would be no legal differences in the national mandatory laws of the Member States. Accordingly, the problem of the distortion of competition would be solved.

Unfortunately, this solution has been ruled out by the European Commission.[56] In fact, full harmonisation, from a practical perspective, is impossible to implement. It faces insurmountable political challenge. The Member States would be likely to find that full harmonisation is politically difficult to agree and implement because it would eliminate domestic laws and legal traditions. Objections to this option arise from the legal profession in all Member States. The Majority of Member States who responded to the Green Paper consultation rejected this option outright. The European Commission, therefore, concluded that

> overall, although the full harmonization would eliminate legal differences in the Member States and transaction costs for cross-border trade, it would create other substantive costs, which would not only be of monetary value. From a holistic perspective, taking all the costs (monetary or otherwise) into account, these costs outweigh by far the benefits of the full harmonization.[57]

The last policy choice is the optional instrument, which was proposed recently and is preferred by most contract scholars.[58] An optional Common European Contract Law would be set up as a 'second regime' within each Member State's national law. It would be a comprehensive set of contract law rules with a high level of consumer protection that would stand on its own and could be chosen by the parties as the law applicable to their cross-border contracts.[59] In other words, rather than reducing twenty-seven contract laws in Europe, the optional instrument adds a new contract law, which becomes the twenty-eighth contract law in the EU. However, when firms make cross-border transactions, they could can either the new European contract code or a national contract law to govern their transactions. The legal rules in the

55 European Commission, *Commission Staff Working Paper, Executive Summary of the Impact Assessment*, Brussels, 11.10.2011, SEC (2011) 1166 final, at p. 4.

56 European Commission, *Proposal for a Regulation of the European Parliament and of the Council on a Common European Sale Law, Brussels*, 11.10.2010, COM (2011) 635 final, 2011/0284, pp. 44–8.

57 *Id.*, at 48.

58 *Id.*, at 32.

59 Hans Schulte-Nölke, *The Way Forward in European Consumer Contract Law: Optional Instrument Instead of Further Deconstruction of National Private Law* in EUROPEAN UNION PRIVATE LAW, cit, n 53, 131–46; Christian Twigg-Flesner, *Good-Bye Harmonisation by Directives, Hello Cross-Border Only Regulation?* 7 EUROPEAN REVIEW OF CONTRACT LAW, 235–56 (2011).

European contract law would be mandatory for consumer contracts, but they would be default rules for commercial contracts.

Can this 'new' optional instrument effectively solve the 'old' problems caused by the different national contract laws in the EU? The rationale behind this approach is valid. The 'old' minimum harmonisation has turned out to be very troublesome. Rather than reducing legal complexities and divergences in the national contract laws, it has led to more differences, making the areas which have been harmonised more fragmented. At the other extreme, the full harmonisation is just implausible because of political and economic obstacles. This optional instrument appears as a welcome balanced approach. Nonetheless, it is unlikely to work.

The optional instrument aims to solve the legal problem caused by Rome I Regulations, which set up the mandatory rules to govern the choice of the applicable law. If Firm A in state A sells the goods to party B in state B, even though State A's law is chosen as the applicable law, those mandatory rules in State B's national law still apply. The parties cannot exclude mandatory rules in a national law. It means that there are twenty-seven different mandatory laws on the same legal issue. This makes conditions very uncertain and costly for the party to a cross-border transaction.

The optional instrument can solve this problem. Like a Directive, the uniform European contract law would set the minimum level of mandatory rule, which would apply to all of the Member States. If the parties to a cross-border transaction choose it as the applicable law, they do not need to worry about the mandatory laws in the state in which their transactions take place.

But there are a number of problems with the optional instrument. Firstly, will each Member State be willing to accept this European contract code? There is a subtle difference between the minimum harmonisation through Directives and the optional instrument. Under the minimum harmonisation, legal differences are allowed to remain. In the Member States where national law provides higher legal protection than required by the Directive, the contracting parties must comply with it. Therefore, the Member States offering higher legal protection can always be guaranteed that the Directive cannot downgrade the legal standard in their mandatory laws. But this cannot be achieved under the optional instrument. The optional contract law only sets up the minimum legal duty which the parties have. If its mandatory rules differ from the national law, and the parties choose the optional contract law as the applicable law, the mandatory rules in the national law will not bind the parties anymore. In fact, the optional contract law code downgrades the higher legal protection in the Member State. This is indeed a serious policy problem for the Member States whose national laws provide higher legal protection than the optional contract code to adopt the optional instrument. There is a possibility that the optional European contract law may not be adopted by all of the Member States.

Secondly, the optional contract code is supposed to be a self-contained and exclusive code to govern all of the cross-border transactions. This idea has its origin in the civil law tradition. However, this would be highly problematic for the harmonisation of mandatory rules. As noted previously, mandatory rules exist in both contract law and regulatory law. The harmonisation of mandatory rules in contract law is only a partial solution to the problem; the divergences in the national regulatory laws still remain.

Thirdly, even though the optional contract code is a good idea, it is only the first step towards the successful harmonisation of the European contract law. To succeed, it must overcome two other challenges, namely, implementation and legal innovation. The implementation of the optional contract code would have to overcome the immense challenge of inconsistent and conflicting interpretations of the law produced by national courts of the Member States. Conflicting legal interpretations can give rise to uncertainty and increase the transaction cost for cross-border trade. Therefore, the question whether this problem can be effectively solved significantly influences the success of the harmonisation of the European contract law via the optional instrument. One possible solution to this problem is to rely on the Court of Justice of the European Union (CJEU). When different and contradictory interpretations appear, the case should be referred to the CJEU for the final and ultimate ruling, since this has the highest legal authority, prevailing over all of the competing versions of legal interpretation produced by national courts. Clearly, this is a nice solution, but how efficiently can the CJEU perform this function? To judge by past experience, the CJEU often takes enormous amounts of time to deliver its judgment. In other words, it is appropriate to expect that there would still be many competing versions of legal interpretation for the time being because of the inefficient and slow response of the CJEU. This undoubtedly undermines the effectiveness of the optional contract code.

Finally, legal innovation is another challenge. The optional contract code is, by nature, a piece of European legislation. Any amendment or revision has to go through the strict legislative procedure of the EU law. This requires compromises, negotiations, and political and economic dialogues among the member states. This would become a potential obstacle for the revision of the optional contract code in the future. Given the reasons noted, it is unlikely that the optional instrument can be an effective strategy for the harmonisation of mandatory rules.

VI. CONCLUSION

A huge amount of resources and effort has been devoted to the study of the harmonisation of European contract law. As an academic topic, the legal harmonisation is undoubtedly one of the most fascinating questions for legal scholars. It is also valuable to investigate both theoretically and empirically every key questions in relation to the harmonisation of European contract law. But the European contract law must not be adopted officially unless it can be proved empirically that different national contract laws impair cross-border trade and that the European contract law can effectively solve the problem. As discussed in this chapter, there is still insufficient empirical evidence to support both arguments. More importantly, even if the arguments were true, the harmonisation of European contract law would still be unable to solve the problems.

It is more likely that the problem for cross-border trade is mainly attributable to the different mandatory laws in the Member States. The full harmonisation is necessary to solve this problem. Mandatory rules in both contract law and regulatory laws need to be harmonised. Unfortunately, this is unachievable in practice because of insurmountable political challenges. Therefore, the distortion of competition resulting from legal differences in the Member States is inevitable.

The analysis in this chapter provides a cautionary note. It is still too early to suggest that the European contract law should be adopted officially. There are many crucial questions left unanswered. Unless and until we find satisfactory answers to those questions, it is better that the harmonisation of European contract law remain an academic topic rather than a policy suggestion for legal reform.

21

Europeanisation of Contract Law and the Proposed Common European Sales Law

Hector L. MacQueen

This chapter reviews the Proposed Common European Sales Law (CESL) from a number of perspectives: first, whether there is a need for harmonisation in European Internet trading and whether the CESL serves that end; second, whether two national laws on a given subject can co-exist. It uses the example of the evolution of Scottish sales law in relationship to English sales law. Third, it compares the proposed CESL with the UK Sale of Goods Act. In the end, Professor MacQueen sees the CESL as a useful experiment in European private law harmonisation – "It would provide an interesting experiment with which to test the claim that the variety of domestic laws in the European Union is a barrier to the achievement of a single market." It could serve as a means of filling the need to reduce obstacles to cross-border trading by Internet and small- and medium-sized business enterprises. Because of the CESL's optional nature, the chapter concludes that no harm would be caused with its passage while significant benefits would be obtained if businesses widely elected to opt-in to the law.

F.B.A., F.R.S.E.; Commissioner, Scottish Law Commission, Edinburgh, UK The views expressed in this chapter are personal and not to be attributed to the Scottish Law Commission. The author acknowledges, however, his indebtedness to the joint teams with whom he worked to produce LAW COMMISSION and SCOTTISH LAW COMMISSION, AN OPTIONAL COMMON EUROPEAN SALES LAW: ADVANTAGES AND PROBLEMS: ADVICE TO THE UK GOVERNMENT, published only online at http://www.scotlawcom.gov.uk/news/advice-on-european-sales-law or http://www.justice.gov.uk/lawcommission/publications/1698.htm (10 November 2011) (hereinafter, JOINT ADVICE). I have also benefited greatly from participation in the AHRC-funded research project THE COMMON FRAME OF REFERENCE FOR EUROPEAN CONTRACT LAW AND ITS INTERACTION WITH ENGLISH AND GERMAN LAW, led by Stefan Vogenauer (Oxford) and Gerhard Dannemann (Berlin). The results of the project will be published by Oxford University Press as a collection of essays, the present author's contribution to which (co-authored with Barbara Dauner-Lieb and Peter W. Tettinger) is entitled *Specific Performance and Rights of Cure*. Finally, my understanding was much helped by attendance at two events in November 2011 – the first a conference mounted in Warsaw, Poland, by the Polish Presidency on the Common European Sales Law proposal; the other a panel on contract law at a meeting of the Ius Commune Research School held in Utrecht, Netherlands. All URLs cited in this chapter were last checked on 14 January 2012.

I. INTRODUCTION: PROPOSED COMMON EUROPEAN SALES LAW

On 11 October 2011, the European Commission published its Proposal for a Regulation on a Common European Sales Law (CESL).[1] Whatever one's view of the proposal's merits, it was a momentous day for contract law in Europe. Sale, in a familiar phrase, is the master form of contract, and the proposed CESL clearly contains much general contract law as well as sales law. While the proposed instrument takes an 'optional' approach[2] and involves neither the harmonisation nor the replacement of the domestic laws of the European Union's Member States, it is apparent that at least some in the commission envisage further such optional instruments in other areas of contract law, such as insurance and perhaps service contracts.[3] If so, the general contract parts of the proposed CESL could readily be adopted for use in these contexts. Moreover, the chosen form of law-making – a Regulation – gives the proposal the potential to become law in all Member States, so that it would go further than the Vienna Convention on the International Sale of Goods (CISG) and reach even those states which do not incorporate the latter into their domestic law (that is, the United Kingdom, Ireland, Portugal, and Malta). If it is enacted, then for the first time there will be in place a genuinely European-wide contract law.

This perception is reinforced when the historical development of the text of the proposed CESL is considered. In reverse chronological order, the CESL text is first derived from one prepared as a Feasibility Study by an Expert Group from May 2010 to its publication in May 2011.[4] The Feasibility Study was in turn drawn from the text known as the Draft Common Frame of Reference (DCFR), published in its final version in February 2009.[5] Funded by the European Commission, the DCFR is a joint production of a number of mainly academic groups, each of which had previously been working in its own way for some time on statements in a code-like form of European private law, in particular contract law. The most important of these groups were the Study Group on a European Civil Code, led by Professor Christian von Bar (Osnabrück), and the 'Acquis' Research Group on Existing EC Private

1 Proposal for a Regulation of the European Parliament and of the Council on a Common European Sales Law, Brussels, 11.10.2011, COM(2011) 635 final (hereinafter, Reg-CESL).

2 See *infra* note 17 and accompanying text.

3 See Commissioner Viviane Reding's comments on 21 September 2011, available at http://europa.eu/rapid/pressReleasesAction.do?reference=MEMO/11/624&format=HTML& aged=0&language=EN&guiLanguage=en.

4 *A European Contract Law for Consumers and Businesses: Publication of the Results of the Feasibility Study Carried Out by the Expert Group on European Contract Law for Stakeholders' and Legal Practitioners' Feedback*, available at http://ec.europa.eu/justice/contract/files/feasibility_study_final.pdf).

5 PRINCIPLES, DEFINITIONS AND MODEL RULES OF EUROPEAN PRIVATE LAW: DRAFT COMMON FRAME OF REFERENCE (DCFR) (6 volumes, Christian von Bar, Eric Clive & Hans Schulte-Nölke eds., Sellier: Munich 2009).

Law, led by Professor Hans Schulte-Nölke (at the time Bielefeld, now Osnabrück as well). The focus of the Acquis Group, as its name suggests, was the systematisation of the Directives related to contract law already produced in the European Union, while the Study Group sought to produce a series of legislative-style texts on various private law subjects under the overall title, Principles of European Law.[6] The foundation of the Study Group's efforts, the Principles of European Contract Law (the PECL, completed 2003), was yet another product of an academic group, one which had begun its work in 1982, the Commission on European Contract Law led by Professor Ole Lando (Copenhagen).[7] The Study Group's subject matter was mostly specific contracts – sale and lease of goods, services, loan, mandate and donation, for instance – but non-contractual areas such as civil liability for damage caused (tort or delict), unjustified enrichment, trusts and transfer of property were also within its scope. The DCFR drew the various parts of the two groups' work together in as systematic a fashion as possible, with the end result looking rather like at least the first draft of part of a civil or private law code.

This brief history reveals that the starting point of the work leading to the proposed CESL was the general law of contract as embodied in the PECL. It was only at the point when the Expert Group was commissioned to produce the Feasibility Study that the objective became the production of a sales law rather than a general contract one. The Feasibility Study and the proposed CESL are thus based primarily on texts that were developed with sale as an add-on to general contract material, rather than the other way around. This may have led to the appearance in the CESL text of elements that are in some respects unusual in a sales law, but more significantly it may well also mean that the basic general contract law rules in the CESL can be used later for future instruments on other types of contracts. Insurance contracts are often mentioned as another subject for an optional instrument. It is worth noting that the academic group that published the Principles of European Insurance Contract Law (PEICL) in 2009 also took the PECL as its starting point.[8]

The genealogy of the proposed CESL leads back to the CISG. Professor Ole Lando has explained the 'considerable influence' which the CISG had on the development

6 Eight of the projected 12 volumes have so far been published: see for up-to-date details the Web site of the publisher, Sellier, at http://www.sellier.de/pages/en/buecher_s_elp/europarecht/454.htm.

7 PRINCIPLES OF EUROPEAN CONTRACT LAW (2 volumes, Ole Lando and others eds., Kluwer Law International: The Hague, 2001–3). For Professor Lando's account of the origins of the idea of a European contract law project see his articles, *Eight Principles of European Contract Law*, in MAKING COMMERCIAL LAW: ESSAYS IN HONOUR OF ROY GOODE (Ross Cranston ed., Clarendon Press: Oxford, 1997), 103, 103–6 (hereinafter Lando, *Eight Principles*); and *My Life as a Lawyer*, 10(3) ZEITSCHRIFT FÜR EUROPÄISCHES PRIVATRECHT 508, 519–21 (2002) (hereinafter, Lando, *My Life*).

8 PRINCIPLES OF EUROPEAN INSURANCE CONTRACT LAW (Jurgen Basedow and Project Group, eds., Sellier: Munich 2009), Preface, p. xxxii; see further Introduction, p. liii.

of the PECL, with the latter often providing the same rules.[9] He himself participated as an observer for the International Chamber of Commerce in the last two weeks of the Diplomatic Conference in Vienna in 1980 at which the text of the CISG was finalised.[10] The existence of the CISG may have promoted agreement amongst the members of the multi-national Lando Commission in drafting the PECL, given the growing international acceptability of the CISG rules as evidenced by the steadily growing number of European countries ratifying the Convention during the 1980s and 1990s.[11] There were also important personal and intellectual links between the CESL and the contemporaneous UNIDROIT project that led to the publication in 1994 of the Principles of International Commercial Contracts (PICC). This too 'follow[ed] the solutions found in [the CISG]' on the basis of their world-wide acceptance,[12] and the membership of its editorial team enjoyed a significant overlap with that of the Lando Commission.[13] Given that the CISG coverage of contract law principles was not comprehensive – in its own words, it governs only formation of contract and the rights and obligations of buyers and sellers, including remedies for non-performance[14] – new rules had to be developed for both the PECL and the PICC, sometimes working from the more limited material in the CISG. The overlap in the working membership of the two groups again led to some commonalities in the solutions eventually achieved.[15]

The scheme of the CESL proposal is innovative in many ways. As already mentioned, it takes the form of an 'optional instrument', meaning that it is a set of rules applying to sale of goods and supply of digital content contracts that the parties can choose to govern their particular transaction.[16] At one level, there is nothing

9 Lando, *My Life*, 520–1.

10 Personal e-mail to the author from Ole Lando dated 11 January 2012.

11 Lando, *Eight Principles*, 105.

12 Principles of International Commercial Contracts (UNIDROIT: Rome 1994), introduction, p. viii; see also Commentary on the UNIDROIT Principles of International Commercial Contracts (Stefan Vogenauer and Jan Kleinheisterkamp eds., Oxford University Press: Oxford, 2009), 10 (para 22). The PICC has been extended in versions published by UNIDROIT in 2004 and 2010.

13 Apart from Lando himself, other persons who contributed to both sets of Principles include Michael Joachim Bonell, Ulrich Drobnig, Arthur Hartkamp and Denis Tallon.

14 Article 3 CISG.

15 See Michael Joachim Bonell, *The UNIDROIT Principles of International Commercial Contracts and the Principles of European Contract Law: A Comparison*, in Making Commercial Law, *supra* note 7, 91; Ole Lando, *Principles of European Contract Law and Unidroit Principles: Similarities, Differences and Perspectives* (Centro di studi e recherché di diritto comparator e straniero, Saggi, Conferenze e Seminari 49: Rome, 2002).

16 The application of the proposed CESL to supplies of digital content is not covered in this chapter. See Marco Loos, Natali Helberger, Lucie Guibault and Chantal Mak, *The Regulation of Digital Content Contracts in the Optional Instrument of Contract Law*, 19 European Review of Private Law 729 (2011). The report by the authors to which this chapter refers is now published and available at http://www.ivir.nl/publications/helberger/digital_content_contracts_for_consumers.pdf.

unusual about this; contracting parties are generally free to choose the law that will govern their contract. Parties can choose the law of a jurisdiction with which they have no other connection and in which no aspect of the contract will be performed. If the parties make no explicit choice, then the rules of international private law will determine which law applies. In the European Union those rules are now to be found in the Rome I Regulation of 2008.[17] What the CESL provides is a choice additional to those that already exist. But this alternative has a rather different character. As a Regulation, the proposed CESL will be directly applicable to Member States and become part of their domestic laws, operating alongside those laws insofar as it does not supplant them. If it goes into effect, therefore, it will do so as part of French, German, English or Scots law as the case may be. This, as we shall see in more detail later,[18] has crucial effects for consumer sales in particular. Above all, it means that the consumer protection regime applying in such sales is that provided by the CESL, rather than that established by purely domestic legislation.

The choice of the CESL is also restricted by the scope of the instrument itself. First, it limits its application to cross-border contracts in which at least one of the countries involved is a Member State of the European Union.[19] There are several implications here, and space allows only brief reference to some of them. A transaction is cross-border when the parties are located in different countries at the time of contracting, but not if the parties are merely of different nationalities. So, for example, a shop in Edinburgh's Royal Mile may target tourists from the Continent by offering only foreign language guides and newspapers for sale, using these languages rather than English (or Scots) as appropriate in dealing with individual customers, and giving prices in euros rather than pounds, but any contract of sale resulting will be a domestic one under Scots law or some choice of law other than the CESL. The likeliest scenario for a consumer transaction to be governable by the CESL is one of distance selling, most probably by way of the Internet.[20] But if a party from Scotland orders goods from an Internet trader based in England, the transaction is not cross-border for CESL purposes. On the other hand, an Internet trader based in the United States targeting the European market with its Web site is coverable under the CESL.

The next limitation of the CESL's scope is that the seller must be a trader; if the buyer is also a trader, then one of the parties must be a small- or medium-sized

[17] Regulation (EC) No 593/2008 of the European Parliament and of the Council of 17 June 2008 on the law applicable to contractual obligations (Rome I), OJ 4.7.2008, L 177/6 (hereinafter, Rome I).

[18] See, text accompanying notes 46–53.

[19] Article 4 Reg-CESL.

[20] See further the JOINT ADVICE, Parts 2–4. As the JOINT ADVICE also points out (paras 5.2–5.27), several practical difficulties confront telephone sellers under the proposed CESL.

enterprise (SME).[21] Hence, the CESL may be deployed in business-to-business (B2B) or business-to-consumer (B2C) sales, but it may not be used when neither party is a trader. Finally, while the CESL applies to sales of goods and service contracts related to sales transactions, it excludes 'mixed-purpose' contracts that include any element beyond sale of goods and related services.[22] Some of these restrictions are, however, in their turn subject to choices that can be made by Member States.[23] They can decide to have no requirement that at least one party be a SME in a B2B transaction governed by the CESL. They may also choose to make the CESL available for entirely domestic transactions without any cross-border element.

All this helps to differentiate the proposed CESL from the CISG. While the CISG too applies to cross-border sales of goods and may be made applicable to domestic transactions as well by its Member States,[24] it is confined to B2B transactions,[25] without, moreover, any requirement that one of the businesses be an SME. The CISG is thus wider in scope than the CESL in this regard but on the other hand has no application in B2C transactions. Again, a CISG Member State will have the Convention as its applicable law for cross-border B2B transactions[26] and does not have any option to provide a parallel system of its own devising. But where the proposed CESL is an 'opt in' for the parties to a contract, the CISG allows parties in jurisdictions where it is the applicable law to 'opt out', in whole or in part, and choose another law.[27] In this rather different way, then, the CISG too is an optional instrument. The alternative to it could be the domestic sales law of the Member State with which the contract otherwise has its closest connections, or the law of some non-CISG jurisdiction, such as England. Opting out of the CISG is common in commercial practice, raising the question of whether business parties in Europe and their advisers are any more likely to 'opt in' to the proposed CESL.

The CISG is, however, by no means a dead letter, and the evidence about its use does not preclude the possibility that, over time, the CESL might also gain a degree of business credibility. Two aspects of the proposal may be helpful in this regard. One is that as part of a European Union Regulation, the CESL, unlike the CISG, will have a court – the Court of Justice of the European Union (CJEU) – in which issues about its interpretation can be authoritatively determined for all the jurisdictions in which it applies.[28] The other potentially useful aspect of the CESL is its slightly wider coverage by comparison with the CISG. The latter does not cover 'the

[21] Article 7(2) Reg-CESL provides a definition of an SME. For difficulties see Joint Advice, para 6.47.
[22] Article 6(1) Reg-CESL.
[23] Article 13 Reg-CESL.
[24] Article 1 CISG.
[25] See Article 2 CISG.
[26] See Article 99 CISG.
[27] See Article 6 CISG.
[28] But note the cautionary words of Joint Advice, paras 7.18–7.21.

validity of the contract or of any of its provisions'.[29] In contrast, the CESL devotes an entire chapter to the issue of validity.[30] The CESL also provides rules relating to the contents and effects of contracts and unfair contract terms. Provisions on unfair terms also apply to unfair terms in B2B contracts.[31] There is very little overlap here with anything in the CISG.[32] The CESL also provides additional content to some of the rules in the CISG, including remedies for non-performance, such as specific performance, and the seller's right to cure.[33]

On the other hand, the proposed CESL does not any more than the CISG have rules on the transfer of ownership from seller to buyer, which might be thought a surprising omission of one of the defining characteristics of a sale.[34] A businessman may also think that some of what the proposed CESL adds to the CISG is too open-textured and uncertain, making litigation the only possible way of resolving disputes on legal (as distinct from factual) issues.[35] In general, greater likelihood of litigation is reinforced in the case of the CESL. For example, where the CISG famously requires only 'regard … to be had to … the observance of good faith in international trade' in its own interpretation,[36] Article 2 CESL affirms that each party has an un-excludable duty to act in accordance with good faith and fair dealing, breach of which may not only preclude a party from exercising or relying on a right, remedy or defence it would otherwise have, but also make that party liable for any loss caused by the breach of duty to the other party.[37] Good faith and fair dealing are recognized throughout the CESL, and not only in connection with consumer protection. In B2B transactions, the duty of good faith covers pre-contractual disclosure of information about the main characteristics of the goods to be supplied,[38] in what is to be

[29] Article 4(a) CISG.

[30] Chapter 5 CESL, consisting of Articles 48–57.

[31] Chapters 7 and 8 CESL. Section 3 of the latter chapter deals with unfair terms in B2B contracts.

[32] Note, however, that Article 9 CISG on usages is broadly paralleled by Article 67 CESL on usages and practices in contracts between traders.

[33] See further Sonja Kruisinga, *The Seller's Right of Cure in the CISG and the Common European Sales Law* 19 European Review of Private Law 907 (2011); MacQueen, Dauner-Lieb & Tettinger, *Specific Performance and Rights of Cure*, in The Common Frame of Reference for European Contract Law and its Interaction with English and German Law (Stefan Vogenauer & Gerhard Dannemann eds. Oxford University Press) (hereinafter, MacQueen, *Specific Performance*).

[34] Article 2 Reg-CESL defines 'sales contract' as 'any contract under which the trader ('the seller') transfers or undertakes to transfer the ownership of the goods to another person ('the buyer'), and the buyer pays or undertakes to pay the price thereof'.

[35] See too the criticisms in Joint Advice, paras 7.53–7.99.

[36] Article 7(1) CISG.

[37] Note, however, Recital 31 CESL, providing that good faith should not be used "as a tool to amend the specific rights and obligations of parties as set out in the specific rules.… In transactions between traders, good commercial practice in the specific situation concerned should be a relevant factor…." It is unclear how far this may limit Article 2 CESL.

[38] Article 23 CESL.

regarded as a relevant matter in interpreting any contract,[39] in the implication of terms,[40] and in the regulation of unfair terms in B2B contracts.[41]

A contract may also be avoided by a party who made a mistake of fact or law existing at the time of formation and who would otherwise not have entered the contract or would have done so only on fundamentally different terms, and the other party knew or could be expected to have known of the mistake but failed to point out the relevant information where good faith and fair dealing would have required such disclosure.[42] The same Article limits a party's disclosure duty where the mistaken party assumed the risk of mistake or should, under the circumstances, bear that risk, but the issues raised by this are of a type that could probably only be resolved by going to court. Again, Article 89 CESL requires parties to re-negotiate their contract 'where performance becomes excessively onerous because of an exceptional change of circumstances', also enabling them to ask a court to adapt or terminate the contract should such negotiations fail. This may also be seen from a business perspective as undermining certainty of performance. A party to a losing or hard bargain may strategically attempt to escape the contract or have it adjusted to be more favourable. It is left unclear how the duty to re-negotiate might be enforced. Once more the spectre of ending up in court looms large over all aspects of this Article.

Some of this at least can be avoided by using the freedom of contract principle proclaimed in the first Article of the proposed CESL, which also allows parties to 'exclude the application of any of the provisions of the [CESL], or derogate from or vary their effects'. So it might be possible, for example, to exclude Article 89 CESL, or to provide explicitly that a party assumes the risk of a mistake so that there is no option of avoidance if a mistake is actually made. But there are limits to this – Article 1 CESL says that exclusion or variation of the provisions of the CESL is not allowed where the provisions themselves so state, as, for example, with the non-excludable duty of good faith in Article 2 CESL. Most of the other mandatory provisions in the proposed CESL favour consumers, and the B2B transaction is little affected by them. But the duty of good faith and dealing is a potentially far-reaching one. Furthermore, the more that business parties choose to exclude, vary or derogate from many of the CESL provisions, the less useful or practical the CESL becomes as an opt in law.

Overall, as the Law Commissions pointed out in their Joint Advice to the United Kingdom government on the CESL proposal (published in November 2011), the most likely B2B setting in which the proposed CESL could prove attractive is where

39 Article 59 CESL.
40 Article 68 CESL.
41 Article 86 CESL.
42 Article 48 CESL.

SMEs are dealing with each other.[43] Such businesses lack the resources to negotiate the detailed, professionally drafted contracts that are characteristic of transactions between large businesses and tend to rely instead on either pre-prepared standard forms or the default rules of whatever may be the governing law. If, however, standard forms are used on each side, there is the hazard of the 'battle of the forms', or the possibility that the other side's form somehow comes to be the basis of the contract; if there is reliance on the governing law, it is crucial to have confidence about what that law is as well as its content. The proposed CESL contains a solution to the 'battle of the forms' as well as regulating B2B standard form terms 'of such a nature that [their] use deviates from good commercial practice, contrary to good faith and fair dealing'.[44] On parties' confidence about the governing law, the Law Commissions referred to a case called to their attention in which the conclusion of an otherwise straightforward negotiation for a contract between a Scottish and a Polish company was held up for weeks as the parties debated what the governing law should be. The parties knew nothing of each other's laws, neither of which was available in any language that they knew well enough. Had the proposed CESL been in force, it would have been available in all the languages of the European Union, and, provided the parties were happy with what they read, their problem could have been resolved without much delay and expense.[45]

Turning to the B2C transaction, freedom of contract is constrained, not only by the mandatory provisions on consumer protection, but also by a provision in the Regulation that 'in relations between a trader and a consumer the Common European Sales Law may not be chosen partially, but only in its entirety'.[46] What this prevents, however, is not the exercise of the freedom provided within the proposed CESL itself, to vary or replace the rules in particular Articles, but the alternative possibility, known as *depeçage* in the world of international private law, of changing non-mandatory CESL rules by a choice of some other system's parallel but different rules. In the consumer context, in other words, the contract is to be governed by the CESL and those rules that the parties formulate for themselves when they are free to do so, rather than by a mixture of bits of the CESL and reference to bits of other laws. But the argument from the silence of the Regulation on this possibility in the B2B context leaves business parties free to pick and choose the CESL rules that will be applicable to their contract.

Article 11 of the CESL Regulation provides that 'where the parties have validly agreed to use the [CESL] for [their] contract, only the [CESL] shall govern the

43 See Joint Advice, paras 6.19–6.50, 7.35–7.52, 7.64–7.66, 7.94–7.99.

44 Article 39 CESL (conflicting standard contract terms), Article 86 CESL (meaning of 'unfair' in contracts between traders). See on the battle of the forms Joint Advice, paras 7.39–7.43.

45 Joint Advice, para 6.31.

46 Article 8(3) Reg-CESL.

matters addressed in its rules'. This provision suggests that the CESL's mandatory consumer protection provisions preclude the application of parallel rules found in the consumer's normal domestic law. This will not matter if the CESL rules afford the same or a higher protection compared with those of the consumer's normal domestic law, but it will be very important if the latter is in fact better. Then the effect of a choice of the CESL will strip from the cross-border consumer the benefits of the Rome I Regulation, which says, simply put, that a choice of law other than one a consumer would normally enjoy may not deprive that party of mandatory domestic consumer protections.[47] For this reason above all, consumer groups in Europe are largely hostile to the CESL proposal. This is although the proposal, as first published, incorporates all the major relevant European Union consumer protection measures. There is perhaps a not wholly rational fear that existing protections may be whittled down in the negotiating process before the CESL text is finalised, or, more intelligibly, that once the CESL is enacted, Member States may lower their existing protections to conform to the CESL or avoid any further measures of expansion in order to enable their domestic law to compete more effectively with other national laws to remain "legally" competitive. In other words, consumer protection in Europe could either become frozen at its present levels or begin to diminish in a 'race to the bottom'.

Another key point in the area of choice of law is that the decision whether or not to use the CESL in consumer transactions will primarily be made by the supplier, not the consumer. The most probable scenario is that a trader seeking to attract cross-border customers will by way of the Internet declare the CESL as governing law by a notice or appropriate symbol on its Web site. This allows the trader to be governed by a single law unless dealing domestically. So the consumer will be in a 'take it or leave it' position with regard to the CESL, protected only by the Regulation's requirement that the consumer be notified by the trader in advance by means of a "Standard Information Notice" and by separate agreement with the trader supplying the consumer with a confirmation of that agreement in a durable medium.[48] Thus, consumers in need of the trader's goods will effectively have no choice but to give up whatever advantages may be afforded them by applicable domestic law.

The argument in favour of a single EU sales law is that sales by Internet traders are hampered by the Rome I rule that consumers' domestic protections apply because those protections vary across the European Union with its multiplicity of jurisdictions and Member States.[49] A particular cause of concern is the costs of information and privacy duties – given numerous EU languages, the cost of meeting which in

[47] Article 6(2) Rome 1.

[48] Articles 8, 9 Reg-CESL.

[49] Further on the effect of Rome I see JOINT ADVICE, paras 2.6–2.32.

terms of the languages and the variability of the requirements themselves is prohibitively high. It is certainly a common experience to find Internet traders declining to do business with someone in another Member State because of language differences, translation issues, payment and delivery difficulties.[50] Even the Internet giant Amazon divides its Web sites along national lines in the European Union, with different sites for the United Kingdom (amazon.co.uk), France (amazon.fr), Germany (amazon.de), Italy (amazon.it) and the Netherlands (amazon.nl), and so forth. In all these jurisdictions, it may be noted, Amazon currently trades under the law of Luxembourg, but in each of them Rome I ensures that nonetheless Amazon customers at whom these sites are directed retain the benefit of the relevant local consumer protection laws.

A further point to be made is that not all domestic consumer protection laws will be displaced by the CESL, only those which apply directly in relation to the sale of goods. For example, United Kingdom consumers would remain protected by connected lender liability under section 75 of the Consumer Credit Act of 1974. There is no direct equivalent to this elsewhere in the European Union, which does not require Member States to go so far.[51] Its existence partly explains the relative confidence of British consumers in using their credit cards to pay for Internet purchases compared to what is found elsewhere in Europe. Ultimately, the credit card supplier is liable if the goods or services are faulty, even if the goods are purchased outside the United Kingdom.[52] The section's continued operation is extremely important to the electronic marketplace with or without the CESL as applicable law. A strong argument can be made that the European Union should facilitate electronic commerce by making connected lender liability a Union-wide form of consumer protection.[53]

II. A HISTORICAL SCOTTISH PERSPECTIVE

Viewed historically, the story of harmonising and unifying sale of goods law to aid in the promotion of a single market between countries with different laws is a familiar one in the United Kingdom, which was created as a result of the Treaty of Union between Scotland and England in 1707. About a century before then, the great Scottish jurist Thomas Craig, writing in the optimistic light created by the 1603

[50] See further JOINT ADVICE, paras 2.57–2.61.

[51] See further JOINT ADVICE, paras 4.37–4.40.

[52] See *Office of Fair Trading v Lloyds TSB Bank* [2007] UKHL 48, [2008] 1 A.C. 316; also BBC News Business, 5 December 2011 ('UK Shopping Habits Transformed by Technology, says KPMG,' available at http://www.bbc.co.uk/news/business-16024079); also UK CARDS ASSOCIATION, A DECADE OF CARDS 2000–2010 … AND BEYOND (September 2011), at 3, 12 (available at http://www.theukcardsassociation.org.uk/files/ukca/documents/press_releases/decade_of_cards_final.pdf).

[53] See Article 15 of the Consumer Credit Directive (Council Directive 2008/48/EC, 23.4.2008).

union of the Scottish and English Crowns in the person of King James VI and I, had argued, in a passage striking for its market liberalism, that to bring the kingdoms themselves together would require changes in the law:

> It must also be permitted to every man born in the island to live where he likes, and to enjoy the rights and privileges of citizenship, to pursue whatever trade and livelihood he pleases, just as though his parents had been born and brought up there. It ought to be open to all to better their position and means, to acquire real property, personality, landed property, in the country and in the towns, by every title recognised by the law of nations, by will or under an intestacy, by purchase, sale, exchange, gift, auction, and by any other form of contract enforceable at civil or municipal law.... Both [Englishmen and Scotsmen] must also be free from taxes or customs duties, by which it has been usual to distinguish between the subjects of one kingdom and the other, so that wherever they are they may be able to buy provisions at their charges, and with no greater liability to duties and exactions than they would have if native born.[54]

The 1707 Union when it eventually came about was clearly concerned with much more than simply the creation of a single Crown and Parliament for a united kingdom, primary objectives although these too undoubtedly were (Articles II and III). The root of the Union was economic and commercial, and many of the desiderata of a more perfect Union as adumbrated by Craig were picked up again in 1707. Article IV says that 'all the subjects of the United Kingdom of Great Britain shall from and after the Union have full freedom and intercourse of trade and navigation to and from any port or place within the said United Kingdom'. Article VI lays down that 'all parts of the United Kingdom for ever from and after the Union shall have the same allowances, encouragements and drawbacks, and be under the same prohibitions, restrictions ands regulations of trade, and liable to the same customs and duties on import and export'. Articles VII–XV provide for a uniform tax regime, while Article XVI sets up a common currency and Article XVII a common weights and measures system. Most significantly of all in the present context, Article XVIII goes on to provide for 'the laws concerning regulation of trade, customs and excises' to be the same in Scotland and England. This of course did not abolish either Scots or English law but instead made them both alterable by the new Parliament of Great Britain. However, the Article distinguished between public and private law, with the former being liable to change simply to make it the same throughout the United Kingdom, whereas change to private law could not be made 'except for evident utility of the subjects within Scotland'.[55]

[54] Thomas Craig, De Unione Regnorum Britanniae (C. S. Terry, ed., Scottish History Society: Edinburgh 1909), f. 258.

[55] For discussion of the meanings of public and private right see John D. Ford, *The Legal Provisions in the Acts of Union* 66 Cambridge L.J. 106, 108–18 (2007); John W. Cairns, *The Origins of the Edinburgh Law School: The Union of 1707 and the Regius Chair* 11 Edinburgh L.R. 300, 313–26 (2007).

The 1707 Union was undoubtedly successful in establishing in Great Britain a single market that survives and, the vagaries of the economic cycle notwithstanding, thrives down to the present day. What is also interesting, however, is to observe not only the evolution in the areas in which the 1707 Union helped create similar laws, but also the developments in those areas which were left untouched. By and large, 'single market law' can be identified from that experience as including tax, welfare, companies and business associations, employment, intellectual property, financial services including insurance, and consumer protection.[56] In all these areas today it is clear that we can talk about United Kingdom law.[57] The fields where Scots and English law remain distinct are in the classical private law subjects of persons, family, succession, property and obligations, and where these areas interact, such as rights in security, bankruptcy, and trusts.[58] Even within these subjects a good deal of convergence has taken place, most notably in the law of delict and in particular negligence,[59] but also in large parts of contract law.[60] This has not been a one-way process; Scots law has moved in an English direction in a number of respects, and in a number of areas English law has moved closer to Scots law.[61]

The United Kingdom does therefore provide a still-working example of how a reasonably large and active single market can develop, thrive and function despite internal diversity of law. Since the laws of both England and Scotland have developed fairly pragmatically since 1707, whether development was legislative or judicial, their history over that time can reasonably be examined to see what problems were thought to require a unified response, and where diversity of law could remain. Of course, the lessons to be drawn from this experience for the much larger and more complex task of creating a single market in Europe are limited, but the evidence is at least interesting and suggests questions that should be asked about the current effort to unify European sales law.

The development of sale of goods law was quite distinct in Scotland and England before 1707 and, indeed, afterwards for a considerable time. Unlike English law, Scots law following Roman law and the civilian legal tradition treated the law of sale

[56] For a study of the post-Union development of one branch of law see Hector L. MacQueen, *Intellectual Property and the Common Law in Scotland c.1700–c.1850*, in THE COMMON LAW OF INTELLECTUAL PROPERTY: ESSAYS IN HONOUR OF PROFESSOR DAVID VAVER (Catherine W. Ng, Lionel Bently and Giuseppina D'Agostino eds., Hart Publishing: Oxford, 2010), 21–43.

[57] Indeed, increasingly since 1973, European Union law.

[58] See in general A HISTORY OF PRIVATE LAW IN SCOTLAND (Kenneth G. C. Reid and Reinhard Zimmermann eds., 2 volumes, Oxford University Press: Oxford 2000).

[59] Hector L. MacQueen and W. David H. Sellar, *History of Negligence in Scots Law*, in NEGLIGENCE: THE COMPARATIVE LEGAL HISTORY OF THE LAW OF TORTS (Eltjo J. H. Schrage ed., Duncker & Humboldt: Berlin 2001).

[60] Hector L. MacQueen, *Scots and English Law: The Case of Contract*, 54 CURRENT LEGAL PROBLEMS 205 (2001).

[61] E.g., the development of a principle against unjust enrichment in the law of restitution, or the abolition of privity in the Contracts (Rights of Third Parties) Act 1999.

as a unitary subject whether the sale was for land or goods.[62] The major differences from English law so far as goods were concerned lay in the rules relating to the seller's guarantee of the quality of the goods (with Scots law much less informed by the caveat emptor principle than its English counterpart), the transfer of property (dependent on delivery rather than contract in Scotland), and the apportionment of risk between the parties (connected not to transfer of property, but to the conclusion of contract in Scotland).[63] In 1853, however, a Royal Commission was established to 'inquire and ascertain how far the Mercantile Laws of the different Parts of the United Kingdom … may be advantageously assimilated'. The organisation of the Commission seems to have been the result of pressure applied by business interests, including those in Scotland.[64] In the context of sale of goods, this pressure was likely sparked by rapid economic growth and technological development in an expanding single market where mass manufacturing had become well established, a consumer market was expanding, postal and telegram services were enabling rapid communication between previously remote parts of the kingdom, and the new railways permitted the bulk transit of goods as well as people across the country.[65] All the same, as Alan Rodger remarks, 'When the Commission asked about the practical difficulties encountered by businessmen as a result of the differences among the various legal systems, the witnesses could give them few actual examples'.[66]

Once the Commission reported, legislation rapidly followed in Scotland with the passage of the 1856 Mercantile Law Amendment Act. Speaking from the throne at the opening of the Westminster Parliament the previous year, Queen Victoria had declared:

> The difference which exists in several important particulars between the commercial laws of Scotland and those of the other parts of the United Kingdom has occasioned inconvenience to a large portion of my subjects engaged in trade. Measures will be proposed to you for remedying this evil.[67]

[62] William M. Gordon, *Sale*, in 2 A History of Private Law in Scotland 305–32 (hereinafter Gordon, *Sale*).

[63] See Gordon, *Sale*, 314–25.

[64] Alan Rodger, *The Codification of Commercial Law in Victorian Britain*, 108 Law Quarterly Review 570, 573–4 (1992), from whence the quotation (hereinafter Rodger, *Codification*).

[65] Available recent accounts of these developments include Judith Flanders, Consuming Passions: Leisure and Pleasure in Victorian Britain (Harper Press: London 2006); Duncan Campbell-Smith, Masters of the Post: The Authorized History of the Royal Mail (Allen Lane: London 2011); Tom Standage, The Victorian Internet: The Remarkable Story of the Telegraph and the Nineteenth Century's Online Pioneers (Weidenfeld & Nicolson: London 1998); and Christian Wolmar, Fire & Steam: How the Railways Transformed Britain (Atlantic Books: London 2007).

[66] Rodger, *Codification*, 575.

[67] As quoted in Elaine E. Sutherland, *Remedying an Evil? Warrandice of Quality at Common Law in Scotland*, 32 Juridical Review 24, 24–5 (1987).

In fact, though, so far as sale of goods was concerned, there were only two major changes in the 1856 act, one regarding transfer of property and the other relating to the seller's warranty of quality. Neither produced a unified regime of rules applying throughout the United Kingdom; indeed it was said that the act had changed the laws of both jurisdictions without making them the same.[68] As Professor Gordon remarks, 'The aim was to assimilate Scots and English law on the matters dealt with in their practical effect but by means of piecemeal, not radical, change'.[69] Indeed, the Scottish courts seem to have been reluctant to apply the new rules in anything more than the narrowest of fashions.[70]

Pressure for assimilation, unification and, increasingly, codification of commercial law continued from both business and at least some lawyers. Alan Rodger has shown the inspiration of the German Common Commercial Code of 1862 that lies behind the extension to Scotland of the Bills of Exchange Act 1882, the Factors Act 1889, and the Partnership Act 1890, as well as, eventually, the Sale of Goods Act 1893. All these began as England-only pieces of legislation but by dint of lobbying and some modicum of amendment became also part of Scots law.[71] What became the Sale of Goods Act of 1893 was introduced into Parliament as a Bill in 1888. It essentially codified existing English law, which was substantially different from its Scottish counterpart. Over the next five years, the Bill was successively abandoned, then reintroduced, and then abandoned again. Amendments to extend the Bill to Scotland seem first to have been put forward in 1891 with the support of the House of Lords Judge Lord Watson, the Scottish bar (the Faculty of Advocates), and solicitors in commercial practice in Glasgow. Businessmen from the Scottish Chambers of Commerce also lobbied actively on the matter. The Bill finally passed on 20 February 1894 with retrospective effect to the preceding New Year's Day.[72]

The long-sustained pressure from Scottish business interests to obtain a unified Sale of Goods Act and other assimilating and codifying legislation in commercial law raises the question, What were the difficulties caused by the preceding, non-unified system laws found in Scotland and England? While Rodger doubts the reality of such difficulties except perhaps in connection with bills of exchange,[73] it must be said that business people do tend to engage with legal questions only where they feel adverse effects from the status quo. Likewise, politicians and managers of parliamentary business usually embark on technical legislation only if convinced that it is

[68] Rodger, *Codification*, 574–5.
[69] Gordon, *Sale*, 326.
[70] *Id.*, 327.
[71] Rodger, *Codification*, 578–81
[72] For accounts of the passage of the Sale of Goods Bill, see Rodger, *Codification*, 581–83; Gordon, *Sale*, 328–30.
[73] Rodger, *Codification* at 587.

needed.[74] That Scottish business took the lead in campaigning for a unified law may have owed something to the fact that they were the ones most often doing business in foreign legal territory, while English-based businesses and lawyers would for the most part never have had to confront the issue of deciding the applicable law. But it may be that even in Scotland the supporters of assimilation and codification were simply the more vocal and active members of their communities, with the silent remainder at best passively acquiescent or unbelieving that change on such a scale would ever actually take place. Rodger notes that at the last minute the Faculty of Advocates withdrew its support for the Sale of Goods Bill and speculates that 'this was the voice of the ordinary members of Faculty that had never spoken yet'.[75]

A contemporary's view was that the Sale of Goods Act 1893 made 'important and almost revolutionary changes ... upon the principles and practice of the Scottish law of sale'.[76] Professor Gordon summarises the effect of the act as making the law 'largely British [which] meant largely English'. It was not however 'a total surrender'.[77] The key changes for Scots law were to the rules on transfer of property and risk,[78] and to the seller's implied obligations, which were now set out in English law terminology and were in substance much narrower than the pre-1856 common law.[79] But the buyer's remedies in Scots law for the seller's breach were largely preserved. The right to reject faulty goods remained dependent on the materiality of the seller's breach rather than on the characterisation of the term breached as a condition or a warranty.[80] The existing Scottish common law rules on the remedy of specific implement were explicitly maintained by the act; the accompanying provisions defining more particularly when a court might grant a specific performance order were intended primarily to encourage the English courts to follow the Scottish example and be more liberal in granting such orders.[81] In a converse direction the act also allowed a buyer under Scots law to retain faulty goods and sue the seller for damages, a remedy previously refused by the nineteenth-century Scottish courts.[82] In this regard at least, the act could be said to have effected an important improvement in Scots law.

No one at the time or since seems to have assessed the economic impact of the unification of sales law in the United Kingdom. Did cross-border traffic in goods

74 Cf. *id.*, 588 ("Because the evils were not acute, politicians did not give a high priority to formal assimilation"). But four major statutes were passed in not much more than 10 years.

75 *Id.*, 583 & 589.

76 Richard Brown, Notes and Commentaries on the Sale of Goods Act 1893 (W Green & Sons: Edinburgh, 1895), introductory note.

77 Gordon, *Sale*, 331.

78 See Sale of Goods Act 1893 (hereinafter, SOGA 1893), ss. 16–20.

79 See SOGA 1893 ss. 12–15.

80 SOGA 1893 s. 11(2).

81 SOGA 1893 s. 52.

82 SOGA 1893 s. 11(2). See further Robin Evans-Jones, *The History of the Actio Quanti Minoris in Scots Law*, 36 Juridical Review 190 (1991).

increase after 1894? Did businesspeople cease to suffer the difficulties resulting from the differences between Scots and English law that were said to exist prior to 1894? Quite possibly the answer to both these questions is yes, but the further question, whether that would be attributable to the new law or not, remains unanswered. It may be significant that, although the Sale of Goods Act has been much criticised and, in the last three decades of the twentieth century, significantly amended,[83] there has been no serious suggestion from either the business or the increasingly important consumer lobby for a return to a system of separate rules in the two jurisdictions.

The lessons for the CESL proposal are various. One lesson is that a uniform sales law is more likely than not in a single market that embraces more than one jurisdiction, each with its own legal system.[84] The uniform sales law is, however, much more likely to be achieved if it has backing from business interests and today, it may be suggested, also consumer groups. Lawyers will probably be divided in their views, between the idealists with a vision of a perfect law, and the pragmatists who prefer the status quo because at least they know, more or less, how to deal with its problematic aspects, but in the end that division of opinion will not be decisive.

III. COMPARING THE PROPOSED CESL WITH THE UK SALE OF GOODS ACT

If businesses are to make the choice between the CESL and a domestic law, they and their advisers will first have to compare the two and see which one better promotes their interests. Consumer groups will wish to do likewise in considering the merits of their concerns that the proposed instrument diminishes their hard-won protections. With this in mind, this section of the chapter compares the proposed CESL with present law in the United Kingdom – the Sale of Goods Act 1979 – on the closely linked topics of the seller's obligations with regard to the quality of the goods and the buyer's remedies when the goods fall below the required standard of quality. Both are of central importance to seller and buyer concerns. The reader should bear in mind the cross-border context and assume a scenario of a business trading into the United Kingdom, whether with another business or a consumer. A British trader selling to consumers outside the United Kingdom is unlikely to be able to impose its own law apart from the CESL. Only if the transaction is with another trader

83 See the Supply of Goods (Implied Terms) Act 1973; Consumer Credit Act 1974; and the consolidation in the Sale of Goods Act 1979, which was in turn amended by the Sale and Supply of Goods Act 1994, the Sale of Goods (Amendment) Act 1995, and the Sale and Supply of Goods Regulations 2002 (S.I. 2002/3045, implementing Directive 1999/44/EC of the European Parliament and of the Council on certain aspects of the sale of consumer goods and associated guarantees, i.e., the Consumer Sales Directive).

84 Another example is Article 2 of the Uniform Commercial Code in the USA.

located in a different Member State will it be possible to consider the alternatives of the CESL, English, and Scots law. There remains, of course, the possibility that the United Kingdom will use its option to extend the CESL to all domestic sales, in which case the choice of law would become all the more significant.

A. *Implied Terms or Rules*

The Sale of Goods Act's approach to the issue of the implication of terms and rules is still coloured by its origins as a codification of commercial custom in nineteenth-century England, although it has been heavily modified over the last thirty-five years in order to protect consumers better.[85] The rules on the seller's obligations are expressed as a series of implied terms – that is, as rules that can be set aside by the agreement of the parties,[86] or where there is an express term inconsistent with the implied terms.[87] One has to look outside the Sale of Goods Act altogether – to Sections 6 and 20 of the Unfair Contract Terms Act 1977 – to find rules making these implied terms mandatory in consumer contracts. Under the same act, exclusions of the implied terms in non-consumer cases are allowed but are subject to a fairness and reasonableness test. So the 'implied terms' are now effectively consumer protection rules. Exclusions may also be regulated in commercial contracts, although not many cases illustrate that possibility.

Under the proposed CESL, the seller's obligations are expressed in a rather stronger way than as implied terms. The seller *must* ensure that the goods are in conformity with the contract, which, of course, consists not only of its express terms, but also of usages and practices, terms implied from the nature and purpose of the contract, the circumstances in which it was concluded, and the non-mandatory rules of the CESL that apply in the absence of any agreement of the parties to the contrary.[88] But the rules on quality are non-mandatory, and so they can be varied or excluded by agreement. The protection for the consumer is that any agreement derogating from the seller's conformity obligations is valid only if at the time of the conclusion of the contract the consumer knew of the specific condition of the goods and accepted them as being in conformity with the contract at the time of formation.[89] This of course encourages pre-contractual disclosure by the seller. But probably, along with the mandatory general CESL rules on unfair terms,[90] it also means that

[85] *Supra* notes 68–83 and accompanying text.
[86] Sale of Goods Act 1979 (hereinafter, SOGA 1979), s. 55(1).
[87] SOGA 1979, s. 55(2).
[88] Article 66 CESL.
[89] Article 99(3) CESL.
[90] Chapter 8 CESL, sections 1 and 2.

usually the rules on conformity will operate in protection of the consumer, since the CESL requires the consumer's subjective knowledge of the condition of the goods. But still, unlike the Sale of Goods Act, there is *some* possibility of excluding quality obligations in consumer sales, which may account for some of the business support for the CESL.

In a B2B contract, however, the approach is much more in favour of caveat emptor: the seller is not liable for any lack of conformity if at the time of the conclusion of the contract the buyer knew or could not have been unaware of the lack of conformity from an objective perspective.[91] These rules are slightly more demanding in character than their equivalent in the Sale of Goods Act. The latter has no implied term about the quality of the goods in relation to a matter specifically drawn to the buyer's attention before the contract is made, or if the buyer's examination of the goods *before the contract is made* ought to have revealed the defect in question.[92] Under these rules (which also apply to B2C contracts), knowledge that a buyer held despite not being informed by the seller or not making a pre-contractual examination of the goods would not prevent the implication of a quality term, whereas these factors may prevent the buyer from complaining of a non-conformity under the proposed CESL.

B. *Quality Defined*

The implied terms of the Sale of Goods Act were recast more than once in the latter decades of the twentieth century to become more protective of buyers, especially consumers. For example, the original Sale of Goods Act concept of 'merchantable quality', a reflection of the nineteenth century, has now been replaced by the more anodyne 'satisfactory quality', which is the implied condition in every sale where the seller is acting in the course of a business. Satisfactoriness is defined in terms of what a reasonable person would regard as satisfactory, taking account of any description of the goods, the price (if relevant) and all other relevant circumstances.[93] The factors considered in determining the quality of goods in B2C contracts include (in implementation of the Consumer Sales Directive[94]) any public statements on the specific characteristics of the goods made by the seller or the producer, particularly in advertising or labelling.[95] There is a non-exclusive list of 'aspects of the quality of

[91] Article 104 CESL.

[92] SOGA 1979, s. 14(2C).

[93] SOGA 1979, s. 14(2A).

[94] Directive 99/44/EC on certain aspects of the sale of consumer goods and associated guarantees.

[95] SOGA 1979, s. 14(2D). Section 14(2E)–(2F) contains further provisions on this point.

goods', most of which are responsive to issues that had arisen under the earlier law, especially in relation to consumers.[96] The list includes:

(a) Fitness for all the purposes for which goods of the kind in question are commonly supplied;
(b) Appearance and finish;
(c) Freedom from minor defects;
(d) Safety;
(e) Durability.

Perhaps the key idea to note here is 'fitness for purpose'. It is clear from the subsequent items on the Sale of Goods Act list that this 'fitness for purpose' is not a purely functional requirement; non-functional aspects of the goods, such as 'appearance and finish', are included. This is important in consumer cases in particular. So for example in the leading case of *Rogers v Parish (Scarborough) Ltd*,[97] which arose from the sale of a new motor vehicle, it was held that in assessing the buyer's reasonable expectations,

> one would include … not merely the buyer's purpose of driving the car from one place to another but of doing so with the appropriate degree of comfort, ease of handling and reliability and, one may add, of pride in the vehicle's outward and interior appearance.[98]

But it is quite possible for non-functional aspects to be relevant in commercial sales as well.[99]

There are three other implied terms under the Sale of Goods Act:

(1) a requirement that goods must correspond with any description applied to them, in the contract or otherwise[100];
(2) where the buyer makes a particular purpose known to the seller who is in the course of a business, the goods must be reasonably fit for that purpose, whether or not it is a purpose for which such goods are commonly supplied, unless the circumstances show that the buyer does not rely, or that it would be unreasonable for him to rely, on the seller's skill or judgment[101]; and finally

[96] SOGA 1979, s. 14(2B).
[97] [1987] Q.B. 933.
[98] *Id.*, 944 (Lord Justice Mustill).
[99] P. S. Atiyah, The Sale of Goods (12th ed. J. N. Adams and H. L. MacQueen, eds., Pearson: Harlow 2010), 178–82.
[100] SOGA 1979, s. 13.
[101] SOGA 1979, s. 14(3).

(3) in contracts for sale by sample, that the bulk will correspond with the sample and the goods will be free from any defect making their quality unsatisfactory which would not be apparent on reasonable examination of the sample.[102]

The requirement of the Sale of Goods Act that the seller be acting in the course of a business, not only in relationship to the fitness-for-particular-purpose obligation, but also under the satisfactory quality standard, means that in cases where the seller is not acting in the course of a business, the dis-satisfied buyer is forced into bringing his complaint under the implied term corresponding with the product description, leading to unsatisfactory debates about the difference between description and quality.[103]

The CESL's Article 100 provides an extended list of criteria for conformity of the goods, which can be paraphrased as follows:

The goods must

(a) be fit for any particular purpose made known to the seller at the time of the conclusion of the contract, except where the circumstances show that the buyer did not rely, or that it was unreasonable for the buyer to rely, on the seller's skill and judgement;
(b) be fit for the purposes for which goods of the same description would ordinarily be used;
(c) possess the qualities of goods which the seller held out to the buyer as a sample or model;
(d) be contained or packaged in the manner usual for such goods or, where there is no such manner, in a manner adequate to preserve and protect the goods;
(e) be supplied along with such accessories, installation instructions or other instructions as the buyer may reasonably expect to receive;
(f) possess the qualities and performance capabilities indicated in any pre-contractual statement about the characteristics of the goods made by the seller, or third parties in earlier links of the business chain before the sale, to the buyer or publicly, and which forms part of the contract terms under Article 69 of the CESL; and
(g) possess such qualities and performance capabilities as the buyer may reasonably expect.[104]

It is clear that the dominant idea here, as in the Sale of Goods Act's implied terms rule, is a fitness-for-purpose requirement, whether the purpose is particular to the buyer or one generally to be expected. The proposed CESL, however, lacks a direct

[102] SOGA 1979, s. 15.
[103] See Atiyah, Sale of Goods, *supra* note 99, 152–4.
[104] Article 100 CESL.

statement that its concept of purpose extends beyond the functional to such non-functional matters as appearance and finish. Criterion (g) probably means that it can be taken as encompassing this as well as safety and durability. The CESL rules on the time available to the buyer to complain of non-conformity seem entirely compatible with the last quality in particular. There is little doubt too that defective packaging and defective instructions in relation to installation or use can make the goods themselves unsatisfactory under the Sale of Goods Act, as part of the 'state or condition' of the goods, especially if they affect safety.[105] In further provisions, however, the proposed CESL goes beyond anything to be found in the Sale of Goods Act, reflecting something of the realities of the twenty-first century. In consumer contracts, lack of conformity resulting from incorrect installations of goods – for example, the faulty fitting out of a new kitchen in which all the component parts conform to the contract requirements – is deemed to be a lack of conformity of the goods if the installation was by the seller or under its responsibility, or if the installation was by the consumer but its incorrectness resulted from shortcomings in the installation instructions.[106]

The proposed CESL's equivalent to the 'correspondence with description' obligation in the Sale of Goods Act is criterion (f), which itself also has a direct parallel in the latter's provision about public statements as a relevant circumstance in assessing whether or not goods are satisfactory in consumer sales. The CESL rule is, however, not confined to the B2C transaction. Much of the United Kingdom's complexity in distinguishing between 'description' and 'quality' might be straightened out if it followed the CESL model in this regard. The remaining difficulty would be that the quality obligations under the Sale of Goods Act only arise if the seller is in the course of a business. This means that the correspondence with description obligation, which does not have the same pre-condition, is important for sales where neither seller nor buyer is acting in the course of a business. But there seems to be no good reason why the quality obligation should be excluded from such sales. The proposed CESL of course applies as a whole only if the seller is a trader, whether one selling to another business or a consumer.

C. *Time of Conformity*

The relevant time for determining conformity under the CESL provisions is when the risk passes to the buyer.[107] This varies according to whether the contract is B2B

[105] *Gilbert Sharp & Bishop v Wills & Co* [1919] S.A.S.R. 114; *Niblett v Confectioners' Materials Co Ltd* [1921] 3 K.B. 387; *Wormell v R.H.M. Agriculture (East) Ltd* [1987] 1 W.L.R. 1091 (C.A.); Atiyah, Sale of Goods, *supra* note 99, 175 & 190. See also, *id.*, 202).

[106] Article 101 CESL.

[107] Article 105(1) CESL. The passage of risk means that the buyer must pay for the goods, unless the loss or damage resulting from the materialisation of the risk is due to an act or omission of the seller.

or B2C. In B2B contracts risk generally passes when the buyer takes delivery of the goods.[108] In B2C contracts, the risk passes to the consumer at the time when the latter acquires physical possession of the goods.[109] There is a special provision for consumers which states that any lack of conformity that becomes apparent within six months after the passing of risk to the consumer buyer is presumed to have existed at that time of delivery unless this is incompatible with the nature of the goods or of the lack of conformity.[110] In the case of goods requiring installation, conformity is tested when the installation is complete.[111]

The time of conformity under the Sale of Goods Act is normally taken to be at the time of delivery. This has to be inferred, however, from section 34 of the act, under which the seller must on delivery afford the buyer a reasonable opportunity to examine the goods for the purpose of ascertaining whether they are in conformity with the contract. The proposed CESL thus has the advantage of clarity and explicitness on this point. A problem can also arise under the Sale of Goods Act provisions that tie the passage of risk to the transfer of ownership, thus enabling it to occur in some cases *before* delivery, for example, on conclusion of a contract for the sale of specific goods (where ownership will be transferred unless otherwise agreed).[112] Thus, where the goods deteriorate between the passage of risk and delivery, there may be an issue as to whether a defect of quality is a breach of obligation for which the seller is liable or simply the materialisation of a risk allocated to the buyer. It has been suggested that a solution to this problem is provided by the concept of 'constructive delivery' of the goods occurring when risk passes, which is then the point at which the conformity of the goods is judged, including their compliance with any requirement of durability[113]; but this fictional approach is not especially attractive by comparison with the CESL approach, under which generally risk only passes when buyers actually take over the goods whether or not they had previously become owners of the goods.[114]

Section 33 of the act states that where the seller agrees to deliver the goods at his own risk at a place other than that where they were sold the buyer must, unless

For critical comment on the CESL risk rules see Kare Lilleholt, *Passing of Risk and the Risk of Mystification: Some Drafting Issues*, 19 EUROPEAN REVIEW OF PRIVATE LAW 921 (2011).

108 Article 143 CESL. Articles 144–6 CESL contain further rules on the transfer of risk when goods are placed at the buyer's disposal, or transported by a carrier, or sold in transit.

109 Article 142(1) CESL.

110 Article 105(2) CESL.

111 Article 105(3) CESL.

112 See SOGA 1979, ss. 18, 20; Atiyah, SALE OF GOODS, *supra* note 99, 343.

113 *Id.*, 141–2. The suggestion is that of Professor Atiyah and is not necessarily supported by the current editors.

114 See further *id.*, 346–7 (arguing that in general risk should pass only on delivery because the party in physical possession is the most appropriate person to insure the goods); also SOGA 1979, s. 20(4) (under which in consumer sales goods remain at seller's risk until delivery to the consumer, i.e., the CESL position).

otherwise agreed, take any risk of deterioration in the goods necessarily incident to the course of transit, which is not the same as deterioration of the goods caused by an innate lack of the necessary quality. A different problem was presented by the case of *Mash and Murrell v Joseph I Emmanuel*,[115] where sellers in Cyprus sold potatoes to be shipped to the buyers in Liverpool. Under the contract, the risk passed to the buyers on shipment. The potatoes were sound when loaded into the ship but had rotted by the time of arrival in Liverpool. It was held at first instance that the sellers were liable for the defect on the basis that the goods must be loaded in 'such a state that they could endure the normal journey and be in a merchantable condition on arrival'.[116] The court reasoned that the risk of deterioration in the course of transit that arises as a result of the defective condition of the goods at the commencement of the transit is not the buyer's responsibility.[117] This approach is now reinforced by the statutory reference to durability as an aspect of quality mentioned previously. The proposed CESL provides a different answer in stating that generally where a B2B contract of sale involves the carriage of goods risk passes to the buyer when the seller hands over the goods to the carrier.[118] This is, however, a non-mandatory rule that can be varied by the parties' agreement.

D. *Termination: The Right to Reject*

In the proposed CESL, the buyer's exercise of remedies in respect of non-conforming goods under a B2B contract is governed first by an expectation that the goods will be examined 'within as short a period as is reasonable not exceeding 14 days from the date of delivery of the goods'; otherwise the right to rely on any lack of conformity may be lost.[119] In addition, the buyer is required to give notice of the non-conformity to the seller within a reasonable time if it wishes to take action upon the defect.[120] The reasonable time for giving notice to the seller runs from when the goods are supplied or, if it is later, from the time when the buyer discovered, or could be expected to have discovered, the non-conformity.[121] Thus, a latent defect not detected shortly after the buyer takes delivery of the goods may still give rise to non-conformity and a claim thereon once it emerges or is found by the buyer. There is a long-stop or limitation period, however: the business buyer loses the right to rely

[115] [1961] 1 All E.R. 485.

[116] *Id.*, 485 (Justice Devlin).

[117] The decision was reversed on its facts in the Court of Appeal, but not on the law: [1962] 1 All E.R. 77. See also *Lambert v Lewis* [1982] A.C. 225 and Atiyah, Sale of Goods, *supra* note 99, 182 & 346.

[118] Article 145 CESL. Under Article 142(4) CESL, a consumer has the risk of goods being carried only if it has arranged the carriage of the goods.

[119] Article 121(1) CESL.

[120] Article 122(1) CESL.

[121] Article 122(1) CESL.

on a lack of conformity if no notice is given to the seller within two years of the goods being handed over to the buyer in accordance with the contract.[122]

The crucial point which emerges from this summary is that throughout this two-year period the business buyer can exercise any of the remedies for non-performance that are available under the proposed CESL, including termination of the contract as well as specific performance, withholding performance, price reduction and damages.[123] But the position of the consumer buyer who wishes to complain about non-conformities is different since the requirements of examination and notice do not apply.[124] Thus, all the remedies mentioned, including termination of the contract (plus a right to repair or replacement of the faulty goods), continue to be available to the consumer, regardless of examination or notification, until the lapse of the prescription period found in chapter 18 of the proposed CESL. Chapter 18 provides that the right to enforce performance of an obligation and any ancillary right thereto is extinguished two years from the time when the buyer has become, or could be expected to have become, aware of the facts as a result of which the right can be exercised.[125] The consumer is thus able to terminate for non-conformity for an even longer period than the business buyer, who has the same period of two years but starting from the point of hand-over rather than of knowledge of the non-conformity. Beyond this the only long-stop is provided by a second prescriptive period of ten years from the time the buyer took physical possession of the goods.[126]

All this contrasts significantly, not only with the present rules under the Sale of Goods Act, but also with the approach of the Law Commissions, in a report published in 2009 relating to the reform of the rules in consumer transactions. The current law confers upon any buyer taking delivery of goods a right to examine them in order to ascertain whether they are in conformity with the contract.[127] Failure to exercise this right has, unlike its CESL counterpart, no stated effect upon the buyer's entitlement to complain subsequently of non-conformity. Instead, what is fatal for the buyer's right to reject the goods, after an examination of them, is either to tell the seller that they are accepted or after delivery to do any act in relation to the goods inconsistent with the seller's ownership of the goods.[128] But the consumer buyer cannot be deprived by agreement, waiver or otherwise, of this requirement of examination before acceptance is constituted; the effect is that the consumer's right to reject is not lost before the goods have been examined.[129] Retaining the

[122] Article 122(2) CESL.
[123] For the buyer's remedies in general overview see Article 106 CESL.
[124] Article 106(3)(b) CESL.
[125] Articles 178, 180, 185 CESL.
[126] Article 186(2) CESL.
[127] SOGA 1979, s. 34.
[128] SOGA 1979, s. 35(1), (2).
[129] SOGA 1979, s. 35(3).

goods without intimating rejection to the seller before the lapse of a reasonable time constitutes an acceptance, however, whether or not the buyer is a consumer, and whether or not there has been an examination.[130] There is no specification of what a reasonable time may be, but the case law suggests that it is not usually more than a matter of a few months in either commercial or consumer cases, and certainly not often as long as the two-year period provided in the CESL.[131]

The most recent case, *Douglas v Glenvarigill Co. Ltd.*,[132] in which the buyer of a defective car was held not entitled to reject it more than two years after purchase, confirms the general approach. The Law Commissions have proposed that in consumer cases the buyer's right of rejection should generally be confined to a period of thirty days from the date of purchase, delivery or completion of the contract, whichever is later.[133] This, it is said, would give a reasonable opportunity to inspect the goods and to test them for a period in actual use. It would also provide both sides with a greater degree of certainty, which is thought to be particularly useful in the consumer context. The recommendation is, however, in even sharper contrast than the current law with the position under the proposed CESL. If implemented, it is more likely to be attractive to businesses dealing with consumers than the CESL.

The Sale of Goods Act has since 1994 provided that a buyer is not deemed to have accepted the goods merely because repair is asked for or agreed by arrangement with the seller.[134] This was considered a pro-consumer protection, but a lacuna was exposed in a House of Lords commercial case, where the question was whether the buyer who had agreed to repair of defective goods by the seller could still exercise a right of rejection after a repair had been carried out but after the seller refused to explain what had been done to effect the repair. The decision was that the buyer could still reject the goods in these circumstances.[135] It would seem that under the proposed CESL the buyer might still be able to terminate after a cure in the circumstances found in this case. The buyer may withhold its own performance during an attempt at cure, but otherwise its rights are *suspended* so far as inconsistent with the supplier's right of cure. Even if cure is achieved, the buyer may claim damages for delay and other losses caused by the cure process. It would, therefore, seem that the buyer might still be able to terminate after a cure, the buyer's rights

130 SOGA 1979, s. 35(4).

131 See the survey of modern cases in LAW COMMISSION AND SCOTTISH LAW COMMISSION, JOINT REPORT ON CONSUMER REMEDIES FOR FAULTY GOODS (Law Com. No. 317, Scot. Law Com. No. 216, 2009), paras 2.11–2.19.

132 [2010] CSOH 14, 2010 S.L.T. 634.

133 LAW COMMISSIONS, CONSUMER REMEDIES FOR FAULTY GOODS, *supra* note 131, paras 3.36–3.95.

134 SOGA 1979, s. 35(6).

135 *J. & H. Ritchie v Lloyd Ltd.* [2007] UKHL 9; 2007 S.C. (H.L.) 89; [2007] 1 W.L.R. 670 (H.L.).

there reviving after the seller refused (possibly in breach of the duties of good faith and co-operation?)[136] to explain the steps taken to achieve the cure, or if the cure was unsuccessful.

The proposed CESL includes the consumer remedies of repair or replacement first put forward under the Consumer Sales Directive and implemented in the United Kingdom by amendments to the Sale of Goods Act in 2002.[137] The decision of the CJEU that replacement in relation to consumer goods installed in good faith by the buyer – tiles in one case, a washing machine in another – means not only replacement but also reinstallation of the goods in question, or meeting the costs of removal and reinstallation, makes it likely that the remedy should be seen as of fairly wide scope.[138] The certainty and precision of the rules are increased by the proposed CESL. The seller must complete repair or replacement within a reasonable period not exceeding thirty days from the time the consumer requires it; otherwise the consumer may resort to other remedies.[139] While then the consumer is not obliged to seek repair or replacement before termination under the proposed CESL (as was the case under the Consumer Sales Directive), the choice of the former means that the latter is precluded during the repair/replacement period. There is no maximum or minimum period within which the claim to repair or replacement must be made other than the periods of prescription under the proposed CESL,[140] but the consumer is not obliged to pay for any use made of a replaced item prior to its replacement.[141]

The discussion of the remedy of repair or replacement in United Kingdom courts has taken place in the long shadow cast by the buyer's remedy of rejection. The implementation of the Consumer Sales Directive is simply additional to the existing scheme of remedies under the Sale of Goods Act and did not replace it. Accordingly, the established right of immediate rejection of faulty goods by a buyer was not displaced by the directive scheme in which 'rescission' could only follow an unsuccessful attempt at repair or replacement.[142] A trader considering whether or not to deal with consumers on the basis of the proposed CESL rather than the present English

136 See Articles 2 and 3 CESL.

137 See now SOGA 1979, ss. 48A–48E.

138 Cases C-65/09, C-87/09, *Wittmer v Gebr GmbH; Putz v Medianess Electronics GmbH* [2011] 3 CMLR 27.

139 Article 111(2) CESL.

140 See Chapter 18 CESL generally.

141 Article 112(2) CESL. A repaired item will, however, have to be paid for. Note that the consumer who terminates may have to pay for the use of the goods before termination: Article 174(1)(c) CESL.

142 See *Douglas v Glenvarigill Co. Ltd.* [2010] CSOH 14; 2010 S.L.T. 634; *Lowe v W. Machell Joinery Ltd* [2011] EWCA Civ 794. Neither case applies the repair or replacement remedy, concentrating instead on the buyer's right of rejection. See further, Martin Hogg, *The Consumer's Right to Rescind under the Sale of Goods Act: A Tale of Two Remedies*, Scots Law Times (News Section) 277 (2003); Atiyah, Sale of Goods, *supra* note 99, 522–6; MacQueen, *Specific Performance*.

or Scots law might therefore note that, while exposed to a longer period of risk of the buyer's rejection of the goods under the proposed CESL, offering repair or replacement as a remedy does head off that risk to a significant degree, albeit also putting the trader under the pressure of a fairly tight time limit (thirty days) within which to give effect to the remedy. Neither the proposed CESL nor the present law in the United Kingdom prevents the consumer from terminating straightaway in response to a problem. However, both laws do give that party a modicum of bargaining power in dealing with the trader not found in the Consumer Sales Directive's scheme of remedies.[143]

E. *Overview*

As to the major issue of the buyer's right to reject, the businessperson considering the choice between the proposed CESL and the present law in the United Kingdom is likely to select the latter, given the lengthy period of time for which a consumer buyer remains able to reject the goods under the former. The present law's advantage in this respect will be confirmed if the Law Commissions' proposals, including restricting the consumer's right to reject to a thirty-day period, are implemented into legislation. The slightly greater power of a seller to exclude its quality obligations under the proposed CESL may not be a sufficient offset. For the rest, including B2B transactions, it is a fairly equal choice, with the CESL perhaps presenting a bit more clarity than the Sale of Goods Act in its current form.

IV. CONCLUSION

What are the prospects for the passage of the proposed CESL? The proposal was published at an unpropitious moment as Member States struggled desperately to prevent the collapse of one of the EU's vital symbols, the common currency. The chances of the CESL's making its way successfully through even the qualified majority voting process is no more certain than those of the Herculean labours to save the euro. The European Commission, under the slogan 'Justice for Growth', sees the CESL as the means to free up a hitherto latent online market worth an extra 26 billion euros to the European economy.[144] The proposal has survived a rather absurd challenge to

[143] See also *O'Farrell v Moroney* 2008 G.W.D. 35–533 (Edinburgh Sheriff Court, 17 October 2008), in which it was held that the goods (a young peregrine falcon, which died 25 days after sale) had been conform to contract so that the issue of remedy (presumably replacement) did not arise. Termination would certainly not have availed the unfortunate purchaser.

[144] European Commission, DG Justice, "Common European Sales Law to Boost Trade and Expand Consumer Choice" (11 October 2011) (press release and accompanying documentation), available at http://ec.europa.eu/justice/newsroom/news/20111011_en.htm.

its compliance with the EU subsidiarity principle.[145] Further, it has received support not only from the European Parliament,[146] but also from representatives of Internet traders and SMEs.[147] Some of the pre-conditions for a successful outcome to the reform process are thus in place. On the other hand, there is significant opposition from consumer and legal professional groups,[148] and it is highly uncertain whether enough Member States can be persuaded to vote for what some undoubtedly see as a challenge to domestic law, despite its being a purely optional law.

As already noted, the United Kingdom government asked the English and the Scottish Law Commissions to advise it on the subject.[149] That advice accepted the view that the European single market was indeed potentially divided in the online consumer context, and that a common European sales law might indeed be beneficial there. But, at the same time the commissions were sceptical about whether certain aspects of the CESL proposal would solve the perceived problems. Were the proposal to be focused more clearly or exclusively on the problems of Internet trading its chances of success would likely improve. The commissions were also doubtful about whether the proposed CESL met the needs of SMEs in contracting across borders. The commissions argued, however, that if the CESL were adopted, the United Kingdom should consider making it an option available for domestic as well as cross-border online consumer transactions, since Internet traders would find it problematic to trade under different laws based upon the residence or location of the consumer. Likewise, if the CESL were to be adopted for B2B transactions, the United Kingdom should make it available in the purely domestic marketplace

[145] For details see Eric Clive, *European Private Law News* [blog], 4 January 2012 ('Common European Sales Law Easily Survives First Subsidiarity Challenge,' available at http://www.law.ed.ac.uk/epln/blogentry.aspx?blogentryref=8844).

[146] See European Parliament, Report on Policy Options for Progress Towards a European Contract Law for Consumers and Businesses (2011/2013(INI)), 18.4.2011, available at http://www.europarl.europa.eu/sides/getDoc.do?pubRef=-//EP//NONSGML+REPORT+A7–2011–0164+0+DOC+PDF+V0//EN&language=EN; European Parliament resolution of 8 June 2011 on policy options for progress towards a European Contract Law for consumers and businesses (2011/2013(INI), available at http://www.europarl.europa.eu/sides/getDoc.do?type=TA&language=EN&reference=P7-TA-2011–0262).

[147] See, e.g., the reaction of the British Retail Consortium, press release 11 October 2011, 'Plan for Single EU Online Shopping Law Good for Customers and UK Retailers,' available at http://www.brc.org.uk/brc_news_detail.asp?id=2060&kCat=&kData=1); and the U.K. Federation of Small Businesses, press release dated 14 October 2011, 'Figures Show the New EU-Wide Sales Law Will Make It Easier for Small Firms to Trade within the EU' (available at http://www.fsb.org.uk/News.aspx?loc=pressroom&rec=7344).

[148] See, e.g., BEUC: The European Consumers Organisation, press release 10 October 2011, 'New "Optional" EU Sales Law Makes Consumer Protection a Guessing Game', available at http://www.beuc.org/BEUCNoFrame/Docs/4/HNCPKOECADFHJGKNIGIHLELHPDWY9D7WWN9DW3571KM/BEUC/docs/DLS/2011–09816–01-E.pdf and the comments of the Law Society of England and Wales, 'EU Common Sales Law: Law Society Considers Contract Proposals', available at http://international.lawsociety.org.uk/node/10660.

[149] See generally JOINT ADVICE.

and not exclude its use by non-SMEs. In essence, the market should be allowed to decide the fate of the CESL, rather than the government or vested interests such as the legal professions. Should it fail, then no one would be damaged; success might, on the other hand, contribute to recovery in Europe, whether or not at the levels rather optimistically forecast by the European Commission.[150]

This chapter must end on the uncertain note that passage through the European legislative process is in doubt. Such a failure would be a matter for regret. The optional nature of the instrument would provide an interesting experiment with which to test the claim that the variety of domestic laws in the European Union is a barrier to the achievement of a single market. No one would be harmed by its passage due to its optional nature. But the benefits would be substantial if Internet traders and SMEs in sufficient numbers elect to use it as a means to expand their markets more widely in Europe. These benefits would surely outweigh the rather theoretical risk of a certain loss of consumer protection.

[150] See also Hector MacQueen, *European Private Law News* [blog], 11 November 2011 ('The UK Take on Cross-Border Internet Trading and Growth?', available at http://www.law.ed.ac.uk/epln/blogentry.aspx?blogentryref=8784).

22

Harmonization of International Sales Law

Larry A. DiMatteo

This chapter reviews the relative success of the United Nations Convention on Contracts for the International Sale of Goods (CISG) in harmonizing international sales law. It questions the worth of the CISG when private parties often opt out of its coverage. It begins first at the grass roots of law application and asks – Have the CISG text and principles, and their application, set the foundation for a relative uniformity of application? Has there been a convergence in CISG jurisprudence towards more uniform interpretations? What remain as the key issues in dispute? What are the current trends in CISG jurisprudence? Can we speak of majority and minority views? Rule and principle applications often generate a list of factors that the courts look to in their application. What factors analyses have been developed to guide the courts and arbitral tribunals in applying CISG Articles to different real world contexts? Have implied principles and implied default rules been developed to fill in the gaps in the CISG text?

The chapter asks what are the possible "future" roles of the CISG in harmonizing international sales law. The areas to be analyzed include whether there will be a (1) continuance of current trends towards substantive convergence, (2) further increase in operational usefulness, (3) increased use as customary international law? (4) continued use of it as a model for modernization of domestic sales and contract law. Question (1) builds on the first part of the chapter, that shows a substantive convergence of divergent, autonomous interpretations of CISG articles. Question (2) deals with the problem of private ignorance and avoidance of the CISG through the exercise of the right to opt out. The obvious solution to this problem will be explored: the education of the legal and business communities on the benefits of using the CISG as choice of law (opting in) and how it can be used strategically on behalf of buyers and sellers.

I would like to thank my co-editors Qi Zhou and Séverine Saintier, whose hard work, perseverance, and collegiality helped us overcome a very trying manuscript editing process. I thank them for helping preserve my sanity.

Question (3) deals with the lackluster use of the CISG as evidence of international customary law, with a focus on its use as such by arbitral tribunals. Question (4) may in the end be the most important – the impact of the CISG as a model for the modernization of domestic contract law.

I. INTRODUCTION

The United Nations Convention on Contracts for the International Sale of Goods (CISG)[1] has been heralded as the most successful substantive private law convention in history. In some respects this has been true; however, by some measures it has failed its intended purpose of harmonizing international sales law. This chapter examines the success of the CISG on a number of different metrics. The first section looks at the written document itself and examines the internal obstacles to international sales law harmonization. It looks at the substantive shortcomings of the CISG, the problem of reservations, and finally its widespread adoption. Even though these areas have been widely discussed, it is important to mention these issues before moving on to the central issue of uniformity of application, or the lack thereof. The second section examines the issue of the uniformity of application and the "problem" of variant interpretations. The section asks whether, despite the existence of divergent interpretations, the principle of uniformity as espoused in the CISG has been sufficiently advanced by courts and arbitral tribunals. The American Uniform Commercial Code (UCC) and its evolution will be used by analogy to discuss the problem of a uniform text's being applied in multiple independent court systems. The final section questions the relevancy of the CISG despite its widespread adoption. A best practice methodology will be used throughout the chapter to illustrate how the parties – knowledgeable in the reach of the CISG – would be able to overcome many of the obstacles of non-uniform interpretation and application of the CISG

II. GOAL OF HARMONIZING INTERNATIONAL SALES LAW

The goal of the CISG, as with any uniform or model law, is to promote the harmonization of law across jurisdictions. This is a true in countries of federated states like the United States. For example, the American Law Institute (ALI)[2] and the National Conference of Commissioners of Uniform States Laws (NCCUSL)[3] have

1 Adopted in Vienna on 11 April 1980 and entered into force in 1988, 1489 UNTS 3, available at www.cisg.law.pace.edu.

2 For a list of American Law Institute's model acts, principles and Restatements see, http://www.ali.org/doc/past_present_ALIprojects.pdf (accessed 7 March 2012).

3 See http://www.nccusl.org. NCCUSL and the ALI have been co-sponsors of the Uniform Commercial Code and its subsequent revisions, except for the failed revision of Article 2 sale of goods (accessed 7 March 2012).

created well over two hundred model laws and instruments for adoption by the fifty American states.[4] The Hague Conference on Private International Law[5] and the United Nations Commission on International Trade Law (UNCITRAL)[6] have created numerous international conventions. UNCITRAL was the sponsor of two highly successful international conventions: CISG and Convention on the Recognition and Enforcement of Foreign Arbitral Awards (New York Convention).[7]

A. *Substantive Shortcomings*

The CISG expressly states that it provides limited coverage of sales law – formation of sales contracts and sellers'-buyers' obligations and rights. Many issues relevant to sales law and core contract principles are missing from CISG coverage. Thus, the CISG's goal of harmonizing sales law is a non-starter. The result of a decidedly non-comprehensive code is an array of definitional, coverage, and scope problems. For example, the CISG does not define what a "good" is or for that matter what a "sale" entails. These definitional shortcomings have resulted in a debate as to whether software transactions are covered by the CISG.[8] Is the transaction a sale of a good or a licensing of intellectual property? Is the selling of an exclusive license and use of a copy of protected software tantamount to a sale of that copy? Or, even where there is a sale of an exclusive use of a copy of software, is it a sale of a good or a sale of information (non-good)? Finishing this stream of thought, does the commodification of information render the compilation of that information a good?

Another example of a core sales law area left uncertain by the CISG is the law of warranty. The CISG fails to provide a theory of warranty.[9] It simply deals with the issue of conformity or non-conformity of goods. However, this coverage is limited

4 The official archive of NCCUSL acts and drafts is located at the University of Pennsylvania Law School at http://www.law.upenn.edu/bll/archives/ulc/ulc.htm (accessed 7 March 2012).

5 Hague Conference on Private International Law lists 38 Conventions created under its auspices. See http://www.hcch.net/index_en.php?act=conventions.listing.

6 See http://www.uncitral.org.

7 The New York Convention is the most successful of private law conventions with 146 signatory countries. See United Nations Treaty Collection at http://treaties.un.org/Pages/ViewDetails.aspx?src=TREATY&mtdsg_no=XXII-1&chapter=22&lang=en (accessed 9 March 2012).

8 The general consensus is that standard or mass-produced software is covered by the CISG. See Peter Schlechtriem & Petra Butler, UN LAW ON INTERNATIONAL SALE 30 (Springer-Verlag: Berlin 2009). However, Professor Hiroo Sono has argued the contrary view that the CISG does not apply since software is a licensing transaction and not a sales transaction. Hiroo Sono, *The Applicability and Non-Applicability of the CISG to Software Transactions*, in SHARING INTERNATIONAL COMMERCIAL LAW ACROSS NATIONAL BOUNDARIES: FESTSCHRIFT FOR ALBERT KRITZER 512–26 (C. Andersen & U. Schroeter eds., Wildy, Simmonds & Hill Publishing: London 2008).

9 Henry Deeb Gabriel, *An American Perspective on the United Nations Convention on Contracts for the International Sale of Goods*, 9 INTERNATIONAL TRADE & BUSINESS L. REV. 1, 15 (2005).

to the recognition of the warranty of merchantability and warranty for a particular purpose. It fails to provide any governance on how the seller can disclaim such warranties. The lack of comprehensiveness of the CISG leads to increased complexity – antithetical to the mission of simplification and harmonization – because national laws are used to fill in the gaps in coverage. This intermixing of the CISG – born of the civil and common laws – with idiosyncratic rules of national contract or sales law is not always a good fit. For example, the CISG expressly abdicates the right to specific performance to national law. Under CISG rejection-avoidance rules, the buyer is limited in its ability to reject defective goods by its fundamental breach rule. At the same time, the national law being applied may fully recognize the buyer's right to specific performance.[10] How does the right to specific performance relate to the rule of fundamental beach?

1. Problem of Reservations

There are numerous reservations provided for in the text of the CISG that allow countries to opt out of Parts and Articles of the CISG.[11] Article 92 CISG allows a ratifying country to declare that it will not be bound by Part II (Formation of Contract) or Part III (Obligations of Sellers and Buyers; Conformity; Remedies; Delivery; Passing of Risk; Damages). In particular, Denmark, Finland, Norway and Sweden declared, in accordance with Article 92 CISG, that they would not be bound by Part II of the Convention (contract formation). They, along with Iceland, also declared, pursuant to Article 94 CISG, that the Convention would not apply to contracts of sale where the parties have their places of business in Denmark, Finland, Iceland, Norway, or Sweden.[12] Professor Ramberg has noted that the presumed rationale for the reservation was "the desirability to avoid a two-track system for the formation of contracts which would tend to create confusion if contracts falling under the CISG were subject to different rules with respect to formation than other [types of] contracts."[13] In fact, Ramberg argues that the Nordic countries have had little difficulty in applying the CISG formation rules when it is the law of the case. This recognition undercuts the rationale for opting out of Part II.

Similar arguments may apply to those declarations lodged under Article 95 CISG, which allows for the exclusion of the application of the CISG under its Article 1(1)(b) jurisdiction. Article 1(1)(b) is one of the two pillars of CISG jurisdiction. It provides

[10] *Ibid.*, at 16.

[11] Harry M. Flechtner, *The Several Texts of the CISG in a Decentralized System: Observations on Translations, Reservations and other Challenges to the Uniformity Principle in Article 7(1)*, 17 Journal of Law & Commerce. 187, 188 (1998).

[12] Iceland's declaration under Article 94 CISG extends as well to the formation of contracts of sale, as Iceland did not exclude the application of Part II of the CISG.

[13] Jan Ramberg, *The Nordic Countries*, in Global Challenge of International Sales Law (L. A. DiMatteo ed., Cambridge University Press: New York 2013).

that when private international law rules (conflicts of law) direct a court to the law of a country that has adopted the CISG, then the CISG is applicable law despite the fact that the other party is from a non-CISG country. This reservation was entered into by several States, including the Czech Republic, the People's Republic of China, Singapore, Slovakia and the United States. A rationale that the CISG should not be forced upon an unsuspecting party whose country has not adopted the CISG is a weak one. First, the CISG is the substantive law of the country making the Article 95 declaration and is not any less transparent than any other law of that country. Second, the freedom of contract rationale argues that the parties can simply avoid the CISG through an explicit choice of law clause. There is no strong rationale for such a declaration. Withdrawal of Article 95 declarations would decrease the complexity of CISG jurisdictional issues and at the same time incentivize countries to adopt the CISG or, at the very least, encourage parties to write clearer contracts.

Another important reservation is provided for in Articles 12 and 96 of the CISG. It allows countries to opt out of the "no writing" rule found in Article 11. In such cases, if the law of the reserving country applies, then its writing and other formality requirements would apply. The rational for abandoning this reservation has been stated by Luca Castellani of UNCITRAL:

> States may reconsider their declaration under articles 12 and 96 CISG, requiring the contract to be in written form. This is particularly relevant for economies in transition. In fact, the written form declaration was originally introduced to address concerns about the correct implementation of central plans in Socialist economies. Countries such as Hungary, Latvia and Lithuania have now changed their economic system and have become European Union members.[14]

Because that transition has moved to a more mature stage, for the sake of lesser complexity, those countries, as well as other countries that have made Article 96 declarations, should consider withdrawing their reservations, as has already been done by Estonia.

2. Problem of Translation

There are six official language versions of the CISG.[15] Professor Germain notes that "words used in one language may have a different meaning from the ones in another language, even though the CISG drafters aimed to create a neutral, independent legal language."[16] Germain suggests the creation of "an international

[14] Luca G. Castellani, *The CISG in Context: Work in Process and Complimentary Texts*, in Global Challenge of International Sales Law (L. A. DiMatteo ed., Cambridge University Press: New York 2013).

[15] The six official CISG languages are Arabic, Chinese, English, French, Russian and Spanish.

[16] Claire M. Germain, *CISG Translation Issues*, in Global Challenge of International Sales Law (L. A. DiMatteo ed., Cambridge University Press 2013).

sales law thesaurus," which would promote accessibility and uniformity of interpretation through the use of a "controlled vocabulary."[17] Thus, when confronted with the neutral language (non-nation-specific) the interpreter can use the thesaurus to interpret words like "avoidance," "non-conformity," and "time extension." The thesaurus would act as "a uniform international sales law indexing language."[18] The thesaurus concept would be a tool to greater understanding of the CISG. However, understanding aside, the simplest way to avoid translation issues would be a best practice approach in which the parties expressly state the language of the contract and the official language of the CISG to be applied. By selecting the language of the CISG, the contracting parties would preclude the need for a court to compare different language versions. But, for the party or court whose native language is different than the chosen language, the problem of translation persists. This is where the idea of an international CISG thesaurus can be of assistance. The parties in their contract could refer to the thesaurus much as a trade term references the ICC Incoterms manual. In the end, the translation problem may be intractable between parties who speak and contract using different languages.

B. *Uniformity of Application and National Law Bias*

This section reviews a number of issues that have appeared during the interpretive phase of CISG development. The topics reviewed include the problem of national bias and divergent interpretations, scarcity of CISG jurisprudence in certain areas, scarcity of case law in the common law countries, and disregard of the CISG at the judicial and practice levels of the law.

1. Nationally Biased Interpretations

The "problem" with an international convention that is a product of common and civil law scholars is that it requires the presiding judge to detach herself from her respective legal tradition and to provide autonomous interpretations. For some, this is near an impossible task. The result has been numerous nationally biased interpretations of the CISG. If this is a persistent occurrence, then the goal of harmonization is not attainable. One scholar notes that "a convention cannot be regarded as a successful harmonizing instrument if there is a homeward trend in its interpretation

[17] Vikki M. Rogers & Albert H. Kritzer, *A Uniform International Sales Law Terminology*, available at http://www.cisg.law.pace.edu/cisg/biblio/rogers2.html; Camilla Baasch Andersen, *The Uniform International Sales Law and the Global Jurisconsultorium*, 24 Journal of Law and Commerce (2005) 159–79; http://www.cisg.law.pace.edu/cisg/biblio/andersen3.html.

[18] Claire Germain, *CISG Translation Issues*, in Global Challenge of International Sales Law (L. A. DiMatteo ed., Cambridge University Press 2013).

and application."[19] The problem of national legal bias or homeward trend bias has been well documented.[20] The CISG allows for a resort to national law and cases, but only as a last resort. CISG interpretive methodology requires interpretations to be made – including, filling in gaps in areas covered by the CISG – by the use of express and implied underlying principles. Homeward or national bias refers to the premature reliance on domestic law to interpret the CISG by not correctly applying CISG interpretive methodology.

In homeward bias cases, a perceived gap in the CISG is often too quickly construed as being outside the scope of the CISG. Before resorting to national law, seeking guidance from foreign case decisions and scholarly commentary is a more appropriate methodology for filling in these gaps. National law biased interpretations of the CISG create divergent interpretations not within the spirit of the underlying purposes of the CISG. The premature resort to domestic law concepts and rules results in a second problem – the narrowing of the scope and reach of the CISG.[21] Misinterpreting the scope of the CISG, in order to rely on a national legal tradition, arbitrarily narrows the intended scope of CISG coverage.

2. Uniformity Principle and the Problem of Divergent Interpretations

The scholarly literature expounds on the cases in which different national courts, and sometimes the courts of a single country,[22] have given variant interpretations to CISG rules and words. One commentator notes that "it is still – or more and more it seems – extremely hard work to achieve even a basic level of uniformity in

[19] Sieg Eiselen, citing Franco Ferrari, *CISG Case Law: A New Challenge for Interpreters?* 17 JOURNAL OF LAW AND COMMERCE 245–61(1999); Lisa Ryan, *The Convention on Contracts for the International Sale of Goods: Divergent Interpretations*, 4 TULANE JOURNAL OF INTERNATIONAL AND COMPARATIVE LAW 99, 101 (1995).

[20] See Franco Ferrari, *Homeward Trend: What, Why, and Why Not?* in CISG METHODOLOGY 171–206 (A. Janssen & O. Meyers eds., Sellier European Publishers: Munich 2009); Franco Ferrari, *Have the Dragons of Uniform Sales Law Been Tamed?* in SHARING INTERNATIONAL COMMERCIAL LAW ACROSS NATIONAL BOUNDARIES – FESTSCHRIFT FOR ALBERT H. KRITZER ON THE OCCASION OF HIS 80TH BIRTHDAY 134–67 (C. Andersen & U. Schroeter, Wildy & Hill Publishing 2008); Larry A. DiMatteo, et al., INTERNATIONAL SALES LAW: A CRITICAL ANALYSIS OF THE CISG 174–7 (Cambridge University Press: New York 2005).

[21] See Ingeborg Schwenzer, *Divergent Interpretations of the CISG*, in GLOBAL CHALLENGE OF INTERNATIONAL SALES LAW (L. A. DiMatteo ed., Cambridge University Press: New York 2013).

[22] E.g., two American federal circuit courts rendered different findings on the applicability of the parol evidence rule to CISG contracts: *Beijing Metals & Minerals Import/Export Corp. v. American Bus. Ctr., Inc.*, 993 F.2d 1178 (5th Cir. 1993) (held that the parol evidence rule is a procedural rule and thus applies in the interpretation and application of the CISG in American courts); *MMC-Marble Ceramic Center v. Ceramica Nuova D'Agostino, S.P.A.*, 114 F. 3d 1384 (11th Cir. 1998) (held that the parol evidence rule is a substantive contract law rule and does not apply to CISG-governed contracts). The second ruling is undoubtedly the correct one.

the application and interpretation of the CISG."[23] An example is found in the area of implied warranties in Article 35; some courts have held that the use of express warranty language in a contract automatically disclaims any implied warranties of quality.[24] Professor Flechtner has noted that other courts have held that the implied warranties in Article 35 are cumulative in nature.[25] As such, express language of warranty does not preclude their implication in determining the conformity of goods.[26] Clearly, the "harmonising effect" of the CISG is maximized when the adopting countries "diverge as little as possible from the model law."[27] A best practice approach suggests that the parties – if it is their intention – expressly limit or disclaim liability for non-conformity of goods including expressly derogating from the implied warranties of Article 35.

Uniformity of application is an expressed principle of the CISG.[28] However, the principle of uniformity is undefined by the CISG. Given the previous discussion of the problem of divergent interpretations, has the CISG failed to improve the uniformity of international sales law? The answer to that question has been debated in depth.[29] This debate can be reduced to a definitional issue.[30] Whether or not the

[23] Ingeborg Schwenzer, *Divergent Interpretations of the CISG*, in GLOBAL CHALLENGE OF INTERNATIONAL SALES LAW (L. A. DiMatteo ed., Cambridge University Press: New York 2013).

[24] See, e.g., Supreme Court, Czech Republic, 29 March 2006, available at http://cisgw3.law.pace.edu/cases/060329cz.html (reference to a specific type of contract prevented the implication of the implied warranties of quality).

[25] Harry Flechtner, *CISG Conformity and Notice Provisions*, in GLOBAL CHALLENGE OF INTERNATIONAL SALES LAW (L. A. DiMatteo ed., Cambridge University Press: New York 2013). See also, Harry M. Flechtner, *Excluding CISG Article 35(2) Quality Obligations: The "Default Rule" View vs. the "Cumulation" View*, in INTERNATIONAL ARBITRATION AND INTERNATIONAL COMMERCIAL LAW: SYNERGY, CONVERGENCE AND EVOLUTION: FESTSCHRIFT FOR LIBER AMICORUM ERIC BERGSTEN ON THE OCCASION OF HIS EIGHTIETH BIRTHDAY 571 ff. (S. Kroll, L. A. Mistelis, P. Perales & V. Rogers eds., 2011).

[26] See, e.g., Arbitration Institute of the Stockholm Chamber of Commerce, Sweden, 5 June 1998, available at http://cisgw3.law.pace.edu/cases/980605s5.html (provisions in a contract that only describe positive factors relating to the quality of goods and not language of disclaimer do not exclude the imposition of the implied warranties in Article 35).

[27] Sieg Eiselen, *CISG as Bridge between Common and Civil Law Divide*, in GLOBAL CHALLENGE OF INTERNATIONAL SALES LAW (L. A. DiMatteo ed., Cambridge University Press: New York 2013).

[28] CISG Article 7(1) states that there is a need when interpreting the CISG "to promote uniformity in its application."

[29] See John Honnold, *The Sales Convention in Action – Uniform International Words: Uniform Applications?* 8 JOURNAL OF LAW & COMMERCE 207 (1988); Franco Ferrari, *Uniform Interpretation of the 1980 Uniform Sales Law*, 24 GEORGIA JOURNAL OF INTERNATIONAL & COMPARATIVE LAW 183 (1998); Camilla B. Andersen, *The Uniform International Sales Law and the Global Jurisconsultorium*, 24 JOURNAL OF LAW & COMMERCE 159 (2005).

[30] See Roderick Munday, *The Uniform Interpretation of International Conventions*, 27 INTERNATIONAL AND COMPARATIVE LAW QUARTERLY 450 (1978); Camilla Baasch Andersen, *Defining Uniformity in Law*, 12 UNIFORM L. R. 5–57 (2007); Paul B. Stephan, *The Futility of Unification and Harmonization*

CISG has advanced unity or harmony in sales law depends on what measure is used to determine an acceptable level of uniformity of application. One scholar offers this definition, or better stated the scholar offers a method of reaching a definition: "We can define 'uniformity' as the varying degree of similar effects on a legal phenomenon across boundaries of different jurisdictions resulting from the application of deliberate efforts to create specific shared rules in some form."[31] This can be seen as something an empiricist could determine. But the review of the data (cases) would be very much a subjective undertaking and is rather a useless exercise because the normative question remains – what is an acceptable level of uniformity? The general opinion is the standard is something less than absolute uniformity of application.[32] Possibly, the most that can be hoped for is that the CISG is itself "a standard of common discourse."[33]

Despite the quixotic nature of the quest for uniformity of application among CISG countries, interpretive uniformity should remain an aspirational goal. It provides a normative framework in which to justly decide disputes between parties from different countries. This framework alerts the courts and arbitral bodies that ad hoc application of the CISG is not consistent with its underlying principles and purposes. This framework should guide the interpreter to contemplate future cases or fact scenarios that may be affected by her interpretation. This normative quest is the very purpose for the creation of the CISG. Descriptive reality argues that such a normative goal is an illusion. The facts seem supportive of this conclusion. The lack of a CISG supranational appellate court and the existence of divergent interpretations, on the surface, support the view that the application of the CISG has failed to advance the principle of uniformity. However, a number of scenarios can be constructed to challenge such a view. In some cases, one of the interpretations may be unreasonable. In practice, unreasonable interpretations tend to work themselves out of the subsequent case law in favor of well-reasoned interpretations. A second scenario would be the case of two reasonable autonomous, but divergent interpretations of a CISG rule. In the case of reasonable alternative interpretations, commentators

in International Commercial Law, 39 Virginia Journal Of International Law 743 (1999).

[31] See Camilla Baasch Andersen, *Defining Uniformity in Law* in 12 Uniform L. Rev. 5 (2007); Camilla Baasch Andersen, Uniform Application of the International Sales Law (Kluwer, 2007); Eric Bergsten, *Methodological Problems in the Drafting of the CISG*, in CIGS Methodology 5–31 (A. Janssen & O. Meyer eds., Sellier European Publishers: Munich 2009); Camilla Baasch Andersen, *Macro-Systematic Interpretation of Uniform Commercial Law: The Interrelation of the CISG and Other Uniform Sources*, in CIGS Methodology 5–31 (A. Janssen & O. Meyer eds., Sellier European Publishers: Munich 2009), ("varying degrees of similar effects").

[32] Jan Smits, *Problems of Uniform Laws*, in Global Challenge of International Sales Law (L. A. DiMatteo ed., Cambridge University Press: New York 2013).

[33] Larry A. DiMatteo, et al., International Sales Law: A Critical Analysis of CISG Jurisprudence 2 (Cambridge University Press: New York 2005).

speak of majority and minority views. This suggests a degree of uniformity where critics see only non-uniformity. The fact that numerous national court and arbitral decisions coalesce around majority and minority views is, in itself, within the realm of relative uniformity.

One way of understanding the problem of uniform laws and non-uniform applications across multiple jurisdictions is by analogizing the CISG to the evolution of the American UCC. The stated purpose of the American UCC is to "simplify, clarify, modernize, and unify" the commercial law of the United States. Professors James White and Robert Summers in their seminal work on the UCC declared, despite divergent interpretations among the states, that "judged by its reception in the enacting jurisdictions, the Code [UCC] is the most spectacular success story in the history of American law."[34] The purpose of the CISG is the facilitation of international trade.[35] The hoped for outcome of the CISG is that the replacement of private international law with an international sales law "would contribute to the removal of legal barriers in international trade and promote the development of international trade."[36] Both codes – UCC and CISG – make the harmonization of law across jurisdictions the principle goal of their respective instruments.[37]

Article 2 (Sale of Goods) of the UCC has been adopted by forty-nine of the fifty American states.[38] The CISG has been, at the time of this writing, adopted by seventy-eight countries. There is no national appellate system to unify UCC law or an international appellate court to unify CISG law. Although the UCC is applied in the federal court system, there is no federal common law of sales relating to the interpretation and application of Article 2. The federal court "receives" the sales law by taking the state law of the case and how it has been interpreted by the courts of that state. Additionally, neither Article 2 nor the CISG was intended to be or to represent a comprehensive code. In the case of a gap in the UCC or CISG, courts should look to the UCC or CISG as a whole and through analogical reasoning to provide a solution or rule to fill in the gap. This of course assumes that the gap is within the scope of the instrument (internal gap). In the case where the gap is not within the scope of the UCC or CISG, the interpreter will need to look outside of the instrument to fill in the gap. The default law in the case of the UCC is the common law of contracts. Section 1–103(b) states that "unless displaced by the particular provisions of [the UCC], the principles of law and equity ... supplement its provisions." Non-coverage in the CISG (external gap) include specific exclusions of

[34] James J. White & Robert S. Summer, HANDBOOK OF THE LAW UNDER THE UNIFORM COMMERCIAL CODE 5 (2d ed., West Publishing: St. Paul, MN 1980).

[35] CISG, Article 7(1).

[36] CISG, Preamble, ¶ 3.

[37] James J. White & Robert S. Summer, HANDBOOK OF THE LAW UNDER THE UNIFORM COMMERCIAL CODE 3 (2d ed., West Publishing: St. Paul, MN 1980) ("a major objective of the 'uniform acts' had been to promote uniformity").

[38] State of Louisiana's sale law is rooted in the French Napoleonic Code.

coverage, such as Article 96 declaration opting out of the "no writing" requirement of CISG Article 11; Article 92 allows countries to opt out of Part II (formation of contract rules) and Part III (obligations of buyers and sellers).

The UCC does something that is not done in the CISG – it provides a set of rules of interpretation. It provides that "the [UCC] shall be liberally construed and applied to promote its underlying purposes and policies – simplify, clarify and modernize the law governing commercial transactions";[39] permit the continuance of the "expansion of commercial practices through custom, usage and agreement of parties";[40] and "make uniform the law among the various jurisdictions."[41] It further states that the reasonableness standard (of commercial practice) "may not be disclaimed by agreement but the parties may by agreement determine the standards by which the performance of such obligations is to be measured if such standards are not manifestly unreasonable."[42] Elsewhere it states that its remedies provisions "shall be liberally administered."[43] White and Summers argue that this language in the UCC is an express rejection of the statutory canon that statutes are to be narrowly construed.[44] Comment 1 to Section 1–102 implies that analogical reasoning within the UCC should be used in the quest for meaning whether that leads to a narrow or broad construction based upon underlying purposes and policies: "The text of each section should be read in light of the purpose and policy of the rule or principle in question, as also the Uniform Commercial Code as a whole, and the application of the language should be construed narrowly or broadly, as the case may be, in conformity with the purposes and polices involved."[45]

One test offered in relationship to the "lack" of uniformity in the application of the UCC is simply: Would a lawyer attempting to solve a commercial law problem in 1938 and then again in 1998 not find the law to be more uniform? The answer, given the breadth of the UCC – as compared to the patchwork quilt of narrow, uniform acts existing in the early twentieth century – is a resounding yes. Applying this test to the CISG, Would an international transactional lawyer attempting to solve a sales law problem in 1965 and then again in 2012 not find the law to be more uniform? The very existence of the CISG, especially in its wider use in Europe, requires a "yes" answer when comparing it to the private international law regime that preceded its adoption.

In the end, given the open-textured nature of CISG rules, with the substantial use of the standard of "reasonableness," as well as some of its more general principles

39 UCC §1–102(1)(a).

40 UCC §1–102(1)(b).

41 UCC §1–102(1)(c).

42 UCC §1–102(3).

43 UCC §1–106(1).

44 *Supra note* 34, White & Summer, at 18.

45 UCC §1–102, Cmt. 1.

(good faith) and terms (impediment, fundamental breach), the likelihood of variant interpretations out of national courts is a foregone conclusion. Ultimately, as these divergent interpretations become acknowledged, the importance of the choice of law clause heightens in importance. Sophisticated practitioners, knowledgeable about these divergent interpretations may, as a matter of best practice, expressly choose the state of application, such as "the CISG as interpreted and applied by the courts of Germany."

C. *Widespread Approval and Widespread Disregard*

The adoption of the CISG as the law of seventy-eight countries[46] – which conduct three-quarters of the world trade[47] – is used as a surrogate to demonstrate the importance of the CISG. This linking of accession to the CISG to its actual use as applicable law in a large number of international sales transaction is tenuous. One scholar states the obvious: "The CISG technically is the applicable law for international contracts of sale in jurisdictions which represent [three-quarters] of international trade, [however,] it is exempted and disregarded and opted out in part or in whole in so many contracts"[48] Another commentator, in reviewing the use of the CISG in New Zealand, concludes that "regrettably, even though the Convention has been a part of New Zealand law for 15 years, there are both an unusual lack of awareness and application of the Convention in practice."[49] This statement can be applied to many countries including, the United States.

One scholar offers the following rationale for the discrepancy between the CISG's adoption as law and use in practice:

> In so far as commercial parties have a choice between various legal systems that can be applicable to their contract, they are likely to choose the legal system they know best, or that (in their view) provides them with most legal certainty. True, in an ideal world they would probably prefer to have one law applicable to all their transactions, no matter where they take place. However the general problem of uniform laws is that they never provide a truly self-standing jurisdiction that completely

[46] On 8 January 2012, Benin became the seventy-eighth country officially to place the CISG into effect as the law of its nation. This list of adopting countries can be found in the United Nations Treaty Collection, which is the official depository of the CISG. See http://treaties.un.org/Pages/ViewDetails.aspx?src=TREATY&mtdsg_no=X-10&chapter=10&lang=en (accessed 7 March 2010).

[47] See World Trade Organization, *Leading Exporters and Importers in World Merchandise Trade (2009)*, in INTERNATIONAL TRADE STATISTICS 2010 (World Trade Organization: Geneva 2010).

[48] Camilla Baasch Andersen, *The CISG in National Courts*, in GLOBAL CHALLENGE OF INTERNATIONAL SALES LAW (L. A. DiMatteo ed., Cambridge University Press: New York 2013).

[49] Petra Butler, *New Zealand and the CISG – Who Will Awaken Sleeping Beauty?* in GLOBAL CHALLENGE OF INTERNATIONAL SALES LAW (L. A. DiMatteo ed., Cambridge University Press: New York 2013).

> excludes the applicability of national law. In this sense, the creation of a uniform sales regime can even complicate matters: it means that parties are no longer governed by one law, but by several fragments consisting of national rules and of the rules of the CISG.[50]

This may be a good rationale for parties to opt out of the CISG, but it is not necessarily a rationale for attorneys to suggest that their clients opt out. An attorney should only opt out of or into a legal regime after gaining a sufficient level of understanding of the competing laws. An example illustrates this point. From the seller's perspective the fundamental breach rule as defined in CISG Article 25 and the extended right to cure a defective performance under CISG Article 48(1) are extremely pro-seller. A seller shipping goods around the world incurs greater risks than one sending goods domestically. Under the CISG, the buyer does not have the discretion to reject goods as he would under the UCC's perfect tender rule.[51] Instead, the buyer is forced to accept defective goods unless the defects amount to a fundamental breach. Along the same lines, retrieving goods from another country is more costly than transshipment domestically. The CISG allows the seller the right to cure the defects beyond the contractual date of delivery unless the buyer can show that the delay in delivery was unreasonable or caused unreasonable inconvenience or uncertainty.[52] Not advising a seller-client of these benefits before opting out of the CISG is borderline malpractice. This is more unforgivable since CISG Article 6 allows for derogation from any CISG provisions that the attorney may deem to be "anti-seller."

III. UNIFORMITY IN PRACTICE AND THE PROBLEM OF SCARCITY

One commentator in reviewing CISG case law refers to the CISG's "quieter domains."[53] These are the Articles of the CISG that have not developed a surrounding critical mass of jurisprudence. This scarcity of cases can be understood in a number of ways. First, these are relatively clear, uncontroversial, or minor provisions. This is a difficult argument to support given that many of these provisions deal with issues that are often litigated under national laws. A second explanation is that the scarcity of cases is proof of the failure of the CISG to become relevant in international commercial transactions. Either way, the lack of jurisprudence interpreting and applying some CISG Articles is problematic. Until that jurisprudence evolves, the meaning of the CISG remains unfulfilled.

50 Jan Smits, *Problem of Uniform Laws*, in GLOBAL CHALLENGE OF INTERNATIONAL SALES LAW (L. A. DiMatteo ed., Cambridge University Press: New York 2013).

51 UCC § 2–601.

52 CISG Article, 48(1).

53 Olaf Meyer, *CISG – Three Decades of (More or Less) Success*, in GLOBAL CHALLENGE OF INTERNATIONAL SALES LAW (L. A. DiMatteo ed., Cambridge University Press: New York 2013).

A. *Civil-Common Law Divide*

A more troublesome issue is the great disparity of CISG jurisprudence between civil and common law countries. The Pace Law School's CISG Database's "Country Case Schedule" of court and arbitral decisions provides some cursory insight into the overwhelming influence of the civil law countries in the interpretation of the CISG.[54] Of the 2,718 reported cases, 1,364 were from eight European countries: Germany (477), the Netherlands (203), Switzerland (182), Belgium (142), Austria (128), France (100), Spain (83), and Italy (49). As important as the quantity of cases is the fact that a majority of the cases are substantively reasoned judicial opinions. In contrast, the common law countries has yielded only 200 cases: United States (151), Australia (19), Canada (16), New Zealand (11), and United Kingdom (3). These numbers are overinflated given the fact that a good number of the early American cases were instances when the CISG was dismissed as inapplicable law.

The civil-common law division and the differences in the degrees of application of the CISG among civil law countries are again reflected by the number of cases that reached the highest court in the respective judicial systems. Two hundred and forty-one cases reached civil law countries' supreme courts. CISG-related cases reached the Austrian Supreme Court (Oberster Gerichtshof) an astonishing seventy-eight times, or 32 percent of all Supreme Court cases worldwide. Germany was next with thirty-five, followed by France with twenty-seven, Switzerland with twenty-six, Italy with twenty-one, Spain with thirteen, and The Netherlands with eleven cases. In contrast, there are no instances of a case applying the CISG as applicable law that reached a supreme court of a common law country.

B. *German Role in CISG Jurisprudence*

Despite the CISG's being the law of seventy-eight countries, its interpretation has been delegated by default to a handful of European countries. German courts have provided numerous interpretations of CISG provisions in cases of first instance. Thus, the predominant force in shaping and interpreting the CISG has been the German court system. This is represented in a number of ways. First, is the sheer quantity of German cases interpreting the CISG. The Pace Law School database shows that the largest body of CISG case law has been produced by the German court system.[55] Second, a substantial number of cases have reached the German

[54] See http://www.cisg,law.pace.edu.

[55] As of 23 February 2011, there are 477 German cases listed on the Pace CISG Database. This is out of a total of 2,751 judicial and arbitral decisions listed in the database, or 17.3% of all cases. The People's Republic of China ranks second with 426 cases. However, a majority of these cases were held in front of the China International Economic and Trade Arbitration Commission (CIETAC). See

Federal Supreme Court (Bundesgerichtshof), which is widely recognized as providing well-reasoned decisions.[56] A 2007 Swiss case in determining the promptness of a notice of non-conformity noted that "according to German jurisprudence, a time for notification of one month is reasonable in these cases."[57]

The question is, what are the positive and negative consequences of the German dominance of CISG jurisprudence? One example is found in the application of the principle of good faith. The doctrine of good faith in contract law interpretation and enforcement is a core element of German jurisprudence – more so than in the common law legal system or in most other national civil law systems.[58] CISG Article 7 states the interpretation of its provisions should reflect " the observances of good faith in international trade."[59] Taken literally the CISG only requires that its provisions be interpreted in good faith.[60] Nowhere does the CISG recognize a duty of good faith in the performance or enforcement of a sale of goods contract, as is done in the German BGB[61] or the American UCC.[62] The majority view, however, favours a wider application of good faith despite the legislative history of Article 7.[63] Schlechtriem states: [64]

> But similar to the irresistible force of fundamental laws of nature such as the law of gravity, the principle that not only the interpretation of the Convention, but also the evaluation of the relations, rights and remedies of the parties, should be

http://www.cisg.law.pace.edu/cisg/text/casecit.html#arb. The Russian Federation ranks third with 294 cases, but all of these are decisions of arbitral panels, most notably the Tribunal of International Arbitration at the Russian Federation Chamber of Commerce and Industry, as well as the High Arbitration Court (or Presidium of Supreme Arbitration Court) of the Russian Federation. In contrast, the German decisions are reasoned decisions of judicial courts. See http://www.cisg.law.pace.edu/cisg/text/casecit.html#russian.

56 Thirty-five decisions of the German Federal Court are listed in the Pace CISG Database (accessed 15 March 2012), available at http://www.cisg.law.pace.edu/cisg/text/casecit.html#Bundesgerichtshof.

57 Switzerland 6 September 2007 *Kantonsgericht* [District Court] Appenzel Ausserhoden (*clothing case*), available at http://cisgw3.law.pace.edu/cases/070906s1.html.

58 See Basil Markesinis, Hannes Unberath & Angus Johnston, THE GERMAN LAW OF CONTRACTS 119–33 (2nd ed., Hart Publishing: Oxford 2006); Werner Ebke & Bettina Steinhauer, *The Doctrine of Good Faith in German Contract Law*, in GOOD FAITH AND FAULT IN CONTRACT LAW 171–90 (J. Beatson & D. Friedmann eds., Oxford University Press: New York 1995).

59 CISG, Article 7(1).

60 This has been confirmed by Peter Schlechtriem: "The drafters of the CISG debated for a long time whether the obligation to act in good faith should also apply to the parties. However, they rejected the advancement of good faith on party conduct in the end." Peter Schlectriem & Petra Butler, UN LAW ON INTERNATIONAL SALES 49 (Springer: Berlin 2009).

61 BGB, § 241.

62 UCC, § 1–304.

63 Ulrich Magnus, *Staudinger's Kommentar zum Bürgerlichen Gesetzbuch UN Kaufrecht* 170 & 175.

64 Peter Schlechtriem, *Good faith in German Law and in International Uniform Law*, in Centro di studi e ricerche di diritto comparato e straniero-diretto da M. J. Bonell, Saggi, Conferenze e Seminari No. 24 (February 1997), available at http://cisgw3.law.pace.edu/cisg/biblio/schlechtriem16.html.

subject to the principle of good faith and fair dealing has found its way into the Convention, its understanding by the majority of legal writers and its application by the courts.

It would seem, however, that the majority of cases and commentators favouring the general application of good faith are from civil law jurisdictions, whereas most common law commentators have been more guarded in their approach and provide a more limited role to the principle.[65]

C. *Understated Role of Unreported Arbitration Cases*

Ingeborg Schwenzer has argued that many judicial decisions applying the CISG often involve disputes that end up in the awarding of less than one hundred thousand dollars.[66] She surmises that sophisticated parties, whose disputes involve higher damage claims, generally use private arbitration that result in unpublished and, at times, unreasoned decisions. The role of the CISG in this private domain is unaccounted for, but it may be where it shows its real worth. The reported arbitration cases may be just a tip of the iceberg in the use of the CISG in international sales disputes. About seven hundred arbitral cases have come from the Russian Federation (285) and the People's Republic of China (424). Again, in Serbia, 60 of the seventy case decisions came from the Foreign Trade Court of Arbitration attached to the Yugoslav Chamber of Commerce.

In fact, 835 of the 2,754 documented cases in the Pace CISG database were arbitral awards. André Janssen and Matthias Spilker have noted that due to the private nature of arbitral proceedings there are likely a far greater number of arbitral cases that have used the CISG.[67] They note that Loukas Mistelis estimates that less than 5 percent of arbitration awards are published.[68] On that basis he concludes that the CISG was applied in about 4,250–5,000 arbitration cases by the end of 2008.[69]

[65] Peter Schlechtriem & Hachem *Commentary Art 7* in Uniform Law for International Sales Under the 1980 United Nations Convention paras 16 & 17 (J. O. Honnold ed., 3rd ed. Kluwer: The Netherlands 1999); Sieg Eiselen & Albert Kritzer, International Contract Manual para 85:10. Cf. Bruno Zeller, *Good Faith – the Scarlet Pimpernel of the CISG* at http://www.cisg.law.pace.edu/cisg/biblio/zeller2.html.

[66] Ingeborg Schwenzer, *Divergent Interpretations of the CISG*, in Global Challenge of International Sales Law (L. A. DiMatteo ed., Cambridge University Press: New York 2013).

[67] André Janssen & Matthias Spilker, *CISG and International Arbitration*, in Global Challenge of International Sales Law (L. A. DiMatteo ed., Cambridge University Press: New York 2013).

[68] Loukas A. Mistelis *in* UN Convention on Contracts for the International Sale of Goods (CISG) Article 1, Paragraph 18 (S. M. Kröll, L. A. Mistelis & P. P. Viscasillas eds., C. H. Beck, Hart & Nomos: Munich 2011).

[69] Loukas A. Mistelis, CISG and Arbitration, in CISG Methodology 375, 387 (A. Janssen & O. Meyer eds., Sellier European Law Publishers: Munich 2009).

D. *Summary*

Despite the CISG's own self-imposed obstacles – lack of comprehensiveness, vagueness, and the allowance of reservations – the CISG still has the potential to evolve into a more meaningful instrument than it has at the present moment. Currently, its success has been measured by numerous scholars and the large group of member countries including, most of the world's major trading countries – North America, Continental Europe, People's Republic of China, Russia, and, in the near future, Brazil. The reality of this success is that in practice the CISG is the applicable law of a fraction of transborder sale of goods transactions. At present, substantively it has had only modest success, not so much due to the existence of nation-biased or divergent interpretations as due to the disregard of its existence or express exclusion in international sales contracts.

Ultimately, the success of the CISG in harmonizing international sales law is a matter of practice. One commentator notes that "the familiarity and acceptance of a law arise, in the long term, from its use and positive experiences. If a law is not applied, the chance is let slip by the practitioners to make use of, or at least experience, the advantages preached about the law in the literature, with the result that any incentive to apply the law fails to arise."[70] Alternatively stated, it is in the teaching of the CISG in law schools and at the bar that will determine whether the CISG is a watershed event or a symbolic marker in the march towards uniform transactional law. In the short term, it is unclear whether the CISG will achieve even a modicum of its goal to harmonize international sales law. The adoption of the CISG was revolutionary, but its success will be determined through a long-term, evolutionary process. The direction of that progression can only be a matter of conjecture at the present time.

IV. VALUE OF THE CISG OUTSIDE THE CONTEXT OF INTERNATIONAL HARMONIZATION

The goal of the CISG is to become a widely accepted "hard" law that would harmonize the law of international sales and replace the complexity of private international law rules. However, failure to achieve this ambitious goal does not in itself render the CISG a failure. The use of the CISG as a "soft" law or model law may become equally important factors in its legacy. One commentator has noted that the CISG is already "being used as a benchmark for international sales law and practice in different contexts: as a blueprint for new laws, as a contract checklist for negotiating,

[70] Martin F. Koehler, Survey regarding the relevance of the United Nations Convention for the International Sale of Goods (CISG) in legal practice and the exclusion of its application (October 2006), available at http://www.cisg.law.pace.edu/cisg/biblio/koehler.html.

and as a benchmark for good commercial practice."[71] This part will examine the use of the CISG in these different contexts

A. *CISG as Customary International Law and as Soft Law*

The use of the CISG by arbitral tribunals, as is done with soft law instruments, is a natural fit. In cases where the parties' contracts fail to include a choice of law or the parties have agreed to disregard the chosen law for purposes of arbitration – such as in cases of *ex aequo bonos*[72] and *amiables compositeurs*[73] – then the CISG can be used as a tool by the arbitrators in reaching a just decision. The CISG, given its history as a product of civil and common law drafters, can be recognized as international trade usage in filling in gaps of a contract or in the interpretation of ambiguous contractual language. Of course, courts regularly make use of soft law instruments, especially in the area of international business contract disputes.[74] A British court, in *ProForce Recruit Ltd v Rugby Group Ltd.*,[75] used the CISG in that capacity. Lady Justice Arden noted that:

> It may be appropriate to consider a number of international instruments applying to contracts. It is sufficient to take two examples. The UNIDROIT Principles of International Commercial Contracts give primacy to the common intention of the parties and on questions of interpretation requires regard to be had to all the circumstances, including the pre-contractual negotiations of the parties (article 4.3). The UN Convention on Contracts for the International Sale of Goods (1980) provides that a party's intention is in certain circumstances relevant, and in determining that intention regard is to be had to all relevant circumstances, including preliminary negotiations.

This case did not involve a sale of goods. It was a purely domestic transaction, and was in front of a court in a country, which had not adopted the CISG. The case

[71] Camilla Baasch Andersen, *The CISG in National Courts*, in Global Challenge of International Sales Law (L. A. DiMatteo ed., Cambridge University Press: New York 2013).

[72] Latin for "according to the right and good" or "from equity and conscience." In arbitral proceedings, it refers to the power of the arbitrators to dispense with consideration of the law and consider solely what they consider to be fair and equitable in rendering a decision.

[73] Clauses in arbitration agreements allowing the arbitrators to act as "*amiables compositeurs*" permit the arbitrators to decide the dispute according to the legal principles they believe to be just, without being limited to any particular national law. See William Tetley, *Glossary of Conflict of Law*, available at http://www.mcgill.ca/maritimelaw/glossaries/conflictlaws.

[74] See, e.g., Michael J. Bonell, The UNIDROIT Principles and CISG – Sources of Inspiration for English Courts? Uniform L. R. 305 (2006) (potential use of CISG as soft law by English courts).

[75] *ProForce Recruit Ltd v Rugby Group Ltd.*, United Kingdom 17 February (2006) Court of Appeal (Civil Division), available at http://cisgw3.law.pace.edu/cases/060217uk.html. See also, *The Square Mile Partnership Ltd v Fitzmaurice McCall Ltd*, available at http://cisgw3.law.pace.edu/cases/061218uk.html; Iran-U.S. Claims Tribunal, award of 28.07.1989, available at http://cisgw3.law.pace.edu/cases/890728i2.html.

involved a contract for the supply of temporary workers between an employment company and a cement company. The lower court had barred the admission of pre-contractual negotiations "in aid of the construction of a 'preferred supplier status' term in the agreement." Arden disagreed and proposed the use of the CISG as soft law to support the admission of the evidence.

In an early International Chamber of Commerce arbitration case, the arbitral panel disregarded the domestic law of the case and used the CISG as evidence of international customary law or trade usage.[76] At the time neither party to the dispute was from a country that had adopted the CISG. The panel stated that "as the applicable provisions of the law of the country where the seller had his place of business appeared to deviate from the generally accepted trade usage reflected in the CISG in that it imposed extremely short and specific requirements in respect of the buyer giving notice to the seller in the case of defects, the tribunal applied the CISG."[77] Thus, the arbitral panel used the CISG as international customary law to trump the application of the national law of the case.

B. *Use as a Model National Law*

The CISG purpose was to provide a single set of rules that would be adopted by member countries in order to harmonize international sales law. A somewhat unintended consequence has been the use of the CISG by individual nations as a template, or more minimally as a source, in the revisions of national sales and contract laws. This has been the case in revisions undertaken in Germany (BGB, 2002), People's Republic of China, New Dutch Civil Code, and in the current revision process for a new French Code Civile. Professor Sonja Kruisinga acknowledges the influence of the CISG on the law of obligations in the New Dutch Civil Code or *Burgerlijk Wetboek* (BW): "It is difficult to overestimate the influence of the CISG on [Dutch] national sales law."[78] In regard to the German BGB, the revised sections on domestic sales law and the general remedies for breach of contract are based on CISG concepts.[79] As a consequence, practicing lawyers are much more familiar with CISG's concepts, removing one of the biggest obstacles to its application."[80]

[76] *Seller v. Buyer*, International Commercial Arbitration, No. 5713 (1989), reprinted in, 15 YEARBOOK OF COMMERCIAL ARBITRATION 70 (1999).

[77] *Ibid.*

[78] Sonja A. Kruisinga, *The Netherlands*, in GLOBAL CHALLENGE OF INTERNATIONAL SALES LAW (L. A. DiMatteo ed., Cambridge University Press: New York 2013).

[79] In the official statement accompanying the proposal for the revision of the German law, it was explicitly mentioned that the law should be oriented upon the principles of the CISG; see Bundestags-Drucksache 14/6040, p. 86.

[80] Stefan Kröll, *Germany*, in GLOBAL CHALLENGE OF INTERNATIONAL SALES LAW (L. A. DiMatteo ed., Cambridge University Press: New York 2013).

Professor Sörren Kiene notes that "as in the laws of many other countries,[81] the reformed German Civil Code is now consciously based on UN Sales."[82]

Professor Li Wei asserts that the CISG has served to supplement Chinese law and – the General Principles of the Civil Law of People's Republic of China and the Common Contract Law (CCL) (law governing contracts for international sale of goods), which were enacted on 1 October 1999. The CCL contains many provisions similar to the rules in the CISG and UNIDROIT Principles. The new laws symbolized the "switch from a planed economic regime to a socialist market economy." Furthermore, Li Wei notes that the CISG "deeply affects Chinese legal practice" as it has become a "familiar business instrument of the Chinese law practitioner."[83]

The CISG has also been used to revise national laws, in places where the CISG has been adopted, but not embraced. Egypt provides an example; Professor El-Saghir writes that the:

> CISG has limited judicial applications in Arab Countries; it has significantly influenced the Egyptian legislature in the enactment of the New Commercial Code, Law No. 17 of the year 1997. The Code entered into force on October 1, 1999, replacing the old Commercial Code that was enacted in 1883. The New Code regulates commercial sales in a way that significantly differs from the way the Civil Code regulates non-commercial contracts. The Code incorporated as domestic law many CISG concepts and rules.[84]

In sum, the CISG, as a "model law," has proved to be remarkably cross-cultural in its role in the revision of national contract and sales laws in Asia, Europe, and Africa.

V. CONCLUSION

This chapter assesses the role of the United Nations Convention on Contracts for the International Sale of Goods (CISG) in harmonizing international sales law. It ventures to answer the following question: To what degree has the CISG been successful in harmonizing international sales law and in advancing the principle of uniformity? The answer is an equivocal conclusion that it has been partially successful

[81] The Dutch "*Burgerlijk Wetboek*," the Chinese reform of the law of contract and Scandinavian sales legislation have also been based on UN sales law; see the references in Sörren C. Kiene, Vertragsaufhebung und Rücktritt im UN-Kaufrecht und Bgb 23 et. seq. (Nomos Verlag: Baden-Baden 2010).

[82] Sörren Kiene, *Germany II*, in Global Challenge of International Sales Law (L. A. DiMatteo ed., Cambridge University Press: New York 2013).

[83] Li Wei, *People's Republic of China*, in Global Challenge of International Sales Law (L. A. DiMatteo ed., Cambridge University Press: New York 2013).

[84] Hossam A. El-Saghir, *The Implementation of the CISG in Islamic Countries: The Case of Egypt*, in Global Challenge of International Sales Law (L. A. DiMatteo ed., Cambridge University Press: New York 2013).

in accomplishing its stated goal of creating a uniform international sales law. On the surface, at the level of adoption, it has been extremely successful with its adoption by seventy-eight countries to date. In the area of uniformity in application or practice, its success has been, at best, mixed. It has not been embraced by the common law countries that have made the CISG part of their domestic laws. The paucity of case law in the common law countries is due, in part, to ignorance of its existence and, in part, to indifference or fear of the unknown. The result has been that many contracts opt out of the CISG. This is unfortunate since many of the decisions to opt out appear not to be based upon any substantive shortcomings of the CISG. Instead, opting out has generally been a product of the parties', or more importantly their lawyers', familiarity of national law and the lack of an effort to become knowledgeable of the contents of the CISG.

On the other hand, the adoption of the CISG has led to a number of unintended, but beneficial consequences. It has been used as a template in the revision of a number of national contract and sales laws. In this way, international sales law has become more harmonized not by the uniform application of the CISG, but by the harmonizing of sales law at the level of domestic sales law. It has also been used by arbitration panels – both as mandatory law and as evidence of international customary law. Finally, it is a source for the drafting of international contracts and as a compromise choice of law.

The drafting and application of the CISG, and the debates over the appropriateness of common and civil law rules to international business transactions, as well as the overwhelming amount of commentaries and scholarship generated by the adoption of the CISG, has surely heightened the awareness of the similarities and differences found in these two major legal traditions. This in turn has resulted in less misunderstanding relating to the meaning of applicable contract law and the contents of international contracts. This in a way has led to increased harmonization of international sales law – not at the level of supranational law per se, but at the grassroots of individual business transactions.

Index